PERSECUTION, POLEMIC, AND DIALOGUE

Essays in Jewish-Christian Relations

JUDAISM AND JEWISH LIFE

ACADEMIC
STUDIES
PRESS

PERSECUTION, POLEMIC, AND DIALOGUE

Essays in Jewish-Christian Relations

DAVID BERGER

Boston
2010

Library of Congress Cataloging-in-Publication Data

Berger, David, 1943-
  Persecution, polemic, and dialogue : essays in Jewish-Christian relations.
    p. cm.—(Judaism and Jewish life)
  Includes bibliographical references and index.
  ISBN 978-1-934843-76-5 (hardback)
1. Judaism—Relations—Christianity. 2. Christianity and other
religions—Judaism. 3. Christianity and antisemitism—History.
4. Antisemitism—History. I. Title.
  BM535.B4655 2010
  296.3'96—dc22
            2010017685

Book design by Ivan Grave

Published by Academic Studies Press in 2010
28 Montfern Avenue
Brighton, MA 02135, USA
press@academicstudiespress.com
www.academicstudiespress.com

For Pearl

CONTENTS

Modern and Contemporary Times

INTRODUCTION

Like Jewish identity itself, which is rooted in a complex, tangled skein of religion and peoplehood, Jewish-Christian relations as a field of inquiry resists easy definition. On the one hand, its focus is narrower than the totality of the Jewish experience in Christian lands; on the other, its reach extends beyond the examination of quintessentially religious interactions. The studies in this volume, while remaining well within the parameters of any reasonable definition of the field, range from religious polemic to images of the Other to the waxing and waning of anti-Semitism, often seen through the prism of ever-changing historiographical perceptions.

My interest in this subject emerged out of a religious matrix. As I noted in the review essay of Robert Chazan's *Barcelona and Beyond* reprinted in this collection, I was especially fascinated by Nahmanides' account of his 1263 disputation when I read it as a high school student drawn to a text defending Judaism against a Christian critique. As a senior in Yeshiva College, I attended a class in medieval history taught by Norman Cantor, who supplemented his work at Columbia University with a course at Yeshiva. Since I had majored in classical languages, I chose a paper topic that would enable me to use Latin—and, I suppose, to show off my ability to do so. Because of a stray line in Cantor's *Medieval History* to which I made a brief allusion in that paper, I decided to write about the attitude of St. Peter Damian (with whom I was of course entirely unfamiliar before that year) toward the Jews. The paper questioned the validity of Cantor's remark, and his single comment was both gratifying and sobering: "A+. Merits publication. Still, I think you miss the point." To a significant degree, this undergraduate study, which revealed a key source of Damian's polemic against the Jews and was published a year later in the journal of an Orthodox Jewish student organization, served as the underpinning of my subsequent work in this field. The readers of this collection will have more than enough data to determine whether or not I continue to miss the point.

Since Cantor served on the admissions and fellowship committee of Columbia University's graduate History Department, to which I was admitted during that academic year, the course that I took with him no doubt had another, even more crucial effect on my subsequent career. As a graduate student at Columbia working with the guidance of Gerson Cohen, I wrote a Master's thesis on Nahmanides that had nothing to do with his disputation. But in a course with the semi-retired Salo Baron, I wrote a paper on St. Bernard of Clairvaux and the Jews modeled in part on the article about Damian; years later, it became my first scholarly publication after the completion of my doctorate. As I faced the daunting task of choosing a doctoral dissertation topic, a college classmate named Sidney Hook gave me a soft cover volume recently published for teaching purposes at the Hebrew University in Jerusalem. It consisted of a photo-offset of a medieval polemic against Christianity entitled *Sefer Nizzahon Yashan*, or *Nizzahon Vetus*, taken from Johann Christoph Wagenseil's 1681 collection *Tela Ignea Satanae*. The *Nizzahon Vetus*, with its intriguing amalgam of Scriptural polemic, attacks on the New Testament and Christian doctrine, critique of Christian morality, and uninhibited (or almost uninhibited) vituperation, captured my attention and imagination. The edition, translation and commentary that emerged not only led to a PhD but launched me on a lifelong study of Jewish-Christian interaction along the widest thematic and chronological spectrum.

As I indicated in an essay providing personal reflections on the value of academic Jewish Studies,[1] scholarly inquiry into medieval relations between Christians and Jews grew into engagement with contemporary issues of remarkable weight and controversy. One of

---

[1]   "Identity, Ideology, and Faith: Some Personal Reflections on the Social, Cultural and Spiritual Value of the Academic Study of Judaism." In *Study and Knowledge in Jewish Thought*, ed. by Howard Kreisel (Beer Sheva, 2006), pp. 11–29. That essay, scheduled to reappear in a companion volume published by Academic Studies Press, provides an account of the trajectory of my scholarly interests that supplements and elaborates the brief remarks in this Preface.

these issues, despite a novel formulation and setting, was a reprise of the polemics of old. Pursuant to a request from a Jewish organization, Michael Wyschogrod and I wrote a booklet responding to the arguments of "Jews for Jesus" and similar missionary organizations.[2] The tone and approach of this work are more respectful, sensitive, and polite than the typical tracts of the past, but there is no avoiding the fact that many of the issues would have been familiar to participants in medieval disputations. Nonetheless, as the title of the present volume implies, a dramatic and welcome transformation has moved the center of gravity of Jewish-Christian interaction from persecution and polemic to often friendly dialogue, although the burdens of the past and the challenges of the present render the new relationship complex, challenging, and strewn with minefields. Some of my forays into this arena appear in the latter section of this book, but I have also been compelled to engage significant challenges that have not made their way into print.

To take just the most recent example, the United States Conference of Catholic Bishops issued a statement in July 2009 objecting to a remark in a 2002 Catholic document entitled *Reflections on Covenant and Mission*. *Reflections*, in a passage that its authors surely regarded as entirely uncontroversial, had affirmed that "Catholics participating in inter-religious dialogue, a mutually enriching sharing of gifts devoid of any intention whatsoever to invite the dialogue partner to baptism, are nonetheless witnessing to their own faith in the kingdom of God embodied in Christ. This is a form of evangelization, a way of encouraging the Church's mission." The 2009 statement found fault with this position: "*Reflections on Covenant and Mission* proposes inter-religious dialogue as a form of evangelization that is 'devoid of any intention whatsoever to invite the dialogue partner to baptism.' Though Christian participation in inter-religious dialogue would not normally include an explicit invitation to baptism and entrance into the Church, the Christian dialogue partner is always giving witness to the following of Christ to which all are implicitly invited."

Jews involved in dialogue with Christians were taken aback, even stunned, by what appeared to be a redefinition of the objective of

---

2   *Jews and "Jewish Christianity"* (New York, 1978). Russian translation by Mikhail Ryzhik (New York, 1991). Reprinted as *Jews and "Jewish Christianity": A Jewish Response to the Missionary Challenge* (Jews for Judaism: Toronto, 2002).

interfaith dialogue so that it now affirmed a Catholic intention to issue an implicit invitation that their Jewish partners embrace Christianity. As a member of a delegation of the Rabbinical Council of America and the Union of Orthodox Jewish Congregations of America that holds regular discussions with representatives of the USCCB, I formulated a friendly, respectful, but vigorous letter asserting that we could not continue business as usual as long as these two sentences remained.[3] Shortly thereafter, I was the primary author of a briefer letter sent to the USCCB by five Jewish organizations making a similar point.[4] It is an understatement to say that I was pleasantly surprised when the bishops, after weeks of deliberation and several unpublicized interchanges, removed the problematic sentences from the official document. This affair illustrates the continuing tensions in even the most amicable sphere of Jewish-Christian relations, but it also demonstrates an unprecedented level of sensitivity to Jewish concerns.

On a lighter note, Sister Mary Boys, who is both an academic and an ecumenical leader, told a memorable story many years ago in her response to a talk that I was invited to deliver at Boston College on the history of Jewish-Christian relations. She was present, she reported, at an ecumenical Passover Seder (perhaps a few days before the holiday itself). It is worth remembering that several hundred years ago participation in a Seder would have subjected a Christian to a charge of Judaizing and in the case of a *converso* could have been grounds for burning at the stake. When the time came for the first of the four required cups of wine, several Catholic participants asked Sister Boys a question. The Seder was being held during Lent, and the questioners had taken it upon themselves to abstain from alcoholic beverages during that season. Must they consequently refrain from drinking the wine? She thought for a moment and responded, "Tell me. St. Patrick's Day also falls during Lent. Do you drink on St. Patrick's Day?" The answer was affirmative. If so, ruled Sister Boys, the Passover Seder may be granted the same status as St. Patrick's Day. After her presentation, I told her that it was worth coming to Boston to hear this story, although I would have ruined it by suggesting that they drink grape juice. Amusing as this wonderful

3   The letter is available on the websites of both organizations. See http://www.rabbis.org/ news/article.cfm?id=105461 and http://www.ou.org/public_affairs/article/orthodox_ response_to_catholic_bishops_statement_on_mission_dialogue/.

4   This letter is available at http://www.adl.org/Interfaith/usccb_letter.asp.

story is, it provides a striking, very serious illustration of the dawning of an age that—for all its abiding conflicts and sometimes profound difficulties—would seem as strange to medieval Jews and Christians as Alice's Wonderland.

Though this collection includes the lion's share of what I have written about this topic, I have not incorporated everything. Relatively short book reviews, even if they make substantive points beyond the assessment of the book itself, have been omitted.[5] So has an article that, while not written as a review, is focused on a specific mistranslation and its implications for the interpretation of a key historical document.[6] Articles in newspapers and a non-academic journal commenting on Catholic-Jewish relations, the legacy of John Paul II regarding Jews, and the controversy over the text of the Tridentine mass have also been excluded.[7]

Then there are three substantial articles that I have left out after some inner struggle. The first is an overview of the history of the Jewish-Christian debate omitted because it seemed inappropriate to include an encyclopedia article and because much, though by no means all, of its content is represented elsewhere in the book.[8] The other two are directed largely to an Orthodox audience, although they decidedly have wider implications. One of these is a review essay of a work by one of the most important ecumenical thinkers in the Jewish community, where I express both considerable admiration and profound disagreement.[9] Finally, at a meeting of The Orthodox Forum, which takes place annually

[5]   These include reviews of Daniel J. Lasker, *Jewish Philosophical Polemics Against Christianity in the Middle Ages*, Association for Jewish Studies Newsletter 22 (March, 1978): 16–17, 19; Jeremy Cohen, *The Friars and the Jews*, American Historical Review 88 (1983): 93; Hyam Maccoby, *Judaism on Trial: Jewish-Christian Disputations in the Middle Ages*, Jewish Quarterly Review 76 (1986): 253–257; Gavin Langmuir, *History, Religion and Antisemitism*, American Historical Review 96 (1991): 1498–99; B. Netanyahu, *The Origins of the Inquisition in Fifteenth-Century Spain*, Commentary 100:4 (October, 1995): 55–57.

[6]   "*Cum Nimis Absurdum* and the Conversion of the Jews," *Jewish Quarterly Review* 70 (1979): 41–49.

[7]   "The Holocaust, the State of Israel, and the Catholic Church: Reflections on Jewish–Catholic Relations at the Outset of the Twenty-First Century" (in Hebrew), *Hadoar* 82:2 (January, 2003): 51–55; "A Remarkable Legacy," *Jerusalem Post*, March 11, 2005; "Let's Clarify the Purpose of Interfaith Dialogue," *Jerusalem Post*, Feb. 16, 2008.

[8]   "Jewish-Christian Polemics," *The Encyclopedia of Religion* 11: 389–395.

[9]   "Covenants, Messiahs, and Religious Boundaries," a review essay of Irving Greenberg, *For the Sake of Heaven and Earth: The New Encounter between Judaism and Christianity*, Tradition 39:2 (2005): 66–78.

under the auspices of Yeshiva University, I wrestled with texts about non-Jews in classical Jewish sources that pose ethical problems for the sensibilities of many contemporary believers. The article that emerged from that effort is simultaneously scholarly, religious, and deeply personal. Readers are invited to peruse it, but I did not think that it belonged in this volume.[10]

I am grateful to Simcha Fishbane for inviting me to publish this collection of essays and to Meira Mintz, whose preparation of the index served as a salutary reminder of the thoughtfulness and creativity demanded by a task that casual observers often misperceive as routine and mechanical. Menachem Butler was good enough to produce PDF files of the original articles that served as the basis for the production of the volume. I can only hope that the final product is not entirely unworthy of their efforts as well as those of the efficient, helpful leadership and staff of Academic Studies Press among whom I must single out Kira Nemirovsky for her diligent and meticulous care in overseeing the production of the final version.

I am also grateful to the original publishers of these essays for granting permission to reprint them in this volume.

Finally, when publishing a book that represents work done over the course of a lifetime, an author's expression of gratitude to wife and family embraces far more than the period needed to write a single volume. Without Pearl, whose human qualities and intellectual and practical talents beggar description, whatever I might have achieved would have been set in a life largely bereft of meaning. And then there are Miriam and Elie—and Shai, Aryeh and Sarah; Yitzhak and Ditza—and Racheli, Sara, Tehilla, Baruch Meir, Breindy, Tova, and Batsheva; Gedalyah and Miriam—and Shoshana, Racheli, Sheindl, and Baruch Meir. Each of these names evokes emotions for which I am immeasurably grateful and which I cannot even begin to express.

10 "Jews, Gentiles, and the Modern Egalitarian Ethos: Some Tentative Thoughts." In *Formulating Responses in an Egalitarian Age*, ed. by Marc Stern (Lanham, 2005), pp. 83–108.

SPANNING
THE
CENTURIES

ANTI-SEMITISM

An Overview

From: *History and Hate: The Dimensions of Anti-Semitism* (Jewish Publication Society of America: Philadelphia, 1986), pp. 3–14.

We shall never fully understand anti-Semitism. Deep-rooted, complex, endlessly persistent, constantly changing yet remaining the same, it is a phenomenon that stands at the intersection of history, sociology, economics, political science, religion, and psychology. But it is often the most elusive phenomena that are the most intriguing, and here fascination and profound historical significance merge to make this subject a central challenge to Jewish historians.

Despite its nineteenth-century context and its often inappropriate racial implications, the term *anti-Semitism* has become so deeply entrenched that resistance to its use is probably futile. The impropriety of the term, however, makes it all the more important to clarify as fully as possible the range of meanings that can legitimately be assigned to it. Essentially, anti-Semitism means either of the following: (1) hostility toward Jews as a group which results from no legitimate cause or greatly exceeds any reasonable, ethical response to genuine provocation; or (2) a pejorative perception of Jewish physical or moral traits which is either utterly groundless or a result of irrational generalization and exaggeration.

These definitions can place an atypical and sometimes unwelcome burden on historians, who must consequently make ethical judgments a central part of historical analysis. When is a cause legitimate or a provocation genuine? At what point does a generalization become irrational or a response exceedingly unethical? Most anti-Semites have unfortunately made such evaluations very simple, but, as Shaye Cohen indicates in his contribution to this volume, these questions become particularly acute when one deals with anti-Semitism in antiquity.

The earliest references to Jews in the Hellenistic world are positive ones, and the attraction of Judaism for many pagans continued well into the Christian era. When anti-Jewish sentiment arises, it can usually be explained by causative factors of a straightforward sort: Jewish refusal to worship local gods, missionizing, revolutionary activity, dietary separatism, and marital exclusivity. Some of these, at least, can be perceived as "legitimate" grievances, although a number of the pagan reactions so violate the requirements of proportionality that they cross the threshold into anti-Semitism. In any event, we have no reason to believe that we are dealing in this case with a phenomenon that resists ordinary historical explanation. If one were to insist on defining anti-Semitism as a pathology, then its existence in the ancient world has yet to be demonstrated.

As pagan antiquity gives way to the Christian Middle Ages, we confront the first crucial transition in the history of anti-Semitism. Much has been written about the question of continuity and disjunction at this point: Did Christianity, for all its original contributions to the theory of Jew-hatred, essentially continue a pre-existing strand in classical thought and society, or did it create virtually *de novo* a virulent strain that bears but a superficial resemblance to the anti-Semitism of old? Despite the sharpness of the formulation, the alternatives posed in this question are not, in fact, mutually exclusive. It would violate common sense to deny that classical anti-Semitism provided fertile soil for the growth of the medieval variety, and despite the demise of the ancient gods and the waning of Jewish missionizing and rebelliousness, some of the older grievances retained their force. Nevertheless, if ancient paganism had been replaced by a religion or ideology without an internal anti-Jewish dynamic, it is likely that the anti-Semitism of the classical world would have gradually faded. Instead, it was reinforced. The old, pedestrian causes of anti-Jewish animus were replaced by a new, powerful myth of extraordinary force and vitality.

Medieval Christian theology expresses a profound love-hate relationship with Judaism. Of all religions in the world, only Judaism may be tolerated under the cross, for Jews serve as unwilling, unwitting witnesses of Christian truth. This testimony arises from Jewish authentication of the Hebrew Scriptures, which in turn authenticate Christianity, but it also arises from Jewish suffering, whose severity and duration can be explained only as divine retribution for the sin of the crucifixion. Hence, the same theology that accorded Jews a unique toleration required them to undergo unique persecution.

In the early Middle Ages, it was the tolerant element in this position that predominated. With the great exception of seventh-century Visigothic Spain, persecution of Jews in pre-Crusade Europe was sporadic and desultory; the regions north and west of Italy had no indigenous anti-Semitic tradition, and Christianity had not yet struck deep enough roots in mass psychology to generate the emotional force necessary for the wreaking of vengeance on the agents of the crucifixion. Early medieval Europeans worshipped Jesus, but it is not clear that they loved him enough.

This is not to say that the course of medieval anti-Semitism is to be charted by reference to religious developments alone, although religion is almost surely the crucial guide. The deterioration of Jewish security in the high Middle Ages and beyond corresponds to transformations in economic, political, and intellectual history as well; indeed, the fact that a variety of changes that may well have affected anti-Semitism unfolded in rough synchronism makes it difficult to untangle the causal skeins but at the same time provides a richer and more satisfying explanatory network.

Christian piety widened and deepened, and the spectacular outbreaks of Jew-hatred during the Crusades were surely nourished by pietistic excess. As mercantile and administrative experience spread through an increasingly literate and urbanized Christian bourgeoisie, the economic need for Jews declined precipitously; it is no accident that in the later Middle Ages Jews were welcome primarily in less-developed regions like thirteenth-century Spain and, even later, Bohemia, Austria, and Poland. To make matters worse, the remaining economic activity in which Jews came to be concentrated was a natural spawning-ground for intense hostility: Moneylending may be a necessity, but it does not generate affection. In the political sphere, the high Middle Ages saw the beginnings of a sense of national unity at least in France and England; although this fell short of genuine nationalism in the modem sense, it sharpened the perception of the Jew as the quintessential alien. Finally, despite the centrifugal effects of individual nationalisms, the concept of a monochromatic European Christendom also grew, and with it came heightened intolerance toward any form of deviation.

At a time of growing friction with ordinary Christians, Jews were obliged to look for protection to kings and churchmen. Since riots against Jews violated the law and undermined public order, appeals for royal protection were sometimes heeded. Of equal importance, kings had begun to look upon Jewish holdings—and even upon the Jews themselves—as property of the royal treasury, with the ironic result that protection might well be forthcoming to safeguard the financial interests of the king. Alternatively, however, the process of fiscal exploitation and confiscation could just as easily culminate in outright expulsion.

Appeals to the clergy produced similarly mixed results. The theoretical position of canon law concerning Jewish toleration was no longer a self-evident assumption governing the status of the Jews in a relatively tolerant society; it required constant reaffirmation in a Europe where it had frequently become not only the last line of Jewish defense but also the first. It was for this reason alone that St. Bernard of Clairvaux, who had little affection for Jews, intervened to save Jewish lives during the second crusade, and it is symptomatic of the new circumstances that a Jewish chronicler considers it noteworthy that he took no money for this intervention. Moreover, fissures were developing in the theory of toleration itself. The Talmud was investigated in Paris and burned at the behest of the Church; on occasion, even expulsions came to be regarded as not altogether inconsistent with a policy of toleration, since they fell short of the shedding of blood. Only the innate conservatism characteristic of any system of religious law protected the core of the position from concerted attack, so that Jews could continue to hope—ever more wistfully—for the protection of an increasingly hostile Church.

As the Middle Ages drew to a close, a new specter began haunting the Jews of Europe—the specter of demonology. The growing importance of the devil and his minions in late medieval Europe far transcends the Jewish question. Nevertheless, plague, war, and depression created an atmosphere, especially in northern lands, in which the explanation for terror and tragedy was sought in the alliance between the Jewish adversary and the Adversary himself. Jews, it was said, perpetrated ritual murder, consuming the blood—and sometimes the hearts—of their victims; Jews poisoned wells and Jewish doctors poisoned patients; consecrated hosts were stolen, pierced, and beaten; the Jewish stench and other unique illnesses and deformities underscored the alienness and dubious humanity of the lecherous vicars of Satan. It was not only the folk imagination that could depict a Jewish woman who gives birth to swine; fifteenth-century intellectuals from Spain to Bohemia could speak of Jews as the offspring of a liaison between Adam and demons or as the product not of the patriarchs' seed but of their excrement. The vulgar fulminations in the late works of Luther did not arise *ex nihilo*.

The perception of Jews as forces of darkness in the most fearsome and tangible sense was especially conducive to the expulsions and brutalities that mark late medieval Jewish history, but the belief that Jewish alienness transcends religious differences was important in another context as well. When Jews converted to Christianity singly or in tiny groups, it was relatively easy to accept them unreservedly with the full measure of Christian love. In fourteenth- and fifteenth-century Spain, however, Christians had to deal with the new phenomenon of mass conversion. This, of course, created economic tensions that are not generated by individual conversions, but it must also have produced a psychological dilemma: It is extraordinarily difficult for a society to transform its attitude toward an entire group virtually overnight. There were, it is true, plausible arguments that the religious sincerity of these new Christians left something to be desired; nevertheless, the reluctance to accord them a full welcome into the Christian fold went beyond such considerations. Despite the absence of a prominent demonic motif, the Marranos faced at least an embryonic manifestation of racial anti-Semitism, which served as a refuge for a hostile impulse that could no longer point to palpable distinctions.

This figure of the hated new Christian adumbrates the hated acculturated Jew of later centuries and points the way toward the crucial transition to modern times. Like the passing of pagan antiquity and the emergence of Christian dominance, the waning of the Middle Ages was marked by fundamental ideological change. By the eighteenth century, Christianity began to lose its hold on important elements of the intellectual elite, and once again there seemed to be potential for the eradication or radical weakening of anti-Semitism. The transition of the eighteenth century, however, was far more complex than that of the fourth.

First of all, the old ideology did not disappear. There were areas of Europe, most notably in the east, where the commitment to traditional forms of Christianity retained its full force into the nineteenth century and beyond. Even in the west, large sectors of the early modern population remained immune to the impact of Enlightenment and secularization, so that old-style hostility to Jews could continue to flourish. A second complicating factor is that this time there are periods and places in which anti-Semitism *did* wane, and analysis of its modern manifestations must balance explanations for persistence against reasons for decline. Finally, the stated reasons for modern Jew-hatred are more varied and mutable than their medieval equivalents. In the Middle Ages, whatever the role of economic and political factors, the religious basis for anti-Semitism was a constant throughout the period, forming a permanent foundation that served as both underlying reason and stated rationale. In the modern era, on the other hand, we are presented with a shifting, dizzying kaleidoscope of often contradictory explanations: The Jews are Rothschilds and paupers, capitalists and communists, nationalists and deracinated cosmopolitans, religious separatists and dangerous free thinkers, evil geniuses and the possessors of superficial, third-rate minds.

We must beware of easy psychological reductionism, which excuses the historian from a careful examination of the complexities of modem anti-Semitism. Nevertheless, this list of grievances against Jews suggests that by the modem period anti-Semitism had reached the level of a deeply rooted pathology. It is precisely because Jews were the only significant minority in medieval Christian Europe that the fear and hatred of the alien became fixed upon them; a fixation that develops over a millennium is not uprooted merely by the slow weakening of its major cause. Hence, the arguments proposed by modern anti-Semites—and by historians who try to understand them—reflect a complex interweaving of reason and rationalization, of genuine cause and shifting, often elusive excuse.

With the passing of Christian dominance, anti-Semitism in the modern West came to be associated with other ideological issues that in large measure replaced Christianity as the focus of European concerns. The first of these was nationalism. At first glance, the egalitarian spirit of the French Revolution appears utterly incompatible with the persistence of Jewish disabilities, and the emancipation of the Jews was, in fact, achieved. But the increasing power of the national state—and its increasing demands—provided ammunition for a new, exceptionally powerful argument against such emancipation. The eighteenth-century state demanded not only its residents' toil and sweat but also their hearts and souls: full loyalty, total identification, fervent patriotism. Moreover, the breakdown of the old regime's corporate structure required the citizen to engage in an unmediated relationship with the centralized state. Jews, it was said, failed these tests. In descent and behavior, in communal structure and emotional ties, Jews were an alien nation, a state within a state, no more deserving of citizenship than Frenchmen in Germany or Germans in France. Since the nature of the state had changed so much that retention of medieval status was hardly a realistic option, this analysis posed no small threat to Jewish security.

The only viable response, it seemed, was the denial of Jewish nationhood. So Jews denied it—and they denied it sincerely. There is at least faint irony in Jews' declaring that they are not a nation while anti-Semites vigorously affirm that they are, but the gradual spread of Jewish emancipation through much of nineteenth-century Europe awakened feelings of genuine, profound patriotism that led to the defining of Judaism in the narrowest confessional terms. Until late in the century, this sacrifice—which most western Jews considered no sacrifice at all— appeared to have achieved its goal. Barriers crumbled, discrimination eased, redemption-in-exile appeared at hand.

Nevertheless, like so many earlier, more traditional instances of messianic aspirations, this one too was doomed to disappointment. The more Jews behaved like Christians, the stranger it seemed that they would not become Christians, and even in a more secularized age, conversion remained the symbol and *sine qua non* of full entry into Gentile society. On occasion, an act of acculturation and rapprochement would paradoxically lead to increased tensions. Reform Judaism, for example, de-emphasized ritual while stressing ethics, much as liberal Protestantism had elevated ethics and downgraded dogma. However, in the absence of conversion of Reform Jews, this agreement on content led to an acrimonious dispute as to which religion had the legitimate claim to the ethical message preached by both sides, and Christian denigration of Jewish ethics became a theme that bordered on anti-Semitism. In a broader context, even Christian supporters of Jewish emancipation had generally expected it to bring about the gradual disappearance of the Jews, and the failure of most Jews to cooperate left a sense of disquiet and frustration. Additionally, as Todd Endelman stresses in this volume, the resurgence of anti-Semitism in the late nineteenth century was part of a general rebellion against the liberalism and modernity that were responsible for emancipating the Jews.

In a world of acculturated Jews, how was this new anti-Semitism to be expressed? Many of the anti-Semitic political parties pressed economic and religious grievances of a quite traditional sort, but there were difficulties in arguing that the Jews of France and Germany were so different from Christians that they posed a genuine, alien threat. There was, however, a more promising approach—explosive, sinister, closer to the psychic wellsprings of popular anti-Semitism, and immune to the argument that Jews were, after all, "improving." Racial categories were prominent and universal in nineteenth-century European thought; to some degree they had been used against Jews from the earliest days of emancipation, and Jews themselves evinced no hesitation in assigning special characteristics—sometimes even physical ones—to the Jewish "race." For anti-Semites—and it is in this context that the term was coined—the "polluted" racial character of the Jews served, as it had in the Marrano period, as a basis for hating people whose distinctiveness could not readily be discerned. The unacculturated Jew was a visible enemy; the acculturated one—despite caricatures of Jewish physical traits—was insidious, camouflaged, coiled to strike at European society from within. Jewish acculturation was no longer a promise; it was a threat.

It is no accident that the worst manifestation of Jew-hatred in history was built upon this foundation. Nazi anti-Semitism achieved such virulent, unrestrained consequences precisely because it stripped away the semi-civilized rationales that had been given in the past for persecuting Jews and liberated the deepest psychic impulses that had been partly nurtured but partly suppressed by those rationales. Although the Nazis used the standard political, economic, and sometimes even religious arguments for persecution, their central message was that Jews were alien, demonic creatures, subhuman and superhuman at the same time, who threatened "Aryans" with racial corruption and with profound, almost inexpressible terror. Such feelings were probably a part of the anti-Semitic psyche for centuries, and I have already argued that the deeply rooted fear and hatred of the alien had become fixed upon the Jews; nevertheless, these feelings had not been given free reign. The persecution of political enemies, economic exploiters, and religious deviants must still be governed by a modicum of civilized restraint; although this restraint must have seemed invisible to the victims of the Crusades, it reappears, however dimly, when seen through the prism of the Holocaust. On the other hand, malevolent demons, racial aliens, and malignant vermin can be extirpated with single-minded, ruthless ferocity.[1]

One of the most significant reactions to the new anti-Semitism was the rise of Jewish nationalism. To many observers—including many Jews—this was an abrogation of the original, unwritten contract granting Jews emancipation; nevertheless, the Zionist movement did not play a major role in the upsurge of European anti-Semitism in the decades before the Holocaust. Its impact on anti-Semitism came in different, quite unexpected ways: in the grafting of western Jew-hatred onto the traditional patterns of discrimination in the Muslim world, and in providing a new outlet and a new camouflage for the anti-Semitic impulse.

Pre-modern Jews had flourished and suffered under Islam, but anti-Jewish sentiment rarely reached the heights that it attained in the Christian world. This was partly because Jews were never the only minority in the Muslim orbit, but it was also because Judaism did not play the crucial role in Islam that it did in Christianity. The frequent Christian obsession with Jews was nourished in large measure by resentment toward a parent with whom intimate contact could not be avoided; Islam's relationship with Judaism lacked that intimacy and hence failed to generate the sort of tensions that explode into violence. Persecutions of Jews in the Muslim world should not be minimized, but they are not of the same order of magnitude as anti-Jewish outbreaks in the Christian West.

However persuasive the claim of the Jewish people may be to its ancestral homeland, the failure of Arabs to embrace the Zionist immigrants was hardly unexpected and is not in itself grounds for a charge of anti-Semitism. But offended nationalist sentiments and old-style denigration of Jews combined to make the Arab world receptive to anti-Semitic propaganda ranging from *Mein Kampf* to *The Protocols of the Elders of Zion*. (The assertion that Arabs, as Semites, cannot be anti-Semitic is, of course, an overliteral and usually disingenuous argument.) Moreover, extreme forms of anti-Zionism outside the Arab world serve as a vehicle for anti-Semitic sentiments that are no longer respectable

[1] Much of the language in this paragraph is borrowed from my "Jewish-Christian Relations: A Jewish Perspective," *Journal of Ecumenical Studies* 20 (1983): 23.

in their unalloyed, naked form. Here again there are genuine problems of definition, but "anti-Zionist" literature in the Soviet Union and the widespread application to Israel of an egregious double standard make it difficult to deny that anti-Zionism and anti-Semitism are not infrequently synonymous. The positions of the emancipation period have been reversed: Jews now lay claim to a nationhood that their enemies deny.

Anti-Semitism is no longer an acknowledged pillar of western thought and society. The distinguished medievalist R. W. Southern, in evaluating the normalcy or eccentricity of a major medieval churchman, correctly classified his "deep hostility toward the Jews" among the arguments for normalcy; had the subject of his evaluation been a contemporary western figure, such a classification would have been more than dubious. Despite the unspeakable agonies of twentieth-century European Jewry, anti-Semitism has not been wholly intractable.

At the same time, the nineteenth-century mixture of hope and expectation that Jew-hatred would fade away has proved to be a fantasy, and few indeed continue to indulge such dreams—surely not the Jew at a recent conference who confided his fears of the aftermath of nuclear war. He does not fear radiation, or climatic change, or wounds crying vainly for treatment; he worries instead that the war will be blamed on Einstein, Oppenheimer, and Teller.

Macabre Jewish humor, no doubt, or simple paranoia.

And yet . . .

THE
MIDDLE
AGES

FROM CRUSADES TO BLOOD LIBELS
TO EXPULSIONS

Some New Approaches to Medieval Anti-Semitism

The Second Victor J. Selmanowitz Memorial Lecture. Touro College
Graduate School of Jewish Studies (New York, 1997).

Despite ubiquitous, ritualized gestures of obeisance toward Salo
Baron's rejection of the "lachrymose conception" of Jewish history,
most historians of medieval Jewry continue to employ a periodization
structured by patterns of toleration and persecution. On the whole, the
Jewish condition in the early Middle Ages emerges as relatively stable
and secure, while the later period is marked by a growing hostility which
finally erupts into libels, pogroms and expulsions.

Sweeping generalizations are, of course, always vulnerable to attack,
and this one more than most. Even if limited, as it is, to Christian Europe,
it characterizes the treatment of a dispersed group across a thousand
years and a multitude of political and cultural boundaries. Thus, all
observers make an exception for the persecution of Jews in seventh-
century Visigothic Spain. Beyond this instance, some historians have
raised more general questions about what they see as a rose-colored
perception of the early period. Kenneth Stow, for example, challenges
the view that Jews were treated so well in the early Middle Ages that one
can justly speak of an alliance with Christian rulers or even of Jewish
political power.[1] Although his rejection of this position unquestionably
has concrete ramifications for our perception of early medieval Jewry,
what he substitutes for a political alliance which ultimately breaks down
is a legal status which ultimately becomes anomalous. The fundamental
periodization remains intact.

---

[1]   Kenneth R. Stow, *Alienated Minority: The Jews of Medieval Latin Europe* (Cambridge,
       Mass., 1992), pp. 3–4.

Within this general framework, the effort to locate more precise transitions immediately raises the specter of the crusade of 1096, an event which looms large in the Jewish popular imagination as well as in the works of historians. In his important studies of the catastrophe which befell the Jews of the Rhineland, Robert Chazan has argued against the position that it was a watershed, primarily on the grounds that Northern European Jewry in the following century achieved economic growth and extraordinary cultural creativity in an environment of relative toleration.[2] The transforming significance of the first crusade can also be challenged from the other direction—by underscoring evidence of significant persecution in Northern Europe beginning with the early years of the eleventh century.

One item of such evidence is the series of attacks around the year 1010 to which we shall presently return. No less significant are the indications of routine violence against eleventh-century Jews, but here we face a methodological question of great interest and wide application. In a brief passage marked by his typical erudition and care, Avraham Grossman has noted a number of sources in which Jews report looting of Jewish homes, roads so dangerous that "no Jew comes or goes," and fear that a city-wide tragedy would generate attacks on the Jewish community.[3]

The problem here is to distinguish the generic unrest of an extremely violent society from "bias crimes" directed specifically against Jews. Grossman is not insensitive to this point. On one occasion, for example, he argues that a reference to the looting of "the houses of all the Jews" makes it clear that the violence was targeted. While he may well be correct in this case, the argument is not decisive, and the reference to dangerous roads is even less compelling. Members of a minority group with a powerful self-consciousness of their subordinate position tend to perceive attacks in personal terms even if the identity of the victim was irrelevant or marginal in the eyes of the perpetrator; sometimes, they may make specific reference to Jews simply because that is the universe of discourse of both the writer and his audience.

---

[2]   Robert Chazan, *European Jewry and the First Crusade* (Berkeley, Los Angeles, and London, 1987), pp. 197–210; Chazan, *In the Year 1096: The First Crusade and the Jews* (Philadelphia and Jerusalem, 1996), pp. 127–132. In a forthcoming article on the fast of 20 Sivan, David Wachtel has made some valuable observations on the deep impact that must nonetheless be attributed to these events.

[3]   Avraham Grossman, *Hakhmei Ashkenaz ha-Rishonim* (Jerusalem, 1981), pp. 12–13.

In his very recent *Communities of Violence*, an excellent work concentrating on the later Middle Ages in the South of Europe, David Nirenberg has noted the problem of classifying violent crimes on the basis of unproven religious motivations. He presents the issue extremely well but puts it aside on the grounds that the medievals' legal perception of violence across religious boundaries, at least in the Crown of Aragon, saw it through the prism of those boundaries.[4] This does not resolve the question if we are interested, as we are here, in the motivation of attackers who were neither lawyers nor theologians. As contemporary authorities have discovered while struggling to determine whether a particular mugging should be classified as a bias crime, it is no easy task to decide whether even the racist who shouted, "Nigger!" as he relieved his victim of his wallet was motivated primarily by greed, primarily by bigotry, or by an equal measure of each. It is a foregone conclusion that the victim in that case would see himself as the object of a racially inspired attack, and such feelings may exist—at times justly, at times not—even when no epithet was heard. Standing alone, sporadic Jewish testimony to anti-Jewish violence must be utilized with care.

Nirenberg also raises a much larger question which stands as a challenge to the fundamental enterprise addressed in this lecture. The overarching patterns limned by "teleological, *longue durée*" history tend to disappear, he says, when one looks closely at individual events. The point is of central importance provided that we apply it with due moderation. *Longue durée* history should indeed not allow us to forget that Jews could live in relative security well beyond a "turning point," and that a horrific event can be followed by a return to normalcy. Eleazar Gutwirth, for example, has recently argued that the Jewish community of Spain remained creative and even optimistic well after the "watershed" pogroms of 1391.[5] Local conditions, which depend on a multitude of factors, will often be decisive for a particular community, and even in the midst of a massive wave of persecutions such as those spawned in Franconia from 1298 to 1300 by the host desecration charge, "the universal narrative was always told and unfolded within the immediate context of power and politics of a town and its region."[6]

---

4   *Communities of Violence* (Princeton, 1996), pp. 30–32.
5   E. Gutwirth, "Towards Expulsion: 1391–1492," in *Spain and the Jews: The Sephardi Experience, 1492 and After*, ed. by Elie Kedourie (London, 1992), pp. 51–73.
6   Miri Rubin, "Desecration of the Host: The Birth of an Accusation," in *Christianity and Judaism*, ed. by Diana Wood (Oxford, 1992), p. 184.

The same caveat applies on the wider canvas of national rather than local politics. In 1992, I organized a session at the conference of the Association for Jewish Studies on medieval expulsions of Jews in comparative perspective. Robert C. Stacey and William C. Jordan discussed the expulsions from England and France respectively. Despite the fact that these events took place in neighboring countries less than two decades apart and both analyses focused on relations between the king and the local aristocracy, the explanations proposed were so disparate that one could easily have come away with the sense that the proximity of both geography and chronology was entirely coincidental.[7]

This was of course not the case, as both participants took pains to note, and their feeling of unease at such a perception illustrates the dangers of too dismissive an approach to *longue durée* history. We cannot allow the trees, or even the groves, to persuade us that there is no forest. In the final paragraph of his book, Nirenberg concedes that cataclysmic events like those of 1391 can "indelibly alter the world in which they occurred, refiguring the field of meaning in their ritual lexicon."[8] Changes of perception, whether they result from cataclysm or more gradual developments, fundamentally transform the psychology of a society, so that courses of action that would never have been entertained as anything but a fantasy or an intellectual exercise become real, even seductive options. To take a narrow example, an unhappy marriage in a society in which divorce, though legal, is almost unthinkable is far more likely to last than the same marriage in an environment where relationships are routinely dissolved. The same local or national conditions can engender very different results; an environment in which massacres or expulsions are seen as realistic possibilities is far more likely to produce them.

The second half of the Middle Ages, then, generated physical attacks, conversionary efforts, economic restrictions, the badge, campaigns against the Talmud, the three major accusations of ritual murder, host desecration, and well poisoning, and widespread expulsions. This is a real shift, and it legitimately calls for large scale explanatory efforts,

---

7   Stacey's analysis has now appeared in a Hebrew version. See his "Yahadut Angliah ba-Me'ah ha-Yod-Gimmel u-Be'ayat ha-Gerush" in *Gerush ve-Shivah: Yehudei Angliah be-Hillufei ha-Zemannim*, ed. by David Katz and Yosef Kaplan (Jerusalem, c. 1993), pp. 9–25.

8   *Communities of Violence*, p. 249.

always disciplined by the considerations of which Nirenberg so effectively reminds us.

It is far from clear that the primary explanation for such shifts lies in the specifics of the relationship between the dominant society and the particular minority group. Most contemporary Jews recoil at the suggestion that objectionable Jewish behavior produces, let alone justifies, anti-Semitism, though the instinct which generated movements for moral self-improvement as a weapon against hostility has not faded into total oblivion. But if it is not offensive Jewish behavior which engenders hatred, we need not assume that any concrete Jewish action or characteristic, or even a historical event involving Jews, is the key to understanding the transformation that we confront.

We might profitably pursue this point through a passing glance at a recent, benign development in the relationship between Christians and Jews. The received wisdom informs us that the Second Vatican Council's declaration in *Nostra Aetate no. 4* that contemporary Jews bear no responsibility for the crucifixion and that Judaism retains spiritual value resulted from introspection which was occasioned by the Holocaust and encouraged by Jewish ecumenicists. While these factors were surely real, I believe that they were decidedly secondary.

Vatican II was convened in a post-colonial age marked by a new regard for self-determination and a new respect for cultural diversity—including religious diversity—as well as minority rights. Exclusivist claims did not sit well in this environment, and harsh punishment, even divine punishment, for religious dissent surely did not. A telling expression of the inner struggle triggered by the clash of this liberal, humanistic sensibility with a narrower, more forbidding tradition was formulated by a playwright hostile to Catholicism whose bitter work, *Sister Mary Ignatius Explains It All To You*, nonetheless has its very funny moments. Sister Mary, an old-fashioned nun teaching in the aftermath of Vatican II, defines "limbo" for her classroom/audience. If I remember correctly, she displays a picture of a baby trapped behind the bars of a crib and declares, "Limbo is the place where unbaptized infants went before the Ecumenical Council."

The historical and theological precision of this statement may leave something to be desired, but it brilliantly captures a central feature of the ideological atmosphere of the Council, which had nothing to do with Jews and next to nothing to do with the Holocaust. It was this spirit that animated the adoption of a more positive attitude toward Islam and the religions of the East, the assertion that salvation is possible outside the Church—and *Nostra Aetate no. 4*. One who locates the fundamental impetus of the historic declaration on the Jews in the specifics of the Jewish-Catholic relationship loses sight of the larger process and misses the key point.

— II —

For medieval Europe, the most important recent effort to subsume the transformation of attitudes toward Jews under the rubric of a much broader change is R. I. Moore's *The Formation of a Persecuting Society*.[9] Moore's essential argument proposes that economic, political, and cultural developments in the eleventh and twelfth centuries produced a new class or group of classes which needed to consolidate power in the face of elements which posed a threat to the evolving order. Thus, heretics, Jews, even lepers, began to face exclusion and persecution at approximately the same time; somewhat later, male homosexuals and witches faced a new level of hostility for similar reasons. As we shall see, even Moore cannot refrain altogether from an analysis of certain characteristics of medieval Jewry, if only to establish the plausibility of a Jewish threat, but the thrust of his argument points away from the particularities of Christian attitudes toward Judaism and Jews.

Though Nirenberg dislikes Moore's approach as an example of the suspect *longue durée* mode of historiography, his own analysis, for all its specificity, also marginalizes the particularities of the Jewish-Christian relationship. Through a comparative examination of the treatment of Jews and Muslims in Aragon, he reminds us, to take a single example, that not only the former were accused of poisoning wells. Thus, we can see Jews as a vulnerable group whose specific Jewishness is almost irrelevant.

In very recent years, we have witnessed the revival of a long-rejected interpretation of eleventh-century Europe which also sees Jews as one of several groups victimized by a larger transformation. Richard Landes' *Relics, Apocalypse, and the Deceits of History*,[10] which has been

---

9   Oxford, 1987.
10   Cambridge, Mass., 1995.

described as probably "the best of a number of recent studies forcing reassessment of the central Middle Ages,"[11] maintains that eschatological expectations surrounding the millennium gripped the imagination of the European populace, generating a wide variety of religious and social movements. In an article specifically addressing the persecution of Jews, Landes has now argued for harmonizing Jewish and Christian accounts of persecutions which he dates in 1010 to produce a picture of sustained violence whose aetiology he locates in apocalyptic frenzy.[12]

Landes' stimulating presentation merits careful attention, though I remain more skeptical than he about the dating and reliability of the major Jewish source describing these events.[13] It is a virtual certainty that noteworthy attacks against the Jews of Northern Europe took place in approximately 1010; that these resulted from millennial eschatology is a possibility that has been restored to the historiographic map but continues to strike me as highly speculative. Should we embrace this possibility, we would then face a second, larger challenge which applies to Moore's position as well. Do these interpretations purport to explain only the *genesis* of anti-Jewish violence by identifying the spark which kindled a conflagration but which, like the God of the Deists, did its deed and—in the words of a caustic observer—then went to Florida? Or is it possible that apocalyptic tension and a Jewish threat to the position of Christian elites persisted beyond the period of their initial appearance and provided an ongoing impetus to medieval Judeophobia?

---

[11] *The American Historical Review* 102 (1997): 433.

[12] Richard Landes, "The Massacres of 1010: On the Origins of Popular Violence in Western Europe," in *From Witness to Witchcraft: Jews and Judaism in Medieval Christian Thought*, ed. by Jeremy Cohen (Wiesbaden, 1996), pp. 79–112. Landes credits two earlier studies, which have in his view been unjustly ignored, with looking at these developments from the proper perspective. See Hans Liebeschütz, *Synagoga und Ecclesia* (Heidelberg, 1938, 2nd ed., 1983), and L. Dasberg, *Untersuchungen über die Entwertung des Judenstatus in 11. Jahrhundert* (Paris, 1965).

[13] The most hostile treatment of the reliability of that source is Kenneth Stow, *The "1007 Anonymous" and Papal Sovereignty: Jewish Perceptions of the Papacy and Papal Policy in the High Middle Ages* (Cincinnati, 1984). I have reservations about important aspects of Stow's argument, which he strengthens in one instance by unjustifiably conflating two disparate quotations in his source; see Robert Chazan's review in *Speculum* 62 (1987): 728–731. At the same time, I am largely persuaded by his uneasiness at finding a strong and sophisticated Jewish presentation of the doctrine of papal sovereignty in an allegedly eleventh-century text.

Landes himself describes a "millennial generation" lasting in acute form until 1033, which is the thousandth anniversary of the Passion, and sees close links between this atmosphere and that of the late-eleventh-century crusade. This is self-evidently an important historiographic contention, but we cannot plausibly extend such a factor indefinitely, though it can surely make further appearances.[14] Later medieval anti-Semitism will have to seek other sources of nourishment.

In Moore's case, the process by which a new, literate elite established itself extends over a longer period of time than a millennial generation, but here too the explanation must lose its force after a decent interval. And once again, the initial contention itself bears scrutiny: Moore sees the Jewish threat to this elite as both economic/professional and intellectual/religious. Jews, he says, had a tradition of literacy and economic experience which stood in the way of aspiring Christian merchants and bureaucrats, and they had a developed understanding of Scripture which raised questions about the theological and exegetical enterprise which Christians were beginning to pursue with renewed sophistication.

With respect to the first point, it is difficult to agree that the tiny Jewish population of Northern Europe, however overrepresented it might have been in commerce, constituted the sort of obstacle to Christian entrepreneurs or government functionaries that would produce widespread persecution. The second assertion is particularly difficult to test. I have argued elsewhere that European Jews, especially in the North, did challenge Christian beliefs with surprising aggressiveness,[15] but references to the challenge posed by Judaism do not appear with sufficient frequency in Christian literature to persuade me that it was a factor so compelling that it played a major role in the formation

---

[14] See, for example, Jeremy Cohen, *The Friars and the Jews: The Evolution of Medieval Anti-Judaism* (Ithaca and London, 1982), pp. 246–247, for references to Joachite eschatology as a possible secondary factor in the development of anti-Jewish attitudes in the thirteenth century. For the sixteenth century, see Heiko A. Oberman, *The Roots of Anti-Semitism in the Age of Renaissance and Reformation* (Philadelphia, 1984; German original, 1981), pp. 118–122; Kenneth Stow, *Catholic Thought and Papal Jewry Policy 1555–1593* (New York, 1977).

[15] David Berger, "Mission to the Jews and Jewish-Christian Contacts in the Polemical Literature of the High Middle Ages," *The American Historical Review* 91 (1986): 576–591.

of a persecuting society. Ironically, Moore's deemphasis of Jewish particularity in the development of medieval anti-Semitism requires him to attribute enormous importance to their role in European society so that they may fit into his larger explanatory scheme.

— III —

Other approaches to our problem appeal to factors which began in the eleventh or twelfth century but persisted through the end of the Middle Ages. There is nothing new about the view that increased piety at all levels of society played a critical role in the rise of hostility toward Jews. In an essay in which I shamelessly attempted to interpret the entire history of anti-Semitism in twelve pages, I noted this point by observing that before the eleventh century "Christianity had not yet struck deep enough roots in mass psychology to generate the emotional force necessary for the wreaking of vengeance on the agents of the crucifixion. Early medieval Europeans worshipped Jesus, but it is not clear that they loved him enough."[16]

Jeremy Cohen, in a major study which has deservedly become central to the discussion of medieval anti-Semitism, emphasized the role of Christian belief but shifted the focus from the piety of the masses to the theology of the elite. *The Friars and the Jews*[17] argues that the very foundations of toleration were undermined by growing Christian familiarity with the Talmud. Through the efforts of Nicholas Donin, a thirteenth-century French Jewish convert to Christianity, Christians came to realize that (to borrow the sharp formulation of an acquaintance of mine) the Jews are the people of the book—but the book is not the Bible. Though Donin and others attacked the Talmud for blasphemy and hostility to Christians, Cohen sees the primary thrust as the argument that the Talmud was "another law." Since one of the cornerstones of the theology granting Jews toleration was the assumption that they preserve the law of the Hebrew Bible not only in their libraries but in their behavior, this argument was fraught with the most dire consequences.

---

[16] See my "Anti-Semitism: An Overview," in *History and Hate: The Dimensions of Anti-Semitism,* ed. *by* David Berger (Philadelphia, 1986), pp. 3–14 (quotation on p. 5).

[17] See note 14.

Key aspects of Cohen's argument convince me, while others do not. I believe that Donin really was intent upon reversing the Church's fundamental policy of toleration and that the "other law" argument was his most important weapon. I also believe that this effort, in the long run, was not wholly ineffective; later medieval friars were greatly tempted by the blandishments of the argument, and by the end of the Middle Ages, some Christian scholars were saying things about forcible conversion that would have been inadmissible in earlier centuries.[18]

At the same time, the analysis does not place sufficient emphasis on the impact of Donin's other arguments, and, far more important, it does not accord appropriate consideration to the profound conservatism that marks all law, and particularly religious law. Later attacks on the Talmud, including arguments for rescinding toleration of Jews because of it, drew primarily upon allegations of hostility toward Gentiles (which, to the extent that it is embedded in Talmudic Law, could not easily be removed by censorship), secondarily upon assertions of blasphemy against Jesus (which could be more readily deleted), and only marginally if at all upon the contention that Jews are adherents of "another law."[19]

The deeper problem is that toleration of Jews was a matter of settled doctrine in medieval canon law. It was hard to avoid the impression that Donin was arguing that Church authorities from Augustine through a long line of Popes were simply mistaken about a key issue. In the thirteenth century, at least, the inadmissibility of such a conclusion was so clear that it was in the Jewish interest to argue that banning the Talmud was tantamount to banning Judaism, and this point appears to have carried considerable weight in the ultimate decision to permit the pursuit of Talmudic study. In a very recent article which addresses the question of why Jews, who were widely associated with witchcraft, were hardly ever prosecuted for their sorcery, Anna Foa alludes to this point. It may be, she suggests, that the Church avoided prosecuting Jews for the "heresy of witchcraft" for the same reason that the "new law" argument was abandoned: either step would have resulted in the

---

[18] See, for example, R. Po-Chia Hsia, *The Myth of Ritual Murder: Jews and Magic in Reformation Germany* (New Haven, 1988), pp. 111–131.

[19] See my "Christians, Gentiles, and the Talmud: a Fourteenth-Century Jewish Response to the Attack on Rabbinic Judaism," in *Religionsgespräche im Mittelalter*, ed. by Bernard Lewis and Friedrich Niewöhner (Wiesbaden, 1992), pp. 115–130.

classification of "all the Jews, qua Jews," as heretics, thus breaking down the fundamental conceptual barriers that made the traditional toleration of Jews possible.[20]

As time passed, however, the force of the doctrine of toleration eroded even as it was ritualistically affirmed. The tepid reaction of the Church to anti-Jewish massacres and the evolving sense that expulsions do not violate accepted doctrine are cases in point. A striking illustration of the gaping inconsistencies that arose out of the tension between a tolerant doctrine and an intolerant society—not excluding the clergy themselves—leaps out at the reader of R. Po-Chia Hsia's account of the report of a papal commission on the trial of Jews for the ritual murder of Simon of Trent. Here the protective doctrine is not the overarching Augustinian argument for tolerating Jews but the Church's determination that the blood accusation is a libel.

On June 20, 1478, a papal bull was published pursuant to the commission's report.

> [Pope] Sixtus IV cleared Hinderbach [the prince-bishop involved in the case who was urging approval for the cult of Simon] of all suspicions; the commission of cardinals, who had diligently examined all pertinent records, concluded that the [torture-ridden] trial had been conducted in conformity with legal procedure. Sixtus praised the bishop's zeal but admonished Hinderbach, on his conscience, not to permit anything contrary to the 1247 Decretum of Innocent IV (which prohibited ritual murder trials) in promoting devotion to Simon nor to disobey the Holy See or canonical prescriptions. Moreover, Sixtus forbade any Christian, on this or any other occasion, without papal judgment, to kill or mutilate Jews, or extort money from them, or to prevent them from practicing their rites as permitted by law.[21]

In other words, Jews do not commit ritual murder, ritual murder trials are illegal, this ritual murder trial was conducted in accordance with

---

[20]   Anna Foa, "The Witch and the Jew: Two Alikes that Were Not the Same," in *From Witness to Witchcraft*, pp. 373–374. On "the persistence of traditional behavior," see also Stow, *Alienated Minority*, pp. 242–247. Alexander Patschowsky has reacted to Cohen's thesis by pointing to the fourteenth-century suggestion at high levels of the Church that killers of Jews be prosecuted as heretics; see his "Der 'Talmudjude': mittelalterlichen Ursprung eines neuzeitlichen Themas," in *Juden in der christlichen Umwelt während des späten Mittelalters*, ed. by Alfred Haverkampf and Franz-Josef Ziwes (Berlin, 1992), p. 22.

[21]   R. Po-Chia Hsia, *Trent, 1475: Stories of a Ritual Murder Trial* (New Haven, 1992), p. 127.

legal procedures, and one may promote devotion to Simon of Trent, whose only claim to devotion is that he was martyred in a ritual murder, provided that one does not affirm the reality of ritual murder.

Thus far, I have presented Cohen's thesis in terms that are narrowly focused on Christian familiarity with a Jewish text, but there is a broader dimension as well. Decades ago, Salo Baron proposed a relationship between national unification and medieval anti-Semitism, arguing that "single nationality states," driven both by incipient feelings of nationalism and the intolerance of a monolithic society toward outsiders, were far more likely to be hostile to their Jews. Since such states tended to develop in the central and late Middle Ages, it was in that period that anti-Semitism peaked.[22] Though Baron's thesis may help us understand national differences in the treatment of Jews, its arguably anachronistic appeal to nationalism and its failure to address the degree to which the transformation cut across national boundaries has marginalized it as a major explanatory strategy.

Cohen invokes a different sort of unity—the unity of Christendom as a whole. Thus, his emphasis on the Talmud is complemented by the argument that the friars' inclination to exclude the Jews was nourished by the growing sense that all of society is an organic Christian body. When the primacy of the Church as a unifying force began to decline, this inclination was not undermined; on the contrary, "the defensiveness characteristic of declining empires" reinforced the predisposition "to scrutinize the substance of contemporary Judaism and develop the theory of Jewish heresy."[23] I am somewhat uneasy about adopting a speculative argument which draws the same conclusion from an ascendant Church as from a declining one, particularly since at least some of the friars were severe critics rather than defenders of Rome. In any case, there is no intrinsic connection between the larger picture drawn by Cohen and the more specific argument which is the core of his extremely valuable study. Though both factors could of course be significant, the bulk of the work creates the impression that familiarity with the Talmud was the driving force behind the reevaluation of Jewish status. The concluding

---

[22] Salo W. Baron, *A Social and Religious History of the Jews*, 2nd ed., vol 11 (New York, London, and Philadelphia, 1967), pp. 192–201. This section of Baron's magnum opus summarizes a thesis that he had first proposed much earlier.

[23] *The Friars and the Jews*, pp. 248–264 (quotation on p. 255).

chapter appears to suggest that it was primarily Christian unity which inspired the impulse to exclude Jews, and the Talmud was the available means to do so.

— IV —

If only because of the prominence of the Jewish moneylender in popular images of the Jew, economic explanations of medieval anti-Semitism have always enjoyed considerable prominence. The central Middle Ages witnessed the development of a profit economy. To the extent that Jews had owned significant lands—and it is very difficult to assess the dimensions of such ownership—they tended to become urbanized and eventually engaged in moneylending to a degree considerably disproportionate to their numbers. Despite the unquestionable value of Joseph Shatzmiller's revisionist *Shylock Reconsidered*, which documents friendly relations between a beleaguered Jewish moneylender and his Christian customers, there is no doubt that this profession was not conducive to feelings of warmth and amity.[24]

Moreover, the transformation of the economic landscape was accompanied by the growth of a literate class. We have already encountered Moore's emphasis on the competition that this development engendered with the established literate class of the Jews. Even if we hesitate to speak of fierce competition, we can certainly recognize the impact of this change on the society's economic or administrative need for an increasingly marginalized minority. To the extent that even the undeveloped economy of the early Middle Ages had some need for an educated class—and it did—that need was partially met by Jews; the profit economy required a greater number of educated people, but it generated a sufficient supply from within the Christian community itself. This consideration may well loom large in explaining the welcome granted late medieval Jews in the economically and culturally undeveloped lands of central and Eastern Europe in the late Middle Ages, well after they had worn out their welcome in the developed countries of the West.

---

[24] J. Shatzmiller, *Shylock Reconsidered: Jews, Moneylending, and Medieval Society* (Berkeley, Los Angeles and London, 1990). Cf. William C. Jordan's beautifully formulated reservations in an essentially appreciative review: see *The Jewish Quarterly Review* 82 (1991): 221–223.

In his *Religious Poverty and the Profit Economy in Medieval Europe*,[25] Lester K. Little has attempted to weave a psychological explanation of anti-Semitism into the fabric of economic change. Christians, he says, experienced wrenching moral conflicts in confronting the profit economy. Guilt over usury, pawnbroking, even the sale of religious objects and outright theft was projected on to the Jews, who became "scapegoat[s] for Christian failure to adapt successfully to the profit economy." Jews were limited "to occupations thought by Christian moralists to be sinful and then harass[ed] . . . for doing their jobs."[26] It is unfair to ask for hard evidence for this sort of psychological assertion, and historiography would be a far less interesting, fecund, and instructive enterprise if we systematically refrained from such speculations. Still, in the absence of evidence one can react to this suggestion only by putting the question to one's informed intuitions. Since the Christian masses did not engage in the economic "sins" of which the Jews were accused, my own instincts do not permit me more than a whispered "perhaps."[27]

— V —

The most widely discussed theory of medieval anti-Semitism in the last few years is undoubtedly the one presented by Gavin Langmuir in his very impressive twin volumes, *History, Religion, and Anti-Semitism*, and *Toward A Definition of Anti-Semitism*.[28] Here too we find a psychological explanation, but it is rooted in much different considerations involving a redefinition of anti-Semitism itself and careful but creative speculation about the reaction of Christians to new developments in their own religion.

To Langmuir, hostility toward Jews before the twelfth century was an unremarkable version of ordinary xenophobia. Like all forms of bigotry, it exaggerated, distorted, and generalized real characteristics of the hated group. In the twelfth and thirteenth centuries, however, something frighteningly special occurred: Jews came to be subjected to accusations of a wholly chimerical sort. The entire group was stigmatized

[25] Ithaca, New York, 1978.
[26] *Religious Poverty*, pp. 54–56.
[27] It is true that Little (p. 54) also speaks of the projection of guilt feelings for violence, which the masses did perpetrate, but violence predates the central Middle Ages, and an appeal to specifically anti-Jewish violence raises the specter of circularity.
[28] Berkeley, Los Angeles, and London, 1990.

as ritual murderers, consumers of human flesh and blood, desecrators of hosts, and poisoners of wells despite the fact that not one Jew had ever been observed in the act of committing a single one of these crimes. Such accusations—and only such accusations—deserve the unique appellation "anti-Semitism."

What could have caused this new departure? Langmuir believes that Christians in the High Middle Ages, faced with profoundly difficult doctrines like transubstantiation, began to entertain grave doubts about the irrational demands made upon them by their evolving faith. One solution was to deflect these doubts by attributing irrational beliefs and behavior to Jews, whose very presence was a disturbing challenge to the dogmas with which Christians were struggling. It was not Christians, then, but Jews who came to embody irrationality *par excellence*.

There can be little question that some Christians were deeply troubled by the doctrine that the object which looked, felt, and tasted like bread was in fact the body of Jesus, and there is much plausibility in the suggestion that the host desecration charge, which in some cases implied that Jews themselves recognize the numinous character of this bread, could help to allay such doubts. As Miri Rubin put it in a study of this accusation, "The tale's force derived from the rich world of eucharistic knowledge and myth which was being imparted at the very heart of the religious culture, and it was bolstered by an ongoing tension between the eucharistic claims and the realities or appearances which most people apprehended in and around it."[29]

Langmuir, however, goes much further by placing the "chimerical" accusations in a separate category and connecting all of them to the inner doubts of Christians. Several scholars have noted that the sharp distinction between normal xenophobia and accusations without a shred of empirical basis is highly problematic. In lengthy reviews of Langmuir's book, Robert Stacey argued persuasively that by medieval criteria, the evidence that Jews commit ritual murder was not without rational foundation, and Marc Saperstein made the even stronger point that we cannot be certain even today that no Jew ever desecrated a host.[30]

---

[29] "Desecration of the Host," p. 184.

[30] Robert C. Stacey, "History, Religion, and Medieval Anti-Semitism: A Response to Gavin Langmuir," *Religious Studies Review* 20 (1994): 95–101; Marc Saperstein, "Medieval Christians and Jews: A Review Essay," *Shofar* 8:4 (Summer, 1990): 1–10. See also Chazan, *In the Year 1096*, pp. 143–146.

Indeed, although obtaining a consecrated host was no simple matter and there is no reason to believe that any medieval Jew bothered to take the risk, I have little doubt that if such a Jew had found himself in possession of this idolatrous object symbolizing the faith of his oppressors, it would not have fared very well in his hands.[31] Any definition whose validity is entirely dependent on the assumption that a particular act never happened even once is likely to find itself in a precarious position.

Moreover, as I noted in a much briefer review, even if we attribute antisemitic accusations to psychic insecurity—and the evidence for this is quite thin—that insecurity need not take the form of religious uncertainty. The turbulent world of late medieval Europe was not incapable of producing other forms of emotional dislocation. "Indeed, [Langmuir's] parallel discussion of modern times inevitably refers to inner tensions involving self-esteem and the role of the individual in society rather than traditional religious doubts."[32] Most recently, Anna Sapir Abulafia, without rejecting Langmuir's thesis for some Christians, argues that others were genuinely persuaded that the proper use of reason demonstrates the truth of Christianity so clearly that the Jews' failure to see this calls their very humanity into question. She sees no real evidence to regard this position as a result of "irrationality caused by suppressed doubts," and I think that she is right.[33]

Finally, let me emphasize that whatever my reservations about Langmuir's analysis, I do not reject on principle the position that the doctrine of transubstantiation may have had a significant effect on Jewish insecurity beyond the host desecration charge itself. Indeed, I am

[31]   In "Mission to the Jews," p. 589, I alluded to the story in Joseph Official's *Sefer Yosef ha-Meqanne*, ed. by Judah Rosenthal (Jerusalem, 1970), p. 14, which describes a Jew who was seen urinating on a cross and proceeded to produce a clever justification. See also Joseph Shatzmiller, "Mi-Gilluyeha shel ha-Antishemiyyut bi-Yemei ha-Beinayim: Ha'ashamat ha-Yehudim be-Hillul ha-Zelav", in *Mehqarim be-Toledot Am Yisrael ve-Erez Yisrael*, vol. 5 (Haifa, 1980), pp. 159–173, and the observations on the relationship between host desecration charges and other accusations of Jewish acts of desecration in Friedrich Lotter, "Hostienfrevelvorwurf und Blutwunderfälschung bei den Judenverfolgungen von 1298 ('Rindfleisch') und 1336–1338 ('Armleder')," in *Fälschungen im Mittelalter*, vol. 5 (Hannover, 1988), pp. 543–548. Yisrael Yuval, "Ha-Naqam ve-ha-Qelalah, ha-Dam ve-ha-'Alilah," *Zion* 58 (1992/93): 52, n. 77, properly endorses Lotter's position that not every accusation that Jews desecrated Christian sancta should automatically be rejected as unfounded.

[32]   *The American Historical Review* 96 (1991): 1498–1499.

[33]   Anna Sapir Abulafia, "Twelfth-Century Renaissance Theology and the Jews," in *From Witness to Witchcraft*, pp. 128–132. In general, see her *Christians and Jews in the Twelfth-Century Renaissance* (London and New York, 1995).

inclined to think that the belief that the body of Jesus was regularly sacrificed in Christian ritual greatly increased Christian receptivity to the assertion that Jews sacrificed his surrogates in their own perverted fashion. Where the belief in the "real presence" waned, the blood libel found considerably less fertile soil.

— VI —

If Langmuir's thesis has generated the broadest discussion of our issue in the last few years, a more narrowly focused article about the ritual murder charge has produced the most explosive one. About five years ago, Yisrael Yuval published a lengthy Hebrew essay with the intriguing title, "The Vengeance and the Curse, the Blood and the Libel."[34] What he had to say generated fascination, controversy, even anger, to the point where the journal in which the study appeared devoted a double issue to multifaceted responses followed by the author's rejoinder.[35]

In ruthlessly compressed form, Yuval's thesis makes the following argument:

1. The vengeance: A great divide separated Ashkenazic and Sephardic perceptions of the fate of Gentiles at the end of days. The former anticipated a vengeful redemption, the latter a proselytizing one. While Sephardim envisioned a world in which all nations will recognize the God of Israel, Ashkenazim elaborated a tradition attested in midrashic and liturgical texts which described how the blood of Jewish martyrs splatters and stains the royal cloak of the Lord until the time when He will avenge that blood in a campaign of devastation and annihilation against the Gentile world which had shed it. Despite the dearth of typical Messianic movements among Ashkenazim, they looked forward to this event with acute eschatological anticipation.

2. The curse: On the Day of Atonement and during the Passover Seder, the Ashkenazic liturgy was marked by curses against the Gentiles. This too is a manifestation of the specifically Ashkenazic vision of redemption and should probably be seen as a quasi-magical effort to hasten the much-awaited moment of divine vengeance. Northern European Jewry was not without its unique form of Messianic activism.

---

[34] "Ha-Naqam ve-ha-Qelalah, Ha-Dam ve-ha-'Alilah," *Zion* 58 (1992/93): 33–90.
[35] *Zion* 59: 2–3 (1994).

3. The blood: During the first crusade, some Rhineland Jews killed their own children. While the motive of preventing forced apostasy is self-evident, one chronicle approvingly recounts the story of a Jew who killed both himself and his children after the crusading army had already left as an act of atonement for his conversion during the earlier attack. To the chronicler, personal atonement is only part of the story. A key element in the narratives of such killings is the capacity of the victims' blood to arouse divine vengeance and hence hasten the redemption. In the later discourse, if not in the events themselves, the martyrs' death "was intended (*no'ad*) not merely to sanctify God's name but to arouse Him to revenge."[36]

4. The libel: No satisfactory explanation exists for the genesis of the ritual murder accusation. The widely held perception that it was born in England with the death of William of Norwich in 1144 is erroneous. A careful examination reveals that it originated in Würzburg in 1147 or even in Worms in 1096, that is, in Germany during the first or second crusade, while the earliest suggestion that William was killed by Jews did not emerge until 1149. There is good reason to speculate that a major impetus for this false accusation was the real behavior of Jews in killing their own children. Christians were probably aware of some aspects of points 1, 2, and 3, and they transformed the Jewish belief in divine eschatological vengeance and the "blood sacrifice" designed to arouse the Lord to carry out that vengeance into a libel in which the hostility of known child killers is directed toward more logical victims, namely, the children of the hated Christians themselves. The accusation of ritual murder, utterly false as it is, was extrapolated from genuine Jewish behavior.

This is a provocative thesis provocatively formulated. "The [Christian] narrative," writes Yuval, "sets forth Jewish murderousness and desire for revenge. These two motifs are not fabrications *ex nihilo*; rather, they follow from a distorted interpretation of Jewish behavior during the persecutions in 1096 and of the ritual of vengeance which was part of the Jews' eschatological conception. "This lie," he concludes, playing on a Rabbinic aphorism, "had legs."[37] It is hardly surprising that the article evoked a sharp response.

---

36   "Ha-Naqam," p. 70.
37   "Ha-Naqam," p. 86.

Let me react, once again with ruthless brevity, to the four elements of Yuval's thesis.

1. The vengeance: As Yuval's critics pointed out, and as he himself conceded in a clarification, even Ashkenazic Jews did not envision the complete liquidation of non-Jews at the end of days. In my view, the subject is more complex and more interesting than either Yuval or his critics have indicated, and I have elaborated in some detail in a forthcoming Hebrew article.[38] At the end of the day, however, the motif of eschatological vengeance is more than strong enough to sustain the initial step of the first element in Yuval's argument.

Nonetheless, significant obstacles stand in the way of his use even of this first element. To begin with, there is no concrete evidence that twelfth-century Christians, who never mention a Jewish belief about the eschatological destruction of Gentiles, knew anything about it.[39] Moreover, the real Ashkenazic doctrine, as Yuval concedes and even insists, was entirely passive; vengeance is the Lord's. Yuval's point is that this shift from the passive expectation of divine vengeance to active, eschatologically motivated revenge is precisely the Christian distortion. This is surely not impossible, but a speculative connection in the absence of any evidence that Christians even knew of the belief in question would be considerably more plausible if the hypothesized link were straightforward. The more distant the real conception is from its use by Christians, the less convincing the speculation becomes.

Yuval does point to one early Christian text which indeed connects Jewish murderousness with redemption, and it is none other than Thomas of Monmouth's account of the alleged ritual murder in Norwich. Here we are told that it is recorded in ancient Jewish writings that "without the shedding of blood the Jews can neither obtain their liberty nor ever return to their ancestral land." Standing alone, this sentence

---

[38] "'Al Tadmitam ve-Goralam shel ha-Goyim be-Sifrut ha-Pulmus ha-Ashkenazit," in *Yehudim mul ha-Zelav: Gezerot Tatnu Ba-Halakhah, Ba-Historiah, u-ba-Historiographiah*, ed. by Yom Tov Assis et al. (Jerusalem, 2000). [An English translation appears in this volume.]

[39] Let me make it clear that a request for evidence to support this and related hypotheses is not predicated on the antiquated assumption that the culture of Ashkenazic Jews and that of their Christian neighbors were sealed off from one another. I have discussed this interaction with references to recent scholarship in Gerald J. Blidstein, David Berger, Shnayer Z. Leiman, and Aharon Lichtenstein, *Judaism's Encounter with Other Cultures: Rejection or Integration?*, ed. by Jacob J. Schacter (Northvale, New Jersey and Jerusalem, 1997), pp. 117–125.

must surely capture the attention of a reader who has been introduced to the "vengeful redemption," though even at this point there is a sense of profound dissonance since God's eschatological destruction of Gentiles is not a condition of redemption but a part of the final scenario.

Whatever connection may nonetheless be entertained is profoundly shaken by the continuation of Thomas's account:

> Hence it was decided by them in antiquity that every year they will sacrifice a Christian in some part of the world to the most high God to the scorn and disgrace of Christ, so that in this fashion they will avenge their suffering on him whose death is the reason why they are excluded from their homeland and are exiled as slaves in foreign lands.[40]

By this point, we realize that the text knows nothing of a Jewish belief that Gentiles will be killed *en masse* at the end of days. Though Yuval cites Thomas's report as a reflection of the vengeful redemption, he might have been better advised to see it primarily as a distortion of the belief that the death of Jewish martyrs arouses divine wrath against Gentiles, though here too only the first sentence is even of potential value. By the end of the passage, it becomes evident that we have no indication that Christians knew anything of this belief.

To utilize this text, then, Yuval must assume multiple distortions: With respect to the vengeful redemption, killing by God becomes killing by Jews, eschatological killing becomes contemporary killing, mass killing becomes the annual killing of one person; with respect to "the blood ritual," Jewish children become Christian children, and killing to arouse divine wrath becomes killing to counteract the effect of Jesus' death. Again—all this is possible, but the larger the magnitude and quantity of the distortions, the weaker the argument. It requires a monumental stretch to maintain that even this text is evidence of Christian familiarity with either of the Jewish beliefs in question.

2. The curse: As Yuval indicates, the earliest evidence that Christians knew of the liturgical curses dates from 1248, a full century after the beginning of the ritual murder accusation. It is not even clear, especially in light of Yuval's response to one of his critics, that in the final analysis he even argues that this component of the "ritual of vengeance" played

---

[40]   *The Life and Miracles of St. William of Norwich*, ed. by A. Jessop and M. R. James, (Cambridge, 1896), Book 2, pp. 93–94. (I have made some modifications in Jessop and James's translation.) Yuval discusses the passage in "Ha-Naqam," p. 82.

a role in creating the accusation;[41] in any event, it is the least important element in his argument.

3. The blood: Christians certainly knew that some crusade-era Jews had killed their own children. The force of Yuval's argument, however, depends on considerably more than this, namely, that the Jewish chroniclers understood these killings as part of an effort to arouse divine wrath against Christians and thus hasten their eschatological annihilation and that at least some vague awareness of this interpretation penetrated Christian society.

The key issue is that of intent, and there is something of a slippery nature to Yuval's presentation of this issue. If all he means is that the chroniclers believed that the *effect* of the killings would or might be that divine wrath would be aroused, he is on firm ground—but his larger argument is dramatically weakened. We would again have to assume a major distortion—in this case a quantum leap—in the Christian perception of a Jewish belief: Although in fact no Jew ever suggested that martyrs killed children *so that* God would take revenge against those who indirectly precipitated, but did not carry out, the killings, Christians mistakenly assumed that this peculiar logic is what drove the Jews' behavior and then took the next crucial step by making Christians the direct victims.

In fact, Yuval almost surely aims to make the stronger argument by maintaining that the chroniclers did see the killings as *designed* to arouse divine vengeance, that is, that Jews killed their own children—in at least one instance when there was no real need to do so—so that God should get angry at Christians. He writes that the belief in a connection between the blood of Jewish martyrs and such vengeance "makes it possible to hasten [the redemption]."[42] We have already encountered his assertion that the death of martyrs "was intended . . . to arouse [God] to revenge."[43] And he speaks about "such intentions" attributed to the martyrs by the chroniclers.[44]

Both Ezra Fleisher and, even more clearly, Mordechai Breuer pointed out the absence of any evidence that the chroniclers assigned

---

41   See his remarks in *Zion* 59 (1994): 399–400.
42   "Ha-Naqam," pp. 65–66.
43   "Ha-Naqam," p. 70. *No'ad* can just possibly have the softer meaning of "was destined," but this does not appear to be the sense of the passage.
44   "Ha-Naqam," p. 68.

this motivation to the martyrs. In his responses, Yuval appears to miss the crucial distinction between the motivation of martyrdom and its eschatological effect, so that he believes that he has refuted the criticism by pointing to the motif of the stained robe which arouses God to action.[45] Although the chroniclers call upon God to avenge the blood of his people, there is not the slightest indication that they believed that Jews killed their children for the purpose of eliciting this vengeance, nor does any Christian source ever hint at such a motive.

4. The libel: Though Yuval does point to some Christian sources that draw a connection between the Jewish belief in eschatological vengeance and the blood libel, these are extremely late. Once the accusation existed, Christians attempted to buttress it using whatever means were available to them; as early as the thirteenth century we find citations of biblical "proof texts" which no one would seriously identify as factors in generating the libel.[46] Yuval's argument for shifting the locus of the earliest ritual murder accusation to Germany is suggestive but far from compelling. As for the early Christian reactions to the killing of Jewish children, some were unrelievedly hostile, but some were remarkably understanding.[47]

In sum, early Christian sources make no reference to the Jewish belief in eschatological vengeance, a belief which in any event did not involve Jewish activism. There is no evidence that twelfth-century Christians knew of the curse, which is in any case the least significant element in Yuval's thesis. There is no evidence that they knew that Jews kill their

---

[45]   *Zion* 59 (1994): 383–384, 398.

[46]   See the *Nizzahon Vetus* in my edition, *The Jewish-Christian Debate in the High Middle Ages* (Philadelphia, 1979; softcover ed., Northvale, New Jersey, 1996), #16, Hebrew section, pp. 14–15, English section, p. 54, and *Sefer Yosef ha-Meqanne*, pp. 53–54.

[47]   A survey of the Christian material was presented by Mary Minty, "Qiddush Hashem be-'einei Nozrim be-Germaniah bi-Yemei ha-Beinayim," *Zion* 59 (1994): 209–266.

The most insightful Christian remark appears in a fourteenth-century text, but its force was somewhat obscured by a mistranslation in the article. *The Cronica Rheinhardsbrunnensis* (*MGHS* 30/31, Hannover, 1896, p. 642) reads as follows: "Dicitur eciam, quod dum Iudei viderent non posse evadere manus occisorum, quod pro quadam sanctitate secundum legem ipsorum, ne traderentur in manibus incircumsorum, se mutuo interfecerunt." Minty (p. 216) translates: "It is also said that once the Jews saw that they could not save themselves from their killers, they voluntarily killed one another for a certain sanctity rather than fall into the hands of the uncircumcised." The word "voluntarily" is not in the Latin. What the text says is that "they killed one another for a certain sanctity in accordance with their own law," an absolutely accurate presentation of the martyrs' view that they were dying to fulfill the halakhic requirement of sanctifying the name of God.

children to hasten the vengeful redemption (or that Jewish chroniclers believe this), and there is good reason for them not to know this since it is not true. They do know that Jews killed their children in order to prevent their conversion to Christianity. And that is all. Is this enough to allow a historian to speculate that such knowledge could have contributed to producing the accusation of ritual murder? Yes. But it is a speculation that could have been—and was—offered before Yuval's argument,[48] and it is a far weaker speculation than the article attempts to present.

While I remain unpersuaded by the central thesis of this essay and recoil from some of its rhetoric, I would be ungrateful if I did not acknowledge how much I learned from it. Rarely has an article generated as much stimulating discussion—some of it sterile, but some of it fructifying—of a crucial subject in the history of medieval Jewry.

— VII —

Finally, we need to look at a large question which cuts across the boundaries of the varying interpretations that we have examined. Did the upsurge in anti-Semitism in the latter half of the Middle Ages move from the top down or from the bottom up? Part of the problem arises from the difficulty of defining "top" and "bottom." Relevant components of medieval society include popes and kings, canon lawyers and upper clergy, mendicant friars and parish priests, knights and bureaucrats, merchants, serfs, and the urban poor. Cohen's emphasis on theology clearly points to the upper, educated end of the spectrum, while Landes makes a point of stressing the popular nature of the eleventh-century hostility.[49] Moore has been particularly sharp in his denunciation of the view that anti-Semitism was "popular" in origin, but because he sees knights and lower clergy as distinct from the "populus," his denial that the masses played a key role in the development of Judeophobia does not necessarily become an emphasis on society's elite. The distinction between the highest echelons of the Church and the lower clergy is well illustrated by their respective attitudes to the charge of ritual murder; the official Church resisted it, but the accusation in Norwich as well as the first genuine blood libel, which occurred in Fulda in 1235,

48 See his gracious comment (*Zion* 59 [1994]: 392) acknowledging a tentative suggestion by Ivan Marcus in *Jewish History* 1 (1986).
49 "The Massacres of 1010," pp. 93–96.

resulted in large measure from the initiatives of clerics.[50] As to the "populus," the association between the Devil and the Jews, complete with physical deformities and Jewish stench, gives off the odor of mass superstition.[51]

It is especially important to recognize that once a belief has entered society, it takes on a life of its own. It spawns new beliefs. It may be an effect, but it becomes a cause. Self-evident as this may be, failure to respect this point has led to historiographic anomalies of the most serious sort, not least of which was the refusal of classical Marxism to recognize non-economic causes in history. Even if certain ideologies were spawned by class interests, it violates common sense to argue that children brought up with a set of beliefs cannot be motivated by them. In our own area of concern, it seems to me that Langmuir's theoretical discussion in *History, Religion, and Anti-Semitism* is marred by a refusal to recognize this possibility. Thus, he argues on principle that it is inherently problematic to appeal to religious belief—rather than "normal empirical explanation"—to account for historical developments such as anti-Semitism, as if such beliefs, even if initially generated by "normal, empirical" causes, cannot produce further effects.[52]

Moore correctly observes that "once a pattern of persecution has been established and its victims identified," it is easy to understand why popular sentiment would demand appropriate action.[53] Similarly, Stacey pointed out in his lecture on the expulsion from England that people who believed that Jews regularly kidnapped and murdered Christian

50   On Fulda, Yuval (*Zion* 59 [1994]: 397, 399) points to the study by B. Diestelkampf, "Der Vorwurf des Ritualmordes gegen Juden vor dem Hofgericht Kaiser Friedrichs II. in Jahre 1236," in *Religiöse Devianz*, ed. by D. Simon (Frankfurt/M, 1990).

51   In the absence of new interpretations of the Jewish association with Satan, I have not addressed the subject here. This does not mean that I do not consider it highly significant; see my brief remarks in *History and Hate*, pp. 7–8, 11–12. For my reaction to B. Netanyahu's recent work on anti-Semitism in late medieval Spain (*The Origins of the Inquisition* [New York, 1995]), see my review in *Commentary* 100:4 (October: 1995): 55–57.

     Two important, recent books which address Christian anti-Semitism in the Middle Ages did not fit into the parameters of this lecture, but I would be remiss if I did not acknowledge them. Mark Cohen's *Under Crescent and Cross: The Jews in the Middle Ages* (Princeton, 1994) draws upon its author's great expertise in the Islamic world to place our subject in a comparative context, and the first volume of Steven T. Katz's *The Holocaust in Historical Context* (New York, 1994) contains a book-length treatment of medieval anti-Semitism which is balanced, comprehensive, and remarkably erudite.

52   See *History, Religion, and Anti-Semitism*, p. 9, and esp. pp. 42–46.

53   *Formation of a Persecuting Society*, p. 108.

children clearly had every reason to want those Jews as far removed from their families as possible. We readily recognize that by modern times, Jew-hatred had become so deeply ingrained that for many people, the evaporation of old "causes" required the substitution of new ones. In the Middle Ages as well, new resentments would naturally be directed at familiar enemies, and these resentments would reinforce the enmity. Precisely because causes produce effects which produce further effects, we *may* be able to speak of a primary cause for an eleventh or twelfth or thirteenth century transformation, but we cannot speak of *the* cause, perhaps not even the primary cause, of the increased hostility to Jews in a period as extensive as the late Middle Ages.

An intensification of popular piety, a changing economic reality, political, social and economic struggle among nobility, kings, and popular movements, Christian familiarity with post-biblical Jewish texts, the growing prominence of the Devil and his minions, naked fear, millenarian expectations and a triumphalist Christian mission, perhaps the exclusiveness produced by national or Church-centered unity and the anxiety engendered by the doctrine of transubstantiation—all these contributed to the erosion of the security of the Jews. Of course we need to evaluate the relative significance of one or another factor in specific environments, whether chronological, geographic or personal, and sometimes we may conclude that a particular proposal is simply wrong. But embracing all those that we deem relevant is not a counsel of despair or a failure of nerve. Not only does history resist controlled experiments in which we can isolate one factor to see if it works; large historical developments are rarely moved by isolated factors to begin with. We would do well to remember Burke's analogy—proposed for quite different purposes—between the complexity of society and that of the human organism. A candid look at the tangled web of our own psyches is a salutary reminder of the humility with which we need to approach the explanation of so durable, so protean, and so daunting a phenomenon as anti-Semitism in medieval Christian Europe.

A GENERATION OF SCHOLARSHIP ON JEWISH-CHRISTIAN INTERACTION IN THE MEDIEVAL WORLD [1]

From: *Tradition* 38:2 (Summer, 2004): 4–14.

To what extent has research in the past three decades changed our understanding of Jewish-Christian interaction in the pre-modern period?

To what degree has the assumption that Jewish-Christian relations were dominated by the facts of irreconcilable theological differences, legal discrimination, and outbreaks of violence obscured the complexities of these relations?

How have insights from other disciplines shed new light on Jewish-Christian interactions? In particular, how has the scholarly awareness of differences between "high" and "low" culture contributed to interpretation of these relations?

How have the Holocaust, on the one hand, and the founding of the State of Israel, on the other, affected modern historiography of Jewish-Christian relations?

Which aspects of Jewish-Christian relations remain least understood?

This assignment has been a salutary and humbling experience. We all pay lip service to the recognition that history is rewritten in every generation, but if we did not believe that something of our own contributions would endure, we would, I think, lose much of the drive that impels us to do our work. The study of medieval Jewish-Christian relations is after all a relatively small field, and yet a hard look at the

---

[1]   At the conference of the Association for Jewish Studies in December, 2001, I was one of three historians of medieval Jewish-Christian relations asked to address a series of questions about the state of the field. It is a pleasure to present a written, annotated version of my remarks as a tribute to Rabbi Emanuel Feldman, whose learning, commitment and stylistic flair have preserved and enhanced the tradition of this distinguished journal.

state of that field three decades ago reveals a dramatically different, often thoroughly alien landscape.

This is especially true of Northern Europe in the Middle Ages. Truly great scholars of the late nineteenth and early twentieth centuries— people whose command of classical Jewish and Christian sources renders us all *ammei ha-aretz* by comparison—had begun to examine the relationship through a historical lens: Heinrich Graetz, Avraham Berliner, David Kaufmann, Samuel Krauss, Adolf and Samuel Posnanski, and more. By 1970, which happens to be the year I received my doctorate, Yitzhak Baer's work on *Hasidei Ashkenaz* and Northern France,[2] Judah Rosenthal's editions and studies of polemical works,[3] Solomon Grayzel's volume on papal documents,[4] Bernhard Blumenkranz's collection and analysis of pre-crusade Christian materials,[5] several chapters of Salo Baron's *History*, the early studies of Frank E. Talmage,[6] and Jacob Katz's seminal, remarkably insightful, though largely impressionistic *Exclusiveness and Tolerance* had begun to set a new agenda. Nonetheless, I think it is fair to say that the prevailing impression of Northern European Jewry in the High Middle Ages continued to be one of an insular community, hostile to and ignorant of the society that surrounded it.

Both new information and new methodologies have produced a significant reassessment. In the last generation, arguments have been presented for a variety of theses that would have seemed implausible thirty years ago: that Northern European Jews discussed biblical texts with Christians in non-polemical contexts,[7] that Jewish exegesis was

---

2   "Ha-Megammah ha-Datit-Hevratit shel Sefer Hasidim," *Zion* 3 (1938): 1–50; "Rashi ve-ha-Meziut ha-Historit shel Zemanno," *Tarbiz* 20 (1949): 320–332, and more.

3   Jacob ben Reuben, *Milhamot Hashem* (Jerusalem, 1963); Joseph Official, *Sefer Yosef ha-Meqanne* (Jerusalem, 1970); the studies collected in Rosenthal, *Mehqarim u-Meqorot* (Jerusalem, 1967), and more.

4   *The Church and the Jews in the XIIIth Century* (Philadelphia, 1933). See now the expanded version edited by Kenneth Stow (New York, 1989).

5   *Les Auteurs Chrétiens Latins du Moyen Age sur les Juifs et le Judaisme* (Paris, La Haye, 1963); *Juifs et Chrétiens dans le Monde Occidental, 430–1096* (Paris, 1960).

6   "Rabbi David Kimhi as Polemicist," *Hebrew Union College Annual* 38 (1967): 213–235; "An Hebrew Polemical Treatise, Anti-Cathar and anti-Orthodox," *Harvard Theological Review* 60 (1967): 323–348. These and some of his later studies have now been collected in Frank Ephraim Talmage, *Apples of Gold in Settings of Silver: Studies in Medieval Jewish Exegesis and Polemics*, ed. by Barry Dov Walfish (Toronto, 1999).

7   Aryeh Grabois, "The Hebraica Veritas and Jewish-Christian Intellectual Relations in the Twelfth Century," *Speculum* 50 (1975): 613–634.

profoundly influenced by both the Jewish-Christian confrontation and the intellectual atmosphere of the Twelfth-Century Renaissance,[8] that sharp polemical exchanges, sometimes initiated by Jews, took place on the streets and even in homes,[9] that Jews were sorely tempted by Christianity and converted more often than we imagined,[10] that Jewish religious ceremonies arose and developed in conscious and subconscious interaction with Christian rituals,[11] that martyrdom itself reflects a religious environment shared with the dominant culture and even an awareness of its evolving theology,[12] that the crusades were not a significant turning point,[13] and that images of self and other were formed through constant, shifting interaction.[14]

This incomplete list concentrates on the North and refers almost exclusively to Jewish reactions to Christian society. If we expand our purview to Spain and to Christian perceptions and policies, a different set of suggestive, largely new questions emerges. Were the conversos really crypto-Jews?[15] How did Jews utilize their growing historical

8   A mini-literature has grown up around this theme. See the overall argument presented in Elazar Touitou, "Shitato ha-Parshanit shel ha-Rashbam al Reqa ha-Mezi'ut ha-Historit shel Zemanno," in *Iyyunim be-Sifrut Hazal ba-Mikra u-be-Toledot Yisrael: Muqdash li-Prof. E. Z. Melamed*, ed. by Y. D. Gilat et al. (Ramat Gan, 1982), pp. 48–74. For a particularly good discussion containing some important methodological observations, see Avraham Grossman, "Ha-Pulmus ha-Yehudi ha-Nozri ve-ha-Parshanut ha-Yehudit la-Miqra be-Zarfat ba-Meah ha-Yod-Bet," *Zion* 91 (1986): 29–60.

9   See my "Mission to the Jews and Jewish-Christian Contacts in the Polemical Literature of the High Middle Ages," *American Historical Review* 91 (1986): 576–591.

10 Avraham Grossman, *Hakhmei Zarfat ha-Rishonim* (Jerusalem, 1995), pp. 502–503.

11 Ivan G. Marcus, *Rituals of Childhood* (New Haven, 1996); Yisrael Yuval, *Shenei Goyim be-Bitnekh: Yehudim ve-Nozrim—Dimmuyim Hadadiyyim* (Tel Aviv, 2000), pp. 219–266.

12 See most recently Shmuel Shepkaru, "To Die for God: Martyrs' Heaven in Hebrew and Latin Crusade Narratives," *Speculum* 77 (2002): 311–341.

13 Robert Chazan, *European Jewry and the First Crusade* (Berkeley, 1987), pp. 197–222.

14 See my "Al Tadmitam ve-Goralam shel ha-Goyim be-Sifrut ha-Pulmus ha-Ashkenazit," in *Yehudim mul ha-Tselav: Gezerot Tatn'u ba-Historiah u-ba-Historiographiah*, ed. by Yom Tov Assis et al. (Jerusalem, 2000), pp. 74–91. Cf. Robert Chazan, *Medieval Stereotypes and Modern Antisemitism* (Berkeley, 1997). On this and related matters, see now Ivan Marcus, "A Jewish-Christian Symbiosis: The Culture of Early Ashkenaz," in *Cultures of the Jews: A New History*, ed. by David Biale (New York, 2002), pp. 449–518.

15 This question has produced a significant body of historiography since the late 1960's, especially in the wake of B. Netanyahu's *The Marranos of Spain from the Late XIVth to the Early XVIth Century According to Contemporary Hebrew Sources* (New York, 1966). For a brief statement of my own perspective, see my review of Netanyahu's *The Origins of the Inquisition in Fifteenth Century Spain* (New York, 1995) in *Commentary* 100:4 (October, 1995): 55–57.

sophistication, developed in significant measure through exposure to Christian thought, in responding to Christianity?[16] Can we still speak of fifteenth-century Spanish Jewry as a community suffering decline and demoralization?[17] Does Christian familiarity with the Talmud explain policies of intolerance?[18] Does the charge of ritual murder emerge out of a Christian interpretation of real Jewish behavior?[19] Must our understanding of the treatment of Jews be rethought in light of attitudes toward other "others": Muslims, witches, lepers, heretics, homosexuals, even a non-other other—women?[20] Is there a deep difference between Crusade-era hostility toward Jews and the arguably irrational sort manifested in charges of ritual murder, host desecration, and well poisoning?[21] Does the close examination of specific histories require us to jettison our perception of an overarching pattern in which the condition of Jews deteriorates from the early to the late Middle Ages?[22]

All these questions and contentions were first framed—or framed in significantly new forms—during the last three decades. I cannot, of course, address them all in the purview of this presentation, and so let

---

[16]   Ram Bar Shalom, *Dimmuy ha-Tarbut ha-Nozrit ba-Toda'ah ha-Historit shel Yehudei Sefarad u-Provence (Ha-Me'ah ha-Shtem-Esreh ad ha-Hamesh-Esreh)*, Ph. D dissertation (Tel Aviv University, 1996). See too my "On the Uses of History in Medieval Jewish Polemic against Christianity: The Search for the Historical Jesus," in *Jewish History and Jewish Memory: Essays in Honor of Yosef Hayim Yerushalmi*, ed. by E. Carlebach, J. M. Efron, and D. N. Myers (Hanover and London, 1998), pp. 25–39. On Jewish-Christian interaction in Spain, see now Benjamin Gampel, "The Transformation of Sephardic Culture in Christian Iberia," in *Cultures of the Jews* (above, n. 13), pp. 389–447.

[17]   Eleazar Gutwirth, "Towards Expulsion: 1391–1492," in Elie Kedourie, ed., *Spain and the Jews* (London, 1992), pp. 51–73.

[18]   Jeremy Cohen, *The Friars and the Jews* (Ithaca and London, 1982). Cf. my review in *American Historical Review* 88 (1983): 93.

[19]   Yisrael Yuval, "Ha-Naqam ve-ha-Qelalah, ha-Dam ve-ha-Alilah," *Zion* 58 (1992/93): 33–90, and the reactions in *Zion* 59:2–3 (1994).

[20]   R. I. Moore, *The Formation of a Persecuting Society* (Oxford, 1987).

[21]   Gavin Langmuir, *History, Religion and Antisemitism* and *Toward a Definition of Antisemitism* (Berkeley, 1990). For reactions to this thesis, see Robert C. Stacey, "History, Religion and Medieval Antisemitism: A Response to Gavin Langmuir," *Religious Studies Review* 20 (1994): 95–101; Marc Saperstein, "Medieval Christians and Jews: A Review Essay," *Shofar* 8:4 (Summer, 1990): 1–10; Robert Chazan, *In the Year 1096: The First Crusade and the Jews* (Philadelphia, 1996), pp. 143–146; David Berger, *From Crusades to Blood Libels to Expulsions: Some New Approaches to Medieval Antisemitism*. The Second Victor J. Selmanowitz Memorial Lecture, Touro College Graduate School of Jewish Studies (1997), pp. 14–16.

[22]   David Nirenberg, *Communities of Violence* (Princeton, 1996).

me concentrate on just a few central points regarding cultural interaction that may be methodologically fruitful.

Influence is notoriously difficult to pin down. To return to Northern European Jews, we can now take it for granted that they were acutely aware of many Christian ceremonies and symbols. Festive religious processions wended their way through the streets, and routine, everyday activities brought Jews into contact with Christian discourse. Popular, hostile euphemisms for Christian sancta—chalice (*kelev*), priest (*gallah*), sermon (*nibbu'ah*), church (*to'evah*), saints (*kedeshim*), the host (*lehem mego'al*), baptismal water (*mayim zedonim*), the holy sepulcher (*shuha*), not to speak of Peter (*Peter Hamor*), Jesus (*ha-Taluy*), and Mary (*Haria*)—testify to the ubiquitous presence of these symbols in the daily life of Ashkenazic Jews. The very hostility in these terms leads anyone attempting to assess Christian influence on expressions of Jewish culture and thought into a methodological thicket where psychology, halakha, and theology meet.

I do not believe that any medieval Jew, Ashkenazic or Sephardic, would have explicitly said, even to him or herself, *Kammah na'ah avodah zarah zo*: "How lovely is this quintessentially Christian religious practice or idea; let us import it into our faith." The refusal to do this was rooted only secondarily in formal strictures prohibiting imitation of Gentile statutes; it spoke to elemental instincts.[23] Moreover, I am not persuaded that Ashkenazic Jews—even those who specialized in interfaith confrontations—actually read Christian literary works other than the New Testament. They do not cite such works either explicitly or by convincing implication, and this silence counts. Even the Southern French case that I noted in the early 1970s—Jacob ben Reuben's familiarity with a polemical collection, including selections from Gilbert Crispin—is exceptional and results from his having been handed the collection by his Christian interlocutor.[24] The familiarity with Christian works in the writings of R. Elhanan b. Yaqar of London is so atypical that it is nothing less than stunning.[25]

---

[23]   On the importance of instincts in this discourse see my "Jacob Katz on Jews and Christians in the Middle Ages," in *The Pride of Jacob: Essays on Jacob Katz and his Work*, ed. by Jay M. Harris (Cambridge, Mass., 2002), pp. 41–63.

[24]   See my "Gilbert Crispin, Alan of Lille, and Jacob ben Reuben: A Study in the Transmission of Medieval Polemic," *Speculum* 49 (1974): 34–47.

[25]   G. Vajda, "De quelques infiltrations chrétiennes dans l'oeuvre d'un auteur anglo-juif du XIIIe siècle," *Archives d'Histoire Doctrinale et Littéraire du Moyen Age* 28 (1961): 15–34.

Thus, we must be cognizant of a complex of questions when we approach the issue at hand: Is the practice or belief or symbol or exegetical approach likely to have been known to Jews? How evident was it to an outsider? How clear would its religious, i.e., its specifically Christian, character be? In this particular instance, can we plausibly posit unconscious influence? Would this practice be expected to trigger reflexive Jewish aversion if its Christian character were understood? If the religious character of the practice is evident, do classic Jewish texts nonetheless provide enough basis for adopting it that a Jew attracted by it could persuade himself and others that it is really Jewish after all? Perhaps a Jewish text weighs so powerfully in favor of this practice or belief that Jews really affirmed it for internal reasons—not through Christian influence but *despite* full awareness of its Christian resonance. Does a Jewish practice change the Christian original sufficiently that intentional religious competition or symbolic inversion can plausibly be proposed? Since Jews and Christians examined history, studied sacred texts, and molded their religious lives in the context of a common biblical tradition and essentially monotheistic theology, can the phenomenon under discussion be reasonably understood as a result of independent development?

Much more rarely, such questions can even be relevant where our focus is on Christian behaviors or beliefs. Thus, the assertion that Christians developed their views about Jewish ritual murder in response to Jewish actions during the Crusades and even to Jewish prayers and eschatological conceptions requires a prior assessment of the likelihood that Christians were aware of these conceptions at the relevant time. If such awareness seems implausible, so do conclusions drawn from it.[26]

To some degree, these criteria generate a question that might be described as an analytical chicken and egg. Even if I have no independent knowledge that Jews knew a Christian doctrine, and even if I would consider such knowledge intrinsically implausible, I may still be persuaded by connections that seem so striking that I will posit such knowledge. Still, in such a case the burden of argument (there are few "proofs" in this discourse) is heavily on the advocate of the hypothesis of influence or reaction. It must be acknowledged, of course, that if I am indeed

---

[26] See my observations on Yuval's "Ha-Naqam ve-ha-Qelalah" in *From Crusades to Blood Libels to Expulsions*, pp. 16–22.

persuaded by striking connections in more than a few instances, I would have to reassess the threshold of probable influence when examining new questions.

So far, all this has been highly abstract, and I have to provide some concrete examples to flesh out these principles, though to dwell on any of them is beyond the scope of this presentation.

With respect to *Hasidei Ashkenaz*: The movement itself is now seen as a manifestation of a largely internal Jewish dynamic.[27] Penances, however, are a different matter. Christian self-mortification was almost certainly known to Jews, its Christian character was clear enough to raise warning flags, there were enough Jewish sources to make the argument for the Jewishness of the practice but not enough for this to be an internal, immanent development, and it could serve subconsciously and perhaps even consciously as an affirmation of superior Jewish religious devotion in the face of Christian piety. Weighing all this, I am inclined to think that influence, or response, is highly likely.[28]

With respect to biblical exegesis: Both Jews and Christians were sufficiently familiar with the approaches of the other for influence—in both directions—to be plausible. Religiously neutral aspects of the twelfth-century Christian cultural efflorescence have sufficient affinities to certain predilections of *pashtanim* (e.g., interpreting according to *derekh eretz*) to have inspired them without their seeing these predilections as deriving from a specifically Christian environment. I am convinced that polemical encounters were considerably more common, even among ordinary people, than we used to think, and Jews may well have so internalized their polemical insistence on straightforward interpretation that they applied this approach ruthlessly even in works directed at their own coreligionists.

In matters of exegetical detail, polemical motives are occasionally obvious, occasionally likely, and occasionally asserted implausibly. When a Jewish commentary is alleged to counter a Christian interpretation never (or hardly ever) cited by Jewish polemicists, and not prominent

---

27 Haym Soloveitchik, "Three Themes in the Sefer Hasidim," *AJS Review* 1 (1976): 311–57. See too Ivan Marcus, *Piety and Society* (Leiden, 1981).

28 See Talya Fishman, "The Penitential System of Hasidei Ashkenaz and the Problem of Cultural Boundaries," *The Journal of Jewish Thought and Philosophy* 8 (1999): 201–229. Cf. my remarks in *The Jewish-Christian Debate in the High Middle Ages* (Philadelphia, 1979), p. 27, and in "Al Tadmitam ve-Goralam shel ha-Goyim" (above, n. 13), pp. 78–79.

in Christian exegesis of the period, we would do well to be wary. Here is an example proposed in the scholarly literature that strikes me as a close call: Did Rashbam's assertion that Moses dropped rather that threw down the tablets result from his desire to counter the view that the first tablets represent the Old Law, which is to be superseded? The Christian interpretation is not particularly prominent; it is not, however, altogether obscure either, and Rashbam's comment does say *"darsheni."* To take another concrete example, this time from a passage where polemical sensibilities are obvious, I do not accept the widespread view that Rashi adopted a vicarious atonement reading of Isaiah 53 as a result of historical considerations relating to the first Crusade.[29] Here, vicarious atonement is adopted despite its evident Christological valence because of internal exegetical considerations reinforced by sufficient rabbinic precedent to justify the doctrine itself.

With respect to the Tosafists: The similarity between the dialectical methods they used and those of more or less contemporary Christian theologians and canon lawyers are striking indeed, but significant Christian familiarity with talmudic discourse or substantial Jewish knowledge of scholastic discussions and the concordance of discordant canons appears very low. If one were to be persuaded of influence, this would be a case of being swept away by a parallelism that is difficult to attribute to coincidence. Conflicting, very powerful considerations leave us in limbo.

With respect to popular practices and rituals: My inclination, for reasons already noted, is to privilege immanent development, but here too I take very seriously the possibility of influence and response where the Christian parallel, as in the case of certain "rituals of childhood,"[30] was not glaringly evident to the medieval Jew. Here "high" and "low" culture intersect, but the essential methodology does not, I think, change fundamentally even though one's verdict in a specific case must consider the knowledge and sensibilities of the presumed objects of influence.

I have already alluded to the complex interaction between attraction and hostility. Here as elsewhere I am inclined to think that the most

---

[29] Joel Rembaum, "The Development of a Jewish Exegetical Tradition Regarding Isaiah 53," *Harvard Theological Review* 75 (1982):289–311.
[30] Marcus (above, n. 10).

relevant discipline outside history is psychology, where an understanding of the dynamics of fascination and hate, of self and other, is central to illuminating our concerns. Since both history and psychology are among the most imperialistic of disciplines—there really are no humanistic or social scientific pursuits that are not part of the historian's craft, and no study of human activity is alien to psychology—this assertion may be a truism. But whatever disciplinary labels we assign—cultural studies, anthropology, social history—we are considerably more sensitive to the crucial insight that in certain circumstances subcultures can interact and influence one another despite a sense of existential difference, even of mutual hatred.

With respect to Christian attitudes to Jews, I will be much more brief, relying on my essay on new approaches to medieval anti-Semitism.[31] Still, it is self-evident that psychological assertions play a central role in this discourse as well. A case in point is the distinction put forth in the last decade between irrational and other forms of medieval anti-Semitism.[32] Even if we can satisfy ourselves that late medieval Christians were insecure in their beliefs, a proposition that seems plausible with respect to transubstantiation but much less well established on a larger scale, the assertion that they coped with the perceived irrationality of their own faith by attributing irrational behavior to Jews does not follow ineluctably. I do not know whether such coping mechanisms can be firmly established through psychological research, but the possibility of such investigation—even though it would not be wholly determinative for our purposes—is intriguing.

With respect to anti-Jewish attitudes and policies, the question of high and low culture has played a particularly significant role. Approaches that privilege—or blame—the former include the assertion that Christian intellectuals reacted to a perceived Jewish challenge,[33] the emphasis on the Christian discovery of the Talmud,[34] and concentration on the evolution of Church law regarding Jews.[35] Low culture takes center stage in analyses emphasizing economic grievances, satanic fantasies, and,

---

[31] *From Crusades to Blood Libels to Expulsions* (above, n. 20).
[32] Langmuir (above, n. 20).
[33] Moore, *The Formation of a Persecuting Society* (above, n. 19).
[34] Cohen, *The Friars* (above, n. 17).
[35] This is a significant motif in Kenneth Stow's *Alienated Minority: The Jews of Medieval Latin Europe* (Cambridge, Mass., 1992) and in many of his other studies.

more ambiguously, millennial upheavals[36] and enhanced piety. Since high and low culture constantly interact, and in the case of the very important lower clergy cannot even be clearly distinguished, I am inclined to see a sharp division between these categories as misleading.

Then there is the question of *longue durée* patterns in the treatment of Jews. Despite important work calling traditional periodization into question,[37] I continue to believe that a pattern of decline from early to late Middle Ages remains a reality. Sometimes increasing historical sophistication along with additional information can blur differences between communities and periods so that things that "everyone knew" about continuities and discontinuities now appear questionable. Usually, however, if everyone knows something is true, it is true, or at least more or less true. This is a point that concerns me in many areas and periods, some well out of my field of specialized expertise. At the risk of revealing my own lack of sophistication, here is a partial list of old-fashioned views that I think deserve some defense against revisionist critiques that have in some instances become the new orthodoxies: Despite everything, Ashkenazic culture *was* more insular than that of Spanish Jewry; sixteenth-century Jewish messianism and historiography *are* noteworthy; rabbinic Judaism in the early Christian centuries *was* a more direct continuation of Second Temple Judaism in all its forms than Christianity; Orthodox Judaism in modern times *is* a more direct continuation of medieval Judaism than Reform Judaism; the eastern Haskalah *did* begin later than that of the West; and the condition of late medieval Jewry under Christendom *was* more precarious than that of the Jews of the earlier Middle Ages.

A final word on the question about Zionism: The impact of Zionism on twentieth-century Jewish historiography is beyond question, and beyond the scope of this presentation. At this moment in history, I do not think that the relevant fault lines, to the extent that they exist, are along Israel-Diaspora lines. If they do exist, they may reflect religious commitments, so that historians with traditionalist sympathies or beliefs may be less inclined, for example, to endorse connections between Jewish behavior during the Crusades—behavior lionized in

---

36   Richard Landes, "The Massacres of 1010: On the Origins of Popular Violence in Western Europe," in *From Witness to Witchcraft: Jews and Judaism in Medieval Christian Thought*, ed. by Jeremy Cohen (Wiesbaden, 1996), pp. 79–112.

37   Nirenberg, *Communities of Violence* (above, n. 21).

the liturgy—and stories of ritual murder. Both Israeli and diaspora historians live in societies where anti-Semitism in its medieval form has receded, and this liberates everyone from some of the constraints of the past, notwithstanding the virulent resurgence of attacks against both the Jewish people and its State in the last several years. I must confess to having experienced some uneasiness when translating the *Nitzahon Yashan*'s anti-Christian invective into English and listing a medieval Christian's bill of particulars against the Talmud in an English article,[38] but, for better or worse, I overcame that uneasiness. That queasy feeling, however, has its own historiographic benefits. It enables us better to understand the often wrenching struggles of Jews from R. Yehiel of Paris to the participants in the Napoleonic Sanhedrin to balance candor and self-interest in presenting the teachings of their classical texts. I do not react well when people speak with bemused condescension about the quaint notes in old editions of *selihot* affirming that the gentiles of the poet are the Visigoths or the heathens of old. There is not a scintilla of doubt that the condescending critic would have done the same thing had he or she been put in the same position.

I end where I began. The chastening effect of considering the monumental changes that have been effected during the last three decades in the historiography of medieval Jewish-Christian relations makes me loath to draw up a list of areas requiring further study, though it is not difficult to list such areas: interaction in the economic sphere, in folk beliefs, in perceptions of the role of women,[39] and much more. The greatest changes, I am afraid, may well come in areas that I think I understand best.

---

[38] "Christians, Gentiles, and the Talmud: A Fourteenth-Century Jewish Response to the Attack on Rabbinic Judaism," in *Religionsgespräche im Mittelalter*, ed. by Bernard Lewis and Friedrich Niewöhner (Wiesbaden, 1992}, pp. 115–130.

[39] See now Avraham Grossman, *Hasidot u-Mordot: Nashim Yehudiyyot be-Eropah bi-Yemei ha-Beinayim* (Jerusalem, 2001); Elisheva Baumgarten, *Mothers and Children: Jewish Family Life in Medieval Europe* (Princeton, N.J., 2004).

JACOB KATZ ON JEWS AND CHRISTIANS
IN THE MIDDLE AGES

From: *The Pride of Jacob: Essays on Jacob Katz and his Work,*
ed. by Jay M. Harris (Harvard University Press: Cambridge, Mass., 2002),
pp. 41–63.

Few scholars indeed have produced seminal works of abiding value in areas outside their primary field of expertise. Jacob Katz's *Exclusiveness and Tolerance*, which is precisely such a work, is remarkable testimony to the power of wide learning, penetrating insight, and exceptional instincts to overcome significant lacunae in the author's command of relevant material.[1] Katz was not a medievalist; he was not deeply conversant with Christian sources; and he did not study the full range of Jewish texts relevant to the relationship between medieval Christians and Jews. Thus, Christian works play virtually no role in any facet of his analysis. His discussion of the motivation of Christian converts to Judaism, for example, makes no reference to the one memoir by such a convert that addresses this question explicitly, and his assertion that the doctrine of Jewish toleration was not fully worked out until Aquinas provides a somewhat misleading impression that probably results from lack of familiarity with earlier texts by churchmen of lesser renown. Apart from the famous Paris disputation, to which he devotes an important chapter, he makes virtually no use of Jewish polemical literature, so that we find precisely one reference to *Sefer Yosef ha-Meqanne*, the central polemical text in thirteenth-century France, and no reference at all to the *Nizzahon*

---

[1]   The English version was published by Oxford University Press in 1961. The Hebrew, *Bein Yehudim le-Goyim* (Jerusalem, 1960), appeared earlier but, according to the preface, was written later and hence, says Katz, takes precedence. In a number of quite important instances, the Hebrew is superior not because of revisions but because at that point Katz's command of written English was not fully adequate to the task and whoever assisted him did not always capture the necessary nuances.

Vetus, a major compilation of anti-Christian arguments in medieval Ashkenaz, which is the sphere of culture standing at the center of his work.[2] Yet this little volume described by Katz himself as a collection of essays rather than a sustained study, has deservedly become the starting point for all serious discussion of Jewish approaches to Christianity in medieval Europe.

When a scholar writes a book about a subject that he is not fully trained to address, the question of motivation arises in more acute fashion than usual. I strongly suspect that Katz was drawn to this theme as a result of a religious concern that he acknowledges and an ethical one that he downplays. His autobiography describes the inner struggles of Orthodox Jewish university students in interwar Germany. "The dilemma for most of my fellow students seemed to be rooted in a sense of contradiction between the Jewish tradition by which they lived and the scientific concepts and universal values encountered during their academic studies. The apologetic efforts of Orthodox Judaism . . . were aimed at creating an ideology to bridge this abyss."[3] He maintains, however, that he himself was not bothered by the discrepancy between traditional Judaism and an "external system of concepts and values"; his concern was with evidence for historical development within a purportedly closed, unitary tradition whose authority seemed to rest on its imperviousness to change.

Although I do not doubt that Katz was disturbed by the latter tension, I doubt very much that he was unconcerned about the former. It cannot be unalloyed coincidence that the theme of *Exclusiveness and Tolerance* unites both issues by examining the development of Jewish law with respect to the standing of Gentiles, perhaps the quintessential area in which Judaism was accused of violating the requirements of universal values. Rabbi David Zvi Hoffmann, the leading German rabbi in the late-nineteenth and early twentieth centuries, was impelled to write an apologetic work on Jewish attitudes toward believers in other faiths.[4]

2   Although *Sefer Yosef ha-Meqanne* had not yet been published in its entirety, much of the work was available in print. See Judah Rosenthal's summary of the publication history in his edition (Jerusalem, 1970), Introduction, p. 32. The *Nizzahon Vetus* had been published by Johann Christoph Wagenseil, *Tela Ignea Satanac*, vol. 2 (Altdorf, 1681), pp. 1–260.
3   Jacob Katz, *With My Own Eyes: The Autobiography of a Historian* (Hanover and London, 1995), p. 82.
4   *Der Slulchan-Aruch und die Rabbinen über das Verhältnis der Juden zu Andersgläubigen* (Berlin, 1894).

We now know that Rabbi Jehiel Jacob Weinberg, the distinguished leader of the Berlin Rabbinical Seminary at the very time that Katz studied in Frankfurt, was profoundly troubled by this problem.[5]

Moreover, Katz himself provides us with several indications of his own sensitivities and sympathies. He argues that a historian has the right to use the term "shortcoming" as an expression of moral judgment with respect to earlier societies without violating the principle that later values alien to those societies should not be imposed in the process of historical assessment. His justification for this position rests on the argument that even the medievals had some sense of a universal humanitarian standard, although they would regularly suspend it in the face of what they perceived to be the demands of their religion; it is precisely their awareness of such a standard that allows a historian to render judgment as to the degree of their fealty to it. One cannot help but wonder if Katz would really have avoided all moral judgment if he were studying a society that he considered bereft of any universal humanitarian concern. He appears to be straining to find an academically plausible argument allowing for the infiltration of an explicitly ethical prism into his historical analysis, thereby satisfying both his moral and his historical conscience.

In the last few lines of the preface to the Hebrew version, he allows us a fleeting glimpse into his hope and conviction that the book is not irrelevant to the issues of the day.

> The roots of contemporary problems extend to the far reaches of the past, and Jewish-Gentile relations even today cannot be understood without knowing their earlier history. A historian is permitted to believe that when he distances the reader from the present, he does not sever him from it; rather, he provides him with a vantage point from which he can more readily encompass even the place where we now stand.[6]

In *Exclusiveness and Tolerance* as well as his other essays on our theme, Katz saw himself as a rebel against dubious apologetics. He does not hesitate to state flatly that a key contention of Hoffmann's work arguing that medieval Jews had declared their Christian contemporaries free of

---

5   See Marc B. Shapiro, *Between the Yeshiva World and Modem Orthodoxy: The Life and Works of Rabbi Jehiel Jacob Weinberg 1884–1966* (London and Portland, Oregon, 1909), pp. 182–183.

6   *Bein Yehudim le-Goyim*, p. 8.

idolatry is misleading.[7] In the wake of Katz's analysis, it is difficult for us to recapture an environment in which excellent scholars affirmed that Ashkenazic Jews of the Middle Ages had utterly excluded Christianity from the category of *avodah zarah*, the technical term imprecisely translated as idolatry. Katz reminds us that such assertions were made not only in explicitly apologetic works; Hanokh Albeck, for example, in a major study of the Mishnah, asserted that the views of medieval Jewish authorities are encompassed in the position of R. Menahem ha-Meiri, which is, in fact, striking in its atypical liberalism.[8] At the same time I do not doubt that Katz was impelled to study ha-Meiri's posture, which he describes as "undoubtedly a great achievement,"[9] precisely because it afforded him the opportunity to highlight Jewish tolerance without sacrificing scholarly integrity.

Whatever Katz's motivations, it is time to turn to the substance of his work. I would like to examine the scope of his interest in medieval Jewish-Christian relations, his methodology, his contribution to the state of the question when he wrote, the validity of his arguments in and of themselves, and the degree to which they stand up in light of later scholarship and the sources he failed to examine.

One of the hallmarks of Katz's approach, which has little if any precedent in earlier historiography, is the great significance that he assigns to instinct. Visceral reactions, he argues, can weigh more heavily than texts. Thus, Jewish revulsion at Christian rituals and symbols is no less important than formal halakhah in determining that Christianity is *avodah zarah* and inspiring the decision of martyrs.[10] Katz ascribes this emotional reaction to Ashkenazic Jews—correctly, in my view— despite his awareness that pawnbroking put them into contact with Christian *sancta* and produced serious temptations to relax taboos against benefiting from such presumably idolatrous objects.

Sensitivity to a different sort of popular instinct plays a major role in a later work in which Katz examined the evolution of legal approaches

7   "Sheloshah Mishpatim Apologetiyyim be-Gilguleihem," reprinted in Jacob Katz, *Halakhah ve-Qabbalah* (Jerusalem, 1984), p. 285. "Misleading" is an accurate but not quite adequate translation of the stronger original (*eino ella mat'eh*).

8   On this point Katz notes that even Hoffmann recognized the uniqueness of ha-Meiri's approach. See Katz, "Sovlanut Datit be-Shitato shel R. Menahem ha-Me'iri ba-Halakhah u-be-Pilosofiah," in *Halakhah ve-Kabbalah*, p. 191, n. 1.

9   *Bein Yehudim le-Goyim*, p. 128 (my translation); *Exclusiveness and Tolerance*, p. 128.

10   *Bein Yehudim le-Goyim*, p. 34; *Exclusiveness and Tolerance*, p. 23.

to the use of Gentiles for work on the Sabbath. Here again, he argues that texts can occasionally be subordinated to "ritual instinct," so that ordinary Jews will ask for permission to violate serious prohibitions that do not repel them while refraining from seeking dispensation to engage in behavior that is less objectionable to the legal mind but unthinkable in light of deeply entrenched emotions.

Standards tor evaluating assertions about instinct can be elusive. Thus, I will sometimes be discussing my instinct about Katz's instinct about the instinct of medieval Jews. Evidence, of course, is not irrelevant to this enterprise, nor was it irrelevant in medieval discourse. One of Katz's great strengths is that he recognizes this. For all his emphasis on the primacy of emotions, instinct, and a sense of social identity, he is not carried away by his insight. It is only on the rarest of occasions that he loses sight of the interplay of these factors with more disciplined intellectual pursuits, whether theological or halakhic. Except in those rare moments, his work is a model of balance, as a supple and subtle mind reconstructs the delicately poised interweaving of unexamined, primal reactions, economic and social needs, and the reasoned examination of authoritative texts.

Even Katz's marginal, poorly informed discussion of polemic reveals this strength. Thus, he appreciates the significance of the intellectual dimension of what many observers have seen as static and uninteresting ritual combat and he points to the internalizing of anti-Christian exegesis as evidence of the deep Jewish sensitivity to Christian arguments. Thus, he says, both R. Joseph Bekhor Shor and R. Isaac Or Zarua assert that Deuteronomy 6:4 affirms not merely that the Lord is God but that He is *our* God, thereby proclaiming that no other nation can claim Him as its own.[11] Still, Katz does not regard intellectual arguments as the Jews' primary line of defense. They were decidedly secondary to the emotions of group identification and the attraction of Judaism's entrenched symbols.[12]

Katz underscores this approach in his more detailed discussion of martyrdom. Ordinary Jews, he says, martyred themselves not because of familiarity with the niceties of their halakhic obligations but because they had been reared on *stories* of heroic self-sacrifice.[13] Despite these

---

11   *Bein Yehudim le-Goyim*, p. 30. The English version (*Exclusiveness and Tolerance*, p. 19) is so
       truncated that the point is almost completely lost.
12   *Bein Yehudim le-Goyim*, p. 32; *Exclusiveness and Tolerance*, p. 21.
13   *Bein Yehudim le-Goyim*, p. 91; *Exclusiveness and Tolerance*, pp. 84–85.

observations, historians debating the roots of Ashkenazic martyrdom—and other instances of extreme behavior—are not as sensitive to this point as they should be. To take an example outside the purview of medieval Ashkenaz, a Christian writer tells the story of Moses of Crete, a fifth-century Messianic pretender, who persuaded all the Jews to jump into the Mediterranean with the assurance that the sea would split to facilitate their journey to the Promised Land. Historians have retold the story with a sense of amazement at such mass credulity or skepticism as to the historicity of the account.[14] Although I am by no means prepared to assert confidently that these events occurred, the plausibility of the narrative increases dramatically once we appreciate the impact of stories about heroic faith absorbed from childhood.

A well-known rabbinic legend relates that the Red Sea split only after Nahshon ben Aminadav of the tribe of Judah demonstrated his unquestioning faith by leaping into the roiling sea.[15] Today, every school child receiving a traditional Jewish education is familiar with this story. We cannot know if this was the case in fifth-century Crete, but if it was, the probability that Jews could have been capable of such behavior is enhanced exponentially. In the safety of a classroom, there is no price to pay for expressions of smug disdain for the lack of faith displayed by pusillanimous skeptics standing at the edge of the sea. But as the Jews of Crete looked out at the Mediterranean facing a potentially deadly choice, the natural resistance to irrational action would be sorely

[14] Salo Baron expressed both reactions, the first in a general discussion of messianic figures and the second in a more detailed account of Moses. The reasons for skepticism, he says, are the Christian author's emphasis on Jewish credulity and his assertion that those saved by Christian fishermen accepted baptism. See *A Social and Religious History of the Jews* (New York, London, and Philadelphia, 1960), vol. 3, p. 16, and vol. 5, pp. 366–367. Gerson Cohen, who excluded messianic movements attested only in Christian sources from his analysis of the messianic stances of medieval Jewish communities, remarked during a Columbia University colloquium in the mid-1960s that his own skepticism about the historicity of this account is rooted in the fact that the Jews' credulousness regarding false messiahs combined with their rejection of the true one is a standard, polemically useful Christian topos. Cohen's policy of excluding messianic accounts by non-Jews has recently come under attack. See his "Messianic Postures of Ashkenazim and Sephardim," in *Studies of the Leo Baeck Institute*, ed. by Max Kreutzberger (New York, 1967), p. 123, n. 11, and Elisheva Carlebach, *Between History and Hope: Jewish Messianism in Ashkenaz and Sepharad. Third Annual Lecture of the Victor J. Selmanowitz Chair of Jewish History* (New York: Touro College, 1998), pp. 12–13.

[15] See the references in Louis Ginzberg, *The Legends of the Jews* (Philadelphia, 1928), vol. 6, pp. 75–79 (n. 388).

challenged by a lesson ingrained from the inception of their religious consciousness.[16]

Let us now return to the martyrs of Ashkenaz. A vexed question central to recent historical debate asks if the justification for suicide and the killing of others emerged out of almost routine analysis of texts or if it was molded by emotional considerations and the need to justify the actions of sainted ancestors. This is not the occasion to survey the state of this question in its fullness. Nonetheless, there remains much to be said both for Katz's general approach and for his specific observations. He noted, for example, a highly unusual formulation in *Tosafot* that persuasively underscores the impact of martyrdom's extraordinary emotional resonance on halakhic discourse. The tosafists remark that the ordinary processes of halakhic reasoning appear to yield the conclusion that it is permissible to commit idolatry under threat of death provided that the act does not take place in the presence of ten Jews. *Tosafot* does not merely reject this position. Rather, we are witness, at least initially, to what Katz properly describes as an extraordinary phenomenon—a *cri de coeur* instead of an argument. "God forbid that we should rule in a case of idolatry that one should transgress rather than die."[17]

In the current debate, Avraham Grossman and Yisrael Ta-Shma have taken issue with Haym Soloveitchik's position that the willingness of Ashkenazic authorities to justify suicide and even the killing of children in the face of enforced idolatry cannot have emerged from a straightforward application of legal reasoning but rather from the need to justify the

[16] Lest I be accused of equating Moses son of Amram with Moses of Crete and ignoring the earlier miraculous events that presumably justified Nahshon's decision, let me put these obvious distinctions on the record. They do not, in my view, undermine the essential psychological observation.

[17] *Tosafot Avodah Zarah* 54a, s. v. *ha be-zin'a*. See *Bein Yehudim le-Goyim*, pp. 90–91; *Exclusiveness and Tolerance*, pp. 83–84. I have a personal stake in this argument. Without any conscious memory of the passage in Katz's book, I was struck by precisely the same formula while studying that *tosafot* for reasons unrelated to history, and I presented his point as my own when writing the introduction to *The Jewish-Christian Debate in the High Middle Ages* (Philadelphia, 1979) in the mid-1970s. While the book was in press, I re-read Katz and discovered to my combined pleasure and disappointment that my "discovery" had already been made. The printed version (pp. 25–26), therefore, contains a footnote attributing the point to *Bein Yehudim le-Goyim* with the observation that the English version is so bland that "the emotional force of the argument is virtually lost." (It renders *has ve-shalom*, which I have translated "God forbid," as "Far be it from us.") When I related the story to Katz years later, he told me how pleased he had been with this insight when it had originally struck him.

behavior of the martyrs. Soloveitchik's argument rests in part on the resort of these authorities to aggadic sources; his critics, however, assert that Ashkenazic Jews drew no material distinction between halakhah and aggadah, so that their arguments from texts that Soloveitchik would place out of bounds are entirely consistent with their own worldview.[18]

I think it is fair to say that even in medieval Ashkenaz, the first resort of rabbinic decisors would be to texts that we would describe as halakhic. At the same time, I do not believe that they would dismiss evidence from an aggadah by saying, "I do not recognize this genre as authoritative in a legal discussion." Thus, when mainstream authorities issue a problematic ruling based entirely on aggadic material, we are justified in asking pointed questions about motivation, as long as we do not insist that the resort to aggadah demonstrates in and of itself that highly unusual processes must be at work. In short, our antennas should be raised, though we may ultimately decide that nothing extraordinary is happening.

With respect to our issue, I am not even certain that it is appropriate to characterize all the sources adduced in the medieval discussion as aggadic;[19] nonetheless, I am strongly inclined to think that a deeply emotional need to validate the heroism of the martyrs did play an important role in Ashkenazic decision-making. Katz's *tosafot* is highly relevant here, but an even more significant text has not, in my view, been given its due by either side in this controversy, even though all the parties know it very well.

Rabbi Meir of Rothenburg, the great thirteenth-century decisor, was asked whether atonement is necessary tor a man who had killed his wife and children (with their consent) to prevent their capture by a mob demanding conversion to Christianity. He responded that suicide can be defended in such a case, but it is much more difficult to find a justification for the killing of others. Nonetheless, he rose to

---

18 See Haym Soloveitchik, "Religious Law and Change: The Medieval Ashkenazic Example," *AJS Review* 12 (1987): 205–221; Avraham Grossman, "Shorashav shel Qiddush ha-Shem be-Ashkenaz ha-Qedumah," in *Qedushat ha-Hayyim ve-Heruf ha-Nefesh: Kovetz Ma'amarim le-Zikhro shel Amir Yekutiel*, ed. by Isaiah Gafni and Aviezer Ravitzky (Jerusalem, 1993), pp. 99–130; Israel Ta Shma, "Hit'abbedut ve-Rezah ha-Zulat al Qiddush ha-Shem: Li-She'elat Meqomah shel ha-Aggadah be-Masoret ha-Pesiqah ha-Ashkenazit," in *Yehudim mul ha-Zelav: Gezerot Tatn'u ba-Historiah u-ba-Historiographiah*, ed. by Yom Tov Assis et al. (Jerusalem, 2000), pp. 150–156.

19 See the following note.

the challenge by proposing an original extension of a rabbinic midrash on a biblical text. Defenders of martyrdom by suicide had long cited the assertion in *Bereshit Rabbah* 34:19 that the word "but" (*akh*) in Genesis 9:5 limits the scope of the prohibition against suicide that immediately follows.[20] R. Meir suggested that this word, and hence this limitation, also governs the remainder of the verse, which prohibits murder. It follows that killing others may be permitted under the same circumstances that justify suicide. He prefaced this suggestion with the observation that "the position that this is permissible has spread widely, for we have seen and found many great men who slaughtered their sons and daughters," and he followed it with the powerful assertion that "anyone who requires atonement tor this is besmirching the name of the pious men of old."

Though large questions of this sort cannot be settled definitively by a single source, this responsum, it seems to me, is as close to a smoking gun as we could ever expect. An Ashkenazic rabbi of the first rank tells us that (1) it is a challenge to find grounds for permitting the killing of others; (2) the reason for seeking such grounds is the fact that the practice has been widespread among great rabbis; (3) one can permit this by an [unattested, innovative] expansion of a rabbinic midrash on a biblical verse [a very rare procedure in thirteenth-century halakhic discourse];[21] and (4) anyone who disagrees with this original proposal to accomplish an admittedly problematic task is besmirching the name of the pious men of old.

Soloveitchik himself cites this responsum only to underscore its tragic character and to note that R. Meir "was hard put to find a reply" to the question. He goes on to assert that "for the murder of children few could find a defense, and almost all passed that over in audible silence." The lengthy footnote to this sentence makes no reference to R. Meir, and

20   Even though *Bereshit Rabbah* is an aggadic text, this passage has the sound and feel of halakhah, so that Soloveitchik's argument that suicides were justified by aggadah pure and simple probably requires qualification. It would be going very far indeed to expect Ashkenazic Jews to shrink from relying upon an explicitly legal formulation solely because it appears in a non-halakhic midrash.

21   In my "Heqer Rabbanut Ashkenaz ha-Qedumah," *Tarbiz* 33 (1984): 484, n. 6, I made the point that R. Meir's determining a halakhah on the basis of a partially original midrash on a biblical verse is highly unusual among medieval authorities. In private conversations, two learned scholars insisted that they do not consider such a practice strikingly atypical, but I am not persuaded.

readers are given no indication of the main point of his responsum.[22] Even though he never wrote the words, "This is permitted," it is beyond question that this is the thrust of R. Meir's ruling. The greatest decisor in thirteenth-century Germany composed an emotion-laden responsum that provides powerful evidence for Soloveitchik's—and Katz's—position.

Despite R. Meir's initial reluctance to extend the permission to commit suicide to include the killing of others, the unhesitating readiness of some Ashkenazic Jews to do so is not, I think, an impenetrable mystery. Once again, I am inclined to assign pride of place to instinctive and emotional considerations. But let me begin by proposing a formal argument that may well have been taken for granted though it is unattested in the medieval sources and has not been noted in the current debates. A much-cited passage in *Da'at Zeqenim mi-Ba'alei ha-Tosafot* to Genesis 9:5 indicates that unnamed Ashkenazic Jews had clearly and apparently unself-consciously applied the passage in *Bereshit Rabbah* not only to suicide but to the killing of children as well. If we turn to that midrashic passage, we find that it points to the death of Saul as one of the paradigmatic exceptions to the prohibition against suicide. But Saul initially asked a servant to kill him; it was only after the servant refused that the king killed himself. (I leave aside the more complicated issue of the subsequent story in II Samuel 1 where an Amalekite tells David that Saul's suicide attempt was not wholly successful and that he acceded to a royal request to complete the task.) The reader of the midrash has every right to assume that the exception made for Saul includes his initial request as well as his final action.[23]

At the same time, I do not believe that such arguments went through the minds of Jews preparing to commit suicide in the blood-stained arenas of Mainz and Worms. Let us imagine the scene. A large group of

---

22 "Religious Law and Change," pp. 209–10.
23 Cf. Radak's commentary to I Samuel 31:4, which states—citing our midrash—that Saul did not sin, without proffering the slightest hint that the initial request, reported in the very same verse, was improper.

Shortly after I submitted this article to the editor, Prof. Ephraim Kanarfogel called my attention to his discussion in a forthcoming article of Rabbenu Tam's position on the fear of succumbing to torture as a halakhic justification for suicide. See Kanarfogel's "*Halakhah and Meziut (Realia) in Medieval Ashkenaz: Surveying the Parameters and Defining the Limits,*" scheduled to appear in *Jewish Law Annual* 14 (2001), where he analyzes the relevance of the talmudic assertion (*Ketubbot* 33b) that Hananiah, Mishael, and Azariah would have bowed to the statue made by Nebuchadnezzar had they been beaten. I thank Prof. Kanarfogel for affording me the opportunity to read the typescript.

Jews is facing the certainty of death or conversion. To save themselves from slaughter at the hands of the crusading hordes—or from the prospect of descending into the maelstrom of idolatry in the face of torture—they decide to take their lives. They know that they will be instantaneously transported to a world of eternal light at the side of Abraham, Isaac, Jacob, and Rabbi Akiva. Do they take their children with them to eternal bliss or do they leave them to wander among the bloody corpses of their parents until they are found and raised to live a life of idolatry? I am tempted to say that the choice is clear. In fact, it is not. The choice to slaughter your children is never clear, and the agonies of that choice are evident in the chilling chronicles of those terrible events. Nonetheless, the choice was made, and I think it far more likely that it was made on the basis of an instinctive reaction than on the basis of textual analysis. Once it was made, subsequent Jews, at least for the most part, had little emotional choice but to react like R. Meir of Rothenburg, though he agonized over the question far more than most, and his transparent struggle has much to teach us about the interaction between heart and mind.

One element in Katz's own formulation of the martyrological psychology of Ashkenazic Jews may even be too weak. He poses the medievals' question as to the permissibility of suicide or the killing of children "to avoid religious compulsion and the temptation to apostasy." He goes on to say that "the answer of Ashkenazic rabbis was inclined toward stringency from the outset . . . , and it is clear that they were not concerned that this stringency fell into the category of a decree that the masses are unprepared to withstand."[24] In other words, not only the rabbis but even the masses were inclined toward such a response. If so, we may well ask ourselves about the propriety of the term "stringency" here. The question posed was whether suicides and killings were permissible, and the answer was in the affirmative. In any other context, an affirmative answer to a question beginning, "Is it permissible?" would be characterized as lenient, not stringent. For all his deep understanding of the psyche of medieval Ashkenazic Jews, Katz could not avoid the unconscious imposition of his (and our) instincts upon theirs by transforming a *qulla* into a *humra*, a leniency into a stringency. Difficult

---

[24] *Bein Yehudim le-Goyim*, p. 91. The English version (*Exclusiveness and Tolerance*, p. 84) does not quite convey the point.

as it is for us to fathom, these medieval Jews *wanted* the answer to be, "It is permissible."

Many years ago, my interest in the centrality of martyrdom for the Ashkenazic psyche was piqued by a passage in the *Nizzahon Vetus*, which impelled me to draw attention to both Katz's *tosafot* and R. Meir of Rothenburg's responsum. That passage, which would surely have caught Katz's sharp eye had he read the text, transmutes the story made famous by Judah Halevi's *Kuzari* into a celebration of the willingness to be martyred as the hallmark of the true faith. As in the *Kuzari*, the soon-to-be-converted ruler is impressed by the fact that Judaism is the second choice of both Muslim and Christian, but he is even more impressed when the Jew is prepared to sacrifice his life where the others are not.[25]

Finally, Katz makes the telling observation that the talmudic concept of *parhesia* describing a public act underwent an illuminating transformation in the Middle Ages. For the talmudic sages, an act fell into the category of *parhesia* if it was done in the presence of ten Jews. In the formal, legal sense, this did not change, but when medieval Jews described the death of martyrs in a public setting, they usually referred to the intent to sanctify God's name by projecting devotion to the non-Jewish world. It was this confrontation that gave the act of martyrdom its critical context and its transcendent purpose.

In citing concrete evidence for this important and penetrating insight, Katz can, nonetheless, overreach. The Hebrew version contains a footnote asserting that the intent of the martyrs to have Christians recognize the truth of Judaism is made explicit (*nitparesh*) in a comment by R. Solomon b. Shimshon.[26] The comment cited certainly expresses the Jews' fervent expectation that Christians will recognize that truth, but the instrument of this recognition is not Jewish martyrdom but the Lord's eschatological vengeance against Christendom. Because of this divine punishment, Christians will perceive the outrageous injustice that they had perpetrated by spilling the blood of Jewish babies in the name of a false belief.

Both the Ashkenazic variant of the Kuzari story and the hope for eschatological Christian enlightenment bring us to Katz's discussion

---

25   *The Jewish-Christian Debate in the High Middle Ages*, pp. 26–27, 216–218.
26   *Bein Yehudim le-Goyim*, p. 97, n. 41.

of converts. Once again, his instincts guide him very well even in the absence of an extensive evidentiary base. He understands, of course, the full spectrum of motivations tor Jewish conversion to Christianity, from pragmatic interests to genuine conviction. His tendency, however, predictably inclines toward social explanation: in a profoundly religious age, Jews attracted by the values of Christian society would express this attraction by embracing the religious form in which those values expressed themselves.[27] Though I would assign somewhat more force than did Katz to the attraction of Christian arguments, I am, nonetheless, inclined to think that his emphasis is correct. He intuits this psychological process despite the fact that his entire discussion of the motivations of Jewish apostates takes place with virtually no reference to Christian sources, which appear in one footnote containing a reference to a few pages in two secondary works.[28] I have already alluded to the fact that our one detailed personal memoir of the conversion experience by a Jewish convert to Christianity, Herman of Cologne's *Opuscula de Conversione Sua*, is entirely absent from the analysis—an inconceivable omission for anyone with real familiarity with Latin materials. And yet, Herman's account strikingly reinforces Katz's point, subordinating, though not ignoring, intellectual arguments, and emphasizing an attraction to the values of simple piety.[29]

Similarly, Katz argues with no concrete evidence that the reason why medieval Ashkenazic Jews persisted in converting Christians despite

---

27   *Bein Yehudim le-Goyim*, p. 83; *Exclusiveness and Tolerance*, p. 76.

28   *Bein Yehudim le-Goyim*, p. 83, n. 46; *Exclusiveness and Tolerance*, p. 75, n. 6.

29   Gerlinde Niemeyer, ed., *Hermannus quondam Judaeus opusculum de conversione sua, Monumenta Germaniae Historica: Quellen zur Geistgeschichte des Mittelalters*, vol. 4 (Weimar, 1963), esp. p. 108. (The text had been published twice before Niemeyer's edition.) See Jeremy Cohen, "The Mentality of the Medieval Jewish Apostate: Peter Alfonsi, Hermann of Cologne, and Pablo Christiani," in *Jewish Apostasy in the Modern World*, ed. by Todd Endelman and Jeffrey Gurock (New York, 1987), pp. 20–47; and Karl F. Morrison, *Conversion and Text: The Cases of Augustine of Hippo, Herman-Judah, and Constantine-Tsatsos* (Charlottesville and London, 1992), which also contains an English translation. Well after Katz wrote his book, Avrom Saltman argued that the *Opusculum* is, in fact, a fictitious work by a born Christian; see his "Hermann's *Opusculum de Conversione Sua*: Truth or Fiction?," *Revue des Etudes Juives* 47 (1988): 31–56. The most recent discussion of this question is Jean-Claude Schmitt, *Die autobiographische Fiktion: Hermann des Juden Bekehrung* (Kleine Schriften des Arye-Maimon Instituts 3: Trier, 2000). Since no one had doubted the authenticity of this work when Katz wrote, I have referred to it as Hermann's in my discussion. As Schmitt argues, many relevant insights can be gleaned from it even if it is essentially fiction.

the obvious difficulties is that they saw every instance of conversion to Judaism as a proof and declaration of the truth of the Jewish religion to the outside world.[30] The *Nizzahon Vetus* strikingly confirms this intuition—not only in the story of the Emperor that we have already encountered but also in a passage dealing frontally with the implications of conversion writ large.

> With regard to their questioning us as to whether there are proselytes among us, they ask this question to their shame and to the shame of their faith. After all, one should not be surprised at the bad deeds of an evil Jew who becomes an apostate, because his motives are to enable himself to eat all that his heart desires, to give pleasure to his flesh with wine and fornication, to remove from himself the yoke of the kingdom of heaven so that he should fear nothing, to free himself from all the commandments, cleave to sin, and concern himself with worldly pleasures. But the situation is different with regard to proselytes who converted to Judaism and thus went of their own free will from freedom to slavery, from light to darkness. If the proselyte is a man, then he knows that he must wound himself by removing his foreskin through circumcision, that he must exile himself from place to place, that he must deprive himself of worldly good and fear for his life from the external threat of being killed by the uncircumcised, and that he will lack many things that his heart desires; similarly, a woman proselyte also separates herself from all pleasures. And despite all this, they come to take refuge under the wing of the divine presence. It is evident that they would not do this unless they knew for certain that their faith is without foundation and that it is all a lie, vanity, and emptiness. Consequently, you should be ashamed when you mention the matter of proselytes.[31]

Katz's related argument that the generally positive attitude toward converts in the Middle Ages reflects an active quest for Jewish triumph[32] is less than compelling in and of itself, but is in my view confirmed by the pervasive tone of Jewish polemic and considerable evidence from Christian sources, none of which played any role in forming Katz's conclusion. Although I do not believe that we should go so far as to speak of a medieval Jewish mission, there is strong reason to believe that Jews confronted Christians on the streets of Europe to pose

---

[30]   *Bein Yehudim le-Goyim*, p. 85. The English version (*Exclusiveness and Tolerance*, p. 77) is considerably less forceful.

[31]   *The Jewish-Christian Debate in the High Middle Ages*, # 211. English section, pp. 206–207.

[32]   *Bein Yehudim le-Goyim*, p. 88; *Exclusiveness and Tolerance*, p. 81.

religious arguments and took great satisfaction in producing a sense of discomfiture or defeat in the mind of their interlocutor.[33]

That Jews reviled apostates is self-evident, and yet they insisted that such converts retain the legal status of Jews. Katz devoted an article to the application of the talmudic formula "even though he sinned he is an Israelite" to the abiding Jewishness of the apostate.[34] He proved the validity of an earlier suggestion that Rashi was responsible for the use of this expression to establish the standing of apostates as Jews; then he proceeded to examine the larger social context of the new understanding and wide popularity of this formula. The explanation, he says, is neither halakhic logic in itself nor Rashi's personal predilections but the real struggle carried on by the Jewish community against conversion and forced apostasy.[35]

On the one hand, there are legal and psychological advantages in seeing the apostate as non-Jewish. He does not generate a levirate relationship, so that his widowed, childless sister-in-law can marry without asking him for a release; you can lend him money at interest; you can indulge your utter rejection of him. In this connection, Katz makes another acute observation about the transformation of a talmudic term. For the Sages, one who habitually violated a particular injunction was a *mumar* with respect to that injunction (*mumar le-x*); for medieval Jews, *mumar le-* became simply *mumar*—an apostate whose very essence is the transgression of the Torah.

But there were countervailing concerns of considerable, ultimately decisive emotional and pragmatic impact. Jews wanted to demonstrate that baptism has no force, that it could not effect a transformation of identity, and they also wanted to encourage converts to return to Judaism.[36] To these considerations I would add a third: Jews wanted to see all the sins of apostates as sins. To be sure, the conversion itself, barring future repentance, sealed their fate. Nonetheless, as long as they remain Jews, every desecration of the Sabbath, every taste of forbidden food increases the temperature of the hellfire prepared for them.

---

33   See my "Mission to the Jews and Jewish-Christian Contacts in the Polemical Literature of the High Middle Ages," *American Historical Review* 91 (1986): 576–591.

34   "Af al Pi she-Hata Yisrael Hu," in *Halakhah ve-Qabbalah*, pp. 255–269.

35   "Af al Pi she-Hata Yisrael Hu," p. 262.

36   "Af al Pi she-Hata Yisrael Hu," pp. 262–265.

Katz's instincts about Jewish attitudes toward Christianity can sometimes not be tested at all. He asserts, for example, that Ashkenazic Jews were sincere both when they prayed for the peace of the government and when they prayed for its ultimate destruction.[37] I am inclined to believe that he is right, but I cannot think of an easy way to prove it. The complex interaction of attraction and revulsion toward the Christian world is particularly difficult to pin down. Citing the work of Yitzhak Baer, Katz affirmed that we now know that religious phenomena in both communities emerged out of a common trend, but the medievals themselves, he argued, did not know this. For them, these very religious impulses strengthened the instinct to recoil from the other religion.[38] With all the substantial progress that has been made since *Exclusiveness and Tolerance* to enhance our understanding of both the openness and the hostility of Ashkenazic Jewry to its Christian environment,[39] Katz's assessment has, in the main, withstood the test of time.

Katz places great emphasis on the Jewish instinct that Christianity is *avodah zarah*, asserting that any economically motivated change in this perception would appear to stand in absolute contradiction to the

[37] *Bein Yehudim le-Goyim*, p. 60; *Exclusiveness and Tolerance*, p. 51. The difference between the Hebrew and English versions of this passage is so striking that for all Katz's insistence that he spurned apologetics, it is difficult to avoid the impression that he or his English stylist softened the formulation for a non-Jewish audience. The Hebrew reads, "The vision of the end of days signifies the overturning of the current order, when the dispersed and humiliated people will see its revenge from its tormentors. The hope for a day of revenge and the prayer for the arrival of that day may be considered as conflicting with a profession of loyalty to the government . . . " Here is the English: "A reversal of the existing order was envisaged in the messianic age, when the dispersed and humiliated Jewish people was to come into its own. The entertaining of such hopes, and the prayer for their fulfillment, might well be considered as conflicting with a profession of loyalty . . . "
On the much debated question of whether Ashkenazic Jews looked forward to Christian conversion or annihilation at the end of days, see my "Al Tadmitam ve-Goralam shel ha-Goyim be-Sifrut ha-Pulmus ha-Ashkenazit," in *Yehudim mul ha-Zelav* (above, n. 18), pp. 74–91.

[38] *Bein Yehudim le-Goyim*, pp. 98–99; *Exclusiveness and Tolerance*, pp. 93–94.
[39] See my discussion and references in Gerald J. Blidstein, David Berger, Shnayer Z. Leiman, and Aharon Lichtenstein, *Judaism's Encounter with Other Cultures: Rejection or Integration?*, ed. by Jacob J. Schacter, pp. 117–125, as well as in "Al Tadmitam ve-Goralam shel ha-Goyim" (above, n. 37). See also Ivan Marcus, *Rituals of Childhood: Jewish Acculturation in Medieval Europe* (New Haven and London, 1996); Israel J. Yuval, *Shenei Goyim be-Bitnekh* (Tel Aviv, 2000); and much relevant discussion in Avraham Grossman's *Hakhmei Ashkenaz ha-Rishonim* (Jerusalem, 1981) and *Hakhmei Zarfat ha-Rishonim* (Jerusalem, 1995) and in Ephraim Kanarfogel, *Jewish Education and Society in the High Middle Ages* (Detroit, 1992).

classic perception that the world is unconditionally divided between Israel and the nations.[40] A bit later he argues that retaining this perception was necessary to safeguard the community against absorption and conversion.[41] There is certainly much truth in this, but to test it one would have to introduce at least some comparative dimension. How did Jews under Islam handle this problem? They surely regarded Muslims as part of "the nations," and with sufficient effort it was possible to classify them as idolaters;[42] nonetheless, neither Maimonides nor the great majority of rabbinic authorities took this step. Though Katz makes no reference to Islam in this context, he does allude to the small size of Ashkenazic communities and the intense missionary efforts exerted by Christians as factors that increased the Jewish need for self-defense. I do not believe that this is enough to explain the different reactions under Christendom and Islam, particularly since the intensity of missionary efforts in Northern Europe through the twelfth century is very much in question.[43] Katz acknowledged that the theological chasm separating Judaism from Christianity played some role here, and in this instance I think that the actual content of Jewish and Christian beliefs deserves pride of place. We shall soon encounter the emphasis by R. Menahem ha-Meiri on the deep and genuine divide between Christianity and paganism, but in the final analysis it is a daunting task to argue that worship of Jesus of Nazareth as God is not *avodah zarah* by the standards of Jewish law.

In his final work, Katz did utilize medieval Jewish-Muslim relations as a tool for evaluating the causes of the tense relationship between Jews and Christians in the same period.[44] Here he endorsed the position that tensions were much greater in the latter case because the truth of one religion depended on the falsehood of the other only in the Jewish-Christian relationship. This stray remark requires elaboration. As I wrote on another occasion with respect to polemical literature,[45] the Jewish-

---

40 *Bein Yehudim le-Goyim*, p. 36; *Exclusiveness and Tolerance*, p. 25. The formulation in the English version is not as sharp.

41 *Bein Yehudim le-Goyim*, p. 46; *Exclusiveness and Tolerance*, p. 37.

42 So the anonymous rabbi attacked by Maimonides in his *Epistle on Martyrdom*; see Abraham Halkin and David Hartman, *Epistles of Maimonides: Crisis and Leadership* (Philadelphia, 1993), pp. 16, 21. Cf. also *Hiddushei ha-Ran to Sanhedrin* 61b. (The author is not Rabbi Nissim Gerondi but a somewhat earlier Spanish talmudist.)

43 See my "Mission to the Jews" (above, n. 33).

44 *Et Lahqor ve-Et Lehitbonen* (Jerusalem: 1999), p. 54.

45 "Jewish-Christian Polemics," *The Encyclopedia of Religion* 11: 389.

Christian encounter was more stressful because of both its greater intimacy and its greater difference. Since the Hebrew Bible played a considerably less important role in Islam than it did in Christianity, arguments over its meaning, including, of course, the identity of True Israel, were incomparably more significant in the Jewish-Christian interaction. With regard to theology, it was the greater gap between Jews and Christians that was decisive in exacerbating tensions. "Islamic monotheism left no room for the creative rancor that produced the philosophical dimension of Jewish-Christian discussions, which addressed such issues as trinity and incarnation."[46] In our context, sharper terminology may be in order. Christianity was *avodah zarah*; Islam was not.

A comparative dimension might also have been useful in testing one aspect of Katz's controversial hypothesis about the difference between medieval Ashkenazim and their sixteenth- and seventeenth-century counterparts. Katz asserts that by the seventeenth century, Ashkenazic Jews had spiritualized the ideal of martyrdom and were far less aggressive in confronting Christianity. These changes, he says, resulted from greater insularity. Christianity had become less of a psychological reality, and the sense of spiritual threat or temptation had diminished.[47]

This is not the forum to address the controversy over this thesis in detail. I think that Katz was wrong about spiritualization and right about aggressiveness, but his reason for the decline in aggressiveness is highly speculative. We would do well to ask why medieval Provencal, Italian, and Spanish Jews were less aggressive than those of Northern Europe in their anti-Christian works. Were those Jews less tempted by Christianity? Was it less of a psychological reality for them? In these societies, it is likely that differences in cultural attitudes and norms of expression were at work. But then, as the Middle Ages wore on, there was fear. This is certainly evident in late medieval Spain, where the Tortosa disputation took place in a profoundly different atmosphere from the one that had prevailed in Barcelona a century and a half earlier, but there were similar transformations in Ashkenaz as well. Rabbi Yehiel of Paris did not dare to address Nicholas Donin in the manner that his contemporary Ashkenazic coreligionists wrote or even, I am inclined to think, still spoke to Christians on the street. Later—but still well before

---

46   "Jewish-Christian Polemics," 389.
47   "Bein Tatn'u le-Ta'h Ta't," in *Halakhah ve-Qabbalah*, pp. 311–330 .

the period identified by Katz—Yom Tov Lipmann Muehlhausen was much less caustic than Joseph Official, and he found it necessary to deny the obvious meaning of pejorative Jewish terms applied to Christian *sancta*.[48] The public aggressiveness of Ashkenazic Jewry changed because it had to change.

Katz's social explanations for the stance of medieval Jews on legal issues in the Jewish-Christian relationship always make intuitive sense, but on rare occasions his formulation is problematic or the evidence is pushed too hard. Thus, he points to an assertion in *Sefer Hasidim* that penance is needed for a Jew who desecrated the Sabbath to save a gentile and contrasts it to the injunctions in the same work to fight a Jew who is attempting to kill an innocent gentile and to take up arms in support of Christian allies who fulfill their obligations to their Jewish partners. The contrast in these positions certainly requires explanation, and Katz suggests two distinctions that somehow appear to merge. There is a difference, he says, between reflective and spontaneous reactions and between the response to an individual Christian and the approach to Christians as a stereotyped group. The reflective reaction requires penance; the spontaneous one requires you to help. The individual is entitled to your assistance; the representative of the group is not.[49]

In this instance however, these are problematic distinctions. It is hard to see why saving someone on the Sabbath involves less of a direct, spontaneous emotion than saving him from a Jewish murderer, or why the former is a stereotypical Christian while the latter is an individual. I think that Katz is correct in his further assertion that the imperative to help the gentile may well emerge from a direct human reaction that transcends self-interest, but I cannot prove this. Even if this is so, the distinction between the cases can result from the conviction, or even instinct, that indifference to the life of a gentile may—and should—be overridden far more readily than the prohibition against violating the Sabbath.

In another instance, I believe that Katz's intuition is correct, but he presses the evidence to the point of misrepresentation. Medieval Jews had a powerful incentive to permit the deriving of benefit from gentile wine; at the same time, they did not drink it and in most cases did not

---

48   *Sefer Nizzahon* (Altdorf, 1644), p. 194.
49   *Bein Yehudim le-Goyim*, p. 105; *Exclusiveness and Tolerance*, pp. 100–101.

want to drink it. As Katz presents it, Rabbenu Tam permitted benefit on the basis of an argument that should logically have permitted drinking as well. When Ri objected by pointing to this implication, Rabbenu Tam withdrew his argument and produced a different one that would not lead to the unwanted conclusion. Katz points out that the Talmud itself makes no distinction between benefit and drinking, so that only the extra-halakhic concern prevented Ri and Rabbenu Tam from endorsing a consistent position.[50]

In a footnote found only in the Hebrew version, Katz concedes that R. Tam's statement "can be interpreted to mean that his ruling was reported inaccurately, but even if this is so one can still wonder why Ri would have been upset by the conclusion that Rabbenu Tarn reached in the form it was reported to him."[51] First of all, R. Tam's statement cannot just be *interpreted* to mean that his position was misreported; that is the only thing it can mean. Second, although the Talmud does not generally distinguish between deriving benefit from Gentile wine and drinking it, in a critically relevant line in this discussion it does. Ri objected to a permissive ruling that was both unprecedented and contrary to accepted practice. What is really striking is R. Tam's reaction, "God forbid," to Ri's assertion in his name, a reaction that powerfully supports Katz's fundamental thesis about the depth of the instinct at work here. We have already seen an instance in which Katz was acutely sensitive to the significance of this formula. In this case he did not pick it up, apparently because he was committed to the position that R. Tam had changed his mind. The deep aversion of Ashkenazic authorities to permitting the drinking of gentile wine really does emerge here, but Katz has constructed a misleading scenario regarding both the unfolding of R. Tam's position and its presumed inconsistency.[52]

---

50 *Bein Yehudim le-Goyim*, pp. 55–56; *Exclusiveness and Tolerance*, pp. 46–47.

51 *Bein Yehudim le-Goyim*, p. 56, n. 36.

52 After writing this, I had the benefit of reading the typescript of Haym Soloveitchik's study, "Sahar bi-Stam Yeinam be-Ashkenaz—Pereq be-Toledot ha-Halakhah ve-ha-Kalkalah ha-Yehudit bi-Yemei ha-Beinayim," which will have appeared before the publication of this article. I am grateful to Prof. Soloveitchik for providing me with this typescript, which contains an important analysis of the exchange between Ri and Rabbenu Tam and argues persuasively for the existence of a deeply ingrained instinctive revulsion among Ashkenazic Jews at the prospect of drinking gentile wine.

Katz's report of a tosafist position in another case also requires correction, but the misleading formulation is only slightly off the mark. He tells us that Ri permitted taking

In his analysis of the perception of Christianity as *avodah zarah*, Katz frequently reiterates what he presents as a fundamental characteristic of halakhic literature: the limited, local application of a principle mobilized to deal with a particular problem. The point is that formulations implying that medieval Christians are not idolaters were not generalized beyond the narrow context that produced them. I do not doubt that this characteristic of halakhic literature, which Haym Soloveitchik has called "halakhic federalism,"[53] is real, and Katz uses it convincingly to refute scholars who equated the tosafists with the Meiri by attributing to them a principled denial that medieval Christians worship *avodah zarah*. But on a matter so fundamental to the self-perception of Ashkenazic Jewry and its relationship with its environment, we are entitled to ask whether the overwhelming instinct that Christianity is *avodah zarah* should inform our understanding of the local contexts themselves. Did medieval Ashkenazic halakhists ever mean to say—even in narrow applications—that Christianity is not *avodah zarah*?

The answer to this question may very well be no. In some of those cases, Katz appears willing to interpret the relevant statements so narrowly that they do not make any assertion about the Christian religion itself. Thus, the declaration that the gentiles among us (or "in this time") are not worshippers of *avodah zarah* means only that they are not particularly devout.[54] The most important example of this issue, *Tosafot's* assertion that "association" (*shittuf*) is not forbidden to non-Jews, elicits a more ambiguous treatment. Katz's own presentation in an earlier article, as well as in his book, indicates that he understands the term to refer to worship of God along with something else. Thus, Christianity would not be *avodah zarah* for gentiles. This principle, however, was applied only in the narrow context in which it arose, to wit, accepting an oath from a Christian in a business

interest from gentiles beyond the requirements of bare sustenance, because Jews were now a minority among the gentiles (*Bein Yehudim le-Goyim*, p. 40; *Exclusiveness and Tolerance*, p. 30). This is a category Katz uses to explain a larger pattern of halakhic adjustment. So he mobilizes it here, when in fact Ri grounded his permissive ruling not on the numerical status of the Jews but on the related fact that they are subject to economic persecution.

53 *Halakhah, Kalkalah, ve-Dimmuy Azmi* (Jerusalem: 1985), pp. 79–81.

54 "Sheloshah Mishpatim Apologetiyyim be-Gilguleihem," in *Halakhah ve-Qabbalah*, p. 284.

dispute.[55] In the article, however, he proceeds to discuss "meticulous jurists" (*baalei halakhah dayqanim*) who understood the tosafists to mean only that gentiles may take an oath in God's name while also thinking of another entity; they never meant to suggest that gentiles may associate God with something else in worship. Nonetheless, Katz does not retract his earlier interpretation, and in the Hebrew version of the book he reiterates it without going on to discuss the meticulous jurists. If, as is very likely, *tosafot* never meant to say that Christian worship is not *avodah zarah* for gentiles, there is no example of narrow application here. There was never any principle that could have been generalized.[56]

One of the weaknesses of halakhic federalism is that it cannot easily survive scrutiny. When exposed to the light, it withers. And so we come to ha-Meiri, where one of Katz's points is precisely that federalism withers, to be replaced by an all-embracing principle excluding Christians from the category of idolaters. Many of Katz's best characteristics emerge in this analysis: sensitivity to language, to pitch, to tone—not just ha-Meiri's new formula describing Christians and Muslims as nations bound by the ways of religions, but the celebratory language and the elimination of other arguments as unnecessary. We find once again a remarkable instinct that cuts to the core of a phenomenon even where hard evidence is thin: in this case, the instinct that philosophy is somehow at work here even though the evidence Katz adduces for this is not utterly compelling and the position to be explained is the opposite of that of Maimonides. In other instances we have seen Katz's intuitions confirmed by polemical works; in this case, Moshe Halbertal has demonstrated the essential correctness of Katz's instincts by reference to philosophical and other texts.[57]

---

55   "Sheloshah Mishpatim" p. 279. Cf. *Bein Yehudim le-Goyim*, p. 163. The English version, *Exclusiveness and Tolerance*, p. 163, omits the reference to worship. As we shall see, this may well be a better understanding of *Tosafot*, but in light of the two Hebrew discussions, I doubt that it represents Katz's true intent at this point in his analysis.

56   There is an additional interpretive option that was proposed to understand this *tosafot* that Katz does not address in the article or in the Hebrew version of the book, but it makes an appearance in the English. *Shittuf* may mean nothing more than the inclusion of references to God and something else—in this case the saints—in the same oath. Christian worship remains *avodah zarah* even for gentiles. I have discussed the various interpretations of this *tosafot* in Appendix III of *The Rebbe, the Messiah, and the Scandal of Orthodox Indifference* (London and Portland, Oregon, 2001).

57   Moshe Halbertal, *Bein Torah le-Hokhmah: Rabbi Menahem ha-Meiri u-Ba'alei ha-Halakhah ha-Maimunim bi-Provence* (Jerusalem, 2000), pp. 80–108. Katz laid special emphasis

Finally, the question of Christianity as *avodah zarah* is intimately connected to the question of the damnation or salvation of Christians. On two occasions, Katz noted a passage in the Hebrew account of the 1240 Paris disputation where R. Yehiel indicated that Christians can be saved if they observe the seven Noahide laws.[58] Katz does not directly address the transparent problem that *avodah zarah* is one of those commandments. Nonetheless, his discussion of this passage and of the disputation as a whole is extremely perceptive, and his insight that the need to respond to Christian attacks on the Talmud could lead to the growth of genuine tolerance has significance beyond the geographical and chronological arena that concerns him in this chapter.[59]

Let us conclude, then, by returning to Katz's introductory comment about the contemporary relevance of his work. Within the medieval universe of discourse, we can unhesitatingly speak of both tolerance and intolerance when discussing the dominant religions. When you have the power to kill or expel—and these options are realistic within your universe of discourse—you exhibit tolerance if you refrain from exercising that power. When you kill or expel one group but not another, you have shown tolerance toward the group that remains. The more tolerant the society, the higher the standard an individual or subcommunity must meet to be considered tolerant.

For a relatively powerless minority, the situation is quite different. We can speak of theoretical tolerance and intolerance, but because the group in question has no authority to enforce its norms, we sometimes slip into a usage in which intolerance becomes synonymous with hostility. This equation, however, blurs important distinctions. Bernard of Clairvaux, for example, was hostile to Jews, even very hostile, but he

---

on ha-Meiri's remarkable assertion that a Jewish convert to Christianity is entitled to the rights accorded to civilized believers, whereas an unconverted heretic is not (*Bein Yehudim le-Goyim*, pp. 124–125; *Exclusiveness and Tolerance*, pp. 123–124). On a similar assertion by Moses ha-Kohen of Tordesillas, see my "Christians, Gentiles, and the Talmud: A Fourteenth-Century Jewish Response to the Attack on Rabbinic Judaism," in *Religionsgespräche im Mittelalter*, ed. by Bernard Lewis and Friedrich Niewoehner (Wiesbaden, 1992), p. 126. Note, too, Yom Tov Lippman Muehlhausen, *Sefer Nizzahon*, p. 193.

58   "Sheloshah Mishpatim," p. 273; *Bein Yehudim le-Goyim*, p. 115; *Exclusiveness and Tolerance* p. 113. See my discussion of this passage in "Al Tadmitam ve-Goralam shel ha-Goyim," pp. 80–81.

59   See my observations in "Christians, Gentiles, and the Talmud," p. 130.

was simultaneously tolerant, even—by medieval Christian standards—very tolerant.[60] No medieval Jew can be judged by this standard, because no Jew was confronted with the temptations or restraints of power.

Powerlessness confers freedom to express hostility without the need for a real confrontation with the consequences. One can curse one's enemies, condemn them to hellfire, list the innumerable offenses for which they should be executed and the many obligations that they must be compelled to discharge—and then go to bed. Power brings responsibility and subjects its bearers to the discipline of governing.[61] Powerlessness provides the luxury of both untested tolerance and untested zealotry. Neither the tolerance nor the zealotry may survive the transition to power.

Whether we frame the issue as hostility versus cordiality or tolerance versus intolerance, Katz's studies reveal how medieval Jews confronting a Christian society dealt with the normative texts that they had inherited. Though their strategies often carried significant practical consequences, the effects were limited by the reality of exile. Katz, on the other hand, wrote in an age of restored Jewish sovereignty. He certainly welcomed this, but he also saw the dangers and no doubt hoped that his work, free of the unhistorical apologetics of an earlier generation, would provide guidance as well as understanding. This dimension of his achievement is difficult to assess. But within the four ells of scholarly endeavor, the impact of his oeuvre is beyond cavil. Every scholar of the Jewish experience is indebted to Jacob Katz for setting a standard of erudition, insight, and clarity that we can only strive to approach.

---

60 See my "The Attitude of St. Bernard of Clairvaux toward the Jews," *Proceedings of the American Academy for Jewish Research* 40 (1972): 89–108.
61 Note the discussion of some of these sometimes surprising complexities in Kenneth R. Stow, "Papal and Royal Attitudes toward Jewish Lending in the Thirteenth Century," *AJS Review* 6 (1981): 161–184.

INTRODUCTION TO *THE JEWISH-CHRISTIAN DEBATE IN THE HIGH MIDDLE AGES*

A Critical Edition of the Nizzahon Vetus with an Introduction, Translation, and Commentary

(Jewish Publication Society of America: Philadelphia, 1979)

I. ON JEWISH-CHRISTIAN POLEMIC

Polemical literature is one of the liveliest manifestations of Jewish-Christian relations in the Middle Ages. At times calm and almost dispassionate, at other times angry and bitter, religious polemic is a reflection of the mood and character not only of the disputants themselves but of the age in which they wrote and spoke. While the tone of the Jewish-Christian debate ranges from somber to sarcastic to playfully humorous, the underlying issues were as serious to the participants as life itself. Failure on the part of the Christian polemicist could encourage Jews in their mockery of all that was sacred and might engender doubts in Christian minds; failure by the Jew could lead to apostasy and, on some occasions, severe persecution and even martyrdom. Religious arguments could be stimulating and enjoyable, but the stakes involved were monumental.

The *Nizzahon Vetus*, or *Old Book of Polemic*, is a striking example of Jewish disputation in its most aggressive mode. The anonymous author collected an encyclopedic array of anti-Christian arguments current among late thirteenth-century Franco-German Jews. Refutations of christological exegesis, attacks on the rationality of Christian doctrine, a critique of the Gospels and Church ritual, denunciations of Christian morality—all these and more are presented in an exceptionally vigorous style that is not especially scrupulous about overstepping the bounds of civility. Although both the style and comprehensiveness of the book are not altogether typical of Jewish polemic, they make the *Nizzahon*

Vetus an excellent and unusually interesting vehicle for the study of this crucial and intriguing dimension of medieval Jewish-Christian relations.

Jewish-Christian polemic begins at the very dawn of Christianity. The reasons for this are built into the essence of the Christian faith, for a religion that was born out of Judaism had to justify the rejection of its parent. Indeed, theological and exegetical approaches which can be labeled polemic can also be seen as the elementary building blocks of the developing faith, since certain early doctrines grew naturally out of a reading of the Hebrew Bible. Isaiah 53, which could easily be read as a reference to the vicarious atonement of a "servant of the Lord," served as an almost inevitable explanation of the paradox of the Messiah's crucifixion. Whether or not Jesus applied such an understanding of this passage to his own career (and he probably did not),[1] this is a case in which a crux of later polemic was read christologically for fundamental, internal reasons.

Some doctrines, of course, did not develop out of the Hebrew Scriptures. Nevertheless, Christian acceptance of the divine origin of those Scriptures, together with an espousal of central beliefs that did not seem to be there, generated a need to explain this omission. Thus, even if Jews had not pressed their opposition to statements concerning the divinity of the Messiah, the virgin birth, or the abrogation of the Law, almost any serious Christian would have tried to find biblical justification for these doctrines. It is, in fact, often difficult to tell when a given Christian argument is directed against Jews and when it is an attempt to deal with a problem raised by the writer's own study of the Bible. This uncertainty applies even to some works ostensibly aimed against the Jews, because the number of such works through the ages seems disproportionate to the threat that Judaism could have posed.[2]

---

[1]   See M. D. Hooker *Jesus and the Servant* (London, 1959); Y. Kaufmann, *Golah ve-Nekhar* (Tel Aviv, 1929/30), 1: 381–389.

[2]   The major anti-Jewish polemics through the twelfth century were summarized by A. L. Williams, *Adversus Judaeos* (Cambridge, 1935). See also B. Blumenkranz, *Les Auteurs Chrétiens Latins du Moyen Age sur les Juifs et le Judaisme* (Paris, La Haye, 1963). J. Pelikan has remarked that as Judaism became less of a threat to Christianity, Christian writers tended "to take their opponents less and less seriously" (*The Christian Tradition, vol. 1, The Emergence of the Catholic Tradition [100–600]* [Chicago and London, 1971], p. 21). There is some validity to this observation, but precisely this fact leads one to ask why Christians continue to write books refuting people that they do not take seriously.

Were Jewish questions, then, the primary factor behind the search for biblical testimonies to Christian truth? Was it, as one scholar has suggested, because of Jewish arguments that Christians became concerned with the conflict between the genealogies of Jesus in Matthew and Luke?[3] Did the incredulous inquiries of Jews inspire the various rationales concerning the need for the incarnation, up to and including Anselm's *Cur Deus Homo*?[4] The extent of Jewish influence is difficult to determine, but it is clear that such issues would not have been ignored in the absence of Jewish disputants. It is surely evident that when Isidore of Seville, in a work on Leviticus, has a Jew ask why Christians fail to bring sacrifices or observe the sabbatical year, he is raising problems suggested by his own reading of the Bible, and yet Peter Damian transferred these passages without change into a polemical work against the Jews.[5] Christians undoubtedly wrote books against Judaism in response to a challenge actually raised by Jews, but they were also motivated by the internal need to deal with issues that were both crucial and profoundly disturbing.

One approach to the puzzling conflict between the Hebrew Bible and Christian beliefs was a frontal attack. Marcion and other Christian heretics rejected the Jewish Scriptures and subjected them to a wide-ranging critique. In one respect this was a simple and straightforward solution since the problem vanishes entirely; there was no longer any need to engage in point by point exegesis of individual passages. On the other hand, this radical solution of one problem created another even more intractable difficulty. The Gospels, after all, clearly recognized the divine origin of the Hebrew Bible; indeed, many of the biblical testimonies central to later polemic are found in the New Testament. The suggestion that offending New Testament passages be emended was hardly palatable to most Christians, and mainstream Christianity rejected the one approach that would have sharply limited the scope of the Jewish-Christian debate.

---

3   See A. B. Hulen, "The Dialogue with the Jews as Source for the Early Jewish Argument against Christianity," *Journal of Biblical Literature* 51 (1932): 61.

4   On the polemical implications of *Cur Deus Homo?* see A. Funkenstein, "Ha-Temurot be-Vikkuah ha-Dat she-bein Yehudim le-Nozerim ba-Me'ah ha-Yod-Bet," *Zion* 33 (1968): 129–132.

5   See my "St. Peter Damian: His Attitude toward the Jews and the Old Testament," *Yavneh Review* 4 (1965): 102–104. The issue of Christian sacrifices in the Middle Ages is raised in N. V. (pp. 207–209), but only in response to a Christian argument.

The Middle Ages

It seems a bit strange to assert that the vigorous anti-Jewish position of the heretics would have minimized polemical activity, but this is indeed the case. Absolute rejection of the Hebrew Bible by Christians would have eliminated much of the wrangling over the meaning of verses which plays such a prominent role in medieval polemic. Moreover, the heretics' reading of the Bible was, in an ironic way, closer to that of the Jews than to that of orthodox Christians, because, like the Jews, they understood it literally. Total rejection eliminated the need for allegory entirely.[6]

In one area, however, such heretics enriched the Jewish-Christian argument. One of the central heretical methods of defending their pejorative evaluation of the Hebrew Bible was to show that it is replete with absurdities and contradictions. In discussions with heretics, orthodox Christians tended to shrink from such arguments, but in debates with Jews they changed their tune. Of course, the arguments were rechanneled; they were no longer proof of the absurdity of the Hebrew Bible, only of the absurdity of literal interpretation. In effect, therefore, Jews found themselves defending their Bible against both heretical barbs and orthodox allegory.[7]

One of the sharpest points of contention in the early confrontation between Jews and Christians—one in which the Christian position was formed by both internal and external factors—was the famous assertion that Christians are the true (*verus*) Israel. Here again, acceptance of the Hebrew Bible led naturally to the need to transform it into a Christian document, and the process through which Israel came to refer to Christians was almost inevitable. In this case, however, powerful forces from the outside combined to make this an argument of extraordinary significance. The pagan accusation that Christianity was an innovation had to be answered because it could affect the very legitimacy of the new faith, and the only effective response was to don the mantle of antiquity through the identification of Christendom with Israel.

Jews could hardly have been expected to suffer such a claim with equanimity. The most succinct summary of the instinctive Jewish reaction to this assertion is the Greek quotation from the *Dialogue*

[6] For a summary of Marcion's attitude towards the Hebrew Bible and his manipulation of the New Testament text, see E. C. Blackman, *Marcion and His Influence* (London, 1948), pp. 42–60, 113–124. Cf. also Pelikan, p. 77.
[7] See appendix 3.

with Trypho which Marcel Simon placed on the cover of his *Verus Israel.* "What?!" said Trypho. "You are Israel?!"[8] After the initial shock wore off, Jews realized that this was a direct assault against the fundamental underpinnings of Judaism, an effort to abscond with the Bible. They pointed with outrage to the arbitrariness of applying all favorable biblical statements about Israel to the church and all pejorative ones to the Jews, and by the high Middle Ages they had assembled passages from the Bible in which favorable and unfavorable references were inextricably intertwined. The same Israel would be exiled and redeemed, and since the church would not suffer the former fate it could hardly lay claim to the latter reward.[9] Whatever the Jewish response, the issue was critical, because it appeared that Christianity could lay claim to legitimacy only by denying it to Judaism. There was no room (at least according to the dominant view) for two spiritual Israels.

The corpus of early Christian works directed against Judaism is, as we have already noted, rather extensive. Anti-Christian works by Jews, on the other hand, are virtually nonexistent before the twelfth century. One reason for this disparity is that Jews had no internal motivation for writing polemics against Christians; in times or places where Christianity was not a threat, we cannot expect Jews to be concerned with a refutation of its claims. Moreover, during much of the so-called Dark Ages, Jews in Christian lands produced no literature that has survived. Consequently, aside from some largely philosophical material in Arabic, our sources for the Jewish side of the discussion consist of scattered references in rabbinic literature,[10] the collections of folk polemic that go by the name *Toledot Yeshu*[11] and quotations in Christian works.[12] The last group of sources is by far the richest, but

---

8   *Ti oun, phesin ho Tryphon, hymeis Israel este?! Dialogue with Trypho,* ch. 123.

9   On the subject of *verus Israel,* see pp. 169–171, and the notes to p. 126. On the typology of Jacob and Esau, see G. D. Cohen, "Esau as Symbol in Early Medieval Thought," in *Jewish Medieval and Renaissance Studies,* ed. by A. Altmann, pp. 19–48, and cf. the notes to p. 55.

10   A list of such references appears in H. H. Ben Sasson's "Disputations and Polemics," *Encyclopaedia Judaica* (Jerusalem, 1971), 6: cols. 81–82.

11   See S. Krauss, *Das Leben Jesu nach Jüdischen Quellen* (Berlin, 1902).

12   See B. Blumenkranz's "Die Jüdischen Beweisgründe im Religionsgespräch mit den Christen," *Theologische Zeitschrift* 4 (1948): 119–147, and his *Juifs et Chrétiens dans le Monde Occidental, 430–1096* (Paris, 1960), pp. 213–289. It is likely that the brief *Sefer Nestor ha-Komer* (Altona, 1875) also predates the high Middle Ages. For a short summary of some sporadic references to other early Jewish polemics, see J. Rosenthal,

determining the authenticity of Jewish arguments cited in some of the purely literary Christian dialogues is a risky procedure. The genuineness of such arguments can usually be tested by their appearance in later Jewish polemic or by their inherent plausibility, and despite the usefulness of these criteria it hardly needs to be said that they are far from foolproof. It is therefore not until the second half of the twelfth century that we can begin to speak with confidence about the details of the Jewish argument against Christianity.

An examination of Jewish-Christian polemic in the high Middle Ages reveals an arena in which most of the battles take place along well-charted lines but where certain new approaches are beginning to make themselves heard. The Christian side is usually on the offensive with respect to biblical verses, although, as I have indicated, there is a fundamentally defensive element in the entire enterprise of searching for biblical testimonies. Indeed, we find Jews arguing that Christianity is so inherently implausible that only the clearest biblical evidence could suffice to establish its validity.[13] Nevertheless, the structure of the Jewish-Christian debate was such that the initiative was taken by Christians in the area of scriptural evidence. On the other hand, Jews usually initiated the discussion of doctrinal questions because they felt that the irrationality of Christianity could be established through such an approach. In each area, however, the initiative could shift; Jews did not refrain from citing specific verses to refute Christian beliefs and Christians did not hesitate to attack Jewish doctrines on philosophical or moral grounds.

The bulk of polemical discussions continued to center around the time-honored issue of christological verses in the Hebrew Bible. Before such discussions could take place, ground rules had to be set up. What is the scope of the Hebrew Bible, and what text can legitimately be cited? Particularly in the early centuries, Christians would have liked very much to include the apocrypha in their arsenal, and they were even

"Haganah ve-Hatqafah be-Sifrut ha-Vikkuah shel Yemei ha-Beinayim," *Proceedings of the Fifth World Congress of Jewish Studies* (Jerusalem, 1969) 2: 354–355. On the degree to which early disputations reflect real encounters, see the summary in A. P. Hayman, *The Disputation of Sergius the Stylite against a Jew*, vol. 2 (Louvain, 1973), Intro., pp. 64*–70*.

13 See J. Rosenthal's introduction to his edition of *Sefer Yosef ha-Meqanne* (Jerusalem, 1970), p. 27.

more anxious to quote certain Septuagint readings. The very nature of this issue, however, forced a resolution in favor of the Jews. It can be very frustrating and unprofitable to argue with someone who simply denies the legitimacy of your quotations, and it was nearly impossible to prove that the apocrypha should be canonical or that Septuagint variants are superior to the Masoretic text (especially when some of those variants were a result of the corruption of the Septuagint text itself). Jerome's respect for the Hebrew text accelerated the resolution of this matter in favor of the Jewish position, and despite the persistence of a handful of apocryphal quotations and a few Septuagint variants, Christians settled down to the task of demonstrating the christological nature of the biblical text accepted by Jews.[14]

This task was pursued on two levels, and it would be useful to draw a distinction between genuine polemic and what could be called exegetical polemic. Genuine polemic involved those verses whose christological interpretation provided a genuine challenge to a Jew. If *'almah* meant virgin, then Isaiah 7:14 really seemed to speak of a virgin birth. Jeremiah 31:31 really spoke of a new covenant that God would make with the house of Israel. What did that mean? Isaiah 53 really did refer to a servant of the Lord who would suffer, despite his innocence, as a result of the sins of others. Who was that servant, and how was such suffering to be explained? If *shiloh* somehow meant Messiah (and many Jews conceded that it did), then Genesis 49:10 could reasonably be taken to mean that Jewish kingship would last until the messianic age and then cease. If the Messiah had not yet come, why was there no Jewish king? Specific rejoinders were necessary to blunt the force of such arguments, and it is no accident that the verses which fall into this category constitute the *loci classici* of polemical literature.

Nevertheless, a great deal of that literature is devoted to a discussion of passages of such weak polemical force that specific refutation was hardly even necessary. Such passages multiplied as a result of Christian exegesis of the Bible, and their christological interpretation was probably not even intended to persuade the nonbeliever. As time passed, however, this type of material began to make its way into polemical works, and the refutation of such "exegetical polemic" became a major

---

14   See the notes to p. 132.

concern of some Jewish writers. Although they used many of the same techniques that were applied to more serious arguments, Jewish polemicists confronted a situation in which the most straightforward response was the observation that there was simply no evidence for the christological assertion. Why should Cyrus in Isaiah 45 be Jesus? On what basis are the heavens in Psalm 19 identified with the apostles? Who says that David in Psalm 17 is Jesus, and why should we assume that the speaker in Psalm 13 is the church?[15] The inclusion of such material blurred the already fuzzy line between polemic and exegesis, and biblical commentaries become a particularly important source of polemical material.

This is true not only of Christian commentaries, which are obviously a major source of exegetical polemic, but of Jewish commentaries as well. When a Jewish exegete reached a passage that was a crux of Christian polemic, he would frequently make an effort, whether implicitly or explicitly, to undermine the christological interpretation.[16] One exegetical tendency that was greatly encouraged by such polemical goals was the denial of the messianic nature of certain biblical passages and the assertion that they referred instead to historical figures. Such a tendency appears in nonpolemical contexts as well, and some scholars have argued that the polemical motivation has been overstated; it is, nevertheless, beyond question that the desire to refute Christian interpretation played some role in the development of this type of exegesis. This is especially clear when surprising historical interpretations appear in overtly polemical works. In the *Nizzahon Vetus*, the most striking use of such exegesis appears in the discussion of Isaiah 11. While the author himself apparently understood that chapter messianically, he made use of a long-standing but clearly radical Jewish interpretation by maintaining that it could be referred to Hezekiah and Sennacherib. This view eliminates any christological reference, but it

---

15 Naturally there are many scriptural arguments that resist neat classification, and not every weak argument should be labeled "exegetical." Nevertheless, these examples are illustrative of Christological interpretations that hardly made any pretense of being demonstrably true. (Isaiah 45 was in a different category during the early stages of its polemical history; see the notes to p. 111.)

16 Some examples can be found in E. I. J. Rosenthal, "Anti-Christian Polemic in Medieval Bible Commentaries," *JJS* 11 (1960): 115–135. Jewish commentaries, of course, deal primarily with what I have called genuine polemic.

also does away with one of the central messianic passages in the Bible. Polemic, then, was at least a factor in stimulating and legitimizing an important development in medieval Jewish exegesis.[17]

Christians were genuinely puzzled at the Jewish failure to accept the overwhelming array of scriptural arguments which they had marshaled. Every major Christian doctrine could be supported by several verses in the Hebrew Bible, and some of these appeared utterly irrefutable. Indeed, a few verses seemed so impressive that the persuasive force of anyone of them should in itself have caused Jews to abandon their faith.[18] Only preternatural blindness or a conscious refusal to accept the truth could account for Jewish resistance, and both of these explanations played a major role in the medieval conception of the Jew.[19]

Jewish refutations of Christian interpretations of the Bible had to proceed on a verse-by-verse basis. There are, nevertheless, certain general principles that were applied time and again, and the most important of these was the argument from context. Jews argued that christological explanations of individual verses could rarely withstand scrutiny from the wider perspective of the passage as a whole, and they constantly cited adjoining verses to demonstrate this point. Perhaps the most important use of this argument was its application to the virgin birth explanation of Isaiah 7:14. This verse was by far the most significant evidence for the virgin birth in the Hebrew Bible, and its importance was enhanced by the fact that it was cited for this purpose in Matthew. Nevertheless, it was only with the greatest difficulty that Christians could respond to the Jewish argument that the birth was clearly expected to take place very shortly after Isaiah's announcement.[20] While the argument from context was not always as effective as it was here, it was the stock-in-trade of any medieval Jewish polemicist.

---

[17] On Isaiah 11, see the notes to p. 108; cf. also p. 125 and the notes there. For a general treatment of medieval Ashkenazic exegesis, see S. Poznanski, *Mavo la-Perush 'al Yehezqel u-Terei 'Asar le-Rabbi Eliezer mi-Balgenzi* (Warsaw, 1913; reprinted Jerusalem, 1965).

[18] So Peter the Venerable with respect to Proverbs 30:4; see his *Tractatus adversus Judaeorum Inveteratam Duritiem*, PL 189: 519.

[19] On blindness, see p. 68 and the notes there. For a possible Jewish reversal of the argument that Jews reject what they know to be the truth, see the notes to pp. 216 and 219.

[20] See the notes to p. 101.

The Jewish posture with respect to the citation of biblical verses was not always defensive. Indeed, the very essence of the Jewish position rested upon certain monumental assertions built upon the straightforward reading of the Hebrew Bible as a whole; It is precisely because of this that Jews were less concerned with the citation of specific controversial verses. A reading of the Bible as a whole leaves the unmistakable impression that the Messiah would bring peace, that he would be a human being, that God is one, and that the ritual law means what it says. The burden of proof that any of these impressions should be modified, elaborated, or rejected was upon the Christians; this was recognized to some degree by the Christian side, and it was one of the fundamental assumptions of Jewish writers. Nevertheless, some Jewish polemicists did compile lists of verses to demonstrate the validity of certain basic Jewish beliefs.[21]

There was another Jewish approach that involved the citation of specific verses, but it is difficult to decide how seriously to take it. The *Nizzahon Vetus*, the earlier *Sefer Yosef ha-Meqanne*, and some other Jewish polemics cite a series of verses which, they say, are aimed directly at Christianity. Several of these constitute clever responses to Christian assertions and are surely not to be taken seriously (e.g., the copper serpent does indeed represent Jesus and that is why Moses was commanded to hang it). I am inclined to think, however, that Jews were entirely serious about some of these quotations. One polemicist, in fact, cited such a verse immediately after a Christian question asking how the Torah could have omitted all reference to Jesus. Thus, the Bible explicitly warned against trusting in a man (Jer. 17:5; Ps. 146:3); it told Jews to punish a man who would claim to have a mother but not a father (Deut. 13:7); and it spoke of the humbling of anyone who pretended to be divine (Isa. 2:11). Such citations were hardly central to Jewish polemic, but they represent an effort by Jews to turn the tables on their opponents by finding "christological" verses of their own.[22]

---

21 The clearest instance of such an approach in pre-fourteenth-century Jewish polemic is Solomon de' Rossi's *'Edut Hashem Ne'emanah*, ed. by J. Rosenthal, *Mehqarim u-Meqorot* (Jerusalem, 1967), 1: 373–430. Jewish arguments based on the non-fulfillment of messianic prophecies of peace were very common; see the notes to p. 107.

22 See pp. 46 and 147 and the notes there. The problem of determining how serious Jews were in their citations of such verses was pointed out briefly by Judah Rosenthal in connection with a sixteenth-century polemic; see his introduction to Ya'ir ben Shabbetai

With respect to doctrinal issues, it was the Jewish side that usually took the offensive. Jews were convinced that some of the central articles of faith professed by Christians were not only devoid of scriptural foundation but were without logical justification as well; to use Christian terminology, they lacked both *ratio* and *auctoritas*.

The trinity, which was an obvious target for logical questions, posed a peculiar problem for Jewish polemicists; they considered it so irrational that they had trouble in coming to grips with it. Although no Jewish writer formulates his difficulties in precisely this fashion, it seems clear that Jews, in effect, asked themselves the following questions: "What do they mean when they talk about a triune God? They say that there are three, and then they say that the three are one. But this is patent nonsense. What, then, do they really believe? Which of these contradictory assertions am I to take seriously and which shall I dismiss as meaningless double-talk? Since they talk about the separate incarnation of one of the three persons, it is apparently the assertion of multiplicity that they really mean. In that case, I shall have to demonstrate to them that there is only one God."

It is only some such line of reasoning that can explain the persistent Jewish efforts to persuade Christians to accept monotheism on both logical and scriptural grounds. Jacob ben Reuben cites philosophical evidence that the world was created by no more than one God. The author of the *Nizzahon Vetus* wants to know what will happen if one person of the trinity makes a decision and another person reverses it. Solomon de' Rossi compiles a list of biblical verses which say that there is one God. Writer after writer reminds Christians that God proclaimed, "I, I am he, and there is no God beside me" (Deut. 32:39). To the Christian polemicist, of course, such arguments were virtually inexplicable and missed the point entirely. Christians, he would reply, believe in monotheism as much as Jews; the question is only the nature

da Correggio's *Herev Pifiyyot* (Jerusalem, 1958), p. 9. Cf. also his citation of several relevant verses in his "Haganah ve-Hatqafah . . . ," pp. 348–349. There is a non-polemical source which may contribute to the impression that there was some degree of seriousness in this enterprise. R. Jacob Tam, we are told, requested divine guidance in a dream to determine whether or not Jesus and Mary are alluded to in Scripture; see A. J. Heschel, "'Al Ruah ha-Qodesh bi-Yemei ha-Beinayim," *Alexander Marx Jubilee Volume*, New York, 1950, Heb. vol., p. 182, n. 27. See also Talmage's note in "Ha-Pulmus ha-Anti-Nozeri ba-Hibbur Leqet Qazar," *Michael* 4 (1976): 71.

of that one God. On this issue, Jews and Christians were operating on different wavelengths, and the essence of the problem was the rationality of the Christian belief.[23]

Christians attempted to defend the plausibility of the trinitarian faith by analogies with physical phenomena or by the identification of the three persons of the trinity with major attributes of God. Such arguments raised complex philosophical questions about divine attributes which transcended the boundaries of the Jewish-Christian debate but did play a role in some of the more sophisticated polemical works. Some Jews tried to undermine this type of explanation by arguing that it could not coexist comfortably with the doctrine of the incarnation which implied the sort of separability among the persons of the trinity that could not be attributed to divine power, wisdom, and will.[24]

The incarnation itself was subjected to a Jewish critique that ranged from the questioning of its necessity to the contention that it is impossible even for an omnipotent God.[25] Christian works quote several Jewish polemicists who became so carried away with the tendency to maintain the impossibility of Christian dogmas that they made such an assertion even with respect to the virgin birth. Here they were on very shaky ground; Christians presented effective rebuttals, and the extant Jewish polemics which discuss the matter concede that God could theoretically have caused a virgin to conceive.[26]

One Christian doctrine that Jews attacked on moral rather than philosophical grounds was the belief in the universal damnation which came in the wake of original sin. They argued that such treatment is clearly unfair and inconsistent with the mercy of God, and at least one Jewish writer made the same argument with respect to the damnation

---

[23] See the notes to pp. 42 (line 12) and 75. The most sophisticated Jewish discussion of the trinity during our period is in Moses of Salerno's *Ta'anot*, and not all Jewish polemicists based their arguments on the undefended assumption that Trinitarianism is simply a polytheism of three. There was, nevertheless, a pervasive Jewish feeling that this is the case. On this topic in general, see D. Lasker, *Jewish Philosophical Polemics against Christianity in the Middle Ages* (New York, 1977), pp. 48–104. (Lasker's important study appeared too late to be utilized systematically in this book; for an assessment, see my review in the *Association for Jewish Studies Newsletter* 22 [March 1978]: 16–17, 19.)

[24] See Appendix 5 for a detailed discussion.

[25] See Appendix 2.

[26] See p. 103 and the notes there.

of the unbaptized, especially unbaptized infants.[27] The terrible consequences of a failure to accept Christianity seemed particularly unjust in light of what Jews considered the unimpressive nature of the miracles associated with Jesus' career.[28] Moreover, some of the central assertions of the Christian faith appeared not only implausible but demeaning to God, and it did not seem right that someone who refused to believe such doctrines should be punished so severely.[29]

For their part, Christians were more than willing to engage in arguments appealing to reason, morality, or fairness. The ritual law, they said, was demonstrably unreasonable. Even where it did not contradict itself, no plausible reasons could be discovered for many of its precepts, and the contention that no reasons need to be given for the divine will is the refuge of desperate, unintelligent men.[30] The very fate of the Jewish people constitutes a rational argument against the validity of Judaism.[31] As for moral arguments, Jews believed that God revealed himself only to them,[32] they apparently thought that only they would be saved,[33] and they possessed a harsh and carnal Law.[34]

Each side, then, was well fortified with arguments from both Scripture and reason, and polemical activity in the twelfth and thirteenth centuries reached new heights. Among Christians, the outpouring of anti-Jewish polemic began in the late eleventh century and reached a crescendo in the twelfth. Peter Damian, Gilbert Crispin, Petrus Alfonsi, Rupert of Deutz, Peter the Venerable, "William of Champeaux," Peter of Blois, Walter of Châtillon, Alan of Lille—these and others made their contributions to the refutation of Judaism. Among Jews, the writing

---

[27]   See the notes to p. 218.

[28]   See especially the notes to p. 146.

[29]   See the notes to p. 222.

[30]   See Appendix 3.

[31]   See the notes to p. 89.

[32]   See Tertullian, *Adversus Judaeos*, PL 2: 599 = Tränkle, p. 4. On Jewish selfishness, cf. also the citations from Bernard in my study, "The Attitude of St. Bernard of Clairvaux toward the Jews," *Proceedings of the American Academy for Jewish Research* 40 (1972): 100.

[33]   So a priest of Étampes quoted by Joseph Official; see the notes to p. 89 for the full quotation and reference. There is, of course, a well-known Talmudic view that righteous Gentiles are admitted into the world to come (*Tosefta Sanhedrin*, ch. 13; B. Sanhedrin 105a), but the definition of righteousness was subject to several ambiguities. Moreover, this priest can hardly be faulted in light of comments made by Joseph Official's own father; see below, p. 68.

[34]   On the carnality of the Law, see p. 80 and the notes there.

of polemic began m the late twelfth century and reached a peak (at least in France and Germany) in the thirteenth. Joseph Kimhi, Jacob ben Reuben, the author of the *Vikkuah le-ha-Radaq*, Meir of Narbonne, Joseph Official (Yosef ha-Meqanne) and his father Nathan, Moses of Salerno, Mordecai of Avignon, Nahmanides, Jacob of Venice, Solomon de' Rossi and, finally, the anonymous author of the *Nizzahon Vetus* were the representatives of a concerted Jewish effort to present the case against Christianity. The renaissance of Christian polemic was as much a result of a general intellectual revival as of a new concern with Jews; the Jewish response, though somewhat delayed, was inevitable, and in two important instances, it was imposed in the form of forced disputations. Confrontations between Jews and Christians were on the increase, and their frequency, their tone, and even their content were being deeply influenced by the political, social, and economic changes of the twelfth and thirteenth centuries.

II. POLEMIC AND HISTORICAL REALITY

The *Nizzahon Vetus*, as we shall see, is a virtual anthology of Ashkenazic polemic in the twelfth and thirteenth centuries, and these centuries constitute a pivotal period in the history of the Jews of France and Germany. In France a major factor in the inexorable decline of the status of the Jews was the growing centralization of power in the hands of an unfriendly monarchy. The growing national unification, together with the increase in mass piety that had been stimulated as early as the eleventh century by the Gregorian reform and the Crusades, sharpened the awareness of the alien character of the Jew both nationally and religiously. The Christian piety of some of the French monarchs, particularly Louis IX, resulted in a major effort to bring about large-scale Jewish conversion, and considerable sums were expended for this purpose.[35] An investigation of the Talmud was pursued in 1240 by means of a Jewish-Christian debate that was really a trial, and the eventual burning of the Talmud shortly thereafter was a devastating psychological and cultural blow to French Jewry.[36] One Jewish source

---

[35] See S. W. Baron, *A Social and Religious History of the Jews* (New York, 1965), 3: 60.
[36] See Ch. Merchavia, *Ha-Talmud bi-Re'i HaNazrut* (Jerusalem, 1970), pp. 227–248.

reports that the king of France encouraged the arrangement of public disputations in 1272–73 by a Jewish convert to Christianity who promised to show the Jews that they were without faith and that, like heretics, they deserved to be burned.[37] Thus, for at least some Jews in thirteenth-century France, religious polemic was simply unavoidable.

Religious motives, however, were not the only factors which undermined the position of the Jews. The French monarchy saw its Jewish subjects as a convenient target for fiscal exploitation, and the economic security of the Jews grew more and more precarious.[38] A feeling of economic insecurity had, in fact, been developing for some time and had even made its way into legal discussions by the twelfth century. The Talmud had recorded a view limiting the amount of interest that a Jew might collect from a Gentile to whatever the Jew needed for bare sustenance. In discussing this passage, some French Jewish commentators argued that such a ruling was of no practical effect under prevailing conditions; since "we do not know how much tax the king will demand," any sum must be regarded as bare sustenance.[39]

Similar evidence of such insecurity can be found in the application of another talmudic law. A Jew who was owed money by a Gentile was not supposed to collect the debt on a pagan holiday unless it was an oral debt; in the latter case, he could collect at any time because he had no assurance that he would be able to collect later. Here again Ashkenazic jurists maintained that under the conditions prevailing in medieval Europe, a debt for which the Jew had written proof (or even a pledge) could be collected on a Christian holiday because there was never any real assurance that even such a debt could be collected at a later date.[40]

---

[37] See A. Neubauer, "Literary Gleanings, IX" *JQR*, o.s. 5 (1893): 713–714; cf. Baron, op. cit., 10: 63–64. See also R. Chazan, *Medieval Jewry in Northern France* (Baltimore and London, 1973), pp. 149–153, for indications that this convert was Pablo C(h)ristia(ni) and that the events may have taken place in 1269.

[38] See Baron, op. cit., 10: 57 ff. On the economic and political decline of French Jewry in the twelfth and thirteenth centuries see esp. Chazan, op. cit., pp. 39–40, 63–96, 100–124, 133–141, 148, 154–186.

[39] See S. Albeck, "Yahaso shel Rabbenu Tam li-Be'ayot Zemanno" (Hebrew), *Zion* 19 (1954): 107–108; cf. *Tosafot Bava Mezi'a*, 70b, s. v. *tashikh.*

[40] *Tosafot Avodah Zarah*, 2a, s. v. *velifroa' mehen.* On Christian efforts to minimize the effectiveness of documents held by Jews which proved Christian indebtedness, see S. Grayzel, *The Church and the Jews in the Thirteenth Century* (Philadelphia, 1933), p. 57, note 78, and pp. 106–107, note 3. The Jewish feeling of economic insecurity is also reflected in the texts in B. Dinur, *Yisrael ba-Golah* II. 1 (Tel Aviv and Jerusalem, 1965), pp. 157–168.

It would, of course, be easy to argue that these rulings were rationalizations to justify widespread violations of the relevant talmudic regulations and that they do not therefore reflect genuine insecurity. The tosafists, however, did not manipulate talmudic law in quite so facile a manner. Whatever their motivations, they were convinced that they were describing their status accurately. It is clear, then, that considerable economic uncertainty was a genuine element in the Jewish psyche as early as the twelfth century, and in the thirteenth such uncertainty must have become more disturbing than ever. Legal attacks against Jewish moneylending were made by both Louis IX and Philip the Bold, while Philip the Fair resorted to outright extortion and eventual banishment in 1306. Even during those periods in the fourteenth century when the Jews were invited back, their security was tenuous. They were subjected to the indirect pressure of the Inquisition, they were vulnerable to the depredations of mobs like the Pastoureaux in 1320, and they were constantly aware of the possibility of another sudden expulsion.[41]

The status of German Jewry in the late thirteenth and early fourteenth centuries was also undergoing a precipitous decline. The most important change involved a new application of the old conception of Jewish servitude. As a theological concept, this doctrine goes back to the early Christian centuries, and it even gave rise to certain practical conclusions. Jews, for example, were not supposed to hold positions that would give them control over Christians, since that would constitute a violation of the biblical injunction (Gen. 25:23) that the older (i.e., the synagogue) must serve the younger (i.e., the church);[42] although honored more in the breach than the observance this rule was not entirely without practical effect. Even the contention that Jews somehow belong to the royal treasury appears much earlier than the thirteenth century. Nevertheless, it was in that century that the fateful phrase *servi camerae* (serfs of the chamber) first appeared, and it was then that the potentially disastrous consequences of that phrase came to be applied in earnest.

---

[41] On the early fourteenth century, see Y. Yerushalmi "The Inquisition and the Jews of France in the Time of Bernard Gui," *HTR* 63 (1970): 317–377. See also R. Anchel, *Les Juifs de France* (1946), pp. 79–91 and Chazan, op. cit. pp. 191–205.

[42] See the notes to p. 55.

Ironically the immediate origins of this expression probably lie in a conflict that had no direct connection with the Jews and affected them at first in the form of an offer of protection. The Jewish question was a peripheral element in the struggle between pope and emperor concerning papal "fullness of power," and the assertion by Frederick II that the Jews were the serfs of his chamber meant, at least initially, that he was their legitimate protector.[43] It did not take long, however, for this doctrine to be transformed into an instrument of severe economic exploitation that reflected an effort to deny to Jews the status of free men.[44] This development was aggravated by recurring blood libels, anti-Jewish riots, local expulsions, and "feudal anarchy";[45] consequently, although German Jews were spared the agony of a nationwide banishment, their legal and social status had sunk to an almost intolerable level.

Polemical works in general and the *Nizzahon Vetus* in particular both reflect and illuminate the historical epoch in which they appear. It is true that many aspects of polemic remained relatively static throughout the Middle Ages, particularly the various arguments and counterarguments regarding the exegesis of specific biblical verses. Nevertheless, the *realia* of any historical period quickly found expression in polemic, and the impact of various political, philosophical, and religious developments can be measured in part by the degree to which they are reflected in this literature. Examples of this can be cited from virtually every period in the development of polemic. The failure of the Bar-Kokheba revolt was reflected almost immediately in Justin's *Dialogue with Trypho*; the problems of "Judaizers" in the church were discussed in the diatribes of John Chrysostom; Agobard's works reflected the challenge of Jewish economic development and political influence; the relatively calm tone of the polemics of Peter Damian and Gilbert Crispin as compared with the vituperation in works of the later Middle Ages mirrored basic differences in Jewish-Christian relations; various

[43]   See Baron, op. cit., 9: 141–147. For a recent discussion of the doctrine of fullness of power see W. D. McCready, "Papal *Plenitudo Potestatis* and the Source of Temporal Authority in Late Medieval Papal Hierocratic Theory," *Speculum* 48 (1973): 654–674.

[44]   See especially G. Kisch, *The Jews in Medieval Germany* (Chicago, 1949), pp. 159–168, and cf. Baron, op. cit., pp. 152 ff.

[45]   Baron, op. cit., pp. 193 ff.

philosophical developments had a major impact on the discussions of the trinity, incarnation, and virgin birth.[46]

In light of the deteriorating status of Ashkenazic Jewry described above, it is particularly interesting that one of the most striking characteristics of the *Nizzahon Vetus* and other Ashkenazic polemics of this period is their aggressiveness, vigor, and vituperation. The Jewish reader is instructed to press his arguments vigorously and not to permit the Christian to change the subject.[47] Christians are told that they will be condemned to hellfire.[48] A rabbi is said to have informed the king of Germany that "if one were to load a donkey with vomit and filth and lead him through the church, he would remain unharmed."[49] Sarcastic stories are told of conversations between Jesus and God,[50] while Jesus, Peter, Mary, and the holy spirit are all referred to in an insulting manner.[51] Some of these comments and witticisms are a reflection of what might be called folk polemic, since such arguments and anecdotes must have enjoyed wide circulation among Jews who were incapable of appreciating more complex and abstract discussions.[52]

Aggressiveness and vituperation were by no means universal among Jewish polemicists of this period and are characteristic primarily of *Sefer Yosef ha-Meqanne* and the *Nizzahon Vetus*, which were written in northern France and Germany. Other writers were far more cautious and restrained. Jacob ben Reuben, for example, prefixed his pioneering critique of Matthew with a diffident, even fearful, introduction. He wrote that Jews should really keep silent on such matters, that he recorded only a few of the errors in Matthew, and that he did even this much only at the insistence of his friends. Moreover, he asked that his

---

[46] There is no really good survey of Jewish-Christian polemic as a whole until the fourteenth century. A few studies, however, do give a picture of some of the areas of interaction between polemic and historical *realia*. See *Ver. Israel; Auteurs; Juifs et Chrét.*; J. Parkes, *The Conflict of The Church and the Synagogue* (London, 1934); I. Loeb, "La Controverse Religieuse entre les Chrétiens et les Juifs au Moyen Age," *Revue d'histoire des Religions* 17 (1888): 311–337; 18 (1888): 133–156 (also printed as a separate monograph); Baron, op. cit. 9: 55–134, 266–307; Funkenstein, op, cit., pp. 125–144.

[47] N. V., p. 169.

[48] Ibid., p. 68.

[49] Ibid., p. 69.

[50] See pp. 43, 77.

[51] See the notes to p. 152.

[52] Nevertheless, Rosenthal (*Jewish Social Studies* 27 [1965]: 121) justly rejects H. J. Schoeps's contention that N. V. stems from "the completely uneducated circles of German Jewry."

name not be mentioned in connection with the critique for fear that Christians would find out.[53] Solomon de' Rossi also counseled restraint at the beginning of his *'Edut Hashem Ne'emanah*. Indeed, he suggested that the Jewish polemicist avoid entirely such subjects as the trinity, incarnation, host, saints, and priesthood—in short, anything that might be offensive. Discussion should be limited to "the coming of the Messiah, the signs of his time, the commandments of the Torah, and the words of the prophets." Moreover, Solomon's advice on the tactics of the Jewish polemicist provides a striking contrast with the above-mentioned instructions given by the author of the *Nizzahon Vetus*. "One who argues with them," says our author, "should be strong willed by asking questions and giving responses that deal with the specific issue at hand and not permitting his antagonist to extricate himself from that issue until it has been completed."[54] Solomon, on the other hand, suggests that if the Jew sees that he is winning the argument, he should not try to appear like the victor but should instead change the subject.[55]

Our author's practical advice to the Jewish polemicist is not the only evidence indicating that the aggressiveness reflected in the *Nizzahon Vetus* was at least partly expressed in actual debate. Agobard accused Jews of blaspheming Jesus in the presence of Christians.[56] In the twelfth century, Jews were said to have challenged Christians to battle in the manner of Goliath.[57] Walter of Châtillon asserted that Jews not only fail to accept the truth of Christianity but actively pose objections to it.[58] The oft-quoted remark of Louis IX that a Christian layman who

---

[53] *Mil. Hashem*, p. 141. While Rosenthal is no doubt correct in suggesting that such factors as the higher philosophical level of *Mil. Hashem* were largely responsible for its less vituperative tone (introduction to *Sefer Yosef ha-Meqanne*, p. 28), this passage shows that fear was also a factor. These observations by Rosenthal revise his earlier judgment that *Mil. Hashem* was the sharpest polemic written by a medieval Jew (introduction to *Mil. Hashem*, p. 19).

[54] N. V., p. 169.

[55] See Solomon de' Rossi, *'Edut Hashem Ne'emanah*, Rosenthal's *Mehqarim*, 1: 378–379. Cf. also the citations in Rosenthal's introduction to *Yosef ha-Meqanne*, p. 17. The contrast between Solomon and N. V. was noted briefly by E. Urbach, "Études sur la littérature polémique au moyen age," *REJ* 100 (1935): 61.

[56] *PL* 104: 71, quoted in Williams, p. 355.

[57] *The Tractatus* in *TNA* 5: 1509 = *PL* 213: 749; cf. M. Guedemann, *Ha-Torah ve-ha-Hayyim bi-Yemei ha-Beinayim* . . . (Tel Aviv, 1968; first printing, Warsaw, 1897), pp. 11–12.

[58] Walter of Châtillon, *Tractatus* . . . , *PL* 209: 424.

is confronted by a Jewish polemicist should refute his adversary by stabbing him assumes that Jews were in the habit of initiating religious discussions.[59] Recent research has revealed that the unflattering explanation of Christian confession proposed in the *Nizzahon Vetus* was actually suggested to a Christian by a thirteenth-century French Jew; the priest, it was said, uses confession to obtain a list of adulterous women whom he can then seduce.[60] In light of this evidence, it appears that the assertiveness and self-confidence of Ashkenazic Jews were remarkable, and the view that most of the sarcastic comments in Jewish polemic were intended for internal consumption should probably be modified though not entirely discarded.[61]

Whether or not vituperative polemical remarks were intended for a Christian audience, such expressions of contempt toward the *sancta* of Christianity became known to the Inquisition. Bernard Gui, who directed the Inquisition in France in the early fourteenth century, referred to

[59] See Anchel, op. cit., pp. 106–107. On "the Jewish mission" through the eleventh century, see also *Juifs et Chrét.*, pp. 159–211.

[60] See J. Shatzmiller, *Recherches sur la communauté juive de Manosque au moyen age* (Paris, La Haye, 1973), pp. 123–127; cf. below, p. 223. Although I find Shatzmiller's analysis quite persuasive, several cautionary remarks should be added. First of all, the text is fragmentary, and Shatzmiller's reconstruction is based in part on the existence of the parallel in N. V. Secondly, the Jew was subjected to a formal accusation as a result of his remarks, and this must obviously temper any conclusions to be drawn from this incident concerning Jewish aggressiveness and freedom of speech. Finally, the Jew denied the charges by presenting a significantly different version of what he had said, and this denial, as Shatzmiller indicates, cannot be dismissed with absolute certainty.

[61] See Urbach, op. cit., pp. 60 ff., for a discussion of this problem. I. Levi had pointed to several sources which reflected Jewish initiation of vigorous religious debate, but he considered this a pre-thirteenth-century phenomenon; see his "Controverse entre un Juif et un Chrétien au XIe Siecle." *REJ* 5 (1882): 238. The view that Provencal Jews "took advantage of their freedom of speech" to a greater extent than other Jews was expressed by Grayzel, *The Church and The Jews in the Thirteenth Century*, p. 29. Baron has even suggested that outspoken polemical remarks may have been inspired by the Official family, and they themselves may have spoken as they did because of their roots in Narbonne, where Jews enjoyed exceptional privileges (op. cit., 9: 277). Many remarks of this type, however, cannot be traced to the Officials, and quite a few are attributed to earlier Ashkenazic figures. The truth probably lies in the most straightforward reading of the evidence, which indicates that the Jews of northern France and Germany did not shrink from outspoken polemic, at least in private conversation, even in the dark days of the late thirteenth century. On the assertiveness that marked Ashkenazic Jewry in the pre-Crusade period, see I. Agus, *The Heroic Age of Franco-German Jewry* (New York, 1969), especially pp. 11–20. Despite certain exaggerations, the main thrust of Agus's portrayal of this characteristic is valid.

a *cemetha* (= *shamta*, or curse) proclaimed by the Jews on the Day of Atonement which indicated through circumlocution that Jesus was the illegitimate son of a prostitute and Mary a woman of voluptuousness. In his study of Gui and the Jews of France, Y. Yerushalmi points to a liturgical poem quoted in *Endecktes Judenthum* that reads: "The nations link your holiness to the yoke of promiscuity, [but] your bethrothed revile the relation to the promiscuous woman (*yihus eshet ha-zimmah*)."[62]

This sort of expression appears in the *Nizzahon Vetus* several times, and Gui's attack points up the danger inherent in the use of such rhetoric even to a Jewish audience. Indeed, Gui was aware of a substantial number of Jewish works and expressions that he felt were directed against Christians or contained blasphemies. Among these were the *Alenu* prayer, Rashi's commentaries, Maimonides' *Mishneh Torah*, R. David Kimhi's commentary on Psalms, and the Talmud itself. Moreover, he was particularly sensitive to the Jewish practice of calling Christians "heretics" (*minim*), a practice that goes back to the Talmud and is reflected frequently in the *Nizzahon Vetus*.[63] Finally, it might be pointed out that a religious disputation actually became part of an inquisitional proceeding in 1320; not surprisingly, the inquisitor emerged victorious in a debate whose ground rules left something to be desired.[64]

The increasing economic exploitation of Jews was reflected all too clearly in the polemical work of Meir of Narbonne. Here the satirical veneer that often concealed Jewish bitterness was dropped, and Meir allowed himself an undisguised outburst which reveals how deeply Jews were hurt by their growing insecurity. The unfair expropriation of property on such a scale "is worse for a man than being murdered. When a person is objected to shame and disgrace, he would rather be

---

62 Yerushalmi, op. cit., pp. 362–363. The phrase *eshet ha-zimmah* is taken from Ezekiel 23:44. See also Merchavia, "Ha-Shamta be-Sifrut ha-Pulmus ha-Nozerit bi-Yemei ha-Beinayim," *Tarbiz* 41 (1971): 95–115; cf. especially pp. 97, 100, where he cites the reading *yihum* rather than *yihus*.
63 See Yerushalmi, op. cit., pp. 350 ff. In the Talmud, *minim* probably referred primarily to Jewish Christians. For the charge that Jews curse Christians in prayer, cf. also Jerome and Agobard cited in Merchavia, *Ha-Talmud bi-Re'i ha-Nazrut*, pp. 82–83. Cf. also the list of pejorative Jewish expressions about Christianity compiled by Christians in 1239 and summarized by Merchavia, p. 278.
64 See S. Grayzel, "The Confessions of a Medieval Jewish Convert," *Historica Judaica* 17 (1955): 89–120, and cf. Yerushalmi, op. cit., pp. 328–333.

dead; moreover, when he loses his money and he and his family remain 'in hunger, in nakedness, and in want of all things' (Deut. 28:48), then he will in fact die before his time." The culmination of this cry of anguish is Meir's anticipation of the day when the Gentiles will have to repay what they stole from the Jews.[65]

Many other aspects of the changing historical situation were also reflected in Jewish polemic. The growing importance of moneylending, for example, led to considerable discussion of its ethics and its biblical justification. Christians not only cited various time honored verses to prove that usury is a moral offense of universal relevance, but were apparently willing to use Jewish typology to buttress their argument. Several Jewish works of this period cite the Christian contention that even if Christians are Edom (a Jewish stereotype), Jews should be forbidden to take interest from them in light of the verses which refer to Edom and Israel as brothers. Moreover, the Jewish response did not restrict itself solely to legalistic refutations; Christian polemicists were charged with hypocrisy on the grounds that Christians themselves were involved in extensive usurious activities.[66]

The truth is that this last accusation is but one expression of the more general contention that Christians behave immorally. Whatever the historical validity of such remarks may be, they are significant for what they reveal about the self-image of the Jews and the use of polemic to strengthen that image. One of the beliefs which sustained medieval Jewry through centuries of adversity was the firm conviction that Jews were clearly superior to their Gentile persecutors. No medieval Jew felt that he was subjected to other nations because they were morally, let alone religiously, superior to him. On the contrary, Ashkenazic Jewry in particular developed the theory that one reason for its suffering was that it was chosen because of its unique qualities to sanctify the divine name through martyrdom.[67] Consequently, martyrdom itself became evidence of the outstanding qualities of the Jews of France and Germany.

Indeed, Ashkenazic Jews were hardly able to discuss the issue of martyrdom, even in a halakhic context, without a passionate, emotional

[65] *Mil. Mizvah*, p. 23b. See also the quotation from Meir in Chazan, op. cit., p. 123.
[66] See pp. 133–134 and the notes there. For discussion of the Christian accusations that Jews engage in extensive usury, see Kisch, op. cit., pp. 327–329.
[67] See H. H. Ben-Sasson, *Peraqim be-Toledot ha-Yehudim bi-Yemei ha-Beinayim* (Tel Aviv, 1958), pp. 174–184. Cf. N.V., p. 70, and the notes there.

response. A remarkable *tosafot*, for example, points out that a certain talmudic passage seems to require a normative legal decision that a Jew is not obligated to resist to the death when forced to engage in a private idolatrous act. But, say the tosafists, "this is difficult," and one expects that this standard formula will be followed by the ordinary kind of legal or exegetical argumentation. Instead, we are confronted, at least initially, by an emotional outburst. "This is difficult, for God forbid that we should rule in a case of idolatry that one should transgress rather than die."[68] A similar reaction appears in a responsum of R. Meir of Rothenburg, who was asked whether atonement is necessary for a man who had killed his wife and children (with their consent) to prevent their capture by a mob demanding conversion to Christianity. Although he concedes the difficulty of finding justification for such an act in rabbinic sources, R. Meir will not even consider seriously the possibility that such behavior is illegal. "This is a matter," he says, "whose permissibility has been widely accepted, for we have heard of many great rabbis who slaughtered their sons and daughters . . . And anyone who requires atonement for this is besmirching the name of the pious men of old."[69]

The *Nizzahon Vetus* supplies additional evidence of the centrality of martyrdom in the thought of Franco-German Jewry in this period. It contains a fascinating passage which illustrates how an Ashkenazic Jew transformed a story that contained no reference to martyrdom into one in which it emerges as the central theme; indeed, it becomes virtually a criterion of religious truth. In Judah Halevi's *Kuzari* a pagan king calls in a philosopher, a Jew, a Muslim, and a Christian so that each can argue the merits of his position. The king is eventually persuaded of the truth of Judaism, partly because both the Muslim and the Christian grant it a certain degree of authenticity. The *Nizzahon Vetus*, on the other hand, tells an elaborate story in which a king threatens a Jew, a Christian, and a Muslim with death unless each one will convert to one of the other faiths. The Jew remains steadfast even at the very edge of the grave,

68 *Tosafot Avodah Zarah* 54a, s. v. *ha-bezin'a*. See J. Katz, *Bein Yehudim le-Goyim* (Jerusalem, 1960), p. 90. (The equivalent passage in the English version [*Exclusiveness and Tolerance* (New York, 1961), pp. 83–84] presents such a bland paraphrase of the *Tosafot* that the emotional force of the argument is virtually lost.)
69 R. Meir of Rothenburg, *Teshuvot, Pesaqim, u-Minhagim*, ed. Y. Z. Kahane (Jerusalem, 1960), 2: 54.

while the other two ultimately lose their resolve and succumb to the king's threats. Both, however, choose Judaism, and "when the emperor heard that the Jew was willing to die for his Torah and would not move from his faith one bit, while the priest and the Muslim both denied their vain beliefs and accepted our faith, he himself chose our religion; he, the priest, and the Muslim were all converted and became true and genuine proselytes." The modification of the *Kuzari* story to make the willingness to die a proof of the truth of Judaism is a truly striking indication of the role martyrdom had come to play in the psyche of the medieval Ashkenazic Jew.[70]

The one aspect of medieval Christian life that challenged the Jewish image of moral superiority was the monastic ideal. At least some Christians, it appeared, were leading pure and ethical lives which could be compared favorably with those of ordinary Jews and perhaps even of rabbinic leaders. It is possible that it was the implicit challenge of monasticism that provoked the vigorous attacks against both the monastic ideal and its practical implementation which are found in Jewish polemic. The author of the *Nizzahon Vetus* argues that at best monks and nuns are overcome with lustful desires that cannot be consummated, and at worst, "they wallow in licentiousness in secret." Only marriage can assure that a person will remain pious and God-fearing. Moreover, monastic orders, some of which were expanding vigorously in the twelfth and thirteenth centuries, were accused of unfair appropriation of land and portrayed as depraved and unethical. Thus, the threat to the Jewish self-image was negated, and Jews were even able to strengthen their conviction of ethical superiority by a partisan examination of monasticism.[71]

It is significant that the relatively recent charge of ritual murder appears in Ashkenazic polemic of the thirteenth century. Whatever the roots of this accusation may be, official church doctrine never sanctioned

---

[70] For further references, see the notes to pp. 216–218.

[71] See pp. 69–70, 98–99, 223, and cf. the notes there. On the alleged immorality of priests, see also Guedemann, op. cit., pp. 42–43, 67–68. My feeling that monasticism posed a psychological threat to the Jewish self-image is almost impossible to substantiate definitively because no medieval Jew would say this openly. There is, however, interesting evidence that some Ashkenazic Jews in the early modern period felt insecure in the presence of genuine priestly celibacy; see the curious legend in *Shivhei ha-Besht* about the Baal Shem Tov's conversation with a priest (D. Ben-Amos and J. Mintz, *In Praise of the Baal Shem Tov* [Bloomington, 1970], p. 248).

it. Indeed, at least the charge of ritual consumption of Christian blood was vigorously condemned by the papacy, and it may even be appropriate to speak of a thirteenth-century rivalry between pope and emperor over the right to protect the Jews against this libel.[72] It is consequently a matter of particular interest to find Christians searching the Scriptures to discover evidence, and rather complicated evidence at that, to prove that Jews eat human beings and drink their blood.[73] This is one of the earliest concrete indications of an attempt at a reasoned defense of the blood libel.

The spread of heresy was one of the most important social and religious developments in this period and had particularly sensitive implications with regard to Jewish-Christian relations. Christians had traditionally labeled members of any schismatic group "Jews," and had occasionally attacked the latter as a means of getting at the former.[74] Moreover, Jews were occasionally accused of harboring heretics, encouraging them, and even of leading orthodox Christians into heresy.[75] Nevertheless, despite considerable scholarly efforts, virtually no hard evidence concerning significant contacts between Jews and medieval heretics has been unearthed.[76]

Precisely such evidence, however, may be found in Jewish polemic. I have argued elsewhere that the *Nizzahon Vetus* contains a refutation of a heretical Christian doctrine, that a thirteenth-century French polemicist makes explicit reference to Albigensians and Bogomils in order to attack orthodox Christianity, and that Jacob ben Reuben's *Milhamot Hashem* may preserve evidence of an even more intriguing nature. Jacob's Christian disputant may have unwittingly quoted the arguments of a friend which were ostensibly aimed at Judaism but were

---

[72] Baron, op. cit., 9: 144–145.
[73] See pp. 54, 229 and the notes there.
[74] So Cassiodorus, *PL* 70: 74D ("Judaei vel Donatistae"); Hadrian I, *PL* 98: 1255–1256. Cf. *Juifs et Chrét.* pp. xvi–xvii and note 11 there. See also Damian's *De Sacramentis per Improbos Administratis*, *PL* 145: 529, and his *Liber Qui Dicitur Gratissimus*, ch. 37, *PL* 145: 153, discussed in my "St. Peter Damian," pp. 86–87, 89–90. Cf. Humbert, *PL* 143: 1093 C. On this practice in the Byzantine Empire, see Parkes, op. cit., pp. 300–303. Cf. also Baron, op. cit., 9: 58–60.
[75] Cf. Baron, op cit., pp. 59, 267–268.
[76] See L. I. Newman, *Jewish Influence on Christian Reform Movements* (New York, 1925); G. Scholem, *Ursprung und Anfänge der Kabbala* (Berlin, 1962), pp. 206–210; F. Talmage, "An Hebrew Polemical Treatise: Anti-Cathar and Anti-Orthodox," *HTR* 60 (1967): 335–337.

really designed to undermine orthodox Christianity. Thus, Christian heretics may have used anti-Jewish polemic as a cover for attacks against the orthodox Christian faith.[77]

The twelfth and thirteenth centuries were also characterized by the broadening of the horizons of Europe that took place in the wake of the Crusades; indeed, the rise of heresy in Western Europe may have been stimulated by the new contacts between East and West.[78] These contacts with the Muslim world aided Jewish apologists in a very old and critical area of polemic, namely, the Christian argument that the success and wide diffusion of Christianity proved its superiority over a religion with a small number of adherents who were growing progressively weaker. Jews could now argue with genuine conviction and greater effectiveness that even by the numerical test alone, Christianity would not prevail; Muslims, they said, rule "half the world," and God's promise to Abraham that all nations of the world would be blessed in him and his seed was certainly not fulfilled through Christianity. Jews even attempted to make Christians feel isolated by arguing that the disgust at eating pork is really a *consensus omnium* with the sole exception of Christians. In fact, even the existence of Christian heresy could be cited as proof of the limited extent of orthodox Christianity. Finally, the failure of the Crusades was cited to show that the alleged success of Christianity was illusory; consequently, Christians would have to admit that temporal success is unrelated to religious truth. Once this admission was made, the old argument against Judaism would have to be abandoned.[79]

One of the most striking characteristics of the polemic reflected in the *Nizzahon Vetus* is the extensive use of the New Testament. The first extant critique of the New Testament by a European Jew is in the eleventh chapter of Jacob ben Reuben's *Milhamot Hashem* (1170);[80] this work, however, deals only with Matthew. On the other hand, *Sefer Yosef ha-Meqanne, Milhemet Mizvah* of Meir b. Simon of Narbonne, and the

---

[77] See my "Christian Heresy and Jewish Polemic in the Twelfth and Thirteenth Centuries," *HTR* 68 (1975): 287–303. See also p. 153 below and the notes there.

[78] On the causes of the rise of heresy, see J. Russell's "Interpretations of the Origins of Medieval Heresy," *Medieval Studies* 25 (1963): 26–53, and his *Dissent and Reform in the Early Middle Ages* (Berkeley, 1965).

[79] See p. 89 and the notes there for specific references and a fuller discussion.

[80] For a discussion of this date, see J. Rosenthal's edition of *Mil Hashem*, introduction, p. viii.

Nizzahon Vetus reflect an intimate knowledge of all the Gospels and some awareness of the other books of the New Testament.[81]

There are certain instructive similarities between Jewish use of the New Testament in polemic and the Christian approach to the Talmud, which became important in the thirteenth century. Both religions had one sacred text—the Hebrew Scriptures—which they held in common, and another sacred body of teaching about whose authority they differed. Traditionally, polemical writings had largely restricted themselves to different interpretations of the text whose authority and divine origin both groups accepted. In our period, however, the usefulness of the New Testament for Jewish polemicists and of the Talmud for Christians began to become evident. There is, in fact, a clear parallelism between the approaches developed by each group to the sacred literature of its adversaries. On the one hand, that literature was subjected to a vigorous critique; on the other, it was exploited to disprove the beliefs of its own adherents.

Thus, beginning in the twelfth century a series of Christian authors attacked the Talmud as a work replete with absurdities, and in the 1230s Nicholas Donin asserted that it contained blasphemies against Jesus which made it a candidate for destruction. The Jewish defense presented at the so-called disputation in Paris in 1240 did not succeed in thwarting Donin's wishes, and within a relatively short time a public burning of the Talmud took place. A few decades later in Spain the Talmud was again the focus of a disputation, but the approach was entirely different. Here, Pablo C(h)ristia(ni) maintained that the dogmas of Christianity could be demonstrated from the Talmud; the rabbis, for example, were said to have indicated that the Messiah had already come and that he is a preexistent being. Significant, though less spectacular, consequences resulted from this disputation as well, and the use of the Talmud to support Christianity became a central element of the Jewish-Christian debate in the centuries to come. Some later Christians even combined

---

[81] Cf. the reference to 1 Corinthians on p. 70. The impression of close familiarity with the New Testament is marred by the frequent attribution of a quotation to the wrong book of the Gospels. See, e.g., pp. 180, 183, 188. These inaccurate ascriptions may offer a partial explanation tor the lack of a systematic order in the section of N. V. that contains a critique of the Gospels. N. V. also contains some non-authentic quotations from Christian literature (e.g., pp. 160, 203) which J. Wakius complained about in a late seventeenth-century refutation. See his *Teshuvat ha-Din al ha-Yehudim sive Recriminatio Actionis in nuperos Christi Accusatores cujus pars prima agit contra . . . librum Nizzachon Vetus* (Jenae, 1699), pp. 20–21, 28–29.

the two approaches, arguing that the Talmud contains both blasphemies and evidence of Christian truths.[82]

The Jewish critique of the Gospels had a similar twofold nature. Jews attacked the Christian Scriptures for their alleged absurdities and contradictions, and at the same time they tried to prove that later Christian dogmas are inconsistent with the Gospels themselves. It was, of course, much easier to maintain both Jewish attitudes at the same time than it was to do the same for both Christian arguments, and the dual approach is used without hesitation throughout the latter section of the *Nizzahon Vetus*.[83]

The knowledge of the New Testament displayed in *Yosef ha-Meqanne* and the *Nizzahon Vetus* was at least partly firsthand since there are a substantial number of Latin quotations in both works.[84] Nevertheless, various citations of the opinions of proselytes leave no room for doubt that some of the familiarity with Christian texts and especially with Christian prayers, festivals, and rituals resulted from contact with these converts; indeed, the Rome manuscript passages that served as a source of the *Nizzahon Vetus* may well have been written by a student of a proselyte's son. Similarly, the Christian awareness of the

[82] Both views were expressed in the Tortosa disputation in the early fifteenth century; cf. the citations in Baron, op. cit., 9: 90, 91. Baron, however, does not note that two originally disparate approaches are represented here. On medieval Christian use of the Talmud through the Donin episode see Merchavia, *Ha-Talmud bi-Re'i ha-Nazrut*, passim. Pablo's approach was adopted by Raymond Martini in his classic *Pugio Fidei* (Leipzig, 1687), which became a manual for Christian polemicists in late medieval Spain. For Donin's approach in thirteenth-century Italy, cf. C. Roth, *History of the Jews of Italy* (Philadelphia, 1946), pp. 99–100.

[83] On the search for contradictions, see, for example, N. V., pp. 167–168 regarding the contradictory genealogies in Matthew and Luke. The argument against Christian dogma through Gospel citations is very common; see especially the notes to p. 183.

[84] There is some discussion of Jacob ben Reuben's Hebrew translations of Matthew in Rosenthal's "Targum shel ha-Besorah 'al pi Matti le-Ya'aqov ben Reuven," *Tarbiz* 32 (1962): 48–66. On Jacob's translation of selections from Gilbert Crispin's *Disputatio* see my "Gilbert Crispin, Alan of Lille, and Jacob ben Reuben: A Study in the Transmission of Medieval Polemic," *Speculum* 49 (1974): 34–47. On Jewish knowledge of Latin see also the references in Merchavia, op. cit., p. 245. The author of the *Dialogus* attributed to William of Champeaux refers to his supposed Jewish disputant as a man expert in Jewish law and "not ignorant" of Christian literature (*PL* 163: 1045). Gilbert Crispin, after whose work "William" modeled this passage, had used an even stronger expression; the Jew "was well-versed (*bene sciens*) in our law and literature" (*Disputatio*, ed. by Blumenkranz, p. 27). Solomon de' Rossi lists such knowledge as one of the requirements for a Jewish polemicist ('*Edut Hashem Ne'emanah*, in Rosenthal's *Mehqarim*, 1: 378).

Talmud stemmed largely from information supplied by Jewish converts. Petrus Alfonsi, for example, had proposed arguments against certain talmudic passages as early as the beginning of the twelfth century,[85] and both Nicholas Donin and Pablo C(h)ristia(ni) were recent converts to Christianity when they began their polemical activities.[86]

Jewish polemic, then, reflects some of the most important social, economic, and intellectual changes that were taking place in the twelfth and thirteenth centuries. Embittered relations, economic exploitation, usury, the expansion of monasticism, martyrdom, the blood libel, Christian heresy, the failure of the Crusades, wider familiarity with the New Testament and the Talmud—all these played a role in the Jewish-Christian debate, and polemical works can frequently supply insights into the impact of some of these momentous developments. Relations between Christians and Jews were indeed deteriorating, but the very symptoms of that deterioration lent greater variety and renewed interest to the vigorous religious discussions that persisted throughout this tragic age in the history of medieval Jewry.

III. THE BOOK AND ITS AUTHOR

Finally, we come to the *Nizzahon Vetus* itself. Some of the basic information concerning the work is either unknown or uncertain, and even the very title has been subjected to varying translations. In this context, the word *nizzahon* probably means polemic rather than victory;[87] the reason that this is the "old *Nizzahon*" is that a more famous polemic of the same name was written by Rabbi Yom Tov Lipmann Mühlhausen at the beginning of the fifteenth century, and the later work came to be the *Sefer ha-Nizzahon* par excellence. Our *Nizzahon* was published in the seventeenth century by a Christian scholar who hesitantly dated it in the twelfth century, because, he said, no one who lived after that time is mentioned in the book.[88]

---

85 See Merchavia, op. cit., pp. 93–127.
86 See below, note 91. On the role of converts, see Blumenkranz, "Jüdische und Christliche Konvertiten im Jüdisch-Christlischen Religionsgespräche des Mittelalters," in Paul Wilpert's *Judentum im Mittelalter* (Berlin, 1966), pp. 264–282, and cf. Guedemann, op. cit., p. 11.
87 See the notes to p. 41.
88 *Tela*, 2: 1.

We now know that at least one or two later figures are named and that the book is probably dependent upon the thirteenth-century *Sefer Yosef ha-Meqanne*;[89] consequently, the most plausible date for the *Nizzahon Vetus* is the latter part of the thirteenth century, and this is the date that has been accepted by most modern scholars.[90] Urbach dates the work in the fourteenth century, apparently because its two major sources are from the second half of the thirteenth; this reasoning, however, does not preclude a late thirteenth-century date.[91] In the absence of clearer evidence, therefore, a cautious approach is advisable, and the book must be dated either in the late thirteenth or early fourteenth century. As we shall see, however, the bulk of its material stems from an earlier period.

Several writers have assumed that the seventeenth-century scholar Wilhelm Schickard reported that the author of the *Nizzahon Vetus* was named R. Mattityahu; moreover, this assertion by Schickard is supposed

---

[89] This work was probably written in the mid-thirteenth century. See the discussion and references in Rosenthal, *Sefer Yosef ha-Meqanne*, pp. 15 ff.

[90] See L. Zunz, *Zur Geschichte und Literatur* (Berlin 1845), p. 85 (cited also in M. Steinschneider, *Catalog der Hebräischen Handschriften in der Stadtbliothek zu Hamburg und der sich anschliessenden in anderen Sprachen* [Hamburg, 1878], p. 72); A. Posnanski, *Schiloh* . . . (Leipzig, 1904), p. 148; J. Rosenthal, "Sifrut ha-Vikkuah ha-Anti-Nozerit," *Areshet* 2 (1960): 173; Baron, op. cit., 9: 294. Zunz dates the work a bit earlier than the others. See especially Rosenthal's introduction to *Yosef ha-Meqanne*, p. 15.

[91] Urbach, op. cit., pp. 60, 76–77. The sources are *Sefer Yosef ha-Meqanne* and the third part of Hebrew manuscript no. 53 in the Vittorio Emanuele library in Rome.

In an unpublished dissertation written after this book was substantially completed (*The Sefer Nizzahon: A Thirteenth Century Defense of Judaism*, New York University, October, 1974), A. Ehrman has argued tor a date between 1220 and 1229 (pp. 4–5) or 1220 and 1235 (p. 163), and in a forthcoming article he has extended the final terminus to 1242. His most important arguments are the author's failure to mention the disputation at Paris in the short final paragraph on the Talmud and the fact that none of the few names that we can identify with certainty belongs to anyone who flourished in the second half of the century. Neither of these arguments strikes me as especially persuasive. That final passage on the Talmud in itself suggests a *terminus a quo* of 1240 or even a bit later, and since the events of 1240 were in France while N. V. is largely an anthology written in Germany, prudence would appear to dictate our allowing a decent interval after that date for its composition. Moreover, there is no internal evidence that *Yosef ha-Meqanne* is an anthology as there is with respect to N. V. (see just below), but if we date N. V. before *Yosef ha-Meqanne*, we would have to assume that much of the Gospel critique in the Rome manuscript version of the latter work was copied from N. V. or its source while the source of N. V. is lost. Finally, our anthology would have to be credited with a whole series of polemical firsts probably originating in lost sources. None of this is impossible, but it hardly seems like the course to choose in the absence of compelling evidence.

to have been repeated by Wagenseil in the introduction to his edition of the book. The very brief introduction to the Jerusalem reprint of the Hebrew section of *Tela Ignea Satanae* attributes this view to Wagenseil, and this attribution has been repeated by at least two other scholars.[92] Judah Rosenthal also pointed to a book by Schickard that refers to a *Triumphator R. Matthias* (which Rosenthal evidently identified with the *Nizzahon Vetus*),[93] and he went on to note Schickard's unfinished *Nizzahon Beli Nezah sive Triumphator Vapulans* (Tübingen, 1623), which he described as a refutation of the *Nizzahon Vetus* that he was unable to consult. Finally, he suggested that the attribution of the *Nizzahon Vetus* to a R. Mattityahu may have resulted from a confusion with the fifteenth-century author of *Sefer Ahituv ve-Zalmon*, which was also called *Nizzahon*.[94]

It can now be asserted with full confidence that Rosenthal's conjecture is correct, but neither Schickard nor Wagenseil were guilty of confusing the two books. The *Nizzahon Beli Nezah*, which is available from the Bibliothèque Nationale in Paris, does not deal with the *Nizzahon Vetus* at all; the book Schickard had in fact was the later *Sefer Ahituv ve-Zalmon*, and his only error was in dating it somewhat too early. It was to this *Triumphator* that he referred in *Jus Regium Hebraeorum*, where he even cited a poetic passage from *Sefer Ahituv ve-Zalmon* that is nowhere in the *Nizzahon Vetus*. Moreover, a careful reading of Wagenseil's introduction shows that he never meant to say that Schickard had begun editing the same *Nizzahon* that he was now publishing. Wagenseil was merely reviewing the history of the publication of Jewish polemics called *Nizzahon*, and he therefore mentioned both Schickard's work and T. Hackspanius's edition of Mühlhausen's polemic.

All references by seventeenth- and eighteenth-century scholars to a *Nizzahon* of R. Matthaeus are to the work utilized by Schickard. Although there was some confusion about the various books called *Nizzahon*, these writers generally knew that Schickard's text was not the same as the book edited by Wagenseil. Nevertheless, neither they nor any subsequent scholar that I know recognized the fact that Schickard's *Triumphator* was the same as *Sefer Ahituv ve-Zalmon*, which some of them

---

92   J. Rosenthal, introduction to *Sefer Yosef ha-Meqanne*, p. 15, note 15; J. Shatzmiller, op. cit., p. 126.

93   See Schickard's *Jus Regium Hebraeorum* (Leipzig, 1764), p. 449.

94   Rosenthal, loc. cit.

list separately.[95] In any event, there is no tradition at all concerning the author of the *Nizzahon Vetus*, and any search for the appropriate "R. Mattityahu" would be futile.

Although the identity of the author himself is unknown, it is very likely that he was a German Jew. The book contains a substantial number of German words as well as a passage that says that the "main body of the Gentiles is called Ashkenazim."[96] There is no evidence for the assumption made by Loeb that the German words are later interpolations;[97] consequently, although there is a great deal (perhaps even a preponderance) of French material in the work, the author himself almost certainly lived in Germany.[98]

The *Nizzahon Vetus* is largely an anthology whose two major identifiable sources were *Sefer Yosef ha-Meqanne* (at least in the section on the Gospels)[99] and the third part of Hebrew manuscript number 53 in the Vittorio Emanuele library in Rome.[100] Its character as an anthology is clear not only from the fact that we have some of its sources but from the occasional repetition of similar material in the same section of the work[101] and from the scattered references to issues that are not found in the book as matters discussed by the author.[102] Nevertheless, the *Nizzahon Vetus* contains a great deal of material for which we cannot identify precise parallels, let alone word-for-word sources, and there is every reason to believe that the author added his own material and revised that of others. Consequently, although he followed the widespread medieval practice of making extensive, often

---

[95]   See T. Hackspanius, *Liber Nizachon Rabbi Lipmanni* (Nuremberg, 1644), pp. 218–219; J. Buxtorf, *Bibliotheca Rabbinica* (Herborn, 1708), pp. 145–147; J. C. Wolf, *Bibliotheca Hebraeae*, vol. 1 (Hamburg and Leipzig, 1715), pp. 738–741, and cf. vol. 2 (Hamburg, 1721), pp. 1051, 1052, 1259; G. B. de Rossi, *Bibliotheca Judaica Antichristiana* (Parma, 1800), pp. 63–64.

[96]   P. 156. Ashkenazim in this passage probably means specifically Germans: cf. the notes there. See also Steinschneider, loc. cit.

[97]   Loeb, op. cit., p. 329.

[98]   So Zunz and Urbach, loc. cit. Posnanski, loc. cit., places the book in either northern France or Germany.

[99]   Cf. below in the discussion of "The Text of the *Nizzahon Vetus*."

[100]   Cf. note 91 and see the section on the text. Urbach (op. cit., p. 77) refers to N. V. as "an anthology of all the [Ashkenazic] polemical literature of the twelfth and thirteenth centuries."

[101]   See especially pp. 48–51; 100–104.

[102]   See, e.g., p. 65, and cf. the notes to p. 122.

verbatim, use of his predecessors' works, he deserves the title of author and not merely compiler.[103]

The array of arguments in the *Nizzahon Vetus* is almost encyclopedic, and the book is therefore an excellent vehicle for an analysis of virtually all the central issues in the Jewish-Christian debate during the twelfth and thirteenth centuries. In the Commentary I have tried to indicate many of the parallels with earlier works,[104] and these similarities leave no

---

[103] On the order of the book, see p. 388.

[104] Both Jewish and Christian parallels have been cited only through the thirteenth century and have usually been arranged chronologically. I have tried to consult all Jewish polemics and what I hope is a representative selection of Christian works. (In some respects, Raymund Martini's *Pugio Fidei* can be regarded as the inauguration of a new era of Spanish polemic, and I have not cited it here even though its appearance toward the end of the thirteenth century makes it technically eligible for inclusion.) Needless to say, the citation of a parallel in the notes is not always intended to show that the author of N. V. was influenced by that particular source.

There is one recurring reference which requires some clarification at this point. The passage in Rome ms. 53, pp. 21a–21b, begins with a report that Pablo C(h)ristia(ni) arrived in Montpellier in 1269 and continues with a summary of Nahmanides' earlier disputation with him; this summary is followed by an unrelated collection of miscellaneous arguments (pp. 22a–25b), some of which are in the standard form of a debate between a "believer" and a "heretic." (A lengthy section of this collection [pp. 22b–23a] is a reworking of a passage from Joseph Kimhi's *Sefer ha-Berit* [Talmage's edition, pp. 26–29].) Most of the material from p. 21a through p. 25a, line 16, was transcribed (though never published) by Adolph Posnanski and attributed by him to Mordecai b. Yehosafah of Avignon, apparently because Mordecai is known to have had a dispute with Pablo. Recently, Judah Rosenthal published this section of the manuscript (through p. 25b) as "Vikkuah Dati Bern Hakham be-Shem Menahem u-bein ha-Mumar ve-ha-Nazir ha-Dominiqani Pablo Christiani," *Hagut 'Ivrit ba-Ameriqah*, ed. by M. Zohori, A. Tartakover, and H. Ormian (Tel Aviv, 1974), pp. 61–74. Rosenthal's ascription of the work to a "Menahem" is based on the remark that "these are the words of Menahem," which appears twice in the final passage (on "true Israel"); that passage, which begins on p. 25a, line 17, was omitted by Posnanski and placed instead in his edition of N. V. (It is clear that Rosenthal was unaware of Posnanski's edition, which is generally superior to his.) There is really no firm basis for any decision about the authorship at this collection (which also contains a note in a different hand that "these are the words of Asher" [p. 22a]), and I have cited it by giving the page number of the Rome ms. followed by references to both Posnanski's "Mordecai of Avignon" ms. and Rosenthal's "Menahem."

Finally—an apology. For a variety of not particularly good reasons, translations of biblical verses are not consistently based on a single translation of the Bible (although I have avoided inconsistent translations of any one verse). The enormous effort that would have been necessary to correct this defect did not seem worth the trouble, and the rabbinic observation that no two prophets prophesy in the same style no longer needs to be restricted to the original Hebrew text. (When the author of N. V. misquotes a verse or understands it in a peculiar fashion, I have, of course, deliberately "mistranslated" it in order to reflect his text or interpretation.)

doubt about the existence of a Jewish polemical tradition. Whether or not the author of the *Nizzahon Vetus* read such works as Kimhi's *Sefer ha-Berit* or Jacob ben Reuben's *Milhamot Hashem*, their influence, or the influence of the tradition upon which they drew, certainly reached him. The argument that the christological interpretation of Isaiah 53:2–3 is inconsistent with the christological interpretation of Psalms 45:2–3 is not likely to have been made independently in *Milhamot Hashem* and the *Nizzahon Vetus*.[105] Our author's discussion of signs in connection with the Immanuel prophecy is clearly indebted to a tradition represented in *Sefer ha-Berit*, in Meir of Narbonne's *Milhemet Mizvah*, and in Moses of Salerno.[106] The fact that at least five Jewish polemicists cite the argument from the limited diffusion of Christianity specifically in connection with Psalms 72:11 is no coincidence.[107] These examples can easily be multiplied, and it is clear that both Christians and Jews had polemical traditions that drew upon the past but which remained flexible enough to accommodate, and sometimes even influence, new social, political, religious, and philosophical realities.

---

[105] See the notes to p. 115.

[106] See the notes to p. 101. Note immediately that parallels between *Mil. Mizvah* and Moses of Salerno's *Ta'anot* result from the fact that much of the nonphilosophical section of the *Ta'anot* consists of verbatim copying from Meir's work. See page correlations in Joel Rembaum, "The Influence of *Sefer Nestor Hakomer* on Medieval Jewish Polemics," *Proceedings of the American Academy for Jewish Research* 45 (1978): 167, note 54. (Those correlations require two corrections: "41–55" should be "40–55," and the material on Isa. 7:14 in *Mil. Mizvah*, pp. 111a–112a, should be listed as appearing on pp. 33–34 of the Posnanski ms. Although I had noted almost all the relevant parallels between these two works, I had not realized the full extent of the copying before reading Rembaum's article.) Most of the remaining material in this section of the *Ta'anot* is found in the Rome ms. version of *Yosef ha-Meqanne* and in N.V.; see the notes to pp. 180, 192, 193 and 198.

[107] See the notes to p. 159.

ON THE IMAGE AND DESTINY OF GENTILES
IN ASHKENAZIC POLEMICAL LITERATURE

From: *Facing the Cross: The Persecutions of 1096 in History and Historiography*,
ed. by Yom Tov Assis et al. (The Hebrew University Magnes Press: Jerusalem,
2000), pp. 74–91 (Hebrew). Translated by Gabriel Wasserman.

The hostile attitude toward Christian society found in medieval Ashkenazic literature is quite well known, and hardly needs to be demonstrated. Expressions of bitter animosity toward Christianity and its adherents are found throughout this literature, most especially in liturgical poetry, even before the catastrophe of the First Crusade in 1096. Israel Yuval has recently argued that these expressions of animosity are not merely reactions to medieval persecutions, but rather are rooted in an ancient, more comprehensive worldview, associated with apocalyptic ideas about the ultimate redemption.[1] However, he admits that the bloody incidents in 1096 certainly made this animosity harsher, and strengthened the Jews' desire for vengeance.[2] The unprecedented attacks and the martyrdom of thousands of Jews became implanted in the collective, long term Ashkenazic consciousness, and they reinforced the feelings of revulsion toward the murderous enemy and his false religion.

The Hebrew chronicles that deal with these events are filled with curses and expressions of reproach toward the Christian faith and its founder. Such expressions are found not only during the emotionally charged time of the catastrophe itself; in the years following 1096, too, Ashkenazic literature contains many terms of extreme derision and

[1] Y. Y. Yuval, "Ha-Naqam ve-ha-Qelalah, ha-Dam ve-ha-Alilah," *Zion* 58 (1983): 37-44. See also A. Grossman, *Hakhmei Ashkenaz ha-Rishonim* (Jerusalem, 1981), p. 99, n. 100.
[2] Yuval, p. 41.

degradation for all that Christianity considers sacred. This phenomenon is found most especially in polemical literature.[3]

This literature focuses primarily on the question of the true religion. The personality, practices, and fate of the followers of false religions occupy only a secondary place in these writings. However, from the historian's point of view, these topics deserve special attention, for they shed light on a wide range of social contacts between the Jewish and Christian communities, and sometimes even directly affect the very heart of the polemical issue.

Our point of departure here will be Ashkenazic polemical literature, as expressed in its three major representatives: *Sefer Yosef ha-Meqanne*, *Sefer Nizzahon Yashan* (*Nizzahon Vetus*), and the disputation of R. Yehiel of Paris. However, our analysis will broaden from time to time, and we will deal with polemical literature from other areas and later periods, and other branches of medieval Jewish literature.

---

[3]   See D. Berger, *The Jewish–Christian Debate in the High Middle Ages: A Critical Edition of the Nizzahon Vetus with an Introduction, Translation and Commentary* (Philadelphia, 1979), pp. 20–24, 302; A. Sapir Abulafia, "Invectives against Christianity in the Hebrew Chronicles of the First Crusade," in *Crusade and Settlement*, ed. by P. W. Edbury (Cardiff, 1985), pp. 66–72. A list of several of the Jewish derogatory terms for Christian concepts can be found in an appendix to M. Breuer's edition of *Sefer Nizzahon Yashan* (Ramat Gan, 1978), p. 195. Amos Funkenstein incorrectly states that derogatory terms towards Christianity, which must have been common in the daily spoken language, are rare in polemical literature and are mainly attested in sources such as Tosafot. He seems to have come to this erroneous conclusion by comparing the extremely bitter expressions in Ashkenazic commentaries and halakhic works, on the one hand, to those found in polemical writings from Spain and southern France, on the other. It would have been far more fruitful for him to have compared the expressions found in Ashkenazic commentaries and halakhic works to those found in *Sefer Yosef ha-Meqanne* and *Sefer Nizzahon Yashan*, and similar polemical works from northern Europe. See A. Funkenstein, *Perceptions of Jewish History* (Berkeley, Los Angeles and Oxford, 1993), p. 171.

The general lack of acquaintance with the standard Ashkenazic derogatory terms for Christian concepts has led scholars to misunderstand a line in a *qinah* (elegy) for the Ninth of Av about the 1096 massacres. The poet writes: *nit'orer goy az doresh shuhah*— a fierce nation arose, seeking a pit; or, according to a variant text, *koreh shuhah*—digging a pit. See *Seder ha-Qinot le-Tish'ah be-Av*, ed. by D. Goldschmidt (Jerusalem 1968), p. 84. Goldschmidt and others prefer the smoother reading, "digging a pit," an expression which is also found in other liturgical poems. Apparently, these scholars found the reading *doresh shuhah* ("seeking a pit") so difficult that even the principle of *lectio difficilior* was unable to rescue it. Nevertheless, it is clear that this is the correct reading, and in fact it is not difficult at all. The term *shuhah* (pit) was the standard Ashkenazic expression for the holy sepulcher. (See, for example, *The Jewish–Christian Debate in the High Middle Ages*, Hebrew section, pp. 61 and 63: the Arabs came to Jerusalem and "defiled the *shuhah*.") The crusading armies were precisely "a fierce nation, seeking the *shuhah*."

THE IMAGE

There are many dimensions to the image of "the other," but the first (often neglected in scholarly literature) is the physical dimension. An oppressed minority tends to adopt and internalize the values of the general culture to a certain extent. The Jews of the Middle Ages attempted to resist this tendency as far as religious and spiritual values were concerned—but a strange, gripping passage from *Yosef ha-Meqanne*, which appears in a different formulation in *Sefer Nizzahon Yashan*, shows that on the aesthetic/physical plane, this process did affect the Jews:

> "Therefore have I also made you contemptible and base before all the people" (Malachi 2:9). A certain apostate said to R. Nathan: "You Jews are uglier than any people on the face of the earth, whereas we are very beautiful." He responded: "What is the color of the blossom of the *shveske* which are called *prunelles*, which grow in the bushes?" The apostate replied: "White." The rabbi asked: "And what color is the blossom of the apple tree?" The apostate replied: "Red." The rabbi explained: "Thus, we come from clean, white seed, so our faces are black; but you are from red seed—from menstruants—and therefore your faces are yellow and ruddy." But the real reason is that we are in exile, as it says in the Song of Songs, "Look not upon me, because I am black, because the sun has gazed upon me: my mother's children were angry with me; they made me the keeper of the vineyards; but my own vineyard have I not kept" (Song of Songs 1:6). However, when I used to keep my own vineyard, I was quite beautiful indeed, as it is written, "And your renown went forth among the heathen for your beauty" (Ezekiel 16:14).[4]

R. Nathan's response is representative of the classic polemical approach arguing that an apparent defect is actually an asset: physical inferiority is a direct result of ethical superiority. However, the author himself says that in fact, it is the exile that is truly responsible for the physical unattractiveness of the Jews.[5] Either way, the Jewish partner in the debate is affirming the aesthetic judgment made by the gentiles. Since

---

[4]   *Sefer Yosef ha-Meqanne*, ed. by Y. Rosenthal (Jerusalem, 1970), p. 95.

[5]   This explanation appears also in a manuscript which Rosenthal quotes in his note ad loc.: "If a gentile should say to you, "We are beautiful, and you are not," you should reply: "Before our Temple was destroyed, we were more beautiful; . . . and when our Temple was destroyed, our beauty was taken away from us . . . . In the future, God is going to give it back to us." Cf. *Mishnah Nedarim* 9:10.

the criteria for attractiveness are largely subjective, the Jews' agreement with the gentile assessment has deep psychological significance.

Haim Hillel Ben-Sasson already noted this point in connection with the parallel passage in *Sefer Nizzahon Yashan*.[6] However, there is a major difference in that text:

> The heretics [i.e., the Christians] ask: Why are most Gentiles fair-skinned and handsome while most Jews are dark and ugly? Answer them that this is similar to a fruit; when it begins to grow it is white but when it ripens it becomes black, as is the case with sloes and plums. On the other hand, any fruit which is red at the beginning becomes lighter as it ripens, as is the case with apples and apricots. This, then, is testimony that Jews are pure of menstrual blood so that there is no initial redness. Gentiles, however, are not careful about menstruant women and have sexual relations during menstruation; thus, there is redness at the outset, and so the fruit that comes out, i.e., the children, are light. One can respond further by noting that Gentiles are incontinent and have sexual relations during the day, at a time when they see the faces on attractive pictures; therefore, they give birth to children who look like those picture, as it is written, "And the sheep conceived when they came to drink before the rods" [Gen. 30:38–39].[7]

Sefer Nizzahon Yashan retains the same aesthetic judgment as *Yosef ha-Meqanne*; however, unlike *Yosef ha-Meqanne*, this author is unwilling to forego the consolation of reversing the gentile's argument even in his second explanation. Thus, the exile disappears entirely, and the second response provides a different version of the connection between physical ugliness and ethical beauty. *Sefer Nizahon Yashan* is a very aggressive work; in other passages, it argues that Jews are superior even on the physical level: "This is the interpretation of the statement, 'You have saved us from evil and faithful diseases,' in which we thank God for saving us from being afflicted with impure issue, leprosy and skin disease, as they are."[8] This comment only reinforces the impact of the passage

---

6   H. H. Ben-Sasson, *Toledot Yisrael bi-Yemei ha-Beinayim* (volume II of *Toledot Am Yisrael*) (Tel-Aviv, 1969), p. 168.

7   *The Jewish–Christian Debate in the High Middle Ages*, p. 224.

8   *The Jewish–Christian Debate*, p. 211. As I note there (p. 340), this passage supports S. Baron's claim that the relative silence about lepers in medieval Jewish sources is evidence that the Jews suffered from this ailment to a lesser degree than their Christian neighbors. See S. Baron, *A Social and Religious History of the Jews*, volume IX (New York, London, and Philadelphia, 1965), p. 338, n. 14. See also Isaac Polgar's explicit statement in *'Ezer ha-Dat*: "Anyone who examines our Torah will find . . . just and pure laws, such as

regarding beauty. The fact that this author, who is prepared to formulate surprisingly vigorous and aggressive arguments, sees Christian aesthetic superiority as a self-evident truth lends all the more significance to this phenomenon.

The same effort to turn a physical defect into a spiritual asset can be seen clearly in a unique passage which Marc Saperstein published from Isaac ben Yeda'ya's commentary to *Midrash Rabbah*. The author of this passage, who clearly suffered from a sexual problem, attributed this problem to all circumcised men. He writes as a general rule that circumcised men are unable to satisfy their wives' sexual needs; consequently, Jewish women do not receive much benefit from their husbands' presence and are willing to let them go study Torah and wisdom. This is not the case, however, with respect to the wives of the uncircumcised, whose husbands possess highly impressive sexually potency. Consequently, these men expend their time and energy in such activity and remain immersed in the vanity of the physical world.[9]

These attempts to make the bitter sweet sound pathetic to the modern reader, and they were probably not particularly convincing in the Middle Ages either. Now, from the isolated example of Isaac ben Yeda'ya, which deals with very private matters, it is hard to argue that many Jews considered themselves inferior to gentiles in their sexual ability. However, the sources about physical beauty appear quite convincing. In the consciousness of many Jews, ethical and spiritual superiority came at a very high physical and psychological price.

---

the prohibition of sleeping with a woman during her menstrual period, which . . . is the reason that we have been saved from the horrible ailment of leprosy, which is so common in individuals of the nations surrounding us" (*'Ezer ha-Dat*, ed. by J. Levinger [Tel-Aviv, 1984], Part 1, Section 2, p. 36.) These two pieces of evidence—the *Nizzahon Yashan* from Ashkenaz, and Isaac Polgar from Spain—deserve our serious attention.

9   M. Saperstein, "The Earliest Commentary on the *Midrash Rabbah*," in *Studies in Medieval Jewish History and Literature* I, ed. by I. Twersky (Cambridge, Mass. and London 1979), pp. 294–297; idem, *Decoding the Rabbis: A Thirteenth-Century Commentary on the Aggadah* (Cambridge, Mass. and London, 1980), pp. 97–102. Saperstein (p. 100) tentatively suggested that these words might be due to a personal problem of Isaac ben Yeda'ya: "To what extent do passages such as this reflect the personal experience of the author . . . ? To what extent do they seem to be an elaborate rationalization meant to solve personal problems which bothered him greatly?" I have no hesitation in changing Saperstein's tentative suggestion to a definite assertion. Any Jewish man who did not personally suffer from this problem would never have been able to create or affirm the delusional idea that every circumcised male suffers from it.

A famous passage in Isaac Polgar's '*Ezer ha-Dat* reflects the same problem and the same tendency. The topic of this passage is the cause of the suffering of exile—a major, central issue that I shall not address here. However, when Polgar writes that Jews suffer under the yoke of the gentiles because they have forgotten the art of war due to their dedication to the study of Torah and wisdom, the Temple service, and the cultivation of the quality of compassion, he is attempting to transform physical weakness into an ethical-spiritual asset. He does this through a naturalistic analysis whose method is essentially similar to the one which we find in *Yosef ha-Meqanne*, in *Nizzahon Yashan*, and in Isaac ben Yeda'ya's writing, with all the tortuous psychological complexity that this entails.[10]

10   "Because our perfect Torah has forbidden us from going in vain directions, and has prevented us from succumbing to the evil tendency alluded to in general terms by the commandment 'You shall not covet,' and more specifically by our other commandments, this means that we will necessarily be those who are oppressed, and not those who oppress, those who are humiliated and not those who humiliate others. But because physical desires, including this tendency, are not forbidden to the other nations, they are necessarily the oppressors and humiliators . . . When we were on our own land, we were elevated and sanctified above all the other nations that surrounded us. We kept the commandments of our glorious Torah, which forbids and prevents us from indulging all sorts of physical desires, and we broke the yoke of the evil inclination from upon our necks; thus, we refrained from acts of oppression. Moreover, we were commanded to spend our time delving into the Torah and studying other forms of wisdom, all day and all night, and this weakened us physically. Moreover, we had compassion and soft-heartedness impressed upon us at all times. We occupied ourselves with offering sacrifices in the Temple, and forgot how to engage in war . . . But the nations that surrounded us had exactly the opposite attributes from us; their heart was tough and cruel . . . Their way was to tear like wild beasts, bears or lions. They did not speak kindly to us, but gnashed their teeth at us, and gathered together and destroyed our city and our Temple, and took us captive, such that we were spread out all over the earth, with only a few of us surviving in each place. However, because we are certain that we have the truth, and that all physical desire for this world and its delights is vain, we are willing to bear this difficulty on our shoulders, and we trust our God, our rescuer, and he looks down and rescues us, so that we are able to live among our enemies and reside in the tents of those who seek our harm" ('*Ezer ha-Dat* [see above, n. 8], Part 1, Section 5, pp. 55–56.) Needless to say, Polgar's words raise a theological challenge that is not present in the words of *Yosef ha-Meqanne, Sefer Nizzahon Yashan*, or Isaac ben Yeda'ya. A naturalistic explanation for the exile of the Jewish people is considerably more problematic than a naturalistic explanation for unattractiveness or sexual dysfunction, and Polgar himself attempts to blunt the radical sting of his words in the subsequent paragraph in '*Ezer ha-Dat*.
      On Spinoza's claim that Judaism has led to a "softening" of the Jews' nature, see S. Pines, "Histabberut ha-Tequmah me-Hadash shel Medinah Yehudit le-fi Yosef ibn Kaspi u-le-fi Spinoza," '*Iyyun* 14–15 (1963–4): 314–315; in the same article (p. 305), Pines provides a citation to a somewhat similar argument in a letter from Maimonides

Our examination of the physical depiction of the gentiles leads us to an investigation of their ethical depiction. The authors of polemical literature were primarily interested in identifying the true religion, and such identification is not necessarily dependent on the ethical behavior of the community that believes in that religion. Nevertheless, polemicists in various regions and eras felt that there was a connection between a religion of truth and people of truth, between ethical doctrine and ethical praxis. R. Joseph Kimhi pointed to the ethical superiority of the Jews, and his Christian opponent (according to the Jewish record of the debate) was forced to admit that this was correct, but he countered with the response that even such ethical behavior was useless without the proper faith.[11] A re-working of this passage appears in an Ashkenazic manuscript from the fourteenth century, which also includes considerable material from the school of Yosef ha-Meqanne and from the traditions that were incorporated into *Sefer Nizzahon Yashan*.[12] These two polemical works, as well as *Milhemet Mizvah* by

to the rabbis of Marseilles; the difference is that Maimonides says that the Jews stopped studying the art of war because they trusted in astrologically based fantasies. Pines attempts to draw connections between the arguments of Maimonides, Polgar, and Spinoza in another article: "Al Sugyot Ahadot ha-Kelulot be-Sefer *Ezer ha-Dat* le-Yitzhak Polgar ve-Tiqbolot la-hen etzel Spinoza," in J. Dan and J. Hacker (eds.), *Studies in Jewish Mysticism, Philosophy, and Ethical Literature* (Jubilee Volume for Isaiah Tishby) (Jerusalem, 1986), pp. 423–443. The argument that the loss of the art of war among the Jews was due to an entirely positive phenomenon is found only in Polgar. I believe that there is a strong connection between Polgar's argument and one of the theses that appears repeatedly in Solomon ibn Verga's *Shevet Yehudah*. Ibn Verga too is inclined to naturalistic explanations of the suffering of the exile, and he too presents a description of Jews who are unprepared to defend themselves from their enemies. For naturalistic explanations of the suffering of the Jews, see *Sefer Shevet Yehudah*, ed. by A. Shochet and Y. Baer (Jerusalem, 1947), pp. 40–44, 127–128; Ibn Verga discusses the Jews' ignorance of military affairs on p. 44, and their cowardice on p. 28. On the motif of Jewish cowardice, see E. Gutwirth, "Gender, History and the Jewish–Christian Polemic," ed. by O. Limor and G. G. Stroumsa, *Contra Judaeos* (Tübingen, 1996), p. 265.

11 *Sefer ha-Berit u-Vikkuhei Radaq im ha-Nazrut*, ed. by A. Talmage, Jerusalem 1974, pp. 25–28. On this passage, see B. Sh. Albert, "L'image du chrétien dans les sources juives du Languedoc (XIIe–XIVe Siècle)," in *Les Juifs à Montpellier et dans le Languedoc du Moyen Age à nos jours*, ed. by C. Iancu (Montpellier, 1988), pp. 118–119.

12 Y. Rosenthal, "Vikkuah Dati bein Hakham be-Shem Menahem u-bein ha-Mumar ve-ha-Nazir ha-Dominiqani Pablo Christiani," in *Hagut Ivrit ba-America*, ed. by M. Zohori, A. Tartakower, and H. Ormian (Tel-Aviv, 1974), p. 67. Despite the title, the text is not actually a debate between Pablo Christiani and a Jew named Menahem. See the introduction to my book (above, note 3), p. 36, n. 104; and also J. E. Rembaum, "A Reevaluation of a Medieval Polemical Manuscript," *AJS Review* 5 (1980): 81–99.

R. Meir of Narbonne, an Ashkenazic compilation attributed to R. Moses of Salerno, the Tosafistic commentary *Da'at Zeqenim* on the Pentateuch, and Nahmanides' *Sefer ha-Ge'ullah* all view the expression "a degenerate nation" in Deuteronomy 32:21 as referring to the Christians. In the words of *Yosef ha-Meqanne*: "If there were any nation more degenerate than you, it would be the one to subjugate us."[13]

It is specifically in Ashkenazic polemics that special emphasis is placed on the sins of priests, monks, and nuns. As I have noted with great brevity in my introduction to the *Nizzazon Yashan*, it seems to me that this fierce attack flows from a feeling of Jewish discomfort in the face of religious self-sacrifice by gentiles.[14] Of course, abstention from sexual life is problematic from the perspective of Jewish law and the Jewish worldview, but the impressive phenomenon of the ability of Christians to conquer their own natural drives in order to fulfill the will of their creator must have weakened, if only slightly, the Jewish self-image of absolute moral superiority to the degenerate gentile.

This understanding of the polemical sources cannot be proven conclusively from the texts, for one could hardly expect medieval Jews to express such a feeling explicitly and openly. Nevertheless, we find such a psychological reaction expressly attested in other genres of literature, or in later eras. A substantial exegetical tradition regarding the Book of Jonah explained the prophet's flight from God as being due to a concern that the residents of Nineveh might repent, and thus cause disaster to befall the Jews, who stubbornly refused to repent of their evil ways.[15] In the book *Shivhei ha-Besht (The Praises of the Baal Shem Tov)*, we find a story in which the founder of Hasidism succeeds in implanting sinful thoughts into the mind of an old Catholic priest, such that the priest, who has never had such an experience before, has a seminal emission. The Ba'al Shem Tov does this because he has been informed by heaven that the prayers of the Jewish people on Yom Kippur would not be accepted as long as there was still a priest in that area who remained pure.[16] Although no such passage is found in the polemical literature of

---

13 *Sefer Yosef ha-Meqanne*, p. 62; *The Jewish-Christian Debate*, English section, p. 75. References to the other relevant sources can be found in my notes there, English section, pp. 257, 262–263.
14 *The Jewish-Christian Debate*, Introduction, p. 27.
15 See, for example, Rashi's commentary on Jonah 1:3.
16 *Sefer Shivhei ha-Besht*, ed. Sh. A. Horodezky (Tel-Aviv 1947), pp. 163–164.

medieval Ashkenaz, the emphasis on the chasm between the disgusting gentiles and the moral Jews appears quite often in this literature, and leaves little room for doubt that it had great psychological significance for the authors of these texts.[17]

The Jewish argument that the Christian world was engaged in immoral behavior focused mainly on behavior that both Jews and Christians viewed as improper; this is typical polemical method. However, it is evident that Jewish condemnation of Christian immorality also rested on an additional consideration, to wit, the persecution of the Jewish people. And so—Christians believe in a false religion, defile themselves through abominable sins, and persecute the chosen people. What then will be their ultimate destiny?

THE DESTINY

Personal destiny

The question of destiny has two dimensions. On the one hand, there is the personal destiny of each individual Christian after death; on the other, there is the collective destiny of "the Kingdom of Edom" and its inhabitants at the End of Days. In general, the Ashkenazic polemical writers answered the question of the Christian's personal destiny very sharply indeed: a Christian is destined to hell. There is nothing innovative or surprising about this, but we should note the reasoning that is given for it: the Christian deserves this punishment not because he hates the Jews, but because he believes in the Christian faith. In certain periods, when the ideal of tolerance began to develop, some Jews began to consider Christians to be "righteous gentiles," who fulfill the seven Noahide commandments; however, Talmudic tradition includes the prohibition of idolatry among these seven, and in accordance with a straightforward understanding of this prohibition, it is hard to escape the conclusion that one who worships Jesus as a god commits idolatry.

---

[17]   See my observations in *The Jewish-Christian Debate*, English section, pp. 257–258. In a Sephardic polemical work from the fifteenth century, we find a horrifying depiction of Christian immoral behavior; see Hayyim ibn Musa, *Magen va-Romah* (Jerusalem, 1970), pp. 82–83. This passage has recently been noted by Gutwirth (above, n. 10), p. 267. See H. Graetz's *History* in Sh. P. Rabbinowitz's Hebrew translation, *Divrei Yemei Yisrael* (Warsaw, 1906), p. 419.

Sefer Nizzahon Yashan reports a conversation between R. Nathan Official and a group of priests on the topic of the sin of the golden calf. According to the sharp formulation in this report—the version in *Yosef ha-Meqanne* is more moderate—R. Nathan emphasized that the generation of Moses received a harsh punishment because they made the error of believing that "the spirit of God" could enter as pure and clean a substance as gold. Yet the Christians do not understand to what degree

> they will be judged and entrapped in hell. Why, an a fortiori argument applies here: They [the generation of Moses] erred in worshiping a clean thing like gold, and yet their iniquity was marked before God, who said, "When I make an accounting, I will bring them to account for their sins" [Exod. 32:34] and refused to grant them complete forgiveness. Certainly, then, you who err in saying that something holy entered into a woman in that stinking place, . . . will certainly be consumed by "a fire not blown" [Job 20:26] and descend to deepest hell.[18]

It is quite interesting that R. Nathan is not faithful to the Talmudic principle of *dayyo la-ba min ha-din lihyot ka-nidon* (when making an a fortiori argument, one can only argue that the consequences of the severe case are *as severe* as those of the light case, not *more severe*); rather, he jumps straight from the fact that God "refused complete forgiveness" to the worshippers of the calf to the statement that the Christians will "descend to deepest hell." In any event, it is their theological error, or, in other words, their violation of the prohibition of idolatry, that leads the Christians to perdition.

In the Disputation of Paris, there is a discussion of this question that constitutes an exception that proves the rule. Nicholas Donin quoted

---

18   *The Jewish-Christian Debate*, English section, p. 68. It must be emphasized that when R. Nathan says that the worshippers of the calf believed that "the spirit of God" entered it, he is not saying that they believed that the calf was a god. This distinction is explicitly made in *Yosef ha-Meqanne*: "No one ever believed such a thing; they did not err by saying that the calf was a god." Nevertheless, he goes on, "See what happened to them: 'There fell of the people that day about three thousand men' (Exod. 32:28), and it is written, 'In the day when I visit, I will visit their sin upon them'" (ibid., verse 34). And it is written, 'Therefore he said that he would destroy them, had not Moses his chosen stood before him in the breach' (Psalms 106:23) (*Yosef ha-Meqanne*, p. 50). This passage in *Yosef ha-Meqanne* does not speak of hell, but the work does speak of hell elsewhere: "What is your fate? [The answer is,] You shall 'be for burning, for fuel of fire' [Isaiah 9:4]. You shall all descend to hell" (p. 76).

a Talmudic statement condemning heretics (*minim*) to eternal hellfire. When R. Yehiel responded that the passage in question refers not to Christians but to people who deny the validity of the oral Torah, Donin pointed to Rashi's comment on the passage, which considers the disciples of Jesus to be a classic example of "heretics."[19] R. Yehiel replied that there is no need to accept Rashi's comment as determinative, but even if we do accept it, it is speaking of Jesus' original disciples, who were Jewish, and therefore obligated to observe the Torah's commandments. Gentile Christians, on the other hand, "will not suffer *such a severe* hell."

The bishops went on to ask if Judaism believes that Christians could be saved through their religion. "The rabbi responded: 'Let me tell you a way that you can be saved even through your faith. If you observe the seven commandments that you have been commanded, you will be saved through them.' The bishops rejoiced, and responded: 'Indeed, we have ten!'[20] The rabbi replied: 'That is fine with me.' "[21]

We see that even when R. Yehiel was under severe pressure, he refused to say explicitly that Christians have a share in the world to come. He began by saying that the Christians may have a slightly cooler hell than the actual followers of Jesus (who were apostate Jews), and then went on to point out that observance of the seven Noahide commandments are a medium through which gentiles can save their souls, but he avoided an explicit statement as to whether or not a Christian violates one of those commandments, to wit, the prohibition of idolatry, by virtue of his Christianity; he leaves it to the bishops themselves to issue a ruling in their favor. It is true that the expression "you can be saved even through your faith," which R. Yehiel pronounced as if the proverbial demon was compelling him, does indicate that one can believe in Christianity while still observing the seven Noahide commandments, but a careful reading of the passage as a whole nonetheless reveals the deeply entrenched belief of Ashkenazic Jewry that the Christian is condemned to hell.

R. Yehiel, then, avoids a direct engagement with the question of the status of a gentile who believes in Jesus' divinity yet still wants to be counted among those who observe the seven Noahide Commandments.

---

19   *B. Rosh Ha-shanah* 17a, and Rashi ad loc. (See the variants in *Diqduqei Soferim*.)
20   MS Moscow (folio 96b) and MS Oxford (folio 10a) read: "Indeed, they have definitely been commanded to us, and we observe (or will observe) them," though each of these texts has its own scribal error in its presentation of this variant.
21   *Vikkuah Rabbenu Yehiel mi-Paris*, ed. by R. Margoliyot (Lvov [1868]), pp. 22–23.

However, Meir ben Simon of Narbonne was not deterred from confronting the question directly and explicitly. In his book *Milhemet Mizvah*, he reports that a Christian asked precisely the same question that the bishops asked R. Yehiel. In this debate, the Jew responds to the Christian that the gentiles are obligated to observe the seven Noahide commandments, one of which is to believe

> "that the universe has a creator, who is one, true, primeval, and without beginning or end, and that he watches over all his creations, to repay the actions of each one." The Christian responded: "Yes—we, too, believe that." The Jew said: "And yet, if you were to ask one who believes this who this creator is and he would say that he is a certain man, born of a woman, who has undergone all bodily vicissitudes including death, such a believer would be one who denies the creator of the universe if his assertion is untrue, and he would be condemned to hell."[22]

Collective destiny

The picture is much more complicated when we look at the question of the collective destiny of the gentiles at the end of days. Yuval's article paints a sharp, almost polar contrast between the "avenging redemption" in Ashkenazic eschatology versus the "conversionary redemption" in Sephardic eschatology.[23] The Jews of Ashkenaz looked forward to a divine campaign by the Master of the Universe wrapped in his royal robe drenched in the blood of generations of martyrs, a campaign that would visit utter destruction upon all the nations. By contrast, Jews of

---

[22] W. Herskowitz (ed.), *Judeo-Christian Dialogue in Provence as Reflected in Milhemet Mizvah of R. Meir ha-Meili*, D.H.L. dissertation, Yeshiva University, 1974, p. 111. Herskowitz's text is based on MS Parma, 43b. The question of Christianity's status as idolatry comes up in a number of places in Jacob Katz's book *Exclusiveness and Tolerance: Studies in Jewish-Gentile Relations in Medieval and Modern Times* (New York, 1961). See also what I have written in my articles, "Religion, Nationalism, and Historiography: Yehzkel Kaufmann's Account of Jesus and Early Christianity," in *Scholars and Scholarship: The Interaction between Judaism and Other Cultures*, ed. by L. Landman (New York, 1990), pp. 150–153; and "Christians, Gentiles, and the Talmud: A Fourteenth-Century Jewish Response to the Attack on Rabbinic Judaism," in *Religionsgespräche im Mittelalter*, ed. by B. Lewis and F. Niewöhner (Wiesbaden, 1992), pp. 124–127.

[23] Yuval, pp. 34–50. For example, he regards as exceptional the assertion in an Askenazic liturgical poem (by Rabbenu Gershom of Mainz) that "all inhabitants of the universe / will say out loud together: Behold, there is no god in the world / other than that of Israel, whose redeemer is strong" (p. 34).

other regions looked forward to a mass conversion of all residents of the world. In a critical response to Yuval's position, Avraham Grossman pointed to Ashkenazic sources that describe conversion at the end of days; he concluded that Yuval's article does identify a genuine, significant contrast but characterizes it too sharply.[24] In a response to Grossman's review, Yuval clarified his position. When all the dust settled—after the initial article, the critique, and the rejoinder—there emerged a conclusion apparently acceptable to both scholars: although the emphasis on vengeance was much stronger in Ashkenaz, even there the avenging redemption was considered only the first stage of the eschatological process; the second stage is that of the conversionary redemption.

There is certainly a large degree of truth in this conception. Nevertheless, I believe that with respect to a number of fundamental points, it requires clarification, expansion, and qualification. If the impression created by Yuval's initial article was too strong, I think that the position emerging from the subsequent exchange is too mild. In the overwhelming majority of sources, there is no true universal conversion that turns the gentiles at the end of days into "an inseparable part of the Jewish people."[25] The remaining gentiles do adopt a belief in one God, but they remain separate from and inferior to the Chosen People, accept its authority, and serve it. Some sources even speak of the total destruction of an entire sector of the human race, rather than just the death of many gentiles.

Conversion:

We read in tractate *Avodah Zarah*:

> It has been taught: R. Yosi says, "In the time to come, the nations of the world will come and convert." (But will we accept them?) Has it not been taught: In the days of the Messiah proselytes will not be accepted, just as they were not accepted in the days of David or Solomon?—Rather, they will be self-made proselytes. [Rashi comments: they will convert of their own volition, but we will not accept them, because they are converting only

---

24   A. Grossman, "'Ha-Ge'ullah ha-Megayyeret' be-Mishnatam shel Hakhmei Ashkenaz ha-Rishonim," *Zion* 59 (1994): 325–342. Two of Grossman's proof-texts (the *Aleinu* prayer and the liturgical poem *Ve-Ye'etayu kol le-Avdekha*) are cited also in Ezra Fleischer's critical review, "Yahasei Yehudim-Nozerim bi-Re'i Aqum" in the same volume of *Zion*, p. 291.

25   Grossman, p. 340.

because they see the exalted position of the Jewish people]. They will place *tefillin* on their foreheads, *tefillin* on their arms, *zizit* on their garments, and a *mezuzah* on their doorways. When they see the battle of Gog and Magog, they will be asked: "For what purpose have you come?" They will respond: "Against the Lord, and against His anointed one." As it is said: "Why do the heathen rage, and the nations speak vainly?" (Psalms 2:1) At that moment, each one of them will remove his religious object and leave, as it is said: "Let us remove their chains" (Psalms 2:3). [26]

It is true that not every messianic vision must be bound by this Talmudic passage. Maimonides explicitly says: "The Sages did not have an authoritative tradition regarding these matters; rather, they [tried to determine the events of the end of days] from their own understanding of scriptural verses, and they therefore disagreed with each other about these matters."[27] Medieval Jews who envisioned the events of the end of days generally conducted themselves in accordance with this approach, even if they did not consciously embrace it. Nevertheless, the text affirming that proselytes will not be accepted in the time of the Messiah is a halakhic statement, which therefore had a normative status even among the followers of Maimonides' approach. There is one late medieval polemic in which the question comes up explicitly. R. Solomon ben Simon Duran reads certain scriptural verses as indicating that gentiles will convert in the future, and he notices the contradiction between these verses and the rabbinic ruling. He resolves the apparent contradiction by concluding that the verses are speaking not of conversion to the status of *ger zedeq* (one who becomes a full member of the Jewish people), but merely that of *ger toshav* (one who accepts the seven Noahide commandments).[28]

It goes without saying that the halakhic lens is not sufficient to provide a full understanding of the various perspectives on the process of redemption. The citation of the rabbinic ruling in Solomon ben Simon Duran's polemic is exceptional; as we have noted, writers on eschatology did not feel bound by the Talmudic tradition in all its details. Nevertheless, we see from here that the word "proselyte" (*ger*) covers three different categories (true proselyte, *ger toshav*, and "self-made proselyte"), and the verb "to convert" (*lehitgayyer*) does not necessarily mean becoming

[26] B. *Avodah Zarah* 3b; cf. also B. *Yevamot* 24b.
[27] *Hilkhot Melakhim* 12:2.
[28] *Milhemet Mizvah*, published with *Keshet u-Magen le-R. Shim'on ben Zemah Duran* (Jerusalem, 1970), p. 37b.

an integral part of the Jewish people. Moreover, the rabbinic ruling in question does not play a significant role in messianic texts not only because of the ideational flexibility that excused messianic visionaries from confronting problems emerging from the Talmud; the majority of these texts did not need to deal with the halakhic problem because it never occurred to their authors that in the final stage of the redemption all gentiles would become Jews in the full sense of the term.

In another Talmudic passage, we find the position that became the predominant one among medieval Jews:

> Ulla contrasted two scriptural verses: It is written, "He will swallow up death forever; and the Lord will wipe away tears from off all faces" (Isaiah 25:8); yet it is also written: "For the child shall die a hundred years old" (ibid. 65:20). . . . There is no contradiction—this verse [stating that people will be immortal] refers to the Jewish people, and the other verse [stating that people will die only at a ripe old age] refers to the nations of the world. But why will the nations of the world be there? As it is written [or "This refers to those of whom it is written"]: "And foreigners shall stand and feed your flocks, and the sons of the alien shall be your plowmen and your vinedressers" (ibid. 61:5).[29]

The first half of this passage is cited in the Disputation of Paris as an example of contradictory verses in Scripture that force us to turn to the Talmud for a resolution. The second half appears at that point in the margin of the Hamburg manuscript, though with no explicit reference to our question.[30] In any event, this is a Talmudic passage that explicitly poses the question of whether the gentiles will survive at the end of days, and it answers that they—or some of them—will remain alive in order to serve the Jewish people.

In *Sefer Nizzahon Yashan*, which serves, as we shall see, as a source of the most extreme form of the idea of apocalyptic vengeance against the gentiles, we find a sharp passage about the servitude of the gentiles.

---

29   B. *Sanhedrin* 61b. Cf. also B. *Pesahim* 68a, as well as the following passage: "All the gentiles who are still on the earth at the time of the Messiah will go to the Land of Israel, and bring grain and bread and sustenance into the houses of the Jewish people, and make the Jews very wealthy" (*Seder Eliyyahu Rabbah* 20 [Ish-Shalom's edition, p. 113]).

30   *Vikkuah Rabbenu Yehiel mi-Paris*, p. 13; Hamburg ms., p. 73a. (In the manuscript, the Talmudic passage is cited according to the variant, "This refers to those of whom it is written," rather than merely "It is written." This may indicate that only a few gentiles are expected to survive.)

As a reflection of the self-image of Ashkenazic Jewry, this passage is remarkable, for it describes a situation of Jewish social and economic superiority *at the present time*, i.e., in thirteenth-century Ashkenaz, and presents this "fact" as self evident. However, the passage does not limit its discussion to the present; it clearly refers also to the future, when the gentiles will continue (!) to serve the Jewish people. In the merit of their servitude—and in this merit alone—they will have some "slight hope":

> They bark their assertion that it is improper for the uncircumcised and impure to serve Jews. Tell them: On the contrary, if not for the fact that they serve Jews they would have been condemned to destruction, for it is written in Isaiah, "Arise, shine, for your light has come . . . . For the nation and kingdom that will not serve you shall perish; yea, those nations shall be utterly wasted" (Isa. 60:1, 12). On the other hand, as long as they serve Israel they have some hope, as it is written, "And strangers shall stand and tend your flock, and the sons of foreigners shall be your farmers and vintners" (Isa. 61:5); consequently, they should serve us all the time, so that they may fulfill the prophecy, "The elder shall serve the younger" (Gen. 25:23). It was for this reason that the Torah said, "You shall not eat anything that dies of itself; you shall give it to the stranger that is in your gates, that he may eat it, or you may sell it to a gentile" (Deut. 14:21). The Torah told us to sell such meat to gentiles because they will serve us, and God does not withhold the reward of any creature. This, in fact, is what we do; we give over to them the animals which are ritually unfit for our use, and we sell them the hind portions of animals for this same reason.[31]

The hope that the gentiles would serve the Jews can be found outside Ashkenaz as well. In Grossman's above-mentioned article, he cites a salient example from R. Saadya Gaon's philosophical work, which asserts explicitly that "those who correct their behavior by entering into the Torah of Israel" will serve the Jews at the end of days "in their homes . . . in city and village work, . . . in the fields and in the wilderness . . . The rest will return to their own land, but under the dominion of the Jewish people."[32]

There are, it is true, a number of sources, mainly from outside of Ashkenaz, that speak according to their straightforward meaning of a massive conversion to Judaism at the end of days. It is not my wish

---

[31] *The Jewish-Christian Debate*, p. 207.
[32] *Sefer ha-Emunot ve-he-De'ot* (Constantinople [1562]), folio 68b, cited in Grossman, p. 339.

to force all the numerous, varied texts that address the destiny of the gentiles into a procrustean bed and to artificially impose ideological agreement between them, but it is possible that even these sources are not speaking of complete integration of the gentiles into the Jewish people. Rav Hai Gaon, for example, writes, "The remaining nations will convert, as it is said: 'For then will I turn to the people a pure language, that they may all call upon the name of the Lord' (Zephaniah 3:9), and it is said: 'They will say, Come ye, and let us go up to the mountain of the Lord, to the house of the God of Jacob; and he will teach us of his ways, and we will walk in his paths: for out of Zion shall go forth the law, and the word of the Lord from Jerusalem' (Isaiah 2:3). When they come before the Messiah, he will order them to end all fighting and wars."[33] However, Rav Hai was well aware of the Talmudic passage from tractate *Avodah Zarah* ("In the time to come, the nations of the world will come and convert . . . ; they will be self-made proselytes"), and it is quite possible that the gentiles described here are expected to retain their separate national identity.[34]

Even the interesting Ashkenazic sources presented by Grossman do not seem to be examples of texts predicting a conversion so complete that the gentiles become "an inseparable part of the Jewish people." In three places, Grossman himself points out formulations indicating that the gentiles "will not reach the high level of the Jewish people".[35] If we briefly survey the other sources, we will see that the conclusions emerging from them do not contradict this affirmation.

---

[33] Yehuda ibn Shmuel, *Midreshei Ge'ullah* (Jerusalem and Tel-Aviv, 1954), pp. 139–140. Part of this passage is quoted by Yuval, p. 45.

[34] The first source that Yuval cites as an example of "conversionary redemption" is one in which the gentiles accept the beliefs of the Jews, but it does not necessarily refer to "conversion" in the full sense of the word. ("All the nations will accept our faith, and say that they have inherited falsehood from their ancestors . . . for all the nations will turn to belief in the glorious God, after having seen all the wonders that he performs when he rescues us from this exile"—R. Simon of Narbonne, *Milhemet Mizvah*, Parma ms., pp.19b–20a; cited in Yuval, p. 34.) There is one passage in *Derashot ha-Ran* that seems to say that the gentiles will become completely integrated into the Jewish people at the end of days. Even here, I do not think that this understanding of the text is absolutely unavoidable, but the truth is that anyone who wishes to escape this conclusion must provide a forced interpretation. See *Derashot ha-Ran*, ed. by A. L. Feldman (Jerusalem, 1977), p. 121, and D. Schwartz, *Ha-Ra'ayon ha-Meshihi be-Hagut ha-Yehudit bi-Yemei ha-Beinayim* (Ramat-Gan, 1997), p. 182.

[35] Grossman, p. 334 (regarding Rashi on Isaiah 42), and cf. p. 330 (regarding the liturgical poem *Eimat Nore'otekha*) and p. 337 (regarding Rashi on Zechariah 9:1).

Rashi's commentary on Isaiah 14:1 does speak of true proselytes, but it is clear that these individuals are not to be identified with the totality of the gentiles who remain during the final phase of the redemption. On the contrary, the following verse informs us that after the conversion of these gentiles, the remaining nations will take the Jewish people "to [the Jews'] own territory, and the Jewish people will take them as an inheritance upon God's land, as male and female slaves, and they will plunder those who had plundered them, and dominate those who had oppressed them."

Rashi's commentary on Isaiah 56, too, speaks of true proselytes, but it refers to the individuals who convert before the final stage of the redemption, and perhaps even over the course of the years of the exile. This is clear from Rashi's words in his commentary on verse 3: "Let not the foreigner say: 'Why should I convert? Will not God remove me from his people *when he pays them their reward*?'" I believe that R. Joseph Qara's commentary on the chapter should be understood the same way.

Rashi's commentary on Zechariah 13:8–9 does speak of true proselytes, or rather of a group of Judaizing gentiles, a subset of which will ultimately be accepted as true proselytes. However, the initial conversion of these individuals is to take place before "the suffering associated with the birth-pangs of the Messiah and the wars of Gog and Magog." It is precisely through these many tribulations that these converts will be tested. The majority of them "will return to their straying ways, and join with the forces of Gog, as we find in an *aggadah*,"[36] but a minority will survive the test, and become part of the Jewish people. This is hardly a description of a massive conversion of the gentiles after the stage of the avenging redemption.

I must emphasize that the question that I am raising is not the central point in the articles by Yuval or Grossman. Yuval is interested in the contrast between the sources that foresee the destruction of the gentiles and those that foresee their acceptance of the faith of the Jews, and Grossman is interested in proving that even the Ashkenazic vision of the redemption does not affirm that the gentiles will be totally destroyed. In neither case is the nature of the "conversion" the central point; indeed,

---

[36] Rashi appears to be referring to the passage in *B. Avodah Zarah* 3b, which I have already quoted above.

from a narrow vantage point, it is not relevant at all to their concerns. However, there is no doubt that this question is of great importance for a deep understanding of the relationship between the Jews and their neighbors, and a reader who has been following the scholarly exchange sparked by Yuval's initial article will be exposed to an inaccurate impression that envisions the utter erasure of the boundaries between Israel and the nations at the end of days. In fact, the Jews of the Middle Ages felt at the deepest level of their consciousness that the uniqueness of the Jewish people would remain even at the end of days.

Punishment:

According to the common conclusion that Yuval and Grossman have reached at the current state of their exchange, even the Ashkenazim did not hope for the total destruction of all gentiles. In Grossman's words: "The Jews did not believe that all of their gentile neighbors were destined to be wiped out. There was a core of good people ensconced among them, who would ultimately convert to Judaism, either personally or through their descendants."[37]

Here, too, I think that there are sources meriting renewed attention that will not undermine this assertion entirely but will add a sharper and more hostile perspective. Let us begin with a passage from the *Tanna de-Bei Eliyyahu*:

> I was once travelling from one town to another, and I found a certain old man. He asked me: "Master, will there be gentiles at the time of the Messiah?" I told him: "My son, all the nations and kingdoms that tormented and oppressed the Jewish people will come and see the happiness of the Jews, and turn to dust, and never return, as it is said: 'The wicked shall see it, and be grieved' (Psalms 112:10); and it is said: 'And you shall leave your name for a curse unto my chosen' (Isaiah 65:15). And all the kingdoms and nations that have not tormented or oppressed the Jews will come and serve as farmers and vineyard-keepers for the Jews, as it is said: 'And strangers shall stand and tend your flock, and the sons of foreigners shall be your farmers and vintners . . . and you shall be called the Lord's priests' (Isaiah 61:5–6); and it is said: 'For then will I turn to the people a pure language' (Zephaniah 3:9); and it is said: 'And he will call his servants by a different name' (Isaiah 65:15)—these verses refer to those gentiles worthy of living

---

[37] Grossman, p. 340.

in the time of the Messiah. You might think that because they are going to remain alive in the time of the Messiah, they will also merit the World to Come. You must, therefore, set aside the words I have just spoken and give heed to the words of the Torah, which are more severe than the words that I have just said. The Torah says: 'No uncircumcised individual shall eat of [the paschal sacrifice]' (Exodus 12:48). If this is so of such a minor matter as the paschal sacrifice, surely it should be so of the World to Come, which is the holiest matter of all. No uncircumcised individual shall ever, ever eat in it, nor ever, ever, dwell in it."[38]

We see then that according to the first approach cited here, the more "liberal" one, the nations that have oppressed the Jews will completely perish; and according to the second, more severe approach, all of the gentiles—or perhaps only all of the uncircumcised gentiles—will disappear from the world.[39]

As an example of the avenging redemption, Yuval cites an abbreviated version of a passage from *Sefer Nizzahon Yashan* that according to its straightforward meaning describes the total destruction of all the gentiles. Here is the full passage:

The heretics harass us by noting that God has delayed the end of this exile longer than those of the others. But this is not surprising, for God does not punish a nation until the measure of its sins has been filled, as it is written, "In a measure, when it is sent forth you will contend with it" (Isa. 27:8). Similarly, he told Abraham, "And the fourth generation shall return here, for the iniquity of the Amorites is not yet complete (Gen. 15:16), and I do not wish to destroy the Amorites until their measure has been filled." That is why that exile lasted only four hundred years, for in that period of time the measure of two nations—the Egyptians and the Amorites— was filled, and they became deserving of destruction; it should be noted, furthermore, that it took a long time for it to be filled since it dates back to the generation when nations were separated. Now, until the generation when the Babylonian exile ended there was no further destruction of any

---

[38]   *Seder Eliyyahu Rabbah* (22) 20 (Ish-Shalom's edition, pp. 120–121). Cf. also above, n. 29.

[39]   Ish-Shalom (ad loc., note 13) expresses the view that the text is referring only to uncircumcised gentiles. For another example of such a distinction, see *Tosafot* on *Avodah Zarah* 10b, s.v. *Vai lah le-ilfa*. Cf. also *Yosef ha-Meqanne*, p. 17, on Ezekiel 32. In verse 29 there, Ezekiel informs us that Edom will descend into a pit full of uncircumcised men ("There is Edom . . . and all its princes"), and the author of *Yosef ha-Meqanne* points out: "The Jews, the circumcised nation, will not be there." Here, the distinction is clearly between the Jewish people and the gentiles, not between circumcised and uncircumcised gentiles.

nation, and that redemption was also not accomplished "with a high hand"; indeed, that is why the exile lasted only seventy years. This redemption, however, will involve the ruin, destruction, killing, and eradication of all the nations, them, and the angels who watch over them, and their gods, as it is written, "The Lord shall punish the heavenly host in heaven and the kings of the earth on earth" (Isa. 24:21). Jeremiah too said, "Fear not, my servant Jacob, said the Lord, for I am with you; for I will make a full end of all the nations whither I have driven you, but with you I will not make a full end" (Jer. 46:28).[40]

It is true that we have seen above that the author of *Sefer Nizzahon Yashan* does speak of a "slight hope" for the gentiles who will serve the Jewish people, but the book is largely an anthology of anti-Christian arguments from various sources, and it is hard to escape the conclusion that whoever wrote our passage looked forward to the total destruction of all the gentiles. The author no doubt recited *Ve-ye'etayu kol le-ovdekha* (see note 21) in the High Holiday service, but when he wrote these lines, this element of the eschatological vision disappeared entirely from his consciousness.[41]

Though the expectation that all the gentiles would be utterly destroyed was rare even in Ashkenaz, the hope for the total destruction of the Kingdom of Edom, i.e., Christendom, was undoubtedly quite common—and not just in Ashkenaz.

---

[40]   *The Jewish-Christian Debate*, p. 227. It is possible that the use of the word *kelayah* ("destruction") with reference to the Egyptians, who were not completely destroyed, can mitigate the impression created by this passage. However, the tone of the passage is so strong that I hesitate to suggest a moderate interpretation.

[41]   In Rashi's commentary on *Sanhedrin* 111a, s.v. *amar Resh Laqish* and s.v. *la niha lehu*, he suggests two explanations of the Talmudic passage: one in the name of his teacher, and one which he thinks is preferable. The first explanation raises the possibility that all the gentiles will perish, and only (part of) the Jewish people will survive. We need to be very careful about reaching any conclusions about the worldview of a commentator from his remarks on a difficult passage that he is struggling to interpret. Nevertheless, we may not completely ignore the fact that this commentary explicitly states that such a total destruction is in the realm of possibility. (Even if Rashi is not the author of the commentary on this chapter of Sanhedrin that is attributed to him, it was definitely written in the Ashkenazic sphere of culture no later than the twelfth century.) See also *Yosef ha-Meqanne*, p. 58: "A priest from Etampes once asked me, 'Do you really believe that the entire population of the world will perish, and you, the smallest nation, will merit life in the World to Come?' I replied, 'Is it not written: "It was not because you were more in number than any of the peoples that the Lord set his love on you or chose you, for you were the fewest [of all peoples]" (Deut. 7:7)?'"

We find the following in a passage in *Sefer Nizzahon Yashan* that is partly parallel to the one we have just cited:

> You have no shame in saying of him who spoke and the world came to be, of him who lives forever, that he accepted death and suffering for you. Why, Moses said in the name of God, "Lo, I raise my hand to heaven and say: As I live forever . . ." (Deut. 32:40), and David, Elijah, and Daniel all swore by the life of God. Moreover, it is written, "See then, that I, I am he; there is no god beside me" (Deut. 32:39); yet you say that he has a partner, that there are two, nay, three gods. Know clearly that God will exact revenge from you, as it is written, "For the Lord will vindicate his people and take revenge for his servants . . . O nations, acclaim his people! For he will avenge the blood of his servants" (Deut. 32:36, 43). And Jeremiah said, "But fear not, O my servant Jacob, and be not dismayed, O Israel . . . for I am with you; for I will make a full end of all the nations whither I have driven you, but I will not make a full end of you" (Jer. 46:27–28; 30:10–11). Furthermore, he promised us, "But fear not, O my servant Jacob, and be not dismayed, O Israel, for, behold, I will save you from afar off and your seed from the land of their captivity; and Jacob shall return and be in rest and at ease, and none shall make him afraid" (Jer. 46:27; 30:10), but none of the house of Esau shall remain or escape (cf. Obadiah 1:18).[42]

Here, too, we find a description of total destruction, but this time it is specifically directed toward the House of Esau. In this context, we should pay attention to the full citation from Jeremiah: "all the nations *whither I have driven you.*" It is difficult to conjecture what the author's attitude might have been regarding the fate of the inhabitants of the Lands of Ishmael to which God had driven Jews—it is doubtful that the question entered his mind when he wrote these words—but it is clear that he did not believe that the gentiles in the far-off islands, where no Jews lived, would be destroyed. To resort to a formulation in *Ve-ye'etayu kol le-ovdekha*, those straying peoples who will learn wisdom at the end of days "will tell of your righteousness in the islands"—but not in Europe. In the Christian world, there will be total destruction. This will occur for two reasons. The primary reason, according to this passage, is Christian theology—God will not tolerate the embarrassment caused to him by the people who declare that he has a partner, or that he has undergone death and suffering. The line "God will exact revenge from

---

42   *The Jewish-Christian Debate*, pp. 75–76.

you" at first seems to be referring to revenge for this embarrassment, but the passage immediately quotes a scriptural verse about vengeance with a different motive—avenging the "blood of His servants." In another passage, the author of *Sefer Nizzahon Yashan* says to the Christians: "'The Lord your God will place these curses upon your enemies and foes who have persecuted you' (Deut. 30:7)—you [Christians] are included among these, and therefore we cannot become one people, for we are inscribed for life, and you for death, for you are our enemies and persecutors."[43] Persecution of Israel and idolatrous audacity directed at God go hand in hand to lead Christians to their ultimate destruction.

It seems to me that a passage from the Ashkenazic *Treatise concerning the Date of the Redemption* quoted in Yuval's article as an example of the anticipation of "the destruction of all the nations" in fact reflects a distinction between the nations in general and Edom in particular. The passage does begin by speaking of vengeance against "the nations," but the continuation is revealing::

> During those thirty-five years (1317–1352 CE), there will be a fulfillment of the scriptural passage, "You will be raised up next to princes, and kings will serve you as nurses" (cf. Isaiah 49:22–23)—for the kings of the nations will see the vengeance that God has carried out against them for the sake of the Jewish people, and they will see the ingathering of the exiles . . . . And in that year . . . which is the year 5112 (1352 CE), this nation will entirely disappear, and Jerusalem will be built.[44]

In this passage, God takes "vengeance" against the nations in general, but brings total destruction to "this nation."

---

43   Ibid., p. 127. Similarly, *Yosef ha-Meqanne* (p. 87) writes that the punishment of Edom, mentioned at the end of the prophecy of Obadiah, will follow from "the afflictions and persecutions that you impose on us in each generation." Compare also the collection of scriptural verses at the beginning of the book (pp. 15–25) promising consolation to Israel and punishment to the gentiles. There is an Ashkenazic penitential poem for the Eve of Rosh Hashanah that looks to the day when the people of Edom will be destroyed as a consequence of both their idolatry and their persecution of the Jewish people: "May haughty Edom and Moab be blotted out from the book of life, / for they bow before a block of wood, and declare it divine. / Let the wicked oppressor receive no mercy; may he be condemned to destruction, / for he has taunted the legions of the living God." (In D. Goldschmidt, *Seder ha-Selihot ke-Minhag Lita u-Qehillot ha-Perushim be-Eretz Yisrael* [Jerusalem, 1965], p. 91.)

44   A. Marx, "Ma'amar al Shenat ha-Ge'ullah," in *Ha-Zofeh le-Hokhmat Yisrael* 5 (1921): 197, cited by Yuval, pp. 44–45.

This position appears explicitly in *Sephardic* sources from the late Middle Ages. Simon ben Zemah Duran writes that the prophets envisioned

> the destruction of each of these religions [Christianity and Islam] . . . in a manner commensurate with the degree that it has strayed from the truth. For regarding the Christian nation, which pronounced blasphemies against God, the verse says: "And the House of Jacob shall be a fire . . . and not leave any remnant of the House of Esau" (Obadiah 1:18) . . . But we are assured that the Muslim nation, which has humiliated our people and cast truth to the ground, will be humiliated before us as its mother [Hagar] was humiliated before our mother [Sarah].

He goes on to present a long list of scriptural verses reporting how the nations will be abased before Israel at the end of days.[45]

A similar distinction between Edom and the other nations is made in R. Isaac Abravanel's *Ma'yenei ha-Yeshu'ah*; however, for exegetical reasons, he includes Ishmael as well in the group that will be totally destroyed. The main target of God's wrath is Christianity: "The ultimate decree against [the people of Rome, the Fourth Beast in Daniel's vision] will be not on account of their evil deeds, but on account of the strange

---

[45] P. Murciano, *Simon ben Zemah Duran, Keshet u-Magen: A Critical Edition*, Ph.D. dissertation, New York University, 1975, pp. 107–108. Yuval (p. 69) points out that "as far as we can tell, the distinction between the Ashkenazim and the Sephardim becomes progressively smaller toward the end of the thirteenth century." On eschatological vengeance against the gentiles in a fourteenth-century Sephardic polemic, see Y. Shamir, *Rabbi Moses ha-Kohen of Tordesillas and his Book Ezer Ha-Emunah: A Chapter in the History of the Judeo–Christian Controversy* II (Coconut Grove, Fla., 1972), pp. 83, 84, and cf. p. 86. All the essential components—the decree that Edom will be destroyed, the humiliation of the nations, and their recognition of the God of Israel—appear together in an Ashkenazic liturgical poem, but they are less explicit there. In the poem *Ototekha Ra'inu* by R. Simon bar Isaac, we read that the following will take place on the day of the redemption: "He will visit complete destruction upon Edom . . . when he makes great, eternal joy [for the Jews] . . . . He will remove the enemy, and humiliate it, / and pastor his flock in his shadow, / and fell the mighty horns of the gentiles. / They will tell of his loftiness and his military might, / and all will be united to serve him, / when the universe and its fullness will praise him." (See J. Fränkel, *Mahzor Pesah* (Jerusalem, 1993), pp. 504–505.) If we take the expression "He will visit complete destruction upon Edom" literally, then the poem is speaking of the total destruction of the Christian world. If so, the enemy who is merely humiliated must be understood as the Muslim world or other gentile nations. However, there is room for one who disagrees with this understanding to argue that the expression, "He will visit complete destruction upon Edom" is poetic exaggeration that allows for some subjugated, monotheistic Christians to appear in the continuation of the passage.

and harsh words and beliefs that the small horn [in Daniel's vision], which refers to the Pope, and the sect of the priests of Jesus, pronounce against God, may he be blessed."[46] Abravanel continues with a stunning interpretation of Psalms 50:16–23, a passage which he understands as being an admonition to Christian Edom: "Who are you to declare my statutes, or express my covenant in your mouth, seeing that you hate instruction, and cast my words behind you?" (verses 16–17). The Christians will be punished for their perversions of the scriptures, for casting the words of the prophets that refer to the future redemption "behind them," that is, for interpreting them as referring to the past (!). A further punishment will befall them because "You speak against your brother; you slander your mother's son" (verse 20), i.e., they have persecuted the Jewish people, which is called Edom's brother. However, Scripture continues, "These things you have done, and I kept silent. You thought that I was altogether such a one as yourself: I will reprove you and confront you with charges" (verse 21). The "great punishment" will befall Edom on account of the second, "truly monumental sin—that they have spoken against God by attributing humanity and corporeality to him, as if he were one of us."[47]

The first three beasts in Daniel's vision are punished in careful proportion and measure, but the fourth beast, Edom, is punished with "utter extinction," "to be destroyed to the very end." "The Kingdom of Rome—the nation of Edom and the nation of the Ishmaelites who have entered under their governance—will all perish from the face of the earth, and those nations will be totally destroyed."[48] Abravanel's analysis does not provide a sufficient religious-ethical explanation for why the Ishmaelite nation should be destroyed. The Muslims are completely innocent of the decisive sin that causes the destruction of Edom. However, to their great misfortune, Abravanel is forced to include them in "the Kingdom of Edom," for Daniel's vision includes only four beasts, and not five. It is this exegetical difficulty that sends them to their destruction.[49]

---

[46] *Ma'yenei ha-Yeshu'ah, Ma'ayan* #8, *Tamar* #8, in Abravanel, *Perush al Nevi'im u-Ketuvim* III (Tel Aviv, 1960), pp. 346–347.

[47] P. 348.

[48] P. 347.

[49] Abravanel gives a historico-exegetical justification for his inclusion of Ishmael in the Edomite nation in *Ma'ayan* #2, *Tamar* #3, p. 290.

The presence of a vision of vengeance and destruction alongside a vision of subjugation and recognition of the faith of Israel expresses a tension between two types of prophecies, two traditions, and two psychological needs. On the one hand, there is the desire for radical, absolute, ultimate vengeance against the oppressor; on the other hand, there is the desire to see one's opponent admit his error not for a passing moment but for untold generations. Apparently, the yearning for vengeance occasionally became so powerful that it led to a willingness to forego the desire for an ongoing admission of error entirely. The most prevalent solution, which took varied forms, envisioned the destruction of entire nations or many individuals of those nations, and the survival of the rest in a more or less inferior status, after they recognize that the Lord, God of Israel, is king, and his rule dominates all. Medieval Christian theology viewed the Jews as unwilling witnesses to the truth of Christianity, whereas the Jewish messianic vision viewed the remaining gentiles of the end of days as willing witnesses to the truth of Judaism.[50]

Over the course of this article, we have seen some small sampling of the complex relations between the Jews and their neighbors in the crucible of Christian Europe: images of superiority and inferiority mixed together, visions of destruction on the one hand and of a united faith on the other. We have focused here on hostile relations, but we should not forget that there were also friendly relations in daily life that left their mark even on Ashkenazic polemical literature, especially *Sefer*

[50] This comparison of the Jewish eschatological vision to the Augustinian doctrine appears in Yuval's article in a slightly different form and is described as the position of the "non-Ashkenazic world" alone. He explains that the survival of non-Jews is "necessary . . . in order to prove the truth of Judaism." If he means that it is *logically* necessary along the lines of the Christian theory, it is hard to accept his statement, for in the days of the Messiah, the truth will be completely clear without any need of external proofs. However, if he means that it is *psychologically* necessary for the persecuted Jews—whether Sephardic or Ashkenazic—I think that his statement has much truth in it. See Yuval, p. 48. It is not impossible that the Christian position that the Jews must be kept alive as living witnesses of the truth of Christianity sheds light on a stanza in a penitential poem recited during the days between Rosh Hashanah and Yom Kippur: "We have fallen low, and cannot arise, . . . We sit like false witnesses, / unable to raise our heads" (Goldschmidt [see above, n. 43], p. 179.) It is indeed possible that this is a routine simile asserting that the Jews in exile are as embarrassed as a false witness who has been found out. However, if we read the line in light of the Augustinian doctrine, which an educated Jews would surely have known, the line becomes an impassioned cry, full of pathos.

Yosef ha-Meqanne, and certainly on other genres of literature.[51] Jews and Christians alike were delighted to discern the defects in the other group, but they also, however unwillingly, saw the positive characteristics as well. In the downtrodden Jewish community, both their self-image and their image of the other were formed out of deep personal struggles, and their visions of the ultimate fate of the gentiles reflected a range of theological, exegetical, historical, and psychological considerations that arose out of the depths of the soul of an exiled people. The ironclad faith that the Jew would ultimate be victorious at the end of days made it possible for an oppressed minority to maintain itself even in its contemporary condition, and an examination of the various paths that this faith took can help us understand the remarkable phenomenon that manifests itself before our eyes—not the survival of the gentiles at the end of days, but the survival of the Jews in medieval Europe.

ADDENDUM

About three years after the publication of this article, Reuven Kimelman's excellent study of the mystical meaning of the *Lekhah Dodi* prayer appeared (*Lekhah Dodi ve-Qabbalat Shabbat: ha-Mashma'ut ha-Mistit* [Jerusalem, 2003]). Kimelman, who had not seen my article, devoted a chapter to the stanza beginning, "You shall burst forth to the right and to the left," arguing that it expresses the expectation that Esau and Ishmael will convert to Judaism at the end of days. (All the references cited in this addendum can be found in that chapter.) My first impression was that the sources that he cites provide a body of evidence demonstrating that the expectation of full conversion was more common than I had thought. More careful examination, however, reveals that the dominant

---

51   For an excellent example from the Provençal community, see J. Shatzmiller, *Shylock Reconsidered* (Berkeley, Los Angeles and Oxford, 1970), pp. 104–122. In this context, let me emphasize a particularly significant point that has emerged from the exchange between Fleischer and Yuval: the vengeance that the Ashkenazim envisioned in their apocalyptic predictions is not carried out by the Jews against their enemies; rather, it plays itself out as an eschatological mission of the God of Israel, who avenges himself and his people. For an evaluation of the central thesis of Yuval's article, see my discussion in *From Crusades to Blood Libels to Expulsions: Some New Approaches to Medieval Antisemitism* (Second Annual Lecture of the V. J. Selmanowitz Chair of Jewish History, Touro College Graduate School of Jewish Studies, New York, 1997).

view in those sources is precisely that of the texts that I had analyzed: the nations of the world will recognize the validity of Judaism without full conversion and persist in a state of subordination to Jews.

One quotation in Kimelman's chapter does appear to look forward to full conversion. The late-thirteenth-century R. Moses of Burgos writes, "All the nations will return to the worship of our Creator may he be blessed and convert so that they will come under the wings of the divine Presence, observing his Torah and serving him wholeheartedly as one . . . for they will all convert for the sake of the Lord, the Eternal God." All the other sources, however, though often using the terms conversion or union with Israel, tell a different story.

Thus, R. Bahya ben Asher in his commentary to Deuteronomy 30:7 asserts that Edom and Ishmael "are destined to join us by converting and becoming one nation, and it is not even necessary to say that the authority and the kingship will return to us." Kimelman's paraphrase merely underscores the tension in this position. "All," he writes, "will convert, and Israel will rule." Shem Tov ben Shem Tov appears to maintain that only Ishmael will convert "because they are closer," a position with which we are of course familiar. Moses de Leon affirms that all nations—indeed all existence—will become one, and yet he goes on to say that all the nations will enter the holy covenant without losing their identity.

R. Shlomo Alkabetz writes that when God will subdue the "princes" (i.e., the cosmic powers) in charge of the nations, those princes will not be destroyed entirely. On the contrary, the nations (as Zechariah prophesies) will come to celebrate the festival of *Sukkot*. They will be enveloped by sanctity, "for the nations are branches and wings for Israel."

The tension is even more explicit in *Sefer ha-Peli'ah*. "Not one of the seventy princes will be uprooted or destroyed; rather, weakness and dryness will develop in them, and the mistress will once again become the mistress and the maidservant a maidservant. For if even one of the seventy princes is uprooted, you have left no possibility for the survival of the world. All the nations will return to bow to our God . . . after they convert." The nations convert—and remain maidservants. And here is ibn Gikatilla: "Because of their great desire to cleave to the Lord may He be blessed they will serve Israel," and they will be united in the faith of Israel.

Thus, as in the some of the texts analyzed in my article, terms like conversion and even union can coexist with servitude and separate national identity.

Finally, after citing Shem Tov's expectation that it is specifically Ishmael who will convert, Kimelman notes without elaboration Abravanel's *Mashmia Yeshu'ah* (*Perush al Nevi'im u-Ketuvim* III, p. 566a). This passage will repay more detailed analysis in light of the author's rather different position in his commentary to Daniel (*Ma'yenei ha-Yeshu'ah*), with which we are already familiar. We recall that in the latter work, Abravanel maintained that although logically Christians and not Muslims should be destroyed at the end of days, the latter will be destroyed as well because the Book of Daniel, as Abravanel understood it, subsumes them under the fourth beast, which is doomed to annihilation. The exegetical imperative overcame the appropriate ethical-religious assessment and condemned Ishmael to destruction.

In *Mashmia Yeshu'ah*, a work of messianic theory, Abravanel was removed from the immediate impact of Daniel and was consequently liberated to follow moral logic to its proper conclusion. Thus, he makes a striking observation about the prophet's famous assertion, "Then I will make the nations pure of speech so that they all invoke the Lord by name and serve him with one accord" (Zephaniah 3:9). The verse, he says, does not say "all the nations." The reason for this is that "the nation of Edom is not included in this promise, for they are the enemies of God and his Torah and will not see the [open manifestation] of God's majesty. But the other nations from the descendants of Ishmael who did not pervert the fundamentals of the Torah as much—they will be granted the merit of accepting the divine faith." He makes clear, however, that they too will not reach the level of the Jewish people.

Finally, it is of no small interest that Abravanel goes on to assert that once the dead are resurrected, even the far-flung pagan nations will recognize the true God and serve him. It is the monumental miracle of the resurrection that will enable even those nations who knew nothing of the Torah to take this otherwise inexplicable step. I suspect that Abravanel had in mind Maimonides' well-known affirmation at the end of his *Mishneh Torah* that God brought about the rise and spread of Christianity and Islam to familiarize the nations with the Torah so that they would have the minimal preparation necessary to appreciate and internalize the Messiah's message when he comes. Without this preparation, even eschatological acceptance of the true faith is a monumental challenge, and it is only the witness of the resurrection that makes it possible. Though the Maimonidean passage underlies Abravanel's remarks, it is noteworthy that the function assigned to Christianity in the *Mishneh Torah* is marginalized or even neutralized entirely once one envisions the eschatological destruction of all Christians.

What is particularly striking about Abravanel's affirmation that pagans will embrace the true faith is that his argument for the destruction of Edom—expressed more fully in *Ma'yenei ha-Yeshu'ah*—was that Christians reject pure monotheism in favor of an essentially idolatrous belief. By this criterion, pagans too should suffer utter annihilation, and yet they will not. "Innocent" idolatry is one thing; the idolatry of "the enemies of God and his Torah" is quite another. Pagans never recognized the God of Israel; Christians did—and turned him into a human being, perverting Scripture along the way. Thus, even the vision of masses of pagans acknowledging the true God cannot mitigate Abravanel's vengeful vision of the fate of Christians.

Despite this argument for the special sinfulness of the Christian faith, it remains difficult to accept the proposition that a cold calculation would have persuaded a medieval Jew that in purely theological terms, the sin of Trinitarian Incarnationism is worse than that of full-fledged polytheism, complete with all the abominations that Scripture associates with it. In the deep recesses of Abravanel's psyche, God's reckoning with Christendom at the end of days will almost surely be driven by concern not only for his own honor but for that of the expelled and persecuted people who suffered so long and so grievously at the hands of the Kingdom of Edom.

ON THE USES OF HISTORY IN MEDIEVAL JEWISH POLEMIC AGAINST CHRISTIANITY

The Quest for the Historical Jesus

From: *Jewish History and Jewish Memory: Essays in Honor of Yosef Hayim Yerushalmi*, ed. by E. Carlebach, J.M. Efron, and D.N. Myers (New England University Press: Hanover and London, 1998), pp. 25–39.

"History" is not a simple term, and the uses of "history" are even more diverse than its meanings. Historical investigation can mean the critical examination of sources, often with a measure of empathy, always with a skeptical eye, to refine our image of the personalities and events of the past. But it can also be a didactic enterprise, accepting of unscrutinized data, highlighting heroes and villains, mobilizing past and present in the service of an overarching end. It is a commonplace that the first approach is most characteristic of post-Enlightenment historiography, while the second was the hallmark of the medieval mind.

Like most commonplaces, this one is essentially true. At the same time, the boundaries between the approaches are hardly impermeable. We have long abandoned—perhaps too eagerly—the historicist fantasy that contemporary historians work in a rarefied atmosphere of wholly objective truth. With respect to the Middle Ages, we will indeed search in vain for a systematic application of critical historical perspectives, but some intellectual challenges produced insights foreshadowing the historiographical orientation that became increasingly evident first during the Renaissance and ultimately in modern times.

Within a Jewish context, critical comments by biblical exegetes, debates about the antiquity of kabbalistic works, historical reasons proposed for the commandments, and halakhic approaches to changing conditions have sharpened our awareness of medieval sensitivity to textual, theological, and social change. Jewish polemic against Christianity is a particularly promising field for the pursuit of this inquiry.

Christianity emerged out of Judaism in historical times; its founder was a Jew; its sacred text is largely a collection of purportedly historical narratives about that Jew and his immediate successors; its fundamental claim speaks of the end of one age and the birth of another; it pointed to the historical condition of contemporary Jews as a confirmation of that claim, while Jews pointed to the unfolding of history in a patently unredeemed world as its most effective refutation. We usually identify exegesis and philosophy as the core of the Jewish-Christian debate, but the role of history was no less central.

This role took many forms. Historical context could help determine the plausibility of a scriptural argument; historical analysis could shed light on talmudic references to Jesus and to gentiles; the history of the Jewish people in exile demanded explanation—often theological but sometimes naturalistic; the larger pattern of history might reveal the character of the age in which medieval Jews and Christians lived. While I hope to examine all these issues and more in a fuller study, this essay will concentrate on a basic concern of many Jewish polemicists, which can be described without serious anachronism as the search for the historical Jesus. From late antiquity through the early seventeenth century this quest moved from hostile legends to unsystematic criticism, both naive and penetrating, and finally produced flashes of genuine historical reconstruction. In the course of their investigations, Jews honed their sense of historical skepticism while remaining checked by an invisible hand that prevented them from taking steps that sometimes appear self-evident to the modern eye. An inquiry into both the breakthroughs and the inhibitions of these polemicists can provide a fascinating look at the historical *mentalités* of medieval and Renaissance Jews.

Medieval Jewry was heir to two sets of internal sources about Jesus: a handful of scattered remarks in rabbinic texts and the various versions of the counter-Gospel known as *Toledot Yeshu*.[1] There is little we can say about the image of Jesus held by early medieval Jews, although there is no reason to doubt that many of them accepted as simple truth *Toledot*

---

[1] For a list of the rabbinic passages, see H. H. Ben Sasson, "Disputations and Polemics," *Encyclopedia Judaica* 6; cols. 81–82. The standard collection and discussion of *Toledot Yeshu* material remains Samuel Krauss, *Das Leben Jesu nach Jüdischen Quellen* (Berlin, 1902).

Yeshu's depiction of an idolatrous enticer and bastard sorcerer who was hanged from a stalk of cabbage.[2]

By the twelfth century, when European Jews began to write polemical works, they had far more information, which made their task easier in some respects and more complex in others. Polemicists were familiar with at least parts of the New Testament, and they were also in possession of a short Jewish work written in Arabic by an unknown author and translated into Hebrew as *Sefer Nestor ha-Komer*.[3] *Nestor* already contains, in however embryonic a form, some of the key points about Jesus that Jewish polemicists were to make for the remainder of the Middle Ages and into modern times.

The relationship of Jesus to Judaism is most critically defined by two issues: his attitude toward the laws of the Torah and his own self-perception. While *Nestor*, which is a work containing several redactional layers, criticizes Jesus for violating the Law and asserting that he and his Father are one, the most sustained passage argues for his loyalty to the classic positions of Judaism with respect to both points. In his programmatic declaration in Matthew (5:17–18), Jesus affirmed that the Torah must be observed, and in several other passages he made it perfectly clear that he did not consider himself God. Thus, he maintained that he did not know the time of the resurrection because such knowledge is confined to God alone (Mark 13:32), and he refused to be called righteous because such a term is reserved for God (Mark 10:18). "Know," continues *Nestor*, "that you have deviated greatly by forsaking the deeds which he performed: circumcision, Passover, the Sabbath, the great fast, the ten commandments, indeed, all the commandments."[4]

---

2   Later Jews quite familiar with the Gospels had no trouble accepting this information at face value. See the *Nizzahon Vetus* (henceforth N. V.) in my *The Jewish-Christian Debate in the High Middle Ages* (Philadelphia, 1979; reprint, Northvale, N. J., 1996), sec. 202, p. 202 (English) = 141 (Hebrew); sec. 205, pp. 203–204 (English) = 142 (Hebrew), and my notes to both passages.

3   Daniel J. Lasker and Sarah Stroumsa, *The Polemic of Nestor the Priest: Qissat Mujadalat al-Usquf and Sefer Nestor Ha-Komer* (Jerusalem, 1996). On the impact of this work, see Joel Rembaum, "The Influence of *Sefer Nestor ha-Komer* on Medieval Jewish Polemics," *Proceedings of the American Academy for Jewish Research* 45 (1978): 155–185.

4   On violations of the Law, see *Nestor*, paragraphs 127, 135. On the identity of Jesus and his Father, see paragraphs 68, 145, and cf. the assertion in paragraph 150 that he contradicted himself on this point. On Jesus' loyalty to the positions of Judaism, see paragraphs 35–57, 63, 105. I have translated a version of paragraph 63 (on circumcision, Passover, etc.) which appears only in the Hebrew section (p. 124) of Lasker and Stroumsa's edition.

Despite this approach and its manifest polemical utility, Jews could not readily embrace the simple proposition that Jesus was a perfectly good Jew. First of all, Jewish tradition itself spoke of his sinfulness and well-deserved execution. Second, both psychological and polemical reasons impelled Jews to criticize Jesus rather than embrace him. Finally, the New Testament material, with which Jews were increasingly familiar, presented a bewildering array of conflicting evidence, particularly with respect to the law but to some degree even with respect to the question of divinity. Not only did this create genuine historical perplexity; it presented an opportunity for criticizing the Christians' sacred text no less tempting than the chance to denounce its hero.

The polemicists of Northern Europe made no attempt to produce a coherent portrait of Jesus but were satisfied with ad hoc criticisms. The critique of the New Testament in the standard version of Joseph Official's thirteenth-century polemic consists of a series of snippets.[5] The more elaborate discussions in the *Nizzahon Vetus* and an alternate version of *Yosef ha-Meqanne* are far more interesting, not only because of the richness of the argumentation but precisely because they confirm the narrow focus and the absence of any effort to come away with a comprehensive picture.

In discussing the New Testament, the *Nizzahon Vetus* repeatedly maintains that Jesus denied he was divine; in other sections of what is admittedly an anthology, the author reiterates on several occasions that Jesus made himself into a god.[6] In one passage where the polemicist points to Jesus' use of the term "son of man," his point is not primarily that Jesus had no pretensions to divinity. It is, rather, that if Jesus were God, it would have been wrong of him to use this term. In fact, the passage continues, Jesus would be lying in his assertion (Luke 9:58) that he has no place to lay his head, when the Psalmist testifies that "the earth is the Lord's, and the fullness thereof" (Ps. 24:1), and Jesus himself said elsewhere, "Dominion is given unto me in heaven and in earth" (Matt.

---

5   *Sefer Yosef ha-Meqanne*, ed. by Judah Rosenthal (Jerusalem, 1970), pp. 125–138.
6   N. V., sec. 194, p. 200 (English) = 138–139 (Hebrew); secs. 197–199, p. 201 (Eng.) = 140 (Heb.); sec. 207, pp. 204–205 (Eng.) = 143 (Heb.). Contrast with sec. 9, p. 46 (Eng.) = 7 (Heb.); sec. 50, p. 75 (Eng.) = 34–35 (Heb.); sec. 67, p. 86 (Eng.) = 44 (Heb.). On N. V. as an anthology (at least in part), see my discussion, *Jewish-Christian Debate*, pp. 35–36. For the alternate version of the *Yosef ha-Meqanne* critique of the New Testament, see Judah Rosenthal, "Bikkoret Yehudit shel *ha-Berit ha-Hadashah* min ha-Meah ha-Yod-gimel," in *Studies in Jewish Bibliography, History, and Literature in Honor of I. Edward Kiev*, ed. by Charles Berlin (New York, 1971). Heb. sec., pp. 123–139.

28:18).[7] To the extent that this text, which also appears in modified form in both versions of *Yosef ha-Meqanne* and in another Ashkenazic collection,[8] presents a straightforward argument, it is not that Jesus did not consider himself divine but rather that, for someone who claimed to be God, he made some peculiarly inappropriate remarks.

An even less clear but nonetheless similar impression emerges from a different discussion in the standard text of *Yosef ha-Meqanne*, which cites two New Testament verses in which Jesus appears to deny his divinity: the above-cited statement in Mark that only God can be called good and a verse in John (probably 12:49). The author's formulation does not address Jesus' self-perception. Rather, he asks why Jesus would say these things if he was God (not if he thought he was God), much as he goes on to ask why he was hungry and thirsty if he was God.[9]

With respect to the law, the fullest array of Northern European arguments appears in the *Nizzahon Vetus*. On the one hand, we are repeatedly presented with the evidence of Matthew 5:17–18 that Jesus declared his intention to complete (*lehashlim*) or to fulfill (*leqayyem*) the law, not to destroy it. The author argues that the Christian assertion that the new covenant of Jeremiah replaces the old Torah contradicts the Gospel passage. Despite this, Christians maintain that Jesus "caused the Torah of Moses to be truncated by abolishing circumcision, observance of the Sabbath, and many commandments."[10]

---

7   N. V., sec. 168, p. 181 (Eng.) = 119 (Heb).

8   *Sefer Yosef ha-Meqanne*, p. 132; *Kiev Festschrift*, p. 125 (without the reference to Matt. 28:18). By "another Ashkenazic collection," I refer to the non-philosophical section of *Liqqutei R Mosheh ben Shlomoh mi-Salerno*, unpublished edition by A. Posnanski, p. 35 (including the reference to Matt. 28:18). I am now convinced that this section of the work, which differs dramatically from the philosophical material published by S. Simon (*Mose ben Salomo von Salerno und seine philosophischen Auseinandersetzung mit den Lehren des Christentums* [Breslau, 1932]), is a Northern European polemical mélange.

9   *Sefer Yosef ha-Meqanne*, p. 134. Cf. p. 54 for an indication that Jesus did claim divinity.

10 N. V., sec. 71, p. 89 (Eng.) = 47 (Heb.). The verse about not coming to destroy the law was also cited by Meir of Narbonne, Parma ms., p. 4a, and "Moses of Salerno," Posnanski ms., p. 33. Peter Damian's *Dialogus inter Judaeum Requirentem et Christianum e Contrario Respondentem* (pt. 2 of his *Antilogus-Dialogus*) begins with a series of ten Jewish questions, each of which is prefaced by the phrase, "If Christ did not come to destroy the law but to fulfill it" (*PL* 145: 57–59). However, as I showed in detail in "St. Peter Damian: His Attitude toward the Jews and the Old Testament," *Yavneh Review* 4 (1965): 99–104, this section of Damian's polemic is borrowed from an essentially exegetical work by Isidore of Seville (*Quaestiones in Leviticum, PL* 83: 336–339); it consequently proves nothing about actual Jewish citations of this verse.

The same Matthean passage, reinforced by the author's version of Luke 16:17 ("Even if heaven and earth shall pass, the words of Moses and the other prophets shall not pass"), refutes the antinomian Christian interpretation of Isaiah's declaration that God hates the Jewish festivals (Isa. 1:14); Jesus, after all, "accept[ed] the Jewish religion—circumcision, the Sabbath, indeed, the entire religion—all the days of his life."[11] Jesus' circumcision along with his observance of the Sabbath and festivals ("for he did observe all these commandments"), particularly in light of his statement in Matthew, surely establishes a precedent that Christians should follow.[12]

Elsewhere, however, the *Nizzahon Vetus* presents a rather different picture. In discussing the assertion that baptism has replaced circumcision, the author begins with his usual response that this would contradict Matthew. He continues, "It would follow then (*nimza*), that Jesus annulled the law of Moses and thereby gave the lie to his own Torah where he wrote, 'Not one thing will pass from the Law,' *for he added and diminished from the law in several places*" (emphasis added).[13] This appears to go further than the earlier citation, which said only that Christians attributed such deviations to him.

Other passages surely go further. In a discussion that also appears in both versions of *Yosef ha-Meqanne*, the *Nizzahon Vetus* uses one of the most clearly nomian passages in the Gospels as a foundation for an attack on Jesus for his violations of the law. After curing a leper, Jesus instructs him to bring a sacrifice of purification "as Moses has commanded in the Torah" (Matt. 8:4). One expects a Jew to pounce on this passage as further evidence of Christian failure to emulate Jesus' devotion to the Torah. But the Northern European polemicists find themselves in a particularly churlish frame of mind: "Now, I am surprised at his commanding the leper to go to the priest and bring his sacrifice. Once he was cured by Jesus why should he have to go to the priest? Moreover, from the time of his birth we don't see that he commanded the observance of any other commandments in the Torah, such as those regarding the Sabbath, circumcision, pork, and the mixing of species, and several others which, in fact, he permitted people to transgress

11 N. V., sec. 79, p. 96 (Eng.) = 52 (Heb.).
12 N. V., sec. 158, p. 173 (Eng.) = 110 (Heb.), and see also sec. 104, p. 191 (Eng.) = 129 (Heb.), and sec. 221, p. 215 (Eng.) = 150 (Heb.).
13 N. V., sec. 157, p. 172 (Eng.) = 109–110 (Heb.).

after his advent. Indeed, even this commandment was not observed from that day on."[14]

Shortly thereafter, the author criticizes Jesus for permitting work on the Sabbath by justifying his disciples' plucking of corn (Matt. 12:1–12) and asks how this squares with his instructions to the leper.[15] Finally, along with one version of *Yosef ha-Meqanne* and the above-cited Ashkenazic collection, he objects to Jesus' instructing a man to carry his bed on the Sabbath.[16] Thus, as in the case of Jesus' self-perception, the polemical need, or even whim, of the moment appears to prevail. Jesus is a loyal adherent of the law, a man awash in contradiction, or a systematic, committed violator.

It is tempting to proffer the highly tentative suggestion that this is precisely the sort of approach we should expect from Ashkenazic Jews in the High Middle Ages. The genius of this culture did not lie in integrative works. Its relative lack of interest in philosophy left its literature even more focused on exegesis, whether biblical or talmudic, than that of other Jewish centers. Even in works whose primary purpose was harmonization of conflicting evidence drawn from a vast corpus, broad applications were often avoided in the absence of a concrete motivation. The ad hoc character of Ashkenazic pronouncements about Christianity has been analyzed in Jacob Katz's classic discussion, and this is only one example of a wider phenomenon.[17] In our context, the search for contradictions that so characterized the initial step of the Tosafist approach to the Talmud became the final step as well. There was no motive for Jews to seek the concord of discordant passages in the New Testament even on

---

[14]   N. V., sec. 166, p. 178 (Eng.) = p. 116 (Heb.). See too *Sefer Yosef ha-Meqanne*, p. 131; *Kiev Festschrift*, p. 129. Cf. *Nestor ha-Komer*, par. 127.

[15]   N. V., sec. 171, pp. 182–183 (Eng.) = 120 (Heb.). Cf. Meir of Narbonne's citation of the leper story as contradicting the Christian assertion that Jesus annulled the commandments (*Milhemet Mizvah*, Parma ms., p. 97b).

[16]   N. V., sec. 169, p. 181 (Eng.) = 119 (Heb.); *Kiev Festschrift*, p. 125; "Moses of Salerno," Posnanski ms., p. 40.

[17]   See Jacob Katz, *Exclusiveness and Tolerance* (New York, 1961). Also see Haym Soloveitchik's comments in *Halakhah Kalkalah ve-Dimmuy 'Azmi* (Jerusalem, 1985), p. 36, and for a somewhat later period, the discussion on pp. 79–81, where he speaks of "Halakhic federalism." See also his possibly relevant observation in "Can Halakhic Texts Talk History?" *AJS Review* 3 (1978): 155, n. 2. Though the sources analyzed there are primarily Ashkenazic, the issue is the tendency of law, not just Ashkenazic halakhah, to "prefer local definitions"; still, a culture trained primarily in law is more likely to reflect this orientation in other contexts.

an ad hoc basis, and Northern European polemicists evince little interest in penetrating the psyche of Jesus of Nazareth.

The concentration on specific texts coupled with the absence of a wider perspective stands in sharp contrast to Maimonides' approach to the history of deviations from the true faith. In his account of Christianity and Islam in *The Epistle to Yemen* and more strikingly in the history of idolatry in his code, Maimonides is interested precisely in the large picture, the critical deviations, and the underlying causes.[18] It matters little if he can point to specific evidence for his contentions; a verse here, an aggadah there constitute sufficient building blocks for a structure that rests upon ideology and theory far more than on texts and testimony. Maimonides' vistas are too broad; his historiographic weaknesses are those of a philosopher. The vistas of the Northern European polemicists are too narrow; their drawbacks are those of legists and exegetes.

The earliest European Jewish polemic, the Provencal *Milhamot Hashem* by Jacob ben Reuben, also attempts no resolution of key contradictions, but it does not fall prey to inconsistency in quite the same degree and reflects a somewhat greater concern with understanding Jesus. From a polemical perspective, it is difficult to decide which is better—to fault Jesus himself for self-contradiction or to question the reliability of Christian tradition and the basis of Christian practice by emphasizing his devotion to the law. Jacob resolves the problem by doing both. Like his successors in the North, who may well have borrowed the argument from him, he criticizes Christians for saying that Jesus did not come to add to the law or to change it and then citing Jeremiah's prophecy of a new covenant to defend precisely such a change. Elsewhere, he blames Jesus for inconsistency, but he does not leave this as an ad hoc assertion here and there. Rather, he views Jesus neither as an uncompromising upholder of the law nor as an antinomian ideologue. Inconsistency is precisely what characterizes him. In the very same sermon in which he declared the law eternal and unchanging, he changed it, and such vacillation is evident in other passages about the law as well as in his changing position regarding the public revelation of his miracles. With respect to the law, "he did not maintain a single stance but rather followed

[18] Maimonides, *Epistle to Yemen*, in Abraham Halkin and David Hartman, *Crisis and Leadership: Epistles of Maimonides* (Philadelphia, 1985), pp. 98–99: *Mishneh Torah, Hilkhot 'Avodah Zarah.*

a variety of approaches," and with respect to self-revelation, "no one can determine his position because whatever he said on one occasion he contradicted on another."[19]

In the fourteenth century a work partially dependent upon *Milhamot Hashem* reflects the persistence of this tension even as it reaffirms Jesus' observance of the law. Moses ha-Kohen of Tordesillas also responded to the Christian interpretation of Jeremiah's "new covenant" by pointing to Jesus' exhortations affirming the eternity of the law, but he translated "I have not come to destroy but to fulfill [*plerosai; adimplere*]" as "I have not come to take away but to add [*lehosif*]." Thus, Jesus may have added to the law by requiring baptism in addition to circumcision, but he never abolished the earlier obligation. Moses' comment that Jesus observed "many" of the commandments of the Torah may also reflect some reservations about his full commitment, although there is no question that the fundamental thrust of the passage ascribes to him a deep loyalty to the Torah.[20]

The breakthrough toward a Jewish picture of Jesus that attempted to account for all the New Testament evidence in a coherent fashion came at the end of the fourteenth century in Profiat Duran's *Kelimat ha-Goyim*, which reflects a maturity that owes much to the accumulation of polemical experience, the cultural breadth and sophistication of Spanish Jewry, and the stellar qualities of the author. For the first time, a Jewish polemic reflects more than just extensive familiarity with Christian sources; it handles those sources with a sense of confidence and command.[21] With

---

19   Jacob ben Reuben, *Milhamot Hashem*, ed. by Judah Rosenthal (Jerusalem, 1963), pp. 81, 146, 148–149; cf. 151, 152–153. Joseph Kimhi's *Sefer ha-Berit* was written at about the same time as *Milhamot Hashem* and hence shares its distinction as a pioneering work.

20   *'Ezer ha-Emunah*, ed. by Yehuda Shamir (*Rabbi Moses Ha-Kohen of Tordesillas and His Book 'Ezer ha-Emunah—A Chapter in the History of the Judeo-Christian Controversy, Part II* [Coconut Grove, Fla., 1972]), p. 93. Moses' translation of *adimplere* is particularly interesting in light of the fact that Jacob ben Reuben twice asserted that Jesus declared that he had not come to add to the Torah of Moses (*Milhamot Hashem*, pp. 81, 148). There are two readings of the Talmudic citation of this passage (*B. Shabbat* 116b): either "I have not come to take away from the Torah of Moses or (*ve-lo*) to add to the Torah of Moses" or "I have not come to take away from the Torah of Moses but (*ella*) to add to it." The first version, which corresponds to Jacob ben Reuben's citation, is also quoted by Simon Duran in his *Keshet u-Magen* (see n. 24, below), p. 4.

21   *Kelimat ha-Goyim*, in *Kitvei Pulmus li-Profiat Duran*, ed. by Frank Talmage (Jerusalem, 1981). Eleazar Gutwirth, in an article which makes the general point that polemic helped produce a critical historical sense, discussed *Kelimat ha-Goyim* as his prime example;

respect to the law, Duran was not content to point to the well-worn passage from the Sermon on the Mount that Jesus did not come to destroy but to fulfill. (Duran, like *Nestor ha-Komer* and one passage in the *Nizzahon Vetus*, translates *adimplere* as "to complete" (*lehashlim*), which stands somewhere between "to fulfill" and Moses ha-Kohen's "to add"). He made a concerted, impressive effort to explain all contrary evidence from the Gospels to accord with his portrait of a nomian Jesus. To take a particularly difficult example, the assertion that what goes into the mouth does not defile a man (Matt. 15:11) cannot mean that forbidden foods are permitted, since we can prove that Jesus' own disciples refrained from eating such food (a historical argument of continuing relevance). Rather, Jesus must have meant that the food is not intrinsically unclean; it is only the divine command that renders it so.[22]

Profiat Duran's proof texts that Jesus advocated observance of the law include the verse in which he instructs his disciples to do what the scribes and Pharisees say because they sit on the seat of Moses (Matt. 23:2–3); the passage, however, is not explicitly utilized to make the point that Jesus has thereby endorsed the oral as well as the written law.[23] Influenced by *Kelimat ha-Goyim*, R Simon Duran repeated the citation in his *Keshet u-Magen*, again without drawing the explicit conclusion about the oral law, although several lines later he argued that Jesus' disciples were scrupulous even about rabbinic injunctions.[24] Simon's son Solomon, however, took this development to its logical conclusion in a highly charged context. His *Milhemet Mizvah* is devoted to a defense of the Talmud against an increasingly dangerous Christian attack. Here the citation from Matthew demonstrates that an attack on the Talmud is an attack on Jesus himself, and Solomon proceeds with additional

---

see "History and Apologetics in XVth Century Hispano-Jewish Thought," *Helmantica* 35 (1984): 231–242, which also contains several observations about Simon Duran. For a discussion of the context that produced Duran's approach, see Jeremy Cohen, "Profiat Duran's *The Reproach of the Gentiles* and the Development of Jewish anti-Christian Polemic," in *Shlomoh Simonsohn Jubilee Volume* (Tel Aviv, 1993), pp. 71–84. Cohen's well-argued thesis, which sees Duran's approach as a response to Raymund Martini's *Pugio Fidei*, is, I think, partly correct, but I would formulate the polemical context somewhat differently.

22   *Kelimat ha-Goyim*, pp. 24–25. (The discussion continues through p. 34.) Needless to say, my encomium to Duran does not mean that I necessarily endorse his interpretation.
23   Ibid., p. 25.
24   Simon ben Zemah Duran, *Keshet u-Magen: A Critical Edition*, ed. by Prosper Murciano (PhD. diss., New York University, 1975), pp. 3–4; cf. p. 45.

arguments that the oral law underlies several of Jesus' legal dicta.[25] The contradictory New Testament passages of Joseph Official and the *Nizzahon Vetus*, the inconsistent Jesus of *Milhamot Hashem*, and the partially nomian figure of Moses ha-Kohen have given way to a Jesus thoroughly committed to the written and oral law so cavalierly rejected by his putative medieval disciples.

To reinforce the contrast between contemporary Christians and the founder—or presumed founder—of their faith, the later polemicists also portrayed a strongly "Jewish" Jesus with respect to the question of his self-perception. We have already seen the contradictory assertions of some of the Ashkenazic authors on this issue. Here too, Profiat Duran resolved the issue in favor of the option that is most compatible with traditional Judaism, and he provided an overarching explanation to account for any contrary evidence. Jesus, we know, used poetic language and spoke in parables. Through a careful examination of specific texts, Duran concluded that when Jesus said that he and his Father were one or called himself Son of God, he meant to affirm nothing more than a special relationship with God, not to describe himself as "the First Cause and Creator of the world."[26]

More subtle shifts in matters of detail also demonstrate Duran's changing emphasis. Jewish polemicists had regularly pointed to the story of Jesus' cursing the fig tree when he discovered it had no fruit as evidence that he could not have been divine. The primary argument, of course, was that God would have known from the outset that he would find no fruit. Several polemicists added the rather amusing point that the curse contradicts Jesus' exhortation to love one's enemies, and Meir of Narbonne argued that instead of making the tree wither he should have commanded it to produce fruit.[27] Although one manuscript tradition of *Kelimat ha-Goyim* contains the standard argument about Jesus' ungodlike ignorance, Duran's first (and perhaps only) use of this story is to argue that the disciples' amazement at the miraculous withering of the tree demonstrates that they did not believe that Jesus was divine.[28]

---

25   *Milhemet Mizvah*, appended to *Keshet u-Magen*, Makor reprint (Jerusalem, 1970), pp. 28b–29a.

26   *Kelimat ha-Goyim*, p. 7 (full discussion on pp. 4–10).

27   *Milhamot Hashem*, p. 151; *Kiev Festschrift*, p. 126; Meir's *Milhemet Mizvah*, Parma ms., pp. 90b, 222a–b; N. V., sec. 181, pp. 188–189 (Eng.) = 126–127 (Heb).

28   *Kelimat ha-Goyim*, p. 5.

Duran was surely interested in showing that Jesus was not God, but he was more interested in the historical assertion that neither he nor his disciples thought he was.

Simon Duran cited the arguments from Jesus' ignorance and the disciples' amazement in one breath,[29] and his general treatment of Jesus is more complex and more problematic than that of *Kelimat ha-Goyim*. Simon attempted a fairly ambitious reconstruction of Jesus' life and ideas, utilizing rabbinic as well as Christian sources. The methodology is essentially that rabbinic information is always correct, that in many important matters the Jewish sources correspond to what we learn from Christian works, and that instances of irreconcilable difference reveal errors in Christian tradition. After all, he says, even the reports of Jesus' disciples in the Gospels "are not in agreement with respect to all matters; there is contradiction and difference among them whether as a result of forgetfulness or as a result of the desire to make matters look more attractive."[30]

Occasionally, this approach can yield flashes of very interesting historical skepticism. Simon describes the connection that Christians made between Micah 5:1 and Jesus' presumed birth in Bethlehem, shows that the verse cannot refer to this, and then argues that the rabbinic name "Jesus of Nazareth" indicates that he was not born in Bethlehem at all. The force of the rabbinic evidence here seems weak, and it appears that Simon uses it as a peg on which to hang a skeptical look at the Gospel report. Later, he argues that talmudic sources indicate that Jesus indeed went to Egypt but not under the circumstances described in Matthew 2. Finally, Simon expends considerable effort to reconstruct Jesus' lineage and associations utilizing the full array of sources at his disposal. In this discussion, the primary purpose of New Testament citations is not to criticize them but to use them constructively to buttress and clarify rabbinic sources. The result has much in common with Christian efforts to harmonize the Gospels, except that one set of sources is in the final analysis not authoritative.[31]

The effort to coordinate rabbinic and Gospel evidence in the context of a "Jewish" portrayal of Jesus' views raised the question of how to assess his overall character and mission. Needless to say, the assertion

---

[29] *Keshet u-Magen*, p. 24.
[30] Ibid., p. 16.
[31] Ibid., pp. 15–21. I hope to examine the mixture of skepticism and credulousness with which Jews approached Christian sources on another occasion.

that he observed the commandments and did not consider himself God was by no means sufficient to generate an enthusiastic evaluation, and it was hardly feasible for medieval Jews—for reasons both emotional and talmudic—to produce a literature of *laudes Jesu*.

For Jews like the Durans, one solution was to depict Jesus as a pietistic fool (*hasid shoteh*). Jacob ben Reuben had already described him as an ignoramus preaching to ignoramuses. Isaiah 30:20, which speaks of a presumably great teacher, cannot, said Jacob, refer to Jesus, who taught "rustics and fishermen because he was as devoid of understanding as they."[32] To Profiat Duran, the ignorance of Jesus and his disciples is evident from the many errors in their citations of the Bible as well as from Jesus' apparent belief that reward and punishment in the afterlife are physical.[33] The balance between a Jesus who did not affirm the key theological errors of Christianity but was nonetheless very far from a role model appears in particularly striking fashion in Duran's analysis of a lengthy passage in John (6:47–66) in which Jesus promises eternal life to whoever eats his flesh and drinks his blood. "Although this statement points to his foolishness and insanity, as the Jews indicated—and, in fact, many of his students were taken aback by it—it does not necessarily follow from it that the intention was that they actually eat his flesh and drink his blood."[34]

Simon Duran repeated Profiat's assessment, citing the same evidence of errors in biblical citation, and described most of the Sermon on the Mount as a quintessential example of pietistic foolishness.[35] A century and a half later, Yair ben Shabbetai da Correggio was prepared to regard Jesus as a learned man who had studied with R. Yehoshua ben Perahiah but continued to insist on the ignorance of his disciples: "If he taught wisdom to his students, a negligible number actually absorbed it, because they were not men of culture."[36]

An ignorant, foolish, even insane Jesus may have satisfied the psychic needs and resolved some of the historical questions of medieval Jews, but a key problem remained unresolved. Ignorance, foolishness, and insanity

32 *Milhamot Hashem*, p. 96.
33 *Kelimat ha-Goyim*, pp. 49–59, 20–21, 24. See also p. 40 for the assertion that John the Baptist, like Jesus, was a *hasid shoteh*. Gutwirth's suggestion ("History and Apologetics," p. 237) that the term "may reflect an association with the historical sect of 'Hasidim' in Talmudic times" seems to me highly improbable.
34 *Kelimat ha-Goyim*, p. 39.
35 *Keshet u-Magen*, pp. 38–39, 56–61.
36 Yair ben Shabbetai, *Herev Pifiyyot*, ed. by Judah Rosenthal (Jerusalem, 1958), p. 65.

are not grounds for execution. Since the Talmud as well as the Gospels assign responsibility for Jesus' execution to his own people, Jews were impelled not only to acknowledge responsibility but to argue that the decision was justified. What did a man who observed the Torah and never claimed to be divine do to deserve his fate? For the compartmentalizing polemicists of thirteenth-century Ashkenaz, this was no problem. Not only was Jesus a sorcerer; he also claimed to be God. In other contexts, as we have seen, they said that he disclaimed divinity, but this was not the place for that position. As it happens, however, it was precisely a Jew from thirteenth-century France who opened the door to a different, if highly problematic solution—and then refrained from walking through that door with more than one foot.

It is well known that when R. Yehiel of Paris was confronted in 1240 with the argument that the Talmud should be banned partly because of blasphemies against Jesus, he maintained that the Jesus of the Talmud and the Jesus of the Christians are two different people. The actual presentation, however, is far more complicated. R. Yehiel was initially confronted with a talmudic passage about a "Yeshu" who is punished in the afterlife with boiling excrement for mocking the words of the sages. Because the passage does not say "Jesus of Nazareth" (*Yeshu ha-Nozri*) and does not mention the latter's more serious sins, R. Yehiel denies that the two are one and the same. He then responds to a talmudic citation about the execution of Jesus of Nazareth for sorcery and for leading Jews into idolatry with a concession that this is the Christian Jesus. However, in the discussion of yet a third passage he concludes, on the basis of chronological considerations, that the Christian Jesus is never mentioned in the Talmud at all. Now, if his argument that the Jesus of the boiling excrement is not the Talmud's Jesus of Nazareth still stands, then R. Yehiel has not two Jesuses but three, two of whom came from Nazareth, and this is in fact strongly implied in the Christian response recorded in the Oxford manuscript of the Hebrew text and is explicitly stated in the Moscow manuscript.[37]

This position would have made it possible to argue that the execution of the Christian Jesus was primarily the responsibility of the Roman authorities or that only a handful of Jews were involved; in short, all the options of modern Jewish apologetics became available once

---

[37] *Vikkuah R. Yehiel mi-Paris*, ed. by R. Margaliyyot (Lwow, n.d.), pp. 15–17.

rabbinic statements about Jesus' villainy and execution had been made to vanish into thin air. But R. Yehiel does nothing of the sort, and the edited Hebrew version retains his initial statement about the Christian Jesus as an inciter to idolatry. Whatever one thinks of the sincerity of the multiple Jesus theory, R. Yehiel found a way to neutralize some dangerous rabbinic statements, and yet the essential Ashkenazic evaluation of Jesus remains even in the text of this disputation.

In the fourteenth century, Moses ha-Kohen of Tordesillas made much stronger use of the theory of the two Jesuses in defending Judaism and the Talmud against renewed attack. For Moses, the lack of identity between the Talmud's Jesus and the hero of the New Testament is demonstrated not only by the chronological problem raised by R. Yehiel but by an additional, striking point. The Jesus of the Talmud erected a brick and bowed to it (*B. Sanhedrin* 107b), while the Jesus of the Gospels was an uncompromising monotheist![38]

And so we return to our original question. Why was an observant Jew who made no claims of divinity executed by Jewish authorities?

Profiat Duran addressed this question only in passing as part of his argument that Jesus did not annul the law. "If the crucifixion stories about him are true, you will find that they condemned him to death not for destroying the Torah but for saying that he is the son of God and the Messiah."[39] Duran, who was not a halakhist, does not seem disturbed by the fact that these accusations in themselves—given the assumption that "son of God" was not meant literally—do not clearly generate a death sentence according to Jewish law.[40] It would be much too facile

---

38 *'Ezer ha-Emunah*, pp. 141–142. Cf. my "Christians, Gentiles, and the Talmud: A Fourteenth-Century Jewish Response to the Attack on Rabbinic Judaism," in *Religionsgespräche im Mittelalter*, ed. by Bernard Lewis and Friedrich Niewöhner (Wiesbaden, 1992), p. 128.

39 *Kelimat ha-Goyim*, p. 25, a statement repeated by Simon Duran in *Keshet u-Magen*, p. 4. (The reference is to the account in Matthew 26:63–66.) Elsewhere, Profiat Duran maintained that Jesus considered himself superior even to Moses (p. 4). Again, cf. the reiteration of this passage by Simon Duran, *Keshet u-Magen*, p. 25.

40 See my remarks in "Religion, Nationalism, and Historiography: Yehezkel Kaufmann's Account of Jesus and Early Christianity," in *Scholars and Scholarship: The Interaction between Judaism and Other Cultures*, ed. by Leo Landman (New York, 1990), p. 167:

Kaufmann argues that Jesus could properly have been executed as a false prophet, even according to Mishnaic law, for refusing to provide a sign authenticating his messianic claims. In fact, a person who refused to provide a sign might well forfeit his right to be believed, but he would not forfeit his life. Only a prediction or sign that did not materialize would be grounds for execution, and nothing in the

to solve this problem by suggesting that Duran's declared methodology of refuting Christianity from its own sources (*ke-fi ma'amar ha-omer*) means that he really did not believe what he said about Jesus and that his ultimate loyalty was to the talmudic reports about an inciter to idolatry. His entire discussion of the historical development of Christianity, which is beyond the purview of this essay, shows that he took New Testament evidence seriously and that he regarded both idolatry and the rejection of the law as later developments. In discussing when Jesus lived, he accords rabbinic tradition great respect but does not appear unequivocally bound by it. Thus, after examining Christian sources, he concludes that the statement of the "true sages" (*hakhmei ha-emet*) that Jesus was a student of R. Yehoshua ben Perahiah "appears [*yera'eh*] to be the truth."[41] I suppose one could insist on a literal translation of *yera'eh emet* as "is seen to be the truth," but I doubt very much that this is correct. In the final analysis, Profiat Duran's Jesus is that of a critical reading of the Gospels, not of a straightforward reading of the Talmud.

R. Simon Duran, who was a preeminent halakhist, could not avoid the question of Jesus' capital crime, nor could he marginalize talmudic traditions, and the problem appears to have created a tension in his image of Jesus almost reminiscent of earlier Ashkenazic contradictions. In a lengthy passage borrowing many of Profiat Duran's arguments, Simon maintained that Jesus made no claim of divinity and that the term "son of God" means the most exalted of men.[42] In his general reconstruction of Jesus' biography, however, the emphasis differs. There, the New Testament report that Jesus was executed for describing himself as the son of God is connected with the talmudic assertions that he led Israel astray (*hesit ve-hiddiah*, which is really a *terminus technicus* for encouraging idolatry) and that he set up a brick to which he bowed. This rabbinic report, which does not contend that Jesus claimed divinity for himself, is the historical truth, while the Gospel assertion that he was executed for claiming to be the son of God is a confused reflection of his

sources indicates that this had occurred. If Jesus claimed to be the Messiah but refused to produce a sign, the only evidence strong enough to justify his execution would be the fact that he died without redeeming the world. Jews presented that evidence to the court of history, but it was too late to present it to a court of law.

41 *Kelimat ha-Goyim*, p. 63. This discussion makes it perfectly clear that Duran gave no credence to a theory of two Jesuses.

42 *Keshet u-Magen*, pp. 22–25.

condemnation for incitement to idolatry.[43] Through the miasma of New Testament misunderstanding, one can nonetheless glimpse the kernel of truth that reinforces talmudic tradition.

Thus, Profiat Duran's assertion that "son of God" in the Gospels does not denote divinity is a key element in the depiction of Jesus as a monotheist who never condoned idolatry. Simon Duran, while accepting his predecessor's understanding of the Gospels' "son of God," sought what was for him the best of both worlds: a Jesus who never endorsed the Christian doctrine that he himself was God (a position confirmed by both Talmud and Gospels) but who incited Jews to worship a different, old-fashioned form of idolatry (the stone cult that the Talmud calls *Merqulis*) and who worshipped it himself—all this while affirming the eternity and inviolability of the Torah! In Simon Duran's case it may be that the assertions of Jesus' devotion to the law are indeed a purely tactical use of Christian evidence. ("We have cited their words verbatim to speak for us against those who believe in him by demonstrating that they have been untrue to Jesus' intention.")[44] Nonetheless, it is hard to come away from much of *Keshet u-Magen*, including the discussion of the apostles, without assuming that Duran was serious about the argument that Jesus observed the law, and this is a position that is very difficult to square with his endorsement of the talmudic account of an inciter to idolatry.

As the Middle Ages gave way to the Renaissance and early modern times, access to historical sources, interest in history, and a critical sense of the past changed the face of at least some historical literature. It is hardly necessary to say that among Jews, the quintessential example of these developments is the sixteenth-century Italian scholar Azariah de' Rossi, and it should come as no surprise that the next level of sophistication in the polemical reconstruction of the historical Jesus was reached by an Italian Jew of the seventeenth century.

Leone da Modena's *Magen va-Herev* reflects philosophical sophistication, thorough familiarity with Christian literature, and an unusual degree of historical acumen. This last characteristic is manifest in Leone's analysis of the development of Christian doctrine, which cannot detain us here, but it is also evident in a brief chapter that attempts to paint a portrait of Jesus' beliefs and the unfolding of his career. Like Simon

43   Ibid., pp. 13–15.
44   Ibid., p. 4.

Duran, Leone tells us that he will utilize Christian and Jewish sources to produce his reconstruction, but the difference in both methodology and conclusions illustrates strikingly the differences of time, place, and author.

Leone begins with a vehement dismissal of an unnamed Jewish version of Jesus' career, which is surely *Toledot Yeshu*. "For various reasons, it is a disgrace for any Jew to believe it." He goes on to say with great confidence that from perusing "our books and theirs," he has attained an understanding of Jesus "which I believe to be as firmly true as if I had lived in his generation and sat with him." Jesus observed the Torah. If he had not done so, he would have had no credibility at all in that society. Rather, he rejected a number of minor practices, one of the first of which was the ritual washing of hands with a blessing, which probably accounts for a talmudic statement that whoever is lax with respect to this ritual is uprooted from the world (*Sotah* 4b).

We must remember, continues Leone, that this was a period of sectarian diversity, which has been described in historical works ranging from *Josippon* to Caroli Sigonii's *De Republica Hebraeorum*.[45] That Jesus himself identified with the Pharisees, who were the bearers of the true tradition, is evident from his statement that they sit on the seat of Moses. Despite this indication that he acknowledged both the written and the oral law, his minor deviations alarmed the Sages, who feared that Sadducees, Boethusians, Essenes, and others would soon be joined by an additional sect. In response to their opposition, Jesus strengthened himself by claiming the mantle of son of God. This is not a claim of divinity but of a status higher than that of the prophets. Jesus was no fool; he knew perfectly well that even the masses would have stoned him had he made the preposterous assertion that a man who was seen to eat, drink, sleep, and defecate was God. He certainly could not have anticipated the incredible truth: that after his death people would actually concoct arguments to affirm such absurdities.[46]

For all its spirited partisanship, this is serious history. It attempts to account for all the evidence; it utilizes secondary as well as primary historical literature; it dismisses contemptuously the fantasies of *Toledot Yeshu*; it examines historical context; it speculates in sober,

---

45   Bologna, 1582.
46   *Magen va-Herev*, pp. 43–45.

informed fashion about the possible motivations, concerns, even the personal development of the major protagonists. Leone really cares about understanding the hero of the Gospels, so that his Jesus is not a stick figure; he has a texture that even Profiat Duran's Jesus lacks.

In light of Azariah de' Rossi's well-known skepticism about some historical material in the Talmud, the role of rabbinic traditions in Leone's reconstruction is particularly intriguing. He declares that he reached his conclusions on the basis of "our books and theirs," but the only Jewish material explicitly cited is Josippon and a single talmudic reference to washing one's hands. Even if we recognize the relevance of other rabbinic sources to his portrait of sectarianism, the absence of any reference to R. Yehoshua ben Perahiah's idolatrous student or to the man executed for sorcery and incitement to idolatry is striking. When Simon Duran produced a portrait of Jesus on the basis of our books and theirs, these talmudic passages took center stage. Unless we assume that Leone endorsed the two-Jesus theory, which strikes me as improbable in the extreme, he has silently rejected the historicity not only of *Toledot Yeshu* but of the major rabbinic sources as well.[47]

Whatever one thinks of the number of Jesuses in antiquity, no one can question the multiplicity of Jesuses in medieval Jewish polemic. Many Jews with no interest at all in history were forced to confront a historical/biographical question that continues to bedevil historians to our own day. Once the issue was joined, it produced a series of analyses that reflect profound differences among varying Jewish centers in different periods, and it demonstrates a development in which Jews who deal with history in grudging, limited fashion, as if compelled by the proverbial demon, give way to polemicists who, within the limits of their time, seem inspired by the historical Muse.

---

[47] Because Profiat Duran's work explicitly focused on Christian sources exclusively, his ignoring of the crucial Talmudic assertions is considerably less striking than Leone's. I am not suggesting that dismissing rabbinic material is the mark of a good historian. What is genuinely significant, however, is the transformation that allowed a rabbinic figure to place all the sources, including those in the Talmud, into the crucible of critical historical assessment.

CHRISTIANS, GENTILES, AND THE TALMUD

A Fourteenth-Century Jewish Response
to the Attack on Rabbinic Judaism[1]

From: *Religionsgespräche im Mittelalter*, ed. by Bernard Lewis and Friedrich Niewöhner (Otto Harrassowitz: Wiesbaden, 1992), pp. 115–130.

The Jewish-Christian debate underwent a momentous transformation in the thirteenth and fourteenth centuries. From time immemorial, Jews and Christians had argued about the alleged Christological meaning of verses in the Hebrew Bible, and in the high middle ages Jews began to exhibit growing sophistication in their philosophical critique of the central dogmas of Christian faith. Since the thirteenth and fourteenth centuries mark the maturation of the philosophical debate, their centrality to the history of polemic could well be defended on this basis alone.[2] Nonetheless, these centuries were also marked by the growth of another, more innovative approach, which was fraught with acute danger for medieval Jewry. Christian polemicists began to study the Talmud.

---

[1]   The writing of this article began and ended under dramatically different circumstances. Most of the text was written when I was teaching, on two weeks notice, at the inaugural semester [late February-early April, 1989] of the Moscow yeshiva founded by Rabbi Adin Steinsaltz, which opened as the first officially recognized institution of higher Jewish education in the Soviet Union (The Judaica Section of the Academy of World Civilizations). The last few pages of text were written on the plane returning to New York, slightly after the deadline for submission of the preliminary version before the conference [in Wolfenbüttel, Germany, where it was presented]. The only relevant books available to me were the Bible, the Talmud, and *'Ezer ha-Emunah*, although the inspiration provided by the extraordinary devotion of the yeshiva's students was more than sufficient compensation.

The footnotes, on the other hand, were written in the fall semester of 1989, when I was a fellow in the Eden-like environment of the Annenberg Research Institute in Philadelphia. It is a pleasure to thank the administration and staff of the Institute and of its library for providing the conditions for a rare and rewarding experience.

[2]   See Daniel J. Lasker, *Jewish Philosophical Polemics Against Christianity in the Middle Ages* (New York, 1977).

Adumbrations of the Christian use of Rabbinic literature can be found before the thirteenth century, but these are at best a faint, barely audible accompaniment to the main themes of the debate, and in most polemics they are nowhere to be found. In the 1230's, however, Nicholas Donin began to press a threefold assertion: The Talmud contains absurdities, insults against Christians, and blasphemies against Jesus. His further assertion that it is another law replacing that of the Bible had potential consequences of the highest magnitude, but the real impact of that argument appears to have been contained and is in any case peripheral to our present concerns.[3] Several decades later, Pablo Christiani refined and popularized an array of arguments purporting to demonstrate the truth of Christian dogmas from the Talmud itself. However disparate the two approaches may appear, medieval Christians did not regard them as contradictory: Rabbinic texts, despite their theological obtuseness and hostility toward Christianity, preserved elements of the ancient, pre-Talmudic traditions which, like the Hebrew Bible itself, affirmed the validity of Christian beliefs.

In his confrontation with Donin, R. Yehiel of Paris denied the identification of the Talmud's Jesus with that of the Christians, distinguished between the Gentiles of old and the Christians of today, and even remarked briefly that the *aggadah*, or non-legal material in Rabbinic literature, does not have the same binding force as Talmudic law.[4] The key points, however, were not fully developed, and it was left for later Jews to pursue the argument against an increasingly sophisticated Christian attack. The issue of *aggadah* was especially critical in dealing with Pablo's approach, and Nahmanides proffered the famous and controversial classification of Rabbinic texts in which *aggadot* are merely *sermones* that can be accepted or rejected at the discretion of the reader.[5]

---

3   See Ch. Merchavia, *Ha-Talmud bi-Re'i ha-Nazrut* (Jerusalem, 1970); Jeremy Cohen *The Friars and the Jews* (Ithaca, 1982); Joel Rembaum, "The Talmud and the Popes; Reflections on the Talmud Trials of the 1240's," *Viator* 13 (1982): 203–223; Robert Chazan, "The Condemnation of the Talmud Reconsidered," *Proceedings of the American Academy for Jewish Research* 55 (1988): 11–30; cf. also my brief review of *The Friars and the Jews* in the *American Historical Review* 88 (1983): 93.

4   *Vikkuah Rabbenu Yehiel mi-Paris*, ed. by S. Gruenbaum (Thorn, 1873). The point about *aggadah* is on p. 2.

5   *Kitvei Rabbenu Mosheh ben Nahman*, ed. by C. D. Chavel (Jerusalem, 1963), I, p. 308; Bernard Septimus, "Open Rebuke and Concealed Love': Nahmanides and the Andalusian Tradition," in *Rabbi Moses Nahmanides (Ramban): Explorations in his Religious and Literary*

Nahmanides himself, though he clearly legitimated the simple rejection of an *aggadah*, also spoke of deeper meanings, which often enabled the Jewish polemicist to deflect a Christian argument without imputing error to the Talmudic sages.

With respect to Donin's attack, the crucial issue was the distinction between ancient gentiles and medieval Christians, and this point achieved its fullest development outside the context of polemic. In the late thirteenth and early fourteenth centuries, R. Menahem ha-Meiri of Perpignan built upon the scattered, *ad hoc* remarks of various earlier halakhists and established a category which he called "nations bound by religious mores"; the central thrust of this classification appears to be that these nations behave in a civilized fashion, but ha-Meiri also asserted that they are free of idolatry. In the case of Christians, he explicitly maintained that although they have an erroneous conception of the Deity, they are monotheists nonetheless. While ha-Meiri did not extend the practical halakhic consequences of his distinction much beyond established precedent, he spoke with a passionate conviction which is absent from his sources and creates a powerful impression of sincerity. Moreover, ha-Meiri appears concerned with more than the unpleasant economic consequences that would result from applying certain Talmudic regulations to medieval Christians; he was also motivated by a sensitivity to the moral problem inherent in a legal code that forbids the returning of a lost item to a gentile and permits the retention of funds that came into one's possession because of miscalculation by a non-Jew. Such regulations, he argued, were never intended to apply to civilized monotheists and are hence irrelevant in contemporary practice.[6]

Virtuosity, ed. by Isadore Twersky (Cambridge, Mass., 1983), pp. 20–22; my review of "Maccoby's *Judaism on Trial*," *Jewish Quarterly Review* 76 (1986): 253–257 (esp. 254–255); Marvin Fox, "Nahmanides on the Status of Aggadot: Perspectives on the Disputation at Barcelona, 1263," *Journal of Jewish Studies* 40 (1989): 95–109. For a general discussion of attitudes toward *aggadah*, see Marc Saperstein, *Decoding the Rabbis* (Cambridge, Mass., and London, 1980), pp. 1–20.

6   See Jacob Katz, *Exclusiveness and Tolerance* (London, 1961), pp. 114–128; Ephraim E. Urbach, "Shitat ha-Sovlanut shel R. Menahem ha-Meiri—Meqorah u-Migbeloteha," in *Peraqim be-Toledot ha-Hevrah ha-Yehudit bi-Yemei ha-Beinayim u-Va-'et ha-Hadashah—Muqdashim Li-Professor Y. Katz* (Jerusalem, 1980), pp. 34–40; J. Katz, "Od al Sovlanuto ha-Datit shel R. Menahem ha-Meiri," *Zion* 46 (1981): 243–246; Yaaqov Blidstein, "Yahaso shel R. Menahem ha-Meiri la-Nokhri—Bein Apologetiqah le-Hafnamah," *Zion* 51 (1986): 153–166.

In the 1370's, a Spanish Jew named Moses ha-Kohen of Tordesillas was confronted by the new Christian critique of the Talmud in all its force. By this time, Christian polemicists had begun to absorb and apply the arguments in Raymond Martini's massive, late-thirteenth-century *Pugio Fidei*, and the works of the learned Jewish convert Abner of Burgos had become a major force in Jewish-Christian relations. Moses ha-Kohen had participated in a disputation forced upon the Jewish community of Avila, and subsequently wrote a polemical work entitled *'Ezer ha-Emunah* (*The Aid of Faith*) which no doubt reflected some of the arguments in the public disputation. The most important part of his work, however, bears no relation to that disputation. He informs us that a Christian student of Abner of Burgos approached him with a demand that he respond in private to a series of criticisms of Talmudic Judaism. Should he refuse, the Christian would preach a sermon that would be attended by both Christians and Jews in which he would impute "to the Jews every evil in the world in the presence of the Christian audience; he would list all the objectionable *aggadot* in the Talmud, and indicate that we curse them every day." Moses, then, was presented with an "offer" he could not refuse, and the final section of *'Ezer ha-Emunah* is the first large scale example of a Jewish response to the mature Christian attack on the Talmud.[7]

Though the primary context of this discussion is the threat to reveal an intolerable level of hostility to Christians, Abner's student utilized the full range of Christian approaches to the Talmud, including the discovery within its pages of support for Christian doctrine. Thus, we find the midrashic passage already cited by Pablo that the Messiah was born on the day of the Temple's destruction (*Lamentations Rabbah* 1:16, #51), a passage that presumably demonstrates that he must have already come, reinforced by the Rabbinic statement, made so many centuries ago, that he has been sitting in the gates of Rome (*B. Sanhedrin* 98a). Indeed, says the Christian, the Talmud even has positive things to say about

---

[7] The text was edited in part II of Yehudah Shamir's dissertation, *Rabbi Moses Ha-Kohen of Tordesillas and his Book 'Ezer Ha-Emunah—A Chapter in the History of the Judeo-Christian Controversy* (Coconut Grove, Florida), 1972 (henceforth *E. H.*). Part I, which contains Shamir's analysis, was later republished with the same title (Leiden, 1975); on the marginal value of this analysis, see Daniel J. Lasker's review, *Association for Jewish Studies Newsletter* 20 (June, 1977): 22, 24. The threat by Abner's student is described in *E. H.*, p. 127.

Jesus himself (*Yer. 'Avodah Zarah* 40d).[8] The contention that the Talmud can be scrutinized for doctrinally useful assertions despite its essential falsehood comes into bold relief when the Christian cites the famous view of R. Hillel that "Israel has no Messiah, for he has already been consumed in the days of Hezekiah" (*B. Sanhedrin* 99a). The second half of the statement, we are told, is untrue, but the first half demonstrates that Jews should abandon their vain hope that the Messiah is yet to come.[9] Moreover, the Christian cites several Messianic calculations in the Talmud which point to a period nearly a millennium earlier than the fourteenth century (*B. Sanhedrin* 97a–b).[10]

The most interesting argument that the Talmud undermines belief in the future advent of the Messiah comes in the citation of two enigmatic passages from *Sanhedrin* (98a and 97a). The first of these asserts that "the son of David will not come until someone searching for a small fish for a sick person will be unable to find one," while the other says that he will not come until pockets will have been emptied of their very last penny.[11] Moses' adversary argues that neither of these conditions could ever be met, and therefore the Talmudic passages must be hinting at a message that differs from their superficial meaning: "Just as all this cannot happen, so the Messiah cannot come." Since the major Jewish line of defense was to explain *aggadot* non-literally, it is striking to find a Christian polemicist exploiting precisely such an approach, even if only to a very limited degree.

Abner's student goes on to cite Talmudic remarks that express what he regards as objectionable beliefs or which reflect badly on the status of Jews. Thus, the Rabbis assert that God encourages belief in idolatry so that He might punish idolaters (*B. 'Avodah Zarah* 55a), and they allegedly understand the scapegoat in Leviticus 16 as a sacrifice to a power other than God (*Pirkei de-Rabbi Eliezer* 46). One Talmudic sage said that from the time the Temple was destroyed, an iron barrier has separated the people of Israel from their Father in heaven (*B. Berakhot* 32b), and another passage maintains that whoever persecutes Israel attains the highest office (*B. Gittin* 56b and *B. Sanhedrin* 104b).[12]

---

8   *E. H.*, pp. 153, 156, 154–155.
9   *E. H.*, p. 131.
10   *E. H.*, pp. 132–133.
11   *E. H.*, p. 133.
12   *E. H.*, pp. 146, 148, 157, 143.

All these arguments, however, are secondary to the crucial assertion: The Talmud is replete with passages that reflect such hostility toward Christians that the toleration of Jews in a Christian society must be called into the most serious question. Because of the important work of Jeremy Cohen, we have become accustomed to regarding the "other law" argument as the most dangerous to the fundamental toleration of Jews; if Jews do not really observe the Hebrew Bible, one of the standard rationales for tolerating them would be jeopardized. On the other hand, the arguments from blasphemy and the like, however threatening they may have been, could be dealt with in the final extremity through the censorship of a handful of Talmudic texts. In fact, however, if Jewish security was not seriously undermined by these attacks, the Jewish sense of security certainly was. Of the various factors that may have motivated the later Luther to advocate hair-raising forms of persecution against Jews, I am persuaded that an important consideration was his reading of Margaritha's *The Whole Jewish Faith*, which detailed attacks against Christianity in Jewish texts and ritual.[13] In our case, Moses ha-Kohen's adversary explicitly and repeatedly raised the question of Christian toleration of people who curse and deride the majority faith; the threat raised at the outset of the discussion was never allowed to fade.

The list of the Talmud's offenses included a variety of disturbing allegations. While Christians actually pay a higher fine for assaulting a Jew than for striking a fellow Christian, the Talmud says that a gentile who hits a Jew is guilty of a capital offense (*B. Sanhedrin* 58b) while a Jew who strikes a fellow Jew would clearly be treated less harshly. Such discrimination also extends to liability for damage to property (*M. Bava*

---

13   The point is not merely that Luther used Margaritha but that the material in *The Whole Jewish Faith* may have helped transform his attitude toward the Jews. For a survey of the literature on Luther and the Jews, see Johannes Brosseder, *Luthers Stellung zu den Juden im Spiegel seiner Interpreten* (Munich, 1972), and for a recent analysis see Mark U. Edwards, Jr., *Luther's Last Battles: Politics and Polemics, 1531–1546* (Ithaca, 1986). See also the studies of Heiko A. Oberman, which tend to emphasize the continuities in Luther's stance (*The Roots of Anti-Semitism* [Philadelphia, 1984], pp. 93–137; *Luther: Man Between God and the Devil* [New Haven and London, 1989], pp. 292–297). For the argument that Luther changed his position on the Jews primarily because of the impact of new information, see Gerhard O. Forde, "Luther and the Jews: A Review and Some Preliminary Reflections," in *Luther, Lutherans, and the Jewish People: A Study Resource, 1977*, prepared by the American Lutheran Church, pp. 6–20. Despite the apologetic context of the publication (which does not mention Margaritha), and despite the undoubted relevance of other considerations, the argument deserves to be taken seriously.

Qamma 4:3) and to the ruling that the obligation to return a lost item is applicable only if the owner is a Jew (*M. Makhshirin* 2:8; cf. *B. Bava Mezi'a* 24a–b). The Rabbis maintain that the best of the gentiles deserves to be killed (*Yer. Qiddushin* 66c). Jews dare to call Christian holidays "days of catastrophe" (e. g., *M. 'Avodah Zarah* 1:1) while living in Christian lands; they curse Christians, their Churches, their governments, even their cemeteries (*B. Berakhot* 58b). The blessing upon seeing a Jewish king is "Blessed is He who has granted a portion of His glory to those who fear Him"; for Gentile kings the final phrase becomes merely "to flesh and blood" (*B. Berakhot* 58a). Jews are told not to rent homes to gentiles (*M. 'Avodah Zarah* 1:8) and not to sell arms to the very people who protect them (*Tos. 'Avodah Zarah* 2:4). They compare Gentiles to dogs (*Mekhilta Mishpatim* 20) and assert that the contamination that the primeval serpent inserted into Eve was eliminated from the Jews at Sinai but not from other nations (*B. 'Avodah Zarah* 22b and *B. Yevamot* 103b).[14]

It is evident from this summary that the Christian attack was based upon both the legal and the non-legal material in the Talmud—upon the *halakhah* as well as the *aggadah*. Hence, if the labeling of this section of the book as "the debates concerning the *aggadot*" is the work of Moses himself rather than of a copyist, it is particularly interesting. Although Moses never denies the authoritativeness of Talmudic *halakhah*, he would like to create the impression that the entire dispute revolves around passages that do not stand at the center of the Talmudic corpus. The question of the binding force of *aggadah* had been introduced into the Barcelona disputation by Nahmanides in an effort to undermine the fundamental thrust of Pablo's argument. The issue, however, is an extremely sensitive one, since the Jewish polemicist runs the risk of vanquishing his Christian opponent only to discover that his Jewish audience has lost respect for the Talmudic rabbis. Moses ha-Kohen's polemic is an early, revealing example of the delicate line that Jews had to tread in confronting an extraordinarily complex challenge.

Moses begins with an affirmation of faith in all of Rabbinic literature which becomes steadily more ambiguous as his discussion continues and ultimately encompasses sharp disagreements with Rabbinic assertions. "I believe," he writes, "that all the words of the sages are true. Nonetheless, the Talmud is not a homogeneous work." The Rabbis said that one does

---

14   E. H., pp. 134, 154, 134–136, 144–145, 151, 144, 154.

not refute *aggadah*, and the reason is that there is no point in disagreeing with material that does not contain binding instruction.

Moses continues with an interesting typology of *aggadot* and an even more interesting application of that typology. 1. Some *aggadot* result from the teacher's desire to lift his students' spirits before teaching them. 2. In other cases, he needed to wake them up by making astonishing remarks, as in the observation that a single Jewish woman during the Egyptian bondage would give birth to six hundred thousand children (*Mekhilta Beshallah, Massekhta de-Shira* 9). 3. A rabbi may have wished to make a profound observation inappropriate for the masses, and so he cloaked it in a parable that would be taken literally by the ignorant and figuratively by the wise. For such a genre, no less a work than the Song of Songs serves as a legitimating precedent. 4. A sage who had a dream bordering on divine inspiration would sometimes recount the experience as if he had been awake. 5. Finally, the Talmud contains extravagant stories and assertions that may have a deeper meaning or may simply be exaggerations along the lines of the Scriptural passage that speaks of the cities of Canaan as "large and fortified to the heavens" (Deuteromy 1:28).[15]

This typology is followed by a carefully calibrated, almost exquisitely poised formulation: "With respect to all these *aggadot* that I have mentioned, if it is an *aggadah* that appears reasonable, I will believe it as is; if, on the other hand, it is highly unreasonable, then if I wish I will defend its wisdom by believing that its author intended a meaning that eludes me, and if I wish I will not believe it, since the author may have said it for one of the reasons that I have listed above."[16] The key point here is that disbelief is not disbelief and error is not error. The decision not to believe is specifically placed within the framework of the author's typology, and none of his categories include error or even genuine falsehood. Neither exaggerations nor parables nor intentionally astonishing statements are unqualifiedly false, and prophetic dreams are among the highest forms of truth. The analogies to the Song of Songs and the verse in Deuteronomy demonstrate even to Christians that the word of God itself contains surface falsehoods; rejection of the literal meaning of a text hardly undermines its standing and authority. At this stage, Moses' concession is no concession at all.

[15]   *E. H.*, pp. 128–129.
[16]   *E. H.*, p. 129.

Nevertheless, as the discussion progresses and becomes more specific, the willingness to reject *aggadot* gradually grows until it reaches remarkable proportions. A particularly striking aspect of Moses' argument is that he will oppose an aggadic statement to a biblical one and triumphantly assert that the aggadic passage stands refuted. In the context of Christian arguments about the absurdity of the *aggadah*, such an approach appears self-defeating, but where Christians cite the Talmud to demonstrate Christianity or refute Jewish beliefs, this is an argument of great, ironic force. In the final analysis, do Christians prefer the Bible or the Talmud?

The first, relatively moderate example of this argument comes in response to the Christian citation of a Talmudic passage describing the names in Isaiah 9:5 as names of the Messiah. Since medieval Jewish exegesis avoided a Messianic understanding of a verse that arguably spoke of a child named "Mighty God" and "Eternal Father," this passage gave considerable aid and comfort to a Christian polemicist. Moses refutes the argument in predictable fashion by pointing to an alternative Rabbinic position and arguing that even the cited view does not require belief in the Messiah's divinity. But he also maintains that "even if the *aggadah* were as you say, I should surely believe the prophecy of Isaiah including the verses in that very same passage which indicate without a doubt that this was said of Hezekiah rather than the aggadic statement of a Talmudic sage." Similarly, in response to Christian citations of Talmudic statements suggesting that the Messiah must already have come, Moses provides alternative interpretations, but he also suggests that the citations are in any case irrelevant in light of biblical evidence that the Messianic age is yet to be.[17]

Later in the work, Moses cites biblical verses to undermine the Talmudic observation that the persecutors of Israel attain the highest office even though that observation was itself buttressed by the citation of Lamentations 1:5. In this case, however, the tactic was reinforced by another clever but forced assertion. In *B. Gittin* 56b, the deceased Titus, in the midst of his richly deserved suffering in the afterlife, advises a questioner that despite Israel's pre-eminence in the world to come, joining the Jewish people is too difficult. The sensible course, then, is to attain high station in this world by persecuting them. Moses quotes a series of verses to demonstrate that oppressing Israel brings

---

[17]   *E. H.*, pp. 130, 133.

punishment even in this world, but he formulates this as a refutation not of the Talmud but of Titus. "I should surely believe the prophets rather than the wicked Titus, who was our enemy and destroyed our Temple and our city." The problem, as Moses is well aware, is that R. Yohanan and not Titus made the identical remark in *B. Sanhedrin* 104b. In an aside to the reader, Moses suggests that if a Christian should quote the latter passage, he should be told that R. Yohanan was discussing the past rather than the present or future. The persecutors of Israel "attained"—not "attain" —the highest rank (*kol ha-mezer le-Yisrael na'asah*—not *na'aseh*—*rosh*). This ploy was unavailable to Moses in dealing with the passage in *Gittin* since Titus was currently giving advice on the basis of this verse; in *Sanhedrin*, where the refuted party would have to have been R. Yohanan, it was available, and Moses did not hesitate to use it.[18]

In this passage, then, Moses was not willing to reject the words of a Talmudic sage on the basis of biblical evidence. Elsewhere, however, he does—or almost does—precisely that in surprisingly sharp fashion. In *B. Berakhot* 32b, R. Eleazar cites Ezekiel 4:3 to demonstrate that since the destruction of the Temple an iron barrier has separated Israel from its Father in heaven. Since the proof-text refers to a barrier outside the city of Jerusalem and not to a partition between God and Israel, "R. Eleazar," says Moses, "could not legitimately adduce the slightest evidence for his position from this verse, not even by way of an *asmakhta* [i. e., a biblical citation utilized to support a point without reference to the straightforward meaning of the verse]." He softens the blow slightly as he continues, but only after reiterating his thorough, unequivocal rejection of the Talmudic rabbi's exegesis: "This verse, then, constitutes no evidence whatsoever for R. Eleazar's statement . . . ; but since I am concerned with his words and with his honor, I will explain his statement, but in a way that deviates from his own reason." Thus, we do not quite have the rejection of a Rabbinic statement on Scriptural grounds, but we do have the rejection of a Rabbinic interpretation of the Bible on the grounds that it cannot be sustained by a careful examination of the text. And despite Moses' effort to explain R. Eleazar's essential statement, the reader surely finishes the discussion with the unmistakable impression that rejection of that statement is a viable, legitimate option.[19]

---

[18]   *E. H.*, pp. 143–144.
[19]   *E. H.*, pp. 157–158.

Finally and remarkably, Moses is prepared to utilize the Bible to reject even the sort of *aggadah* that the Christian cites to demonstrate the objectionable beliefs in the Talmud. As we have already seen, this appears to be a self-defeating concession to the Christian argument. Apparently, however, Moses regarded such an attack primarily as an effort to attribute these beliefs to Judaism itself, and he was therefore prepared to disassociate himself from them with a vigor that is almost heedless of the impact upon the Talmud.

Moses' Christian interlocutor had cited the Talmudic assertion that God encourages idolaters in their folly so that He may destroy them. Moses begins his reply with the standard remark that *aggadot* have no legal consequences and often represent the opinion of a single scholar. In this case, he continues, he does not believe this *aggadah* in accordance with its plain meaning because it contradicts the Bible, "and I believe the words of Jeremiah and David rather than the *aggadah*." Again, "How can I abandon belief in the words of a prophet of God and believe an *aggadah* that says the opposite of the prophecies?" What follows is a telling example of the inner turmoil caused by this issue. Moses had begun by denying his belief in the "plain meaning" of the *aggadah*, and continued with the very strong language contrasting the Talmudic statement and the Bible. Under the impact of his argument, he then allows himself to make the remarkable assertion that the Talmudic rabbi said "something improper" (*davar shelo ke-hogen*). Immediately, however, he continues with a partial defense of the "improper" statement; on various occasions, after all, the Bible tells us that God helps the already wicked on their road to disaster.[20] Is the statement, then, improper? Is it true? Does it have a deeper meaning? Does it contradict the Bible? At various points in a very brief passage, Moses appears to give an affirmative answer to all these questions. Clearly, he preferred transparent and logically dubious tergiversations to the painful alternatives of a full defense or a candid rejection of this *aggadah*. The strategy asserting that *aggadot* are not binding while nonetheless attempting to explain each problematic passage was sensible and often effective, but it did not always obscure the tensions that beset Moses both as a polemicist and as a believing Jew.

Whatever the difficulties raised by Christian citations of Talmudic passages to demonstrate either Christian truth or Rabbinic error, they

---

[20]   *E. H.*, pp. 146–147.

do not compare in their level of danger with allegations of extreme hostility toward Gentiles (read: Christians) in classical Jewish texts. For the most part, such passages were halakhic rather than aggadic and could consequently not be dismissed as non-authoritative. The central Jewish response, then, rested on the distinction between ancient pagans and medieval Christians, and Moses utilized this approach in a consistent, extreme, and intriguing fashion.

The terms "Gentile" (*goy*) and "Noahide," he says, do not apply to Christians, who are called *Nozrim* and not *goyim*.[21] On one level, this is simply a linguistic assertion, which gains credibility from the fact that Christians occasionally used the term Gentile to mean a non-Christian. Thus, when Moses transliterates the word gentiles into Hebrew as the proper translation of *goyim*, he is, I think, consciously evoking this Christian usage. The assertion that "Noahide," whose plain meaning is clearly inclusive, refers only to non-Christians is even more difficult to defend. On one occasion, Moses makes it with no effort at a reasoned argument; elsewhere, he notes the Rabbinic observation that the Noahides violated their commandments, and he may be implying that Christians observe these obligations and are hence excluded from the Talmudic category.[22] Nonetheless, even in that passage, the assertion that Noahides are called gentiles (and hence non-Christians) is apparently made independently of this implicit argument. If the Talmud meant *Nozrim*, it would have said so.

Moses' argument, however, goes well beyond language. One of the central contexts in which halakhists had distinguished between the gentiles of the Middle Ages and those of the Talmudic period concerned the prohibition against doing business with non-Jews on their holidays. Jacob Katz has argued persuasively that the permissive rulings on this issue before the Meiri involve *ad hoc* assertions that do not reflect a fundamental reevaluation of Christianity.[23] Moses ha-Kohen, however, did not read Katz's work, and he responds to the Christian complaint that Jews call Gentile holidays "days of catastrophe" by reference to halakhic authorities who excluded medieval Christians from this prohibition.

[21]   *E. H.*, pp. 134–135.
[22]   *E. H.*, pp. 134, 154.
[23]   *Exclusiveness and Tolerance*, pp. 33–36, 44–45.

He begins by pointing to a Talmudic remark that "gentiles outside the land of Israel are not idolaters but merely follow the custom of their ancestors" (*B. Hullin* 13b). In the standard text of the Talmud, the word "gentiles" in this passage is *nokhrim*; Moses, however, quotes it as *goyim* and explicitly refers it to Christians. The irony in this quotation is therefore nothing less than excruciating. The linchpin of Moses' fundamental approach has been that the term *goyim* necessarily excludes Christians, while here he could not resist citing an extremely tempting Talmudic passage where he must ignore, indeed contradict, the core of his argument.[24]

Moreover, says Moses, Rashi explicitly asserted in this context that Christians are not idolaters. Thus, the permissive halakhic ruling becomes the basis for a theological reevaluation of Christianity on the grounds that such a reevaluation must have been the basis of the ruling. Moses then continues with an argument which, in a different form, plays a key role in a famous ruling of the Tosafists. Christian holidays, he says, are dedicated. to "the disciples of Jesus and those who accepted suffering or death for his faith. You do not, however, render them divine by believing in them; rather, you believe in God alone."[25] Until the last phrase, this argument is analogous to the Tosafist assertion that a Jew needn't be concerned about entering a business arrangement that may lead a Christian to take an oath. Christians, after all, swear in the name of saints to whom they ascribe no divinity.[26] *Tosafot*, however, raises the further question that Christians also swear in the name of God while having Jesus of Nazareth in mind. Here the Tosafists provide the dual reply that Jesus is not named explicitly and the intention is in any case to the Creator of heaven and earth. The second part of the answer cannot apparently stand on its own; had Jesus been mentioned explicitly, Jews would have been forbidden to bring about such an oath. Elsewhere, I have described this tension-laden position as the perception

---

24 *E. H.*, pp. 35–36. One could imagine an assertion that if the *goyim* outside of the land of Israel are not considered idolaters, this is true of Christians *a fortiori*. Moses, however, would probably have been puzzled by the suggestion that genuine idolaters somehow cease to be idolaters because of a change of location.

25 *E. H.*, p. 136.

26 *Tosafot Sanhedrin* 63b, s. v. *asur*; *Tosafot Bekhorot* 2b, s. v. *shemma*. The best text of the passage is in R. Yeruham b. Meshullam, *Sefer Toledot Adam ve-Havvah* (Venice, 1553), 17:5, p. 159b.

of Christianity as idolatrous monotheism or monotheistic idolatry.[27] Moses' discussion certainly retains some of this tension. Though Christians serve God alone, he considers it important to note that the holidays are dedicated to saints rather than to Jesus. At the same time, the phrase "You believe in God alone" is considerably stronger than *Tosafot's* "their intention is to the Creator of heaven and earth." It is, in fact, so strong that the reader is left wondering about the need to make the point about the saints at all.

Elsewhere, Moses' assertions of Christian monotheism are so emphatic that they evoke the most extreme passages in ha-Meiri. The Talmudic curse against pagan temples, he says, has no application to Christian Churches because "you do not worship idolatry, as I have already written. In your houses of worship, you pray to God alone, for Jesus said . . . , 'You may not bow down to another God,' and he also said, 'And Him shall you serve.' And the truth is that you are careful about idolatry."[28] It is a matter of no small interest that Jewish polemicists who cited such remarks by Jesus generally did so to attack contemporary Christianity for failing to heed the admonitions of its founder; here we find precisely the reverse.

Moses then goes even further. Katz regards ha-Meiri's insistence that Jewish heretics are worse than Jewish converts to Christianity as the most remarkable assertion that he makes, one with "no parallel in the whole of medieval Hebrew literature." In *'Ezer ha-Emunah*, the same argument is made—at least implicitly—to deflect the allegation that the curse against heretics in the Jewish liturgy is directed against contemporary Christians. Moses' antagonist first cites the text as "Let there be no hope for the apostates (*la-meshummadim*), and let the informers (*malshinim*) be destroyed in a moment"; he comments that the first clause refers to Jewish converts to Christianity and the second to Christians, whom Jews call heretics (*minim*) and enemies. Later, Moses himself cites the second clause as "Let the *minim* be destroyed in a moment," which is almost certainly the correct reading in the earlier citation of this passage as well. In his response, he argues that although

27 See my "Religion, Nationalism, and Historiography: Yehezkel Kaufmann's Account of Jesus and Early Christianity," in *Scholars and Scholarship: The Interaction Between Judaism and Other Cultures*, ed. by Leo Landman (New York, 1990), p. 152.

28 *E. H.*, p. 137.

meshummadim indeed refers to converts in popular parlance, its proper technical meaning is Jews who habitually commit certain transgressions, as in the phrase, "a *meshummad* with respect to that transgression." The technical term for a convert is a *memir*. In other words, a habitual sinner deserves to be cursed; a convert to Christianity does not.

As for the *minim* who should be destroyed in a moment, this refers to those "who do not believe in the Creator, who deny reward and punishment, hell and heaven, and who possess no Torah and commandments. You, on the other hand, have a powerful faith in the Creator; the difference is only that you believe in the trinity, which we reject in favor of absolute unity. Moreover, you are the possessors of Torah and commandments." This is a passage that could have been (and may have been) taken directly from ha-Meiri, who also spoke of Christianity as a non-idolatrous religion which is flawed by a misunderstanding of the precise nature of God.[29] Ha-Meiri's position remains more significant because of its chronological priority, its distinguished provenance, and its non-polemical context, but Moses' work reflects the impact and polemical utility of this approach. I am also inclined to think that despite the implausible arguments that occasionally emerge in the discussion, we are dealing with a position which Southern European Jews had begun to internalize and which—at least in its fundamental outlines—Moses sincerely believed.

In some contexts, Moses limits the definition of "gentile" even further by referring it to the seven nations of ancient Canaan. The Talmud had derived a prohibition against selling homes to gentiles in the land of Israel from Deuteronomy 7:2, which indeed refers to the Canaanites, and proceeded to add a Rabbinic prohibition against rentals as well. Moses' interlocutor cites the passage without the limiting condition about the land of Israel. Moses points out the condition, notes that the matter is disputed in the Talmud itself, and then argues that the biblical context requires us to restrict this law to pagans of the past. The reasons that the Rabbis cite for this prohibition, says Moses, are that the gentile brings in idols and that the home would then be without a *mezuzah*. Although the first explanation would appear to apply to all idolaters and the second to all non-Jews, Moses nonetheless quotes these reasons and immediately asserts, "You have, then, clear evidence that all these matters were said

---

29   See *E. H.*, pp. 136, 138; *Exclusiveness and Tolerance*, pp. 121–124.

only about the seven idolatrous nations." The biblical context and the polemical need are more than sufficient to sweep aside all ambiguity.[30]

Moses proceeds to introduce the seven nations even into a context where the supporting biblical argument is considerably less clear. The Bible recommends that non-kosher meat be given to dogs or sold to gentiles. Since the type of meat given to the former is regarded as superior to the type sold to the latter, a Rabbinic text draws the apparently logical conclusion. Moses' outraged antagonist asks why the Jews do not delete such a passage from their literature in order to save themselves from acute danger. Here again Moses is not content to refer the remark to ancient idolaters in general. Both the Bible and the Rabbis, he says, were discussing the people who are called *Cananeos*. It is impossible not to speculate that the sudden use of the Latin term may be intended to underscore the relationship between Canaanites in particular and dogs (*canes*). That the biblical Canaanites, who were marked for destruction, were the intended recipients of this food is far from self-evident, but the genre that we are examining is hardly disinterested biblical exegesis.[31]

Whatever the plausibility of Moses' biblical argumentation, the emphasis on the Bible which we saw in the discussion of *aggadah* persists in these passages as well. It is his standard practice to demonstrate that the rabbinic statements under attack are supported by proof-texts, and all biblical proof-texts obviously predate Christianity.[32] Since the Rabbis must have referred to the same people that the biblical author had in mind, Christians are consistently and conveniently excluded.

Finally, no list of Talmudic passages offensive to Christianity could be complete without reference to the assertion in B. *Gittin* 57a that Jesus is being punished in boiling excrement. Here, Moses' response is

---

[30] E. H., pp. 145–146. See B. *'Avodah Zarah* 20a, 20b–21a. Had Moses omitted the two reasons that he cites and restricted himself to the concern that rentals might lead to sales, his argument that the law is restricted to Canaanites would have been far more plausible and effective.

[31] E. H., pp. 151–152, footnoted passage. See Exodus 22:30 and the *Mekhilta* there; Deut. 14:21. Cf. the *Nizzahon Vetus* in my *The Jewish-Christian Debate in the High Middle Ages* (Philadelphia, 1979), #212, Eng. sec., p. 207 = Heb. sec., p. 145, where the author applies the biblical text to contemporary Christians with a sense of dismissive superiority remarkable even for that work; see also the notes ad loc. (p. 329). For a humanitarian explanation arguing that the non-kosher food given to dogs is unhealthful to human beings, see Ibn Ezra's citation (to Exodus 22:30) of an earlier Moses ha-Kohen.

[32] See, for example, the two citations in E. H., p. 154, and cf. p. 140.

of extraordinary interest. First, he proffers the old argument of R. Yehiel of Paris that the chronological context of the Talmudic discussion of Jesus demonstrates that the Rabbis were not referring to the founder of Christianity. Not only did this Jesus live too early; he was executed in Lydda rather than Jerusalem. Moses then produces a response which fits perfectly into his own extremely positive evaluation of the theology of Christianity and of Jesus, but which is simply startling to the reader of earlier Jewish polemic. The Jesus of the Talmud erected a brick and bowed to it (*B. Sanhedrin* 107b [uncensored version]); the Jesus of the Christians, as Moses has already noted, was an uncompromising monotheist who insisted on the worship of God alone. Moses proceeds to further attenuate the impact of the passage by assigning a symbolic meaning to the medium of Jesus' punishment. If Jesus is not Jesus and boiling excrement is not boiling excrement, there is not much left for Christians to criticize.[33]

The assertion that the Talmud attacks Christians in general and Jesus in particular goes back, as we have seen, at least to Nicholas Donin. *'Ezer ha-Emunah* testifies to the sharpening of this assertion by the addition of the allegation that Christian kings are a particular object of attack. Yosef Yerushalmi has pointed out the special role played by the royal image in the consciousness of late medieval Iberian Jewry. Jews came to recognize that their one source of protection in the face of an increasingly hostile populace was a sympathetic king.[34] In light of this development, the danger of this new charge can scarcely be exaggerated.

Moses' antagonist makes a special point of maintaining that the curse against "the wicked kingdom" is aimed at Christian kings.[35] He distinguishes, as we have seen, between the blessings recited upon seeing a gentile and a Jewish king.[36] In the passage concerning gentiles and

33   *E. H.*, pp. 140–143.
34   *The Lisbon Massacre of 1506 and the Royal Image in the Shevet Yehudah* (Cincinnati, 1976), esp. pp. 35–66. Note too A. Gross's observation that late medieval Iberian exegetes of the Book of Esther tended to view Ahasuerus favorably in light of their general attitude toward royalty. See his "Hishtaqqefut Gerushei Sefarad u-Portugal be-Perush Megillat Ester," *Proceedings of the Ninth World Congress of Jewish Studies*, 1986, sec. 2, vol. 1, p. 155. A similar phenomenon was pointed out in a recent Master's thesis by my student Hershel Bessin on R. Joseph Hayyon's commentary to Esther (Bernard Revel Graduate School, Yeshiva University, 1989).
35   *E. H.*, p. 134.
36   *E. H.*, p. 144.

dogs, he goes out of his way to say, "Thus, you have regarded us as dogs, and this includes our king."[37] For his part, Moses not only responds to such explicit charges; he too introduces references to the king where there appears to be no compelling need to do so. The Christian use, or misuse, of the Rabbinic statement that the best of the gentiles should be killed can once again be traced to Donin, and Moses deals with it in standard fashion. But his initial reaction—and one suspects that it is based upon such a Christian understanding of the statement—is that Jews are suspected of wanting to kill the king, who is the best of the gentiles.[38] He consequently asserts that it is inconceivable that Jews should want to do this. Not only does the Mishnah instruct us to pray for the welfare of the kingdom; without the protection of the king, we are subject to slaughter and despoliation.

"God forbid," Moses writes elsewhere, "that we should curse our king, who serves as our shield, protector and savior from all adversity, for the Jews have no salvation except from the Creator, may He be blessed, and from the kings and princes. If we were in the hands of the masses who would be without fear of the king and princes, we would not have the slightest hope of survival or salvation."[39] Even though God has placed a barrier between Himself and His people, he has inspired kings and princes to feel compassion toward us.[40] As for the blessings, here too the Talmud is speaking about ancient pagan kings; indeed, since the blessings for Jewish and gentile rulers were presumably introduced simultaneously, the latter blessing must have been intended for gentiles who ruled at a time when there were also Jewish kings.[41] Did Moses really recite the blessing, "Who has granted a portion of His glory to those who fear Him" (rather than "to flesh and blood") when seeing Christian kings? Despite my inclination to regard his position as essentially sincere, that would be scanned.

---

[37]   *E. H.*, p. 151.

[38]   *E. H.*, p. 134.

[39]   *E. H.*, p. 136: cf. also p. 134. Note too the sentiments expressed by the Ashkenazic author of the *Nizzahon Vetus*, who refused to admit that Jeremiah's curse (17:5) against anyone "who trusts in man" could refer to anything other than the attribution of divinity to a human being. It is, after all, impossible not to place one's reliance on kings and princes. Despite the polemical usefulness of the argument, the underlying sentiment seems real enough. See *The Jewish-Christian Debate*, #67, Eng. sec., p. 86 = Heb. sec., p. 44.

[40]   *E. H.*, p. 158.

[41]   *E. H.*, p. 144.

'Ezer ha-Emunah is not a great polemical work, but it is an exceedingly important one. Few books illustrate so well the transition from an assertive, confident, sometimes almost celebratory Jewish polemical literature to one of fear, defensiveness, and caution. Ashkenazic polemic in particular had almost reveled in the sharp denunciation of Christians and their faith, and the far more polite disputation of Nahmanides is still marked by the boldness and serene confidence not only of a great man but of an age which is just beginning to feel the cutting edge of a new and deadly attack. In the fourteenth century, Iberian Jews were faced with a massive paradox that they could not exploit. Hostile, intolerant Christians attacked Jews for being hostile and intolerant. It is not a pleasant sight to watch Moses ha-Kohen's attempt to reevaluate Talmudic material while conceding by his silence—and sometimes by more than silence—the kindness and benevolence of late medieval Christian society. And this paradox may be eclipsed by an even greater one. The pressures of the new Christian attack may well have been instrumental in broadening and deepening a sincere Jewish reinterpretation of sacred texts in a direction that created a genuinely more positive attitude toward the religion of the oppressor. The transition so painfully evident in *'Ezer ha-Emunah* is a transition not only in the history of polemic but in medieval Jewish history at large. Rarely has a polemical work so captured the spirit of an age.

MISSION TO THE JEWS AND JEWISH-CHRISTIAN CONTACTS IN THE POLEMICAL LITERATURE OF THE HIGH MIDDLE AGES

From: *American Historical Review* 91 (1986): 576–591.

Spreading the good news has been a principal objective of Christianity since its infancy. Nevertheless, after the initial Jewish rejection of the Christian message, the expansionism of the church was directed mainly toward the pagan world, and it is by no means clear that even those patristic works that were directed *adversus Judaeos* were marked by realistic missionary objectives.[1] Jews, moreover, were granted unique toleration in Christian Europe on the theological grounds that they served, however unwillingly, as living testimony to Christian truth and that their conversion at the end of days was required by biblical prophecy. At the same time, no one doubted that the acceptance of Christianity by individual Jews was devoutly to be wished. Thus, at its core, the fundamental theory governing Jewish status in early medieval Europe was marked by tension and ambivalence—a result of the contradiction between the theoretical goals of a universal Christian mission and an argument for toleration that came close to discouraging Jewish conversion.

Christian polemic against Jews is a crucial genre for the study of missionary intentions, and the theoretical tension that I noted is clearly reflected in the assessment of that literature in the standard study of Jewish-Christian relations before the First Crusade. Bernhard Blumenkranz devoted much of his *Juifs et Chrétiens dans le monde*

---

[1]   See David Rokeah, *Jews, Pagans, and Christians in Conflict* (Jerusalem, 1982), pp. 40–48. Also see my brief discussion in David Berger, *The Jewish-Christian Debate in the High Middle Ages: A Critical Edition of the Nizzahon Vetus with an Introduction, Translation, and Commentary* (Philadelphia, 1979), pp. 4–5.

occidental, 430–1096, to the issues of polemic and mission.[2] On the one hand, he indicated that pre-crusade polemic against Jews was intended for Christian disputants in a context that did not involve a direct and immediate mission.[3] On the other hand, he stressed the persistence of the missionary ideal as a motive for polemical activity: Christians were impelled by a natural desire to persuade others of the truth, by the aspirations of believers in a majority faith to make that faith the exclusive one, and by the great Christian expectation of seeing all humanity "assembled under the scepter of Christ." To a significant degree, then, Blumenkranz perceived pre-crusade literary polemics as the result of a missionary objective.[4]

If this assessment of the relatively sparse polemical literature written before 1096 is sound, the much richer material from the following century should reflect a similar motive. But, even if one remains skeptical about a significant missionary impulse in the early period, a number of considerations require a fresh and careful look at the possibility of missionary objectives in the elusive twelfth century. First, the resurgence of polemic, which produced almost twenty works from the late eleventh through the twelfth century, suggests prima facie a more aggressive Christian attitude toward conversion of Jews. Second, we know that mission to the Jews had become an important goal of many Christians by the mid-thirteenth century,[5] and the suddenly numerous polemical works of the previous century are a tempting and reasonable place to look for the roots of this phenomenon. Third, the widely admired First Crusade, with its bloody attempt at the forcible conversion of the Jewish communities in the Rhineland, could have been responsible for placing mission to the Jews on the agenda of a newly expansionist and assertive Christendom, and the upsurge of anti-Jewish works could be understood as a product of that expansionism. Finally, the crucial turning point in the Christian attitude toward mission to Islam occurs in the twelfth century.

---

2   Blumenkranz, *Juifs et Chrétiens dans le monde occidental, 430–1096* (Paris, 1960).

3   Ibid., p. 75. On Blumenkranz's complex position, see, especially, note 72, below.

4   Ibid., pp. 67–68, 152, 216.

5   Although I have some reservations about Jeremy Cohen's conclusions concerning the shift from tolerance to intolerance of Jews in the thought of the thirteenth- and fourteenth-century friars, his thorough description of their missionary objectives is correct. See Cohen, *The Friars and the Jews* (Ithaca, N.Y., 1982). For my review, see *AHR* 88 (1983): 93.

Benjamin Z. Kedar's recent study of this question has pointed to an utter indifference to converting Muslims during the early Middle Ages that gave way by the mid-twelfth century to a strong feeling that they should be made Christian. From that point on, there appears to have been little question of the desirability of mission, and the controversy was confined to the debate between advocates of force and of persuasion.[6]

This question is but one aspect of the broader challenge that the twelfth century has posed for Jewish historians. The early Middle Ages, with the exception of Visigothic Spain, were a period of relative peace and opportunity for Europe's Jews. Only in the eleventh century did some distinct signs of deterioration in their status begin to emerge, although questions remain about both the extent and the cause of that decline.[7] The century culminated, of course, in the crusade, and by the late thirteenth century the Jews of Northern Europe were subject to expulsions and persecution. Can a more or less straight line be drawn from the First Crusade to the expulsions, or was it only in the thirteenth century that relatively new forces emerged that moved the history of medieval European Jewry toward its tragic denouement? In the twelfth century, the Second Crusade swept through the Rhineland, the ritual murder accusation was born, and yet the Jewish community continued to function in a hostile but relatively stable environment. From a cultural perspective, the period was one of dazzling achievement. Even the acute contemporary observer would not have seen a people poised at the edge of a precipice.[8]

---

6   Kedar, *Crusade and Mission: European Approaches toward the Muslims* (Princeton, N.J., 1984), esp. pp. 57–74.

7   See Lena Dasberg, *Untersuchungen über die Entwertung des Judenstatus im 11. jahrhundert* (Paris, 1965). Compare the remarks of Amos Funkenstein, "Basic Types of Christian Anti-Jewish Polemics in the Later Middle Ages," *Viator* 2 (1971): 377. Also see Gavin Langmuir, "From Ambrose of Milan to Emicho of Leiningen: The Transformation of Hostility against Jews in Northern Christendom," *Gli Ebrei nell'Alto Medioevo, Settimane di Studio*, 26 (Spoleto, 1980), pp. 313–368; and Avraham Grossman, *Hakhmei Ashkenaz ha-Rishonim* (Jerusalem, 1981), pp. 12–13, 163. Compare the remarks in my review, *Tarbiz* 53 (1984): 480. Also see Robert Chazan, "1007–1012: Initial Crisis for Northern European Jewry," *Proceedings of the American Academy for Jewish Research* 39 (1972): 101–118; and Kenneth R. Stow, *The "1007 Anonymous" and Papal Sovereignty: Jewish Perceptions of the Papacy and Papal Policy in the High Middle Ages* (Cincinnati, Ohio, 1984).

8   For a vigorous argument that 1096 was not a watershed in Jewish history, see Robert Chazan's *European Jewry and the First Crusade* (forthcoming [subsequently published, Berkeley, c. 1987]).

With regard to the question of mission, the historiographical problem posed by the twelfth century emerges in all of its tantalizing ambiguity in an intentionally cautious and ambivalent formulation by Salo Baron. "In the Roman and Byzantine empires, and even in western Europe before the age of the Crusades, the numerous tracts 'Against the Jews' primarily had Christian audiences in mind. Now, on the contrary, the Church viewed the apologetic literature as but another weapon in its march toward world domination. The new offensive, seized particularly by the preaching orders, also infused new vigor and introduced novel facets into the polemics which, together with the vastly expanding missionary sermons and oral disputations, tried to persuade the Jews of the 'foolishness' of their stubborn perseverance."[9] At first, this passage suggests that a change in Christian attitude occurred at the beginning of "the age of the Crusades," but almost immediately the emphasis shifts to "the preaching orders," which belong to the thirteenth century. Once again, the twelfth century is left in a sort of limbo. Was it a watershed in the use of polemic as a weapon in the church's "march toward world domination," or does this questionable distinction belong to the age of the friars?[10]

I believe this question can be answered unequivocally. Despite the proliferation of Christian polemics in the late eleventh and twelfth centuries, the evidence is overwhelming that these works were not rooted in a new or continuing missionary impulse. An examination of the reasons that polemicists gave for writing their tracts reveals a remarkable need to apologize for engaging in an activity considered improper on ideological grounds, and, even when there is no apology, hesitation, or refusal, the reasons given almost invariably do not include the idea that Christians should attempt to proselytize Jews.

If this conclusion is correct, then two potential explanations for the upsurge of Christian polemic remain. First, the primary impulse for this literature may have come from outside the arena of Jewish-Christian relations and resulted, instead, from the overall cultural renaissance of the late eleventh and twelfth centuries. Since no Christian engaged in

---

[9]   Baron, *A Social and Religious History of the Jews* (2d edn., New York, 1965), vol. 9, p. 101.

[10]   Amos Funkenstein did not take a clear position on this question in his studies of twelfth-century Christian polemic. See "Ha-Temurot be-Vikkuah ha-Dat she-bein Yehudim le-Nozrim ba-Meah ha-Yod-Bet," *Zion* 33 (1968): 125–144, and "Basic Types," 373–382.

a careful examination of the sacred texts and doctrines of Christianity could have avoided a confrontation with Judaism, apologetic writings could have been an inevitable consequence of an internal Christian dynamic.[11]

On the other hand, the impetus for these works may lie in Jewish-Christian interaction of the most vibrant sort. There is no longer any question that some Jews in Northern Europe were involved in discussions of biblical and other issues with Christian scholars.[12] The polemical literature contains considerable evidence that ordinary Jews and Christians held lively, informal debates about sensitive religious matters, and the authors of Christian polemics speak of the need for a response to aggressive Jewish questions. Such debates no doubt predated the High Middle Ages, but they may well have intensified as a result of the growing intellectual sophistication engendered by the cultural revolution that transformed both Jewish and Christian society in this period. The renaissance of the High Middle Ages surely facilitated the literary expression of these confrontations by both sides. The Christian assertions that Jews posed provocative questions with frequency and vehemence must be taken seriously. Christians were not confronting Jewish missionaries, but they faced a genuine, vigorous challenge from a proud and assertive Jewish community.[13]

Eleventh- and twelfth-century Christian intellectuals had profound reservations about mission to the Jews. Perhaps the most striking illustration of this position is the outright refusal of Adam of Perseigne (d. 1203) to accede to a friend's request that he write an anti-Jewish polemic. First, it seemed to him that his friend was motivated more by the desire to dispute than by zeal for the truth; second, Christians, he believed, should not be contentious on general principles (2 Tim. 2:23–24). Third—and for us most important—the Jews would remain blind and hard-hearted "until the fulness of the nations will come in" (Rom. 11:25).

---

[11] At one time, I regarded the influence of internal Christian developments as slightly more central to the upsurge in polemic than I do now. See my brief remark in *The Jewish-Christian Debate*, p. 16.

[12] For an important summary of the evidence, see Aryeh Grabois, "The *Hebraica veritas* and Jewish-Christian Intellectual Relations in the Twelfth Century," *Speculum* 50 (1975): 613–634.

[13] I discuss the state of this question later in this article.

The famous verse from Romans, then, predicts the futility of missionary efforts and may even intend to discourage them; Jewish conversion is reserved for the *eschaton*. Later, Adam added a further consideration: Christians should not pollute themselves with discussions of falsehood but should study Christian doctrines with pure heart and hands and simple eyes.[14] Since Adam could have written a brief compendium of standard anti-Jewish arguments with little more effort than it took him to write this letter, I doubt that he was concocting excuses for a refusal motivated by laziness; this is a genuine, antimissionary ideology.

In one of the earliest polemics of the period, hesitation is followed by acceptance of responsibility. Peter Damian (d. 1072) mentioned Jewish conversion as a reason for writing polemic, but almost as an after-thought following an exhortation to concentrate on more important things than arguing with Jews. Damian was responding to a request from a churchman named Honestus to provide material refuting Jewish arguments, and he began by suggesting that, "if you wish to be a soldier of Christ and fight for him courageously, then take up arms . . . against the vices of the flesh, the contrivances of the devil—an enemy who will clearly never die—rather than against the Jews, who will soon be virtually destroyed from the face of the earth." Nevertheless, he agreed to provide the material because it was disgraceful (*inhonestum*) to remain silent while Christianity was insulted, such silence could arouse doubts in Christian minds, and, finally, Jews might be converted by well-presented Christian arguments.[15] A reluctant missionary indeed.

Peter of Blois (d. 1200) provided an even stronger prolegomenon before finally acquiescing and writing his polemic. He addressed the work to a Christian who complained that he was surrounded by Jews

---

14 Adam of Perseigne, *Epistola ad amicum, Patrologia Latina*, ed. J. P. Migne (hereafter, *PL*) 211: 653–659. It bears noting that Adam considered a bad Christian worse than a Jew, who acted in ignorance; ibid., 657, 659. This reference should be added to Jeremy Cohen's valuable discussion of the question of Jewish ignorance and culpability in Christian thought. See Cohen, "The Jews as the Killers of Christ in the Latin Tradition, from Augustine to the Friars," *Traditio* 39 (1983): 1–27.

15 Peter Damian, *Antilogus contra judaeos, PL* 145: 41. See my discussion in "St. Peter Damian: His Attitude toward the Jews and the Old Testament," *Yavneh Review* 4 (1965): 83–84. Blumenkranz's references to this work illustrate his tendency to emphasize missionary motivations. He first cited Damian's hope for conversion, two pages later he indicated the rather different need to assist Honestus, and considerably later he referred to the *Antilogus* without qualification as a "missionary work;" *Juifs et Chrétiens*, pp. 69, 71, 153.

and heretics and was unequipped to answer the tricky arguments raised by the Jews in their disputations. It was unwise, Peter said, for someone without good polemical aptitude to debate with a heretic or a Jew; such disputes, in fact, tended to turn the inexperienced Christian into a heretic himself. And it was surely absurd to debate a subject like the Trinity. In effect, Peter argued that Christians need not worry about educating the heretic or Jew: beasts were not permitted to touch Mount Sinai, and pearls were not to be cast before swine.[16] Moreover, if one defeats an enemy of the cross in debate, he will in any event not convert in his heart. As for the Jews, they cannot be converted because God has set them an end that cannot be advanced. One might, it is true, make an occasional convert, but the rest will persist in their stubbornness.[17] Apparently, the missionary enterprise was not sufficiently justified by the handful of souls that might be saved.

Peter, of course, did relent and write polemic, and suspicious historians may be tempted to conclude that this introductory show of reluctance is a disguise for missionary zeal. In determining twelfth-century attitudes toward mission, however, what he wrote is decisive, and underlying motives are of secondary significance as signposts of future developments. In a sense, the point would even be strengthened, since Peter was apparently embarrassed to be pursuing an objective that any Christian would have been expected to applaud. It seems probable that discouraging mission to the Jews was an ideology that arose as a rationalization to explain centuries of relative indifference to Jewish conversion or even as a direct reaction to protracted Jewish stubbornness. Nevertheless, the reluctance to proselytize among Jews remains both surprising and significant.

Peter relented, he said, because the request came from a person beset (*obsessum*) by Jews and heretics. A similar defensive motive is proffered in an anonymous twelfth-century polemic whose author maintained that he wrote for simple people and in simple faith, not for the sake of dialectical disputations. Jews, he said, should not be able to mock Christian ignorance (*imperitia*)—those Jews "who taunt [*insultant*] us all day and say with Goliath, 'Choose someone from among you who will

16 In light of the context of this phrase in the Gospels, its use as an argument against preaching to Jews is painfully ironic.
17 Peter of Blois, *Contra perfidiam Judaeorum*, PL 207: 825–827.

engage in a one-on-one battle with us.'"[18] Similarly, Walter of Châtillon introduced his polemic with the remark that the Jews "not only fail to acquiesce in the truth of the new grace but even, like retrograde planets, attempt to oppose the firmament of our faith and pose objections to Christians from the authority of the Pentateuch. Hence, mindful of their ignorance [again, *imperitia*, this time about the Jews], we decided to write a book with arguments so compelling that even . . . [an] ass will not be able to contradict them."[19] Once more a defensive motive appears. Whether the conditions described by Peter, Walter, and the anonymous author of the *Tractatus* reflect historical reality is an issue to which I shall presently return, but the reiteration of such defensive claims underscores the absence of explicit missionary goals.

Rupert of Deutz (d. 1135), like Adam and the two Peters, wrote in response to a request. Rudolph of St. Trond, at that time abbot of St. Pantaleon in Cologne, is reported to have had frequent contact with Jews, and he not only requested Rupert's polemic but subsequently wrote a letter asking for material that would demonstrate the triune God and the incarnation and discuss the evidence from Gen. 49:10.[20] Rudolph may have been interested in mission, but Rupert, who did not accede to the request immediately, would not have written polemic on his own initiative.[21]

---

[18]   *Tractatus adversus Judaeum*, PL 213: 749. The effectiveness of Jewish debaters is also attested in Bartholomew of Exeter's unpublished "Dialogus contra Judaeos" (early 1180s), which warns against engaging in public controversies with them. At the same time, Bartholomew remarked (if only in a subordinate clause) that "we hold discussions with them for their own salvation." There is, then, a missionary intention blunted by fear of the consequences of disputation. For the relevant passage, see R. W. Hunt, "The Disputation of Peter of Cornwall against Symon the Jew," in *Studies in Medieval History Presented to Frederick Maurice Powicke*, ed. by R. W. Hunt et al. (Oxford, 1948), pp. 147–148.

[19]   Walter of Châtillon, *Tractatus sive dialogus contra Judaeos*, PL 209: 424–425.

[20]   "Ein Briefes Chronisten Rudolph von St. Trond an Rupert von Deutz," *Neues Archiv* 17 (1892): 617–618. This letter influenced the writing of *De glorificatione Trinitatis* and perhaps part of *De gloria et honore Filii hominis*. See J. H. Van Engen, *Rupert of Deutz* (Berkeley and Los Angeles, 1983), pp. 246–247, 354–355; and *Hermannus quondam Judaeus opusculum de conversione sua*, Monumenta Germaniae Historica: Quellen zur Geistgeschichte des Mittelalters, vol. 4, ed. by G. Niemeyer (Weimar, 1963), p. 5 n. 3, and pp. 41–43. Rudolph's letter sounds like the request of a man who had read Fulbert of Chartres's *Tractatus contra Judaeos*, which deals precisely with the topics specified, and found it inadequate in real discussions with Jews.

[21]   Rupert of Deutz, *Anulus sive dialogus inter Christianum et Judaeum*, in M. L. Arduini, *Ruperto de Deutz e la controversia tra Cristiani ed Ebrei nel secolo XII* (Rome, 1979), esp. p. 184. The work is also in *PL* 170: 559–610.

In addition to Peter Damian's *Antilogus*, the other anti-Jewish polemics written in the eleventh century also contain motives that have little to do with mission. Fulbert of Chartres maintained that his intention was to speak of the errors of nonbelievers in general; he began with Jews because they agreed with Christians in their monotheistic faith and disagreed with respect to several clearly defined issues: the Trinity, the divinity of the Messiah, and whether or not he had come.[22] Gilbert Crispin introduced his enormously influential disputation by saying that it reflected amicable discussions that he had had with a Jewish acquaintance who came to him frequently on business and other matters, at which times they conversed about the Scriptures and issues of faith. He did note that a Jew present at such discussions converted and became a monk, but he seemed to regard this as something of an unanticipated bonus rather than the purpose of the conversation and gave no indication that his book was to be used in any special effort to convert Jews.[23]

In the following century, an author once thought to be William of Champeaux produced a sharper version of Crispin's disputation and introduced a reference to missionary intentions into his paraphrase of Crispin's introductory passage. "I was acquainted with a certain Jew because of a business affair; as time passed, I was moved by love to urge him frequently to abandon Judaism and become a Christian."[24] Although this work does not, of course, reflect a real experience, the author's remark is not insignificant, but his assertion is limited to a specific Jew whom he was allegedly motivated to convert because of personal friendship. No interest in a broader mission is either stated or implied. At the end of a work directed mainly at Christian heretics, Alan of Lille appended a chapter on the Jews also derived largely from Crispin. In this case, the structure as well as the content make it abundantly clear that the author, who also added a chapter on Islam, did not write out of a missionary zeal directed at Jews.[25]

---

[22]   Fulbert of Chartres, *Tractatus contra Judaeos*, PL 141: 308.

[23]   *Gisleberti Crispini disputatio Judaei et Christiani*, ed. by Bernhard Blumenkranz (Utrecht, 1956), pp. 27–28. The work is also in *PL* 159: 1005–1036.

[24]   Pseudo-William of Champeaux, *Dialogus inter Christianum et Judaeum de fide Catholica*, PL 163: 1045. On the tone of this work, see Israel Levi, "Controverse entre un Juif et un Chrétien au XIe Siècle," *Revue des Etudes Juives* 5 (1882): 244.

[25]   *De fide Catholica contra haereticos*, PL 210: 305–430, bk. 3, PL 210: 399–422. See my "Gilbert Crispin, Alan of Lille, and Jacob ben Reuben: A Study in the Transmission of Medieval Polemic," *Speculum* 49 (1974): 34–47; and M. H. Vicaire, "'Contra Judaeos'

Similar attitudes appear in two early twelfth-century polemics concerning the incarnation. Odo of Cambrai addressed his work to a monk who had been present at a lecture by Odo on the incarnation and had urged him to put it in writing. Odo was finally persuaded to do so, but, before he wrote his book, he had a discussion on the subject with a Jew. Consequently, it seemed appropriate to Odo to record his remarks in the form of a dialogue. "Now, then, I invoke the Holy Spirit so that whatever inspiration it gave me for the purpose of convincing a Jew it might give me once again for the instruction of a faithful monk."[26] Odo then described how the Jew Leo visited him after his midday nap and initiated the discussion that he recorded. Once again, the question of historicity can be postponed; the immediate point is that Odo proffered no missionary intention at all and explicitly directed his work to a Christian audience motivated by a desire to understand the incarnation.

Guibert de Nogent's *Tractatus* on the incarnation *contra Judaeos* was actually directed against a count of Soissons who, Guibert said, cultivated the views of Jews and heretics. To Guibert, it was tolerable when someone who never accepted Christianity rejected it; the Jews, after all, grew up with this attitude, implanted in them since their forefathers crucified Jesus. What was intolerable was for people who called themselves Christians to attack the faith. To make matters worse, the count dared to proclaim nefarious ideas that Jews themselves were afraid to utter aloud. The Jews, in fact, considered him insane, because he extolled their sect while ostensibly following Christianity.[27] Although Guibert said that four years after writing the book he used it to strengthen the faith of a Jewish convert, there are no missionary overtones whatever in the reason he gave for its composition. The Jews, in fact, are used almost as a foil for the real object of Guibert's attack, and the implication is that he would not have written to expose the longstanding errors of a tolerated Jewish community.

Even the three polemics by pre-thirteenth-century converts to Christianity do not reflect the systematic missionary zeal that we might

méridionaux au début du XIIIe siècle: Alain de Lille, Evrard de Béthune, Guillaume de Bourges," in M. H. Vicaire and B. Blumenkranz, eds., *Juifs et judaïsme de Languedoc* (Toulouse, 1977), pp. 269–287.

[26] Odo of Cambrai, *Disputatio contra Judaeum*, PL 160: 1103.

[27] Guibert de Nogent, *Tractatus de Incarnatione contra Judaeos*, PL 156: 489–490; and *De vita sua*, PL 156: 949–950.

expect. The work by "Samuel of Morocco," though it deals with some broader issues, is couched as an explanation of the exile addressed to a Jew named Isaac, and it is hard to decide whether the work is a polemic with a limited missionary purpose or an *apologia pro conversione sua*.[28] Petrus Alfonsi explicitly described the dialogue with his own former Jewish persona as a reaction to attacks questioning the motives and sincerity of his conversion,[29] and the fascinating little book by Herman of Cologne is an autobiographical account of his experiences on the road to conversion rather than a true polemic.[30]

A final work that fits this pattern is essentially *sui generis*. Peter Abelard wrote a dialogue involving a philosopher, a Christian, and a Jew in which the relevant discussion takes place between the Jew and the philosopher, not between the Jew and the Christian. The irenic tone as well as the structure make it improbable that missionary zeal was Abelard's reason for writing.[31]

The overall impression gained from these works is not merely that they fail to explicate a missionary intention. If the absence of proselytism were the only common feature, one might assume that the motive to convert was so integral to polemic that the authors took it for granted. Instead, work after work presents ideological reservations about mission, reluctance to engage in debate, defensive explanations for writing polemical works, and justifications based on the need to combat heresy and to instruct a Christian audience—all of which point to a striking lack of interest in a missionary program. Either mission was a secondary motive or not a motive at all or else these authors felt uncomfortable asserting it. In either case, the ideology they expressed—at the very minimum—attached little importance to conversion of Jews.

There are, however, three twelfth-century works that contain signs of things to come. The first, emerging from the school of Abelard, is known

---

28 The work of "Samuel of Morocco" may well be a pseudepigraph of the fourteenth century. See M. Marsmann, *Die Epistel des Rabbi Samuel an Rabbi Isaak: Untersuchung und Edition* (Siegen, 1971). The epistle also appears in *PL* 149: 337–368.

29 Petrus Alfonsi, *Dialogus Petri, cognomento Alphonsi, ex Judaeo Christiani, et Moysi Judaei*, *PL* 157: 535–672, esp. 538.

30 Niemeyer, *Hermannus quondam Judaeus opusculum de conversione sua*.

31 Peter Abelard, *Dialogus inter philosophum, iudaeum, et christianum*, ed. by Rudolf Thomas (Stuttgart, 1970), pp. 44–85. Richard of St. Victor's *De Emmanuele* was directed against Andrew of St. Victor's Judaizing commentary on Isa. 7:14 and is surely not a missionary tract. See *PL* 196: 601–666.

for its striking use of Hebrew as a tool in the debate with Jews, but, in light of the objectives of earlier polemics, the motive it suggests for disputation is at least equally interesting. Sometime between 1139 and 1148, an obscure cleric named Odo wrote the *Ysagoge in theologiam*. In the introduction to the section on Jews, he made the following assertion: "For if it is proper for us to exhort those who are fashioned in the faith to live better, surely we should recall the Jews from their erroneous, disbelieving sect."[32] If such an attitude were common, this would have been an utterly routine sentence. The editor of the *Ysagoge*, for example, wrote that "the conversion of the Jews was one of the great preoccupations of Christian intellectuals in the twelfth and thirteenth centuries," and Odo was a participant in this movement.[33] In fact, a statement like this before the middle of the twelfth century was not routine but sharply polemical; it was a pointed *a fortiori* argument directed against the then-dominant view of the upper clergy that efforts at conversion of Jews were improper or unimportant.

The later attitude of aggressive mission to the Jews is adumbrated with particular clarity by Peter the Venerable. The reader of the prologue to his polemic finds himself in a different, unfamiliar world. No hesitation here, and no apology. How can Jews, he wrote, alone in all the world, deny Jesus? They are stiff-necked, without celestial or terrestrial glory, but, if they convert, they, too, can be saved.[34] Later in the work, Peter expressed doubts about his prospects for success. With the arrogance and belligerence typical of this polemic, he noted that his arguments from both authority and reason would satisfy any human being, but he was not so sure that Jews, whose reason appeared "extinct" and "buried," could be called human beings and not animals.[35] Whatever the tactical wisdom of his denunciatory tone, and whether or not Peter ever had contact with his prospective converts, there is in his work at least some expression of a hope of conversion.[36]

---

[32] *Ysagoge in theologiam*, ed. Arthur M. Landgraf, *Ecrits théologiques de l'école d'Abélard* (Louvain, 1934), pp. 126–127. Also see Avrom Saltman, "Ha-Ysagoge shel Odo—Shitah Hadashah ba-Pulmus ha-anti-Yehudi," *Biqqoret u-Parshanut* 13–14 (1979): 265–280.

[33] *Ecrits théologiques*, xlvii.

[34] Peter the Venerable, *Tractatus adversus Judaeorum inveteratam duritiem*, PL 189: 507–509.

[35] Ibid., 602.

[36] It may be more than coincidence that both Odo and Peter, who were interested in genuine mission, used tools borrowed from the Jewish armory—in the first case linguistic and in the second Talmudic.

Finally, later in the century, we come to an author whom we might well expect to find in any list of exceptional figures: Joachim of Fiore. Nevertheless, not all of his discourse is exceptional. Joachim began with the familiar assertion that response to the Jews is necessary because otherwise one gives occasion to the enemies of Christ to insult the faith and confuse the simple believer. He went on, however, to a consideration peculiar to his own well-known speculations about the imminence of a new age. An additional reason for the work, he said, was his feeling that the Jews would soon experience the divine mercy as the time of their consolation and conversion arrived.[37] At that time, all Jews would convert. Joachim, however, wanted some to see the light just before the period of general salvation, and he broke into prophetic exhortation: "And now, O Jewish men, hear my voice this day, and do not persist in hardening your heart."[38]

These exceptions are few in number, and there is less to them than meets the eye. The relevant section of the *Ysagoge in theologiam* is a manifestly atypical work by an insignificant author, and Joachim of Fiore is a profoundly idiosyncratic figure whose position on Jewish conversion flows precisely from his most important idiosyncrasy. As for Peter the Venerable, his bitter pessimism about the prospects of persuading the Jews drastically tempers the impression of missionary zeal that his remarks may create, and the *Tractatus* remains far more a work of denunciation than of mission.

In the thirteenth century, sentiments for proselytism continued to grow, and ultimately they prevailed. Peter of Cornwall's disputation, completed in 1208, describes at great length his successful effort to convert a Jewish acquaintance, although, as in the reworking of Crispin's polemic, the object of this effort is a single individual.[39] In the 1230s, William of Bourges wrote that, shortly after his conversion to Christianity,

---

37 Joachim of Fiore, *Adversus Judaeos di Gioacchino da Fiore*, ed. by Arsenio Frugoni (Rome, 1957), p. 3.

38 Ibid., pp. 85–89. The points in this paragraph were made by Frugoni in the introduction to his edition (pp. xxxii–xxxvii). I hesitate to include Hildebert of Lavardin's short sermon "Against the Jews Concerning the Incarnation" among these exceptional polemics, despite its apostrophe to the Jews urging their conversion. The entire work is a few paragraphs long, was delivered to a Christian audience, and merely lists a handful of the standard verses on the incarnation with virtually no argumentation. See PL 171: 811–814.

39 The prologue to Peter's *Liber disputationum contra Symonem Iudeum* was published by Hunt; "Disputation of Peter of Cornwall," 153–156.

he was urged to use his knowledge of Hebrew to compose a work to refute the Jews. After all, Jesus himself fought against both Sadducee heretics and other Jews, and, if Christians truly love him, they should do battle against his enemies. Ominously, William's proof text is "Shall I not hate those who hate you, O Lord?" (Ps. 139:21).[40] Whether the motivation was hate or love, by the mid-thirteenth century a Christian campaign to convert the Jews was gathering momentum,[41] and the theoretical desirability of such a program was not again seriously questioned until modern times.

The polemical works that I have examined do more than reveal the absence of a missionary ideology; they also make assertions about frequent discussions between Jews and Christians at and especially below the level of the upper clergy. Such information, if authentic, is of extraordinary historical value. Assessing authenticity is, of course, no easy task. We are dealing in many of these instances with a literary genre of fictitious debate, which led one scholar to regard virtually all of the major polemics besides Crispin's as possessing "no historical interest."[42] There are, however, ways of evaluating this evidence.

First, the requests for polemical material were genuine. It would require a perverse level of skepticism to assume that Adam of Perseigne invented a request so that he could explain why he turned it down. Peter Damian's entire personal history and psychology indicate that he was sincere in asserting that one should concentrate on battling the vices of the flesh and that his reluctant agreement to enter the lists against the Jews resulted from a letter of request.[43] In Rupert's case, a somewhat later request from his correspondent exists. One cannot be certain about Peter of Blois, but the evidence in the other cases places the burden of proof on the skeptic. It appears that the lower clergy, precisely because of greater contact with the outside world, felt a need for works that would assist them in the religious discussions that were apparently a common feature of everyday life.

The evidence, moreover, does not allow the assumption that these discussions were necessarily initiated by proselytizing Christians. The

---

40   Guillaume de Bourges, *Livre des guerres du Seigneur*, ed. by Gilbert Dahan (Paris, 1981), pp. 66, 68.
41   Cohen, *The Friars and the Jews*.
42   Lévi, "Controverse," 239.
43   See my discussion in "St. Peter Damian," 83.

assertions of Jewish aggressiveness in the works of Peter of Blois and Walter of Châtillon and in the anonymous *Tractatus* may be exaggerated, but they would constitute silly, almost self-defeating bombast if they did not have some basis in reality.[44] Furthermore, the testimony in these polemics is borne out to a striking extent by thirteenth-century Jewish works. Whether Jews or Christians initiated these exchanges, the indications are overwhelming that they were real and frequent. The nature of some of the arguments as well as circumstantial evidence support this conclusion.

The most detailed account of a Jewish-Christian debate in a Christian work is that of Herman of Cologne. Here a Jewish youth in early twelfth-century Germany listens to a Christian sermon that describes Jews as animals who understand only the letter of the law, in contrast to Christians, who are human beings who use reason to understand the spirit of the law.[45] He is directly exhorted to give up the heavy yoke of the Mosaic law and take up instead the easy burden offered by Jesus (Matt. 11:30),[46] and at one point he initiates a conversation with no less a figure than Rupert of Deutz himself.[47] Local churchmen provide him with books, and he maintains that he succeeded in teaching himself Latin so that he could read them.[48] Nevertheless, he insists that what really clinched his decision to convert was his observation of the

---

[44] The remarks by Peter and the author of the *Tractatus* were noted by Lévi, and many historians have cited Louis IX's comment that a Christian layman approached by a Jewish polemicist should respond by stabbing him. See Lévi, "Controverse," 238. Also see my brief discussion in *The Jewish-Christian Debate*, pp. 22–23. Compare the somewhat weaker impression given by Peter Damian that Honestus was confronted by a Jewish challenge, and see Bartholomew of Exeter's comments cited in note 18, above. Guibert's remark that the Jews hardly dared whisper what the count of Soissons said aloud does reflect some Jewish caution, but it must also be read in light of Guibert's strategy to use the Jews as a foil for the heretical count.

[45] Niemeyer, *Hermannus quondam Judaeus opusculum de conversione sua*, p. 74. This image appears in the work of Walter of Châtillon and, more clearly, in the polemic of Peter the Venerable. Also see my "The Attitude of St. Bernard of Clairvaux toward the Jews," *Proceedings of the American Academy for Jewish Research* 40 (1972): 103.

[46] Niemeyer, *Hermannus quondam Judaeus opusculum de conversione sua*, p. 75. Such an argument by Christian missionaries may have partially inspired and surely lent force to the Jewish contention that conversion to Christianity proved nothing more than the convert's desire to experience the pleasures of the flesh; *Nizzahon Vetus*, in *The Jewish-Christian Debate*, p. 206, and, in the Hebrew section, p. 144.

[47] Niemeyer, *Hermannus quondam Judaeus opusculum de conversione sua*, pp. 77–83.

[48] Ibid., p. 76.

prayerful devotion of simple nuns.[49] The strong impression that emerges from his work is not that of an intellectual poring over sophisticated tracts or even disputing with people like Rupert; rather, we see a Jew who maintains regular, intimate contacts with ordinary Christians and lower clergy and who is eventually won over to the dominant religion by an accumulation of such experiences. Although Herman reported that a Jew chastised him for excessive association with Christians,[50] the impression of frequent religious discussions between ordinary Jews and Christians is by no means negated by the undeniable fact that Herman went too far. The atmosphere of the memoir is compelling.

The reality of such contacts emerges from a number of other Christian works as well. Rudolph of St. Trond, the abbot who requested Rupert of Deutz to write his polemic, is reported to have "frequently held mild discussions with Jews without disputation or reproach; rather, he softened the hardness of their heart by stroking and massage . . . . For this reason they loved him so much that even their women came to see him and speak with him."[51] The general tone and content of Crispin's disputation has convinced most scholars of its essential authenticity as a work arising out of friendly, informal meetings between the author and a Jewish acquaintance.[52] Odo of Cambrai's assertion that he had an unplanned discussion with a Jew is highly plausible because he has another explicit motive for writing his work: the addressee, as we recall, had requested that he record his lecture on the incarnation.

Moreover, Odo's polemic ends with a fascinating sentence that suggests not only the reality of such discussions but also their context.

[49] Ibid., pp. 107–108.
[50] Ibid., p. 93.
[51] *Gesta abbatum Trudonensium*, quoted by Niemeyer, in his introduction to *Hermannus quondam Judaeus opusculum de conversione sua*, p. 5 n. 3.
[52] In composing such a work, an author naturally expands and "improves" the discussion; hence, certain implausibilities in the exchange do not in themselves undermine the likelihood of an encounter, and even R. J. Zvi Werblowsky, who expressed serious reservations about the recorded disputation, did not doubt Crispin's statement that he held amicable discussions about religion with a Jewish acquaintance. See Werblowsky, "Crispin's Disputation," *Journal of Jewish Studies* 11 (1960): 73. The reworking of Crispin presents a fictitious exchange, and I would therefore treat it more cautiously than did Aryeh Grabois, who said that the work "clearly attests" frequent, informal meetings among intellectuals. Nevertheless, the author's assertion that he had such discussions, even though it too is borrowed from Crispin, presumably reflects a milieu in which such a report would sound plausible. See Grabois, "The *Hebraica veritas*," 634.

"These . . . are the reasons that I gave the Jew concerning the coming of Christ, having been forced to dispute all the more subtly by certain Christians who took the part of the Jew."[53] Thus, as in Crispin's case, there was an audience, and here some Christians attending were prepared to challenge the arguments of the Christian protagonist. Even if these Christians were advocates of an explanation of the incarnation that differed from Odo's, such intervention would be inconceivable in a debate whose serious goal was the conversion of the Jew. These confrontations were ultimately very serious indeed, but the atmosphere appears to have been one of a duel of wits—almost a form of intellectual entertainment.

Guibert's polemic, which does not reflect a real confrontation, ends with a miracle story also pertinent to this discussion. He heard an account of a disputation in a home (*in quadam domo*) in which a cleric was unable to contest the perfidious bombast of a Jew, so the cleric offered to hold the burning part of a firebrand in order to prove his position. The Jew made no effort to dissuade him, and the cleric grabbed hold of the flame and did not burn. The Jew marveled but was nonetheless not impelled to convert.[54] The miracle here is not especially miraculous, and the story could be true. Even if it is not, however, it suggests that such discussions were routine.

Finally, both Peter of Blois and the author of the anonymous *Tractatus* proffered practical advice on pinning down the slippery and elusive Jewish disputant, who was likely to change the subject whenever he encountered difficulty.[55] Once again, works that do not record actual disputations suggest that Jews and Christians expected to confront one another in the field of religious combat.

Thus far, I have examined only Christian works, but the impression created by those works is confirmed by Jewish polemics as well. This literature does not begin until the late twelfth century, and one of the earliest works, authored by the southern French polemicist Jacob ben Reuben, reports an encounter whose essential historicity has never

---

53   Odo of Cambrai, *Disputatio contra Judaeum*, PL 160: 1112.

54   Guibert de Nogent, *Tractatus de Incarnatione contra judaeos*, PL 156: 528. For an eleventh-century proposal to prove Christianity through ordeal by fire to an audience of similarly unimpressed Muslims, see Kedar, *Crusade and Mission*, p. 45.

55   Peter of Blois, *Contra perfidiam Judaeorum*, PL 207: 870; and *Tractatus adversus Judaeum*, PL 213: 749.

been questioned.[56] The tone is cordial, the arguments rigorous, and the agenda—which includes a discussion of the book of Matthew—unusually broad. In the thirteenth century, Meir of Narbonne recorded what were surely genuine exchanges with influential Christians on sensitive questions,[57] and Moses of Salerno described philosophical discussions of unusual sophistication with Italian churchmen.[58] These were not formal disputations of the sort that were held in Paris and Barcelona; Jacob, Meir, and Moses described what were for the most part informal discussions that took place in the course of everyday life.[59]

Finally, there is fascinating and somewhat problematical evidence from northern Ashkenaz in Joseph Official's *Sefer Yosef HaMeqanne*[60] and the anonymous *Nizzahon Vetus*.[61] On the one hand, the sharpness of some of the exchanges in these works invites skepticism about their authenticity. Once again, however, the atmosphere of constant interaction is compelling, and it is almost inconceivable that these accounts are not essentially authentic. Most of the arguments are introduced by phrases like "a certain *cordelier*" or "a certain apostate asked." Specific priests are identified by their towns, and arguments are placed in specific settings.

Moreover, the aggressiveness of the tone of both works makes it difficult to reject Christian assertions that Jews often initiated debate. It is true that one of the most distinguished students of this literature has urged us to differentiate between "audacity in confronting

---

56   *Milhamot Hashem*, ed. by Judah Rosenthal (Jerusalem, 1963), esp. pp. xxii, 4–5.

57   *Milhemet Mizvah*, Biblioteca Palatina Parma, ms. 2749. A substantial part of the manuscript was transcribed by William Herskowitz. See Herskowitz, "Judaeo-Christian Disputation in Provence as Reflected in Milhemet Mitzva of R. Meir HaMeili" (D.H.L. dissertation, Bernard Revel Graduate School, Yeshiva University, 1974). On Meir's work, see Siegfried Stein, *Jewish-Christian Disputations in Thirteenth-Century Narbonne* (London, 1969). Also see the studies by Robert Chazan in *Harvard Theological Review* 67 (1974): 437–457; *Hebrew Union College Annual* 45 (1974): 287–305; and *Proceedings of the American Academy for Jewish Research* 41–42 (1973–74): 45–67.

58   *Ta'anot*, in Stanislaus Simon, *Mose ben Salomo von Salerno und seine philosophischen Auseinandersetzung mit den Lehren des Christentums* (Breslau, 1931).

59   It is worth noting that in the Barcelona disputation of 1263, Nahmanides commented that "there is not a single priest or child" who does not ask the Jews about Ps. 110. See *Kitvei Ramban*, ed. by C. Chavel (Jerusalem, 1963), vol. 1, p. 317.

60   Joseph Official, *Sefer Yosef ha-Meqanne*, ed. by Judah Rosenthal (Jerusalem, 1970).

61   See *The Jewish-Christian Debate*. The *Nizzahon Vetus* was also edited by Mordechai Breuer; *Sefer Nizzahon Yashan* (Jerusalem, 1978).

Christianity" and the initiation of disputation,[62] and in some instances this is a useful caveat. But the assertiveness of the Ashkenazic polemics must undercut skepticism about the validity of Christian reports concerning Jewish initiatives. Jews who urged their readers to tell Christians that Jacob sat on a cross,[63] who reported (falsely or not) that a Jew urinated on a cross in the presence of a churchman and then produced a clever justification,[64] who clearly suggested to their readers that they raise embarrassing questions with Christians[65]— Jews who said such things and more cannot be assumed a priori to have shrunk from initiating religious discussions with Christian acquaintances. Even if the authors—despite the plain meaning of their exhortations—expected discretion from their Jewish readers, not all readers would have obliged. In short, the existence of such polemics practically guarantees that Jews who took them literally would act on their advice, and, while the worst excesses of these works may never have been translated into practice, it is hard to deny that a number of readers would have been impelled to challenge Christians to defend their faith. There were, of course, cautious Jews,[66] but bold, even reckless, disputants, especially in northern France and Germany, appear to have constituted far more than a lunatic fringe.

Even Jewish familiarity with Christian books often resulted from these discussions since the access of Jews to such works normally came through Christians who owned them. Herman of Cologne was given Latin books, and Jacob ben Reuben said that his Christian friend gave him a work that apparently was—at least in part—a polemical anthology.[67] Although sections of some Jewish polemics appear to have

---

62   Frank Talmage, *Commentary*, June 1975, p. 23.

63   This is a delicate paraphrase of the original. See *Nizzahon Vetus*, in *The Jewish-Christian Debate*, p. 59, and, in the Hebrew section, p. 20.

64   Joseph Official, *Sefer Yosef ha-Meqanne*, p. 14. There is some ambiguity in the story as to whether the Jew was aware that the Christian would see him.

65   See *The Jewish-Christian Debate*, sects. 156, 161, 188, 206, 210, 229.

66   The most striking example of a cautious polemicist is Solomon de' Rossi. See Frank Talmage, "Christianity and the Jewish People," in his *Disputation and Dialogue* (New York, 1975), p. 240. Here Solomon's position is presented as more or less typical. Also see *The Jewish-Christian Debate*, pp. 21–22, and n. 55. In addition, it should be kept in mind that the greatest figures of medieval Jewry, at least in the period with which we are concerned, did not write polemical works. (Nahmanides' coerced involvement in Barcelona is, of course, not germane to the present discussion.)

67   See my discussion in *Speculum* 49 (1974): 36–37, 46–47.

been composed to refute written Christian exegesis,[68] most of the points were debated in lively and frequent discussions.

It is difficult to characterize with precision the current state of scholarship on this question. Some skepticism remains about Jewish initiation of debate.[69] But scholars who have concentrated on the northern Ashkenazic polemics have found it difficult to discount an impression of authenticity, whatever the degree of their reservations on matters of detail,[70] and this impression is consistent with the general picture reflected in other Jewish sources from Northern Europe.[71] Students of Christian polemic in the High Middle Ages have remarked very briefly on the existence of a genuine Jewish challenge,[72] and here, too, the

---

68 When Jewish works, for example, refute Christological interpretations that are found only in Christian commentaries and not in polemics, we have reason to suspect that the Jewish authors got the information from a literary source, and a systematic investigation along these lines may well prove rewarding. For a clear-cut passage of this sort, note the probably interpolated section in the Munich manuscript of the *Nizzahon Vetus* on Psalms, with its explicit references to Christian translations and to the *glossa* and its concentration on exegesis that no sensible Christian polemicist would have emphasized. See *The Jewish-Christian Debate*, sects. 131–141. The extent to which Jews could have read Latin works depends, of course, on their knowledge of Latin, and, although almost all of the authors of polemical works surely read Latin, we cannot be certain about other Jewish intellectuals. For an argument that the Paris disputation of 1240 was conducted in Latin, see Ch. Merchavia, *Ha-Talmud bi-Re'i ha-Nazrut* (Jerusalem, 1970), p. 245. Grabois's assertion that "Rashi attested that he studied Christian biblical exegesis" is much too strong. Of the two authorities that Grabois noted, Y. Baer presented very little evidence for his assertion that "we may assume that Rashi knew Latin and read widely in Christian works," and E. Shereshevsky explicitly conceded that there is no definitive evidence that Rashi read Latin. See Grabois, "The Hebraica veritas," 632; Baer, "Rashi ve-ha-Meziut ha-Historit shel Zemanno," *Tarbiz* 20 (1950): 326; and Shereshevsky, "Rashi and Christian Interpretations," *Jewish Quarterly Review* 61 (1970–71): 76–86.
69 Talmage, *Disputation and Dialogue*, p. 240; and *Commentary*, June 1975, p. 23.
70 Zadoc Kahn, "Le livre de Joseph le Zélateur," *Revue des Etudes Juives* 1 (1880): 222–246; and 3 (1881): 1–38, esp. 34; Ephraim Urbach, "Etudes sur la littérature polémique au moyen âge," *Revue des Etudes Juives* 100 (1935): 50–77, esp. 60–64; and Mordechai Breuer, *Sefer Nizzahon Yashan*, pp. 20–21. Also see my discussion in *The Jewish-Christian Debate*, pp. 20–23.
71 See, especially, Jacob Katz, *Exclusiveness and Tolerance* (New York, 1960), pp. 98–100. Also see Grabois, "The *Hebraica veritas*." For a vigorous argument, based primarily on Jewish exegetical material, for Jewish-Christian intellectual contacts, see Elazar Touitou, "Shitato ha-Parshanit shel ha-Rashbam al Reqa ha-Meziut ha-Historit shel Zemanno," in *Iyyunim be-Sifrut Hazal ba-Miqra U-be-Toldot Yisrael: Muqdash Li-Prof. Ezra Zion Melamed* (Ramat Gan, 1982), ed. by Y. D. Gilat et al., pp. 48–74.
72 Peter Browe assessed the situation particularly well. See Browe, *Die Judenmission im Mittelalter und die Päpste* (Rome, 1942), pp. 113, 60–64. Also see Hunt, "Disputation of

study of nonpolemical Christian sources confirms the impression of significant interaction.[73] My review of polemic—despite the limitations and inevitably skewed emphasis of the genre—underscores that debate was a central phenomenon in the social and intellectual life of medieval Ashkenazic Jewry. While evidence of extensive debate decidedly does not demonstrate that other developments in the cultural history of Ashkenazic Jews were influenced by Jewish-Christian contacts (particularly since the greatest rabbis were not polemicists), the instinctive resistance that many historians still feel when such assertions are made should be diminished.

One more important point. Jewish aggressiveness and even Jewish initiative do not constitute a Jewish mission. There is no indication that Jews engaged in religious discussions with Christians with the realistic expectation of converting them. Both the Talmud and the status of medieval Jewry militated against such a program, and the occasional evidence of Christian converts to Judaism does not begin to demonstrate a concerted Jewish effort to attract proselytes.[74] Jews challenged Christians as an expression of pride—to raise their own morale and to discomfit their opponents. Joseph Official wrote "to reveal the shame" of Jewish apostates.[75] The author of the *Nizzahon vetus* completed his advice to polemicists by promising that "then you will find the Gentile thoroughly embarrassed; indeed, he will be found to have denied

Peter of Cornwall," 147; and Dahan, *Livre des guerres du Seigneur*, pp. 33–34. Blumenkranz's discussion of "la mission juive" deals mainly with an earlier period; *Juifs et Chrétiens*, pp. 159–211. As I noted, Blumenkranz ascribed a significant missionary motivation to Christian polemic in his period. Elsewhere, however, he argued that the extent of what he described as Christian defense literature demonstrates that Jews must have pursued missionary activity; *Juifs et Chrétiens*, p. 209. In light of his position on the missionary objectives of Christian polemic, this last argument is almost puzzling, and the book, which remains of the first importance, tends to overstate the missionary intentions on both sides.

[73] See Grabois, "The *Hebraica veritas*." Polemical sources are dealt with only in the two concluding paragraphs, pp. 633–634, and on p. 624.

[74] Wolfgang Giese's vehement argument for "intensive Jewish propaganda and missionary activity" is based solely on the existence of Christian converts to Judaism and the efforts made in church councils to limit contacts between Jews and Christians because of the Jews' corrupting influence. See his "In Iudaismum lapsus est: Jüdische Proselytenmacherei im frühen und hohen Mittelalter (600–1300)," *Historisches Jahrbuch*, 88 (1968): 407–18. Also see Baron's remark that "medieval Jews had long given up any missionary aspirations"; *A Social and Religious History*, p. 23.

[75] Joseph Official, *Sefer Yosef ha-Meqanne*, p. 15. See Hosea 2:2.

[Christianity's] central dogmas, while all Israel 'will speak lovely words' (Gen. 49:21)."[76] A chastened Gentile with an enhanced respect for Jews and Judaism—but a Gentile nonetheless.

The absence of a Christian missionary ideology and the presence of frequent Jewish-Christian confrontations establish the likelihood that eleventh- and twelfth-century Christians wrote polemics not out of missionary objectives but largely in response to requests generated by a genuine Jewish challenge. There is, however, a more profound relationship between the disinterest of the upper clergy before the thirteenth century in converting Jews and the existence of lively, regular, often friendly debates between Jews and Christians, which were sometimes begun by the Jewish participant. The tone of these informal contacts and the Jewish willingness to initiate them were possible precisely because the church was not yet deadly serious about the aim of conversion. For Jews, the enjoyment was drained out of these contests in the face of a concerted, formalized Christian mission, and it became foolhardy and dangerous to seek confrontation. During the course of the thirteenth century, the gradual transformation in the Christian position was not immediately reflected in Jewish behavior, and, even later, the spirit never completely departed from Jewish polemicists. Nevertheless, by the late Middle Ages the tone is profoundly different; one begins to see the defensiveness, nervousness, and demoralization of a worried community. Jewish polemic was never the same again.[77]

[76] *The Jewish-Christian Debate*, p. 169, and, in the Hebrew section, p. 108.

[77] The changes in Jewish polemic do not, of course, result solely from increased Christian proselytizing and persecution. Most late medieval Jewish polemic comes from Spanish Jewry rather than from areas where Jewish aggressiveness is most clearly attested in the earlier period. For the decline in polemic and the growing isolationism in the Ashkenazic orbit in the fifteenth, sixteenth, and seventeenth centuries, see Katz, *Exclusiveness and Tolerance*, chaps. 11, 12. On Spain, see the striking personal testimony of an obscure participant in the Tortosa disputation; Frank Talmage, "Trauma at Tortosa: The Testimony of Abraham Rimoch," *Medieval Studies* 47 (1985): 397. I am grateful to Moshe Idel for bringing this last reference to my attention.

THE BARCELONA DISPUTATION
Review Essay

From: *AJS Review: The Journal of the Association for Jewish Studies* 20 (1995): 379–388.

Reviewed work: Robert Chazan. *Barcelona and Beyond: The Disputation of 1263 and Its Aftermath.* Berkeley: University of California Press, 1992, x, 257 pp.

In many respects, Robert Chazan's new book on the disputation of 1263 between Nahmanides and Friar Paul Christian is an excellent and very important contribution to the century-old historiographical debate about one of the most famous events in medieval Jewish history. The Barcelona disputation, where Friar Paul unveiled a relatively new approach appealing to talmudic sources as evidence for the truth of Christianity, was manifestly a moment of high drama, so significant and so thoroughly investigated that we might be pardoned a certain skepticism about the ability of any scholar to say something new about it. To a significant degree, Chazan has overcome this obstacle by providing an overview of the event that forces us to look at the large picture fortified with a healthy infusion of common sense. At the same time, part of the analysis seems to me to stand in tension with itself, and I am inclined to utilize some of the evidence that Chazan presents so lucidly to reach a conclusion different from his.

The book begins with a vigorous and persuasive argument against the widespread, natural inclination to seek clear winners and losers through a close analysis of the partisan records of such disputations. The apt analogy to presidential debates drives home the point that people who see the same event will often perceive the results quite differently depending upon their ideological orientation (p. 14).[1] Even more important, Chazan

---

[1] As Chazan notes (p. 7), the basic observation was made by Isidore Loeb in his classic article, "La Controverse de 1263 à Barcelone entre Paulus Christiani et Moise ben Nahman," *Revue des Études Juives* 15 (1887): 2.

shows how most of the significant discrepancies between the Latin and Hebrew versions of the disputation can be accounted for as different perceptions of the same discussion rather than as purposeful distortions or outright lies. While the argument here is not entirely new, Chazan's analysis is more systematic than that of his predecessors; he evinces greater sympathy for the Latin account than Isidore Loeb or Yitzhak Baer while at the same time reinforcing Loeb's argument that this account rarely makes factual assertions that flatly contradict Nahmanides' narrative. In this crucial respect, the book makes a major contribution.

Despite his effort to understand both versions as essentially honest, though highly tendentious works, Chazan cannot avoid a confrontation with the issue of purposeful distortion or lying, and here he evinces considerable discomfort. On the one hand, he writes that "the royal seal [on the Latin document], . . . Nahmanides' general stature, . . . and above all else, the public nature of the event . . . make . . . out-and-out lying unthinkable" (p. 14). On the following page, however, he affirms that the matter is not so simple. The Latin version's depiction of Nahmanides' confusion and the latter's description of his confident attacks on Christianity are "embellishment and exaggeration" of a sort that "do not seem to me to warrant the accusation of lying. If readers prefer that label to embellishment and exaggeration, so be it."

The problem here is not semantic alone. It goes to the heart of Chazan's vision of the disputation. He explicitly avoids the term "lie," partly because of the analytical difficulties that it would cause him, and partly, I suspect, because he is such a quintessential gentleman. But the brute fact is that Chazan maintains unequivocally that Nahmanides lied about a truly fundamental aspect of the proceedings. At several important moments in the Hebrew account, Nahmanides informs us that he succeeded in presenting certain standard Jewish criticisms of Christian belief, sometimes in sharp language. Chazan regards this as virtually impossible for two reasons that we would do well to examine.

The first of these is the commonsense observation, already noted to some degree by Baer, that it is highly implausible that Nahmanides could have spoken in a public forum about the utter irrationality of the incarnation, the militarism of the Spanish Christian state, the Messiah's future destruction of Rome, or the curses to befall Christians. Nahmanides reports—and a Christian document confirms—that he was granted freedom of speech, but he also reports that he gave assurances of his "good sense to speak properly." No grant of free speech could have extended this far (pp. 48–49, 94–97, 138).

The second reason goes to one of Chazan's most important insights. He argues quite correctly that the use of the Talmud to demonstrate the truth of Christianity provided a structure to the debate between Jews and Christians in which the Christian side could not lose. In an exchange about an allegedly Christological verse in the Bible, a Jew might be able to reverse the argument by showing that the revealed text in fact contradicts Christianity; if, however, the text is talmudic, it has no authority for Christians, so that the Jew can do nothing more than neutralize the citation by showing that it does not support Christian doctrine. "To have developed such a potent new technique and then let it be readily contravened by the Jewish protagonist further strains credulity" (p. 50, and cf. p. 138). Indeed, adds Chazan, evidence from the later Tortosa disputation clearly demonstrates that Christians applying Friar Paul's approach prevented Jews from raising issues that could disturb this one-sided structure (pp. 53–54). Chazan's structural insight, then, impels him to affirm the very strong position that even had Nahmanides spoken with consummate politeness and extreme diffidence, he could not have presented a substantial percentage of the arguments that he reports.

Neither of these points can be dismissed easily. Nonetheless, the second strikes me as a case of anachronistically imposing the Tortosa model on Barcelona, and both must confront a monumental problem that Chazan touches lightly but fails to give its due.

As Chazan indicates, indeed emphasizes, the disputation at Barcelona was a pioneering experiment. I have argued elsewhere that many Jewish-Christian debates of an informal sort had taken place over the generations in an atmosphere of relatively free repartee.[2] It should not be taken for granted that thirteenth-century friars could snap their fingers and change the ground rules abruptly and with total, immediate success to one of ironclad control over the Jewish participant. The ultimate authority during the debate was not the clerics who had constructed the new approach, but the king of Aragon. The king was obviously on the Christian side; nonetheless he may have enjoyed the spectacle of

---

[2]   D. Berger, "Mission to the Jews and Jewish-Christian Contacts in the Polemical Literature of the High Middle Ages," *American Historical Review* 91 (1986): 576–591. To be sure, the strongest evidence comes from Northern Europe, but there is enough from the South to sustain the point.

intellectual jousting, which would have been ruined by the ruthlessly consistent suppression of every new point that Nahmanides wanted to raise. Not only is this scenario not unreasonable; it is, I think, more plausible than Chazan's alternative. Among many other things, Tortosa was a result of lessons learned at Barcelona.

There is, of course, no doubt that Nahmanides worked under severe restraints, and he informs us more than once of initiatives that were thwarted by uneven ground rules. It is self-evident, however, that he would have attempted to broaden the focus of the debate, and there is little reason to believe that at this point in history every such foray was doomed to abject failure. It seems to me that the picture he presents of occasional tolerance and occasional repression is more than credible; it is precisely what we should expect at this transitional point in the medieval Jewish-Christian relationship.

We are left with the sharp formulations and moderately lengthy excursuses that Nahmanides reports, and there is no question that these must give us pause. At the same time, we must keep in mind that a remark can look much sharper on paper than in an oral exchange, where its impact can be mitigated by a disarming smile, a shrug, a softness in tone, particularly if the parties have a cordial relationship, for which there is some external evidence in the case of Nahmanides and the king. More important, our instinctive skepticism must be set against a powerful argument for at least the approximate accuracy of these assertions. Nahmanides probably wrote his account after the dissemination of the Latin summary. He certainly knew that it would be subjected to microscopic scrutiny in an attempt to discredit it. He also knew that James I would surely be informed of any false assertions that audacious and arguably disrespectful statements had been articulated in the royal presence and in two of the crucial instances (about militarism and the incarnation) addressed directly to him. We are, in short, being told that it is hard to imagine that Nahmanides could have said these things in the heat of a debate because he had promised to speak properly and because he knew he would be stopped, but it is perfectly imaginable that he would have lied about saying them in a carefully composed document that would surely be shown to the king.

The core of this point was made already by Loeb. "The friars," he wrote, "could have said and written whatever they wanted with impunity. Nahmanides would have exposed himself to grave dangers had he inserted inexactitudes or lies into his account. He would not have dared to do it."[3] In Baer's critique of the disputation, he ignored this point entirely.[4] Chazan does raise the argument and replies as follows: "The only answer I can supply is that Nahmanides was deeply convinced of the need for such a work and retained some confidence in the capacity of Jewish leverage to protect him, as it eventually did" (p. 98). He goes on to say that the silence of those who heard Nahmanides' alleged remarks would be more problematic than this difficulty (p. 98, and cf. p. 138). By "silence" he presumably means failure to cut off such statements with ruthless efficiency, since the absence of a recorded objection at a particular point in Nahmanides' narrative does not necessarily mean that there was none. Moreover, in a passage that Chazan does his best to explain away at a different point in his analysis (pp. 75–77), Nahmanides informs us that after a day which ended with one of his aggressive comments, he began the next morning's proceedings by asking that the debate be ended because Jews were fearful and Christians, including one whom he identifies by name, had told him that it was inappropriate for him to speak against their faith in their presence.[5]

Chazan is clearly uncomfortable with his reply, and the force of the question is even more powerful than he indicates. A royal document of 1265 reveals that Nahmanides came under attack for "vituperation" against the Catholic faith in what he said at the disputation as well as in what he wrote. This assertion in itself creates intractable problems for Chazan's position, despite his plausible conclusion in light of a papal letter that it was the written work "that set in motion the cycle of prosecution" (p. 98). What is particularly telling is that Nahmanides defended himself

---

3   Loeb, "La Controverse," p. 7.
4   Y. Baer, "Le-Bikkoret ha-Vikkuhim shel R. Yehiel mi-Paris ve-R. Mosheh ben Nahman," *Tarbiz* 2 (1930–31): 172–187.
5   *Kitvei Ramban*, ed. by C. D. Chavel (Jerusalem, 1963), p. 312. Elsewhere (p. 97), Chazan argues that the failure of the Latin account to take Nahmanides to task for his "blasphemies" would be "unthinkable" if he had really spoken as he says. I do not find this silence troubling. The Latin version is very brief and interested primarily in highlighting Nahmanides' ineffectiveness; emphasizing his aggressiveness would have been counterproductive. Moreover, the fact that the king had allowed these statements would have made the charge of blasphemy extremely difficult to level from a political standpoint. It was the publication of the book, which the king had never permitted, that made the attack on Nahmanides politically feasible. It should also be kept in mind that for all his sharp comments, Nahmanides never claims to have said a negative word about Jesus.

by pointing to the freedom of speech granted him by the king at the disputation, a defense that is clearly intended to apply to the written work as well. If we accept the position that the "vituperative" statements had never been made orally, this defense establishes a standard for chutzpah that may even eclipse that of the proverbial parricide who asked the judge for clemency as an orphan. "After all," said Nahmanides to the king, "you granted me freedom of expression at the disputation. Since I ascribed my vituperative statements in the written work to the oral disputation, the grant of free speech applies to them. The fact that this ascription happens to be false is entirely irrelevant."

And even this is not the end of it. No one has ever suggested that the judge accepted the young murderer's argument. In our case, James I resisted the demands of the Church for draconian punishment and proposed milder measures than the ecclesiastical authorities were willing to accept. His reason? "We are certain that the said permission was given to him at that time by us and by Friar R[aymund] of Penyafort" ("cum nobis certum sit, dictam licentiam a nobis et fratre R. de Pennaforti sibi tunc temporis fore datam").[6] Even if we recognize the role of larger policy concerns in the king's position, this scenario does more than strain credulity; it skirts the edges of the inconceivable.[7]

There is some uncertainty as to whether or not the book mentioned in this document, a book which was presented to the bishop of Gerona and allegedly written at his request, is the same as our Hebrew narrative. Chazan's position appears to be that the book given to the bishop could not have been the Hebrew disputation but that it was that disputation which was under attack. I do not understand how this position can be reconciled with the royal document, which asserts with absolute clarity that the book containing the alleged vituperation was given to the bishop; at the same time, it is easy to understand the dilemma which forced Chazan into this uncomfortable stance. On his assumption that Nahmanides could have said virtually nothing offensive at the disputation,

6   Heinrich Denifle, "Quellen zur Disputation Pablos Christiani mit Mose Nachmani zu Barcelona 1263," *Historisches Jahrbuch des Görres-Gesellschaft* 8 (1887): 239.

7   Even Martin Cohen's theory of collusion between Nahmanides and the king would not provide an adequate explanation. For this conspiracy theory, which Chazan rightly rejects, see Cohen's "Reflections on the Text and Context of the Disputation of Barcelona," *Hebrew Union College Annual* 35 (1964): 157–192. (Cohen's close reading of the Hebrew version as a sustained account of Nahmanides' public humiliation at Barcelona is remarkable, if unsettling, testimony to the awesome powers of human ingenuity.)

the following conundrums arise: If the book represented the disputation more or less faithfully, it would have been almost impossible to label it vituperative with any credibility. If the Hebrew narrative existed in 1265 alongside such a faithful report, it is bizarre indeed that the latter rather than the former should have been prosecuted. If the Hebrew narrative did not exist at that time, how can we imagine that after a terrifying brush with severe punishment for writing an accurate account, Nahmanides would proceed to write a much different, far more aggressive, distorted narrative? If, on the other hand, this book was anything like the Hebrew work in our possession, Chazan cannot imagine that Nahmanides would have given it to the bishop; moreover, the claim that the book was covered by the grant of free speech would be quite incomprehensible.

I am inclined to regard this book as very close to the Hebrew disputation though probably not quite identical with it.[8] What remains crystal clear is that Nahmanides wrote a book with arguably vituperative statements against Christianity, that he defended it on the grounds that these statements had been made at the disputation, where he had been granted freedom of expression, and that James I endorsed this defense.

In general, Nahmanides' account has been confirmed by Christian documentation to a degree that we would hardly have had the right to expect. The Latin version, complete with its royal seal, says that Nahmanides ended the disputation by slipping out of town in the king's absence, while the Hebrew text speaks of a friendly leave-taking at which the king gave the rabbi three hundred *dinarim*, a payment which is mentioned in a later royal document. Records that predate the disputation imply the existence of the sort of positive relationship between the royal court and the rabbi of Gerona which emerges from Nahmanides' account. Perhaps most significant of all is the confirmation of the grant of free speech. While reading Chazan's analysis of the iron control exercised by the Christian side and particularly his argument about the implausibility of Nahmanides' assertion that he played some role in formulating the agenda, I began to imagine the scholarly reaction to the rabbi's claim to a grant of free expression had we not possessed the confirming evidence.

---

8   This is more or less Baer's formulation in *Toledot ha-Yehudim bi-Sefarad ha-Nozerit* (Tel Aviv, 1959), p. 93. I assume, for example, that the very sharp introductory paragraph of our Hebrew text, which does not represent anything that Nahmanides said at the disputation, was omitted from the copy prepared for the bishop of Gerona.

Nahmanides, we would have been told, needed to establish a framework in which his blatantly problematic assertions that he criticized Christian beliefs so vigorously and publicly would appear credible. He consequently constructed an exchange in which he extracted a promise that he would be allowed to speak freely. Given the new technique introduced by Friar Paul and his ecclesiastical retainers and surely enforced by their royal sponsor, it is unthinkable that such a dangerous promise could actually have been made. Besides, what leverage did Nahmanides have to elicit such a guarantee? Could he have threatened to go home if the king did not acquiesce? Despite its cleverness, then, this is a transparent ploy which presents one of Nahmanides' least credible claims.

Yet the claim is indisputably true.

None of this means that Nahmanides' oral formulations might not have been somewhat milder than his written version (or even that the book referred to in the royal document might not have been a bit milder than our Hebrew text); it means only that he could not have written something at any stage that he could not have defended as a more or less accurate depiction of what he had said. Needless to say, I am not arguing that the Hebrew account is anything resembling a stenographic record. On the contrary, Chazan is surely correct in his observation that "even a cursory look at the text indicates that it cannot be viewed as a thorough account of the confrontation. The narrative is far too short for that; the reportage on the Christian thrusts is far too restricted; the unfolding of events is far too neat. The Nahmanidean narrative is clearly a carefully crafted record aimed at creating a certain set of impressions in the minds of its readers" (pp. 102–103). It is indeed highly unlikely that the unmediated impression made by the disputation itself even upon Jews was the smashing, devastating victory that the reader of the Hebrew account sees, but Nahmanides' work creates its own impression not by the invention of arguments but by emphasis, allocation of space, rhetorical flourishes, partisan interpretation, and the inevitable clarification, improvement, and elaboration that come with the written formulation of an oral exchange by a highly interested participant.

Chazan devotes an entire chapter to the narrative art of Nahmanides' account. I do not believe that his discussion of the work's "verisimilitude" grants sufficient recognition to the role that verity can play in producing verisimilitude, and where Chazan sees invention I see skillful use of emphasis, characterization, and narration. But I see this largely thanks to

Chazan, and I feel very uncomfortable in leveling even a minor criticism against this marvelous chapter. It is brimming with literary sensitivity, and it enables us to understand the impact that this little work has made upon its readers throughout the generations. One of my clearest teenage memories is reading the *Vikkuaḥ ha-Ramban* for the first time, and I am grateful to Chazan for giving me a better understanding of why I reacted as I did.

There is much more to be said about the issues raised in this book, but this is not the forum to discuss them in detail. Chazan devotes chapters to the authority of rabbinic aggadah, to Nahmanides' brief work on Isaiah 53, and to his more important book on the redemption, *Sefer ha-Ge'ullah*. On the first issue, a careful study of Nahmanides' treatment of aggadot throughout his oeuvre remains a desideratum.[9] On *Sefer ha-Ge'ullah*, Chazan makes a number of valuable observations; still, I would not fully endorse the assertion that "the same Nahmanides who was so conservative and secretive with respect to kabbalistic teachings was explosively original and open with respect to equally dangerous messianic speculations" (p. 186). *Sefer ha-Ge'ullah* is indeed an innovative, important work, but it presents a messianic date that is safely in the future and reflects the author's conservatism in other ways as well. I think that Chazan is quite correct in emphasizing Nahmanides' conviction that the times demanded such a work, and this conviction itself tells us something important about the insecurities of Spanish Jews at the time of Nahmanides' impressive achievement at Barcelona.

And it was an impressive achievement. Near the beginning of his study, Chazan points to the danger of Jewish or Christian partisanship that can affect the study of the disputation and pledges his best efforts to avoid it. I have already confessed to a teenage crush on Nahmanides' narrative, and I write this review with full awareness that I could stand accused of both bias and credulousness. I will confess further that my regard for Nahmanides' moral stature prevents me from lightly dismissing his summary statement, which the structure of his work did not force him to make: "This is the substance of all the debates. In my opinion,

---

9   Bernard Septimus's very brief discussion, to which Chazan makes frequent reference, is still the best treatment of this question; see his "Open Rebuke and Concealed Love': Nahmanides and the Andalusian Tradition," in *Rabbi Moses Nahmanides (Ramban): Explorations in His Religious and Literary Virtuosity*, ed. by Isadore Twersky (Cambridge, Mass., 1983), pp. 20–22.

I have changed nothing in them."[10] Chazan himself, as we have seen, does take account of "Nahmanides' stature" in a related context, and this is no less a legitimate historical consideration than the probabilities of royal or ecclesiastical displeasure at a particular argument. The quest for objectivity may sometimes compel us to brave the appearance of bias, and the critical search for truth can occasionally drive us into the arms of the credulous.

This is an admirable study—careful, learned, sensitive, and insightful. Much of it I can unreservedly endorse. Even where I disagree with a fundamental part of the thesis, one of Chazan's arguments for the position I reject turns out to be a significant contribution to our understanding of the structural impact of Friar Paul's use of the Talmud. Nahmanides' performance in Barcelona was far more forceful, wide-ranging, and effective than this book is prepared to acknowledge, and yet Chazan has provided us the tools for a more sophisticated appreciation of that very achievement.

---

[10] *Kitvei Ramban*, p. 319. A fair reading of this assertion is, I think, quite consistent with the sorts of changes that I believe Nahmanides did make.

CHRISTIAN HERESY AND JEWISH POLEMIC
IN THE TWELFTH AND THIRTEENTH CENTURIES

From: *Harvard Theological Review* 68 (1975): 287–303.

The suggestion that there was meaningful contact between Christian heretics and Jews during the Middle Ages is entirely plausible, quite significant, and generally unproved.[1] That the existence of heresy had some impact upon the status of medieval Jews is, of course, beyond question. Inquisitorial proceedings aimed at heretics affected not only crypto-Jews (whether real or alleged) but members of the established Jewish community as well. Jews were accused of harboring heretics, encouraging them, and even of leading orthodox Christians into heresy. On several important occasions, procedures usually directed against heretical works were turned against the Talmud, the works of Maimonides, and certain sections of the Jewish liturgy. By the end of the middle ages, Jews were very well aware of the Church's lack of affection for heretics.[2]

---

[1]   L. I. Newman's *Jewish Influence on Christian Reform Movements* (New York: Columbia University Press, 1925) is an important study, but it does not succeed in establishing the thesis implied by the title. See the discussion by F. Talmage, "An Hebrew Polemical Treatise," *HTR* 60 (1967): 335–337. See also G. Scholem, *Ursprung und Anfänge der Kabbala* (Berlin, 1962), pp. 206–210. Scholem has noted one clear reference by a Jewish polemicist to Christian "heretics who believe in two gods, one good and one evil" (Meir of Narbonne's *Milhemet Mizvah* [1245], cited in Scholem's "Te'udah Hadashah le-Toledot Reshit ha-Qabbalah," *Sefer Bialik* [Tel Aviv, 1934], p. 152). On this reference, see note 36 below. On the possible relationship between Provencal Kabbalah and Catharism, see also Sh. Shahar, "Ha-Qattarim ve-Reshit ha-Qabbalah be-Languedoc," *Tarbiz* 40 (1971): 483–509.

[2]   For a discussion of the impact of inquisitorial procedures on the Jews in a fairly early period, see Y. Yerushalmi, "The Inquisition and the Jews of France in the Time of Bernard Gui," *HTR* 63 (1970): 317–377. The investigation and burning of the Talmud in the thirteenth

Similarly, heretics were incessantly reminded of the Church's attitude toward the Jews. It was a long-standing practice for Christians to label schismatic groups "Jews" even when the relationship of the particular group to Judaism was tenuous or imaginary. This was the case during several early controversies in the Byzantine Empire,[3] and similar tendencies can be documented in Western Europe throughout the middle ages. Peter Damian, for example, reserved his most bitter anti-Jewish invective for occasions when he was attacking not Jews, but Christian heretics; these heretics, he asserted, are even worse than "the Jewish perfidy itself."[4] St. Bernard, who defended Jewish lives with vigor and courage during the second crusade, nonetheless used Jews as a pejorative standard of comparison for various forms of heresy and sin.[5]

The established Church, then, used each group to attack the other; heretics were Jews, while Jews were guilty of encouraging heresy and even of producing heretical works. But did it ever occur to Jews or heretics to use similar tactics? Did Jews ever cite heresy as a way of attacking the Church, and did heretics ever use Judaism to accomplish the same end? Since Jews and heretics were made acutely aware of one another by the

century has been discussed most recently by Ch. Merchavia, *Ha-Talmud bi-Re'i ha-Nazrut* (Jerusalem, 1970), pp. 227–248. On the burning of the works of Maimonides in the 1230s, see A. Schochet, "Berurim be-Parshat ha-Pulmus ha-Rishon al Sifrei ha-Rambam," *Zion* 36 (1971): 27–60. It is especially noteworthy that a Hebrew manuscript alleges that a Christian missionary in 1272–73 threatened to demonstrate that the Jews have no faith and that, like the Bougres, they deserve to be burned; see A. Neubauer, "Literary Gleanings, IX," *JQR*, o.s., 5 (1893): 714. R. Chazan's suggestion that one of the earliest large-scale persecutions of Jews in the high middle ages was related to the beginnings of heresy in the West is interesting although there is no concrete documentation to bear it out; see his "1007–1012: Initial Crisis for Northern European Jewry," *Proceedings of The American Academy for Jewish Research* 38–39 (1970–71): 101–117. For the charge of harboring heretics as well as a more general bibliographical discussion, see S. Baron, *A Social and Religious History of the Jews* (2d ed.; New York, London, and Philadelphia, 1965), pp. 9, 59, 267–268.

3 See J. Parkes, *The Conflict of the Church and the Synagogue* (London, 1934; reprinted New York, 1969) 300–303.

4 See his *Liber Qui Dicitur Gratissimus*, ch. 37, PL 145: 153, and his *De Sacramentis per Improbos Administratis*, PL 145: 529, discussed in my "St. Peter Damian: His Attitude toward the Jews and the Old Testament," *Yavneh Review* 4 (1965): 86–87, 89–90.

5 See my study, "The Attitude of St. Bernard of Clairvaux toward the Jews," *Proceedings of the American Academy for Jewish Research* 40 (1972): 104–105. See also Cassiodorus, PL 70: 74D ("Judaei vel Donatistae"); Hadrian I, PL 98: 1255–1256; Humbert, PL 143: 1093C. Cf. B. Blumenkranz, *Juifs et Chrétiens dans le Monde Occidental 430–1096* (Paris, 1960), pp. xvi–xvii, and note 11 there, and see Baron, *History*, pp. 58–60.

Church itself, such possibilities must at least be considered. Moreover, if each group was familiar with the doctrines of the other, there may be examples of direct attacks against heretical views by Jews or against Jewish views by heretics without reference to the Orthodox Church. Since very little heretical polemic survives, the place to look for possible verification of these suggestions is the Jewish polemic of the high middle ages. An examination of this literature yields some speculative but intriguing conclusions.

Several years ago, Frank Talmage argued that a short Hebrew polemic attributed to Rabbi David Kimhi (d. 1235) contains three arguments, "apparently unique in Hebrew polemical literature," directed against Cathar or Bogomil doctrines.[6] This position, though plausible and stimulating, cannot, in my view, withstand careful scrutiny; nevertheless, it is possible that one of the heretical beliefs to which Prof. Talmage alludes is found in another, even less likely, Jewish polemic.

The first passage in the so-called *Vikkuah le-ha-Radaq* which is alleged to be directed against Christian heresy reads as follows:

> I, the insignificant one, have seen fit to write briefly concerning some of the notions of those who err in saying that Mary conceived Jesus without normal intercourse. They say too that the annunciating angel, Gabriel, said to her, "Ave Maria, gratia plena, Dominus tecum, etc." At that moment the holy spirit of the Lord entered through her ear so that she conceived. Reply to them that every intelligent person knows that the young of all creatures, whether man, animal, fowl or beast, leaves the mother's body from the place where the semen entered. Therefore, Jesus should have left through the ear through which the Holy Spirit entered her womb. Yet he did not leave from there but from the place where all others [leave].[7]

Prof. Talmage notes that "the concept (of conception through the ear) was employed in orthodox Christianity in the patristic period,"[8] but he adds that "the absolute dualists among the heretics carried this further to prove the noncorporeal nature of Jesus himself." These dualists, however, believed in exit through the ear as well, and the author of the *Vikkuah*

---

6   "An Hebrew Polemical Treatise, Anti-Cathar and Anti-Orthodox," *HTR* 60 (1967): 323–348. The article contains a translation of the treatise; the Hebrew text appears in *Milhemet Hovah* (Constantinople, 1710), pp. 13a–18b and in Talmage's *Sefer ha-Berit u-Vikkuhei Radaq im ha-Nazrut* (Jerusalem, 1974). In his introduction to the Hebrew text (15–16), Talmage reiterates the central thesis of the article.

7   Talmage's translation, 341.

8   He refers to C. Schmidt, *Histoire et Doctrine des Cathares ou Albigeois* 2. 41f.

le-ha-Radaq obviously did not know of that doctrine; hence, says Prof. Talmage, he must have been arguing against "mitigated dualists."[9]

First of all, it is difficult to see what the doctrine of aural entry as opposed to aural exit has to do with dualism in any form. It was not necessary to be a Docetist to believe that an incorporeal spirit had entered Mary; only the doctrine of aural exit supported the Docetist position. Without aural exit, aural entry seems logically irrelevant to any heretical position.

Moreover, there is no question that the doctrine of conception through the ear was widespread among orthodox Christians not only in the patristic period but in the later Middle Ages as well. Many paintings of the annunciation appear to reflect this belief rather clearly.[10] More important, there are unambiguous literary references to such a doctrine. At least seven medieval hymns begin with the lines

> Rejoice, O virgin, mother of Christ,
> Who conceived through the ear
> With Gabriel as messenger
> (Gaude, virgo, mater Christi
> Quae per aurem concepisti
> Gabriele nuntio).[11]

It has been argued, in fact, that no less an authority than St. Bernard refers to this belief,[12] and even if symbolic interpretations can be read into some of these remarks, it is clearly inadmissible to assume that the Christian masses or the ordinary priest who heard such statements would do anything other than take them literally.[13] Consequently,

---

9   "An Hebrew Polemical Treatise," p. 327.
10   See M. Meiss, "Light as Form and Symbol in Some Fifteenth Century Paintings," *The Art Bulletin* 27 (1945): 175–181. Cf. also the brief reference in D. M. Robb, "The Iconography of the Annunciation in the Fourteenth and Fifteenth Centuries," *The Art Bulletin* 18 (1936): 523.
11   Quoted in Y. Hirn, *The Sacred Shrine* (London, 1912), p. 297, and in E. Jones, "The Madonna's Conception Through the Ear," *Essays in Applied Psychoanalysis* (London, 1923; reprinted New York, 1964) 2. 269.
12   *PL* 183: 327, cited in Hirn, p. 298.
13   Cf. Hirn, p. 298. In the fifteenth century, a *converso* monk later suspected of Judaizing asked about the channel through which Jesus was conceived, and one answer suggested to him (apparently by an orthodox colleague) was "per la oreja;" see A. A. Sicroff, "Clandestine Judaism in the Hieronymite Monastery of Nuestra Senore de Guadalupe," *Studies in Honor of M. J. Benardete*, ed. by I. Langnas and B. Sholod (New York, 1965), pp. 105–106.

there is no reason to believe that the reference to aural conception in the *Vikkuah le-ha-Radaq* reflects contact with Cathars or any other Christian heretics.

However, we are not yet finished with this rather interesting doctrine. Joseph Official, a Jewish polemicist from northern France writing in the third quarter of the thirteenth century, makes the following brief comment with respect to the Christian assertion that the speaker in Psalm 22 is Jesus:

> "In thee our fathers put their trust; they trusted, and thou didst rescue them" (Psalm 22:5). Now, did he have fathers? After all, they maintain that he entered her through the center of the head.[14]

Here again, pictorial representations of the annunciation appear to reflect such a view,[15] and references to a belief of this sort in a northern French polemic is interesting in itself. But another Jewish polemic goes even further.

The *Nizzahon Vetus* (or *Sefer Nizzahon Yashan*) was written by a German Jew in the late thirteenth or very early fourteenth century. It is basically an anthology of Ashkenazic polemic against Christianity, and it therefore contains a great deal of French material dating from a somewhat earlier period.[16] In discussing the same Psalm 22, the author writes:

> "I was cast upon thee from the womb; thou art my God from my mother's stomach" (Psalm 22:11); but not in the womb or in the stomach. Moreover, if this were said about the hanged one, the problem would be their assertion

14   *Sefer Yosef ha-Meqanne*, ed. by J. Rosenthal (Jerusalem, 1970), p. 104. This section of Joseph's work had never been published before Rosenthal's edition and was therefore unavailable to Talmage. The belief that Jesus was conceived "through the brain" was also reported by Yom Tov Lipmann Mühlhausen in his *Sefer [ha-]Nizzahon* (written at the very beginning of the fifteenth century; Amsterdam, 1709) section 8, p. 15a. He goes on to argue that Jesus should have emerged through the same passageway, and yet no one has ever maintained that the site of his birth was different from that of other infants.

15   See Jacob Arlow, "The Madonna's Conception through the Eyes," *The Psychoanalytic Study of Society* 3 (1965): 13–25, esp. 20 (pointed out by my colleague at Brooklyn College, Prof. Elizabeth Brown).

16   The work was published with a Latin translation by J. Wagenseil, *Tela Ignea Satanae* (Altdorf, 1681) 2. 1–260. On the date, see E. Urbach, "Études sur la littérature polémique au moyen age," *Revue des Études Juives* 100 (1935): 60, 76–77, and Rosenthal's introduction to *Sefer Yosef ha-Meqanne*, p. 15. See also the introduction to my forthcoming critical edition, translation and commentary.

that he was born out of the forehead of a harlot, for the verse says that he was born out of a woman like all children; thus, your books lie when they say that the spirit entered Mary.[17]

This unusual passage contains two separate refutations of the contention that Jesus is the speaker in this Psalm. First, the verse indicates that the speaker recognized God only after he was born ("*from* my mother's stomach" but not in it); if he were divine from the moment of conception, he would have recognized God even in the womb.[18] Secondly, Christians believe that Jesus was born through the forehead, while the verse says that the speaker was born from the stomach.

Here we finally find a Jewish polemicist referring to an unusual location for Jesus' exit at birth. Several arguments can be posed to mitigate the significance of this statement. The Hebrew text is a little bit awkward, and it is not impossible that the key passage ("Moreover—children") is a gloss; nevertheless, even if this is true (and there is no evidence that it is), it would mean that the glossator was aware of such a doctrine. It could also be argued that the author read the above-quoted remark by Joseph Official and merely assumed that Christians would place the birth at the same site as the entry. This, however, seems improbable, since there are several passages in the *Nizzahon Vetus* which reflect awareness of the orthodox view of Jesus' birth.[19] It is one thing to attack a known alternate view; it is something else entirely to invent a view which contradicts the only Christian belief you have ever heard and then proceed to refute it. The passage in Joseph Official's work may well have reminded the author of an unorthodox view of Jesus' birth, but it is quite unlikely that he would have simply made it up.

---

17   *Tela Ignea Satanae*, p. 167.
18   This argument is more elaborate and explicit with respect to the Christian identification of Cyrus with Jesus in Isaiah 45. See *Tela*, p. 102: "It is written, 'That you may know that I, the Lord, who call you by your name, am the God of Israel' (Isaiah 45:3). Thus, you say that this Cyrus whom you identify with Jesus did not know God until the point when all these things were done to him. In light of this, how can you say that the spirit of God entered Mary and took on flesh? If that were true, he certainly should have known God even before his birth."
19   Cf. *Tela*, pp. 7, 210. See p. 201, where the author is apparently interested in proving from Christian sources that Jesus was born from the stomach; this too may be directed against the heretical view. His evidence consists of a quotation which is apparently an abridged and distorted version of Luke 2:5–11.

Exit through the forehead is, of course, not the same as exit through the ear, and I am unaware of any heretical view which maintained the former position. It is therefore highly probable that the passage in the *Nizzahon Vetus* reflects a distorted awareness of the heretical doctrine of aural exit. The distortion may be a result of Joseph Official's reference to entry through the forehead, or it may result from an uncontrollable urge to use the insulting Biblical phrase "the forehead of a harlot" (Jeremiah 3:3) with respect to Mary; it is not even impossible that some heretics could have distorted the doctrine themselves (influenced, perhaps, by the myth of Athena's birth) and that the *Nizzahon Vetus*, which is generally quite reliable in its descriptions of Christian beliefs and ceremonies, may be reporting such a heretical view accurately.

In any case, this passage indicates Jewish familiarity with a clearly heretical doctrine. That such familiarity should be reflected in a late-thirteenth-century work from Germany is somewhat surprising. Nevertheless, heretics were to be found in northern France and Germany in the late twelfth and early thirteenth centuries,[20] and some of their ideas could have become known to Jews. Otherwise, the argument may have come north through the medium of Jewish polemic itself, but whatever its source, it demonstrates some Jewish contact with Christian heretics.

The second argument in the *Vikkuah le-ha-Radaq* which is supposed to be directed against a heretical belief appears in the following passage:

> It is well known to all, even to fools, that every woman from the age of thirteen on undergoes menstruation, which is the period of the blood of women in confinement which the woman experiences every month. When she becomes pregnant, she does not have this blood, for the foetus is nourished on this blood of confinement during the nine months he is in the womb. Furthermore, when a woman gives birth, that menstrual blood goes to the nipples of the woman several days later and turns into milk. Therefore, when the child sucks the breasts of the mother, she does not have this blood, since it went to the breasts, as we have said.
>
> I shall make an additional point to you. Know that the menstrual blood is a virtually fatal poison. Were a man to drink one cup of it, he would die in a few days or succumb to leprosy, for it is blood which is foul and impure. The wonders of the Lord are so great that the foetus is nourished

---

[20]   See A. Borst, *Die Katharer* (Stuttgart, 1953), pp. 103–104. Cf. also W. Wakefield and A. Evans, *Heresies of the High Middle Ages* (New York, 1969), pp. 38–39.

on that blood for nine months without being harmed. However, it does make the child somewhat weak, so that when he leaves the mother's womb, he does not have the strength to walk on his feet, since he was nourished on that blood all those months he was in the womb. This is not the case with the animals, for as soon as they leave their mother's womb, they walk on their feet. This is so because beasts and animals have no menstrual blood and the foetus is nourished on the blood of the heart which is good, healthy, clean blood. Therefore, when the [young of the animal] leaves the womb of its mother, it walks on its feet immediately. If then Jesus' mother conceived him by the holy spirit, so that he was not nourished in his mother's womb on that corrupt blood, he should have walked on his feet the day he was born and he should have spoken and been as wise as he was when he reached the age of thirty. Rather, he left [her body] from the customary place, was small like other infants, and performed his needs as do other children.[21]

The heretical doctrine at which this passage is allegedly aimed is the view that Jesus did not partake of ordinary nourishment. Since this is so, he would not have been nourished by menstrual blood and would therefore have been born with the ability to walk and talk. Now, this interpretation of the passage may be correct, but there exists an alternative explanation which is at least equally reasonable that does not force us to assume any knowledge of heretical beliefs.

The first crucial observation is that there is no intimation in this passage that Jesus did not eat or drink after his birth. The author's reference to the transformation of menstrual blood into mother's milk is not intended to indicate that the milk is harmful or to show that Jesus' failure to drink it (a heretical view) should have made him stronger than the ordinary infant.[22] The reason for that reference is quite different. The author's argument that the foetus is nourished by menstrual blood depends upon the observation that menstruation stops during pregnancy. He must therefore deal with the obvious objection that it does not begin again immediately after childbirth, particularly when the mother is nursing; his solution to this difficulty is the long-standing view that the menstrual blood becomes milk, but there is no reason to believe that it retains its harmful qualities after its transformation.

[21] Talmage's translation, pp. 341–342.
[22] It is not quite clear to me whether Talmage understood the argument in this fashion. He does express surprise (p. 328) that the author should consider mother's milk harmful when all other medieval writers praise its quality.

The only belief that the author assumes explicitly is that Jesus was not nourished in the ordinary fashion *while in the womb*, and this, I think, was his own deduction rather than his report of a known Christian doctrine. The important clauses read, "If then Jesus' mother conceived him by the holy spirit, so that he was not nourished in his mother's womb on that corrupt blood . . . " The second clause, which contains the heretical view, is a logical inference from the doctrine that Mary conceived by the holy spirit.[23] The basis of this inference is fairly clear. Jews frequently asked Christians why Jesus had to eat or drink if he was divine. After all, Moses had been sustained without food by the Holy Spirit for forty days and nights, and if Jesus possessed the Holy Spirit constantly, he should have had no need of any physical nourishment.[24] The only answer that a Jew might grudgingly accept would be that Jesus made every effort to behave like an ordinary mortal, and so he ate even though he did not have to do so.[25] But this makes sense only after birth; while in the womb, Jesus had no conceivable reason for engaging in a totally useless enterprise, and the author simply takes it for granted that Christians would recognize this.[26]

---

[23] Talmage's translation of the *vav* which introduces the second clause as "so that" is precisely to the point. This is a corollary of the first clause rather than a continuing exposition of the straightforward Christian position.

[24] See Meir ben Simon of Narbonne (thirteenth century), *Milhemet Mizvah*, Parma manuscript, 26b–27a, 89a–b; *Nizzahon Vetus, Tela Ignea Satanae*, pp. 213–215, 217–218, 224–226. The point was raised in connection with Matthew 4:2 in Jacob ben Reuben's *Milhamot Hashem*, ed. by J. Rosenthal (Jerusalem, 1963), p. 144, and in the *Nizzahon Vetus*, p. 200.

[25] Such a Christian argument (although in a different context) is cited without direct refutation in the *Nizzahon Vetus*, p. 173: "You may then argue that he prayed and cried not because he wanted to be saved but because people normally pray when they are in trouble; thus, he too prayed because he behaved like an ordinary mortal in every respect." Cf. Jerome, *In Esaiam (Corpus Christianorum. Series Latina*, 73A), p. 706.

[26] For the argument that Jesus did not have to make pretenses in a private situation involving only "himself and his Father," see the *Nizzahon Vetus*, p. 60. The author there is commenting on the Christian assertion that the addressee in Jeremiah 1 is Jesus (cf. Cyprian's *Testimonia* 15, PL 4: 691). If so, he argues, why does Jesus respond, "Ah, Lord God, I cannot speak," so that God must tell him, "Behold, I have put my words in your mouth" (Jer. 1: 69)? "This implies," he continues, "that up to that time he possessed no such power of speech and certainly not divinity . . . Notice, then, their shame, for he was supposed to have been divine from birth, yet Jeremiah says that the divine word was granted him only now. If the Christian will respond by arguing that Jesus spoke this way [reading *amar ken* with the Munich manuscript rather than *amar lah ken*] because of his humility, refute him by asking why humility should be necessary in a conversation between himself and his Father."

There is therefore no compelling reason for regarding this as a response to a known heretical position.

The third and final reference in the *Vikkuah LehaRadaq* which could be related to heresy is the citation of a Christian view that Adam was promised redemption after five and a half days, which equal 5,500 years. This may have been "an element of Bogomil theology," but, as Prof. Talmage himself points out, it is found in many early orthodox writers.[27] There is, moreover, nothing specifically "heretical" about it. Had the first two indications of familiarity with heresy been convincing, the probability that this concept was learned from heretical sources might have been reasonably high; standing on its own, however, this example cannot demonstrate Jewish contact with heretics.

The *Vikkuah le-ha-Radaq*, then, probably does not reflect Jewish knowledge of heretical doctrines. Surprisingly, the *Nizzahon Vetus* probably does, but the report in that work is bizarre and possibly distorted. On the other hand, we can now turn to a passage in another, unpublished Jewish polemic where the reference to heresy is crystal clear and where the heretical doctrine is reported with complete accuracy. Moreover, unlike the argument in the *Nizzahon Vetus* and the possible arguments in the *Vikkuah le-ha-Radaq*, the purpose in this passage is to attack the Orthodox Church itself.

One of the recurring issues in Jewish-Christian polemic was the numerical superiority enjoyed by Christians. This was cited as evidence of the validity of the Christian faith because it showed that the Jews had been rejected and that various Biblical prophecies (such as Genesis 12:2–3; 15:5; Psalms 2:8; 72:11) had been fulfilled through Christianity. Jews responded to this argument in a variety of ways which ranged from the traditional assertion that they were being temporarily punished for their sins to the claim that their degradation is itself proof of their religious superiority.[28] One of the more interesting Jewish approaches

[27] "An Hebrew Polemical Treatise," pp. 328–329. Cf. also H. A. Wolfson, *The Philosophy of the Church Fathers* (2d ed.; Cambridge, Mass., 1964) 1. 364.

[28] This last argument, based on Dan 8: 12 ("And it cast down the truth to the ground"), was proposed by Meir of Narbonne, *Milhemet Mizvah*, Parma ms., 13b, 22b, 105b; cf. also *Sefer Yosef ha-Meqanne*, p. 113. For Jewish explanations of the exile in polemic, see the additions to Joseph Kimhi, *Sefer ha-Berit*, in *Milhemet Hovah*, p. 36a, the Jew in the *Dialogus* of Rupert of Deutz, PL 170: 606, the *Nizzahon Vetus*, pp. 253–257, and Solomon de' Rossi, *'Edut Hashem Ne'emanah*, in J. Rosenthal, *Mehqarim u-Meqorot* (Jerusalem, 1967) 1. 395–400 (= *Sura* 3 [1948]: 260–264).

to this problem was to reverse it by maintaining that Christians do not constitute a majority of the world's population and that they themselves can be placed on the defensive through the use of a numerical argument.[29]

Another issue in which numbers became relevant was the question of God's fairness in making his revelation known. The argument was first raised by a Christian. Why, Tertullian asked, should we believe that God, who rules the entire world, revealed his law to only one nation and did not grant it to all?[30] Well, said some Jewish polemicists (not in direct response to this question), the alleged Christian revelation is hardly a model of fairness either. The miracles associated with Jesus are not particularly impressive, especially in light of the incredible sort of thing we are supposed to believe about him and the terrible consequences of a failure to believe.[31] With respect to the Jews, Jesus caused more suffering than he alleviated, because it was through him that they are supposed to have committed a sin of unparalleled magnitude.[32] Finally— and here the numerical argument comes into play—if Jesus came to redeem the world from damnation, he didn't do a very good job, since only a minority of the world's inhabitants believes in him; he could have found a way to cause all nations to have faith.[33]

A thirteenth-century polemicist from Avignon by the name of Mordecai ben Joseph put this argument in the following form:

> Moreover, how did he redeem the world by his advent? If you alone are saved, a greater number than you have been damned (lit., lost), such as

[29] This argument was applied to Ps 72: 11 by Jacob ben Reuben (*Milhamot Hashem*, p. 74), Nahmanides (*Vikkuah*, in Ch. Chavel, *Kitvei Ramban* [Jerusalem, 1963] 1. 311), and the author of the *Nizzahon Vetus*, p. 176. See also Meir of Narbonne, *Milhemet Mizvah*, Parma ms., 13b, and Jacob ben Reuben, *Milhamot Hashem*, pp. 38–39, 114. Cf. especially the *Nizzahon Vetus*, pp. 237–238.

[30] "Cur etenim Deus, universitatis conditor, mundi totius gubernator . . . legem per Moysen uni populo dedisse credatur, et non omnibus gentibus attribuisse dicatur?" *Q. S. F. Tertulliani Adversus Judaeos mit Einleitung und kritischem Kommentar*, ed. by H. Tränkle (Wiesbaden, 1964), p. 4 (= *PL* 2: 599).

[31] That Christian miracles should have been more impressive was asserted in Meir of Narbonne's *Milhemet Mizvah*, Parma ms., 121a–b, in the *Vikkuah le-ha-Radaq*, Talmage's translation, pp. 345, 347, and in the *Nizzahon Vetus*, pp. 6, 90, 155, 159. The unfairness of punishing someone who refused to believe in the divinity of Jesus was emphasized by Joseph Kimhi, *Sefer ha-Berit*, *Milhemet Hovah*, p. 228.

[32] *Nizzahon Vetus*, pp. 211, 234–235.

[33] Ibid., p. 238.

Jews and Muslims who do not believe in him. Indeed, many have become Albigensians (*Albigois*[34]) or Bogomils (*Bougres*), for (lit., and) they cannot believe his shame, that he should disgrace himself by entering a woman and having men prevail against him (lit., have power over him). The result is that most of the world goes to hell through his advent.[35]

The heretical doctrines alluded to in this passage are the denial that God entered a woman or that men prevailed against him. The pronouns are ambiguous, and the sentence can even be read as a denial that Jesus entered a woman or that men prevailed against him. I am quite convinced that the first explanation is correct, but either one can yield an accurate description of the beliefs of thirteenth-century occitanian heretics. The Cathars believed that Jesus was not God but an angel; hence, God was neither placed in a woman nor crucified. In a sense, these events were not even applicable to Jesus, because his body was not real; consequently, the crucifixion and even incarnation itself were illusions.[36]

Not only were these beliefs accurately perceived by Mordecai, they are in fact at the center of heretical thought. A medieval writer could easily have defended the statement that people became heretics because of an unwillingness to accept demeaning doctrines about God, and here this assertion is used against the Orthodox Church. Christians are not only outnumbered by a combination of Jews and Muslims, but Christian heretics must also be counted among the unredeemed. For a thirteenth-century writer living in southern France, no argument could have been

[34]   This is the preferable form in thirteenth-century French (the Hebrew transliteration is with a *gimel*); see Hatzfeld and Darmesteter, *Dictionnaire Générale de la Langue Française*, s. v. *Albigeois*.

[35]   *Liqqutim me-Hibburei R. Mordekhai ben Yosef me-Avignon*, ed. by A. Posnanski, Hebrew University manuscript, Shelf Mark Heb 8° 769), p. 26. On Posnanski's unpublished transcriptions of Hebrew polemical manuscripts, see D. Simonsen, "Eine Sammlung polemischer und apologetischer Literatur," *Festschrift für Aron Freiman* (Berlin: 1935), pp. 114ff.

[36]   On these doctrines, see Borst, *Die Katharer*, pp. 162–67; J. Russell, *Dissent and Reform in the Early Middle Ages* (Berkeley, Cal., 1965), p. 203; Wakefield and Evans, *Heresies of the High Middle Ages*, pp. 8, 48. Mordecai's reference to heretics is somewhat more significant than that of Meir of Narbonne (see above, note 1). Mordecai employs the specific terms Albigensians and Bogomils rather than the generic "heretics," and the doctrines he cites are less obvious to the casual observer than the dualism mentioned by Meir. Finally, it is of considerable interest that while Meir contrasted heretics and orthodox Christians to the detriment of the former (Jewish law, he tells his orthodox listener, is far more favorably inclined toward orthodox Christians than it is toward dualists), Mordecai cites heresy with some approval as part of an attack against the Christian mainstream.

more natural, and the passage clearly reveals an awareness of heretical beliefs as well as a willingness to cite them as part of an anti-orthodox polemic.

We now turn to a passage in another Jewish polemic which may shed new light on the tactics of medieval heretics. Jacob ben Reuben's *Milhamot Hashem* (*The Wars of the Lord*) was an epoch-making work. Written in southern France in 1170, it is the first or second extant Jewish polemic from western Europe, and it contains the first Jewish critique of a portion of the New Testament (Matthew), the first Hebrew translation of sizable selections from the Latin New Testament (again Matthew), and what may be the first Hebrew translation of any section of a medieval Latin work (Gilbert Crispin's *Disputatio*).[37] It is, moreover, the product of a genuine discussion between Jacob and a Christian acquaintance.

After lengthy but rather cordial disputes concerning the trinity, incarnation, allegory, and standard Christological verses, Jacob's opponent, who is clearly an orthodox Christian, announces that he has a friend named Paul who has posed two philosophical objections against Judaism. The objections are described, Jacob responds, and the discussion then returns to Biblical verses. There is, however, something suspicious about those objections, and they deserve some very careful scrutiny.

> Paul said: I truly know that the Jews believe in God, and they believe that he is a God who exists and brings everything into being, that he is primeval without antecedent, and that he is in the category of what is and what can be. If so, then the two principles of good and evil, which are what is and what can be, are found in him. He (Paul) also said that since he exists and brings everything into being, then he brings about evil just as he brings about good. He also said that since he is without beginning and without end, all created things, which have a beginning and an end, are in him; therefore, he contains evil as well as good. Indeed, my eyes have thus seen and recognized that the Jews do not believe anything, for even according to

37   On the date and place, see Rosenthal's introduction to his edition of *Milhamot Hashem* (Jerusalem, 1963). The problems cited by Ch. Merhavya (*Kirjath Sepher* 39 [1964]: 144–148) are not sufficient, in my opinion, to cast substantial doubt upon the 1170 date in the colophon. On the translations from Matthew, see Rosenthal's "Targum shel ha-Besorah 'al Pi Matti le-Ya'aqov ben Reuven," *Tarbiz* 32 (1962): 48–66, and on the translation from Crispin, see my "Gilbert Crispin, Alan of Lille, and Jacob ben Reuben: A Study in the Transmission of Medieval Polemic," *Speculum* 49 (1974): 34–47.

their own words they believe in a God in whom there exist two principles—good and evil. Now, one who makes evil has evil in him, as I have shown you on the basis of their type of faith and through that which they concede and believe. I have therefore said that your (read: their?) words have no foundation and that faith has been lost and cut off from their mouths.[38]

This is an amazing objection for the obvious but devastating reason that there is nothing in it that cannot be directed against Christianity itself. Whatever reservations may be expressed about the formulation of the premises of the argument (and Jacob does object to at least one such formulation), the crucial fact is that none of those premises are characteristic of Judaism and not of Christianity. Since Christians also believe that God brings everything into being and that he is without beginning and end, it should follow that they too must concede that there is evil in God. But this is heresy! Indeed, it is the Cathar heresy, or something very much like it.[39]

The 1160s were a turning point in the history of Catharism in southern France; it was in this decade that dualism began to spread and to become a vital force.[40] Needless to say, not every Christian who became attracted to dualism as it began to spread immediately announced that he was a heretic. Under the inquisition, of course, concealment of heresy became crucial, but it was hardly unknown in the earlier period. The temptation is therefore overwhelming to suggest that Paul was a concealed dualist of recent vintage who approached an old friend with some objections against Judaism; his real target, however, was not Judaism at all. Under the guise of giving a lecture about the deficiencies of Judaism, Paul was really sowing seeds that would weaken his friend's faith in orthodox Christianity. A fourteenth-century Christian writes about heretics who pretended to be Jews in order to

---

[38]   *Milhamot Hashem*, pp. 116–117. I have tried to provide an extremely literal translation. Despite Merhavya's suggestion to the contrary (*op. cit.*, pp. 146–147), it is quite clear that this Paul, who is a contemporary of the author, is not the same as the Paul mentioned in several earlier passages of *Milhamot Hashem*. Even if that Paul is not the apostle (and he probably is), he is certainly no contemporary of the disputants since he is mentioned along with Jerome and Augustine as one of the founders of the Christian faith (p. 5).

[39]   Whatever dualist elements may have influenced early Christianity (see Rosenthal's note *ad loc.*), it was clearly unacceptable for a twelfth-century Christian to say that there is evil in God.

[40]   See Borst, *Die Katharer*, pp. 89–108. Cf. also Russell, *Dissent and Reform*, p. 200, and R. I. Moore, "The Origins of Medieval Heresy," *History* 55 (1970): 23.

be free to spread heretical ideas;[41] here we are probably dealing with a heretic pretending to attack Judaism in order to accomplish the same end. Jacob's disputant apparently failed to grasp the implications of the question, or, like a famous fourteenth-century convert to Christianity, he may have concocted an orthodox interpretation of it,[42] and so he passed it on to his Jewish acquaintance. The fact remains, however, that if we take this passage at anything resembling face value, it is urging a dualistic belief based on premises shared by both Judaism and orthodox Christianity.

Paul posed a second objection against Judaism in addition to the first, and an examination of this objection ought to help us confirm or deny the impression that there is something quite unusual about this anti-Jewish polemicist. Here, then, is Paul's second argument.

> Paul continued and said: I truly know that the Jews believe in him who is the Lord, God, Almighty, true, and living, as it is written, "The Lord is the true God; he is the living God and eternal king" (Jeremiah 10:10). And [they believe in him who is] mighty and powerful, as it is written, "Through his great might, his might and power" (Isaiah 40:26). [They] also [believe] in him who is "merciful and compassionate, forbearing and constant in his love" (Psalms 145:8). Now, I know that he is not true by partaking of truth, so that truth would be something other than he; nor does he live by partaking of life as man does, who is alive at one time and dead at another; nor is he powerful by partaking of power as man is, who is powerful at one time and weak at another. The creator, blessed be he, is not that way. Rather, his essence is truth, and his essence is life, and his essence is power, and his essence is merciful, and his essence is God, and his essence is Almighty, and the same is true of all the names that apply to him. Moreover, we certainly know that the principle of strength is not merciful, and the principle "merciful" is not strength, and the principle of life is not truth; even though truth cannot exist without life, life exists as a principle without truth. Thus, each of them is a principle in itself, and each one is the basic essence of the creator, blessed be he. Since this is so, it follows that the one in whom you believe is more than one, for his basic essence includes all these things. Now, there is no one who does not believe that he is the Lord, God, Almighty, merciful, compassionate, and living; and each of these is a principle in itself. This is the truth.[43]

41   See the quotation in Baron, *History*, p. 58.
42   For the assertion by Abner of Burgos that evil in this passage does not mean evil, see Rosenthal's note *ad loc.*
43   *Milhamot HaShem*, pp. 120–121.

This second objection is only slightly less suspicious than the first. Once again, Paul presents a position that is almost incredible coming from an orthodox Christian and is, in fact, a common Jewish and Muslim argument against Christianity.

In this period, Christians often explained the trinity in terms of divine attributes. The identification of the trinity with power, wisdom, and will, or essence, wisdom, and will, is frequently represented in the polemical literature of the period, and Jewish writers cite this argument all the time.[44] Both Jews and Muslims responded with a philosophical explanation of attributes designed to undermine this assertion,[45] but they also did something else which was far simpler and probably more effective. God, they said, has more than three attributes.[46]

Paul's argument, then, is once again most peculiar. He asserts that divine attributes imply a multiplicity of some sort within God, but it is a multiplicity of more than three. The only difference between his argument and that of Jewish polemicists is that he purports to believe in such multiplicity while Jews explicitly assert it just for the sake of argument. By purporting to believe in it, Paul can claim to be attacking the Jewish belief in the absolute unity of God, but the effect of his argument is to undermine the standard philosophical interpretation of the trinity as well. Now, Cathars probably did not believe in this kind of multiplicity within God, but they did not believe in the trinity either,[47] and this sort of argument may well have been designed to erode the faith of the orthodox Christian in the trinity.[48]

[44] See Meir of Narbonne, *Milhemet Mizvah*, Parma ms., 30a–b, 49b–50a, 99a–101a; Moses of Salerno, *Ta'anot*, in S. Simon, *Mose ben Salomo von Salerno und seine philosophische Auseinandersetzung mit den Lehren des Christentums* (Breslau, 1932), Hebrew section, pp. 6, 15; Nahmanides, *Vikkuah*, *Kitvei Ramban*, p. 320; Petrus Alfonsi, *Dialogus*, PL 157: 606ff. On the early formulation of this interpretation of the trinity, see H. Wolfson, "The Muslim Attributes and the Christian Trinity," *HTR* 49 (1956): 1–18.

[45] See the references in Rosenthal's notes *ad loc*. Cf. also Nahmanides' *Vikkuah*, p. 320.

[46] See Simon, *Mose ben Salomo von Salerno* (Heb. sec.), p. 6, and Nahmanides' *Vikkuah*, *loc. cit*. Baron (*op. cit.*, p. 85), while incorrectly stating that Nahmanides did not use this argument, refers to it as a "long-debated" matter. The extension of alleged Trinitarian references in the Bible beyond three was also a rather common Jewish approach; see appendix 1 of my forthcoming edition of the *Nizzahon Vetus*.

[47] See the references in note 36, and cf. also S. Runciman, *The Medieval Manichee* (Cambridge, 1947), pp. 148–149, and C. Thouzellier, *Catharisme et Valdéisme en Languedoc à la Fin du XIIe et au Début du XIIIe Siècle* (Paris, 1966), p. 61.

[48] It might be argued that all Paul meant is that Jews who maintain that there are more than three attributes must believe in extensive multiplicity within God; he himself, however,

Can it be a coincidence that both of Paul's objections to Judaism pose a direct challenge to orthodox Christianity? Perhaps. It may be that he was just an incompetent polemicist who could not refrain from putting his foot in his mouth, or it may be that I have missed something and misinterpreted him. However, because of the time and place of this discussion, because both questions appear to undermine elements of Christianity which the Cathars denied, and because Paul presented his arguments against Judaism to Christians and not to Jews,[49] the possibility looms large that we have uncovered a subtle method of Cathar propaganda.[50]

Jewish polemic, then, appears to shed considerable light upon the unhappy triangle of Jews, Christian heretics, and the Orthodox Church in the high middle ages. It reveals some Jewish knowledge of heretical doctrines and provides insights into the tactics used by Jews and heretics to combat orthodox Christianity. The author of the *Nizzahon Vetus* was apparently aware of a heretical belief which he used to undermine the Christological interpretation of a crucial Psalm and which he later attacked directly on the basis of the Gospels themselves.[51] Mordecai of Avignon knew some central heretical teachings and cited them explicitly and accurately in an attack against the Orthodox Church. Finally, Jacob

believes in only three hypostases. Aside from the fact that he never says this explicitly, his final comment that "there is no one (*ein ehad mi-kol ha-nivra'im*) who does not believe" in all these attributes as well as his remark that "this is the truth" make such a position very difficult to maintain. If Paul was a concealed heretic, these last remarks might have been insincere, but if he was an orthodox Christian, he should not have expressed himself in such a fashion.

Moreover, it should be noted that Paul's assertion of divine multiplicity in connection with the attributes of God (or, if our suspicions are correct, in connection with the attributes of the good God) is analogous to the reported views of a thirteenth-century heresiarch with respect to the evil god; in light of this, it is altogether possible that Paul meant what he said. According to the *Summa* of Rainerius Sacconi, John of Lugio maintained that "the first principle of evil is called by many names in the Holy Scriptures. It is called malice, iniquity, cupidity, impiety, sin, pride, death, hell, calumny, vanity, injustice, perdition, confusion, corruption, and fornication. And he also says that all the evils named are gods or goddesses, that they have their being from the malice which, he asserts, is a first cause, and that this first cause is signified from time to time by the vices named" (Wakefield and Evans, *Heresies*, p. 339.

49   *Milhamot Hashem*, p. 118.
50   In light of the paucity of heretical texts from the middle ages, it seems worthwhile to point out explicitly that if this suggestion is correct, Jacob ben Reuben has indirectly provided what is in effect a medieval heretical document from a relatively early period.
51   Cf. note 19.

ben Reuben may have preserved evidence of the fascinating possibility that heretics used anti-Jewish polemic as a cover for efforts to undermine the traditional Christian faith.

Addendum (published with the original article):

After this article went to press, I decided that Posnanski's identification of the author of the polemic mentioning Albigensians and Bogomils as Mordecai of Avignon (see n. 35) cannot be accepted with certainty. It would have been much safer to ascribe the passage (which comes from Vittorio Emanuele Hebrew MS 53, 23b) simply to "a thirteenth century French polemicist."

Addendum 2:

For further comment on this manuscript, see note 104 of my Introduction to *The Jewish-Christian Debate in the High Middle Ages* reprinted in this volume.

GILBERT CRISPIN, ALAN OF LILLE, AND JACOB BEN REUBEN

A Study in the Transmission of Medieval Polemic

From: *Speculum* 49 (1974): 34–47.

One of the most influential medieval polemics against the Jews was Gilbert Crispin's *Disputatio Iudaei et Christiani*, which was written in the late eleventh century and may reflect a genuine discussion between Crispin and a Jewish disputant.[1] However, the dependence of the third book of Alan of Lille's *Contra Haereticos*[2] upon Crispin's disputation has not been widely recognized. Blumenkranz, for example, in discussing the impact of Crispin's work in the twelfth century, noted the resemblance between the *Disputatio* and the *Dialogus inter Christianum et Iudaeum* ascribed to William of Champeaux,[3] but made no mention of the far closer relationship between Crispin and Alan.[4] Vasoli, in a special study of the *Contra Haereticos*, also overlooked the major source of book three.[5] Even d'Alverny, who noted the relationship between the two works, did not give a precise indication of its extent. Alan, she writes, "was inspired in large measure by the *Disputatio* of Gilbert Crispin and reproduced entire

---

[1]   The work was edited by B. Blumenkranz (Utrecht, 1956) = PL 259: 1005–1086. (All references will be to Blumenkranz's edition.) See also Blumenkranz, *Les Auteurs Chrétiens Latins du Moyen Age sur les Juifs et le Judaisme* (Paris, La Haye, 1962), pp. 279–287.

[2]   *De Fide Catholica Contra Haereticos*, PL 210: 305–480 (*Liber Tertia Contra Judeaos*, cc. 399–422). On its late twelfth century date, see below, note 23.

[3]   PL 163: 1045–1072.

[4]   *Disputatio*, introd., p. 17. Blumenkranz's comments are very similar to those of J. de Ghellinck, *L'essor de la Littérature Latine au XIIe Siècle* (Paris, 1946), p. 164.

[5]   Cesare Vasoli, "Il Contra Haereticos di Alano di Lilla," *Bulletino dell' Istituto Storico Italiano per il Medio Evo e Archivio Muratoriano* 75 (1968): 123–172, esp. 171–172.

passages of this work."[6] In fact, just under forty percent of Alan's polemic is copied almost word for word from Crispin or a previous digest of Crispin. The following table indicates the passages which Alan copied:

Alan (*PL* 210)		Crispin (Blumenkranz's ed.)
Column 401. Lines 16–22[7]	=	Page 33. Lines 15–19
407.20–409.13	=	28.12–33.8
409.14–410.6	=	34.30–36.23
410.43–411.9	=	34.7–28
411.12–53	=	37.9–39.4
413.38–414.5	=	43.7–26
414.20–43	=	46.13–47.4
416.8–22	=	59.7–60.1[8]
416.30–417.24	=	51.17–52.24
418.14–419.48	=	48.12–50.33[9]

Certain significant and rather obvious corollaries result from the recognition of the nature and extent of this dependence. First of all, the utmost caution must be exercised in drawing any conclusions about Alan's thought from the material in these passages; a man who is copying an argument mechanically may include expressions and even ideas which are not fully consonant with what he would have written on his own. Secondly, the text of Alan's work can be corrected in several places once his source is known, particularly since we possess a good critical edition of that source.[10] Finally—and here we tread upon much more dangerous

---

6   Marie-Therese d'Alverny, *Alain de Lille: Textes Inédits, avec une introduction sur sa vie et ses oeuvres* (Paris, 1965), p. 161.

7   In determining line numbers in *PL*, the lines in chapter headings have been counted.

8   This passage contains an alleged Jewish suggestion that the famous *'almah* of Isaiah 7:14 means hidden (*abscondita*). See also Crispin, p. 55, and Alan, c. 415. R. Werblowsky has presented an interesting argument that this is not a genuine Jewish interpretation and that it raises serious questions about the genuineness of the discussion in Crispin's work; see his "Crispin's Disputation," *Journal of Jewish Studies* 11 (1960): 69–77. It is, of course, not impossible that a Jew should have presented such an interpretation even though it is not attested in Jewish sources, but it is certainly true that the references to this interpretation in Alan and in Peter of Blois' *Contra Perfidiam Judaeorum, PL* 207: 841 (neither of which is noted by Werblowsky) are a reflection of Crispin and not of actual Jewish arguments.

9   It is possible that Alan 404.24–29 is based upon Crispin 52.26–53.2, but this may be coincidence.

10 In the first parallel passage, for example, Alan's "nugantes" (401.18) is probably a corruption of the phrase in Crispin (33.16–17) in which "negando" appears. See also below, note 32.

ground—we may be justified in wondering whether the remainder of Alan's work might not also be dependent upon an earlier, written polemic. As we shall see, there may be reason to believe that passages from Crispin's disputation were included in a polemical collection that also contained other material; if Alan used such a collection, then other parts of his work might be dependent upon other sections of his source.[11] This suggestion, however, must remain in the realm of speculation.

One of the passages in Crispin which was reproduced by Alan deals with the allegorical interpretation of Pentateuchal law. This issue was, of course, central to the Jewish-Christian debate, and Christians had argued the case for allegory since New Testament times.[12] What is particularly important about this passage, however, is the hitherto unnoticed fact that it was translated into Hebrew in one of the earliest (and perhaps the very earliest) anti-Christian polemics written by a European Jew—Jacob ben Reuben's *Milhamot Hashem* (*Wars of the Lord*).[13]

Milhamot Hashem was probably written in Provence in 1170,[14] and it contains an epoch-making translation and critique of sections of Matthew. No earlier Hebrew translation of the New Testament from Latin is known with the exception of two small fragments of poor quality, and while we cannot be certain that Jacob did not use an earlier translation, Rosenthal's feeling that he did not is certainly supported by the fact that an additional translation can now be identified in his work.[15]

Indeed, it appears that Jacob ben Reuben can now be credited with breaking even more new ground in the translation of Latin into Hebrew, for the passage to be discussed below may constitute the earliest translation into Hebrew of any section of a medieval Latin work. It is clear, at any rate, that no complete Latin work was translated into

---

11 The most important lines of Alan's third book come at the end of Chapter 10 (c. 410), where a Talmudic passage is cited for the first time to prove the truth of Christianity. See Ch. Merchavia, *Ha-Talmud bi-Re'i ha-Nazrut* (Jerusalem, 1970), pp. 214–217. In light of the minimal effort that Alan put into the composition of this section of the *Contra Haereticos*, it appears likely that this information came his way by accident (perhaps through a convert) or that it was already recorded in the source from which he was copying.

12 Cf. Hebrews 10:1. In general, see B. Smalley, *The Study of the Bible in the Middle Ages* (Notre Dame, 1964), pp. 1–26 and *passim*; M. Simon, *Verus Israel* (Paris, 1948), pp. 104–117, 177–184; Blumenkranz, *Die Judenpredigt Augustins* (Basel, 1946), pp. 130–145.

13 This work was edited by Judah Rosenthal (Jerusalem, 1968).

14 See Rosenthal's introduction, p. viii.

15 See J. Rosenthal, "Targum shel ha-Besorah 'al Pi Matti le-Ya'aqov ben Reuven," *Tarbiz* 32 (1962): 48–66, esp. 50–51.

Hebrew before 1170, and thus Jacob may own the twin distinctions of being the first Jew to translate both a substantial passage of a medieval Latin work and sections of the Latin New Testament into Hebrew.[16]

In his introduction, Jacob ben Reuben informs us that his Christian interlocutor "took in his hand a book by the scholars of their early generations who established their error (i.e., Christianity) firmly. These were three authors; the first was Jerome, the second Augustine, and the third Paul. These three founded, sought out, and established (cf. Ecc. xii 9) the basis of the entire error and set it up. But Gregory prepared instruments for them" (i.e., he added to the system founded by the other three).[17] Now, this statement could refer to a manuscript containing three separate books, but this does not seem likely. First of all, the reference to a book (lit., "one book") does not really give such an impression. Secondly, a manuscript containing a work of Jerome followed by a work of Augustine followed by a Pauline epistle would be rather surprising. Thirdly, the reference to Gregory leaves an ambiguity as to whether or not he too was represented in this "book." In addition, Jacob ben Reuben later quotes a passage from Paul which is nowhere in the New Testament and a passage from Jerome which neither the editor of *Milhamot Hashem* nor I have been able to locate in Jerome's works.[18]

---

[16]   On Hebrew translations of medieval Latin works, see M. Steinschneider, *Die Hebräischen Übersetzungen des Mittelalters und die Juden als Dolmestscher* (Berlin, 1893), pp. 461 ff., 616 ff., and 775 ff. Cf. also Charles Singer, "The Jewish Factor in Medieval Thonght," in *The Legacy of Israel*, ed. by E. Bevan and C. J. Singer (Oxford, 1927), pp. 178–314, and A. S. Balkin, "Translation and Translators (Medieval)," *Encyclopedia Judaica*, Jerusalem, 1971, vol. XV, cc. 1318–1329, esp. c. 1324. H. Gollancz (*The Ethical Treatises of Berachya*, London, 1902, introduction) dated Berechiah ha-Nakdan's free paraphrase of Adelard of Bath's *Quaestiones Naturales* before 1170; see, however, the critical remarks in the *Revue des Etudes Juives* 46 (1908): 285–288. (Gollancz himself thonght that Berechiah's work was based on a French translation rather than the Latin original.) Most recent writers date Berechiah in the late twelfth and thirteenth centuries, thus placing his paraphrase later than *Milhamot Hashem*. See, for example, W. T. H. Jackson in his introduction to M. Hadas, *Fables of a Jewish Aesop*, New York and London, 1967, and A. M. Habermann in his introduction to *Mishlei Shu'alim* (Jerusalem and Tel Aviv, 1946), p. vi, and in his articles on Berechiah in the *Enziqlopediah Ivrit* and the *Encyclopedia Judaica*. It should also be noted that aside from Boethius (see Steinschneider, p. 466), Crispin may be the first medieval Christian to have had a portion of his work translated into Hebrew at any time during the Middle Ages.

[17]   *Milhamot Hashem*, p. 5.

[18]   See *Milhamot Hashem*, pp. 26–27, 28–29. Rosenthal (p. 27, n. 8) does supply a reference to Jerome, but he means only that it deals with the same general subject matter as the passage quoted by Jacob.

Finally and most important, the material from Crispin shows either that Jacob's disputant provided him with an additional book that we were not told about in the introduction or that the same book contained this material as well, and there is a concrete indication that the latter alternative is the correct one. One of the selections from Crispin is repeated, and its second appearance (where the language is closest to that of our Latin text) is separated from the main body of the Crispin passage by the quotation from "Jerome" and is followed immediately by the quotation from "Paul."[19] On balance, then, it appears likely that the book shown to Jacob was a collection of polemical and exegetical material taken from various authors which did not always identify its sources and which occasionally contained inaccurate ascriptions. The possibility that Alan of Lille used a source similar to that of Jacob ben Reuben cannot be dismissed out of hand; in any event, there is concrete evidence for believing that Jacob's text sheds light on otherwise unattested readings in Alan's source, although the relationship between their texts is certainly more hypothetical than the clearcut citations of Crispin in *Milhamot Hashem*.

The passage translated by Jacob contains a short introduction, four questions intended to prove the necessity of allegorical interpretation, and a concluding paragraph.

Introductory Passage

Crispin (p. 29):
> Primum itaque legem bonam et a deo datam dicimus, tenemus, astruimus. Ac proinde, quicquid in ea scriptum est, diuino sensu intellectum suis temporibus obseruatum et obseruandum esse sancimus. Diuino quidem sensu legis mandata intelligenda esse dicimus, quia, si humano ea omnia sensu et ad litteram accipimus, multa sibi inuicem aduersantia et multum repugnantia uidemus.

Alan (col. 407):
> Ad haec primo respondemus legem esse bonam, et a Deo datam dicimus, ac ideo quidquid in ea scriptum est, divino sensu intellectum, suis temporibus observatum et observandum esse sentimus; ea vero divino intellectu intelligenda erant, quae si ad litteram accipimus, multa sibi repugnantia videmus.

---

19   Ibid., pp. 26–29. See below. note 34.

Jacob ben Reuben (p. 24):[20]

The beginning of my statement is to establish in truth and strengthen with validity the proposition that all the words of Moses are true and correct to one who understands them, that his Torah and testimony are faithful, and his word is valid. Intelligent men should examine the words with intellect and observe all the commandments in their time, for if we will examine the words of the Torah only according to the letter, many things will appear difficult to us.[21]

Jacob's translation here probably reflects a slightly different Latin text from the ones we have, although he may have simply added some rhetorical flourishes on his own. The main point, in any case, is that the law was indeed revealed by God but that it must be understood allegorically because a literal reading produces contradictions.[22]

The one peculiarity in Jacob's translation comes in his final phrase, but this can be accounted for by a misunderstanding of the text reflected in Alan. Jacob's translation says, "If we will examine the words of the Torah only according to the letter, many things will appear difficult to us." The Latin text, on the other hand, means, "If we accept (the commandments of the law) according to the letter, we will see many things contradictory (lit., repugnant) to one another (multa sibi repugnantia videmus)." Jacob apparently took "sibi" to mean "to ourselves" rather than "to one another" and thus misinterpreted the final phrase. This misinterpretation, however, is significant because it is possible only on the basis of Alan's text; Crispin's more elaborate statement (with its "sibi invicem adversantia") does not lend itself to Jacob's explanation. It follows, then, that Alan's shorter version reflects not his own abridgement but rather a shorter text which he had before him.[23]

---

20 The translations from *Milhamot Hashem*, are my own; they have generally been kept as literal as possible in order to facilitate a direct comparison with the Latin.

21 *Hahiloti ledabber bi-tehillat devaray leqayyem be-qiyyum ha-emet u-lehazzeq be-hizzuq ha-yosher ki kol divrei Mosheh amitiyyim u-nekhohim la-mevin, ve-torato ve-ceduto ne'emanah u-millato nekhonah. Ve-yesh la-maskilim lehitbonen ba-devarim mi-tokh ha-sekhel ve-lishmor be-'ittam kol ha-mizvot, ki im lo nitbonen be-divrei ha-torah akh ke-fi ha-mikhtav, yiqshu 'alenu devarim rabbim.*

22 For this general argument in earlier Christian polemic, cf. Blumenkranz's references in his notes *ad loc.*, in his *Juifs et Chrétiens dans le Monde Occidental, 430–1096* (Paris, 1960), p. 240, and in his *Auteurs*, p. 98.

23 It should be noted here that Jacob wrote before Alan, and so the Hebrew cannot be a reflection of Alan's work. See Vasoli, *op. cit.*, p. 185, for the estimate that Alan wrote *Contra Haereticos* between 1185 and 1195. Jacob's inclusion of Crispin's second question,

Question 1

Crispin (pp. 29–30):

Cum enim peracta creatione mundi Moyses dicat: Vidit deus cuncta que fecerat et erant ualde bona, quomodo in discretione animalium postea scribit hec munda et illa animalia esse inmunda, his uti permittit, illa non solum tangere, sed eum, qui tetigerit, morte multari et puniri mandat? Quod enim est inmundum, quomodo est ualde bonum? Vbi enim cuncta nominauit et ualde bona esse cuncta dixit, neque hoc neque illud animal excepit. Quomodo igitur deus cuncta creauit ualde bona animalia, et postea uetat comedi hec uel illa animalia, et causam reddit dicens, ea esse inmunda animalia? Nec solum ea prohibuit, que sui natura homini ad uescendum noxia sunt, uerum et multa, que gustu iocunda et usu eque salubria ad comedendum existunt. Aliquid ergo sacramenti hec in se continent, que licet a deo dicta sint tamen a se ad litteram inuicem omnino dissident.

Alan (col. 407):

Cum enim Moyses dicat: Vidit Deus cuncta quae fecerat, et erant valde bona, quid est quod in lege quaedam dicantur munda, quaedam immunda? Ad litteram quidem non est immundum, quoniam est valde bonum: nec solum ea prohibentur in lege, quae sui natura nociva sunt homini ad vescendum, verum etiam quae gestu (read: gustu) jucunda, et aeque salubria ad comedendum existunt. Aliquid ergo sacramenti haec in se continent, quae, licet a Deo dicta sint, tamen a se invicem ad litteram omnino dissident.

Jacob ben Reuben (pp. 24–25):

Moses also wrote in his book, "And God saw everything that he had made, and, behold, it was very good" (Genesis 1: 31). He thus included all his creatures—everything that he had made both above and below— in the category of "very good." Elsewhere, however, in distinguishing between animals, he wrote, "These are they which are unclean to you" (Leviticus 11: 31), "These may you eat" (Lev. 11: 9). Moreover, with regard to the impure animals, he did not warn against eating alone but also against touching, as it is written, "Whosoever touches their carcass shall be unclean until the evening" (Lev. 11: 24). Now, how can those animals which are so disgusting in the eyes of the creator that they are impure to the touch have been included in the category of "very good"? For where he wrote, "And he saw everything that he had made, and behold, it was

which Alan omitted, is a further indication that he did not use *Contra Haereticos* or any work dependent upon it. (The fact that Alan's work is a product of his stay in southern France is also relevant to the suggestion of a relationship between his text and the one used by Jacob.)

very good," once he said "very good" he did not leave anything out. Now, if you examine the Torah according to the letter alone, you should wonder how the creator could have made all the animals "very good" and then declared some pure and others impure. And he did not declare those animals impure which are harmful to man by nature; rather, he prohibited many which are very good to eat. Consequently, we should understand some symbol and allegory in these words. Even though God said them, according to the letter their meanings are inconsistent with one another in accordance with the shell of the statement. It is therefore proper for a man to go into the matter deeply, to penetrate the depths of the intellect, and to reach the heights of knowledge.[24]

The basic argument in this passage is that a literal understanding of the prohibition of certain animals as impure contradicts the statement that "God saw all that he had made, and behold, it was very good" (Gen. 1: 31). As Rosenthal points out, this alleged contradiction was cited for the same purpose by Novatian and Petrus Alfonsi.[25] An even more elaborate use of the same argument is found in a work by Isidore of Seville in which he systematically emphasized the discovery of contradictions as a justification for allegory.[26]

[24]   *'Od katav Mosheh be-sifro: Va-yar Elohim et kol asher 'asah ve-hinneh tov me'od, ve-hevi kol yezurav bi-kelal tov me'od, kol hanivra'im ma'lah u-mattah asher 'asah. U-be-maqom aher be-hilluq ha-behemot katav: Elleh ha-teme'im lakhem, et zeh tokhelu. U-ba-teme'ot lo ba lehazhir ba-'akhilah levad akh gam ken be-magga', she-ne'emar, Kol hanogea' be-nivlatam yitma 'ad ha'arev. Ve-elleh asher nim'asu be-'enei ha-bore lihyotam teme'im le-magga' ha-'adam, eikh nikhlelu bi-kelal tov me'od? Ki ba-maqom she-katav, Va-yar et kol asher 'asah ve-hinneh tov me'od; be-amro tov me'od lo hish'ir davar lehozi min ha-kelal. Ve-yesh 'alekha litmoah, im titbonen ba-torah ke-fi ha-mikhtav levad, eikh yazar ha-bore kol ha-behemot tovot me'od, ve-aharei ken tiher et elleh ve-timme et elleh? Ve-lo timme ha-bore ha-behemot ha-mazziqot la-adam be-'ad ha-toledet, akh rabbot me-hen asher asar ahar she-hen tovot me'od le'ekhol. 'Al ken yesh lanu lehavin ba-devarim ha-elleh dimyon u-mashal. Af 'al pi she-ha-bore amaram, ke-fi ha-mikhtav ein pitronam shaveh zeh 'im zeh be-'inyan qelippat ha-ma'amar. Akh ya'ut la-adam lavo be-tokh ha-'omeq ve-laredet be-mordei mezulot ha-sekhel u-lehagbiah be-govhei madda'.*

    Rosenthal placed a comma after *ve-timme et elleh* and a question mark after *ha-toledet.* This punctuation, however, is inherently dubious and is definitively ruled out by the Latin source

[25]   Novatian, *De Cibus Judaicis*, PL 3: 956; Petrus Alfonsi, *Dialogus*, PL 157: 667. In the same note (*Milhamot Hashem*, p. 27, n. 8), Rosenthal refers to Crispin's use of this one argument, which he was familiar with through the brief summary in A. Lukyn Williams, *Adversus Judaeos* (Cambridge, 1935), p. 376.

[26]   See Isidore's *Liber de Variis Quaestionibus Adversus Judaeos seu Ceteros Infideles* (mistakenly attributed to Raban Maur), ed. by E. Martène and U. Durand, *Thesaurus Novus Anecdotorum* V (Paris, 1717), ch. 64, 68, col. 617–19, 529. (I have been unable to obtain the critical edition of A. C. Vega and A. E. Anspach [Escorial, 1940].) For

Aside from Jacob's reversal of the order of Crispin's first two questions[27] and his supplying of several verses which may or may not have been in his source, there are at least two textual problems here which deserve.further discussion.

First of all, Jacob ben Reuben may have afforded us the opportunity of actually correcting a difficult text in Crispin. The last part of Crispin's first sentence (which is not found in Alan's work) means, "Why . . . did he permit these animals while he not only [prohibited] touching the others but commanded that one who touched them be punished by death?" Blumenkranz has already noted the necessity of introducing the verb "prohibited" in order to make sense of this sentence, but there remains an additional difficulty; there is, in fact, no death penalty mentioned in the Pentateuch for one who touches an impure animal.

Now, Jacob's translation reads as follows: "With regard to the impure animals, he did not warn against eating alone but also against touching." It is extremely tempting to suggest that a phrase rather than just a word dropped out of the text of Crispin and that the section about the death penalty was added by an early copyist in order to complete a meaningless sentence. Specifically, I propose the following: The original text read, ". . . illa non solum comedere vetat sed etiam tangere" (while he not only prohibited eating the others but also touching them). The words "comedere vetat sed etiam" dropped out, and what was left simply meant, " . . . while not only touching the others." (It must be kept in mind that we have to assume that "vetat" dropped out in any case.) A copyist surveying this shambles might have automatically supplied the word "prohibited" in his mind and not realized the need to write it down, but the phrase "not only" required some additional section in the sentence; i.e., Moses not only prohibited touching impure animals, but also did something else, even more extreme than that. Presumably that something else was the imposition of the death penalty upon the transgressor. Thus, it is possible that Jacob ben Reuben has preserved a correct reading in Crispin which is corrupted in all the known manuscripts of the *Disputatio*.

an instance of extensive verbatim copying from Isidore in an anti-Jewish polemic, cf. his *Questiones in Leviticum*, PL 83: 886–889, with Peter Damian's *Dialogus*, PL 145: 57 ff.; see my "St. Peter Damian: His Attitude Toward the Jews and the Old Testament," *Yavneh Review* 4 (1965): 80–112.

27 Alan cannot help us on this point because he omits Crispin's second question entirely.

A second, less significant but rather interesting textual question is raised by Jacob's translation of the last sentence in Crispin and Alan. The Latin means, ". . . granted that these things were said by God, nevertheless, according to the letter they differ from one another (*a se invicem*) entirely." Jacob's translation is peculiar and redundant: "Even though God said them, according to the letter their meanings are inconsistent with one another in accordance with the shell of the statement." "According to the letter" and "in accordance with the shell of the statement" seem blatantly repetitious and extremely awkward. Placing the comma after "letter" in order to minimize the redundancy does not appear to help much and is in any case ruled out by the Latin where "ad litteram" (according to the letter) clearly belongs with the second part of the sentence. Moreover, the phrase "the shell of the statement" is simply missing from the Latin entirely.

The fact is, however, that Jacob was almost certainly working with basically the same Latin text that we have, and his translation is a result of one simple misreading. He (or the man who copied the text he was using) read "inuicem" (one another) as "in nucem" (in accordance with a nut). Now, an unbroken nut was used in twelfth-century polemic as a symbol of literal interpretation; the allegorical meaning was like the kernel of a nut which could be reached only if the shell were broken.[28] On the basis of this misreading, therefore, Jacob had his redundancy in the Latin text: ". . . tamen a se ad litteram in nucem omnino dissident" (nevertheless, they differ from each entirely according to the letter, in accordance with the nut).[29]

---

[28] See the *Dialogus inter Christianum et Iudaeum* aschribed to William of Champeaux, *PL* 163: 1048–1049:

> *Christ.* Propono te tenere nucem in manu tua.
> *Jud.* Fiat, teneo nucem.
> *Christ.* Si hanc nucem infractam ederes, forsitan te strangulares.
> *Jud.* Utique cito contingeret.
> *Christ.* Ergo nux integra non est bona ad comedendum.
> *Jud.* Utique.
> *Christ.* Prius ergo oportet testam frangere et sic pervenire ad nucleum.
> *Jud.* Nullatenus aliter esse potest.
> *Christ.* Audi igitur: non potes nucem integram edere utiliter, nec pervenire ad nucleum nisi prius testa fragatur, sicut non potes pervenire ad novam legem nisi vetus lex conquassetur.

[29] The elimination of "invicem" does not distort the remainder of the sentence because "a se" alone is sufficient to convey the meaning "from one another."

Question 2

Crispin (p. 30):

Item scimus quia dixit deus ad Adam: Ecce, dedi uobis omnem herbam afferentem semen super terram et uniuersa ligna, que habent in semetipsis sementem generis sui, ut sint uobis in escam. Qua igitur ratione deus dedit primo homini uniuersa ligna in escam et statim postea prohibuit, ne de ligno scientie boni et mali sumat in escam? Vbi uniuersaliter uniuersa ligna concessa homini commendat, nullum exceptum lignum fuisse insinuat. Non igitur absque mysterio id aecipiendum est.

Alan:

Omitted.

Jacob ben Reuben (p. 24):

For we have seen that Moses wrote in the book of Genesis that the creator told Adam, "You may eat of all the trees of the garden" (Genesis 2: 16). Now, when he told him "of all the trees of the garden" he left nothing out; he kept nothing from him and permitted whatever he desired. In the next verse, however, he told him, "But of the tree of the knowledge of good and evil, you shall not eat of it, for on the day that you eat of it you shall surely die" (Gen. 2: 17). Now, look into this matter and pay close attention. If we are to understand these verses only according to the letter, how can you reconcile the two of them in a straightforward manner? Your own eyes can see (if you are prepared to admit the truth) that when the creator told Adam, "You may eat of all the trees of the garden," once he said "of all the trees" he did not leave over a single tree of all the trees of the garden to be added. Nevertheless, he subsequently prohibited to him the tree of the knowledge of good and evil, which had been among the other trees of the garden and thus permitted to him. I therefore maintain that the Torah was given for the understanding of other matters and different interpretations which are not superficially evident from the verses.[30]

---

[30] *Ki ken ra'inu she-katav Mosheh be-sefer Bereshit asher amar ha-bore la-adam: Mikol'ez ha-gan akhol tokhel, ve-ka'asher amar lo mikol 'ez ha-gan lo shiyyer kelum velo mana' mimmennu davar akh she-hittir lo ha-kol ke-hefzo. U-va-miqra ha-sheni amar elav: U-me-'ez ha-da'at tov va-ra' lo tokhal mimmennu ki be-yom akhalekha mimmennu mot tamut. Ve-'attah re'eh ve-hitbonen ve-sim libbekha le-davar zeh, im lo naskil ba-miqra'ot ha-elleh akh ke-fi ha-mikhtav, eikh tukhal leyasher et shenehem be-derekh yesharah? She-harei 'einekha ro'ot, im tahpoz lehodot 'al ha-emet, ki be-emor ha-bore el ha-adam, Mi-kol 'ez ha-gan akhol tokhel, keivan she-amar mi-kol ha-'ez lo hinniah'ez ehad mi-kol 'azei ha-gan lerabbot, ve-aharei ken hizhiro 'al 'ez ha-da'at tov va-ra' she-hayah bi-kelal she'ar 'azei ha-gan she-huttar lo. Al ken amarti she-nittenah ha-torah lehaskil 'inyanim aherim u-panim aherot she-lo nir'eh la-'ayin min ha-katuv.*

The essential argument here is that God first gave man all trees for food and then apparently contradicted himself by prohibiting the fruit of the tree of knowledge. The precise texts, however, are somewhat different, and the major difference may give us a clue as to why Alan omitted this argument entirely.

The verse quoted by Crispin to show that Adam was given all trees for food is Genesis 1: 29; in Genesis 2: 17, however, the tree of knowledge is forbidden. This, Crispin argues, constitutes a contradiction. In *Milhamot Hashem*, on the other hand, the verse cited to show that all trees were permitted to Adam is Genesis 2: 16 ("You may eat of all the trees of the garden"); the alleged contradiction is, therefore, in the very next verse, which prohibits eating from the tree of knowledge.

There is little doubt that the text used by Jacob reflects the efforts of an overly eager copyist (influenced, perhaps, by Crispin's "statim postea prohibuit") to "improve" his text by making the contradiction come immediately after the first verse quoted. The truth is, of course, that this change completely vitiated whatever force the original question may have had, because the obvious response is that Gen. 2: 17 does not contradict but simply qualifies 2: 16. As Jacob points out in his answer, you simply cannot write two things at the same time.[31]

Now, Alan of Lille was not in the habit of omitting significant sections in the middle of a passage that he copied, and his omission of one of Crispin's four questions is very peculiar. This omission, however, can be explained very easily if we assume that Alan had before him the same text as Jacob ben Reuben. He left out this question because, in the form in which he had it, it was simply ridiculous.

Question 3

Crispin (pp. 80–81):

> In Exodo, inter alia precepta de faciendo altari, dominus Moysi ita precepit: Altare de terra facietis mihi et offeretis super illud holocausta et pacifica uestra. Et de qua materie alia fieri liceret et quomodo, ita subdidit: Quod si de lapidibus illud edificare uolueris, de non sectis lapidibus illud edificabis. In expletione autem tabernaculi et uasorum atque utensilium tabernaculi ita legitur: Fecit Moyses altare thimiamatis de lignis sethim habens per quadrum singulos cubitos et in altitudine duos. Et post pauca:

31   *Milhamot Hashem*, p. 32.

Fecit et altare holocausti de lignis sethim quinque cubitorum per quadrum et trium in altitudine. Non temerario quidem ausu seu presumptione fiebat, quod tam discreta dimensione altitudinis et quadrature fiebat. Item post aliquanta: Fudit bases eneas in introitu tabernaculi et altare eneum cum craticula sua. Item in fine: Candelabrum stabit cum lucernis suis et altare aureum in quo adoletur incensum coram archa testimonii. Quo modo ergo dominus iubet, ut altare de terra faciatis et super illud holocausta uestra offeratis, econtra Moyses fecit altare thimiamatis ligneum et fecit altare holocausti ligneum, fecit altare eneum, fecit et aureum, fecit aliquando etiam et lapideum? Multum itaque aduersum uidetur, ut aliud et aliter quam dominus per Moysen iubet ab ipso Moyse agatur. Altius ergo quam littera sonat et hec accipi oportet.

Alan (col. 407–8):

In exordio[32] autem, inter alia praecepta, de faciendo altari Dominus Moysi ibi ita praecipit: Altare de terra facietis mihi; in sequentibus autem legitur sic: Fecit itaque Moyses altare thymiamatis de lignis setim. Et alibi: Fundavit bases aeneas in introitu tabernaculi. Multum itaque adversum videtur, ut aliud et aliter quam Dominus per Moysen jubet, ab ipso Moyse agatur. Aliter ergo quam littera sonat hoc accipi oportet.

Jacob ben Reuben (p. 25):

The creator also commanded Moses among the other laws: "An altar of earth shall you make unto me, and shall sacrifice thereon your burnt-offerings and your peace-offerings" (Exodus 20: 21). And at that point he taught him in what way he should make all the other altars that he would make, as it is written, "If you make me an altar of stone, you shall not build it of hewn stones" (Exod. 20: 22). But when he came to the construction of the tabernacle, Moses made the altar of gold and the altar of brass. Now, with respect to one of the altars it says, "And he made the altar of incense of acacia-wood: a cubit was the length thereof, and a cubit the breadth thereof, foursquare; and two cubits was the height thereof; the horns thereof were of one piece with it. And he overlaid it with pure gold" (Exod. 37: 25–26). And afterwards it says, "And he made the altar of burnt-offering of acacia-wood: five cubits was the length thereof, and five cubits the breadth thereof, foursquare, and three cubits the height thereof. And he made the horns thereof upon the four corners of it; the horns thereof were of one piece with it; and he overlaid it with brass" (Exod. 38: 1–2). Now, on the basis of all this I ask you why Moses acted in this manner. After all, I have already noted that the creator told him, "An altar of earth shall you make unto me," and that he warned him, "If you make me an altar of stone, you shall not build it of hewn stones." In light of this, why did Moses do all these things? And

---

32   Read "Exodo" in light of Crispin.

for what reason did he make one a cubit in length and a cubit in breadth, foursquare, and the other five cubits in length and five cubits in breadth? Now, this is a very difficult thing, that we should say of Moses, who was the most faithful of all the prophets, that he did that which the creator did not command him. If you will argue that the creator did command him to do this but it was not recorded since Scripture is generally concise, then this matter would be even more difficult, for we would be asserting that the creator, blessed be he, goes back on his word. I have therefore told you that everything is to be understood allegorically and not in accordance with the letter at all, lest we lose our way and walk in darkness.[33]

The basic elements of this question are that God commanded Moses to make an altar of earth (Exodus 20: 21–22), and yet Moses later made altars of wood and metal (Exodus 37: 25; 38: 1–2; 40: 4–5). With some changes in order and with the elaboration of an argument implicit in the *Disputatio*, Jacob ben Reuben's text is very close to that of Crispin. Alan's shorter version is probably his own condensation of the essential points of the argument.

Question 4

Crispin (p. 31):

Rursum, cum ea omnia humanis usibus deum creasse Moyses dicat, eaque omnia homini subdidisse comemoret, ut presit, inquit, piscibus maris, uolatilibus celi, animantibus terre et omni reptili quod mouetur in terra,

[33] *'Od zivvah ha-bore le-Mosheh bi-she'ar ha-huqqim: Mizbah adamah ta'aseh li ve-zavahta 'alav et 'olotekha ve-et shelamekha, ve-sham moreh 'alav be-eizeh 'inyan ya'aseh kol ha-mizbehot ha-aherim asher ya'aseh, kemo she-katuv, Ve-im mizbah avanim ta'aseh li lo tivneh ethen gazit. Ve-ka'asher higgia' le-ma'aseh ha-mishkan ba Mosheh ve-'asah mizbah ha-zahav umizbah ha-nehoshet. U-ba-mizbeah ha-ehad omer: Va-ya'as et mizbah ha-qetoret 'azei shittim ammah orko ve-ammah rohbo ravua' ve-ammatayim qomato mimmennu hayu qarnotav va-yezaf oto zahav tahor. Ve-aharei ken amar: Va-ya'as et mizbah ha-'olah 'azei shittim hamesh ammot orko ve-hamesh ammot rohbo ravua' ve-shalosh ammot qomato va-ya 'as qarnotav 'al arba' pinnotav mimmennu hayu qarnotav vayezaf oto nehoshet. U-mi-kol zeh ani sho'el elekha lammah 'asah Mosheh ken. She-kevar ra'iti she-'amar elav ha-bore, Mizbah adamah ta'aseh li, ve-ra'iti she-hizhiro, Ve-im mizbah avanim ta'aseh li lo tivneh ethen gazit. Ve-aharei ken mah ra'ah Mosheh she-'asah et kol elleh? U-me-eizeh ta'am 'asah ha-ehad ammah orko ve-ammah rohbo ravua', ve-ha-ehad hamesh ammot orko ve-hamesh ammot rohbo? Ve-davar qasheh hu me'od she-nomar mi-Mosheh she-hayah navi ne'eman 'al kol ha-nevi'im she-ya'aseh mah she-lo zivvahu ha-bore. Ve-im tomar she-habore zivvahu ve-lo nikhtav, ve-derekh ha-katuv leqazzer, kol she-ken yiqsheh ha-davar yoter, ki nomar me-habore she-yahazor be-dibburo. 'Al ken amarti elekha she-ha-kol nittan lehavin be-'inyan mashal ve-lo ke-fi ha-mikhtav kelal, pen nit'eh ba-nativ ve-nelekh ba-hoshekh.*

cur postea uetat, ne homo aret in boue et asino? Onus aliud, quodcunque tibi placet, asino imponere licet, et ponere iugum boui cum asino quare non licet? Ad pascua ducere bouem cum asino licebit, in pascuis ea simul esse et conpasci lex permittit, et arare ea simul prohibet et interdicit. Si autem propterea uetat, quia hoc animal inmundum lex dicit, quare circa illud cetera, que dicta sunt, permittit, solum arare excipit? Equus in lege animal inmundum esse perhibetur et alia multa, nec tamen arare bouem cum equo uel alio animali inmundo in lege prohibetur.

Alan (col. 408):

Item, ad litteram quomodo stare potest, quod Deus prohibet: Ne homo aret in bove et asino? Onus aliud quodcunque tibi placet asino imponere, non vetat lex, et ponere jugum cum asino, quasi non licet, cum ad pascua bovem cum asino ducere licet, in pascuis simul esse, et compasci permittit lex, et arare simul prohibet, et interdicit. Si auctor propterea haec vetat, quia hoc animal immundum esse perhibetur, cur non etiam arare bovem cum equo vel alio animali immundo prohibetur in lege?

Jacob ben Reuben (pp. 27–28):[34]

The creator said, "You shall not plow with an ox and an ass together" (Deuteronomy 22: 10). Thus, he prohibited only plowing. With respect to another burden, the creator did not take pity upon it, but with respect to a yoke, he prohibited you from tying it together with an ass. However, when they graze, he permitted that an ox and an ass be together, but while plowing this is a serious prohibition. Now, if the ass was prohibited by the creator because it is an impure animal, why did he permit an ox and an ass to graze together? He should have prohibited even standing and grazing, and yet he prohibited only plowing. With respect to a horse, the Torah says that it is an impure animal, and so too with respect to a mule and many other animals; nevertheless, the creator did not prohibit them from plowing with an ox nor the ox with any other animal except the ass.[35]

---

34 This passage from *Milhamot Hashem* is taken from the section which presumably gives the Christian interpretation of these verses; in fact, the Christian question is reiterated here in a form closer to that of Crispin and Alan than the form in which it first appears in *Milhamot Hashem* (p. 26). Even Jacob's initial formulation, however, is quite close to the text given here.

35 *Amar ha-bore, Lo taharosh be-shor u-va-hamor yahdav, ve-asar ha-harishah levad, u-le-'inyan massa aher lo has ha-bore 'alav, akh le-'inyan 'ol asar lekha shelo tiqshor oto 'im ha-hamor. Aval ka-'asher yir'u hittir lekha she-yihyu ha-shor ve-ha-hamor yahdav, u-be-'et ha-harishah hu issur gadol. Ve-im ne'esar lekha ha-hamor me'et ha-bore ba'avur she-hi behemah teme'ah, maddua' hittir sheyir'u yahdav ha-shor ve-ha-hamor? Hayah lo le'esor afilu ha-ma'mad ve-ha-mir'eh, velo asar ki im ha-harishah levaddah. U-me-ha-sus amrah ha-torah she-hi behemah teme'ah u-me-ha-pered u-mi-behemot aherot rabbot, ve-'af 'al pi ken lo asaram ha-bore laharosh 'im shor ve-shor 'im behemah aheret huz me-ha-hamor.*

In Crispin, this is a two-part argument. First of all, the Bible says that man would rule over the animals of the earth (Genesis 1: 26), and then it prohibits plowing with an ox and an ass together (Deuteronomy 22: 10). This is an alleged contradiction of the sort that this passage has been discussing all along. Crispin then continues with a series of logical arguments designed to show that the prohibition in Deuteronomy is inherently implausible. Why is only plowing prohibited? And if an ox may not plow with an ass because the latter is an impure animal, why was the ass singled out? There are, after all, quite a number of additional impure animals.

Both Jacob and Alan present only the logical arguments and omit the contradiction entirely. Here again Jacob's text probably reveals that the citation of Genesis 1: 26 was missing from Alan's source. This would have been a reasonable conjecture even without Jacob's translation; it is, after all, unlikely that Alan would have omitted the contradiction on his own since the basic character of this passage leads one to expect the citation of contradictions. Nevertheless, it is only *Milhamot Hashem* which enables us to make this assertion with some confidence.[36]

Concluding Passage

Crispin (pp. 31–32)
   Hanc non solum in his que dicta sunt mandatis, sed in quampluribus aliis legalibus cerimoniis contrarietatem uidemus, nisi ea conpetenti sensu intellexerimus. Discreto itaque et diuino sensu hec discutienda et intelligenda sunt, quia fieri non potest, ut ad litteram sumpta ea omnia impleantur. Si uero legem debito sensu accipimus, omnia legis mandata debita obseruatione obseruare poterimus, quedam ad litteram et sine ullo figurarum uelamine dicta esse accipiendo, quedam uero ad figuram et profundo figurarum uelamine adumbrata esse intelligendo. Quedam ad tempus obseruari iussa sunt, quedam sine ulla temporum determinatione obseruanda sunt. Que enim sacramenti alicuius prenunciatiua erant et ueritatis future figura, suo tempore manifestata rei atque ueritatis presentia, oportuit, ut eorum remaneret prenunciatio et figura. Nam sicut ipso usu loquendi uerborum utimur uicissitudinibus, dicendo 'erit', quamdiu futurum est, et ipsum 'erit' prorsus omittentes in presenti 'est'

---

[36] Christian questions concerning the inherent logic of Biblical commandments in order to set up allegorical exegesis are quoted in other Jewish polemics as well. See Meir ben Simon of Narbonne, *Milhemet Mizvah*, Parma ms., pp. 46a–47a; *Nizzahon Vetus*, in J. Wagenseil, *Tela Ignea Satanae* (Altdorf, 1681), II, pp. 10, 19.

assumimus, quidque ipsum iam preterisse significantes utimur 'fuit', sic in rebus prenunciatiuis alicuius sacramenti, ubi presens manifestatur sacramentum, eius iam superfluo seruaretur seu figura seu signum.

Alan (col. 408):

Hanc non solum in iis quae dicta sunt mandatis, sed etiam in pluribus aliis legalibus caeremoniis contrarietatem videmus, nisi ea competenti sensu intellexerimus. Discreto itaque et divino sensu haec intelligenda sunt et discutienda. Si vero legem debito sensu accipimus, omnia legis mandata debita observatione observare poterimus; quaedam ad litteram et sine ullo figurarum velamine dicta esse accipiendo, quaedam ad figuram et profundo velamine obumbrata esse intelligendo: quaedam ad tempus observari jussa sunt, quaedam sine ulla temporum determinatione. Quae enim alicujus sacramenti praenuntiativa erant, et veritatis figuram faterentur, suo tempore, manifestata rei atque veritatis praesentia, oportuit ut eorum non remaneret praenuntiatio et figura. Nam sicut ipso suo loquendi sensu utimur verborum vicissitudinibus, dicendo, erit, quandiu futurum est ipsum quod erit; prorsus omittentes in praesenti, et assumendo, est; cumque ipsum jam praeteriisse significantes utimur, fuit: sic in rebus praenuntiativis alicujus sacramenti, ubi praesens manifestatur sacramentum, ejus jam superflue servaretur figura, seu signum.

Jacob ben Reuben (p. 28):

Similar strange things can be found in many places in the Torah of Moses. It is therefore proper to interpret and understand in accordance with the profundity of the human intellect, for if we should examine it on the basis of the letter alone, it could never be observed. If, on the other hand, we understand the Torah as it is proper to understand it, we shall be able to observe all the commandments as they are, some just as they are written without any symbolism at all, and others through allegory and symbol. Some were commanded to be observed for all time and have no time limit, while others were commanded to be observed for a fixed time. With regard to those which were commanded for a fixed time, once that time has passed, the commandment has been abolished, just as a man usually says of an event which is to take place in the future, "It will be," for it has not yet come, while after it has come it becomes something which already "was." Such is the case with regard to most of the commandments in the Torah of Moses, which were said for a fixed time; after that time has passed, it is only proper that they be abolished.[37]

---

[37] *Ve-ki-devarim elleh she-hem teimah yesh be-rov meqomot be-torat Mosheh. 'Al ken ya'ut lefaresh u-lehavin me-'omeq sekhel ha-adam, ki im lo nitbonen bo raq ke-fi ha-mikhtav, lo yitqayyem le-'olam. Akh im naskil ha-torah asher ya'ut lehaskil, nukhal leqayyem kol ha-mizvot kullan ka'asher hen, ha-aherot beli shum dimyon ba-'olam ka'asher hen ketuvot, ve-ha-aherot*

This passage is almost identical in the three works. It maintains that there are many other difficulties in the Law if it is interpreted literally and that the commandments may be divided into two groups—some which can be taken literally and others which must be understood allegorically. This was a time-honored position in Christian thought although it raised problems which Jews did not hesitate to exploit.[38]

We have seen, then, the existence of an unsuspected Hebrew translation of a selection of Gilbert Crispin's *Disputatio* which may be the first Hebrew translation of any section of a medieval Latin work. Moreover, this translation may reveal the existence of a polemical collection which circulated in France in the twelfth century and contained extensive quotations from Crispin. In at least one instance, these quotations have apparently preserved a reading in the *Disputatio* which has been distorted in all the known manuscripts. Furthermore, it is at least possible that Alan of Lille used a similar collection of polemic in writing the third book of his *Contra Haereticos*; at the very least, this translation reveals variant readings which probably underlie Alan's version and which are preserved in no other source. Finally, we may conclude that the impact of Gilbert Crispin on the Jewish-Christian debate in the twelfth century was truly pervasive and exceeded even the generous estimates that have hitherto prevailed.

---

be-mashal ve-dimyon. Ha-aherot niztavvu lishmor kol ha-yamim, she-ein lahem zeman, ve-ha-aherot niztavvu lishmor li-zeman qavua'. Ve-otan she-niztavvu li-zeman qavua', ahar she-'avar ha-zeman nitbattelah ha-mizvah, kemo she-adam ragil lomar mi-davar she-'atid lihyot "yihyeh," she-'adayin lo ba, ve-ahar she-ba shav ha-davar lihyot "hayah." Ve-ken rov ha-mizvot she-ne'emru be-torat Mosheh li-zeman qavua', ahar she-'avar ha-zeman din hu she-yevattelu otam.

38   Cf. Eucher of Lyon, *PL* 50: 781, and Leo the Great, *PL* 54: 88–89. For the Jewish argument against allegory, see appendix 3 of my dissertation, *The Nizzahon Vetus: A Critical Edition, with an Introduction and Commentary on the First Part*, Columbia University, 1970.

THE ATTITUDE OF ST. BERNARD OF CLAIRVAUX TOWARD THE JEWS

From: *Proceedings of the American Academy for Jewish Research* 40 (1972): 89–108.

St. Bernard of Clairvaux (1090–1153) was a pivotal figure in the intellectual and political changes that shook Western Christendom in the eleventh and twelfth centuries. Apostle of the Gregorian reformers, Bernard believed not merely in the primacy of religion but in its right to control all political and social phenomena. Consequently, he became the self-appointed conscience of Europe; he chastised kings, advised popes, and exercised an undeniable influence upon the most significant religious and secular decisions of his time.

Bernard was, furthermore, in the forefront of the revolution in Christian piety that had begun in the eleventh century. He practically founded a new and more rigorous monastic order, contributed to the burgeoning Mary cult, and helped to strengthen popular piety. These intellectual and emotional changes certainly played some role in the broadening and intensification of anti-Jewish feeling in the second half of the Middle Ages.

The question we shall try to answer in this paper is whether Bernard himself was impelled by these forces toward a more strongly anti-Jewish attitude than his predecessors. As we shall see, he presents a fascinating case study of the increasing tension between the standard theological rationale for tolerating Jews in its most liberal form and the growing hatred for Jews in twelfth-century Europe.

Bernard is a good example of a Christian who formed his attitude toward the Jews almost entirely on the basis of theoretical and theological considerations, for aside from some knowledge of their usurious activities, his contact with Jews was minimal. Malcolm Hay writes that "not a single word (in Bernard's works) suggests the possibility of friendly personal relations with them."[1] Stephen Harding, Bernard's predecessor as head of the Cistercian movement, had used rabbis to help him with textual problems in the Hebrew scriptures, but there is no evidence at all that Bernard continued this practice, and there are some positive indications that he did not do so systematically.[2]

Consequently, his action during the one time of his life when he was faced with a Jewish crisis is reflective of the effects of official Christian theology rather than of any personal relationship with Jews. This action came during the preparations for the second crusade, a crusade that was preached by Bernard, when a Cistercian monk named Radulph left his monastery and began encouraging the mobs to massacre Jews. Bernard heeded an urgent appeal and wrote a number of letters opposing Radulph; ultimately, he even preached to the mobs in order to prevent the massacres.

Part of the texts of Bernard's letters at this time will serve as an excellent basis for a discussion of some of his central positions on Jewish questions:

> For the rest, not I but the Apostle warns you, brethren, not to believe every spirit. I have heard with great joy of the zeal for God's glory which burns in your midst, but your zeal needs the timely restraint of knowledge. The Jews are not to be persecuted, killed, or even put to flight. Ask anyone who knows Sacred Scripture what he finds foretold of the Jews in the Psalm. 'Not for their destruction do I pray,' it says. The Jews are for us the living words of Scripture, for they remind us of what our Lord suffered. They are dispersed all over the world so that by suffering for their crime they may be everywhere the living witnesses of our redemption. Hence the same Psalm adds, 'only let thy power disperse them.' And so it is: dispersed they are. Under Christian princes they endure a hard captivity, but 'they only wait for the time of their deliverance.' Finally, we are told by the Apostle that

---

1   *Europe and the Jews* (Boston, 1961), p. 40.
2   On Harding, see Watkin Williams, *St. Bernard of Clairvaux* (Westminster, Maryland, 1952), p. 259. As for Bernard, there is one sermon, for example, where he expresses doubt as to whether the phrase "meliora sunt ubera tua vino" (Cant. 1.2) was spoken by the bride or bridegroom. A reference to the Hebrew "dodekha" would have resolved the issue (assuming the acceptance of Massoretic vocalization). See *Sermones super Cantica Canticorum* (henceforth referred to as *SCC*), 9.4, *S. Bernardi Opera*, ed. by J. Leclerq, C. H. Talbot, and H. M. Rochais (henceforth referred to as *LTR*) (Rome, 1957), I, p. 44; *Life and Works of St. Bernard*, tr. by Samuel J. Eales (henceforth referred to as Eales) (London, 1896), IV, p. 45. Translations from *SCC* are, with occasional changes, taken from Eales.

when the time is ripe all Israel shall be saved. But those who die before will remain in death . . . . If the Jews are utterly wiped out [or 'ground down'— *conterantur*], what will become of our hope for their promised salvation, their eventual conversion? If the pagans were similarly subjugated to us, then, in my opinion, we should wait for them rather than seek them out with swords. But as they have now begun to attack us, it is necessary for those of us who do not carry a sword in vain to repel them with force. It is an act of Christian piety both to 'vanquish the proud' and also to 'spare the subjected', especially those for whom we have a law and a promise, and whose flesh was shared by Christ whose name be forever blessed.[3]

In another letter, Bernard wrote:

'Put back thy sword into its place; all those who take up the sword will perish by the sword.' Is it not a far better triumph for the Church to convince and convert the Jews than to put them all to the sword? . . . . Otherwise, when does that saying come in, 'Not for their destruction I pray,' and 'When the fulness of the nations shall have come in, then all Israel will be saved,' and 'The Lord is rebuilding Jerusalem, calling the banished sons of Israel home'?[4]

There are a great number of highly significant statements in these passages. Let us begin with the most basic question: the prohibition of converting Jews at the point of a sword. This prohibition, in the view of Bernard, is based upon two independent considerations. The first is logical and the second Scriptural. The logical argument is what prompts him to say that he would tolerate even subjugated pagans, and this argument appears more clearly elsewhere.

In a famous passage in his *Sermons on the Canticle*,[5] he says that heretics should be taken not by force of arms but by force of arguments. In

---

3   Selections from the Latin of this passage:
    Non sunt persequendi Judaei, non sunt trucidandi, sed ne effugandi quidem ... propter hoc dispersi sunt in omnes regiones, ut dum justas tanti facinoris poenas luunt, testes sint nostrae redemptionis ... Denique cum introiret gentium multitudo, 'tunc omnis Israel salvus erit,' ait Apostolus (Rom. 11:26).
    Epist. 363, *Sancti Bernardi ... Opera*, ed. by Johannis Mabillon, I (henceforth referred to as Mabillon) (Paris, 1719), c. 329–330 = Migne, *Patrologia Latina* (henceforth *PL*) 182: 567. The English is based on Bruno Scott James, *The Letters of St. Bernard of Clairvaux* (London, 1953), Letter 391, pp. 462–463. Henceforth, the enumeration and pagination of letters in James' translation will be placed in parentheses next to the usual number. It should be noted that James translates "poenas luunt" as "*expiating* their crime," but this is unlikely
4   Epist. 365, Mabillon, c. 332 = *PL* 182: 57 (James, 393, p. 466).
5   64.8, *LTR*, II, p. 170, Eales, IV, p. 386.

this he follows the rather obvious insight of Gregory I that only preaching can effect a sincere conversion.[6] However, there is a second, less tolerant step in the reasoning associated with this position. Two sermons later,[7] Bernard adds that though faith is produced by persuasion and not by force, it is better to coerce heretics at sword point than to permit them to "draw away many other persons into their error." This is similar to his argument in Ep. 363 with regard to pagans although there he refers to military attacks rather than pagan persuasion. Thus, the logical consideration operates to grant toleration only to docile pagans and heretics. When they become militant or troublesome, they are to be "coerced by the sword."

The Jews, however, are protected not only by logical argument but also by Biblical injunction. What, may we ask, would be the status of a Jewish people which was attracting Christians away from their faith? Would the Biblical requirement that Jews be tolerated also fall before the fear that they would "draw away many other persons into their error"? There is a passage in his *De Consideratione*[8] where Bernard implies that the Bible would prevail: "Let them [heretics], I say, either be corrected by your zeal in this way lest they perish or be coerced lest they destroy others." He then goes on, apparently dealing with a situation in which they might "destroy others," and says: "But concerning the Jews, time excuses you: They have their own end which cannot be brought earlier. The fulness of the nations must precede it." This is a radical statement of extreme toleration.

Whether or not Bernard would have maintained such a position in the face of a proselytizing Judaism is surely open to question, but the fact remains that his actual statements in this area are extremely tolerant, especially when we compare them with his attitude toward pagans. He writes in a letter, "We utterly forbid that for any reason whatsoever a truce should be made with these peoples [Eastern European pagans] ... until such a time as, by God's help, they shall be either converted or wiped out."[9] In another letter, after quoting the very verse about putting away the sword which he used in letter 365 to defend the Jews, he argues

6   Gregory's Epist. 1.47. Cf. James Parkes, *The Conflict of the Church and the Synagogue* (Cleveland, New York, and Philadelphia, 1961), p. 211.

7   *SCC* 66.12, *LTR*, II, p. 187, Eales, IV, p. 407.

8   III. 1.3, Mabillon, c. 433 = *PL* 182: 759 = J. Leclerq & H. M. Rochais, *S. Bernardi Opera* III (Rome, 1963), p. 433.

9   Epist. 467 (394, p. 467).

that it must sometimes be overridden. "I believe that the time has come for both swords to be drawn in defense of the Eastern Church."[10]

Bernard's letter on the Jews, then, distinguishes them favorably from the pagans and was at least partially effective in halting the massacres. His activity on behalf of the Jews was not forgotten by the beneficiaries, and both the twelfth-century Ephraim of Bonn and the sixteenth-century Yosef ha-Kohen refer to his actions with varying degrees of enthusiasm.[11] Malcolm Hay, however, has recently proferred a much less favorable appraisal of Bernard's action in this matter.[12] He emphasizes the fact that Bernard's reasons for opposing the massacres were not humanitarian but theological, and his language in condemning Radulph is scarcely as strong as it could and should have been. When he condemned the murder of a Christian, Master Thomas, he was far more indignant than he was on this occasion. Furthermore, he ended his letter by freeing all crusaders from exactions of usury,[13] a "consolation," says Hay, "for recruits who were now forbidden to exercise their swordsmanship upon defenseless civilians." It should be added that there is no clearcut evidence for Graetz' apologia that Bernard was forced to remit the interest by Papal pressure.[14]

The fact is, however, that Hay's strictures are more a condemnation of medieval anti-Semitism generally than they are of Bernard. Few medieval leaders waxed eloquent over their deep humanitarian concern for Jews, and while occasional feelings of genuine sympathy do appear, they are hardly characteristic of the period. Moreover, to the extent that appeals to Christian mercy are made with regard to treatment of Jews, such appeals are found in Bernard's letters as well.[15]

---

[10] Epist. 256 (399, p. 471).

[11] Yosef ha-Kohen is more enthusiastic than his predecessor, who had emphasized Bernard's theological motivations. See Ephraim of Bonn's *Sefer Zekhirah* in A. M. Habermann, *Sefer Gezerot Ashkenaz ve-Zarfat* (Jerusalem, 1946), p. 116, and Yosef ha-Kohen's *'Emeq ha-Bakhah*, ed. by M. Letteris (Vienna, 1852), p. 41. There is a reference to the Jewish reaction in Richard S. Storrs' brief and enthusiastic account of Bernard's activities on behalf of the Jews; see his *Bernard of Clairvaux* (New York, 1912), pp. 176–181. See also B. Blumenkranz in K. Rengstorff and S. von Kortzfleisch, *Kirche und Synagoge*, I (Stuttgart, 1968), pp. 121–122.

[12] *Europe and the Jews*, chapter 2, pp. 40 ff.

[13] Epist. 363, Mabillon, c. 330 = *PL* 182: 568.

[14] H. Graetz, *Geschichte der Juden*, third ed., VI, (Leipzig, 1894), p. 148 = *Divrei Yemei Yisrael*, translated by S. P. Rabbinowicz (Warsaw, 1894), IV, p. 190.

[15] One medieval leader who appears to have felt some genuine sympathy for Jews was Pope Alexander II. In a letter written in 1063 regarding the murder of Jews by knights in Spain,

Furthermore, Bernard maintained the most liberal of the views that were possible within the accepted theology. It was, of course, universally maintained that Jews should not be massacred; indeed, Psalm 59:12 ("Do not kill them ... "), which Bernard cites in his letter, was a classical proof-text quoted very frequently to buttress this position.[16] Nevertheless, even so extreme an anti-Jewish measure as expulsion was sometimes considered consistent with this and similar verses. Pope Leo VII had written to archbishop Frederick of Mayence between 937 and 939 that Jews should not be forced to convert but that they may be expelled if they refuse.[17] In addition, Bernard's apparent view that even militant Jews should be tolerated, as well as several opinions that we shall discuss below (e.g., the unusual vigor of his insistence on their ultimate salvation and his view that they retain a special favorable status), clearly serve to classify his practical position on the Jews as extremely tolerant. Indeed, even his suggestion that certain debts be voided appears mild in comparison with Peter the Venerable's proposal on the same occasion that Jewish funds be confiscated for use by crusaders.[18] Finally, it ought to be noted that Radulph was held in very high regard in Germany and that vigorous opposition to his preaching was neither easy nor assured of success.[19]

Now, the same verse which prohibits destruction of the Jews (Psalm 59:12) prophesies their dispersion ("only let Thy power disperse them"). Bernard was strongly imbued with the idea of Jewish serfdom, writing that "there is no more dishonorable nor serious serfdom than that of the

---

he called those knights stupid, avaricious, and madly raging for trying to kill people whom divine *pietas* had predestined for salvation, and in another letter he added, "God does not enjoy the shedding of blood nor delight in the destruction of the wicked." See *PL* 146: 1386–1387. For a less impressive but similar remark by Bernard, see below, note 25.

[16] See H. H. Ben Sasson, *Peraqim be-Toledot ha-Yehudim bi-Yemei ha-Beinayim* (Tel Aviv, 1958), pp. 31–32. Cf. also Peter Damian, whose general outlook was quite similar to that of Bernard: "Unde per Psalmistam dicitur . . . ne occidas eos,'" Epist. 13, *PL* 144: 284–285. On Damian's attitude toward the Jews, cf. my "St. Peter Damian: His Attitude toward the Jews and the Old Testament," *The Yavneh Review* 4 (1965): 80–112.

[17] *PL* 132: 1084–1085.

[18] See *PL* 189: 368, and cf. Ch. Merchavia, *Ha-Talmud bi-Re'i HaNazrut* (Jerusalem, 1970), p. 130, and B. Blumenkranz in K. Rengstorff and S. von Kortzfleisch, *Kirche und Synagoge*, I, p. 121.

[19] See the citations in Carl Neumann, *Bernhard von Clairvaux und die Anfänge des Zweiten Kreuzzuges* (Heidelberg, 1882), p. 35. For a fairly recent discussion of some of Bernard's activities in connection with the crusade, see A. Bredero, "Studien zu den Kreuzzugsbriefen Bernhards von Clairvaux und seiner Reise nach Deutschland im Jahre 1146," *Mitteilungen des Instituts für österreichische Geschichtsforschung* 66 (1958), pp. 331–343.

Jews; they carry it with them wherever they go, and everywhere they find their masters."[20] Furthermore, he used the existence of this servitude as an anti-Jewish argument. "But if that flower [of the Jews] still remains, where, then, is the kingdom? where is the priesthood? where the prophets and the temple? where those mighty wonders etc.?"[21] This argument was common,[22] and in this literary form it is taken straight out of a sermon by Peter Chrysologus who asked, "Where is the temple? Where is the priest? Where is the sacrifice?"[23]

This serfdom is, of course, punishment for that greatest of all crimes, the crucifixion. Bernard mentions the Jews' "viperous venom" in hating Jesus and the bestial stupidity and miserable blindness which caused them to "lay impious hands upon the Lord of Glory."[24]

Nevertheless, in spite of the length and severity of what Bernard considered a richly deserved servitude, he firmly believed that the Jews will be saved at the final judgment. The brunt of his argument against their destruction is that such a destruction would invalidate Scriptural prophecies, such as the oft-quoted verse (Romans 11:26) that "all Israel will be saved." He is so thoroughly convinced of the anti-Scriptural character of Radulph's preaching that he writes, "Are you the one who makes the prophets liars and empties out the treasures of piety and mercy of Jesus Christ?"[25] This form of argument is particularly intriguing, since it was usually used as part of anti-Jewish polemic. Thus,

---

20   *De Consideratione*, I, translated in S. W. Baron, *A Social and Religious History of the Jews* (2nd ed., Philadelphia, 1957), V, p. 129.

21   "First Sermon on the Virgin Mother," *St. Bernard's Sermons for the Seasons and the Principal Festivals of the Year*, tr. by a priest of Mt. Melleray (henceforth *Sermons*) (Westminster, Maryland, 1950), I, pp. 60–61.

22   Cf., e.g., Damian's *Dialogus*, PL 145: 65–66, and Jacob ben Reuben, *Milhamot Hashem*, ed. by J. Rosenthal (Jerusalem, 1963), p. 5. For the Jewish response to the Christian argument from the small number, servitude and degradation of the Jews, see *Sefer Yosef ha-Meqanne*, *Festschrift Berliner's* (Frankfurt A.M., 1903), p. 87; Rosenthal's edition (Jerusalem, 1970), p. 58; Meir ben Simon of Narbonne, *Milhemet Mizvah*, Parma ms. p. 14; Joseph Kimhi, *Sefer ha-Berit*, in *Milhemet Hovah* (Constantinople, 1710), p. 36a; Solomon Ben Moses de Rossi, *'Edut Hashem Ne'emanah*, partly edited by J. Rosenthal, *Sura* 3 (1948): 260–264; *Sefer Nizzahon Yashan* in J. Wagenseil, *Tela Ignea Satanae* (Altdorf, 1681), II, pp. 253–257; Rupert of Deutz, *Dialogus Christiani et Judaei*, PL 170: 606.

23   *PL* 52: 512.

24   SCC 60.4, *LTR*, II, p. 144, Eales, IV, p. 362. See too "Second Sermon for Christmas Day," *Sermons*, I, p. 395. Cf. also Epist. 158 (164, p. 233).

25   "Tune es ille qui mendaces facies prophetas et evacuebis omnes thesauros pietatis et misericordiae Jesu Christi?" Epist. 365, Mabillon, c. 332 = *PL* 182: 571.

Bernard may subtly be arguing that Radulph is no better than the Jews whom he is attacking.[26] In a sermon, he says that the judgment against Israel is only partial (*ex parte*) and quotes the verse that God will not reject them to the end, but will save a remnant ("sed nec repellet in finem, reliquias salvaturus").[27] It would not do to press the contradiction between "all Israel" and a "remnant"; Bernard probably felt that the entire last generation of Jews (= all Israel) would be saved, while "remnant" has the wider perspective of all the generations. In fact, Bernard himself mentions both verses one after the other.[28]

What is especially surprising in this connection is Bernard's use of the verse, "The Lord is rebuilding Jerusalem, calling the banished sons of Israel home," as a prophecy of Jewish redemption. In many places, Bernard understands "Jerusalem" as a spiritual term and "Israel" as Christians. He says that at the second advent, God will "rebuild the Jerusalem of your souls."[29] He refers to the "true Jerusalem,"[30] to the renewal of the "spiritual Jerusalem, the true holy city,"[31] and to the "free Jerusalem which is above and mother of us all.[32] Indeed, this widespread conception goes back to Galatians 4:26: "But the Jerusalem above is free, and she is our mother." Bernard, moreover, agrees with the universal Christian belief that the Christians are *verus Israel*.[33] It would seem, then, that in order to save the Jews, Bernard suppressed what he believed to

26   For the argument that Jews, in effect, proclaim the prophets liars, see John 5: 45–47; *Doctrina Jacobi Nuper Baptizati*, ed. by N. Bonwetsch (Berlin, 1910), pp. 20–21, 65 (*ean ouk elthen ho christos, pseudetai ho prophetes*); *Les Trophées de Damas*, ed. by G. Bardy, *Pat. Orientalia* 15, p. 240 (*ton patriarchan pseusten epoiesas*); Petrus Alfonsi's *Dialogus*, PL 157: 618 (Christians believe in the incarnation because they don't consider the prophets liars); Rupert of Deutz, *Dialogus*, PL 170: 596 ("O Judaee, quaecumque loquuntur Scripturae ut vera sunt aut non; sed dicere quis audeat quia non vera sunt ?").

27   *SCC* 14.2, *LTR* I, pp. 76–77, Eales IV, p. 75.

28   *SCC* 79.5–6, *LTR* II, p. 275, Eales, IV, p. 486. Raban Maur also quoted the verse on all Israel and a verse mentioning the *reliquiae* without noticing a contradiction. Cf. *PL* 110: 582. For other references to Jewish salvation in Bernard, cf. *SCC* 16.15, *LTR*, I, p. 97, Eales, IV, p. 94, and Epist. 467 (394, p.467).

29   "Fifth Sermon for Christmas Day," *Sermons*, I, p. 42.

30   Epist. 469 (395, p. 468).

31   "First Sermon for Septuagesima," *Sermons*, II, p. 60.

32   Epist. 64 (67, p. 91).

33   "Second Sermon for Christmas Eve," *Sermons*, I, p. 317; "Fourth Sermon on the Virgin Mother," ibid., p. 114; "First Sermon for the First Sunday after the Octave of the Epiphany," *Sermons*, II, p. 37; Epist. 397 (429, p. 499); Epist. 288 (410, p. 479). On the history of this conception, see M. Simon, *Verus Israel* (Paris, 1948), esp. pp. 110–111, and B. Blumenkranz, *Die Judenpredigt Augustins* (Basel, 1946), pp. 164–175.

be a perfectly valid interpretation of this verse and referred it instead to carnal Israel.[34] He implies, furthermore, that the ultimate Jewish conversion will take place at least with the consent of the Jews' free will; it cannot be entirely imposed from without.[35] Bernard's view of Jewish salvation, then, was of the most positive nature possible within the framework of medieval Christian thought.

It is a matter of particular interest that Bernard appears convinced that Jews retain some special status even after the crucifixion and that some Biblical promises still apply to them. He writes that the Jew, unlike the Christian, has the right to temporal riches, for he "received the promise of a temporal reward."[36] It is, of course, possible that this is a rationalization to explain the theologically uncomfortable fact that some Jews were quite successful financially, but this possibility does not render Bernard's remark insignificant. Moreover, his above-quoted statement suggesting that Jews are to be spared partly because Jesus shared their flesh reinforces the impression that he was genuinely convinced that even carnal Israel has a special, favorable status.[37]

There are a number of other places in his works where Bernard shows some moderate leanings favorable to Jews. Even the infidel, he feels, can love God, though neither Jew nor pagan can love Him as much as the Christian can.[38] He attributes a chaste custom to the Jews by saying that Mary was betrothed to Joseph because the intended husband would, according to "a Jewish custom," watch over the virtue of his intended wife.[39] In apologizing for Paul's early persecution of Christians, he

---

[34]   It is also possible that Bernard referred this verse to the Jews because of the phrase "banished sons of Israel," and Christians had never been banished. Indeed, this argument was used by Jewish polemicists in connection with the *Verus Israel* question in general. See the *Sefer Nizzahon Yashan* in J. Wagenseil, *Tela Ignea Satanae* (Altdorf, 1681), II, p. 31, and cf. my doctoral dissertation, *The Nizzahon Vetus*, Columbia Univ., 1970, pp. 31, 111.

[35]   *The Treatise of St. Bernard Concerning Grace and Free Will (De Gratia et Libero Arbitrio)*, tr. by W. Williams (London and New York, 1920), pp. 16–17.

[36]   "First Sermon for the Feast of All Saints," *Sermons*, III, p. 338.

[37]   See Epist. 363, Mabillon, c. 330 = PL 182: 567 (James 391, p. 463). It must be granted that he is not being theologically rigorous in this sentence (note his "proof-text" regarding vanquishing the proud and sparing the subjected from the *Aeneid*, a work that was hardly canonical despite Virgil's medieval reputation as a near-prophet).

[38]   *The Book on the Love of God (De Diligendo Dei)*, ed. and tr. by E. G. Gardner (London, 1915), pp. 38, 42, 64.

[39]   "Second Sermon on the Virgin Mother," *Sermons*, I, p. 82. This interpretation, however, is theologically motivated and was current before Bernard.

supplies, perhaps unwittingly, a basis for mitigating Jewish sin, saying, "He 'did it ignorantly in unbelief.'"[40] While interpreting the verse, "Thou shalt not walk upon the asp ...", he avoids an Augustinian interpretation which said that the asp was the Jew.[41] Finally, he says that Christians are worse usurers than Jews, a statement we shall discuss below.[42]

Nevertheless, despite the pro-Jewish tendencies discussed above, the general tenor of Bernard's sermons and letters is strongly anti-Semitic. As a loyal member of an anti-Jewish tradition going back to the classical world, Bernard strongly condemns Jewish exclusiveness. "He desired them [the Gentiles] to draw near; but the Synagogue forbade them . . . For Judah has in abundance the oil of knowledge of God, and keeps it to herself, as a miser . . . She desires to possess alone the worship, the knowledge, the great name of God, not because she is jealous of her own happiness, but because she is envious of mine." He then adds that the Jews desire that "the unction of salvation remain upon Aaron's beard alone."[43]

Bernard's negative assessment of Jewish character is not confined to their rejection of Jesus alone, for he refers to Jewish *perfidia* during the first Jewish Commonwealth.[44] He says, with Acts, that the Jews always resist the holy spirit,[45] and, with the Psalmist, that they are ungrateful and "not mindful of His benefits."[46]

However, Bernard discusses most of the repulsive traits of the Jews in connection with their rejection of Jesus and the circumstances surrounding his advent. He is quite emphatic, for example, in his discussion of their extreme cruelty. Joseph had to hide the pregnant Mary lest "that stiff-necked people . . . , those cruel and incredulous Jews, would have mocked at him and stoned her . . . What would they have done to him whilst yet unborn, on whom afterwards, when glorified by miracles, they did not hesitate to lay sacrilegious hand?"[47] Now, this

40 "Third Sermon for the Feast of SS. Peter and Paul," *Sermons*, III, p. 212.
41 "Fourteenth Sermon on Psalm XC," *Sermons*, I, p. 278 (cf. translator's note).
42 Epist. 363, Mabillon, c. 330.
43 *SCC* 14.1–2, *LTR*, I, pp. 75–77, Eales, IV, pp. 74–75.
44 *SCC* 46.5, *LTR*, II, p. 59, Eales, IV, p. 284: "Ita intonans [propheta] in perfidiam Judaeorum."
45 Epist. 311 (374, p. 445).
46 *SCC* 11.2, *LTR*, I, p. 56, Eales, IV, p. 56.
47 "Second Sermon on the Virgin Mother," *Sermons*, I, pp. 86–87. For the passage from Jerome mentioned next, cf. translator's note, p. 85.

particular passage is motivated by exegetical considerations and is, in any case, inspired by Jerome who wrote that Mary was betrothed so that she might not be stoned by the Jews as an adulteress ("ne lapidaretur a Judaeis ut adultera"). Emphasis on Jewish cruelty, however, appears in numerous other passages in Bernard. He remarks that the Apostles had good reason to fear the Jews even after the crucifixion,[48] and he describes the Synagogue as a "cruel mother" for having "cast forth the child of thy womb [Jesus] with none to receive or to care for him."[49] He makes this criticism even though, in another sermon, he praises Jesus for having "left the Synagogue, his mother, so that you might cleave to him."[50] Elsewhere, he says that the Synagogue acted like a stepmother in crowning Jesus with a crown of thorns.[51]

In various places, anti-Jewish stereotypes color Bernard's vocabulary. Like many writers, he uses the word synagogue as a term of opprobrium. When speaking of the heretic Henry, he writes, "Churches are regarded as synagogues."[52] In another letter, he commends Abbot Warren of the Alps for "destroying those synagogues of Satan, the cells where three or four monks live without order or discipline."[53] On the basis of the conviction that Jews are unusually hard-hearted, he says that Jesus engraves his law on a "heart of flesh, ... that is to say, not hard, not stubborn, not Judaic."[54] We shall later examine another, more significant stereotype

[48] "Fifth Sermon for the Feast of the Ascension," *Sermons*, II, p. 285, and "First Sermon for Pentecost," ibid., p. 289. There was even a Christian view that the major cause of the punishment of the Jews was their persecution of the apostles after the crucifixion. See Pseudo-Bede in *PL* 93 : 460, cited in B. Blumenkranz, *Les Auteurs Chrétiens Latins du Moyen Age sur les Juifs et le Judaisme* (Paris, 1963), p. 138, and esp. Gregory I, *PL* 75: 862, cited in *Auteurs*, p. 86.

[49] "Sixth Sermon for Christmas Eve," *Sermons*, I, pp. 379–380.

[50] "Second Sermon for the First Sunday after the Octave of the Epiphany," *Sermons*, II, p. 46.

[51] "Fifth Sermon for the Feast of All Saints," *Sermons*, III, p. 393.

[52] Epist. 241 (317, p. 388). See L. I. Newman, *Jewish Influence on Christian Reform Movements* (New York, 1925), pp. 134–135. Newman (p. 195) compares the following passage with Bernard's: "Sunt autem Burgares seu 'Burgari' secta Catharorum quorum Ecclesiam vel potius Synagogam memoriat Reinerius." Cf. also p. 230.

[53] Epist. 254 (329, p. 408). The phrase "synagogue of Satan" is based on Revelations 2:9 and 3:9. Cf. also Agobard, *PL* 104: 88, cited in Merchavia, *op. cit.*, p. 83.

[54] "First Sermon for the Feast of the Dedication of a Church," *Sermons*, II, p. 389. See also "Second Sermon for Lent," *Sermons*, II, p. 81; see sec. 65.2, *LTR*, II, p. 173, Eales, IV, p. 394 ("O foolish and hard of heart, filled with the spirit of the Pharisees"). Cf. Peter the Venerable, *PL* 189: 551.

which affects Bernard's vocabulary—that of the Jewish usurer. The final, most common, and least significant stereotype is, of course, that of the proud and hypocritical Pharisee.[55]

Other Jewish characteristics that Bernard criticizes are hypocrisy[56] and envy of Christians.[57] Moreover, in one sermon, he goes so much out of his way to criticize Jews that he begins in the following awkward manner: "My brethren, it seems to me that these assemblies of ours are far from deserving that reproach of the Prophet addressed to the Jews: 'Your assemblies are wicked.' For our assemblies are not wicked."[58]

Does Bernard attribute to the Jews a diabolical hatred of God in explaining their rejection of Jesus, or does he say that they are simply stupid? Both points of view were current at this time, and Bernard does not seem to have chosen between them, for at times he expresses the one and at times the other. He says in one sermon, "But the Jews, ever mindful of the hatred wherewith they hate his Father, take this opportunity to vent it on the Son . . . . What then will these wicked men do to him, the mere sight of whom they cannot bear?"[59] "Judea," he says elsewhere, "hates the light."[60] In another sermon, he explicitly calls the Jews the instruments of Satan.[61] In other places, however, he implies that the Jews reject Jesus only out of blindness, for in attacking the heretic Henry he suggests two possibilities for his heresy: either he is afflicted with Jewish blindness, or he resents the truth.[62] The latter possibility is not attributed to the Jews. Moreover, in a long and famous passage, he attributes the intransigence of the Jews to their stupid and bovine intellect. It is in this passage that Bernard tells the Jews that he is kinder to them than Isaiah, for the latter placed them below the animals

---

55   Epist. 6 (7, p. 28); 94 (91, p. 141); see *SCC* 13.2, *LTR* I, p. 69, Eales, IV, pp. 67–68; "Second Sermon on Lent," *Sermons*, II, p. 91; "Third Sermon for the Feast of the Annunciation," *Sermons*, III, pp. 162, 164; *De Gradibus Humilitatis*, tr. by G. B. Burch (Cambridge, Massachusetts, 1942), pp. 152–154.

56   This, of course, was standard Christian procedure. "Second Sermon for Christmas Eve," *Sermons*, I, pp. 317–318.

57   *SCC* 25.9, *LTR*, I, p. 168, Eales, IV, p. 154 ("aemulis posse respondere Judaeis"); "Third Sermon on the Virgin Mother," *Sermons*, I, pp. 103–104; "Second Sermon for the First Sunday after the Octave of the Ephiphany," *Sermons*, II, p. 45.

58   "Sermon for the Feast of the Nativity of St. John the Baptist," *Sermons*, III, p. 173.

59   "Sermon for the Octave of the Feast of the Circumcision," *Sermons*, I, pp. 438–439.

60   "Third Sermon for the Feast of the Epiphany," *Sermons*, II, pp. 22–23.

61   "Second Sermon for the Feast of St. Andrew," *Sermons*, III, p. 60.

62   Epist. 241 (317, p. 388).

in intelligence. Incredibly, Watkin Williams quotes this statement as an example of Bernard's "peculiarly tender feeling toward the Jews," because he *was* kinder to them than Isaiah.[63]

Bernard strongly criticizes Jewish character in economic matters as well. He proclaims, in an important anti-Jewish statement, that Jews are "coarse, . . . for their action carried them into wars, all their inclinations were devoted to the pursuit of gain (*affectus in lucris totus erat*), their intelligence stopped short in the thick husk of the Law, and their worship consisted in shedding the blood of sheep and cattle."[64] Bernard's other important statement on the Jews in economic affairs (aside from his theological justification of their possession of temporal wealth) is his above-quoted statement that Christian usurers are taking more interest (*pejus judaizare*) than the Jews. Though Bernard is apparently making an anti-Christian statement, Baron maintains that he "introduced a novel term of opprobrium" against the Jews here (*judaizare* = lend at interest) and thus lent authoritative support to the stereotype of the Jew as usurer.[65] By using this term, he managed to focus blame on Jews even while blaming Christians.

Bernard, in fact, commonly used Jews as a standard of comparison for various forms of heresy and sin. A Christian who forgets the sufferings of Jesus becomes "a sharer in the unparalleled sin of the Jews."[66] The heretic Henry is charged with "more than Jewish blindness."[67] Those who sell relics differ from Judas Iscariot only in that they are more

---

[63] *St. Bernard of Clairvaux*, p. 259. See *SCC* 60. 4–5, *LTR*, II, p. 144, Eales, IV, p. 362. The old phrase "bovine intellect" was also applied to the Jews by Peter the Venerable, *PL* 189: 539 (cf. also c. 602); see note 76 below. On Jewish blindness, cf. also Bernard's epist. 365, Mabillon, c. 332 = *PL* 182: 571, where he refers to the Church's prayer that God "will remove the veil from their heart and draw them out from their darkness to the light of truth." Regarding this "veil," see II Cor. 3.13–18, and cf. B. Blumenkranz, *Le Juif Medieval au Miroir de l'Art Chrétien* (Paris, 1966), pp. 52–54, 64, and W. Seiferth, *Synagogue and Church in the Middle Ages* (New York, 1970), pp. 95–109. On the diabolical Jewish rejection of what they know to be the truth, see J. Trachtenberg, *The Devil and the Jews* (New York, 1966), pp. 15 ff., and cf. Parkes, *Conflict*, p. 103.

[64] *SCC* 60.3, *LTR*, II, p. 143, Eales, IV, p. 361. Jews, of course, brought no animal sacrifices in the Middle Ages, but some Christians continued to raise this issue. See my "St. Peter Damian . . . ," *Yavneh Review* 4 (1965): 102.

[65] Baron, *Social and Religious History*, IV, pp. 121, 301. That Bernard was the first to use *judaizare* in this sense had been pointed out by S. Posener, *Encyclopedia Judaica* (Berlin, 1929), IV, p. 294. Cf. also Trachtenberg, *op. cit.*, p. 190.

[66] "Sermon for Spy Wednesday," *Sermons*, II, p. 149.

[67] Epist. 241 (317, p. 388).

avaricious.[68] Jesus "suffers a greater persecution from the man who . . . attempts to wrest from him the souls he has ransomed than from the Jews by whom that blood was shed."[69] The excommunicate is worse than the Jew, the heretic, and the heathen, for the Church prays for the latter and not for the former.[70] It is presumably possible to argue that these remarks represent pro-Jewish tendencies since they argue that at least some groups are worse.[71] Nevertheless, this widespread medieval habit of regarding the Jews as a standard for evaluating all sorts of sinners, heretics, and pagans was hardly a phenomenon at which Jews could rejoice.

Against this background of Bernard's anti-Jewish prejudices, we can approach his role in the Anacletus controversy with greater understanding. In 1130, a schism developed between Gregory, a Cardinal-Deacon of St. Angelo, and Peter Pierleoni, Cardinal Priest of St. Calixtus. The former was elected Pope Innocent II, and the latter, in a slightly later and larger election, Pope Anacletus II. What is significant for us in this affair is that Anacletus was of Jewish descent and Bernard opposed him bitterly. The question we must ask is whether his opposition was based on the Jewish parentage of Anacletus.

Bernard writes that he supports Innocent because "his reputation is more fair and his election more sound."[72] "When the first election has taken place, a second one is no election at all."[73] The fact is, however, that Bernard undermines this argument in the very same letter by saying that the supporters of Anacletus could have demanded immediate reconsideration, but to make a new convention now would cause more faction. This sort of backtracking leads one to suspect deeper motives. Bernard, moreover, uses the most vicious sort of language against Anacletus. "The fruitless growth, the rotten branch has been lopped off,"

---

68 SCC 10.3, LTR, I, pp. 49–50, Eales, IV, p. 50.

69 "First Sermon for the Feast of the Conversion of St. Paul," Sermons, III, p. 75.

70 De Gradibus Humilitatis, 22.56, The Steps of Humility, tr. by Burch, p. 232. For the status of the evil Christian in Bernard, cf. Pierre Dérumaux, "St. Bernard et les Infidèles," Mélanges St. Bernard (Dijon, 1954), p. 74.

71 Agobard, for example, had regarded Jews as worse than pagans: "Judaei . . . nationibus pejores inveniuntur: quia illae quidem nec legem acceperunt, isti vero post datam sibi legem, post missos ad se prophetas, etiam Dei filium occiderunt," PL 104: 96. Cf. B. Blumenkranz, Les Auteurs Chrétiens Latins du Moyen Age sur les Juifs et le Judaisme, p. 166. Cf. the same author's Juifs et Chrétiens dans le Monde Occidental, 430–1096 (Paris and The Hague, 1960), pp. xvii-xviii. See also Merchavia, op. cit., p. 82.

72 Epist. 125 (128, p. 190).

73 Epist. 126 (129, p. 195).

he writes to Peter the Venerable.[74] It may be of some interest that the images of a flower without fruit, of withered grass, and of a fruitless tree are used by Bernard elsewhere about the Jews.[75] In another passage, he calls Anacletus a beast.[76] There can be little doubt that in view of the anti-Jewish prejudices that we have seen in Bernard, his objection to Anacletus' Jewish descent must have been among the complex motives which led to the virulence of his attack. And in an oft-quoted letter, he explicitly mentions that "it is to the injury of Christ that a man of Jewish race has seized for himself the see of Peter."[77] It should, however, be remembered that others were far more virulent in specifically attacking Anacletus' Jewishness. Bishops Arnulf and Meinfredus wrote that in his face he presents a Jewish image, that he is worse than a Jew, and that he is still not free of Jewish leaven.[78] Thus, Bernard was motivated to some extent by Anacletus' Jewishness but was more circumspect than others in emphasizing it. In any event, Baron's remark that "the racial issue was seized upon by Anacletus' enemies as an excuse for, rather than as a major cause of, their opposition" is probably valid at least as far as Bernard is concerned.[79] Moreover, as Vogelstein and Rieger point out, "We have no evidence that the opponents of Anacletus aroused the fanaticism of the mob against the Jews."[80]

A general appraisal of Bernard's actions during the Second Crusade and the reasons he gives for them together with an examination of his anti-Jewish sermons and letters and his role in the Anacletus schism

---

[74] Epist. 147 (147, p. 216).

[75] *Exhortatio ad Milites Templi*, chapter 7, Mabillon, c. 556 = *PL* 182: 930 ("Floris odor fructus saporem praecederit . . . , Judaeisque tenui odore contentis"); "First Sermon on the Virgin Mother," *Sermons*, I, pp. 60–61 ("Jews must be withered as the grass"); SCC 60.3–4, *LTR*, II, pp. 143–144, Eales, IV, pp. 361–362 (the Jews are a sterile fig-tree which had to be pruned).

[76] Epist. 126 (129, p. 195). Peter the Venerable himself was strongly opposed to Anacletus, causing James (*Letters*, pp. xi, 187) to say that "even Peter the Venerable, usually so careful and so moderate," made pejorative statements about Anacletus. James was apparently willing to overlook Peter's strongly anti-Semitic writings. On Peter the Venerable and the Jews, see Merchavia, *op. cit.*, pp. 128 ff., and cf. esp. p. 131 for varying appraisals of Peter's attitude. See also Blumenkranz in *Kirche und Synagoge*, I, pp. 119 ff. It should also be noted that the term *bestia* was often applied to Jews by Peter. See Merchavia, p.132.

[77] Epist. 139 (142, p. 210).

[78] "Petrus iste . . . judaicam facie repraesentat imaginem . . . Jam nec Judaeus quidem, sed Judaeo deterior . . . ." Quoted in Latin in Newman, *Jewish Influence*, p. 250.

[79] *Social and Religious History*, IV, p. 11.

[80] *Geschichte der Juden in Rom* (Berlin, 1896), I, p. 222.

leads to the conclusion that he was an unusually strong opponent of the destruction of Jews, yet an equally strong spokesman for anti-Jewish stereotypes and prejudices. Bernard himself, because of his very strong belief in the Biblical promises which he cites and his devotion to canon law, was able to overcome his prejudices and protect Jews from physical violence, but this achievement was no simple matter.

Indeed, he appears to have been conscious of the inner tension involved in his position toward the Jews, for he points it out quite explicitly in several passages in his sermons. In these passages he combines fierce denunciations of the Jews with a description of the incredible mercy shown toward them by Jesus and the Church.

His "First Sermon for Easter Sunday"[81] includes the following passage: "What will you do now, O ye Jews, who on the day of the crucifixion were wagging your sacrilegious heads before the cross, and heaping insults on Christ . . . O venomous tongues!" He then adds: "He received with humility the blasphemous reproaches of the Jews." In another sermon,[82] he marvels that Jesus did not murmur against "his own peculiar people, from whom he received so much evil in return for so much good" and adds, "You are stones, O ye Jews, but you have struck against a softer stone, calling forth therefrom the sweet sound of mercy and the oil of charity." Jesus, he says elsewhere, is merciful toward the Jews, for "if he had treated them according to their merits, he would inflict judgment without mercy upon those who show no mercy (cf. James 2:13)."[83] The Church wishes the Synagogue to be saved though they are enemies. "This degree of charity would be incredible, were it not that the words of the bride here recorded compel us to believe them."[84] There can be no doubt that a person listening to such sermons would be inspired to hate Jews rather than love them through imitation of Jesus and the Church. *Imitatio (misericordiae) Dei* is no easy task after hearing such invective.

Consequently, Bernard himself was not led to violence by his prejudices, but the hatred which he preached was fanning the flames of violence in lesser men. The great Christian protector of twelfth-century Jewry sowed seeds which would claim the life of many a Jewish martyr.

81   *Sermons*, II, pp. 162–165.
82   "Sermon for Spy Wednesday," *Sermons*, II, pp. 136, 147.
83   SCC 14.2, *LTR*, I, pp. 76–77, Eales, IV, p. 75.
84   SCC 79.5–6, *LTR*, II, p. 275, Eales, IV, p. 486.

ST. PETER DAMIAN

*His Attitude toward the Jews and
the Old Testament*[1]

From: *Yavneh Review* 4 (1965): 80–112.

INTRODUCTION

A cursory examination of the career of St. Peter Damian (1007–1072) would probably yield the impression that his was a significant role in the development of anti-Semitism in the high middle ages. Damian was a powerful force in heightening medieval piety through his advocacy of semi-eremitic monasticism, his stressing the adoration of the Virgin, and his contribution to the tremendous upheaval in early medieval values that culminated in the Gregorian reform. There can be little doubt that a deeper and more widespread piety was a key factor in the tremendous upsurge of Judaeophobia that came with the crusades. Furthermore, Damian wrote the first full-scale anti-Jewish work produced on the continent of Europe in two centuries, and the preserved history of Italian polemics of this nature begins with him. The impression is clear. We must now determine whether or not it is accurate.

Damian, of course, cannot be held responsible for the indirect effect that the cult of Mary may ultimately have exercised in fostering a hatred for Jews. Damian as an individual must be judged on the basis of the attitude that he expresses in his writings, and it is to these writings that we now must turn.

Before doing so, however, we must take cognizance of a most important fact. The attitude of a medieval Christian toward the Jews could be closely related to, and often reflected in, his attitude toward

---

[1]   The term "Old Testament" is used for convenience.

the Old Testament and its law. In Damian's case, there is special reason for interest, because his anti-Jewish works deal almost exclusively with the Old Testament and because he is associated with the replacement of "the judging, wrathful, distant God of the Old Testament . . . by the loving, self-abnegating Son of the New Testament, with his weeping and charitable Mother."[2] How real was this dichotomy in Damian's own eyes, and what were his feelings toward that part of the Bible which he shared with the Jews? These are questions that we shall try to answer in the second part of this paper.

I. DAMIAN AND HIS ATTITUDE TOWARD THE JEWS

The status of the Jews in eleventh century Italy was far from ideal. The scattered references that we possess tell of a number of anti-Jewish accusations. After an earthquake in Rome in 1020 or 1021, Jews were savagely punished for having mocked a crucifix. Rabbi Meshullam ben Kalonymus of Lucca wrote to R. Hai, the Gaon in Babylonia, about an "upheaval" in his town—either a persecution or a defeat by an army. In 1062, Jews in Aterno were accused of committing a ritual outrage on an image of Jesus in their synagogue on Good Friday. An attempt at a program of forced conversion in Benevento (c. 1065) drew a strong protest from Pope Alexander II, but the attempt is significant in gauging the attitude of Italian Christians toward the Jews.[3]

Earlier in this century, the rumor had spread through France and Italy that the Jews were responsible for Moslem persecution of Christians in the Holy Land. In France, this rumor led to a campaign of forced baptisms (1007) which was stopped only through Papal intervention.[4] Such reports could not have passed entirely without effect in Italy, at least in the realm of personal relations between individual Christians and Jews.

Nevertheless, three or four incidents in a century, even granted the paucity of sources, do not constitute a bleak picture of the overall

---

[2] Norman F. Cantor, *Medieval History, The Life and Death of a Civilization* (New York, 1963), p. 308.

[3] See Cecil Roth, *The History of the Jews of Italy* (Philadelphia, 1946), p. 72, for the information in this paragraph.

[4] Bernhard Blumenkranz, *Juifs et Chrétiens dans le Monde Occidental, 430–1096* (Paris, 1960) (henceforth referred to as *Juifs et Chrétiens*), p. 136.

situation. It would appear that the Jews of Italy enjoyed relative tranquillity; anti-Semitic incidents, however, kept them aware of the painful lack of long-term, meaningful security.

There had been a lull in the Jewish-Christian polemic in Europe during the late ninth, tenth, and early eleventh centuries. It is true that Bernhard Blumenkranz maintains that "this polemic is a ringing manifestation of the intellectual vitality of the middle ages. This vitality was not at all limited (to any period) . . . ; we can observe it throughout our period."[5] The fact, however, is that an examination of Blumenkranz's own survey of the literature[6] shows that since 846, when Amolon wrote his *Liber Contra Judaeos*, no major anti-Jewish work appeared on the continent till Damian. The anonymous *Altercatio Aecclesie contra Synagogam*, written between 938 and 966, is probably an English creation.[7] The only other lengthy, major references are in Ratherius' *Qualitatis Conjectura*[8] (tenth century) and three sermons delivered by Fulbert of Chartres in 1009.[9]

In Italy, written polemics simply did not exist in the Middle Ages before Damian. Even oral disputations are mentioned most infrequently. Alcuin (c. 750–760) describes a disputation between a Jew named Julius and a Master Pater of Pisa at Pavia.[10] Ahimaaz of Oria describes how an archbishop called in a Rabbi Hananel for a religious discussion at the end of the tenth century, and the *Vita* of the anchorite Simeon in the *Acta Sanctorum* describes a discussion he had with a Jew on religious matters during a meal at Lucca in 1016. The authenticity of both these sources is open to question.[11]

Damian, then, appears in a time and place where the social situation would not have drawn his special attention to the Jews and where the polemical tradition was weak to say the least. Did he have a desire to change the relationship between Christians and Jews? Did he wish to revive the Judaeo-Christian polemic?

---

5   *Juifs et Chrétiens*, p. xv. The "period" is 430–1096.
6   "Les Auteurs Chrétiens Latins du Moyen Age sur les Juifs et le Judaisme" (henceforth referred to as "Auteurs"), *Revue des Etudes Juives* 9 (109) (1948–49): 3–67; 11 (111) (1951–52) : 5–61; 13 (113) (1954): 5–36; 14 (114) (1955): 37–90; 17 (117) (1958): 5–58.
7   "Auteurs," *REJ* 14 (1955): 76 ff.
8   J. P. Migne, *Patrologia Latina* (henceforth *PL*) 136: 535–537.
9   *PL* 141: 305–318.
10 L. I. Newman, *Jewish Influence on Christian Reform Movements* (New York, 1925), p. 333.
11 *Juifs et Chrétiens*, pp. 68–69 and 71.

Peter Damian became involved in many controversies which he disliked and for which he was temperamentally unsuited. His strongest inclination was toward a semi-eremitic monasticism in which he could "avoid human contact."[12] Patricia McNulty maintains that it was "to his credit that he did not stand aside or refuse to aid the Roman Church in her need."[13] The truth of the matter is that Damian agreed to become a cardinal only under threat of excommunication and constantly requested permission to return to a monastic life. Thus, though Damian's was a highly emotional nature,[14] he would have preferred to utilize his emotions in the relationship between himself and God; only the most compelling necessity drove him to direct them toward society. His advocacy of self-flagellation[15] is but one manifestation of the enormous energies he was willing to devote to his personal monastic life. Basically, then, in the words of R. Biron, "he was a contemplative man by temperament."[16] His involvement in the battle for reform brought him more personal frustration than fulfillment. Why should such a man enter into the acrimonious polemic between Christian and Jew?

First of all, the *Antilogus contra Judaeos* and the *Dialogus inter Judaeum Requirentem et Christianum e contrario Respondentem*[17] were not written through Damian's own initiative; they are in essence a *responsum* to a letter from the Egyptian bishop Honestus requesting material with which to counter Jewish arguments. We shall see later that Honestus did not make a very wise choice in choosing Damian. In any event, the latter was not particularly enthusiastic about fulfilling the task, and he characteristically compared this battle with the far more important struggle undertaken daily by every conscientious monk.

---

12 *De Perfections Monachorum*, ch. 3, PL 145 : 294. Translations from *De Perf. Mon.* are taken from Patricia McNulty, *St. Pietro Damiani: Selected Writings on the Spiritual Life* (London, 1959) (henceforth *Spiritual Life*).

13 *Spiritual Life*, pp. 22–23.

14 J. Gonsette, *Pierre Damien et la Culture Profane* (Louvain, 1956), pp. 16–17.

15 Norman T. Boggs, in *Christian Saga*, vol. 1 (New York, 1931), pp. 374–375, gives great emphasis to this element in Damian's thought.

16 *St. Pierre Damien*, p. 192. Quoted in J. Joseph Ryan, "St. Peter Damiani and the Sermons of Nicholas of Clairvaux: A Clarification," *Mediaeval Studies* 9 (1947): 152.

17 PL 145: 41–68. The *Antilogus-Dialogus* (it is basically one work) was probably composed c. 1070. Damian writes (col. 55) that 1040 years have passed since the fulfillment of Daniel's prophecy. From his general treatment of the passage in Daniel it would appear that fulfillment took place at the crucifixion.

"But," he writes, "if you wish to be a soldier of Christ and fight for him courageously, then take up arms as an illustrious warrior against the vices of the flesh, the contrivances of the Devil—an enemy that will indeed never die—rather than against the Jews who will soon be almost destroyed from the face of the earth."[18]

Nevertheless, he undertakes to do as Honestus requested, and he states three reasons for doing so. First, it is disgraceful (*inhonestum!*) for a churchman to hear calumnies against Christianity and remain silent through ignorance. Second, such silence could arouse doubts in the minds of loyal Christians. And finally, Damian expresses the hope that Jews may be converted by well-presented Christian arguments.[19]

Damian keeps this third purpose in mind throughout the *Antilogus* and *Dialogus*. At the beginning of the *Antilogus*, he writes, "When someone begins a dispute about this matter, he should be warned not to exasperate his opponent with insults or haughtiness. But he should soothe his mind with benevolent charity and most patient gravity, for a stony heart which was able to be all the more stubborn when bitterness was poured forth can perhaps be softened toward belief by modest sweetness of words."[20]

Such confidence in the soft and moderate approach is not new in the history of Christian polemic. Maxim, an Arian bishop (c. 365-c. 430), wrote in his *Tractatus Contra Judaeos*, "We speak thus against them not with a desire to harm . . . We wage a lively battle for people's salvation . . . We seek to save them by conversion . . . Therefore, we who seek the truth do not look for (captious) quarrels."[21] We find a similar attitude in Gregory the Great who said that only preaching can effect a sincere conversion.[22]

At the end of the *Dialogus*, this hope turns into a ringing exhortation to his fictitious Jewish opponent. "Therefore, O Jew, listen now to my advice and you may have God, who is now angry at you, well-disposed toward you . . . Desert the error of Jewish blindness, and direct yourself

---

[18] "Sed si Christi miles esse, et pro eo viriliter pugnare desideras, contra carnis vitia, contra diaboli machinas insignis bellator arma, potius corripe; hostes videlicet qui nunquam moriuntur: quam contra Juadaeos, qui jam de terra pene deleti sunt." *PL* 145: 41.

[19] Loc. cit.

[20] Loc. cit.

[21] Quoted in "Auteurs," *REJ* 9 (1948–49): 11.

[22] Ep. I.47. Quoted in James Parkes, *The Conflict of the Church and the Synagogue* (henceforth referred to as *Conflict*) (Philadelphia, 1961), p. 211.

to the truth of Evangelical grace . . . May the God of your fathers cast aside the old veil of ignorance from your heart, and, with the darkness of error dispelled, he will besprinkle you with the new light of His knowledge."[23]

The basic method that Damian uses to bring about this hoped-for conversion is the accumulation of Old Testament passages which, to his mind, prove that Jesus is the Messiah, that God consists of three persons, etc. "In this truly naive way," write Vogelstein and Rieger, "through the piling up of Biblical passages, does Damian seek to demonstrate the truth of Christianity to the Jews."[24] Actually, this method was the classic Christian approach in dealing with Jews, and it begins in the Gospels themselves. The most influential medieval work of this type was Isidore of Seville's *De Fide Catholica ex vetere et novo testamento contra Judaeos*,[25] and Damian was certainly not alone in considering this the basic method of attack.

The Jews, in fact, could be most thankful for this approach, for it is when Christians became less optimistic and less naive that more virulent and dangerous anti-Semitism appeared. And, indeed, not all Christians were naive. As early as the seventh century, Julian of Toledo felt little hope of converting the Jews and wrote against them mainly for Damian's second reason—confirming Christians in their faith. Julian was closely associated with the anti-Jewish policy of seventh century Spain and wrote in his *De Comprobatione Aetatis Sextae*, that the Jews are a sick part of the body of the Spanish people.[26] His attitude is most clearly reflected by the judgment that the worst thing about France is that it is "a brothel of Jews blaspheming our Savior and Lord."[27] Clearly, Julian's pessimism arose from contact with actual Jews, not merely those mentioned in books. Did Damian retain his optimism despite contact with Jews, or did his hopes result from ignorance?

---

23 "Nunc igitur, Judaee, audi meum consilium ut Deum, quem iratum habes, possis habere propitium... Desere Judaicae caecitatis errorem, et te ad Evangelicae gratiae dirige veritatem... Deus patrum tuorum a corde tuo vetustum ignorantiae velamen abjiciat, et, depulsis errorum tenebris, nova te cognitionis suae luce perfundat." *PL* 145: 66.

24 Herman Vogelstein and Paul Rieger, *Geschichte der Juden in Rom* (Berlin, 1896), p. 268.

25 *PL* 83: 449–538.

26 "Auteurs," *REJ* 11 (1951–52): 34–37. This pessimistic attitude toward conversion of the Jews is reflected in the statement of Freculphe of Lisieux (9th cent.) that the Jews are «naturally inimical to Christian dogma» (*PL* 106: 1199). See "Auteurs," *REJ* 13 (1954): 25.

27 "... quod pejus his omnibus (sc. malis) est, contra ipsum Salvatorem nostrum et Dominum Judaeorum blasphemantium prostibulum habebatur." *PL* 96: 766. Translation by Parkes, *Conflict*, p. 342.

It would appear that the latter is true. Damian does not seem aware of the implications of a polemic with Jews. It should have been obvious to him that the Jews have their own interpretations of the verses he quotes. Yet he writes as if no Jewish commentator had ever dealt with the plural verb in Genesis 1:26 ("Let us make man in our image"). He expects such evidence of the trinity as the thrice-repeated word "holy" in Isaiah 6:3 to carry weight with Jews.

Damian almost never reaches the second stage of debate in the exegesis of a verse. It is true that the problematic character of the Christian case in the area of "testimonies" is partially to be blamed, but certainly an attempt can be made to disprove some of the typical Jewish refutations of Christian interpretations. Let us take, for example, Genesis 49:10,[28] one of the verses where a plausible case can be made for the Christian argument. Damian spends about two or three lines on it[29] without mentioning any possible Jewish explanations. When Fulbert of Chartres, a far superior polemicist, dealt with this verse, he dwelt mostly on the refutation of Jewish exegesis.[30] In only one place did Damian bother to refute Jewish interpretations. This is where he tried to show that certain Psalms must refer to Jesus and not to David or Solomon.[31]

As a whole, then, by neglecting to deal with Jewish exegesis, Damian must certainly have failed in helping Honestus. Furthermore, he did not deal at all (except with regard to the Law) with questions initiated by Jews, e.g., "How could Jesus have been the Messiah if none of the Messianic prophecies have been fulfilled?" We must thus accuse Damian of serious negligence or else conclude that his knowledge of Jews and their arguments was minimal. Since none of his other writings betray a familiarity with Jews, we are led to the conclusion that the latter explanation is correct.

If this is true, then the use of stereotyped anti-Jewish expressions in other theological, exegetical, or homiletical works becomes far less significant. Gregory the Great, for example, who displayed a most humane attitude toward the Jews in his correspondence, is vehemently anti-Jewish in his Biblical commentaries, where Jews are symbolized

---

[28] "The scepter shall not pass from Judah nor a lawgiver from among his descendants *ad ki yavo Shiloh.*"

[29] *PL* 145: 46.

[30] See his three speeches against the Jews, *PL* 141: 305–318.

[31] *PL* 145: 49–53.

by camels, wild asses, and serpents.[32] Damian, who seems to have had hardly any contact at all with Jews, can scarcely be blamed or considered unusual for using phrases that, as we shall see, were a hackneyed part of patristic and early medieval literature.

There are a number of passages in which Damian uses very harsh language about the Jews. Perhaps the most extreme instance is in the *De Sacramentis per Improbos Administratis*[33] where he discusses Jewish accusations that Jesus associated with sinners. These accusations, he says, "are the root and entire matter whence the wild furor of Jewish envy (or "spite") against the Lord grew hot (*unde feralis in Dominum furor Judaici livoris incanduit*); hence did the malice of their poisonous bile conspire toward his death (*hinc in mortem ejus viperini fellis malitia conspiravit*)."

A vituperative passage. But who is the primary object of attack here? Not the Jews, but neo-Donatist Christian heretics. Damian here hit upon a tactic which, as we shall see later, was quite common. First, he succeeds in equating Jews—and the ancient Pharisees at that—with Donatists. The next step is to bitterly malign the Jews (an easy and non-controversial task in a treatise intended for Christians) and let the virulence of these statements apply, by implication, to Donatists as well.

Furthermore, every anti-Jewish term in this passage has a "respectable" history in earlier writings. First, the term "feralis," with its allusion to wild beasts. As early as the fourth century, the Jews are referred to as a "feralis secta."[34] In 387, this image was used by John Chrysostom in his sermons against the Jews, where he stated that Jews are "wilder than all wild beasts."[35]

Taio of Saragossa referred to the "furor (*saevitia*) of the Jews against Christ."[36] The term "livor" appears in the statement of Angelomus of Luxeuil (died c. 855) referring to the "depravity of evil intention which the Jewish perfidy wished to stretch forth from the quiver of its spite (*livor*).[37]

---

32 Cf. Parkes' very perceptive comments on the phenomenon in *Conflict*, pp. 219–221.
33 *PL* 145: 529.
34 *Conflict*, p. 185.
35 The Jews *therion hapanton gegonasin agrioterai. PG* 48: 852. In his sixth speech against the Jews, Chrysostom switches the metaphor and compares himself to a wild beast who has drunk blood (of the Jews) and cannot stop. See *PG* 48: 903.
36 *PL* 80: 778.
37 *PL* 115: 264. Quoted in "Auteurs," *REJ* 13 (1954): 33.

The image of the Jew as a serpent ("viperinus") appears elsewhere in Damian as well. In the *Antilogus*, he asks his Jewish adversary not to behave like "a slippery serpent."[38] Elsewhere, he compares the Jews to an ass, saying that "the ass used by Abraham represents the uncomprehending stupidity of the Jews."[39] We have seen above that both these comparisons are found in the exegetical works of Gregory the Great. In the fourth century, the Synod of Jerusalem complained of "Jewish serpents and Samaritan imbeciles listening to sermons in Church like wolves surrounding the flock of Christ."[40] Of course, Damian's lack of original imagery is largely attributable to the fact that almost every possible negative image had already been applied to the Jews. The key point for this passage is that Damian had a special (anti-Donatist) reason for his vitriol here.

In other passages, the Jew is naturally condemned for his disbelief.[41] Jews are audacious,[42] and, what is most frustrating of all, they are blind.[43] The theme of the Jews' blindness is extremely common in medieval literature. It was especially annoying to Christians, because the Jews after all were the carriers of the testimony of Jesus' advent, yet they could not see what they showed others. Leo the Great (c. 391–461) wrote, "Carnal Israel does not understand what it reads, nor does it see what it shows."[44] This phenomenon troubled a man like Damian greatly, for he seems deeply convinced that the testimonies he quotes are quite irrefutable.

[38] " . . . nisi ut lubricus anguis, cum captus fueris, manus evadere gestias." Earlier he said of this behavior, "ut vester mos est." *PL* 145: 44.

[39] "Asinus autem ille quo tunc utebatur Abraham, insensata erat stultitia Judaeorum." *Sermo de Inventione Sancti Crucis, PL* 144: 603. Tr. by McNulty, *Spiritual Life*, p. 169.

[40] "Nos, nos inquietarent Judaici serpentes et Samaratinorum incredibilis stultitia." *PL* 22 : 769. Tr. by Parkes, *Conflict*, p. 173.

[41] "Erubescat Judaeus infelix, qui negat Christum de Virgine natum." *Sermo de Epiphania Domini, PL* 144: 514. I see no reason for doubting the authenticity of this sermon. Kurt Reindel's reason for such doubts is, to say the least, inconclusive. "Sermon one," he says "in contrast to Damian's other sermons, makes a quite impersonal impression; it is almost entirely constructed out of Biblical quotations." "Studien zur Überlieferung der Werke des Petrus Damiani I," *Deutsches Archiv für Erforschung des Mittelalters* 15 (1959): 29.

[42] "Qua inverecundiae mentis audacia tam claris . . . poteris assertionibus obviare." *Antilogus, PL* 145: 52.

[43] *PL* 145: 47.

[44] "Carnalis Israel non intelligit quod legit, non videt quod ostendit." *PL* 54: 242. Quoted in "Auteurs," *REJ* 9 (1948–49): 23.

In discussing the story of David and Absalom, Damian compares those concubines with whom David would not have relations upon his return to Jerusalem to the Jews. "The concubines . . . are those who persevere in guarding the old law . . . Nor does that celestial bridegroom approach them, for, as it were, he is designated to offer his fellowship to women prostituted by the Devil, and, because they have been polluted by adultery, he gives them a book of repudiation."[45] It is especially interesting and indicative of the extent to which Damian is imbued with Old Testament concepts that in a passage where he assails the old law his entire allegory is based upon divorce—a feature of that law—and that he uses the very term "repudii libellum" of Deuteronomy 24:3. The same phrase is found in the writings of Rabanus Maurus (d. 856) who said, "Understand that the Jews have received a book of repudiation, and have been completely forsaken by God."[46] Damian would have had great difficulty in substantiating the charge of adultery; at most, the Jews may have been frigid. He was, however, impelled to make this charge because of the Biblical story on which he was commenting, for the concubines had had relations with Absalom.

Another instance in which Damian makes an almost incomprehensible anti-Jewish statement because of a Biblical passage he is allegorizing is found in his speech *De Inventione Sancti Crucis*. In discussing the passage in II Kings 1:6–7, he says, "And the axe cut down the trees on the banks of the Jordan because the Wisdom of God deigned to correct the impious Jews by the severity of his preaching, standing on the banks of the river of our mortality, hewing them down like barren trees in the stiffness of their pride . . ."[47] What follows is the descent to hell and the resurrection of Jesus. Certainly no Jews were "hewn down" before the resurrection by the preaching of Jesus. It is even quite difficult to determine just what Damian means. But a commitment to allegory will often drive a commentator to uncomfortable lengths.

45   "Concubinae . . . hi sunt qui in veteris legis custodia perseverant . . . Nec ad eos (Judaeos) coelestis ille sponsus ingreditur, quia tanquam mulierculis a diabolo prostitutis suum praebere contubernium designatur, eisque, quia pollute sunt per adulterium, repudii dat libellum." *Epistola* 13 [*ad Desiderium Abbatem et Cardinalem*], PL 144: 287.

46   "Intellige accipientes Judaeos libellum repudii, et omnino a Domino derelictos." This comes right after an explicit mention of Deut. 24:3.

47   ". . . Dei sapientia, juxta fluidum mortalitatis nostrae decursum, dignata est impios Judaeos suae praedicationis austeritate corripere, et velut infructuosas arbores a statu rigidae superbiae desecare." PL 144: 610. Trans. by McNulty, *Spiritual Life*, p. 174.

There is one strongly anti-Jewish sermon printed among Damian's works, but it is one of nineteen sermons printed there that were written by Nicholas of Clairvaux. This sermon is *De S. Stephano Protomartyre*.[48]

We have seen, then, that almost all of Damian's anti-Jewish references are either stereotyped phrases or results of the exigencies of exegesis. They certainly would not seem to classify him as a significant anti-Semite. Further examination, as we shall see, will reinforce this impression.

Damian knows, of course, that before the birth of Jesus, Jews were religiously superior to Gentiles. At Jesus' birth, "The voice of the angels spoke to the Jews, as to reasonable men; the star of heaven spoke to the Gentiles, since they were like the beasts of wood and field."[49] We have here, incidentally, a most unusual situation—the term Jew (and not Hebrew or Israelite) applied to pre-Christians with the result of its acquiring a non-pejorative connotation. The Jews, as Damian tells us elswhere, then lost their claim to the title Israelite.[50] Nowhere, however, (at least not to my knowledge) does he draw the more radical conclusion that the Jews are now inferior to non-Christian gentiles. Agobard (d. 841), for example, does draw this conclusion, saying, "The Jews are worse than the other nations, for the latter never received the Law, while the former, after having received the Law, after the Prophets had been sent to them, nevertheless killed the Son of God."[51]

Whether Jews are inferior, equal, or superior to heretics, was a contested point in the early middle ages. Agobard and Amolon (d. 853) felt that the Jews were worse, for they entirely reject the Church's

---

[48] For the anti-Semitic embellishments in this sermon, see *PL* 144: 854, where Jews are stupid, Satans, serpents, etc. The verses in Acts (6:9–10) which serve as the basis of this part of the sermon simply say, "Then there arose certain people of the synagogue . . . disputing with Stephen, and they were not able to resist the wisdom and the spirit by which he spoke." For the spurious sermons see Migne's introduction to *PL* 144 and J. Joseph Ryan, "St. Peter Damiani and the Sermons of Nicholas of Clairvaux: A Clarification," *Mediaeval Studies* 9 (1947): 151–161. It is most interesting that many scholars have used these sermons in discussing Damian. McNulty even translates one (on St. Benedict). No. 69—which lists more than seven sacraments— has been quoted very often in Damian's name.

[49] "Judaeus itaque tanquam ratione utentibus loquitur vox angelorum, gentibus vero quasi brutis et jumentis in campis silvae loquitur lingue sive stella coelorum." *PL* 144: 507. Tr. by McNulty, *Spiritual Life*, p. 148.

[50] "Sancti enim apostoli... Israeliticae gentis filii sunt." *Antilogus, PL* 145: 47.

[51] "Judaei... nationibus pejores inveniuntur: quia illae quidem nec legem acceperunt, isti vero post datam sibi legem, post missos ad se prophetas, etiam Dei filium occiderunt." *PL* 104: 95–96.

teaching. Peter Chrysologus, Alcuin, and others considered heretics more reprehensible.[52] In a strongly anti-Jewish passage, Damian tells the Simoniacs that they are worse than "the Jewish perfidy itself" and than any heretical depravity.[53] Thus, at least some heretics are worse than Jews, and there is no indication that any are better.

This passage and the one quoted above from the *De Sacramentis per Improbos Administratis* are without question the most strongly anti-Jewish passages in Damian. In both cases, his wrath was excited not by Jews but by Christian heretics, and in both cases he uses his insults against the Jews as a means of attacking these heretics. This was a widespread and effective method of combating a position or group that one did not like. Thus, Cassiodorus compared Jews to Donatists[54] and Hadrian I used this method against the iconoclasts.[55]

In the same passage in the *De Sacramentis*, Damian maintains that it is no crime to associate and eat with sinners. It is unclear whether or not this would apply to Jews as well. A number of Church councils had forbidden the clergy to eat with Jews.[56] Agobard had written of the Jews, "We must not be joined to them by participating (with them) in food and drink."[57] Thus, it is possible that Damian would disagree with a fairly strong current in Christian tradition and permit association with Jews.

Since we are dealing with an individual who lived so close to the crusades, we should try to determine his feelings about the use of violence toward Jews. It has been said that "the massacre of Jews in 1096 ... found its ultimate authority in the writings of Damian himself."[58] Is there really anything in Damian's writings to indicate approval of such an action?

In his discussion of the Jews' rejection of Jesus, Damian, it would appear, quotes a verse in Deuteronomy (18:19), as follows: "The Lord will raise up a prophet for you from your brothers: anyone who will not listen to that prophet will be exterminated ("exterminabitur") from his

---

52 *Juifs et Chrétiens*, pp. xvii-xviii.
53 *Liber Qui Dicitur Gratissimus*, ch 37. PL 145: 153. Humbert too maintains that we should consider "quanto sceleratiores Judaeis arbitramur istos (sc. Simoniacos)." PL 143: 1093C.
54 PL 70: 74D ("Judaei vel Donatistae").
55 PL 98: 1255–6. See *Juifs et Chrétiens*, pp. xvi-xvii and note 11 there.
56 *Conflict*, p. 320. But compare the *Vita* of Simeon cited above at n. 11.
57 "...non debemus eis conjungi participatione ciborum et potuum." PL 104: 73–74, in *De Insolentia Judaeorum*.
58 *Medieval History*, p. 308.

people.[59] This last part of the verse (from "exterminabitur") is not found in Deuteronomy. The Hebrew is *anokhi edrosh me-immo*, the Vulgate has "ego ultor existam," and the Septuagint gives *ego ekdikeso ex autou.* The general meaning of all three is "I (God) will punish him." Damian's version, in a work intended to combat Jews, is taken from Acts 3:22–23[60] where this much harsher version is found.[61] Nevertheless, it would be quite far-fetched to draw any inferences about violent action toward Jews from this quotation. First, the extermination could be left to God, as in Jewish tradition. Second, Damian himself does not discuss any such implications. And finally, he may simply have been quoting from memory, and the New Testament version stuck in his mind.

We have, moreover, an explicit statement by Damian that the Jews must not be killed. The Jews, he says, live to carry the Old Testament everywhere in the original, and are thus a testimony to the truth of Christianity. "Therefore," he writes, "it is said by the Psalmist, 'My God, show me good things among my enemies. Do not kill them, lest they forget your law.'"[62] The relevant part of the Hebrew text reads *pen yishkehu ammi* ("lest my people forget"). There is no mention of "your law." The Vulgate follows the Hebrew: "populi mei." The best manuscripts of the Septuagint, however, give "your law" (= "legis tuae").[63] If Damian knew both versions, then he made his choice in order to strengthen his point that the Jews have a mission. But be that as it may, Damian is certainly quite emphatic about not killing the Jews. The Augustinian doctrine that the Jews have been dispersed to spread the witness of Christ was quite widespread in Christian thought, and Damian has adopted it as one interpretation.[64]

---

59   *Antilogus, PL* 145: 46.

60   *Estai de pasa psyche hetis ean me akouse tou prophetou ekeinou exolothreuthesetai ek tou laou.*

61   Jewish tradition does state that a transgressor of the commandment in this verse will be killed at a younger age at the hand of God. See Mishnah *Sanhedrin* 11:5. This transgression involves both disbelief (II Kings 7:2, 19–20) and disobedience (I Kings 20:35–36). Cf. D. H. Hoffmann's commentary to Deuteronomy, *ad loc.* This tradition may have influenced the Gospel version.

62   "Unde per Psalmistam dicitur, Deus meus, ostende mihi bona inter inimicos meos, ne occidas eos, ne quando obliviscantur legis tuae" (Psalms 59:11–12 in the Hebrew Bible). *Epist.* 13, *PL* 144: 284–285.

63   Rahlfs, on the basis of the Gallic Psalter, prints *tou laou mou* in his Septuagint, feeling that *nomou sou* came in under the influence of Psalms 119, verses 61, 109, 153.

64   Cf. Cassiodorus, *PL* 69: 415, quoted in "Auteurs," *REJ* 9 (1948–49): 46, and Isidore of Seville, *PL* 83: 226 and 236, quoted in *REJ* 11 (1951–52): 18.

Objections to using violence against the Jews find a very strong expression in one of Damian's best friends, Pope Alexander II. Under Nicholas II, Damian and Anselm of Lucca (the future Alexander II) were sent to administer ecclesiastical affairs at Milan. With the partisans of reform, Damian contributed, on October 1, 1060, to elect Anselm Alexander II.[65] Anselm was one of his allies in the battle against simony, and James F. Loughlin calls Hildebrand, Anselm, and Damian "the saintly triumvirate."[66] At least a part of Alexander's spiritual personality and religious views must have been influenced by his Italian friend.

And Alexander was especially emphatic about not killing Jews. He wrote of certain Spanish Christians who were killing Jews, "They, having been moved by stupid ignorance or perhaps by blind greed, wished to rage for their (the Jews') slaughter, whom divine love has perhaps predestined for safety (perhaps "salvation"—*salus*) ... They (Jews) have been preserved by Divine mercy so that, with their homeland and liberty lost ... having been damned by the prejudice of their fathers [note well] in spilling the Saviour's blood, they may live dispersed through the blows of the world."[67] There is a genuine tone of pity here.

Alexander wrote a similar letter to Berengarius of Narbonne. "Let your prudence know," he writes, "that it pleases us that you protect the Jews who are under your dominion, that they not be killed. For God does not find joy through the spilling of blood, nor does he rejoice in the destruction of evil men."[68] Of course, Damian was not the only influence on Alexander, and we know that the latter's teacher Lanfranc had a rather charitable interpretation of the Jews' responsibility for the crucifixion. We must be very wary of equating Alexander's merciful tone with Damian's rather cold statement that the Jews should not be killed.

---

[65]   See G. Bareille in the article "Damien" in *Dictionnaire de Théologie Catholique*, vol. IV, col. 42–43.

[66]   *Catholic Encyclopedia*, vol. I, p. 286.

[67]   "Illi quippe stulta ignorantia, vel forte caeca cupiditate commoti, in eorum (Judaeorum) necem volebant saevire, quos fortasse divina pietas ad salutem praedestinavit . . . Dei misericordia servati sunt, ut, patria libertateque amissa, . . . patrum praejudicio in effusione sanguinis Salvatoris damnati, per terrarum orbis plagas dispersi vivant." *PL* 146: 1386–1387.

[68]   "Noverit prudentia vestra nobis placuisse quod Judaeos qui sub vestra potestate habitant tutati estis ne occiderentur. Non enim gaudet Deus effusione sanguinis, neque laetatur in perditione malorum." *PL* 146 : 1387.

We must also remember that protection of the Jews did not always imply amicable relations with them. Ratherius of Verona (c. 890–974) wrote, "It is sufficient if they (Christians) let them (Jews) live somehow; they should not let them publicly blaspheme the Lord Jesus Christ. 'We shall live under your shadow,' said the prophet of them. 'We shall live,' he said, not 'we shall enjoy ourselves.' 'And he gave them to mercy'— not to exaltation, not to friendship, not to any honor."[69] Moreover, an alternative to forced baptism was expulsion.[70] One thing, however, is clear. Damian would not have lent his authority to the massacre of Jews.

Damian's general attitude toward the Jews of his time, as far as we have been able to ascertain it, has been outlined. We must now try to determine his attitude toward their future. Where do the Jews fit in to the eschatological picture? Before we can answer this question, we must find his attitude toward a great event in the Jewish past, for all of Jewish history was determined by the rejection of Jesus and the crucifixion.

There were Christian thinkers before Damian who presented more moderate statements of Jewish guilt than might be expected. Bede maintained that though the Jews are guilty, so is every Christian sinner. Every sinner "betrays the Son of Man."[71] Lanfranc in effect conceded a point of many Jewish polemicists. "The sin of the Jews," he wrote, "enriched the world, for had they not crucified the Lord, the cross of Christ, the resurrection and the ascension ... would not have existed in the world."[72]

Damian does not seem to have shared this attitude. He argues in the *Dialogus* that the Jews have been placed in eternal exile because of a crime which transcends all others—the murder of the Son of God. After all, he says, the Jews committed terrible crimes recorded in the Old Testament, yet their worst punishment was a seventy year exile.

---

69 "Suffecerat si eos vivere sinerent utcunque, non permitterent eos Dominum Jesum Christum tam publice blasphemare: "Sub umbra enim tua vivemus" dicit de eis propheta. "Vivemus," inquit, non "oblectabimur." "Et dedit eos in misericordias"—non in extollentias, non in amicitiam, non in ullum honorem." *Qualitatis Conjectura, PL* 136: 536.

70 Leo VII wrote to archbishop Frederick of Mayence between 937 and 939 of the Jews, "Si autem credere noluerint, de civitatibus vestris cum nostra auctoritate illos expellite," but "per virtutem autem et sine illorum voluntate... nollite eos baptizare." *PL* 132: 1084–1085.

71 " . . . Filium hominis tradit." *PL* 92: 271.

72 "Delictum Judaeorum ditavit mundum, quia nisi ipsi Dominum crucifixissent, crux Christi, et resurrectio, et ascensio praedicata et credita in mundo non esset." *PL* 150: 141.

Only a truly horrible crime could explain an exile of over one thousand years, one which Damian feels sure is eternal.[73]

Blumenkranz maintains that with this type of argument, Damian introduced a new concept into medieval polemics—the concept of an argument from reason (*ratio*) in addition to those from authority (*auctoritas*).[74] It is true that Damian states, "With the prophetic passages having been set forth, it pleases us to contend with you by reason alone."[75] But the argument following this statement—the argument set forth in the previous paragraph of this paper—is not novel at all.

Prosper of Aquitaine (d. c. 463) wrote that because of the great sin of killing Christ, "grace deserted the Jews, and their land became sterile and deserted. For all prophecy, all sacrifice and all sacraments ceased, and they passed to the humiliation of the nations."[76] The same statement is found in Peter Chrysologus[77] and in Cassiodorus.[78]

Damian, then, does blame the Jews severely for the crucifixion. What will consequently become of them? Will they ever repent and be forgiven?

Damian introduces a reference to Zechariah 12:10 with the remark, " . . . where a little later is added (a verse) concerning the Jews' damnation."[79] This is an eschatological passage; Damian would thus seem to speak of an ultimate Jewish damnation. There certainly was such a view. Bruno of Wurzbourg (d. 1045) wrote of the end of days: "The impious ones and the Jews will cry out to Christ . . . He will not hear them."[80]

And yet Damian could not have held such a view. The hope which he expresses that the Jews will convert is found, as we have seen above,

---

[73] *PL* 145: 65–66.

[74] *Juifs et Chrétiens*, pp. 217–218.

[75] "Libet adhuc, postpositis scilicet prophetarum exemplis, sola tecum ratiocinatione contendere." *PL* 145: 64.

[76] "Judaeos deseruit gratia, et facta est terra eorum sterilis atque deserta. Quia omnis prophetia, omne sacrificium, omna ibi sacramenta cessarunt, et ad humilitatem gentium transierunt." *PL* 51: 309.

[77] *PL* 52: 512. Quoted in "Auteurs," *REJ* 9 (1948–49): 17.

[78] *PL* 69: 525 and 545. Quoted in "Auteurs," *REJ* 9 (1948–49): 46.

[79] "Ubi etiam paulo post de Judaeorum damnatione subjungitur . . . " It is interesting that Amolon knew that the Jews interpreted this verse in Zechariah in light of their belief in a Messiah the son of Joseph who would precede the Messiah son of David. *PL* 116: 148–9. Mentioned in "Auteurs," *REJ* 14 (1955): 51.

[80] "Clamabunt impii et Judaei in futuro judicio ad Christum . . . non exaudiet eos." *PL* 142: 98.

throughout the *Antilogus-Dialogus*. The answer is probably to be found in an eschatological passage in Rabanus Maurus. The latter quotes a verse in Isaiah (10:22), "If the number of your people Israel will be as the sand of the sea, a remnant of it will return."[81] It is very likely that Damian too felt that some of the Jews would be converted either by persuasion or by God's grace while others would suffer damnation.

In Damian's mind, the Jews and the Old Testament are very closely related. They bear it as testimony, and it is only by appealing to its evidence that one can hope to convert them. Finally, adherence to the ancient law was certainly the clearest mark of a Jew.

The time has come to look at Damian and the Old Testament.

II. DAMIAN AND HIS ATTITUDE TOWARD THE OLD TESTAMENT

Peter Damian was very deeply imbued with a knowledge of the Old Testament; in fact, as McNulty says, he quotes "chiefly from the Old Testament and the Pauline Epistles."[82] He seems extremely well-versed in the Hebrew Scriptures, and they have left a very deep impression upon his writings. Throughout *De Perfectione Monachorum*, for example, he refers to monks as Israelites.

He seems a bit unclear as to the scope of the Jewish Bible. In the *Antilogus*, he quotes a verse from *Baruch* (3:36) to prove to the Jews that Jesus was the Messiah. A book of the Apocrypha would, of course, have no authority with the Jew. Yet this mistake does not originate with Damian, and it is possible that he either copied from a predecessor without giving the matter much thought or else he may have had some defense. Gregory of Tours cited this very verse to the Jew Priscus in a disputation.[83] For a possible Christian defense, we may note Gilbert Crispin's *Disputatio* of the late eleventh century where he replies to the Jew's objections by maintaining that *Baruch* was, after all, written at Jeremiah's dictation.[84]

---

[81]   *PL* 110: 582.
[82]   *Spiritual Life*, p. 50.
[83]   See *Juifs et Chrétiens*, p. 73.
[84]   See Israel Levi, "Controverse entre un Juif et un Chrétien au XIe Siecle," *REJ* 5 (1882): 242.

Whether or not Damian had a clear conception of the precise limits of the Old Testament as defined by Jews, he did have a deep emotional attachment to its contents. And here he found himself confronted by the crucial questions: Is the Old Testament superseded? Is only its Law superseded? Perhaps part of the Law remains valid. Is that part which is superseded to be disregarded completely? If so, why then is it retained in the Bible? Why was it ever given? Did it ever have any value? If it is to be taken allegorically, then was it ever intended to be taken literally?

These problems were central to any serious medieval Christian. Many approaches are found in the long history of Christian grappling with these questions. Let us begin with proponents of the negative attitude.

In the *Dialogue with Trypho*, we find the view that the Law is an unimportant part of Scripture which was added because of the Jews' wickedness. In chapter sixteen, the author states, "Circumcision was given to you as a sign, that you may be separated from other nations and from us and that you alone may suffer that which you now justly suffer." Jerome, in Epistle 121, says that the law was a deliberate deception of the Jews by God to lead them to their destruction."[85]

John Cassian, who must have been read avidly by a monk of Damian's inclinations, draws a sharp contrast between the Old and New Testaments. Surprisingly, rather than showing that the Law is harsher (which the paragraph heading implies), he maintains that the New Testament is more effective in preventing sin. Compare, for example, the ability of sexual abstinence to prevent adultery as against that of marriage.[86]

There are passages in Damian's works which reflect a similar, very negative attitude toward the Law. He says of Jesus, "He did not scorn to be cursed, so that he might free us from the Law's curse."[87] Concerning the Law, he quotes a verse in Ezekiel (20:25), "I gave them laws that are no good and precepts by which they will not live."[88] Here, he seems to feel that, at least when given to the Jews, the Law was a curse and an evil.

There is, however, a much different view of the Law in Christian tradition. It is one that we will do well to examine, for we shall see that

---

[85] See *Conflict*, pp. 83–84 and 101 for the references in this paragraph.

[86] "Gratia," he says, " . . . non ramos tantum nequitiae amputat, sed ipsas penitus radices noxiae voluntatis evellit." *PL* 49: 1214.

[87] "Maledici non respuit, ut nos de maledicto legis absolveret." *PL* 144: 608. *Spiritual Life*, pp. 171–172.

[88] *PL* 144: 605.

there are places where Damian appears much closer to this view than to the one already described.

Perhaps the most complimentary explanation by Christians of their ceasing to obey the Law is in Romans 7:14–25. Paul says that he is too weighed down by sin to observe the spiritual Law.[89]

A second Pauline interpretation is to be found in Romans and Galatians. The law was temporary and meant to be a guide to lead us to "faith in Jesus Christ."[90]

In some places, Tertullian seems to go even farther than Paul and uses the Law as a norm of conduct He forbids the teaching of secular studies, for how can a loyal Christian teach literature when the Law prohibits the pronunciation of the names of the gods?[91] He later states that "the Law prohibits to name the gods of the nations, not, of course, that we are not to pronounce their names the mention of which is required by conversation."[92] And so Tertullian seems to be conducting his life on the basis of at least some of the Law's precepts.

This attitude is reflected in Damian in a number of his works. In *Dominus Vobiscum*, he is concerned with a technical question of monastic ritual. In making his point, he appeals to the authority of both Testaments and then adds, "We do not take away from or add to the authority of the Holy Scriptures because of changing circumstances, but rather the customs of the Church are preserved in them."[93] Thus, the Old Testament is to be appealed to not only in homiletical, but also in legal matters.

A perhaps more significant passage is the eighth chapter of *De Perfectione Monachorum*.[94] Here, Damian is allegorizing the first two seven-year periods during which Jacob worked for Laban. These, he says, are the periods which every person must pass through, for the first seven years correspond to the seven commandments of the Decalogue concerned with love of one's neighbor and the last seven symbolize the seven commandments of the Gospel which he proceeds to enumerate.

---

89 See especially 7:14.
90 See Romans 3:21–22 and Galatians 3:24–26.
91 " . . . fidelis litteras doceat . . . cum lex prohibeat, ut diximus, deos pronuntiari." *De Idolat.* X. Quoted in Saul Lieberman, *Hellenism in Jewish Palestine* (New York, 1962), p. 111, note 78.
92 *De Idolat.* XX. Translation by Lieberman, p. 112.
93 This custom "a Veteris Novique Testamenti auctoritate descendit. Sicut ergo divinarum Scripturarum auctoritati nil pro rerum varietate subtrahitur, nil augetur: sed potius in his ecclesiastica consuetudo servatur." *PL* 145: 234.
94 *PL* 145: 303–304.

Only after passing through these stages can one reach Rachel. It appears from this chapter that certain parts of the Pentateuch—namely, the moral law—are of eternal validity.

This is a time-honored Christian position. Eucher of Lyon (d. c. 450–453) wrote in his *Instructiones* as follows: "Question: What parts of the Old Testament should we abandon and what parts should we observe? Answer: We should observe commandments which pertain to the correction of life and abandon the ceremonies and the rites of sacrifices which brought forth the figures and the shadow of future events."[95] We shall see later that Damian would agree completely with both parts of Eucher's response.

Leo the Great (c. 391–461) wrote that it is necessary to preserve "the moral commandments and precepts (of the Old Testament) just as they were set forth."[96] Eginhard (c. 770–840), when enjoining respect for one's father, wrote, "Though this is ordained in the Old Testament, it is part of the numerous laws which the scholars of the Church have declared as valuable to Christians as to Jews."[97]

This division of the Law into two parts—the moral and the ritual—cannot be accomplished without much difficulty, for the borderline is extremely vague and unsteady. A similar division is found in Jewish philosophy in R. Saadiah Gaon, the division of commandments whose purpose is comprehensible and those which are inscrutable, and this division is open to the same objections. There is, of course, an important difference in the acuteness of the problem. To Saadiah, it is a question of classification; to the Christians, it is a problem of acceptance or rejection. Leo, for example, places the prohibition of idolatry among the moral precepts. This could be defended. But Tertullian's concern with the prohibition of pronouncing the name of a foreign god is a good indication that the division was not entirely along moral-ritual lines. It is true that Damian does not include that part of the Decalogue which precedes "Honor thy father and thy mother," but this could

---

95   "Interrogatio: Quae de veteri Testamento relinquere vel quae observare debemus? Responsio: Debemus observare mandata quae ad corrigendam vitam moresque pertinent: relinquere autem caeremonias ritusque sacrificiorum, quae figuras atque umbram futuris tunc rebus praetulerunt." *PL* 50: 781.

96   " . . . mandata vero et praecepta moralia sicut sunt edita." See *PL* 54: 188–189.

97   Quoted in "Auteurs," *REJ* 13 (1954): 27 from *Monumenta Germaniae Historica, Epist.* 5, 115.

very well be because the seven years forced him to include only seven commandments. In any event, even if Damian wanted to retain a sharp, theoretical boundary between the moral and ritual sections of the Law, the practical difficulties are such that such a position devolves in a good number of instances into an acceptance of statutes one likes and a rejection of those that are not appealing.

Thus, Damian feels that the ritual law is of course superseded. At times, he expresses the view that it was always a curse. At other times, he seems to imply that it was an unpleasant necessity: the instrument of bringing justice into the world.[98] In any case, the contrast between the Old and New is quite strong in this area. We shall see presently that through allegory, even the ritual law can be shown to have eternal value. The moral law is still binding.

Before passing to a detailed treatment of Damian's allegorical explanations of ritual law, we must ask ourselves—what of the rest of the Old Testament? Did Damian feel that the entire Old Testament is infected by the same harshness found in a literal interpretation of the ritual law? Is love to be found only after the advent of the Savior?

We may confidently answer that Damian was not aware of such a dichotomy. Tears and mercy were, to Damian, the most profound expressions of love. And in discussing the efficacy of tears, he shows how the God of Israel was moved to compassion when he saw genuine tears being shed. David, despite adultery and indirect murder, did not lose his kingdom or life—because of tears.[99] Hezekiah and Jerusalem were delivered—because the king wept. "Esther ensured that God would deliver the people of Israel from their common danger of death and that the sentence of hanging ... should be suffered by Haman"—through tears. He quotes *Psalms* 39:13, "Listen to my weeping" to show that tears are efficacious.[100]

"The ark," he writes, "was smeared with pitch within and without, so that she should be outwardly soothed by brotherly sweetness and inwardly united in the truth of mutual love."[101]

---

[98] "Moses, the faithful servant ("fidelis famulus"), brought the commandments of naked justice; Christ, our truly loving ("pius") Lord tempered the harsh severity of the Law." *PL*145: 315, *Spiritual Life*, p. 117.

[99] Cf. *Eliyyahu Rabba* ch. 2.

[100] *De Perf. Mon.*, ch. 12. *PL* 145: 308.

[101] *De Perf. Mon.*, ch. 24. *PL* 145: 326. *Spiritual Life*, p. 134.

Damian traces the eremitic ideal, that highest expression of man's love for God, to the Old Testament. It was of the hermit's cell that Jeremiah said (Lamentations 3:26), "It is good that a man should quietly wait for the salvation of the Lord."[102] It was to this little room that Solomon cried out, "How fair and pleasant art thou, O love, for delights" (Song of Songs 7:7).[103] Clearly, the Old Testament as a whole is a source of love, compassion, and the ideal Christian life.

There does, it seems, remain one part of the Old Testament which is worthless or worse—the ritual law. Yet, as indicated above, there is a way to redeem even this section—the way of allegory.

Immediately after quoting the verse from Ezekiel about statutes by which one cannot live, Damian continues, "Nevertheless, if we join the confession of the cross and the mystery of the Lord's passion to this law, immediately that which was bitter turns into the sweetness of spiritual intelligence."[104] The cross clarifies all the hidden meaning of the Law and thus turns a curse into a source of meaningful teachings.

Allegorical interpretations of the ritual law are found throughout Damian's works. Church bells come from the trumpets of Numbers 10, from "the mystical tradition of the old Law."[105] The incense symbolizes good works; the two women of whom one is loved and the other hated are pleasure and virtue respectively.[106] The beautiful woman captured in war represents secular knowledge.[107]

The one place, however, where Damian carefully and at length allegorizes a series of Old Testament laws is at the beginning of the *Dialogus*. Here he would seem to have made an important contribution to the polemic against Jews and to have enriched Christian exegesis. Blumenkranz, in his treatment of Damian in "Auteurs," does not note any major source of his allegories nor, to my knowledge, does any other scholar.

Yet the entire passage is an almost word for word borrowing from Isidore of Seville.[108]

---

[102] *Dominus Vobiscum*, ch. 19. PL 145: 249. *Spiritual Life*, p. 78.
[103] *Dom. Vob.*, PL 145: 250. *Spiritual Life*, p. 79.
[104] "Cui tamen legi si confessio crucis et Dominicae passionis mysterium copulatur, protinus quod amarum fuerat, in spiritualis intelligentiae dulcedinem vertitur." PL 144: 605.
[105] ". . . ex antiquae legis mystica traditione descendit." PL 145: 315–316. *Spiritual Life*, p. 118.
[106] *De Vera Felicitate et Sapientia*, PL 145: 834–836.
[107] *De Perf. Mon.*, PL 145: 307.
[108] *Quaestiones in Vetus Testamentum—in Leviticum*, PL 83: 336–39.

The magnitude of this copying will become sufficiently evident only by a comparison of the two passages in Latin.

Introduction

Isidore:

> Nunc vero jam de quibusdam caeremoniis quid spiritualiter in his habeatur dicendum est. De quibus etiam et Judaei scrupulosissime quaerunt.

Damian:

> Nunc autem de quibusdam caeremoniis, super quibus saepe scrupulosissime quaeritis... Age igitur.

Problem 1

Why do Christians not practice circumcision? Answer: Baptism takes its place as a promise of the future; it was merely a prefiguration of Christ.

Isidore:

> Quaeritur ergo curjam non circumdatur carne Christianus si Christus non venit legem solvere, sed adimiplere. Respondetur: Ideo jam circumciditur Christianus, quia id quod eodem circumcisione prophetabatur jam Christus implevit. Exspoliato enim carnalis generationis quae in illo tacto figurabatur, jam Christi resurrectione impleta est, et quod in nostra resurrectione futuram est, sacramento baptismi commendatur.

Damian:

> Quaestio 1: Si Christus non venit legem solvere, sed implere, cur carne non circumciditur Christianus? Responsio: Imo jam se ideo Christianus minime circumdidit quia quod circumcisione prophetabatur, Christus implevit. Exspoliato quippe vitae carnalis, quae in veteri lege furat figurata, in Christi jam cernitur resurrectione completa, et quod expectamus in nostra resurrectione futurum, jam in sacri baptismatis mysterio commendatur.

Problem 2

Why don't Christians observe the Sabbath? Answer: Christians rest in Christ.

Isidore:

> Cum quaeritur Sabbati otium cur non observet Christianus, si Christus non venit legem solvere sed adimplere, respondetur: Imo et id propterea

non observat Christianus quia quod ea figura prophetabatur jam Christus implevit; in illo quippe habemus Sabbatum, qui dixit: "Venite ad me, omnes qui laboratis et onerati estis, et ego vos reficiam. Tollite jugum meum super vos, et discite a me quia mitis sum et humilis corde, et invenietis requiem animabus vestris" (Matt. 11:28). Cessationem ergo Sabbatorum jam quidem supervacue ducimus observare ex quo spes revelata est nostrae quietis aeternae.

Damian:

Quaestio 2: Cur omittit Christianus Sabbatum colere, si Christus non venit legem solvere, sed implere? Responsio: A nobis Sabbatum ideo non servatur, quia quod tunc erat in figura praemissum per exhibitionem rei jam videmus impletum... in illo (Christo) toto cordis amore ac devotione quiescimus, ut ab omni vitiorum servili opere ac terranarum rerum ambitione cessemus. Ad quod Sabbatum celebrandum ipse provocat, dum clamat, "Venite ad me... et discite quia mitis sum et humilis corde, et invenietis requiem animabus vestris." Carnalis ergo Sabbati cultum supervacuum ducimus, cum jam illud verum et salutiferum, propter quod institulum est, celebramus.

Problem 3

Why do Christians ignore the dietary laws? Answer: We now distinguish between clean and unclean in morality.

Isidore:

Cum quaeritur quare non observet differentiam ciborum quae in lege praecipitur, si Christus non venit legem solvere sed adimplere, respondetur: Imo propterea non observat eam Christianus, quia quod in illius figuris prophetabatur Christus implevit, non admittens ad corpus (quod corpus in sanctis suis in vitam aeternam praedestina sit) quidquid per illa animalia in moribus hominum significatum est.

Damian:

Quaestio 3: Si Christus non venit legem solvere, sed implere, cur Christianus negligit ciborum differentiam, quae in lege praecipitur observari? Responsio: Imo idcirco haec a Christianis ciborum differentia non admittitur, quoniam a Christo quod per hanc figurabatur, impletur. Immunditia quippe quae tunc cavebatur in cibis, nunc in moribus reprobatur humanis. Sicut enim sancti quique, ac justi transferuntur in corpus Christi: sic ab eo reprobi et inique tanquam cibi repellantur immundi.

Problem 4

Why don't Christians bring sacrifices? Answer: Jesus' sacrifice made them unnecessary. Furthermore, sacrifices were instituted to keep Jews away from idol worship.[109]

Blumenkranz maintains that this question was introduced to instruct Christians, for no Jew would press Christians on this matter.[110] The fact is that there was a heretical sect in eleventh century Italy that did sacrifice.[111] The whole question, however, should be applied to Isidore rather than Damian, and actually these problems do fit more readily in a Biblical commentary.

> Isidore:
>
> Cum quaeritur quare Christianus non, animalibus immolatis, carnis et sanguinis sacrificium offerat Deo, si Christus etc., respondetur: . . . ea quae talibus rerum figuris illi prophetabant immolatione carnis et sanguinis sui Christus implevit. Nam de sacrificiis eorumdem animalium quis nostrum nesciat magis ea perverso populo congruenter imposita, quam Deo desideranter oblata?

> Damian:
>
> Quaestio 4: Si Christus etc. cur et animalium carnibus sacrificium Deo Christianus non curat offerre? Responsio: . . . quidquid in illis hostiis typice gerebatur, totum in immolatione agni, qui tollit peccata mundi, veraciter adimpletur. . . Quis enim nesciat eadem sacrificia potius ad hoc inobedienti populo, ne cum idolis fornicarentur, imposita, quam Deo, tanquam ipse desideraret, oblata.

Problem 5

Why do Christians not eat unleavened bread on Passover? Answer: They have expelled the leaven of the old life.

> Isidore:
>
> Cum quaeritur cur azyma non observet Christianus, si Christus etc. respondetur: . . . quod expurgato veteris vitae fermento, novam viam demonstrans implevit Christus.

[109] Cf. Leviticus 17:7. This idea was made famous in Jewish circles by Maimonides. He, however, believed that they would nevertheless be reinstituted in the time of the Messiah.
[110] "Auteurs," *REJ* 17 (1958): 39.
[111] *Juifs et Chrétiens*, p. 58.

Damian:

Quaestio 5: Si Christus etc. cur Christianus azymam. .. non observat? Responsio: quoniam expurgato veteris vitae fermento, nova conspersio spiritualiter adimpletur.

Problem 6

Why do Christians not sacrifice the paschal lamb? Answer: Jesus' sacrifice made it unnecessary.

Isidore:

. . . Cur de carne agni Christianus pascha non celebret, si Christus etc., respondetur: . . . quia quo illa figura prophetabatur Agnus immaculatus sua passione Christus implevit.

Damian:

Quaestio 6: Si Christus etc. cur Christianus paschalis agni sanguine Pascha non celebrat? Responsio: . . . quia postquam verus ille Agnus . . . qui significabatur, superfluus judicatur.

Problem 7

Why don't Christians observe the New Moon? Answer: It prefigured the new man in Christ.

Isidore:

Quam ob causam neomenias in lege mandatas non celebrat Christianus, si, etc., respondetur: . . . Celebratio enim novae lunae praenuntiabat novam creaturam, de qua dicit Apostolus: "Si qua igitur in Christo nova creatura, vetera transierunt, et facta sunt omnia nova." (II Cor. 5:17).

Damian:

Si etc., cur lege mandatam non celebrat neomeniam Christianus? Responsio: . . . Novae quippe lunae solemnitas novam designat in homine fieri creaturam, de qua dicit Apostolus: "Si qua. . . sunt omnia nova" (II Cor. 5:17).

Problem 8

Why do Christians not perform ritual immersions? Answer: Baptism enables us to participate in Christ's death and resurrection.

Isidore:
> ... Cur illa singularum quarumque immunditiarum baptismata ... non observet Christianus, si etc., respondetur: Venit enim (Christus) consepelire nos sibi per baptismum in mortem, ut quemadmodum Christus resurrexit a mortiis sic et nos in novitate vitae ambulemus.

Damian:
> Si Christus etc., cur Christianus illa ablutionum baptismata . . . non observat? Responsio: Consepulti enim sumus Christo per baptismum in morte; ut quomodo surrexit Christus a mortuis per gloriam Patris, sic et nos in novitate vitae ambulemus.

Problem 9

Why do Christians not observe Tabernacles? Answer: The tabernacle prefigured the Church; furthermore, Christians are the tabernacle of God.

Isidore:
> . . . Qua causa scenopegia non sit solemnitas Christianorum si etc., respondetur tabernaculum Dei fideles esse . . . et . . . jam Christus in Ecclesia sua quod illa figura prophetice promittebat implevit.

Damian:
> Si etc., quid rationis objicitur, ut a Christianis Scenopegiae solemnitas non colatur. Responsio: Tabernaculum Dei societas est populi Christiani, et . . . illud tabernaculum sanctam praefigurabat Ecclesiam.

Problem 10

Why do Christians not observe the sabbatical year? Answer: It prefigures the last judgment.

The texts here are very lengthy. Suffice it to say that again the answers are identical and linguistically extremely close.

Thus, Damian does believe even the ritual law to be of permanent value, provided that it is allegorized in light of the new grace.

CONCLUSION

Peter Damian was not, in any direct way, an important forerunner of the ideas of post-crusade Judaeophobia. Any effect that he may have had on their development took place through his contributions to popular piety rather than through his anti-Jewish writings. Damian, in fact, presents an excellent summation of the pre-crusade attitude toward the Jews, for we have seen that all his statements have a substantial history in the writings of Christians who preceded him.

Damian had very little inclination to write his anti-Jewish works. He chided Honestus for making the request, and he finally wrote the *Antilogus-Dialogus* because he felt that Christians were being humiliated and because of the naive hope of converting the Jews by these arguments. However, it seems evident that these reasons would not have impelled him to write the treatise had not Honestus asked him to.

We have concluded after examining his works that Damian probably had very little knowledge of Jews or contact with them. This ignorance of Jews and their arguments greatly decreased his effectiveness as a polemicist. Thus, the *Antilogus-Dialogus* is quite naive and, significantly, rather conciliatory toward the Jews.

Damian does have harsh things to say about the Jews in a few passages. But we have seen that the two most virulent of these were primarily motivated by hatred toward Christian heretics, and all the anti-Jewish expressions are quite hackneyed.

Damian is very clearly against using violence with respect to Jews. He does blame them quite strongly for the crucifixion, but he probably felt that a significant "remnant" would be saved at the last judgment.

As far as the Old Testament is concerned, Damian studied it closely and loved it deeply. The moral law he considered forever valid. The ritual law may once have been a curse, but a new allegorical understanding of it made possible by the advent of Jesus endows it with sacred and eternal significance.

MODERN AND CONTEMPORARY TIMES

RELIGION, NATIONALISM, AND HISTORIOGRAPHY

Yehezkel Kaufmann's Account of Jesus and Early Christianity[1]

From: *Scholars and Scholarship: The Interaction between Judaism and Other Cultures*, ed. by Leo Landman (Yeshiva University Press: New York, 1990), pp. 149–168.

To open a volume by Yehezkel Kaufmann is to embark upon an intellectual adventure. A stimulating, polemical style draws us into the presence of a creative and probing mind that scrutinized the problems of the Jewish experience from the religious struggles of the biblical period to the Zionist controversies of the twentieth century. One does not read Kaufmann: one confronts him.

Though Kaufmann is best known for his monumental *Toledot ha-Emunah ha-Yisre'elit* (*History of the Religion of Israel*),[2] which presents a strikingly original, sweeping reevaluation of the biblical evidence for the faith of ancient Israel, his earlier *Golah ve-Nekhar* (*Exile and Alien Lands*)[3] examines the even larger canvas of Jewish history as a whole with the broad vision and penetrating brilliance that are the hallmark of his work. The ambitious subtitle, "A Historical-Sociological Study of the Question of Jewish Destiny from Antiquity to the Present," is almost understated: *Golah ve-Nekhar* is probably the only serious effort to construct a detailed philosophy of Jewish history in this century.

Shortly after the publication of the book, Yitzhak Baer expressed puzzlement at the surprisingly lengthy treatment devoted to the rise

---

[1] After this article was submitted for publication, G W. Efroymson's translation of the relevant section of *Golah ve-Nekhar* appeared under the title *Christianity and Judaism: Two Covenants* (Jerusalem, 1988).

[2] 8 vols. Tel Aviv, 1937–56. See also Moshe Greenberg's abridged translation, *The Religion of Israel* (Chicago, 1960).

[3] Tel Aviv, 1929 (hereafter cited as *Golah*). All references are to vol. 1 unless otherwise indicated.

of Christianity, and he attempted to account for it as an expression of Kaufmann's emphasis on the power of a handful of abstract ideas.[4] There can be little doubt, however, that at least two additional motives were at work. First, although Kaufmann made rather promiscuous use of the phrase "of unparalleled interest" in characterizing historical phenomena, the reader cannot avoid the impression that when he described "the formation of a gentile religion out of a Jewish nationalist movement" as "a development full of unparalleled historical interest,"[5] he really meant it. One reason for Kaufmann's lengthy discussion is simply that the subject fascinated him. More important, these chapters are in fact central not only to the major themes of *Golah ve-Nekhar* but to Kaufmann's entire life's work. The mission and destiny of the Jewish people, as Kaufmann understood them, were illuminated by an understanding of the rise of Christianity—indeed, they could not be comprehended without it. Consequently, an examination of his discussion of Jesus and early Christianity will afford us insight not only into one of the major developments in human history but also into one of the most ambitious and perceptive works in modern Jewish historiography.

If Kaufmann was a complex thinker, the rise of Christianity is an even more complex phenomenon, and the work before us demands analysis within an unusually multifaceted context: the history of Jewish attitudes toward Jesus and Christianity, the perceptions of Jesus in nineteenth- and twentieth-century scholarship, the impact of Jewish nationalism on the historiography of the Jews, and Kaufmann's own original and challenging oeuvre. Thus, we shall have to embark upon a lengthy, somewhat superficial, but unavoidable and, I hope, not uninteresting detour before returning to *Golah ve-Nekhar*.

To most medieval Jews, Jesus was a sorcerer justly executed for enticing his compatriots away from the purity of their ancestral faith, while the religion that he founded was idolatry pure and simple. Even in the Middle Ages, however, a variety of factors impelled some Jews to a more nuanced examination of these perceptions. With respect to Jesus himself, a careful reading of the Gospels revealed an anti-Christian argument far more effective than the hurling of insults against "the

4   *Qiryat Sefer* 8 (1931/32): 313.
5   *Golah*, p. 336.

hanged one": it appeared that the very figure whom Christians worshipped had rejected the mantle of divinity and demanded observance of the Torah (e.g., Luke 18:18–19 and Matthew 5:17–18). Medieval Jews who utilized this argument were careful not to depict Jesus in glowing terms, but several of them insisted upon his essential loyalty to both Jewish theology and Jewish law. It was only the tragic distortion of Jesus' original teaching—perhaps by Paul, perhaps by later Christians—that had caused the fateful abyss that now separates the two faiths.[6]

Similar ambiguities are evident in the medieval Jewish evaluation of Christianity. On a theoretical level, there was a need to explain the role of the Christian faith in the divine economy, and a number of Jews—most notably Maimonides—regarded both Christianity and Islam as means of spreading knowledge of Torah in preparation for the messianic age.[7] Although Maimonides considered anyone who accepted Christianity an idolater, he apparently saw no impediment to the belief that God would utilize (even initiate?) an idolatrous faith for a holy purpose. While this position is not paradoxical in any technical sense, the positive role assigned to Christianity could not coexist comfortably with the assessment that Christians were idolaters, and this tension may have contributed somewhat to a more charitable evaluation of Christian faith by later Jews. The medieval Jew most famous for such a reevaluation, Rabbi Menahem ha-Meiri of Perpignan (1249–1316), appears to have been motivated largely by moral considerations. Concerned about talmudic passages that discriminated against gentiles, he argued that they referred only to the barbaric heathens of ancient times; Christians, who adhere to the limits imposed by the mores of civilized faiths, must be treated in accordance with the most rigorous ethical standards. Ha-Meiri also declared that Christians were not idolaters. These declarations, however, are innocent of any theological analysis and appear secondary to the ethical criteria that he established.[8]

---

6   The most important and effective expression of this argument is Profiat Duran's *Kelimat ha-Goyim*. See Frank Talmage, *Kitvei Pulmus li-Profiat Duran* (Jerusalem, 1981).

7   *Mishneh Torah, Hilkhot Melakhim* 11:4, in the uncensored version. See the discussion in Haim Hillel Ben-Sasson, "The Reformation in Contemporary Jewish Eyes," *Israel Academy of Sciences and Humanities, Proceedings* 4, no. 12 (1970): 240–242 = "Ha-Yehudim mul ha-Reformazia," *Divrei ha-Aqademia ha-Leumit ha-Yisre'elit le-Madda'im* 4, no. 5 (1970): 62–64.

8   On ha-Meiri's attitude toward Christians, see Jacob Katz, *Exclusiveness and Tolerance* (Oxford, 1961), pp. 114–128; E. E. Urbach, "Shitat ha-Sovlanut shel R Menahem ha-Meiri—Meqorah u-Migbeloteha," in *Peraqim be-Toledot ha-Hevrah ha-Yehudit bi-Yemei*

The most influential formulation exculpating Christians from the sin of idolatry resulted from economic pressures and had to be thoroughly misinterpreted before yielding its ecumenical meaning. In order to permit certain commercial ventures with Christians, medieval Jewish authorities would sometimes argue that contemporary Christians were not truly attached to idolatry or that they merely followed the customs of their forefathers. In one such discussion, a ruling was issued permitting the acceptance of an oath from a Christian despite the fact that the oath would contain a Christian formula. One element of this ruling is of genuine theological interest. A leading tosafist conceded that Christians might have Jesus in mind when they take an oath in the name of God; nonetheless, he said, Jews need not be concerned about engendering this oath as long as Jesus was not mentioned by name, particularly since the intention of the Christian was "to the Creator of heaven and earth." Thus, while the worship of Jesus presumably remains idolatrous, the God Christians worship is ultimately the true Creator. The sharpest way to formulate this position is through an oxymoron: to at least one tosafist, Christianity is idolatrous monotheism or monotheistic idolatry. This striking perception doubtless resulted from considerations having little to do with a careful analysis of Christian theology, and no medieval Jew expressed it so clearly; nonetheless, I think that it is a fair extrapolation from the text before us.[9]

This section of the ruling, however, had less resonance for later Jews than the following passage, which was the one subjected to a highly significant misinterpretation. Non-Jews, we are told, "were not commanded regarding *shittuf* (" partnership" or "association"). Properly understood, the phrase almost surely meant that when Christians take an oath, they may associate the name of God with that of the saints (who are not divinities even in Christianity),[10] but some early modern Jews

ha-Beinayim u-ba-et ha-Hadashah—Muqdashim li-Professor Y. Katz (Jerusalem, 1980), pp. 34–40; J. Katz, "Od al Sovlanuto ha-Datit shel R. Menahem ha-Meiri," *Zion* 46 (1981): 243–246; Yaakov Blidstein, "Yahaso shel R. Menahem ha-Meiri la-Nokhri—Bein Apologetiqah le-Hafnamah," *Zion* 51 (1986): 153–166.

9 The best text of this discussion is in R. Yeruham ben Meshullam, *Sefer Toledot Adam ve-Havvah* (Venice, 1553), 17:5, fol 159b. See also *Tosafot Sanhedrin* 63b, s.v. *asur*, and cf. *Tosafot Bekhorot* 2b, s.v. *shemma*.

10 This point continues to be widely misunderstood by both historians and talmudists. For what I think is an essentially accurate understanding, see *Mahazit ha-Sheqel* in the standard editions of *Shulhan Arukh Orah Hayyim* 146:2, s.v. *yithayyev*. In at least one

took it to absolve gentiles from the prohibition of believing in a divine partnership. As time passed, this understanding was eagerly embraced by many Jews, not for the old economic reasons, but as a means of fostering improved relations in an atmosphere of mutual tolerance.

Although the Jewish folk attitude toward Jesus continued to be decidedly pejorative, more positive assessments made considerable headway among influential modern Jews. Rabbi Jacob Emden (1697–1776) made the striking assertion that Jesus and even Paul did not aim their message at Jews; rather, their intention was to convince gentiles to observe the laws that Judaism considers obligatory for "the descendants of Noah." Moreover, the distortions of later Christianity should not obscure the fact that in the final analysis this mission was largely successful.[11] Moses Mendelssohn replied to a question by expressing his respect for the moral character of Jesus, though only with the understanding that the latter had made no claims of divinity for himself.[12] Many nineteenth- and twentieth-century Jews discovered that the assertion of Jesus' Jewishness served two remarkably disparate purposes: it fulfilled the old polemical goal by appealing to the authority of Jesus to challenge the Christian rejection of Judaism, and by describing the founder of Christianity with sympathy and even enthusiasm, it could serve as a vehicle for alleviating interfaith tensions.

Ironically, the development of liberal religious trends in the nineteenth century actually served to exacerbate these tensions. Both Reform Jews and liberal Protestants emphasized the uniqueness of their own religion's ethical message, but there was really no substantive difference

edition (currently printed by A. Friedman), the relevant paragraph in *Mahazit ha-Sheqel*, which asserts that trinitarianism is forbidden as idolatry even to gentiles, was deleted, no doubt because of Christian censorship or Jewish fear; in another edition (currently printed by M. P. Press), the word *lo* was mistakenly omitted from the phrase *ben* (or *benei) Noah lo niztavvu 'al zeh.* [Addendum: I am no longer certain of the validity of the interpretation that I endorsed here. It is at least as likely that *Tosafot* meant that gentiles are not forbidden to take an oath in the name of God while having Jesus in mind. I continue to consider it highly unlikely that they regarded Christian worship as permissible for non-Jews. For a survey of interpretations of this passage, see my *The Rebbe, the Messiah, and the Scandal of Orthodox Indifference* (London and Portland, Oregon, 2001), Appendix III, pp. 175–177.]

11 See Blu Greenberg, "Rabbi Jacob Emden: The Views of an Enlightened Traditionalist on Christianity," *Judaism* 27 (1978): 351–363.

12 See Alexander Altmann, *Moses Mendelssohn: A Biographical Study* (Philadelphia, 1973), pp. 204–205.

between the ethical positions of the two groups. Hence, what was once an argument about content had now become an argument about turf. For many Christians who had abandoned fundamentalist beliefs, the need to denigrate Jewish ethics was especially compelling; such Christian scholars, who tacitly and even explicitly conceded the old arguments about dogmas and Christological verses to the Jews, needed to move the center of gravity to the question of ethics, where they could still award victory to Christianity.

With specific reference to the image of Jesus, Christians who had serious doubts about his divinity were impelled to defend his unique role by portraying him as ethical innovator par excellence. To accomplish this, it was necessary to depict first-century Judaism in the darkest possible hues: arid, legalistic, hypocritical, and exclusivist. The superiority assigned to the ethics of Jesus in particular and of Christianity in general became so central in the consciousness of nineteenth-century Christians that it plays a crucial role not only in scholarly works but in the writings of missionaries like Alexander McCaul[13] and in the fulminations of overt anti-Semites. The self-centered Jew, obsessed with legal minutiae and insulated by a particularistic ethic, stood in sharp contrast to the Christian, who was liberated from the stultifying letter and concerned with universal salvation and a morality that taught undifferentiated love for all mankind.

Jewish apologists responded along a broad front. Christians, they said, had distorted the character of rabbinic Judaism out of both ignorance and malice. There is nothing significant in Jesus' ethical pronouncements that cannot be found in rabbinic literature; indeed, the only real novelty in such texts as the Sermon on the Mount is the pushing of certain ethical doctrines *ad absurdum* so that no human being could realistically be expected to comply. Moreover, Christians show no understanding of the power of religious law to produce spiritual inspiration. One of the great ironies in this Jewish response is that Reform Jews, who had rejected many Jewish rituals for deficiencies not so different from those ascribed to them by Christians, now found themselves producing rhapsodic elegies to the spiritual beauties of talmudic law.[14] Finally, Jewish

---

13 See McCaul's *The Old Paths* (London, 1837).

14 See, for example, Israel Abrahams, "Professor Schuerer on Life under the Jewish Law," *Jewish Quarterly Review*, o.s. 11 (1899): 626–627. On the general debate, see the references in Ismar Schorsch, *Jewish Reactions to German Anti-Semitism, 1870–1914*

writers insisted that concern for universal salvation is a manifestation of Judaism far more than of Christianity. It is Judaism that teaches that righteous gentiles who observe the Noahide covenant attain salvation; the Christian impulse to convert the world arose precisely out of the intolerant conviction that all nonbelievers are condemned to the eternal torments of hell.

In the late nineteenth and early twentieth centuries, the image of Jesus as a figure whose raison d'être was ethical reform received a serious jolt from Christian historiography itself. In 1892, Johannes Weiss published his *Die Predigt Jesu vom Reiches Gottes*, which "marks the turning point from nineteenth- to twentieth-century New Testament research."[15] Weiss's emphasis on the eschatological dimension of Jesus' thought and his expectation of a wholly new world[16] was reinforced by Albert Schweitzer's *Das Messianitats und Leidensgeheimnis: Eine Skizze des Lebens Jesu*[17] and further reinforced by the latter's enormously influential survey, *The Quest of the Historical Jesus.*[18] To Schweitzer, Jesus was convinced that a radically new order was upon us and the extreme ethical demands that he made should be understood as an interim ethic to be observed for the briefest of periods until the world as we know it would be supplanted by the new order.

Some Christians, of course, were disturbed not only by the deemphasis of Jesus' ethics, but also by the assertion that his central obsession was a conviction that failed to materialize; nevertheless, the new stress on his proclamation of an apocalyptic kingdom inspired greater interest in his perception of the role that he would play in that kingdom. Thus, the late nineteenth and early twentieth centuries were also marked by a renewed examination of the term "son of man" and its context in Daniel 7:13 and especially in the apocalyptic book of I Enoch; a growing number of scholars came to believe that Jesus' use of this term meant that he may have regarded himself as an angelic savior, the celestial son of man

(New York, 1972), p. 257, nn. 63–65. I have noted some of the points in these paragraphs in my "Jewish-Christian Polemics" in *The Encyclopedia of Religion*, ed. by Mircea Eliade (New York, 1987), vol. 11, pp. 389–395.

[15] R. H. Biers and D. L. Hollard in the introduction to their English translation, *Jesus' Proclamation of the Kingdom of God* (Philadelphia. 1971), p. 2.

[16] See, for example, the English translation, p. 93.

[17] Tübingen and Leipzig, 1901.

[18] London, 1910. German original, *Von Reimarus zu Wrede: eine Geschichte der leben-Jesu-forschung* (Tübingen, 1906).

who would descend with the clouds of heaven to redeem the righteous and inaugurate the Kingdom of God. This conception does not sit well with the belief in a national Messiah from the house of David, but it was regarded by some as an embryonic manifestation of precisely the tensions that culminated in the divine Messiah of mature Christianity.

These developments in Christian historiography coincided with the rise of the modern Jewish historical consciousness, which was especially concerned with the nature of Jewish nationhood and religion and with the special character and mission of Israel. As early as the first half of the nineteenth century, Nahman Krochmal attempted to construct an overarching theory of Jewish history in which Jews would be subject to the normal processes of historical causation while retaining an almost metahistorical uniqueness. Nations, he said, grow, flourish, decline, and die; the Jewish people grows, flourishes, declines—and then begins to grow once more. Since it is ultimately spiritual force that sustains a people, and since the Jewish collective is sustained by unalloyed, "absolute" spirit, it can avoid the inevitable destruction that marks the end of the saga of all other nations.[19] Heinrich Graetz, the greatest Jewish historian of the nineteenth century, was less concerned with abstract philosophy of history, but in his major essay "The Structure of Jewish History," he attempted to delineate the special character of Judaism as an amalgam of a unique religious idea and a political and social theory. In a later work, he spoke of the unfinished mission of spreading the ethical message of Judaism, and his writings are permeated by intense Jewish pride to the point where non-Jews attacked him for parochialism and the German Jewish *Gemeindebund* excluded him from its committee of scholars lest his approach offend the gentile world.[20]

Graetz's most distinguished successor, Simon Dubnow, wrote during a period in which Zionism and other forms of Jewish nationalism moved to center stage on the Jewish agenda. In Dubnow's ideology of autonomism, or diaspora nationalism, the affirmation of Jewish nationhood was essential, but a national homeland was not; indeed, the

---

19 *Moreh Nevukhei ha-Zeman*, chaps. 7–8, in *Kitvei R. Nahman Krochmal*, ed. by Simon Rawidowicz, 2nd ed. (Waltham, Mass., 1961).

20 See Heinrich Graetz, *The Structure of Jewish History and Other Essays*, translated, edited, and introduced by Ismar Schorsch (New York, 1975), editor's introduction, esp. pp. 39, 59. See also Schorsch, *Jewish Reactions to German Anti-Semitism*, p. 45.

need for a land was symptomatic of a lower level of national identity. Although Dubnow was more of a materialist than Graetz, he argued that Jews had transcended the sort of nationality that is based on racial kinship or even the nation state and had attained the rarest and must exalted level—nationality rooted in spiritual-cultural identity.[21]

Though the religious overtones have been eliminated, there are echoes of Krochmal here: the Jewish spirit prevails where lesser nations could not survive. Within the secular context of Dubnow's thought, however, the critical role of religion in Jewish culture became particularly problematic. To a secular Jew who defined Jewish nationhood in largely cultural and historical terms, that defining culture had to be extricated, at least in significant measure, from its traditional religious matrix. Despite fundamental differences, a similar problematic faced cultural Zionists: the national cultural revival that would be facilitated by a Jewish center in the land of Israel would be profoundly different from the religious culture of the exile. In this case, however, the return to the land itself could be cited as both catalyst and justification for the elimination of religious practices whose function was perceived as the temporary preservation of a people in the unnatural state of dispersion.

The quest to define the nature of Jewish nationhood and religion and to identify the uniqueness of the Jewish mission remained at the center of Jewish historiography for much of the twentieth century. Yitzhak Baer began his classic *History of the Jews in Christian Spain* with a controversial introduction of doubtful relevance which set forth his

---

[21]   On Dubnow's views of Jewish history and his relationship to Graetz, see Robert M. Seltzer, "From Graetz to Dubnow: The Impact of the East European Milieu on the Writing of Jewish History," in *The Legacy of Jewish Migration: 1881 and Its Impact* (New York, 1983), ed. by David Berger, pp. 49–60. On levels of nationality, see Dubnow, *Nationalism and History: Essays on Old and New Judaism*, ed. by Koppel S. Pinson (Cleveland, 1958), pp. 86–95, and Oscar I. Janowsky, *The Jews and Minority Rights (1898–1919)* (New York, 1933), pp. 57–60. See also Reuven Michael, "Al Yihudan shel Toledot Yisrael be-einei Jost, Graetz, ve-Dubnov," in *Temurot ba-Historiah ha-Yehudit ha-Hadashah* (Jerusalem, 1987), pp. 501–526, which contains some additional references. On the views of Dubnow and Ahad HaAm on national character and their relationship to Kaufmann, see the discussion in two very similar articles by Laurence J. Silberstein, "Religion, Ethnicity and Jewish History: The Contribution of Yehezkel Kaufmann," *Journal of the American Academy of Religion* 42 (1974): 516–531, and "*Exile and Alienhood*: Yehezkel Kaufmann on the Jewish Nation," in *Texts and Responses: Studies Presented to Nahum N. Glatzer on the Occasion of His Seventieth Birthday by His Students*, ed. by Michael A. Fishbane and Paul R. Flohr (Leiden, 1975), pp. 239–256.

position on the distinctive social message of the sages of the Mishnah as a leitmotif of Jewish history; later, he abandoned Spain with single-minded determination to concentrate on the earlier period, in which the wellsprings of the Jewish character and mission were to be found. Gershom Scholem expanded the historiographical parameters of the Jewish religion itself, arguing that the rationalist inclinations of nineteenth-century historians had created a hostility to mysticism which precluded a true understanding of its vital role in the Jewish experience. Joseph Klausner, whose *Yeshu ha-Nozri* (*Jesus of Nazareth*) was the first significant treatment of Jesus in modern Hebrew, would often judge historical figures by their loyalty to the Jewish national cause which he so fervently advocated. Nonetheless, Klausner regarded his work on early Christianity as a landmark of objectivity; his description of Jesus as "the ethical personality par excellence" was resented by many Jewish readers, but he laid equal stress on the Jewish sources of much of that ethical message as well as the drawbacks of Jesus' exaggerated formulations. In essence, Klausner the nationalist wanted to reclaim Jesus for the Jewish people without exempting him from the critical scrutiny that every Jewish instinct required. Though Klausner himself did not entirely ignore the Middle Ages and was especially proud of his essay on the philosophy of Solomon ibn Gabirol, his concentration on the Second Temple and modern Hebrew literature is symptomatic of an approach that characterized many other Zionist theoreticians: the glories of Jewish history are to be found only in the sovereignty of the remote past and in today's heroic struggle toward a national renaissance.[22]

These themes—Jewish nationhood, religion, and mission—form the core of Yehezkel Kaufmann's work. National identity, he argued, is based essentially on racial kinship and a common language. At the same time, he insisted on the supreme historical importance of the power of ideas; in the case of the Jewish people, it was an extraordinary religious idea that served as the vital force in its formative period and as the key guarantor of survival amidst the stress and distress of exile. *Golah ve-Nekhar* and the later collection *Be-Hevlei ha-Zeman*[23] contain biting

---

[22] Valuable insights into Klausner's ideology and self-perception can be gleaned from his autobiography, *Darki Liqrat ha-Tehiyyah ve-ha-Geullah* (Tel Aviv, 1946; 2nd ed., Tel Aviv, 1955).

[23] Tel Aviv, 1936.

attacks on economic determinism and its denigration of the role of ideas in history. In a particularly striking passage, Kaufmann observes that Marxist materialism itself stems from the driving idea of social justice; ironically, he says, what emerged from this catalyzing force was a system that felt impelled to deny its own idealistic roots.[24]

Not only is the Jewish religious idea central to the history of Israel; it is unique and almost primeval. From the moment the Jewish people emerges on the stage of history, Kaufmann argued, it is driven by a faith unprecedented and unparalleled: there exists but one God, and that God transcends nature, is not subject to magical manipulation, and cannot be grasped in mythological terms. Monotheism is not merely a matter of numbers: the nature of the biblical God is at least as striking and significant as the fact that He is the sole divinity. The ordinary processes of pagan religious development might have produced one god, but only ancient Israel, by an intuitive leap whose etiology must elude historians, produced one God. Moreover, this faith was not the preserve of a small elite. On the contrary, its power and significance rest on the fact that it permeated the consciousness of the people as a whole. Biblical religion was the popular religion of Israel.

Though Kaufmann was far removed from any sort of fundamentalism, there are elements in his thesis that are congenial to traditionalist views,[25] and they are surely conducive to the nurturing of Jewish national pride. The essential core of this position is already present in *Golah ve-Nekhar*, but its classic expression came in Kaufmann's *Toledot ha-Emunah ha-Yisre'elit*. In this work, he inveighed against standard biblical criticism for its blurring of the distinctions between Israelite monotheism and the pagan religions of the ancient Near East, and he argued that concentration on details (occasionally even nonexistent details magically called into being through textual emendation) had blinded scholars to the monumental evidence in the biblical record. It is

---

[24]   *Golah*, pp. 51–55.

[25]   The observation was made by Menahem Haran, "Al Gevul ha-Emunah," *Moznayim* 24 (1967): 52–53. Note too Moshe Greenberg, "Kaufmann on the Bible: An Appreciation," *Judaism* 13 (Winter 1964): 86: "Though himself not a man of faith, Kaufmann leaves room for the answer of faith to the phenomenon of the Bible." It is especially worth noting that the responses to Kaufmann's central thesis have been marked by a striking irony. The desire of traditionalists to affirm the monotheism of ancient Israel produces the inclination to explain away prophetic denunciations of idolatry, while radical critics insist on taking them at face value.

often the absence of a fundamental idea that constitutes a monumental phenomenon, and Kaufmann was keenly sensitive to what he perceived as critical omissions: no magic, no true, deeply rooted mythology, no syncretism, a failure even to understand the theology of paganism and the consequent perception of polytheistic religion as fetishism and nothing more, the absence of charges of idolatry in biblical narratives covering the very periods in which the literary prophets appear to describe rampant polytheism.

Though biblical monotheism arose in a particular ethnic group with a strong sense of national identity, the monotheistic idea could not help but transcend narrow nationalism and assume a universal mission. By the time Christianity appeared upon the scene, Judaism had a long-standing commitment to a doctrine of religious conversion in which prior ethnic identity played virtually no role. Jews had long believed that the knowledge of the universal God could and should be spread throughout the world with no national impediment. Despite the significance of the physical people of Israel in Jewish lore, from a legal perspective the door to conversion was wide open, and many Jews in the Roman world were urging gentiles to enter it. Jewish universalism left nothing to be desired.[26]

Christianity, however, did appear upon the scene with its own version of a universal calling, and it is finally time to turn our attention to Kaufmann's central assertions about its origin, its mission, and its hero. There is a special fascination, he says, in the transformation of Christianity from a sect founded by a Jewish messianic figure into a universal faith that encompassed the world. Jesus was thoroughly Jewish, but his message, ironically, was narrower than that of mainstream Judaism in the first century. In the eschatology of the biblical prophets, which continued to dominate the messianic vision of many Jews, the people of Israel prevail over the nations of the world and are the instrument of universal redemption, but the framework of the present order remains intact. To the increasingly popular apocalyptic mentality, on the other hand, an entirely new world was imminent, and that world was not seen through the prism of national divisions. This, however, did not make its message more universal; on the contrary, apocalypticists tended to envision the utter destruction of the gentiles as well as of most Jews.

[26]   See, for example, *Golah*, pp, 220, 224, 255, 292.

Jesus, then, who was a major representative of this world-view, was not only unconcerned with gentiles and the imminence of their destruction; he was convinced that a majority of Jews would also be doomed in the impending cataclysm. Repentance would save a small sect of Jewish believers, and despite some lovely ethical sentiments, the key moment in that repentance is the acceptance of Jesus himself. Kaufmann argues vigorously that Jesus' forgiving of sins and his performance of exorcisms through his own power demonstrate that he used the term "son of man" in the apocalyptic sense; though he had no pretensions to divinity, he regarded himself as a celestial being destined to redeem the world. The central teaching of Jesus, then, is the imminent kingdom to be ushered in by the apocalyptic son of man who is now among us.

Though this conception largely obscures the national mission of the traditional Jewish Messiah, that mission could not be fully exorcised. Thus, Jesus came to Jerusalem for the purpose of being crowned king of the Jews. His execution, which was an entirely unanticipated disaster, came at the instigation of the Jewish authorities on the grounds of false prophecy and blasphemy. Indeed, many tentative believers may have regarded the threat of execution as the best way to force him to produce the sign that so many had requested. In Kaufmann's typically sharp and felicitous formulation, Jesus was crucified even by those who believed in him.[27]

Within Judaism, belief in a crucified Messiah could survive only in sectarian form, but the mission to the gentiles began to succeed just as the message to the Jews was being largely rejected. Ironically, says Kaufmann, it was precisely the narrowness of Jesus' teaching that led to Christian universalism. The Jewish rejection of the good news was received with special bitterness and perplexity precisely because the Christian message was initially directed only to Israel. Hence, the idea was born that Jewish rebelliousness had led to the transfer of the gospel and the election from carnal Israel to the gentiles.

To Kaufmann, the ultimate success of the Christian mission was not due to ethics, which were neither new nor central; it was not due to the downgrading of ritual, which did not really occur and would in any case have had little impact (circumcision aside) on the attractiveness of the faith; nor was it due to the universal character of Christianity,

[27]   Ibid., p. 384.

which was no greater than that of Judaism. Christianity, like Islam, prevailed because of the power of the Jewish message. It was that message and that message alone which swept away the pagan world. Monotheism could not be accepted directly from the Jews because Judaism, through the accidents of history, had come to be associated with exile and defeat. Thus, it was indeed Jewish national identity that served as a stumbling block for gentiles, but this was not a limitation stemming from the national dimension of Judaism as an idea; rather, it was one that had been created by the fortuitous historical circumstances of destruction and exile. The gentile world could not identify itself with a dispersed and defeated nation. This obstacle needed to be removed, and Christianity and Islam removed it.[28] In the final analysis, however, it is Judaism that conquered the world.[29]

This brief summary does not begin to do justice to Kaufmann's richly textured and brilliantly argued thesis,[30] but it does afford us the opportunity to take a closer look at several salient features of his presentation. In a sense, although Kaufmann's argument owes nothing to Maimonides, he has reproduced the tension of the Maimonidean analysis in a new and sharper form: to both thinkers, Christianity is an idolatrous religion whose essential mission is the destruction of idolatry. In Maimonides, there is no need to mitigate the idolatrous element in Christianity in order to accept this conclusion, since it is solely through the spreading of the Torah that the mission is achieved. Despite the gradualism which is the hallmark of the Maimonidean position, the final transformation of Torah-oriented idolaters into monotheists will come through the intervention of the Messiah *ex machina*, so that Christianity does not have to generate the monotheistic impulse directly.

Kaufmann, on the other hand, wrote after many generations of Jewish efforts to see Christianity in as monotheistic a light as possible, and he was able to utilize this perspective in the service of his central theme without rejecting the classical Jewish perception of Christian idolatry. If the concept of Christianity as idolatrous monotheism is implicit in the

---

[28]   For this crucial discussion, see ibid., pp. 292–301.
[29]   Ibid., pp. 306–314.
[30]   On the day after Kaufmann's funeral, Abraham Malamat told Chaim Potok that Kaufmann's discussion of the rise of Christianity is "one of the most significant chapters ever written on the subject." See Potok, "The Mourners of Yehezkel Kaufmann," *Conservative Judaism* 18, no. 2 (Winter 1964): 3.

tosafists, it is explicit in Kaufmann. It is true that Christianity is a semi-pagan religion. Jesus has been worshipped for centuries as a god,[31] and this idolatrous belief may have grown out of his own grandiose (though nonidolatrous) self-perception. Early Christianity was marked by an increasing emphasis not on ethical values but on the mythological-magical character of Jesus,[32] and it was this emphasis that separated the new religion from Judaism, thus eliminating the barrier that the Jews' defeated condition had erected between them and the world of potential converts. For anyone familiar with Kaufmann, the term "mythological-magical" immediately conjures up the image of pagan religion par excellence. In other words, the monotheistic dimension of Christianity was the positive force that enabled it to prevail, while the polytheistic dimension was the facilitating force that allowed the monotheistic appeal to overcome the obstacle of Jewishness. And so—this idolatrous faith destroyed idolatry; this idolatrous faith spread precisely because its mission was the destruction of idolatry; at its core, this idolatrous faith is not idolatrous at all.

While modern Jews had generally recognized the essentially mono-theistic character of Christianity, they had tended to emphasize its residual paganism and its abrogation of the Torah as the central elements in its success. Otherwise, why should it have prevailed over Judaism? Thus, Kaufmann's *emphasis* on Christian monotheism is unusual in Jewish writing, and his position on this question is essential to the significance of his entire life's work. The bulk of that work was devoted to the Jewish monotheistic idea and its impact on history, and it was crucial to him to insist that this idea had conquered the world not as a secondary, largely obscured element in a system deriving most of its power from other sources, but as the central, driving force of history. Kaufmann was not studying the religion of a Near Eastern people, however important it may have been; he was studying the belief that had changed the world. Though he was, of course, aware that polytheism was not fully uprooted on a global scale (and on rare occasions he speaks of Europe and western Asia rather than the world), the sweeping, almost poetic rhetoric of his perorations on this theme reveal his deep emotional involvement with a universal upheaval that he regarded as the core of his work.

---

[31] *Golah*, p. 375.
[32] See, for example, ibid. pp. 407–408.

Not only does Kaufmann insist that Jewish monotheism was the single positive factor in the success of Christianity; he is concerned to deny even a facilitating role to those characteristics of Christianity that were regularly cited as evidence of its superiority to Judaism. Thus, as we have already seen, he utterly dismisses universalism, ethics, and the discarding of ritual. On the whole, his arguments are forceful and often persuasive, but one of those arguments reflects a methodological problem that besets Kaufmann's work in a variety of contexts. He asserts that the prevalence of ritual in Islam, including even circumcision, constitutes decisive proof that Christianity's deemphasis of ritual cannot have been a major reason for its success.[33] Kaufmann has often been criticized for excessive emphasis on the power of ideas at the expense of a careful, empirical examination of less exalted historical forces, and this is a case in point. Islam spread from the outset in the context of military conquest. Christianity did not. Perhaps ritual is indeed a critical obstacle to the widespread acceptance of a new religion, but it is an obstacle that can be overcome by the sword, Eventually, of course, Christianity too spread through the exercise of concrete pressure, and in a different context, Kaufmann distinguishes between the period in which it converted individuals and the time when it began to convert groups. He does not, however, relate this transition to the ability of the church to mobilize the powers of the state: the distinction between attracting individuals and converting entire groups is analyzed solely in terms of the different ways in which they respond to the power of an idea and to the obstacle of Jewish exile.[34] Despite the probable validity of Kaufmann's essential point about ritual, the methodology of his analogy to Islam reflects a disregard of the sort of specificity that can often be achieved only by a descent from the rarefied heights of the history of ideas into the cluttered trenches of social, political, and military history.

In the service of his thesis, Kaufmann must downgrade the substantive differences between Judaism and Christianity by reducing them almost solely to the question of authority.[35] Although at a later point in his analysis he makes some brief remarks about the religious

---

[33]   Ibid., p. 285.
[34]   Ibid., pp. 422–423.
[35]   Ibid., pp. 314–333.

reasons for Jewish disbelief, the body of his discussion of the "conflict of covenants" gives little consideration to the possibility that substantive theological considerations can underlie the decision to reject the authenticity of a particular Messiah. The failure to fulfill biblical prophecy is not as incidental a concern as Kaufmann indicates; it goes to the heart of one's definition of the Messiah. Nor can it be asserted with serene confidence that the doctrines of later Jewish mysticism demonstrate Jewish flexibility of such magnitude that even belief in a divine Messiah might have been absorbed by mainstream Judaism.[36] There is much to Kaufmann's point that we are dealing largely with a dispute about covenants, but his minimizing of crucial distinctions results from his central theme: Christianity acted as the messenger of Judaism.

As for Jesus himself, Kaufmann's analysis once again reflects elements both old and new. Like his Jewish predecessors, Kaufmann sees little that is new in Jesus' ethics. Many Jews who made this point, however, agreed with Christian scholars that ethics lay at the heart of Jesus' message, and we have already seen Joseph Klausner's emphatic reiteration of this perception. Kaufmann, on the other hand, adopted the image of Jesus as a man obsessed with the apocalypse and his own role in the Kingdom of God.

At this point, we must confront a characteristic of Kaufmann's work which is rather disturbing and is by no means isolated. Kaufmann creates the strong impression that his analysis represents an original break with the portrait of Jesus the ethical preacher that is maintained almost universally by Christian scholars. It is true, he writes, that a small minority of such scholars reluctantly recognize Jesus' messianic claims, but even they attempt to strip those claims of any political dimension. These brief remarks appear at the beginning of the chapter on Christianity.[37] The footnote accompanying them refers to a concession by Wellhausen that there is a bit of truth in Reimarus' assertion of Jesus' messianic self-consciousness, and it continues with the observation that "Eduard Meyer also disagrees" with those who deny the value of the evidence for Jesus' messianism, although he believes that Jesus had "no political intentions."[38] And that is all. Kaufmann's

36 Ibid., p. 315.
37 Ibid., pp. 339–341.
38 Ibid., pp. 340–341, note 1.

crucial subchapter entitled "The Apocalyptic Messiah" is bereft of a single reference to the secondary literature on this theme.[39]

As we have already seen, the issues of the apocalyptic kingdom and the meaning of "son of man" were at the cutting edge of European New Testament scholarship at the time that Kaufmann wrote. Even before the turn of the century, Wilhelm Baldensperger had discussed Jesus' use of the term "son of man" in the context of its apocalyptic use in Daniel and I Enoch, and had even noted the implications of Jesus' forgiving of sins, which is one of Kaufmann's central points.[40] The works of Weiss and Schweitzer moved the apocalyptic kingdom to center stage. Kaufmann's grudging reference to Meyer gives no indication of the substantial discussion in *Ursprung und Anfänge des Christentums* of the possibility that Jesus perceived himself as a celestial apocalyptic "son of man," a possibility that Meyer takes very seriously even though he does not embrace it with conviction.[41] Two years before the publication of *Golah ve-Nekhar*, a major scholarly conference was held in Canterbury which has been described as "the true triumph of apocalyptic in the interpretation of the Kingdom of God in the teaching of Jesus."[42] Not a whisper of this intellectual ferment can be discerned in *Golah ve-Nekhar*.

While Kaufmann may have been only partially aware of the most recent research on the frontiers of New Testament scholarship, he surely knew more than he told his readers. Moreover, this is not an entirely atypical phenomenon in Kaufmann's work. Some scholars have leveled criticisms against his history of biblical religion not only for ignoring developments after Wellhausen that might have required him to shift the focus of his study[43] but also because he pays no attention to scholars whose views came closer to his own.[44] Nonetheless, the positions of those scholars are not close enough to Kaufmann's to sustain an accusation

39 Ibid., pp. 355–379.
40 Wilhelm Baldensperger, *Das Selbstbewusstsein Jesu im Lichte der messianische Hoffnungen seiner Zeit*, 2nd ed. (Strasbourg, 1892), pp. 182–192, and esp. p. 172.
41 Vol. 2 (Stuttgart and Berlin, 1921), pp. 330–352, 446–447.
42 Norman Perrin, *The Kingdom of God in the Teaching of Jesus* (Philadelphia, 1963), p. 56. The proceedings of that conference were published in *Theology* 14 (1927): 249–295.
43 Stephen A. Geller, "Wellhausen and Kaufmann," *Midstream* 31, no. 10 (December 1985): 46.
44 Jon D. Levenson, "Why Jews Are Not Interested in Biblical Theology," in *Judaic Perspectives on Ancient Israel*, ed. by Jacob Neusner, Baruch A. Levine, and Ernest S. Frerichs (Philadelphia, 1987), p. 291.

of unacknowledged dependence or even of an inappropriate failure to cite virtually identical views. With respect to *Golah ve-Nekhar*, however, Laurence Silberstein has noted omissions of major proportions, though he makes the point in muted tones. Thus, "none of the major writings of the historical-sociological tradition are referred to in the pages of *Golah ve-Nekhar* despite the subtitle of the work and the evident influence of this school of thought in a variety of fundamental ways."[45] Again, "Although Kaufmann makes no reference to Durkheim, Rudolf Otto, or Weber, there are many similarities" between his views and theirs.[46] Silberstein deduces from this that although Kaufmann was surely aware of these thinkers, he "came to these issues by way of philosophy."[47] The most likely explanation for this recurring phenomenon probably lies in Kaufmann's penchant for polemical style. The argument in virtually all his works is structured dialectically and builds through a critique of earlier views. In this context, references to thinkers and scholars who anticipated important points in Kaufmann's position is structurally inconvenient, and he succumbed to the temptation of leaving them out. While there is little doubt that the remarkable dramatic impact of his work would have suffered from adherence to the proper conventions of scholarly acknowledgment, there is equally little doubt that in the final analysis this is no excuse.

These observations should not be allowed to obscure the fact that even with respect to the particular point about Jesus' apocalyptic views, the fundamental thrust of Kaufmann's discussion is original. All the Christian scholars who wrestled with the issue remained deeply committed to Christian apologetics, and the reader of Kaufmann's analysis certainly comes away with a perception radically different from those that permeate the works of Baldensperger, Weiss, Schweitzer, and Meyer. Moreover, Kaufmann's deemphasis of the ethical element in Jesus' teaching extends into his discussion of the early church, where he argues for the ethical inferiority of Christianity through a strikingly original argument which is considerably sharper than the usual Jewish observations about the unrealistic extremism of Christian

---

[45] "Historical Sociology and Ideology: A Prolegomenon to Yehezkel Kaufmann's *Golah ve-Nekhar*," in *Essays in Modern Jewish History: A Tribute to Ben Halpern*, ed. by Frances Malino and Phyllis Cohen Albert (East Brunswick, N.J., 1982), p. 181.

[46] Ibid., p. 186.

[47] Ibid., p. 181.

moral ideals. The new religion, he says, was so unconcerned with ethics that it rejected not only Jewish ritual but also the entire corpus of Jewish civil and criminal law—a corpus self-evidently superior to the torture-ridden *corpus iuris* of the Romans with which Christians were perfectly satisfied to live.[48]

The discussion of Jesus' career and particularly his trial demonstrates that Kaufmann had an eye for detail as well. In an important respect, this discussion breaks with the *Tendenz* of modern Jewish scholarship and apologetics and stands firmly rooted in the Jewish Middle Ages. In Kaufmann's view, the Jews did crucify Jesus, or at least they were responsible for the crucifixion. Virtually all modern Jews regarded such a position as inimical to fundamental Jewish self-interest, and Kaufmann's willingness to assert it is a striking indication of remarkable courage and independence. For all its boldness, however, the discussion of this point is marked by a serious flaw. Kaufmann argues that Jesus could properly have been executed as a false prophet, even according to mishnaic law, for refusing to provide a sign authenticating his messianic claims.[49] In fact, a person who refused to provide a sign might well forfeit his right to be believed, but he would not forfeit his life. Only a prediction or sign that did not materialize could be grounds for execution, and nothing in the sources indicates that this had occurred. If Jesus claimed to be the Messiah but refused to produce a sign, the only evidence strong enough to justify his execution would be the fact that he died without redeeming the world. Jews presented that evidence to the court of history, but it was too late to present it to a court of law.

In any case, Kaufmann's Jesus died as a false prophet. He had no unique ethical message, and neither did Christianity. He did not deemphasize ritual, and neither, at first, did Christianity. We have already noted Kaufmann's explanation for the transformation of the Christian message into a universal one, and here his crucial point was not to deny that Christianity developed this characteristic but to insist that Judaism had possessed it for centuries before the dawn of the new faith.

This assertion of Jewish universalism leads to a final, fundamental, and tragic tension in *Golah ve-Nekhar*. Kaufmann was a committed Jewish nationalist who saw the great Jewish mission as the dissemination of

---

48   *Golah*, pp. 405–406.
49   Ibid., pp. 391–393.

the monotheistic idea on a supranational, universal scale. Judaism made this possible by effectively abolishing the criterion of nationality through the establishment of religious conversion. But this sacrifice, if indeed it was a sacrifice, was to no avail, since the impediment of exile reintroduced the obstacle of ethnicity. Thus, the mission could be fulfilled only through the agency of Christianity and, later, Islam. Religion preserved the Jews as a national group, and in an age of nascent nationalisms, there was finally hope for the removal of the albatross of exile. Kaufmann regarded this as a consummation devoutly to be wished, though he wrestled with the dilemma of what would preserve the Jewish nation in a postreligious world.[50] In the deepest sense, however, it is impossible to avoid the feeling that the national redemption of Israel comes too late. The nation's unique mission lies in the past, and its fulfillment has been achieved by proxy.

It is no accident that after completing *Golah ve-Nekhar*, Kaufmann turned his full scholarly attention to the biblical period, when the quintessential insight of the Jewish people was exclusively theirs and when the mission of Israel was still to be fulfilled. Kaufmann was no Toynbee, and his Jewish people, poised on the threshold of a national renaissance, was no fossil. Nonetheless, there is a disquieting sense that the nation's truly heroic age can never be recovered. In the chapter on Christianity, for all its celebratory rhetoric about Judaism's conquest of the world, lies the fundamental tragedy of *Golah ve-Nekhar*.

---

[50] See his "Hefez ha-Qiyyum ha-Leumi," *Miqlat* 4 (June-August 1920): 194, cited by Silberstein in all three of his articles on Kaufmann. (See nn. 20 and 44 above.) See also *Golah* II, p. 427.

THE "JEWISH CONTRIBUTION"
TO CHRISTIANITY

From: *The Jewish Contribution to Civilization: Reassessing an Idea*, ed. by
Jeremy Cohen & Richard I. Cohen (Littman Library of Jewish Civilization:
Oxford and Portland, Oregon, 2007), pp. 80–97.

From the late nineteenth until the middle of the twentieth century, Jews and their sympathizers devoted considerable research, energy, and ingenuity to the documentation of signal Jewish contributions to Western civilization. Whatever objections critics might have raised regarding the extent of the Jewish role, the positive assessment of the discipline, field, or ideal to which Jews had allegedly contributed was not usually a matter of controversy, so that the authors of this literature generally take the intrinsic value of the "contribution" for granted.

In 1921 an American Christian recounting what "the Jew has done for the world" listed patriotism, the prophet Samuel's "argument that battered down the enslaving doctrine of Divine Right of kings," involvement in the discovery of America, science, mathematics, medicine, politics, poetry, philology, and law-abiding behavior.[1] Four years later another book of this genre provided chapters on Jewish contributions to education, folklore, literature, philosophy, the law, scientific research, medicine, chemistry, infant welfare, art, music, drama, athletics, Eastern exploration, and citizenship. Still, even such lists, read at a later time, reveal unsuspected layers of complexity. Thus, a heading that I have skipped, "Jewish Pioneers of British Dominion," was of course seen by the author as unequivocally positive; in our age, with its deep reservations about imperialism, that chapter inadvertently alerts us to the value judgments that underline and potentially bedevil

---

[1]   Madison C. Peters, *Justice to the Jew: The Story of What He Has Done for the World* (New York, 1921), p. 23.

aspects of this enterprise, a point already evident if we contemplate how a seventeenth-century European would have reacted to the assertion that the Jewish Bible undermines the divine right of kings.[2] Indeed, since the Bible is the primary source of the doctrine *affirming* the divine right of kings, the tendentiousness of the argument that a single speech in the book of Samuel establishes Jewish responsibility for undermining that doctrine is particularly striking. As late as 1951 we find a shorter but similar list pointing to Jewish contributions to achievements understood as self-evidently meritorious: democracy, science, medicine, exploration, and the military.[3]

So far, with the exception of the reference to Samuel, we have looked at headings that are relentlessly secular, and even the apparent exception congratulates Jews for a political contribution that liberated its beneficiaries from the shackles of a religious conception. But a discussion of Jewish contributions omitting the religious dimension is a quintessential example of the Hebrew adage *ha-ikkar haser min ha-sefer* ("the main element is missing from the book"). As soon as we turn our attention to that dimension, the valuation assigned to both the Jewish characteristic and its purported consequence becomes anything but self-evident, and we are propelled into a fascinating arena of warring values and competing perceptions.

Nonetheless, even on the religious front, we find efforts to produce lists of Jewish influences on Christianity intended to sound soothing

---

[2] *The Real Jew: Some Aspects of the Jewish Contribution to Civilization*, ed. by H. Newman (London, 1925). Needless to say, this is not the only assumption in such a book that can render a contemporary reader uneasy. Here is a description of Jewish athletic aptitude: "The highly emotional and excitable temperament characteristic of the Jew is singularly adapted to enable the possessor to excel . . . . The alert Jewish mind is well suited to boxing and sprinting. Moreover, the Jewish mentality, the morbid anticipation that precedes competition, the almost uncanny knack of seizing opportunities are admirable. The certainty the Jew has of rising to the occasion . . . his overwhelming self-appreciation and confidence—what qualities can be more calculated to enable a man to achieve high athletic distinction? The Jew born of Jewish parents possesses physical qualities and mental qualities well suited to athletic success" (Harold M. Abrahams, "The Jew and Athletics," in *The Real Jew*, pp. 248–249). On the other hand, Charles and Dorothea Singer, in one of the best books of the "Jewish contribution" genre, assert—albeit with some hesitation—that there is no Jewish race. See their "The Jewish Factor in Medieval Thought," in *The Legacy of Israel*, ed. by Edwin R. Bevan and Charles Singer (Oxford, 1927), p. 180.

[3] *The Hebrew Impact on Western Civilization*, ed. by Dagobert Runes (New York, 1951).

and uncontroversial, describing religions whose essential approaches are the very quintessence of harmony. A Christian writer, in a chapter entitled "The Fountainhead of Western Religion," asserted that "much that came to be called Christian was, in fact, the lengthening shadows of Hebraic ideas and influences." His bill of particulars includes a sense of destiny and the unification of morals and religion, even the identity of Judaism's and medieval Catholicism's list of cardinal sins, to wit, "the shedding of blood, sexual impurity, and apostasy."[4] That "apostasy" for Jews included the embrace of medieval Catholicism goes unmentioned.

Cecil Roth's *Jewish Contribution to Civilization* (1940), a classic work on our theme by a prominent historian, concentrates on the secular areas typical of this genre, but the introductory chapter underlines Jewish contributions to Christianity itself, and through it, to the world at large: monotheism, the value of human life, the sanctity of the home, the dignity of the marital relationship, equality of all before the one God, the messianic vision, prayer, even Christian ceremonial (baptism, Communion [from the Passover *seder*], lectionaries, and the liturgical use of Psalms).[5] Perhaps the lengthiest list of his sort was compiled by Joseph Jacobs in 1919, and despite its general tone of apodictic certainty, it includes occasional qualifications that, once again, provide some hint of the problematics of this enterprise. In the realm of practice: prayer (especially the Psalter), the Mass or Communion, baptism, bishops (from the synagogue position of *gabbai*), charity boxes, ordination of priests, religious schools, the missionary character of early Christianity (borrowed from the missionary spirit of the Judaism of the time), aspects of canon law. In the realm of theology: the kingdom of heaven, original sin ("though it must be allowed that it has received much more elaborate development in Church doctrine", while Judaism mitigated its harshness with "original virtue," to wit, the merit of the fathers), special grace to God's favorites, the Fatherhood of God (and even, to some degree, "the analogous conception of the Son of God"), the chosen people,

---

4 Vergilius Fern, "The Fountainhead of Western Religion," in *The Hebrew Impact on Western Civilization*.
5 Cecil Roth, *The Jewish Contribution to Civilization* (Cincinnati, 1940), pp. 4–13. Leon Roth, *Jewish Thought as a Factor in Civilization* (Paris, 1954), lists the messianic idea, the return to Hebrew Scriptures in Christian Reform movements, the Psalter, even the sense of sin and divine punishment.

resurrection, hell (though Christianity laid greater emphasis on this), repentance, confession of sin, the Messiah, the Golden Rule (though this is more practical in its negative, Jewish form), the dicta of the Sermon on the Mount, the Lord's Prayer, and the importance of the Law to Jesus.[6] Jacobs does add that while the only difference between primitive Christianity and developed Judaism is the vague one of Jesus's personality, three major distinctions eventually emerged: the Law, image worship, and the doctrine of a Man-God.

One suspects that Jacobs was well aware that some items on his list of contributions bore a more mixed message than he acknowledged. Thus, Jewish apologists generally denied the existence of any serious concept of original sin in Judaism, pointing *inter alia* to a Jewish prayer beginning, "My God, the soul that you have given me is pure," and minimizing the lasting effect of the sin of Adam and Eve on the spiritual nature of their descendants. Like Roth, he does not inform us that Jews through the ages, like the early Calvinists, perceived the Catholic Mass as an idolatrous ceremony, whatever its original connection to the Passover *seder*, and he does not acknowledge what Jews saw as the critical distinction between confessing one's sins to God and confessing them to a human being.[7] He was surely not interested in noting the interesting irony that while Jews had decidedly "contributed" the idea of the Messiah to Christianity, Reform Judaism, by abandoning belief in a personal Messiah, had recently moved away from a central element of that concept, which was precisely the one that Christians had placed at center stage. Finally, I suspect that one of the items on his list was intended as a subtle critique of Christianity, though he deliberately left the implication unspoken. For a Jew to include "the chosen people" in an accounting of Jewish contributions to Christianity is to underscore the argument that Christian stereotypes of narrow Jewish particularism versus Christian universalism obscure the reality that Christendom has

6   Joseph Jacobs, *Jewish Contributions to Civilization: An Estimate* (Philadelphia, 1919), pp. 91–100. Some of the last items should arguably have been classified as practice rather than theology. The unelaborated reference to the Sermon on the Mount relies, says Jacobs, on Gerald Friedlander's *The Jewish Sources of the Sermon on the Mount* (New York, 1911).

7   For a particularly sharp medieval example of this Jewish critique of Christianity, see my *The Jewish-Christian Debate in the High Middle Ages: A Critical Edition of the Nizzahon Vetus with an Introduction, Translation, and Commentary* (Philadelphia, 1979), pp. 22–23 and n. 60, 223–224, 339.

identified itself as the new chosen people to the exclusion and perhaps damnation of the rest of humanity.[8]

The tendency of authors writing in this genre to avoid highlighting the Jewish clash with Christianity is sharply illustrated in Louis Finkelstein's classic, monumental *The Jews: Their History, Culture and Religion* (1949). His work is far more than an exemplar of the typical effort to establish a Jewish contribution to civilization, but this is surely a major component of its mission. In its four massive volumes, we look in vain for any serious discussion of the relationship between Judaism and Christianity. The brief allusion to Christian ethics in Mordecai Kaplan's contribution affirms, as we shall see, complete commonality between the two faiths. And the editor's own, even briefer, comment on Jewish attitudes towards Christianity is quite remarkable: "Rabbi Jacob Emden (1697–1771), one of the foremost teachers in the history of Judaism, summarized the general Jewish view regarding Christianity in the following words . . . '[Jesus] did a double kindness to the world by supporting the Torah for Jews and teaching Gentiles to abandon idolatry and observe the seven Noahide commandments'."[9] And that is all. So does one of the most strikingly positive—and highly atypical—Jewish assessments of Christianity ever proffered by a traditional rabbi become "the general Jewish view."

It is worth noting that Jewish scholars and apologists during the period in question frequently affirmed that another atypical Jewish view of Christianity was in fact standard. Rabbi Menahem ha-Meiri of late thirteenth- and early fourteenth-century Perpignan had taken the position that Christianity is not to be seen as idolatry at all and that its adherents are entitled to full equality with Jews in matters of civil law because they are among the "nations bound by the ways of religions." Though elements of this position were shared by other medieval and early modern authorities, it is profoundly misleading to describe it as

---

8   As we shall see more strikingly in our discussion of Leo Baeck, the assertion that Jews contributed the missionary spirit to Christianity is also noteworthy and by no means typical.

9   *The Jews: Their History, Culture and Religion*, 4 vols, ed. by Louis Finkelstein (Philadelphia, 1949), IV, p. 1347. On the rarest of occasions, we find a Jewish scholar writing during the period under discussion who exaggerates Jewish hostility to Christianity. Thus, Samuel Krauss asserts that "Jesus' illegitimate birth was always a firmly held dogma in Judaism" ("The Jews in the Works of the Church Fathers," *Jewish Quarterly Review*, o.s. 5 (1892): 143).

typical. Nonetheless, distinguished Jewish authors, for reasons that are not difficult to discern, often described it as such—sometimes, I suspect, in full sincerity.[10]

If the only dynamic in play were the assessment of the Jewish contribution to civilization, it might have been possible to sidestep the major tensions between the two faiths and affirm the Jewish contribution to Christianity by recording the bland commonalities that we have already noted—or by resorting to the silence and disingenuousness of Finkelstein's work. But during the period in which this enterprise was at its height, a period that I will delineate for the purposes of this chapter as roughly the 1890s to the middle of the twentieth century, a related dynamic was also at its height: the depiction by Christian scholars and theologians of a sharp contrast between rabbinic Judaism and Christianity, and the consequent need for a Jewish response.[11]

---

[10] Cf. my observations in "Jacob Katz on Jews and Christians in the Middle Ages," in *The Pride of Jacob: Essays on Jacob Katz and his Work*, ed. by Jay M. Harris (Cambridge, Mass., 2002), pp. 42–44. On ha-Meiri, see Moshe Halbertal, *Bein Torah le-Hokhmah: Rabbi Menahem ha-Meiri u-Ba'alei ha-Halakhah ha-Maimonim bi-Provence* (Jerusalem, 2000). An English translation of much of the relevant chapter appeared in the online *Edah Journal*, 1 (2000), <http://www.edah.org/backend/JournalAAicle/halbertal.pdf>, accessed 11 Sept. 2006.

[11] A substantial scholarly literature has developed around this confrontation, providing analysis of the earlier part of the 19th century as well as the period of direct concern to us. First and foremost is the brilliant work of Uriel Tal, *Christians and Jews in Germany: Religion, Politics and Ideology in the Second Reich, 1870–1914* (Ithaca, NY, 1975). Susannah Heschel addressed the content and impact of a seminal Jewish figure's perception of Jesus in *Abraham Geiger and the Jewish Jesus* (Chicago, 1998). Christian Wiese's important study, *Wissenschaft des Judentums und protestantische Theologie in wilhelminischen Deutschland* (Tübingen, 1999) is highly relevant in its entirety; chapter 4, which deals with particularism versus universalism, ethics versus law, and love versus fear in the context of the debate surrounding Wilhelm Bousset's *Die Religion des Judentums im neutestamentalischen Zeitalter* (Berlin, 1903), bears most directly on our concerns. (An English translation has now been published: Christian Wiese, *Challenging Colonial Discourse: Jewish Studies and Protestant Theology in Wilhelmine Germany*, trans. by Barbara Harshav and Christian Wiese [Leiden, 2005]). Ismar Schorsch, *Jewish Reactions to German Anti-Semitism, 1870–1914* (Newark, 1972), pp. 169–177, provides a succinct summary of Jewish concerns from an institutional perspective. Overviews of modern Jewish assessments of Jesus and Christianity include Gosta Lindeskog, *Die Jesusfrage im neuzeitlichen Judentum. Ein Beitrag zur Geschichte der Leben-Jesu-Forschung* (Uppsala, 1938); Jacob Fleischmann, *Be'ayat ha-Nazrut ba-Mahashavah he-Yehudit mi-Mendelssohn'ad Rosenzweig* (Jerusalem, 1964); Walter Jacob, *Christianity through Jewish Eyes: The Quest for Common Ground* (Cincinnati, 1974); Donald A. Hagner, *The Jewish Reclamation of Jesus* (Grand Rapids, Mich., 1984).

During the course of the late nineteenth century, the maturation of both liberal Protestantism and biblical criticism produced a concerted attack on classical Judaism. Since many liberal Protestants no longer believed the standard dogmas of Christianity, they shifted their faith's center of gravity to the arena of ethical teaching and an intense spiritual relationship to God. The trajectory of pre-Christian Israelite-Jewish religion came to be seen roughly as follows: The early Pentateuchal documents affirmed by adherents of the newly regnant critical hypothesis reflected a naive, rather primitive perception of a God who was accessible in an immediate, almost tangible sense and whose ethical character left much to be desired. With the rise of the literary prophets, both the moral and theological understanding of God reached unprecedented heights. At the same time, the transcendent theology expressed in what the critics identified as the Priestly document of the exilic period produced a remote Deity and came to be associated with overemphasis on ritual, legalism, and arid genealogies, while in the quintessential cases of Ezra and Esther, late biblical Judaism degenerated into extreme, chauvinistic exclusivism. It is these characteristics that persisted into what came to be described as Late Judaism, that is, the Judaism of Jesus's time. Jesus himself, and Christianity after him, not only restored the highest form of religion found in the Hebrew Bible but transcended it, combining ethical selflessness with a fresh, direct experience of God without sacrificing the essence of monotheism.

Needless to say, Jews could not allow this portrait to go unchallenged. Much has been written about the Jewish indictment of Christian scholars for distorting rabbinic Judaism out of both malice and ignorance, and I will not reiterate this aspect of the argument in detail. These Jewish reactions were not without their effect; nonetheless, the old critique of the rabbis persisted in some circles into the mid-twentieth century despite all the efforts of Jewish apologists and sympathetic Christian scholars. Thus, no less a theologian than Rudolf Bultmann, notwithstanding a few pro forma qualifications, produced a chapter entitled "Jewish Legalism" in his *Primitive Christianity* that could have been written in the 1890s. He informs us that ritual in Judaism became more important than morality, "with the result that men lost sight of their social and cultural responsibilities." Precepts that had become meaningless "still had to be obeyed unquestioningly. . . . Regulations went into detail to the point of absurdity . . . This ritualism . . . sanctified the life of the community, but that sanctity was an entirely negative affair." And on and on.[12]

Consequently, from the late nineteenth century until the middle of the twentieth, Jews faced the delicate, challenging task of balancing a complex of objectives that were often in tension with one another. They surely wanted to demonstrate that Judaism played a central role in the rise of Christianity. After all, no Jewish contribution to Western civilization could be clearer than this. At the same time, they did not want to erase the line between the religions. They did not want to offend Christians, but they did not want to absorb the indictment of Judaism supinely. They wanted to embrace Jesus as their own without accepting him as a Jewish authority or granting Jewish legitimacy to the religion that he founded (or, perhaps, did not found).

In this daunting enterprise, their religious and ethical perspectives came to be deeply engaged. One of the most intriguing aspects of this study is the light shone by the historical and apologetic works of these Jews on their own differing values. What some Jews considered quintessentially Christian, others saw as a Jewish influence; what some saw as an admirable Christian belief, others saw as an unfortunate deviation; what some saw as central to Judaism, others saw as problematic and dispensable. Nonetheless, there are also broad and deep commonalities marking the Jewish assessments of the relationship between the religions.

While the range of issues marking these controversies covers a broad spectrum, several stand out in bold relief. These include the Law, particularism and universalism, ethics, the experience and conception of God, and the view of redemption and redeemer. It is to these that we now turn our attention.

On one level, Jews had long argued—inconsistently to be sure— that Jesus himself did not reject the Law.[13] In the modern period, the perception of a 'Jewish' Jesus became dominant, to the point where the

---

12 Rudolf Bultmann, "Jewish Legalism," in Bultmann, *Primitive Christianity* (New York, 1956). I was first alerted to this chapter in graduate school as a result of a passing remark by Gerson Cohen.

13 See my "On the Uses History in Medieval Jewish Polemic against Christianity; The Search for the Historical Jesus," in *Jewish History and Jewish Memory: Essays in Honor of Yosef Haym Yerushalmi*, ed. by Elisheva Carlebach, John M. Efron, and David N. Myers (Hanover, NH, 1998), pp. 25–39.

distinguished German Reform rabbi Leo Baeck eloquently, though no doubt tendentiously, produced an "original Gospel" consisting entirely of Jewish elements.[14] Beyond this point, Jews needed to defend the role of law in rabbinic Judaism itself. Two of the most distinguished Jewish scholars in Britain turned their attention to this task: Israel Abrahams in his classic essay on Emil Schuerer's caricature of rabbinic law and Solomon Schechter in his encomium to the Sabbath and, more briefly, to the donning of tefillin.[15] Wilhelm Bousset's invidious characterization of Judaism generated several Jewish reactions, most fully and notably by Felix Perles, who underscored the deep spirituality of the rabbinic concept of repentance, the joy attendant upon fulfilling the commandments (*simhah shel mizvah*), and the understanding of the Law as an expression of divine love.[16] The essential argument of these works was repeated decades later in a lesser-known essay by the Edinburgh rabbi Salis Daiches, who remarked that to those who know Judaism from within, depicting it as legalism standing in contrast to spirituality "appears not only unfounded but also unintelligible."[17]

In an ambitious, systematic response to Adolf Harnack's *The Essence of Christianity* (*Das Wesen des Christentums*, 1900), the Berlin rabbi Joseph Eschelbacher not only composed a paean of praise to the halakhah but also formulated a sharp riposte. Scholastic argument, he noted, developed Christian dogmatics through the ages. In our time, Julius Wellhausen has agreed that the basic teachings of Jesus can be found in Jewish sources but has insisted that they are submerged by a legal system in which everything is equal. Well, said Eschelbacher, did not Christian dogmatics do to the message of Jesus precisely what Wellhausen ascribes to the Jewish legal system?[18]

---

[14] Leo Baeck, *Judaism and Christianity* (Philadelphia, 1960), pp. 98–136. This volume, published shortly after Baeck's death in 1956, contains English translations of works written several decades earlier.

[15] Israel Abrahams, "Professor Schuerer on Life under the Jewish Law," *Jewish Quarterly Review*, o.s. 11 (1899): 626–662; Solomon Schechter, "The Law and Recent Criticism," *Jewish Quarterly Review*, o.s. 3 (1891): 754–766.

[16] See Felix Perles, *Boussets Religion des Judentums im neutestamentalischen Zeitalter kritisch untersucht* (Berlin, 1003), and the discussion and references in Wiese, *Wissenschaft des Judentums und protestantische Theologie*, p. 161.

[17] Salis Daiches, "Judaism as the Religion of the Law," in *The Real Jew*.

[18] Joseph Eschelbacher, *Das Judentum und das Wesen des Christentums* (Berlin, 1908), pp. 27–28.

In a different mode, Moritz Guedemann argued in 1892 that the depiction of Jewish adherence to the letter rather than the spirit is itself an unfair caricature. Jewish contemporaries of Paul would not have quarreled with the assertion that "the letter killeth but the spirit giveth life" since the letter of various biblical laws from the *lex talionis* to the year of release were in effect set aside by rabbis in favor of the spirit. While Guedemann had no intention here of fully homogenizing Christian and Jewish attitudes towards the Law, this is a striking instance of taking a liberal understanding of the operation of rabbinic law, placing it into a conceptual framework that the rabbis themselves would not have endorsed—and thereby neutralizing a Christian objection to Jewish legalism.[19]

A disturbing problem for some Jews engaged in apologetics regarding the Law was generated by the fact that some of them adhered to Reform, or Liberal, Judaism, so that they rejected elements of the ceremonial law for reasons not very different from those proffered by Christian critics.[20] In 1907 the Reform rabbi Israel Goldschmidt, in another of the book-length Jewish responses to Harnack, wrote an entire appendix to demonstrate that the differences between Orthodoxy and Reform do not undermine a proper analysis of the contrast between Judaism and Christianity. He provided an abstract, highly philosophical account of those differences, and that account enabled him to argue that the essence of Judaism is unaffected by the Orthodox-Reform divide. For him, the basic difference between the Jewish movements is not the Law per se but Orthodoxy's assertion that the bond between God and Israel was formed in a supernatural fashion versus the Reform understanding that sees it in terms of historical evolution.[21]

This approach, however, by avoiding a direct confrontation with the question of the Law, left the issues raised by the Christian critique unresolved. The most striking example of a Liberal Jewish move in

---

19   Moritz Guedemann, "Spirit and Letter in Judaism and Christianity," *Jewish Quarterly Review*, o.s. 4 (1892): 352–353. Though this article appeared in an English journal, Guedemann resided in Vienna, where he pursued a distinguished rabbinic and scholarly career.

20   I made this point in "Religion, Nationalism, and Historiography: Yehezkel Kaufmann's Account of Jesus and Early Christianity," in *Scholars and Scholarship: The Interaction between Judaism and Other Cultures*, ed. by Leo Landman (New York, 1990), p. 154. See now Wiese, *Wissenschaft des Judentums und protestantische Theologie*, p. 162.

21   Joseph Goldschmidt, *Das Wesen des Judentums* (Frankfurt am Main, 1907), pp. 218–219.

the direction of the Christian position on this issue appears in Claude G. Montefiore's 1927 commentary to the Synoptic Gospels. Not surprisingly, the passage in question was noted both by Lou Silberman in his Prolegomenon to the 1968 Ktav reprint of Montefiore's work and by Donald Hagner in his evangelically oriented analysis of Jewish approaches to Jesus, though neither of them quite captures its full radicalism.[22] The Gospel text in question is Mark 7:15: "There is nothing outside a man, which entering into him can make him unclean, but the things which come out of a man, these are what make him unclean." Montefiore asserted that this is one of the two chief justifications for Liberal Judaism's view of "the old ceremonial law." First, the "old prophets" said that "the true service of God is not ceremonial, but moral." But they dealt with the ceremonial laws that were supposed to affect God. Jesus's observation, on the other hand, deals with those ceremonial laws that were supposed to affect man. "Upon these two doctrines, the doctrine of Hosea . . . and the doctrine of Jesus . . . the new attitude of Liberal Judaism toward the ceremonial Law depends."[23] Montefiore hastened to add that Liberal Judaism takes the further step of retaining the ceremonies that it values; nonetheless, we find here a remarkable citation of Jesus as an authority on a par with Hosea in undermining the binding character of sections of the Torah. While this is extraordinary and atypical, it underscores with ruthless candor a central dynamic in the Reform Jewish discourse on Christianity and the Law.

A secondary but revealing point that emerges from this discussion is Montefiore's distinction between ceremonial laws that were supposed to affect God and those intended to affect man. The former category presumably refers to sacrifices, which are ostensibly subjected to criticism in several notable passages in the literary prophets. It is highly unlikely that any pre-modern Jew would have adopted this classification except in a kabbalistic context, where other commandments as well could affect the upper worlds. Sacrifices, whatever their precise purpose, were designed to affect human beings no less than God. For Montefiore, however, they are a reflection of a primitive religious mentality in which God's behavior is directly changed by propitiatory offerings. The prophets took one step towards a more elevated religious sensibility by decrying

[22] Claude G. Montefiore, *The Synoptic Gospels* (first pub. 1927; New York, 1968), Prolegomenon by Lou Silverman, pp. 11–13; Hagner, *The Jewish Reclamation of Jesus*, pp. 114–115.
[23] Montefiore, *The Synoptic Gospels*, pp. 131–132.

this crude ceremonial practice; it was left for Jesus to discern the triviality and inappropriateness of ceremonies whose theological primitivism is less evident. Perhaps, then, one should say not that Jesus is on a par with Hosea but that he stands on a higher rung than the prophet on the ladder of spiritual development.

It is a matter of no small interest that Martin Buber, who did not have a high regard for the ceremonial law, nonetheless saw both biblical sacrifice and the prophetic criticism directed against it through a very different lens.

> One of the two fundamental elements in biblical animal sacrifice is the sacralization of the natural life: he who slaughters an animal consecrates a part of it to God, and so doing hallows his eating of it. The second fundamental element is the sacramentalization of the complete surrender of life; to this element belong those types of sacrifice in which the person who offers the sacrifice puts his hands on the head of the animal in order to identify himself with it; in doing so he gives physical expression to the thought that he is bringing himself to be sacrificed in the person of the animal. He who performs these sacrifices without having this intention in his soul makes the cult meaningless, yes, absurd; it was against him that the prophets directed their fight against the sacrificial service which had been emptied of its core.[24]

With respect to the central issue before us, Buber's dismissive attitude towards the legal component of Judaism placed him in agreement with the liberal Protestant critique. He dealt with this, as Ekkehard Stegemann has pointed out in a perceptive analysis, by identifying Jesus as a perfectly good Jew who indeed recaptured the prophetic, ethically resonant dimension of Judaism, while describing Paul as one who transformed this message into 'the sweet poison of faith'. Thus, historic Judaism contains whatever is valuable in Christianity and justly rejects that which is distinctively Christian.[25] Through this approach, Buber, at least in his own mind, rendered unnecessary the defense of the ceremonial law that presented such a daunting challenge to Liberal Jewish apologists.

[24]   Martin Buber, "The Two Foci of the Jewish Soul," in *Jewish Perspectives on Christianity: Leo Baeck, Martin Buber, Franz Rosenzweig, Will Herberg, and Abraham J. Heschel,* ed. by Fritz A. Rothschild (New York, 1990), p. 126.

[25]   See Stegemann's introduction to the selections from Buber in *Jewish Perspectives on Christianity,* pp. 15–16.

We have already noted Eschelbacher's structural analogy between the Law in Judaism and dogmatics in Christianity. Montefiore provided the more direct analogy between Jewish law and Christian ritual. Thus, John would have objected to the abolition of baptism and the Eucharist just as Philo objected to the abolition of Pentateuchal Law.[26] Similarly, Yehezkel Kaufmann, whose brilliant and original oeuvre addressed not only biblical religion but the entire span of the Jewish experience, argued that Christianity could not have prevailed over Judaism because of its rejection of the Law since Christianity itself is replete with ritual.[27]

Leo Baeck, however, emphasized not the similarity but the disparity between Jewish law and Christian ritual. Paul left Judaism when he embraced *sola fide* and moved from there to dogma and sacrament. Sacrament is not law in the Jewish sense; it is mystery made tangible. What then is the Law to the Liberal rabbi? In one place it is exemplified by ethics. But at the end of the essay he moves to the Sabbath. "The Law, and quite especially the Sabbatical element in it—has educated that capacity in man which is born of the depth of life—the capacity to be different." From here he returns to his earlier emphasis on Judaism as a special synthesis of mystery and commandment. "This is the gift and possession of Judaism."[28] This last sentence encapsulates perfectly the challenge at the heart of the discourse regarding "the Jewish contribution" to Christianity and perhaps to civilization as a whole. Jews wanted to show that they have provided a gift—but that it is still their special possession. The Sabbath is an ideal vehicle for the realization of Baeck's objectives. It is an embodiment of law, but it can be affirmed without all the details of the Law; it is a gift to the world, yet it remains uniquely Jewish.

While this aspect of Baeck's argument, for all the originality of his formulation, is consistent with the mainstream Jewish attitude towards Christianity, he also proffers a highly unusual approach to the relationship between Judaism and Christian antinomianism. A talmudic statement affirmed that the world would last 6,000 years: 2,000 desolation, 2,000 Torah, and 2,000 the messianic age. Since the late twelfth century, Christians had cited this statement to demonstrate that the Torah would

26   Claude G. Montefiore, "Notes on the Religious Value of the Fourth Gospel," *Jewish Quarterly Review*, o.s. 7 (1895): 46.

27   This is part of a larger analysis of the success of Christianity in Yehezkel Kaufnann, *Golah ve-Nekhar* (Tel Aviv, 1929), pp. 292–301.

28   Baeck, *Judaism and Christianity*, pp. 177, 175, 184.

be annulled in the messianic age, and since the thirteenth, Jews had struggled to show that this conclusion did not follow. Baeck adduced this rabbinic passage along with some other evidence to establish precisely what Christians had affirmed all along—that the messianic age is not an age of Torah. He proceeded to argue that since this was the standard Jewish view in antiquity, Paul's rejection of the Law was deeply Jewish. His only innovation was his conviction that the final age had already arrived. In other words, Paul's belief in Jesus' Messiahship required him—on Jewish grounds—to affirm the abolition of the Law. Christian antinomianism is itself a Jewish contribution to the new faith.[29]

Adherence to the Law was often seen as a manifestation of Jewish particularism. Christians had criticized Jews for this presumed failing as early as the Middle Ages; in early modern times, the issue rose to greater prominence, and by our period it was almost ubiquitous. A central explanation—so it was said—of Christendom's victory over Jewry is that the former bore a universalistic message while the latter was concerned only with itself. Here again Jews and their supporters demurred, but in very different ways. One approach was to emphasize the particularism of Jesus himself, who did not want to cast his pearls before non-Jewish swine and who was sent only to the lost sheep of the House of Israel.[30] With respect to the broader arena, a Christian writing enthusiastically of the Jewish struggle against paganism in a book bearing a philosemitic message would only affirm that Judaism had the *potential* to become a world religion, but, he said, the rabbis robbed it of its vital force through a policy of isolation. Thus, "the role which it might have filled was handed over to Christianity."[31] Yehezkel Kaufmann agreed with the final sentence but strongly rejected the reason. Judaism, he argued, was thoroughly universalist, providing everyone the option to enter the Jewish people through conversion. It was not particularism or even Jewish ethnicity per se that caused Judaism to miss its opportunity. Rather, it was the historical accident of exile that transformed this ethnicity into an insuperable obstacle. Non-Jews would have joined the Jewish people, but not a defeated Jewish people. It was the Jewish message of universalist monotheism—and that message alone—that

---

29   Ibid., pp. 154, 161–164, 241–242.
30   See e.g. Samuel S. Cohon, "The Place of Jesus in the Religious Life of his Day," *Journal of Biblical Literature* 48 (1929): 89, citing also Joseph Klausner and Montefiore.
31   George H. Box, "How Judaism Fought Paganism," in *The Real Jew*, p. 34.

accounted for the sweeping triumph of Christianity and then of Islam. The tragedy of Jewish history is that this victory was achieved only by proxy.[32]

Some Jews went even further by arguing that Judaism is more universalist than Christianity. For Israel Goldschmidt, the concept of a church is particularistic in the extreme. Unlike Christianity, Judaism is a *Schule* or an *Orden*, a school of thought or an order, rather than a *Kirche*.[33] Montetiore, conceding Jewish particularism, dealt with it through his openness to religious development: "Jewish particularism is very objectionable . . . but it was happily not part and parcel of the real Jewish creed. It could be, and has been, easily got rid of." On the other hand, John's division of humanity into saved Christians and damned others is deeply embedded in the creed, and thus harder to exorcise. If the rabbis restricted the dictum "Thou shalt love thy neighbor as thyself" to Jews—at least to some degree—John restricts it to Christians. Is this really an improvement?[34] Similarly, but without any overt reference to Christianity, the British rabbi and scholar Abraham Cohen affirmed that the brotherhood of man, including the salvation of righteous Gentiles, is essential to Judaism, which does not "stipulate the necessity of a uniform creed for all."[35] Needless to say, this argument goes back at least to Moses Mendelssohn and served as the stock in trade of many Jewish apologists throughout modern times.

Montefiore himself took the denial of a relationship between faith and salvation to an extreme that can be explained only by his commitment to Liberal Judaism combined with his desire to maintain what was for him a crucial contrast between Judaism and Christianity:

> To all Jews, presumably to all liberal Christians, the action of God on man is not determined by the accuracy of his belief about God. We do not believe that the relation of God to man is different in the case of a Jew and in the case of a Christian. We realize that varying religious beliefs may and do have varying effects upon character, but so far as God is concerned we do not believe that he has other laws of influence and judgment for those who believe concerning him more truly or less truly, or even for those who have failed to find him altogether. Least of all do we believe that these

[32] See my discussion in "Religion, Nationalism, and Historiography," pp. 159–168.
[33] Goldschmidt, *Das Wesen des Judentums*, pp. vi-vii, 214.
[34] Montefiore, "Notes on the Religious Value of the Fourth Gospel," pp. 41, 43.
[35] Abraham Cohen, "Great Jewish Thoughts," in *The Real Jew*, p. 25.

variations of belief affect the destiny of the soul beyond the grave . . . . But inconsistently, as we believe, with the justice of God and the universalism of his providence, the author of the Fourth Gospel did presumably believe that the result of true belief... is the prerogative of eternal life.[36]

"All Jews," then, in 1895, presumably including the traditionalist masses of eastern Europe and the Muslim world, as well as their rabbinic leaders, rejected Maimonides' assertion that denial of his principles deprived the non-believer of a portion in the world to come. It is hard to envision a more striking example of parochialism than Montefiore's blinkered vision of the Jewish world in which he lived. Moreover, even if his presentation of the theology of his contemporary co-religionists had been accurate, there is a transparent element of unfairness in comparing the views of the Fourth Gospel on a point like this with the Judaism of the 1890s rather than that of the first and second century.

And then there was the argument for Jewish nationalism, which in some sense affirmed the value of parochialism. The paradigmatic exemplar of this approach in our context is Joseph Klausner, a fervent Zionist who regularly utilized his scholarship as a handmaiden of his ideological commitments. Klausner insisted that monotheism itself could be preserved only through Jewish adherence to a particular national identity. Abandonment of that identity would have caused Israel—and its unadulterated monotheism—to have been swallowed up by the far more numerous nations.[37]

The contrast between universalism and particularism is not unrelated to the evaluation of Jewish versus Christian ethics. I have already alluded

---

[36] Montefiore, "Notes on the Religious Value of the Fourth Gospel," pp. 32–33.

[37] Joseph Klausner, *Mi-Yeshu ad Paulus* (Tel Aviv, 1940), vol. 2. pp. 220–221. The full discussion fades, as best as I can see, into near incoherence, but I hope I have captured its recoverable essence. It is no accident that, in a quite different context, the argument from the need for national survival was invoked by the Zionist historian to defend acts that raise moral questions of the most serious sort. The Hasmonean expulsion of pagans and occasional acts of forcible conversion appear unjust, says Klausner, but a different policy would have led to the destruction of Judaea and the end of the Jewish people. Faced with such a prospect, "the moral criterion cannot help but retreat, and in its place there comes another criterion: the possibility of survival." See *Historiah shel ha-Bayit ha-Sheni*, 2nd edn, 5 vols (Jerusalem, 1951), vol. 3, pp. 65–66. I discuss this and other aspects of Klausner's Zionist historiography in "Maccabees, Zealots, and Josephus: The Impact of Zionism on Joseph Klausner's History of the Second Temple," in *Studies in Josephus and the Varieties of Ancient Judaism: Louis H. Feldman Jubilee Volume*, ed. by Shaye J. D. Cohen and Joshua Schwartz (Leiden, 2006), pp. 15–27.

to Mordecai Kaplan's avoidance of any contrast between the ethics of the two faiths in his contribution to Finkelstein's *The Jews*. "The Christian Gospel ... not only retained the confidence the Jews had had in their own way of life, as well as the original emphasis upon the primacy and divine character of the ethical, but it also possessed the irresistible vigor and impetus of a new revelation." Thus, it saved "the ethical emphasis of Judaism from being confined to the Jewish people." Monotheism made Judaism's teachings acceptable to the sophisticated as well as the unlettered, and "the same is true of Christianity."[38]

This irenic, contrast-free presentation is, however, highly atypical. For both liberal Protestants and Liberal Jews, a key factor, perhaps *the* key factor, defining the quintessential character of their respective religions was ethics. Since Liberal Jews were no longer committed to traditional Jewish law, and liberal Christians, as I have already noted, were no longer committed to traditional Christian dogma, it followed that unless their ethical teachings could be distinguished from those of rival religions, their own faith's *raison d'etre* was called into question.

That this dynamic operates even in the absence of any ill will towards the Other was brought home to me with particular force in a contemporary context quite different from that of late nineteenth- and early twentieth-century Europe. The State of California was preparing a religion curriculum for its schools, and a still unfinished textbook in the history of religions prepared for this purpose had elicited criticism from Jewish organizations (and, not surprisingly, from other groups as well). The Jewish concerns centered on the depiction of Judaism in the time of Jesus. I was asked to comment on these criticisms and quickly realized that, *mutatis mutandis*, I had been transported back into the days of Schuerer, Bousset, Harnack, Eschelbacher, Abrahams, Perles, et al. This time not a trace of anti-Semitism could reasonably be attributed to the authors, and yet they faced an intractable dilemma. How are the career and significance of Jesus of Nazareth to be presented in a school textbook? Separation of Church and State precludes the affirmation that he was the Messiah and Son of God who died for our sins. At the same time, the United States is a predominantly Christian country, so that Jesus cannot be presented simply as a charismatic preacher who taught more or less

---

[38] Mordecai Kaplan, "The Contribution of Judaism to World Ethics," in *The Jews*, vol. 2, pp. 686–687.

what his contemporaries taught but somehow so inspired his disciples that they succeeded in founding a religion centered upon him. What remains is precisely what remained for liberal Protestants in Europe a century earlier: a depiction of Jesus as the bearer of an ethical message distinct from that of his surroundings and markedly superior to it. While many of those liberal Protestants went well beyond what this structural dilemma had forced upon them, to a significant degree they had little choice.

Perhaps the most systematic—and one of the most combative—Jewish works arguing that whatever is admirable in Jesus' ethics is Jewish, while the rest is not particularly admirable, was Gerald Friedlander's *The Jewish Sources of the Sermon on the Mount* (1911).[39] It is worth noting in this connection that scholars, both Christian and Jewish, of the early twentieth century were not unaware of a methodological issue that has attained particular prominence in our own generation, to wit, the problem of using rabbinic materials, which have come down to us in a literary form that does not predate the second century, to characterize first-century Judaism. Friedlander cites several Christians who made this point with respect to various concepts, most notably the Fatherhood of God, but he argues vigorously, in part by resort to New Testament criticism, that the evidence of rabbinic texts and liturgy can justly be used to argue for Jewish priority.[40]

Joseph Klausner also asserted that the key ethical categories of Judaism are equal or superior to those of Christianity. Thus, Paul's *agape* is simply Jewish love; indeed, he may have refrained from ascribing the principle of loving one's neighbor specifically to Jesus (Rom. 13: 8–10; Gal. 5: 13–14) precisely because he knew that this emphasis was already that of Hillel. At the same time, excessive emphasis on love can eclipse justice, so that Pauline love may be appropriate for the individual, but it cannot serve as the basis for social or national life. I think it is fair to maintain that Klausner and other Jews saw justice as a quintessential Jewish contribution to civilization but did not see it as mediated through Christianity except perhaps in the technical sense that Christians served as a conduit for the Hebrew Bible. I am tempted to say, in a reversal of the medieval Christian assertion, that Christians served as the book-bearers of the Jews.

[39]   See n. 6.
[40]   Friedlander, *The Jewish Sources of the Sermon on the Mount*, pp. 129–134.

Yehezkel Kaufmann, in his argument that Christian ethics did not provide the attraction that accounted for its victory over Judaism, made the particularly acute point that if Christians were so ethically sensitive they would have chosen Jewish civil and criminal law over the torture-ridden Roman *corpus iuris*.[41] But the most striking Jewish reversal of the argument from Christian ethical superiority was made by Leo Baeck. Christianity, he asserted, is the ultimate romantic religion, and the romantic stays away from law, from commandment, from the sphere of good and evil—and hence from ethical action as the highest ideal. Indeed, for Paul and Luther faith is counterposed to all works, not just the ceremonial. Paul made moral demands because he was rooted in Judaism, but ethics are merely an appendage to his religion as well as to that of later Christians. "In the Church, ethics has basically always caused embarrassment. It was there—it had been introduced by the Old Testament which had been accepted as part of the Bible—but the faith lacked any organic relation to it."[42]

Despite the centrality of the ethical moment, liberal Christians who had forsaken much of Christian dogma did not rest their case for Christianity on ethics alone. Harnack's famous account of the essence of Christianity spoke also of the kingdom of God, the Fatherhood of God, and the infinite value of the human soul, and especially emphasized the immediacy of Jesus' relationship with God. Eschelbacher's is the most detailed, systematic Jewish response to these assertions, appealing both to the biblical prophets and to rabbinic aggadah to establish the vibrancy of the Jewish encounter with the divine.[43]

Buber made a major point of insisting on the reality of the Jew's immediate personal relationship with an imageless God.[44] And Montefiore

[41] Kaufmann, *Golah ve-Nekhar*, vol. 1, pp. 405–406, noted in my "Religion, Nationalism, and Historiography," p. 166.

[42] Baeck, *Judaism and Christianity*, pp. 192–193, 249–251, 256. The standard approach of Jewish apologists in the exchange about ethics is exemplified by Moritz Lazarus, *Die Ethik des Judentums* (Frankfurt am Main, 1898, 1911).

[43] Eschelbacher, *Das Judentum und das Wesen des Christentums*, passim.

[44] Martin Buber, *Two Types of Faith* (New York. 1951), pp. 130–131. A Christian scholar writing in our genre also stressed that "the Fatherhood of God" is a Jewish term, but could not refrain from adding a qualification about the fresh vitality infused into it by Jesus. See Francis C. Burkitt, "The Debt of Christianity to Judaism," in *The Legacy of Israel*, p. 72.

insisted with vigor and eloquence that the doctrine of the Incarnation was not needed to bridge the gap between God and man. Jews "from Isaiah to Jesus and from Jesus to Mendelssohn" did not feel what a Christian writer described as "despair at the seemingly hopeless task of climbing the heavens and finding the unapproachable God." Indeed, says Montefiore in a somewhat different context, the complete incarnation of the Logos at a particular time and place substitutes "something mechanical, sensuous, spasmodic, magical" for the gradual unfolding of God's plan for the world.[45]

Finally, a word about eschatology. That Judaism "contributed" to Christianity its concept of a redeemer hardly needs to be said.[46] Jews through the ages concentrated on stressing the differences between the Jewish criteria for identifying the Messiah and those of Christianity, not the obvious commonalities. Thus, *inter alia*, the Jewish Messiah is a human being, not a denizen of the heavens. But the genre we are examining can produce, as we have already seen, some surprising assertions of influence. In this case, Leo Baeck, while of course rejecting the conception of a fully divine redeemer, insisted that the concept of a supernatural Messiah was indeed borrowed from Judaism. Baeck was convinced that the figure "like a [son of] man" in Daniel 7 who comes with the clouds of heaven is in fact the pre-existent Messiah. Thus, "faith had long raised the figure of the Messiah beyond all human limitations into a supra-historical, supra-terrestrial sphere. He was endowed with the radiance of the heavens and transfigured above the earth." Buber maintained that the son of man in Daniel is a "still indefinite image," and even this is too strong a depiction of a figure who is almost certainly nothing more than a symbol. But Baeck sees him as a supernatural Messiah, so that the basic building block of the Christian messianic conception is not merely in extra-biblical apocalypses but in the Jewish Bible itself.[47] Baeck does, however, make a point of noting that the Greek word *soter*, or savior,

---

45 Montefiore, "Notes on the Religious Value of the Fourth Gospel," pp. 66–67, 40.
46 Burkitt, "The Debt of Christianity to Judaism," pp. 95–96, makes the related observation that "the reality and eternal significance of time," the awareness that reality is a grand drama to be played out but once, is a lesson learned from Judaism by all forms of Christianity.
47 Baeck, *Judaism and Christianity*, pp. 66, 148; Buber, *Two Types of Faith*, p. 112.

which is applied by Luke to Jesus, is a term whose Hebrew equivalent is used in the Jewish Bible about God alone.[48]

No less surprising is Baeck's identification of the Christian missionary spirit as a function of Jewish influence. The modern affirmation of Jewish universalism and tolerance, going back to Mendelssohn's emphasis on the portion of ethical non-Jews in the world to come, led Jews to characterize Christian mission as a function of a regrettably intolerant spirit. Not so Baeck. Romantic religion, he says, looks inward, possessing the promise as a gift. It was the Jewish element in Paul, with its "confidence in the meaning of man's exertions," that gave Christianity its missionary impulse, which remains strongest in those Christian groups who are closest to Judaism and the Old Testament.[49]

The project of demonstrating the Jewish contribution to civilization was simultaneously easiest and most difficult when the object of Jewish beneficence was Christianity. Jews wanted to show that they had enriched the world through their daughter religion, but they did not want to render her as attractive as her parent. What is Jewish and what is not, what is Christian and what is not, what is legalistic and what is not, what is ethical and what is not, what is particularistic and what is not—these questions and more provide a window not only into the dynamics of Judaism's encounter with a dominant faith but into its struggle to define its own contours and to penetrate the depths of its soul.

[48]   I cannot resist noting a personal experience with the term *soter* in the context of Jewish-Christian relations. In 1995 the Open University in Israel distributed an eight-part video of discussions between Yeshayahu Leibowitz and Marcel Dubois about Judaism and Christianity that had taken place in 1992 ("In Two Octaves"). The conversations were held in Hebrew, and the video supplied English subtitles. I was asked to comment on two of the installments when the series was shown on a cable TV channel in New York, and so I read the English carefully. Near the end of the second program, Leibowitz tells Dubois that Paul did a terrible thing by denying halakhah and insisting that everything depends on the *soter*. The term recurs about five times at the end of that installment and the beginning of the third. The translator, who knew Hebrew and English but had no understanding of theology or of Greek, recognized *soter* as a perfectly good Hebrew word, and repeatedly provided the incoherent translation "refuter" or "refutation." When I noted this, I had to struggle to convince the moderator that the translation was incorrect.

[49]   Baeck, *Judaism and Christianity*, pp. 284–289. We recall that Joseph Jacobs had also included Christian missionizing in his lengthy list of Jewish influences on Christianity. See n. 6.

JEWISH-CHRISTIAN RELATIONS

A Jewish Perspective

From: *Journal of Ecumenical Studies* 20 (1983): 5–32.

Our generation has seen some fundamental, even revolutionary changes in the official position of many Christian churches toward Jews and Judaism. Anti-Semitism has been denounced, contemporary Jewish responsibility for the crucifixion denied, missionizing re-examined, text-books revised, and dialogue encouraged. These changes, though welcomed by most Jews, have left many lingering problems unresolved, and, especially in the case of dialogue, they have raised new, complex questions about the propriety and character of interfaith relations.

The most famous Christian statement on the Jews in recent years is, of course, the widely heralded and much debated document issued by Vatican II in 1965 (*Nostra Aetate 4*), which spoke of a special bond between Christians and Jews. Since then, a series of Catholic statements both in Rome and in various national churches has attempted to grapple with the ambiguities and omissions in *Nostra Aetate 4*, and in January 1975, official guidelines were issued for the implementation of the council's declaration and the encouragement of continuing contacts between Catholics and Jews.

Protestant churches have also moved toward a reassessment of their attitudes concerning Jews and Judaism in a number of statements by the World Council of Churches, international conferences of individual denominations, and national organizations. Although the decentralized character of Protestantism makes generalization difficult, most of the major trends in the Catholic declarations appear among Protestants as well, and here, too, the call for interfaith dialogue is a prominent and recurring feature.[1]

To further such contacts, both Christians and Jews have set up institutional mechanisms whose primary function is interfaith relations. The Pontifical Commission for Religious Relations with the Jews and the Consultation on the Church and the Jewish People of the World Council of Churches are major examples of Christian bodies which function on a worldwide scale. In the United States, the Catholic Secretariat for Christian-Jewish Relations, the Committee on Christian-Jewish Relations of the National Council of Churches, and a substantial number of national officials of individual Protestant churches deal primarily with Jewish issues. Jews reciprocate with significant programs for interreligious affairs at the American Jewish Committee, Anti-Defamation League, American Jewish Congress, Synagogue Council of America, Union of American Hebrew Congregations, and elsewhere, while the National Conference of Christians and Jews continues to expand its longstanding efforts. Though the scope and intensity of such activities vary greatly from country to country, some increase in interfaith contacts is noticeable in virtually every Western nation with a significant Jewish population.[2]

This essay will concentrate on some of the substantive issues raised by these contacts: the problem of dialogue itself, mission and covenant, anti-Semitism, the State of Israel, and moral questions affecting public policy. These topics may not exhaust the Jewish-Christian agenda, but

---

[1] The major statements, both Catholic and Protestant, have been compiled by Helga Croner in *Stepping Stones to Further Jewish-Christian Relations* (London and New York, 1977) (hereafter, Croner). For highlights of the developing Catholic position, see Leonard Swidler, "Catholic Statements on Jews—A Revolution in Progress," *Judaism* 27 (1978): 299—307; and Jorge Mejia, "Survey of Issues in Catholic-Jewish Relations," *Origins* 7.47 (May 11, 1978): 744–748. An excellent bibliographical survey has been provided by A. Roy Eckardt, "Recent Literature on Jewish-Christian Relations," *Journal of the American Academy of Religion* 49 (1981): 99–111.

[2] On the current situation in Western Europe, see the summary articles in *Face to Face* 7 (Summer, 1980): 1–16. For obvious reasons, Israel provides a special, atypical environment for Jewish-Christian discussions; in addition to such ongoing groups as the Israel Interfaith Committee, the Ecumenical Theological Research Fraternity, and the Rainbow, the Director General of Israel's Ministry of Inter-Religious Affairs has recently established the Jerusalem Institute for Inter-Religious Relations and Research as a public, nongovernmental body (*Christian News from Israel* 27.2 [1979]: 62). In general, see *Face to Face* 2 (Winter/Spring, 1977).

they play a central role in defining both the progress and the continuing problematic of a relationship which is nearing the end of its second decade and its second millennium at the same time.

THE PROBLEM OF DIALOGUE

At first glance, the case for dialogue is self-evident, straightforward, and deceptively simple. Communication is preferable to isolation; friendship and trust can be established only by people who talk to one another. Nevertheless, although dialogue is often initiated by the Jewish side, the history of Jewish-Christian relations has bequeathed to many Jews a legacy of mistrust and suspicion which makes them perceive the Christian advocacy of such discussions as a subtle and more sophisticated expression of the missionary impulse. We shall have to examine the question of mission later on, but to the extent that this perception could be defended, the argument for dialogue—at least in the eyes of many Jews—would be severely undermined.

The conviction that the motivation for dialogue is a sincere desire for mutual understanding is indispensable for the legitimation of such conversations, but it does not define their content. The most interesting questions, in fact, arise only in the context of a favorable decision about the fundamental enterprise. What should be discussed? Are some subjects too sensitive, or does the exclusion of such topics contradict the essential objective of interfaith dialogue? Should discussants direct their efforts toward the solution of clearcut problems in Jewish-Christian relations, or should they address essential matters of faith as well? If a separation between such issues is desirable, is it in fact possible?

In a thoughtful and perceptive article, Henry Siegman argued that Jews and Christians bring different agendas to what is essentially an asymmetrical discussion.[3] Since Jews can understand their faith without reference to Christianity, there is no internal Jewish need to engage in theological discussion with Christians; Christianity, on the other hand, confronts Judaism the moment it "searches into the mystery

---

3   "A Decade of Catholic-Jewish Relations—A Reassessment," *Journal of Ecumenical Studies* (henceforth cited as *J.E.S.*) 15 (1978): 243–260.

of the Church."[4] The Jewish agenda is historical rather than theological and focuses on such issues as anti-Semitism, the Holocaust, and the State of Israel. Although each side may recognize some value in the other's agenda, the basic impulses leading to dialogue are profoundly different.

Since no one can compel the discussion of any particular issue, inhibitions about the content of interfaith exchanges are likely to be respected. While Christians may be more interested in theology, they have no fundamental objections to a discussion of the "Jewish" themes, and considerations of conscience make a refusal to confront such topics both morally questionable and politically awkward. Many Jews, on the other hand, regard certain theological discussions very warily, and the Jewish agenda has generally prevailed.

A striking example of this Jewish "victory" is the agenda proposed by a Christian writing in the middle of the last decade. Though he expressed hope that "the frequency and scope" of purely theological discussions would be increased, the major elements of his list were the establishment of study groups, recognition that Jews can be saved without conversion, renunciation of missionary work, more effective denunciation of anti-Semitism, curricular changes in Christian seminaries and congregational schools, liturgical revisions, and joint social action.[5] The primary emphasis of this proposal is self-evident.

Some Christians, however, have been more assertive. One leading ecumenist, though referring to Siegman's article as a "now classic" statement, has argued that Jewish theology can be aided by Christian insights on "covenant, mission, peoplehood, [and] the Kingdom," while Jewish "self-articulation" in the Christian period was deeply affected by its relationship with Christianity.[6] Another Christian response to Siegman's analysis put the issue even more sharply. "Full attention to theology and ultimate questions can wait. The point is, can they wait forever?"[7]

---

4   The phrase (which Siegman does not use) is from the first sentence of the Vatican II statement. On the impact of this asymmetry on early Jewish-Christian contacts, see my discussion in *The Jewish-Christian Debate in the High Middle Ages* (Philadelphia, 1979), pp. 4- 8.

5   Paul J. Kirsch, *We Christians and Jews* (Philadelphia, 1975), pp. 122–141.

6   Eugene Fisher, "A Roman Catholic Perspective: The Interfaith Agenda," *Ecumenical Bulletin* 44 (November-December, 1980): 11–12.

7   Edward Flannery, "Response to Henry Siegman," *J.E.S.* 15 (1978): 505. Cf. also David-Maria Jaeger, "Catholic-Jewish Dialogue," *Christian Attitudes on Jews and Judaism* 69 (December, 1979): 1–3.

A look at some very recent Christian proposals for discussion reveals a combination of "historical" and "theological" issues. A German Catholic working paper lists belief in the wake of the Holocaust, the meaning of the State of Israel, the problem of combining belief in salvation and political action, a variety of ethical issues, and the diminishing of the supposed conflict between a religion of law and a religion of grace.[8] In a statement that has aroused considerable attention, the Evangelical Church of the Rhineland suggested a similarly "mixed" agenda: the Holocaust, a common Bible, the standing of Jesus, "the one people of God," justice and love, and the problem of mission to the Jews.[9]

In the eyes of many Jews, these lists present a minefield of sensitive issues. Dialogue is by definition a two-way street, and, if Jews expect Christians to revise certain longstanding perspectives on Judaism, they cannot expect Christians to refrain from entertaining reciprocal expectations. This development emerges with striking clarity in the German Catholic working paper. The Christian, it says, cannot regard the Jew as merely a surviving witness of the period of the "Old Testament" and early Christianity. "Conversely, the Christian partner cannot be satisfied if the Jewish partner thinks that only he has something to say to the Christian which is essential to the Christian's faith, while that which the Christian has to say to the Jew has no essential meaning for the faith of the Jew." The Jew cannot know how Abraham became the father of a multitude of nations without an understanding of Christianity; indeed, dialogue can take place seriously only when Jews assume that Christianity was caused by God and when Christianity interests them "for God's sake." Moreover, "Jews can acknowledge that, for the Christians, Jesus has become the way in which they find Israel's God," and one example of a possible "Jewish interest in Christianity" is Franz Rosenzweig's statement that "whether Jesus was the Messiah, will be shown when the Messiah comes." This sort of expectation—closer to a hope than to a demand—is also reflected in a recent book by the Swiss Catholic scholar, Clemens Thoma, who quotes David Flusser's very similar

---

8   "Basic Issues of the Jewish-Christian Dialogue: A Working Paper of the Workshop on 'Jews and Christians' of the Central Committee of Roman Catholics in Germany," *Encounter Today* 14 (1979): 105–113, 125; and *Service International de Documentation Judéo-Chrétienne* (henceforth cited as *SIDIC*), 13.2 (1980): 28–32.

9   *Zur Erneuerung des Verhältnisses von Christen und Juden* (1980), pp. 12–28. Partial English translation by Franklin H. Littell in *J.E.S.* 17 (1980): 211–212.

remark that "I do not think many Jews would object if the messiah when he came again was the Jew Jesus."[10]

Even with respect to the core issues of trinity and incarnation, Thoma attempts to show from biblical, midrashic, and mystical sources that "a Christological perception of God—apart from its historical realization—is not un-Jewish." On similar grounds, another Christian theologian wants Jews to recognize that the doctrine of the trinity "acquired its depth" from the Jewish Scriptures.[11] In a more oblique fashion, the question was raised by John Sheerin in an article whose major thrust is to persuade Christians to modify their preconceptions about Judaism; dialogue, he says, is made difficult if not impossible by some of these Christian ideas. "Likewise, many Jews feel that they cannot engage in dialogue with Christians because they see the adoration of Jesus as sheer idolatry and they simply cannot bring themselves to discuss it with Christians."[12] Since Sheerin's article is not concerned primarily with this problem, he does not say explicitly what Jews should do about it or whether or not this makes dialogue impossible from a Christian perspective. Nevertheless, it is clear that some Christians are beginning to expect a measure of theological reciprocity if meaningful dialogue is to progress.

Can Jews offer such reciprocity? In most cases, I think the answer is no. Statements like those of Rosenzweig and Flusser about Jesus and the Messiah are thoroughly atypical in the Jewish community, and there is little prospect that this will change; indeed, aside from the subtle pressures of the "dialogue" relationship, there is no moral or intellectual reason for such change. Though many Jews are prepared to say that classical Christian theology does not constitute idolatry for Gentiles, there is a consensus that it is idolatry for Jews. Efforts to make the combined doctrines of trinity and incarnation more acceptable to Jews by citing the *sefirot* of the kabbalists or the *shekhinah* of the rabbis are not likely to bear more fruit today than they did in the late Middle Ages.

---

[10]   *A Christian Theology of Judaism* (New York, 1980), p. 134; citation from Flusser's article in *Concilium*, new series, 5.10 (1974): 71.

[11]   Dom Louis Leloir, "One of the More Burning Issues in Jewish-Christian Dialogue: Unity and Trinity in God" (the title is noteworthy), *Encounter Today* 13 (1978): 101–110. Cf. also note 22, below.

[12]   "Has Interfaith a Future?" *Judaism* 27 (1978): 311.

It is therefore a matter of considerable importance for the future of dialogue that Christians not maintain illusory expectations about significant modifications of such theological positions.[13] At the same time, this situation points up an even more troubling asymmetry in interfaith discussions. Many Christians involved in dialogue have been prepared to modify venerable attitudes toward mission, covenant, the significance of Judaism, and even the historicity of Matthew's account of the crucifixion. Jews are not in a position to make gestures nearly as significant, and this creates a situation in which Jews appear to be demanding change without offering very much in return.

There are, of course, valid reasons for this state of affairs. As Siegman has noted, the fundamental factor that gives Jews the "standing" to suggest certain changes in Christian theology is "the price that [they] have paid for such theology in history."[14] As we shall see in our discussion of anti-Semitism, a modification of those elements in Christianity which may lead to hatred of Jews requires at least a careful look at beliefs which come uncomfortably close to the core of the faith. On the other hand, although there is no denying that a pejorative perception of Christians and Christianity exists among many Jews, such perceptions have not led to any significant Christian suffering in the last millennium; moreover, some of them result at least as much from anti-Semitism itself as they do from Jewish theology. Consequently, the relative absence of a Jewish quid pro quo is in a certain sense justified.[15]

Notwithstanding this justification, there is an uncomfortable imbalance in the structure of Jewish-Christian discussion, and one can only admire those Christian participants who are genuinely interested in revising certain elements of Christian theology without expecting much change on the Jewish side. One way to correct this imbalance, at least to some extent, is for Jews to resist as much as possible the temptation of telling Christians what to believe. This is an extremely delicate question which we shall encounter in specific cases later on, and there are several fine lines on the road from hope to suggestion to expectation to demand.

---

13 This point was made by Richard Lowry in a paper presented to a Catholic-Lutheran-Jewish conference in the fall of 1980.
14 Siegman, "A Decade," p. 257.
15 See, however, Gerald Blidstein's remarks about the need for Jews to reassess the image of Christianity (*Tradition* 11 [1970]: 103–113), cited approvingly by Siegman, "A Decade," p. 254.

Often Jews are simply responding to Christian questions about the effect of certain doctrines, and on such occasions they are acting as what one prominent rabbi has described as a resource for the Christian community. Nevertheless, there is no obligation to answer every question; silence is still sometimes "a hedge around wisdom" (*Mishnah Avot* 3:13).

The classic, extreme formulation of this position, which has theoretically governed official Orthodox involvement (and non-involvement) in dialogue, is Rabbi Joseph B. Soloveitchik's argument that matters of faith are not an appropriate subject for interreligious discussion because they are rooted in the profoundest recesses of the religious experience of both the individual and the faith community.[16] Such Orthodox reservations about dialogue are reflected to a somewhat lesser extent in the attitudes of many Christian fundamentalists and evangelicals. The dangers of dialogue for these Christians emerge with striking clarity from an assertion by two liberal Christians whose devotion to the Jewish people and interfaith discussion is unsurpassed. Alice and Roy Eckardt have argued that insistence on "the divine inspiration of all Scripture . . . cannot escape a proclivity to anti-Semitism" and makes interfaith dialogue very difficult.[17] Their theoretical goal is presumably to persuade fundamentalists to abandon fundamentalism, though the realistic objective is to prevent their "achieving forms of political power and influence." To the extent that this approach to dialogue envisions significant changes in the basic beliefs of the participants, it can appear especially threatening to both Christian fundamentalists and Orthodox Jews.

The issue of Jewish relations with fundamentalist evangelicals has become particularly acute in the United States as a result of the meteoric rise of the Moral Majority and related groups. Jewish reactions have varied widely, because the positions espoused by these groups can arouse both enthusiasm and deep suspicion when examined from the perspective of Jewish interests. On Israel their stand is exemplary. On theological issues, they are oriented toward mission and Christian triumphalism, and denials that they seek a Christian America, while welcome, do not always appear consistent with the policies and behavior of local activists. Remarks by the head of New York's Moral Majority (for which he later apologized) asserting that Jews control the city and the media and

16 "Confrontation," *Tradition* 6 (1964): 5–29.
17 "The Achievements and Trials of Interfaith," *Judaism* 27 (1978): 319.

possess a supernatural ability to make money show not so much conscious anti-Semitism as staggering naïveté and unthinking acceptance of anti-Jewish stereotypes; incredibly, the statement was genuinely intended to demonstrate support and admiration. (Jerry Falwell, who knows better by now, reacted immediately by denying that "you can stereotype any people."[18]) On social issues, most Jews are considerably more liberal than the Moral Majority, but there is no unanimity on these questions; still, school prayer is an example of a major goal of the politically oriented evangelicals which is opposed by virtually the entire spectrum of the Jewish community. Hence, the perceived dangers to pluralism and liberalism have led Jewish leaders such as Alexander Schindler to denounce this movement with exceptional vehemence; the vigorous support of Israel has led some Zionist groups to express enthusiastic approval in a world where offending Israel's friends appears suicidal; and the conservative position on moral issues has led some hasidic figures, for whom interfaith discussions are usually anathema, to support an alliance in the face of a deluge threatening all traditional morality.[19]

With respect to dialogue between Jews and evangelical groups in general (not necessarily the political activists), there has been real progress, and some voices have been raised questioning the general view that Jews are "safer" holding discussions with Christian liberals than with conservatives and fundamentalists.[20] The challenge here will be to establish communication and friendly relations without the expectation of much theological flexibility in the Christian position. In light of the potential tensions in the standard dialogue, this is a situation that deserves to be explored with interest. From the perspective of the "Jewish agenda," the prospect of improving relations without theological change was put forcefully by Yosef Yerushalmi: "After all that has happened, do we still have to await a reformulation of Christian theology before the

---

18 *New York Times*, February 5, 1981. Several months after this was written, the individual involved was removed from his post.

19 *Face to Face* 8 (Winter, 1981) is devoted in its entirety to an important collection of reactions to this movement by both Christians and Jews.

20 Cf. William Harter's paper delivered to the Synagogue Council of America on December 7, 1972 (available at the library of the American Jewish Committee); William Sanford Lasor, "An Evangelical and the Interfaith Movement," *Judaism* 27 (1978): 335–339; M. Tanenbaum, M. Wilson, and A. J. Rudin, eds., *Evangelicals and Jews in Conversation* (Grand Rapids, Mich., 1978); and A. J. Rudin, "A Jewish Perspective on Baptist Ecumenism," *J.E.S.* 17 (1980): 161–171.

voice of Jewish blood can be heard crying from the earth? Is our common humanity not sufficient? In any case, Christian theology is an internal affair for Christians alone."[21]

Nevertheless, most Christian and some Jewish participants in dialogue remain interested in "internal" theological issues, and the inner dynamic of the interfaith process may lead inexorably in the direction of such discussions. The historical agenda does not lead to new frontiers, so that some Christians involved in dialogue for many years have begun to complain of discussions that review the same issues again and again. To the extent that such a perspective is correct, progress can be made by either involving new people or exploring new topics, and even though reaching out to new participants is an essential goal of interfaith programs, there remains the inexorable impulse to keep the dialogue vibrant on all levels. Since the frontier appears to be in the theological arena, there is reason to expect—or to fear—that the "victory" of the Jewish agenda will turn out to be ephemeral. To some extent this development is already evident: Clemens Thoma's book, which demonstrates a genuine, sympathetic understanding of Judaism, has been the focus of a major dialogue; the March, 1981, meeting of the National Conference of Christians and Jews dealt with a Christian theology of Judaism and a Jewish theology of Christianity; a recently published discussion on monotheism and the trinity was held some time ago in Europe; and, on a practical level, the National Council of Churches and the Union of American Hebrew Congregations have prepared guidelines for joint worship.[22]

The dialogue, then, for all its accomplishments on the intellectual and especially human levels, is facing a major challenge. The historical agenda may be losing its freshness and vitality; the theological agenda is fraught with problems of the most serious sort, especially from the Jewish perspective. Advocates of dialogue will have to display a remarkable combination of creativity and caution. An interesting decade lies ahead.

---

21 *Auschwitz: Beginning of a New Era?*, ed. by Eva Fleischner (New York, 1977), p. 106. The case for non-intervention in internal Christian theology was expressed eloquently by Siegman in "A Decade," p. 257.

22 See Pinchas Lapide and Jurgen Moltmann, *Jewish Monotheism and Christian Trinitarian Doctrine* (Philadelphia, 1981); "Jews and Christians in Joint Worship: Some Planning Principles and Guidelines," *Ecumenical Bulletin* 44 (November-December, 1980): 36–39.

MISSION AND COVENANT

Perhaps the most vexing question with a direct bearing on the feasibility of dialogue is the status of the traditional Christian desire to convert the Jews. The point was made with exceptional vigor in a recent article in *The Christian Century*: "Dialogue can never be an attempt at conversion, nor can it occur if one party assumes an objective ultimacy or a superiority for his or her point of view. Dialogue must be an interaction in which each participant stands with full integrity in his or her own tradition and is open to the depths of the truth that is in the other."[23] The last sentence is an exaggeration (a person cannot be entirely open while standing with full integrity in a religious tradition), and if the assumption of objective superiority makes dialogue impossible, then most believers will find it impossible. What is, however, indubitably true is that dialogue cannot be an attempt at conversion; if it is, it automatically becomes disputation or polemic, which is precisely what dialogue is intended to transcend.

What is less clear is whether dialogue is impossible with people who run a missionary program to convert you, provided that this particular discussion is not geared to that objective. What if they hope that you will be converted but have no missionaries? And what if that conversionary hope applies only to the end of days? Answers will differ, but there is certainly something uncomfortable about religious discussions with a partner who is working actively toward the elimination of your faith. Consequently, the "dialogue" relationship has played a role in a reassessment by some Christians of the applicability of the missionary ideal to the Jewish people.

Three approaches characterize Christian attitudes on this question: missionize everyone, including Jews; missionize everyone, especially Jews; missionize everyone except for Jews.[24] The first approach requires no explanation. The second argues that since Jews were the original chosen people, since Jesus was of their flesh and was originally sent to them, and since their conversion is singled out as part of the eschatological drama (Rom. 11:25–26), they should be the special targets of the Christian mission. The third approach is the most recent and the

---

[23]   John Shelby Spong, "The Continuing Christian Need for Judaism," *The Christian Century*, September 26, 1979, p. 918.

[24]   The classification is borrowed from Harold Ditmanson's article in *Face to Face* 3–4 (Fall/ Winter, 1977): 7–8.

most interesting. No one, it is true, can reach the Father except through Jesus (John 14:6), but Jews are already with the Father. The covenant with the original Israel has never been abrogated (Rom. 11:28–29); hence, there is no theological necessity for Jewish conversion, at least not before the end of history.

This so-called double-covenant theory has played a major role in Christian discussions of the standing of the Jewish people and the propriety of missions to the Jews. The central text in Romans leaves room for divergent interpretations and deserves to be quoted in full: "As concerning the Gospel, they [the Jews] are enemies for your sakes, but as touching the election, they are beloved for the fathers' sake. For the gifts and calling of God are without repentance." All this text says clearly is that the Jews are in a certain sense still chosen; it says nothing unequivocal about Judaism. Hence, when a Christian writer says that the Vatican II declaration "makes clear that the Jewish religion has a continuing validity" because of its paraphrase of this Pauline passage,[25] he goes beyond the evidence. On the whole, official and semi-official Christian documents have avoided a clearcut assertion of the double-covenant theory in a way that would ascribe anything like religious equality to contemporary Judaism; such documents tend to remain ambiguous or to acknowledge frankly the existence of divergent views on this question.[26] Explicit recognition that Judaism remains binding for Jews, with its implication that Jewish conversion is not even desirable, remains confined to a relatively small group of interfaith activists.

May Jews legitimately tell Christians that they must abandon the belief that Christianity supersedes Judaism? One Jewish leader has recently described Christian supersessionism as "vainglory (and) a kind of religious arrogance that must be labeled a sin. And that sin . . . needs to be purged from the soul of Christianity."[27] This is an exceptionally strong statement which seems to deny any religion the right to declare its own beliefs true and those of another religion false. As Siegman put it, "Judaism constitutes a denial of the central Christian mystery and its notion of salvation; it cannot at the same time demand that

---

25 Sheerin, "Has Interfaith a Future?" pp. 308–309.
26 Note, e.g., the statements of the World Council of Churches (1968) and the Lutheran Commission on World Missions (1969) in Croner, pp. 79, 91.
27 Daniel Polish, "A Jewish Perspective: This Moment in Jewish-Christian Relations," *Ecumenical Bulletin* 44 (November-December, 1980): 8–9.

Christianity be reformulated to accommodate the 'equality' of Judaism."[28] Nevertheless, it is exceptionally interesting that the World Council of Churches' most recent draft guidelines for Jewish-Christian dialogue discuss supersessionism under the rubric of Anti-Semitism and come very close to the sort of affirmation that most official documents have so far avoided:

> We must be especially attentive to those traditional convictions that have furthered antisemitic stances and attitudes on the part of Christians. Attention should therefore be given to the following points: Judaism should not be presented as a kind of anachronism after the coming of Christ: the Jews are a living people, very much alive in our present time as, for instance, the establishment of the State of Israel shows. Neither should the impression be given that the Church has superseded the Israel of old. The Jewish People continues to be God's People, for God is not unfaithful to those whom he has chosen (Rom. 11:29). As long as Christians regard Israel only as preparation for Christianity, as long as Christians claim the validity of God's revelation to them by negating the validity of God's revelation to the Jewish People, Judaism is denied any theological validity, and it becomes impossible to maintain a common ground for our common hope.[29]

Even this carefully formulated statement does not say that the conversion of Jews is not desirable, and in a later paragraph the document acknowledges differences among Christians concerning the obligations to "bear witness . . . to the Jews." It is when the discussion shifts from the abstract level of covenant to the more concrete plane of "witness" and mission that matters become particularly difficult for both Christians and Jews.

Christian witness is a rather important element in most forms of Christianity, and, in the absence of a fairly extreme position on the covenant question, it is difficult to see why Judaism should be excluded as the object of such witness. At the same time, not only is dialogue made difficult by an affirmation of missionizing, but the consciences of many Christians are troubled by the unsavory history of missionary efforts directed at Jews. The solution has been a distinction between witness, which is obligatory, and proselytism, which is forbidden. What is the

---

[28] Siegman, "A Decade," p. 256.
[29] Paragraph 2.4 of the Guidelines (*Ecumenical Bulletin* 44 [November-December, 1980]: 30). See note 61, below.

difference? In the most important Catholic paper on this subject, Tomasso Federici describes "unwarranted proselytism" as any witness or preaching involving "a physical, moral, psychological or cultural constraint on the Jews . . . that could . . . destroy or even diminish personal judgment, free will, full autonomy to decide, either personal or communitarian." This excludes the offering of "legal, material, cultural, political, and other advantages" and certainly rules out any form of coercion. Finally, since conversion must involve the free religious conscience and come only after inner distress and spiritual transformation, no organization should be set up for the conversion of the Jews.[30]

Now, it is perfectly clear that the reasoning in this last sentence does not apply to the Jews any more than it applies to any other group, and its use in this context points up an important ambiguity in the paper. In an early passage, Federici refers to the survival of God's covenant with the Jews, and he later concludes by encouraging study of the "history and mission of Israel, . . . her election and call, her privileges recognized in the New Testament"; nevertheless, these observations do not appear at the heart of his argument. With the exception of a reference to the unpleasant history of Christian mission to the Jews, the central arguments against "unwarranted proselytism" of Jews appear to be arguments against unwarranted proselytism of anyone. Such a position is naturally commendable, but the impression given by Federici that Jews have special standing in this matter appears more rhetorical than substantive when the concrete arguments are examined.

Catholic reactions to the Federici paper have varied widely. Some conservative figures have condemned it outright and defended the necessity of missionizing Jews.[31] While one account reports that Federici rejected "high pressure evangelism,"[32] another cites his paper along with other Catholic statements as evidence that proselytism, apparently meaning all missionary efforts with respect to Jews, has been rejected.[33] The truth is that some of those other statements speak of rejecting proselytism in the context of dialogue, which is not the same as total rejection, though one or two—particularly a 1973 declaration by the bishops of France—do make the point quite vigorously and in

---

30 "Study Outline on the Mission and Witness of the Church," *SIDIC* 11.3 (1978): 32.
31 *The National Catholic Register*, July 10, 1977.
32 Sheerin, "Has Interfaith a Future?" p. 311.
33 Swidler, "Catholic Statements on Jews," pp. 305–306, citing Croner, pp. 7, 12, 18, 51, 64.

a more general context. In a recent paper, Eugene Fisher attempted to read Federici's work in the most liberal way possible and to go beyond it toward a position in which the permanent value of Judaism would rule out any of the traditional forms of mission to the Jews.[34]

Needless to say, Protestant views reflect at least as wide a range of opinion as those of Catholics. Back in 1968, the World Council of Churches denounced crude missionizing ("cajolery, undue pressure or intimidation") and reported the belief of some Protestants that "service" rather than "explicit words" might be the best way to testify to the Jews. On the whole, the document recognizes the goal of conversion quite frankly and does not renounce active missionary efforts. The Lutheran World Federation in 1973 placed mission to the Jews on an equal footing with mission to all other groups, while the position of the German Evangelical Church in 1975 is a striking example of the studied ambiguity often generated by this question: "We have now come to understand mission and dialogue as two dimensions of one Christian witness. . . . Mission and dialogue as descriptions of Christian witness have an ominous sound to Jewish ears. Christians must therefore reassess the meaning with regard to the Jews of their witness to Jesus Christ as salvation for all mankind, the terms by which to identify their witness, and the methods of procedure."[35]

We have already seen that the most recent draft guidelines of the World Council of Churches continue to report disagreement about the need to witness to the Jews. The guidelines, however, do "reject proselytism both in its gross and refined forms. This implies that all triumphalism and every kind of manipulation are to be abrogated. We are called upon to minimize the power dimension in all encounters with the Jews and to speak at every level from equal to equal." At the same time, the guidelines say that "future work" includes "reaching a common understanding of the nature of divine revelation and thus healing the breach which exists between the Jewish people and the Church." While the precise meaning of these remarks is unclear, they are hardly likely to allay Jewish suspicions about the persistence of missionary intentions in an age of dialogue.

[34] "Mission and Conversion in Roman Catholic History and Contemporary Debate: The Mission to the Jews," presented at the Kennedy Institute Trialogue, October 13, 1980.

[35] Croner, pp. 81, 128–129, 148.

Among American evangelicals, Jews continue to be considered appropriate targets of missionary activity, although Billy Graham noted in 1973 that he has never singled out Jews as Jews and is opposed to "coercive proselytizing."[36] Jews for Jesus and other groups whose *raison d'être* is missionizing Jews receive considerable support from evangelical Christians. Here even Jews who hesitate most about intervention in the internal affairs of Christianity have some mixed feelings. Henry Siegman argues that Jews have no right to demand that Christians abandon such missionary activity but notes that "an active Christian mission to the Jews precludes serious dialogue."[37] Jacob Petuchowski maintains that telling a Christian not to missionize is "an illegitimate attempt by one faith to dictate to the other"; nevertheless, he cannot refrain from going beyond Siegman and adding that he would argue that such efforts are unwise and that perhaps the Jews' conversion should be left to God.[38]

This issue, which is a deeply emotional one for many Jews, can be viewed as a matter of simple self-defense. When Marc Tanenbaum persuaded President Carter's sister not to address a group whose purpose was converting Jews, this was not an assertion of the "subordination of Christianity to Judaism," as the *National Review* described it in a remarkably insensitive editorial, but a reaction to a direct spiritual threat.[39] The Jewish mandate to protect Jews from conversion is no less a religious requirement than any Christian mandate to convert them, and, although my basic sympathies are with the "non-interventionists," in the case of aggressive missionizing aimed specifically at Jews the overriding principle of *pikkuah nefesh*, or danger to life (including spiritual life), may well prevail.

Active missionaries are in any case rarely dissuaded from pursuing their task, and the Jewish response must often take the straightforward form of replies to missionary argument. Such exchanges run the risk of acrimony; in fact, however, they need not be strident or disrespectful. Several years ago, the Jewish Community Relations Council (J.C.R.C.) of New York asked Michael Wyschogrod and me to write a booklet addressing the central issues raised by Jews for Jesus; our fundamental objective

36   Rudin, "A Jewish Perspective," pp. 162–163.
37   Siegman, "A Decade," pp. 257–258.
38   "From the Viewpoint of Contemporary Judaism," *Face to Face* 3–4 (Fall/ Winter, 1977): 13.
39   See *National Review*, June 23, 1978, p. 763.

was to produce a work that would combine frank argumentation with a respectful tone.[40] Whether or not we succeeded is not for me to judge, but the angry denunciation that sometimes marks the Jewish response to this challenge is sometimes inappropriate and usually self-defeating.[41] Even more recently, the New York J.C.R.C. has set up a hotline to advise Jews faced with this problem, and a variety of Jewish organizations have recognized the need for a low-key but carefully prepared program to counter missionary efforts.[42]

The counter-missionary act which has aroused the most resentment among Christians is a recent Israeli law which makes illegal the offering of material inducements to convert. At the same time, several mainline churches have supported American Jews in opposing the misleading propaganda of various "Hebrew Christian" groups which attempt to give the impression—at least initially—that they are simply Jews. Finally, a leading Reform rabbi has recently suggested that *Jews* begin to proselytize. Although he has carefully restricted this proposal to "unchurched" Gentiles, the idea remains unpalatable to most non-Reform Jews, partly because of religious principle, but also because it appears to undercut the moral basis for Jewish opposition to Christian missionizing. Like most issues in Jewish-Christian dialogue, the question of mission is one in which significant progress has been made but which remains extremely sensitive, profoundly difficult, and ultimately unresolved.

ANTI-SEMITISM

Condemnations of anti-Semitism are by now routine in the declarations of most major churches. For some time, the linguistic nuances of such statements were examined with exquisite care, so that it became a *cause celebre* when Vatican II "decried" but did not "condemn" anti-Semitism, when it avoided the word "deicide" in declaring contemporary Jews free of responsibility for the crucifixion, and, more seriously, when it

---

40 See *Jews and "Jewish Christianity"* (New York, 1978).
41 Annette Daum, *Missionary and Cult Movements: A Mini-Course for the Upper Grades in Religious Schools* (New York, 1979) is another example of a response that maintains a civil and respectful tone.
42 The status of this problem in the late 1970s was summarized by Mark Cohen in "Missionaries in Our Midst: The Appeal of Alternatives," *Analysis* 64 (March 1978).

refrained from any recognition of Christian guilt for Jewish suffering. On the whole, these nagging points are no longer a problem. At least one official Catholic statement now "condemns" anti-Semitism, and various quasi-official or local declarations speak of Christian guilt.[43] Among Protestants, the first assembly of the World Council of Churches in 1948 denounced anti-Semitism as a sin; a 1968 statement by its Faith and Order Commission followed the lead of Vatican II by rejecting the ascribing of responsibility for the crucifixion to most Jewish contemporaries of Jesus or to any Jews living today; and the latest draft guidelines speak of an "ashamed awareness of Christian anti-Semitism." In the United States, even conservative churches have no hesitation in declaring anti-Semitism an unchristian phenomenon that must be combated.[44]

This, however, is not the end of the issue. It is here that the "historical" and "theological" agendas become disturbingly, perhaps inextricably, intertwined. Rosemary Ruether has coined what has developed into a classic phrase in this discussion; anti-Semitism, she says, is "the left hand of Christology." In Alan Davies' paraphrase, "The question of anti-Judaism is more than a question of a few notorious Matthaean, Pauline, and Johannine passages, but deals with the basic structure of New Testament theology itself." The problem, he says, is whether or not anti-Semitism is a fundamental part of the essential Christian heritage.[45]

Ruether's own view is that anti-Semitism can be purged from Christianity only by a rather fundamental revision of Christian theology. If she is right, then Jews participating in dialogue face a stark dilemma. On the one hand, the right of self-defense would appear to justify demands for such revision;[46] on the other hand, Jews who ask Christians to respect Judaism cannot at the same time demand that classic Christian

---

[43] Swidler, "Catholic Statements on Jews," pp. 301–302.
[44] Croner, pp. 70, 82–83; Draft Guidelines 2.1; Rudin, "A Jewish Perspective," p. 164.
[45] Rosemary Ruether, "Anti-Judaism Is the Left Hand of Christology," in *Jewish-Christian Relations*, ed. by R. Heyer (New York, 1974), pp. 1–9; Ruether, *Faith and Fratricide* (New York, 1974); idem, "Anti-Semitism and Christian Theology," in Fleischner's *Auschwitz*, pp. 79–92; and Alan Davies, *Anti-Semitism and the Foundations of Christianity* (New York, 1979), p. xv.
[46] The classic sociological study attempting to demonstrate the connection between certain Christian beliefs and anti-Jewish attitudes is Charles Glock and Rodney Stark, *Christian Beliefs and Anti-Semitism* (New York, 1966). Note also the later, much more limited survey by B. Cohen and A. Lacognata, *A Pilot Study on Christian Beliefs and Anti-Semitism*, 1976 (available in the library of the American Jewish Committee).

beliefs be dismantled.[47] Moreover, the problem cannot be easily avoided even if Ruether is wrong, because there still remain those "few notorious passages" in the New Testament which have undeniably bred anti-Semitism in the past. If, for example, the Jews really said that Jesus' blood would be on them and on their children, and if Matthew's report of this statement is read as a theological endorsement (Matt. 27:25), anti-Jewish consequences could not easily be avoided.

Concerned Christians have addressed this problem in various ways. Some are prepared to deny that such passages are binding at all; the solution is to develop a "hermeneutic . . . that is not slavishly dependent on accepting the New Testament *in toto* as the Word of God."[48] A somewhat different formulation is that though the text is divinely inspired, on a certain level it must reflect the political and polemical concerns of its time; nevertheless, when read as a whole, the New Testament cannot be regarded as anti-Semitic.[49] Finally, there are Christians who refuse to reject even one line of the Gospels but nevertheless argue that no antisemitic implications need emerge.

What position should Jews take on these questions? Since the ideal answer is clearly that Jews should not prescribe the nature of Christian faith to their partners in dialogue, the only justification for taking a position is, as we have seen, the need for self-defense. If, however, that objective can reasonably be sought in more than one way, Jews, I think, should choose the approach which requires the least intervention in matters of Christian theology. Thus, Jews should encourage efforts to break the link between certain New Testament passages and anti-Jewish consequences but should avoid instructing Christians not to believe what the Gospels report. Needless to say, Jews do not have to become fundamentalist Christian missionaries, and the position of Christians who have rejected certain of those "notorious passages" can be welcomed. But Jewish preaching against the historicity of the Gospels is not only unseemly in the context of dialogue; it is probably also unwise

---

47   Cf. John Oesterreicher's reaction to Jewish support for Ruether, cited in Siegman, "A Decade," p. 257. For Christian denials of an inevitable link between Christology and anti-Semitism, see Fleischner, *Auschwitz*, pp. 93–94, 195–197.

48   Robert Willis, "A Perennial Outrage: Anti-Semitism in the New Testament," *Christian Century*, August 19, 1970, pp. 990–992. See also note 17, above.

49   Cf. Eugene Fisher, *Faith without Prejudice* (New York, 1977), pp. 54–58. For a general discussion of this issue, see also P. van Box and M. McGrath, "Perspectives: Anti-Jewish Elements in the Liturgy," *SIDIC* 10.2 (1978): 25–27.

from a purely pragmatic standpoint. Fundamentalist Christians are not about to reject the historicity of Matthew because Jewish ecumenists tell them to, and all that will be accomplished is the transformation of dialogue into polemic with all the resentment—and perhaps even anti-Semitism —which this can generate.

The best example I have seen of a sensitive, yet vigorous approach to these problems is the recommendations made by two Christian scholars for changes in the Oberammergau passion play. At the request of the Anti-Defamation League, Leonard Swidler and Gerard Sloyan produced a commentary on the play which, with one or two exceptions, avoids any proposal based on the rejection of the Gospel crucifixion accounts.[50] For example, when dealing with the passage in Matthew wherein the Jews say, "His blood be on us and on our children," they do not insist on deletion, even though that is the solution they would no doubt prefer. Instead they suggest an alternative more palatable to the people of Oberammergau: the crowd should say it once, as in Matthew, and not four times, as in the play, and the choir, which now responds, "It will come on you and on your children," should change just one word: "It will come on you—not on your children."

None of this means that Jewish scholars who are convinced that such a passage is unhistorical should censor their scholarly work. These considerations of restraint apply only to the context of religious dialogue, where respect for the other's faith commitment is the essential element that separates dialogue from disputation. There are, furthermore, certain scholarly issues which belong under the rubric of anti-Semitism that do not address the most sensitive matters of faith and can appropriately be raised in dialogue. These issues were addressed by Charlotte Klein in an excellent study of *Anti-Judaism in Christian Theology*,[51] in which she examined the treatment of Judaism in scholarly works used in European seminaries and universities.

The results were profoundly discouraging. Judaism in the time of Jesus continues to be depicted as a legalistic faith concerned primarily with trivialities; the Jewish people in first-century Israel is described as the Jewish religious community; and the term "late Judaism," with its

50 A *Commentary on the Oberammergau Passionspiel in regard to Its Image of Jews and Judaism* (New York, 1977). See also Swidler's brief guidelines in *Face to Face* 7 (Summer, 1980): 19–20.
51 Philadelphia: Fortress Press, 1978; German original 1975.

implication that the religion came to an end with the rise of Christianity, remains in vogue. Klein's chapter on "Jewish Guilt in the Death of Jesus" is especially depressing. It is not the defensible assertion that Jews were involved in the crucifixion; it is, rather, the motives ascribed to them and to their descendants throughout the generations for their rejection of Jesus. This rejection allegedly results not from understandable or even honest error but from obstinacy, the desire to remain the chosen people, culpable blindness, and the like. Nothing in the Gospels really requires such assertions, and Jewish indignation need not be restrained when confronted with this sort of antisemitic pseudo-history. It is worth noting that the 1975 Vatican guidelines specifically state that "the Old Testament and the Jewish tradition founded upon it must not be set against the New Testament in such a way that the former seems to constitute a religion of only justice, fear, and legalism, with no appeal to the love of God and neighbor."[52] Though the Pope himself violated this guideline in the recent encyclical, *Dives in Misercordia*, it remains an important statement, and the one encouraging finding in Klein's book is that Anglo-American scholarship displays far greater accuracy and sensitivity on these issues.

All the ringing denunciations of anti-Semitism and progressive reassessments of Judaism have little importance if they are confined to an activist elite and have no resonance among ordinary Christians. Liturgical reform and textbook revision are, therefore, key elements in the effort to exorcise the impact of historic Christian anti-Judaism. With respect to liturgy, the most serious problems in at least some churches arise in connection with Holy Week in general and Good Friday in particular, when biblical passages commemorating the crucifixion are read. Some of these passages inevitably convey an anti-Jewish message, and, although thoughtful proposals for retranslation, judicious omissions, and substantial corrective commentary have been made, they all raise serious difficulties and face considerable obstacles.[53] The Good Friday "Reproaches" hymn, which is perhaps the most disturbing single prayer, has now been made optional for American Catholics. In 1976, the Liturgical Commission of the Episcopal Church recommended that the

---

52 Croner, p. 14.

53 John Pawlikowski has presented an excellent summary of both proposals and problems, in Fleischner's *Auschwitz*, pp. 172–178. See also *Face to Face* 2 (Summer/Fall, 1976): 3–8.

hymn be adopted;[54] eventually, the proposal was rejected, but the very suggestion indicates that movement on these matters is not always in the direction that Jews would like.

On the textbook issue, there has been considerable progress, at least in the United States. Though various problems remain, the depiction of Jews and Judaism in both Protestant and Catholic texts has shown marked improvement. The Pharisees are no longer simply hypocrites, and there are some indications that Judaism has remained a living religion despite the advent of Christianity. Since there is a movement away from standardized texts, it is now especially important that teachers and preachers be trained to appreciate and transmit these changing perceptions. This is a gargantuan task, but it is crucial if declarations about anti-Semitism are to have a significant impact in the real world.[55]

The most terrible manifestation of anti-Semitism has taken place in our own time, and the vexing question of Christian responsibility for the Holocaust is a brooding presence hovering over all discussions of anti-Jewish elements in Christianity. Inevitably, assessments of this question vary widely. Some would assign primary responsibility to the legacy of Christian teachings; others absolve Christianity with the argument that Nazism was a neo-pagan revolt against the Christian past; while others take a middle position. My own view is that Nazi anti-Semitism achieved such virulent, unrestrained consequences because it stripped away the semi-civilized rationales which had been given in the past for persecuting Jews and liberated the deepest psychic impulses which had been partly nurtured but partly suppressed by those rationales. The Nazis utilized the standard political, economic, and sometimes even religious arguments for persecution, but their central message was that Jews were alien, demonic creatures, subhuman and superhuman at the same time, who threatened "Aryans" with profound, almost inexpressible terror. Such fear and hatred have probably been a significant component

---

54   T. A. Idinopulos, "Old Form of Anti-Judaism in the New Book of Common Prayer," *Christian Century* 93 (August 4–11, 1976): 680–684; John T. Townsend, "'The Reproaches' in Christian Liturgy," *Face to Face* 2 (Summer/Fall, 1976): 8–11.

55   See Fisher, *Faith Without Prejudice*; *Encounter Today* 13 (1978): 111; W.C.C. Draft Guidelines 3.3; J. Pawlikowski in Fleischner, *Auschwitz*, pp. 162, 171; and David Hyatt, "The Interfaith Movement," *Judaism* 27 (1978): 273. For a pessimistic comment on the situation in France, see *Encounter Today* 14 (1979): 152.

of the antisemitic psyche for centuries, but they have not been given free rein. The persecution of political enemies, economic exploiters, and religious deviants must still be governed by a modicum of civilized restraint; though this restraint must have seemed invisible to the victims of the Crusades, it reappears, however dimly, when seen through the prism of the Holocaust. On the other hand, malevolent demons, terrifying aliens, and malignant vermin can only be extirpated with single-minded, ruthless ferocity.

The key question, therefore, is what role Christianity played in strengthening the image of Jew as demon, and the answer cannot be unequivocal. There is no doubt that the growth of such a perception of the Jew in the late Middle Ages was intimately connected with Christian ideas and served as an important explanation of the Jewish rejection of Christianity. Though this belief was manifested largely in popular anti-Semitism, there was no shortage of clergy who endorsed and propagated it. At the same time, such a view is fundamentally alien to the central teachings of the medieval church, which protected Jewish life and looked forward to both the individual and the collective conversion of Jews. Demons, let alone vermin, are not candidates for conversion. Indeed, one could argue plausibly that it was precisely the weakening of religious grounds for anti-Semitism in the modern period which opened the way for their replacement by the racial, demonic justification.

In sum, the Holocaust is not a Christian phenomenon, but it must weigh heavily on the Christian conscience. Many observers believe that it was this unparalleled catastrophe which led to the reexamination of Christian attitudes toward Jews and Judaism manifested in the last few decades. Several churches have even introduced ceremonies commemorating the Holocaust to coincide with the growing Jewish observance of *Yom Hashoah*, or Holocaust Day,[56] and the subject is a recurring theme in Jewish-Christian dialogues. It is a commonplace that the Holocaust has deprived anti-Semitism of "respectability," at least temporarily, in what passes for civilized discourse, and it has served as an important reservoir of sympathy for the State of Israel. Many Jews, however, have begun to worry that this breathing space has passed, and Christian attitudes toward Israel, though often supportive and sometimes enthusiastic, have become a source of growing concern.

---

[56] See *Face to Face* 7 (Winter, 1980): 11–14, 18–19, 17–19.

THE STATE OF ISRAEL

For nearly two millennia, Christians pointed to the destruction of the ancient Jewish state as proof that God had rejected the Jewish people and replaced them with "true Israel." In the context of such a theology, any manifestation of Jewish nationalism would inevitably be regarded as a defiance of the will of God, and the initial reaction of most Christians to the Zionist movement reflected precisely such an attitude. As Eugene Fisher has noted, however, the position of Vatican II on Jewish responsibility for the crucifixion would appear to render such a reaction obsolete and to leave no theological obstacle to Christian, or at least Catholic, support of the State of Israel.[57]

Fisher's logic is unassailable, and a 1973 statement by the bishops of France declared that the conscience of the world community cannot refuse the Jewish people ... the right and means for a political existence among the nations."[58] Nevertheless, one wonders if the implications of Vatican II have been fully discerned in Rome; the official guidelines of 1975 are marked by a deafening silence concerning Israel, while the Vatican's failure to recognize the Jewish state remains a source of tension in Catholic-Jewish relations. This is an issue in which it is particularly difficult to disentangle politics and theology, but the official reasons, which speak of the ongoing state of war and the uncertainty of boundaries, do not carry much conviction.[59]

That Protestant churches would be divided about Israel is obvious and inevitable. In 1968, the World Council of Churches (W.C.C.) confessed its inability to reach a unanimous evaluation of the formation of the state, which, it said, brought Jews self-assurance and security only at the expense of injustice and suffering for Arabs.[60] This, of course, is a reservation not about borders but about the fundamental existence of the state. The W.C.C.'s most recent draft guidelines are a major step forward in this respect. They acknowledge an "indissoluble bond between

---

57   *Origins* 9.10 (August 16, 1979): 158–160.
58   Croner, p. 63.
59   See Marcel Jacques Dubois, "The Catholic Church and the State of Israel—After Thirty Years," *Christian News from Israel*, vol. 27, no. 2 (1979): 64. Some Catholics have argued that Vatican contacts with Israeli officials constitute de facto recognition. De jure would be an improvement.
60   Croner. p. 76.

the Jewish people and the Land of Israel, which has found expression . . . in the reality of the State of Israel. Failing to acknowledge the right of Jews to return to the land prevents any fruitful dialogue with them."[61]

Just as opposition to Israel can be based on either political or theological grounds, support for the state can also be formulated in secular or religious language. Jews have often spoken to Christians about the religious significance of the connection between Jews and the land, and such discussions can have two objectives. The moderate goal is to give Christians an appreciation of the depth and intensity of Jewish feeling on this matter; the more ambitious goal is to persuade them that Christian theology itself demands that Christians support this manifestation of the ongoing, unbroken covenant between God and the Jewish people. "The gifts of God are," after all, "without repentance" (Rom. 11:19).

For Christians who remain impervious to such persuasion, it can sometimes arouse resentment. One Christian, for example, was moved to make a grotesque comparison between Jewish efforts to convert Christians to friendship toward Israel and Christian efforts to convert Jews to Christianity, as if being asked to abandon your faith is analogous to being asked to revise your political opinions (even when those opinions have a theological dimension). He later modified the statement, but the initial reaction remains eloquent testimony to the potential for friction in this area.[62]

Even when Christians endorse the theological necessity of the State of Israel, some strange and unwelcome things can happen if the justification for its existence is made to shift almost entirely from the political to the theological sphere. A striking example of this phenomenon is a 1970 statement by the Synod of the Reformed Church in Holland. God's covenant with Israel, it says, is still in effect, and this includes the connection between Israel and the land. "Because of the special place

61 Guidelines 5.1. The Protestant Church of the Rhineland (see note 9, above) has recently described the creation of the State of Israel as a "sign of God's faithfulness to his people." In subsequent drafts of the W.C.C. Guidelines adopted well after the completion of this article, this passage—and the one discussed at note 29, above—have been attenuated to a point where they no longer retain the significance I have attributed to them. From a Jewish perspective, the discussion of Israel is no longer a step forward and is, in fact, quite disappointing.
62 See *Christianity and Crisis*, October 28 and December 23, 1974. Cf. also the remark by Willard Oxtoby in *The Christian Century*, October 13, 1971, p. 1193, cited in F. Talmage, *Disputation and Dialogue* (New York, 1975), p. 185.

of the Jewish people we endorse in the present situation the right of existence of the state of Israel." The founding of the state took place in an "all too human way, as is the case with practically every other state." But "the special place of Israel was never based on its moral qualities." God's "covenant-love" is not annulled by sin. "Therefore we ought not to dispute on moral grounds the right of the State of Israel to exist."

The document goes on to note that because of the Jews' special place, the State of Israel must behave in an exemplary way—to teach the world a new understanding of what a state is. The state's boundaries must offer the Jews a dwelling place, but the need to protect that dwelling place "should not induce the Jews to make it into a nationalistic state in which the only thing that counts is military power." In this respect, Israel must be better than other states. Finally, it is also called upon to exercise justice in an exemplary way by recognizing responsibility for the Palestinian refugees and giving Israeli Arabs *de facto* and not just *de jure* equality.[63]

Though Jews are inevitably pleased by a theologically oriented defense of Israel on the part of Christians, this document demonstrates the dangers of relying solely on theological grounds for such support; once the burden of Israel's existence is borne by theology alone, it becomes seductively easy to slip into the apparently unimportant concession that its survival is questionable on other, moral grounds. Such a concession is, of course, devastating to Israel's position in the eyes of anyone who does not share the particular theological perspective of this document. Moreover, the end of the statement is an exceptionally frank expression of the double standard often applied to Israel. To say that Israel is called upon to pass tests of prophetic stature is to make a demand that no state can readily meet; to imply, as this document does, that failure to pass these tests leaves Israel's right to exist untouched is not only of questionable value in the political sphere, but it is also—unfortunately— dubious theology. When the prophets made demands, failure to meet them had consequences. While Jewish title to the land remained in force *sub specie aeternitatis*, God reserved the right to suspend the lease. In short, this statement is destructive of Israel's moral and political position while providing very little theological consolation.

Christians hostile to Israel have applied a double standard in a far more egregious fashion. Daniel Berrigan, for example, made a famous speech

---

63   Croner, pp. 104–105.

after the Yom Kippur War in which he strongly implied that Jews must behave differently from others and denounced their failure to do so with the sort of scathing indignation appropriate only for acts of consummate evil.[64] Very recently, several hundred Christian clergy, including the head of the human-rights commission of the National Council of Churches, called for a reduction in U.S. aid to Israel because of alleged violations of human rights. Now, Israel depends on U.S. aid for its very survival. Its human-rights record is, by any standards, immensely superior to that of its adversaries; considering the circumstances, that record is so good as to be almost unbelievable. This Orwellian document is therefore urging that a state with an excellent human-rights record be placed in jeopardy in the face of a challenge from states with human-rights records ranging from poor to terrible—in the name of human rights![65] The signatories, of course, give the impression that Israel's sins *are* sufficiently severe to deserve comparison with those of notorious offenders, but this is a Big Lie of proportions that would have done Goebbels proud and merely underscores the application of a double standard.

Though the major Christian organizations have issued no statements as disgraceful as this one, a number of recent declarations have aroused considerable concern among Jews. The embrace of the Palestinian cause by third-world nations has not left liberal Christians unaffected, and the National Council of Churches has adopted a statement on the Middle East which pursues evenhandedness to the point where perfectly symmetrical demands are made of Israel and the P.L.O. Both must cease acts of violence, and each must recognize the other (apparently simultaneously); in Israel's case, this recognition must include the Palestinian right to establish a sovereign state. The National Council of Churches refused to single out P.L.O. terrorism or to make recognition of Israel a precondition for any change in Israel's policy. Even more recently, an August, 1980, a statement by the Central Committee of the World Council of Churches denounced Israel's annexation of East Jerusalem,

---

64 *American Report*, October 29, 1973. For Arthur Hertzberg's response, see ibid., November 12, 1973. See also Robert Alter, "Berrigan's Diatribe," *Commentary*, February, 1974, pp. 69–73.

65 *New York Times*, January 8, 1981. For Christian comments criticizing the double standard, cf. Fleischner, *Auschwitz*, pp. 232–233; and Kirsch, *We Christians and Jews*, p. 119. On Christian criticism of Israel, see Judith H. Banki's excellent report, "Anti-Israel Influence in American Churches" (1979), prepared for the Inter-religious Affairs Department of the American Jewish Committee.

equated the city's importance in Christianity and Islam to its importance in Judaism, and called on "member churches to exert through their respective governments all pressure on Israel to withhold all action on Jerusalem."[66]

These statements have virtually no theological content, and we have already seen that Jews have attempted to introduce a theological dimension into the Christian approach to this issue. The central point, however, is not a theological one. Positions of Christian religious groups which reflect indifference or worse toward the fate of Israel are interpreted by Jews as "indifference or even antagonism to the survival of the Jewish people";[67] such positions suggest that, despite protestations to the contrary, the history of Christian anti-Semitism has not sufficiently sensitized even some sympathetic Christians to the specter of the mass destruction of Jews.

This is a strong assertion, and it is important at this point to consider briefly why active *Jewish* anti-Zionism is no longer admissible in the mainstream of Jewish life, despite its respectable antecedents in the first part of the century. There are various explanations, including the Holocaust and a growing pride in Israel's achievements, but the main reason is the new implications of anti-Zionism created almost overnight once the State was established. Before there was a state, the anti-Zionist position simply said that no such state should be established; after May, 1948, active anti-Zionism meant that the existing State should cease to exist. But the only reasonable scenario for its destruction would have to be drenched in torrents of Jewish blood. This dilemma is illustrated sharply in the almost pathetic hope expressed in the fiercely anti-Zionist work of the late Satmar rabbi; Jews, he wrote, should pray that Israel be destroyed—but not through the actions of the nations of the world.[68]

By this time, the critical importance of Israel to Jewish survival extends far beyond its boundaries. So many Jews have become psychologically dependent upon the existence of the State—so many perceptions of Jewish history, Jewish identity, indeed of Judaism itself, have been linked to its success—that the destruction of Israel would mean not only the mass extermination of its inhabitants but the spiritual death

---

66   *Current Dialogue* 1 (Winter 1980/81): 10.
67   Polish, "A Jewish Perspective," p. 9.
68   Joel Teitelbaum, *Sefer va-Yoel Mosheh* (Brooklyn, 1981), p. 8.

of a majority of diaspora Jewry. This is a statement of simple fact, and yet it gives the impression of heated, perhaps overblown rhetoric and consequently exemplifies a serious challenge facing Jews who wish to communicate their apprehension. Many well-intentioned listeners react by attributing such fears to an understandable "post-Holocaust" syndrome which must be respected but which hardly reflects objective reality. In this case, however, the paranoiac has real enemies; ironically, it is the detached observer who distorts the dangers by viewing them through the prism of a seductive psychological construct which appears to diminish them.

Ultimately, then, it is the identity of the consequences of anti-Zionism and anti-Semitism which has created a nearly universal consensus among Jews, whatever their ideology, that protecting Israel must be one of the crucial priorities of the Jewish people, and it is this perception which leads to resentment and even anger at certain Christian statements on the Middle East. A feeling of moral outrage cannot justifiably result from a failure by Christians to develop their theology on Israel in a manner pleasing to Jews; it can and does result from the conviction that routine Christian denunciations of anti-Semitism are virtually meaningless when combined with policies which, in Jewish eyes, jeopardize the security of the State and hence the survival of the Jewish people.

This combination of opposition to anti-Semitism and espousal of positions dangerous to Israel does not necessarily demonstrate hypocrisy. We have already seen that non-Jews often fail to perceive the magnitude of the danger or to recognize the link between the threat to Israel and the threat to both Jewish lives and Jewish survival. There is also, of course, the existence of a conflicting moral claim made in the name of Palestinian Arab nationalism. The attractions of this claim are enhanced by its association with the aspirations of groups who have elicited considerable sympathy in the leadership of both the National Council of Churches and the World Council of Churches (the third world, victims of colonialist oppression, and the like), particularly in light of the categories of liberation theology.[69]

---

[69] See Rael Jean Isaac, "Liberal Protestants versus Israel," *Midstream* 27 (October, 1981): 6–14, especially 12–13. [Addendum: My discussion of Palestinian statehood in this essay reflects the prevailing consensus in 1983 that led supporters of Israel to regard a PLO-governed state as an unacceptable danger. In the wake of the Oslo accords (which I regarded at the time as a risk worth taking) and their tortuous aftermath, this consensus no longer obtains. I wish I could say that the reasons for concern have in fact diminished.]

This is not the appropriate forum to argue the merits of this moral claim in detail. Nevertheless, the moral relevance of several well-known factors is worth noting. There is a Palestinian Arab state named Jordan, which is somehow not accepted as a legitimate locus for the realization of Palestinian national aspirations. Palestinian Arab nationalism was generated in part by the Jewish immigration and has tended to define itself, at least to the international community, only in relation to the territory that Jews happen to control (note the lack of interest in a separate Palestinian West Bank before 1967); that is, once Jews control an area, it becomes a focus of the Palestinian desire for self-determination. In a sense, then, a specific Palestinian nationalism (as distinct from a broader Arab nationalism) originated in resistance to Jewish national self-expression and was nurtured in the bitterness and frustration of a refugee status artificially prolonged by Arab states—precisely because of hostility toward Israel. The moral standing of a nationalism both generated and defined largely by relentless animosity toward the Jewish national presence (not to speak of the moral questions regarding the manner in which this nationalism is being pursued) cannot be accepted uncritically merely because it uses the terminology of self-determination. A positive Palestinian nationalism should be able to achieve fulfillment in Jordan (including, perhaps, much of the West Bank); the sort of Palestinian nationalism which is now dominant, given a mini-state in the West Bank and Gaza, will pose a mortal danger to Israel. Moral considerations surely require that the natural tendency of decent people to sympathize with the powerless be tempered by a reasonable assessment of what is likely to happen should they gain power.

Let me emphasize that this argument does not mean that Jews have the right to express righteous indignation whenever Christians or Christian organizations criticize Israel; Jews themselves are not always reticent in expressing disagreement with Israeli policies, and the self-censorship practiced by some Jews in these matters can hardly be demanded of Christians. I think, however, that a question can be formulated which might serve as a rough criterion for a fair Jewish reaction to Christian statements and for self-scrutiny by Christians professing concern for Jews: "Is this position rejected by at least ninety per cent of Israeli Jews on the grounds of national security?"

Israel is a democracy with a diverse and opinionated population; a positive answer to this question almost surely means that the position rejected is fraught with peril. Christians who find that they espouse such a position, particularly if this occurs with any frequency, are probably deceiving themselves about their concern for Jews; in reality, they are prepared to face the destruction of the Jewish people (not only the State of Israel) with relative equanimity.[70] For their part, Jews can hardly be faulted for reacting with deep disappointment when Christians maintain such views, and the National Council of Churches' statement falls into this category. The usefulness of dialogue is called into question when a major Christian body in the United States takes a stand which jeopardizes the survival of Israel. To make matters worse, this stand is less sympathetic than the position taken by both American public opinion and the policy of the United States government itself. It may be unrealistic to expect dialogue to have produced an attitude more favorable than that of the average citizen in a given country, but if the position of the churches is less favorable, many Jews cannot help but feel disillusioned about the entire process of interfaith discussion.

The picture, nevertheless, is not unrelievedly bleak. Veteran interfaith activists such as Franklin Littell, John Oesterreicher, and the Eckardts remain passionately devoted to the defense of Israel. For theological reasons, many Christian fundamentalists have spoken out on Israel's behalf, and, although we have already seen that many Jews feel ambivalent about this support, others have welcomed it with genuine enthusiasm. Given the discouraging atmosphere on the Israel issue as well as the Moral Majority's recent efforts to shed its antisemitic image, rejection of such support is becoming more difficult to justify, and it is especially noteworthy that Southern Baptists were conspicuous by their absence among the signatories of that document condemning Israel for violating human rights.[71] The irony that precisely those groups which participate least in dialogue are the strongest supporters of Israel should not go unnoticed, but this does not mean that dialogue has not helped produce Christian friends of the Jewish state—some of them quite

---

[70] After this was written, Steven E. Plaut proposed a virtually identical criterion to define "What is 'Anti-Israel'" (*Midstream* 28 [May, 1982]: 3–6).

[71] See the Eckardts' warning against relying on the theological arguments for Israel which provide the underpinning of the evangelical position (*Judaism* 27 [1978]: 320). On the other hand, support for Israel on other grounds than particularistic theology is not unheard of among evangelicals. Cf. Carl Henry in *Face to Face* 3–4 (Fall/Winter, 1977): 17. See especially A. Roy Eckardt, "Toward a Secular Theology of Israel," *Christian Jewish Relations* 72 (1980): 8–20.

influential. Israel is now inextricably linked to the spiritual and physical survival of world Jewry, and Jews must pursue every avenue to ensure its security. Interfaith dialogue is one such approach, and it must be cultivated with both deep sensitivity and uncompromising vigor.

ETHICS AND PUBLIC POLICY

Religion has something to say about social issues, but precisely what is not always clear. Wide differences on these questions exist not only among "religious" people in general but also among members of the same faith or even the same denomination. For interfaith dialogue, such a situation presents opportunities and pitfalls at the same time.

In some contexts, the existence of flexibility, divergent opinions within a single religious tradition, and overlapping views cutting across religious lines diminishes the adversarial relationship that can occasionally threaten the atmosphere of dialogue. In dealing with issues such as poverty and civil rights, all parties share the objective of maximizing social justice in an imperfect world, and discussions can constitute a combined effort to articulate the best means of attaining that end. It is not always clear, however, that such discussions are religious dialogue as much as they are a consideration of proper social policy by individuals who happen to be religious. The fundamental ethical principles are largely shared by all decent people, and choices must be made on the basis of calculations that are not radically different for the person of faith and the secular humanist. In other areas of Jewish-Christian dialogue, theological concerns can become too prominent; here, the specifically religious dimension can become little more than window dressing.

With some exceptions, Jewish and Christian participants in dialogue have tended to be theologically and politically liberal. Until fairly recently, this has made cooperation on social issues in the United States relatively straightforward. In the 1960s, for example, the civil rights movement was fighting for a cause whose justice was unassailable, and Jewish religious leaders were particularly prominent in a struggle which exemplified prophetic ideals and evoked no hesitation or ambivalence.

Things are no longer quite so simple. For reasons involving both ethical ideals and practical self-interest, many Jews have profound reservations about affirmative action quotas, and, even in less sensitive areas, the recent conservative trend has not left Jews unaffected. Since many Christian ecumenists have gone along with the sort of redefinition of liberalism which requires support for quotas, it has become somewhat more difficult to find common ground on a topic that once served as a fruitful, noncontroversial area for interfaith cooperation. There should surely be grounds for satisfaction that the civil rights issue has reached a point where ethical people can legitimately disagree about key policy questions, but from the more parochial perspective of Jewish-Christian dialogue (and Jewish-black relations in general), unanimity has been sacrificed on the altar of progress.

Other problems of public policy are marked by a more direct engagement of religious interests. With respect to public school prayer, which almost all Jews oppose, the liberal orientation of most Christian interfaith activists creates a commonality of opinion with Jews which does not mirror the views of the ordinary American Christian. On the matter of aid to parochial schools, where vigorous Catholic support means that there are deep divisions among Christians, the religiously liberal orientation of most Jewish ecumenists creates an illusion of greater Jewish consensus than really exists. The relative absence from dialogue of Orthodox Jews distorts the picture, and one Catholic leader has told me that awareness of significant Orthodox support for such aid is important in moderating Catholic resentment toward Jews because of this issue.[72]

Finally, there are the sensitive, occasionally explosive moral questions exemplified by the abortion controversy but also including such problems as euthanasia, homosexuality, and pornography. Here, too, the failure of Orthodox Jews to participate actively in dialogue can lead to skewed perceptions of what Judaism has to say about such matters. On abortion, for example, a number of Jewish organizations concerned with interfaith relations have declared that Jewish ethics are in essential conformity with the Supreme Court decision allowing abortion on demand before the last trimester. In fact, however, such a decision would have been rejected by every Jewish authority before the twentieth century, and,

---

[72] For a recent work dealing with a variety of social questions, see *The Formation of Social Policy in the Catholic and Jewish Traditions*, ed. by Eugene Fischer and Daniel Polish (Notre Dame, Ind., 1980).

while Orthodox attitudes are neither monolithic nor entirely identical with Catholic views, they are far more restrictive than the public perception of the "Jewish" position.

On this and related matters, an appreciation of the Orthodox stance would contribute to a relaxation of tensions with both Catholics and fundamentalist Protestants. In any case, developments in biology and medicine have moved forward at such a dizzying pace that all religious traditions must take a fresh look at an almost bewildering variety of questions; in this context, abortion is only the proverbial "tip of the iceberg,"[73] and there is every reason to expect that such problems will receive continuing, urgent attention from theologians.[74] Though interfaith discussions will hardly play a decisive role in this process, they are likely to be stimulated and invigorated by confronting some of the most complex issues facing contemporary religious ethics.

CONCLUSION

No area of Jewish-Christian relations has been left untouched by the fundamental transformations of the last two decades. The revolution inevitably remains incomplete, and both opponents and supporters of the interfaith enterprise can cite abundant evidence for their respective positions. The most straightforward achievement of increased Jewish-Christian discussions is the least controversial; ordinary human relationships inevitably improve in the context of regular, sympathetic contacts. From this perspective, at least, even those with the deepest reservations about interfaith dialogue can only wish the participants well as they confront the theological, political, and moral dynamics of a relationship marked by danger, challenge, and genuine promise.

---

[73] Hyatt, "Interfaith Movement," p. 275.
[74] See "The Bio-Medical Revolution: Applying Jewish Values to Public Policy-Making," *Analysis* 62 (April, 1977).

REFLECTIONS ON CONVERSION
AND PROSELYTIZING IN JUDAISM
AND CHRISTIANITY

From: *Studies in Jewish-Christian Relations* 3 (2008): R1-R8, at
http://escholarship.bc.edu/cgi/viewcontent.cgi?article=1140&context=scjr.
This is a slightly revised version of a talk given at the Presbyterian-Jewish
Consultation, October 30-November 1, 2006, Pendle Hill, PA.

Setting aside disputes regarding the State of Israel, there is no more
sensitive subject in the universe of Jewish-Christian relations than
conversionary aspirations on the part of Christians. The reasons for this
appear obvious—and in large measure they are—but they are also marked
by layers of complexity that we would do well to examine, particularly
in light of the controversy engendered by the revised Tridentine mass
issued by Pope Benedict XVI and a full page advertisement in the *New
York Times* in which prominent evangelical Christians advocated the
targeted proselytizing of Jews.[1]

Contemporary discussions of this issue usually take for granted that
Judaism in principle eschews efforts to proselytize others. Thus, a *locus
classicus* in the Talmud in effect instructs Jews approached by a gentile
expressing an interest in conversion to suggest that the prospective
convert urgently seek out a psychiatrist. Why, after all, would anyone in
his or her right mind join a defeated and persecuted people? Only one
who persists despite this effort at discouragement is eligible to pursue
the goal of becoming a Jew.[2]

Nonetheless, some see this passage not as an expression of an anti-
proselytizing principle but as the reaction of Jews who had lost the
contest for pagan adherents and decided to make a virtue of their failure.
The argument for the position that there were widespread Jewish efforts

---

[1] *The New York Times*, March 28, 2008, p. A15. For my reaction to the new text of the mass,
see "Let's Clarify the Purpose of Interfaith Dialogue," *The Jerusalem Post*, Feb. 16, 2008.

[2] Babylonian Talmud *Yevamot* 47a.

in the Graeco-Roman world to attract converts rests upon the presence of "God-fearing" semi-proselytes throughout that world as well as explicit or near-explicit assertions in several texts. In this forum, the most relevant of those texts is the assertion in Matthew (23:15) that Pharisees compass land and sea to make one proselyte. While the question of ancient Jewish proselytizing remains a lively matter of dispute, it is worth noting the obvious. Whether or not one endorses the plural form "Judaisms" in vogue among some historians, it is evident that ancient Jewish attitudes toward a host of religious questions ranged across a very large spectrum, so that indications of both proselytizing activity and opposition or indifference to such activity do not constitute a puzzling contradiction. Unless there are independent grounds to conclude that conflicting evidence about this issue testifies to historical development, such evidence can easily be read as a reflection of very different approaches to proselytizing that coexisted among Jews in the Hellenistic-Roman-rabbinic period.[3]

As Judaism moved into the Middle Ages, it is evident that an explicit rabbinic text would carry more weight than evidence from Matthew or Graeco-Roman artifacts and literature. Jewish reluctance to proselytize was of course greatly reinforced by the attendant dangers of such efforts in both the Christian and the Muslim worlds. Setting aside the danger, the very fact that Jews were a small, relatively powerless minority rendered the idea that they could win over large numbers of converts unrealistic.

Beyond all this, there was, I think, a fascinating dialectic that played itself out in the Jewish psyche. To become a Jew is to join a people, not just a faith. The concept of Jewish chosenness, of the special sanctity of Israel as a collective, rendered the objective of a mass conversion to Judaism problematic. Even in the *eschaton*, all the nations may call upon God together in a clear voice (Zephaniah 3:9), but they remain discrete nations. In Jewish eyes, those nations would presumably follow the Noahide code, binding in historical times as well as at the end of days, which defines God's expectations of non-Jews in a manner that keeps them separate from Israel. Since obedience to this code provides eternal felicity to its non-Jewish adherents, the drive to convert gentiles to Judaism is diminished even further.

---

3   For a book-length discussion of this issue arguing that Jews did not proselytize before the second century C.E., see Martin Goodman, *Mission and Conversion: Proselytizing in the Religious History of the Roman Empire* (Oxford, 1994).

At the same time, it is far from clear that medieval Jews refrained from missionizing only or even primarily because they saw another route to salvation for gentiles. Given the realities of the medieval Jewish condition, many Jews so resented their persecutors that they had no interest in their salvation; rather, they looked forward to their damnation. While Hitler maintains so unique a position in the history of Judaeophobia that analogies can be dangerous and even offensive, it is nonetheless instructive to consider how Jews would have reacted in the last months of World War II to the prospect of a suddenly repentant Hitler who will enter the World to Come as a righteous man. Distasteful as this analogy is, it provides a graphic means of grasping the psychology of people who yearned for the moment when God would destroy their oppressors and consign them to damnation.[4]

Complicating the issue further is the relationship between Christianity and the requirements of the Noahide code. David Novak has written with considerable plausibility that a case can be made that Christianity is a quintessential fulfillment of that code since it not only establishes the obligatory moral framework but even meets the Maimonidean requirement that non-Jews observe the code out of belief that it is a product of divine revelation.[5] Nonetheless, this position runs afoul of a theological point that was at the forefront of the medieval Jewish psyche, to wit, the status of worship directed at Jesus of Nazareth as a hypostasis of the triune God. Almost all medieval Jews saw this as a form of *avodah zarah*, or worship of an entity other than God, which prima facie violated one of the seven Noahide commandments. During the Paris Disputation of 1240, R. Yehiel of Paris displayed considerable unease when he was more or less forced to imply in response to a direct

---

[4] Some forms of Christianity, at least today, take a position on forgiveness of enemies that can be quite jarring to Jews. During a break at an international meeting in Lower Manhattan between Catholic clergy, primarily cardinals, and Orthodox Jews arranged by the World Jewish Congress, the group walked to ground zero, where Cardinal Lustiger of France recited a spontaneous prayer. I was stunned when I heard the words, "Pardonnez les assassins." I cannot imagine a Jew who would share this sentiment, particularly in light of the fact that the 9/11 murderers left themselves no opportunity to repent. My discomfiture was enhanced later in the day when another cardinal spoke of how we can learn from a Jewish Holocaust survivor who converted to Catholicism and declared that she forgives those who tormented her in the camps.

[5] "Mitsvah," in *Christianity in Jewish Terms*, ed. by Tikva Frymer-Kensky, David Novak, Peter Ochs, David Fox Sandmel, and Michael Signer (Boulder, Colorado, and Oxford, 2000), p. 118.

question that Christians could be saved through their own faith; other medieval Jews unhesitatingly answered this question in the negative.[6]

In sum, then, Jews in the Christian world refrained from missionizing as a result of an extraordinarily complex constellation of theological, historical, and psychological considerations not always consistent with one another: The Jewish people should retain its uniqueness even in eschatological times; non-Jews have an avenue of salvation without joining that people (though that avenue is probably not Christianity); missionizing was dangerous; its chances of meeting with significant success were minuscule; and the persecutors of Israel should receive their just punishment for all that they had done.

Despite all this, the impulse to have Christians recognize the truth was not absent from the medieval Jewish psyche. Members of a minority regularly mocked for their religious error and periodically pressured to renounce it enjoyed a sense of validation and enormous satisfaction when adherents of the majority faith recognized their own error. While this is a point whose psychological validity is almost self-evident, here is a text from the *Nizzahon Vetus*, a late-thirteenth-century Northern European polemic that I edited several decades ago, that spells it out:

> With regard to their questioning us as to whether there are proselytes among us, they ask this question to their shame and to the shame of their faith. After all, one should not be surprised at the bad deeds of an evil Jew who becomes an apostate, because his motives are to enable himself to eat all that his heart desires, to give pleasure to his flesh with wine and fornication, to remove from himself the yoke of the kingdom of heaven so that he should fear nothing, to free himself from all the commandments, cleave to sin, and concern himself with worldly pleasures. But the situation is different with regard to proselytes who converted to Judaism and thus went of their own free will from freedom to slavery, from light to darkness. If the proselyte is a man, then he knows that he must wound himself by removing his foreskin through circumcision, that he must exile himself from place to place, that he must deprive himself of worldly good and fear for his life from the external threat of being killed by the uncircumcised, and that he will lack many things that his heart desires; similarly, a woman proselyte also separates herself from all pleasures. And despite all this, they come to

6 See my discussion in "On the Image and Destiny of Gentiles in Ashkenazic Polemical Literature" (in Hebrew), in *Facing the Cross: The Persecutions of 1096 in History and Historiography*, ed. by Yom Tov Assis et al. (Jerusalem, 2000), pp. 80–81 [translation in this volume].

take refuge under the wing of the divine presence. It is evident that they would not do this unless they knew for certain that their faith is without foundation and that it is all a lie, vanity, and emptiness. Consequently, you should be ashamed when you mention the matter of proselytes.[7]

In this environment, a classic Talmudic commentary cites a medieval French proselyte's interpretation of a rabbinic text declaring converts to be as damaging to Israel as a serious disease. The reason for this, says the proselyte, is that converts observe the Torah with such care that they put born Jews to shame.[8]

It is a matter of no small interest that in addressing the question of the permissibility of teaching Torah to non-Jews, Maimonides took a stringent position with respect to Muslims—even though he saw them as exemplary monotheists—and a more lenient one with respect to Christians, even though he saw them as worshippers of *avodah zarah*. The reason he provides is that unlike Muslims, who consider the text of the Hebrew Bible unreliable, Christians accept the accuracy of that text and are therefore more susceptible to being persuaded of the true faith if they can be made to understand the correct meaning of the Bible.[9] I am not prepared to say that Maimonides advocated a Jewish mission to Christians, but he clearly hoped that in sporadic, personal encounters, Jews might be able to demonstrate the superiority of their faith.

Similarly, I am convinced that in the streets of medieval Christian Europe, some Jews challenged their Christian neighbors with arguments designed to prove the truth of Judaism, though here too these contacts do not add up to a Jewish mission or near-mission. The motive was primarily to reinforce Jewish morale, not to create a cadre of proselytes.[10] This motive also plays a role in moderating my earlier observation about the desire of some medieval Jews for the damnation and destruction of

---

[7] *The Jewish-Christian Debate in the High Middle Ages: A Critical Edition of the Nizzahon Vetus with an Introduction, Translation, and Commentary* (Philadelphia, 1979; softcover edition, Northvale, New Jersey and London, 1996), #211, English section, pp. 206–207. I commented on this passage in "Jacob Katz on Jews and Christians in the Middle Ages," in *The Pride of Jacob: Essays on Jacob Katz and his Work*, ed. by Jay M. Harris (Cambridge, Mass., 2002), pp. 52–54.

[8] *Tosafot* to *Qiddushin* 70b, s.v. *qashim gerim.*

[9] *Teshuvot ha-Rambam*, ed. by Joshua Blau (Jerusalem, 1989), no. 149.

[10] See the argument in my "Mission to the Jews and Jewish-Christian Contacts in the Polemical Literature of the High Middle Ages," *American Historical Review* 91 (1986): 576–591.

their oppressors. Such a desire conflicts with the hope for eschatological vindication, a hope that provides its full measure of psychological benefit only if the deniers of Judaism acknowledge their error at the end of days and proclaim, in the words of the High Holiday liturgy, "The Lord God of Israel is King, and his kingship rules over all."[11]

Jacob Katz argued that by the sixteenth century, the assertiveness that marked medieval Jewish attitudes toward Christianity, particularly in Northern Europe, began to wane, and that this transformation also affected attitudes toward converts and conversion. The Jewish community had turned inward and no longer sought to impress the Christian world with its ability to attract outsiders. But as Jews moved toward modernity, other considerations emerged. Significant authorities began to affirm that Christianity is not considered *avodah zarah* when practiced by non-Jews. Thus, the likelihood that Christians could attain salvation increased exponentially. For Moses Mendelssohn, religious toleration became an almost transcendent ideal, and he famously expressed dissatisfaction with Maimonides' requirement that the Noahide Code confers salvation only upon those who accept it as revelation.[12] R. Israel Lipschutz, an important nineteenth-century commentator on the Mishnah, asserted as an almost self-evident truth that God would not fail to provide heavenly reward to Johannes Reuchlin for his defense of Jewish books against those who would have destroyed them.[13]

If Christians can attain salvation as Christians, the motive for a Jewish mission is markedly diminished. In modern times, this is often taken for granted as *the* reason why Jews have refrained from proselytizing. In other words, Jewish opposition to mission is a function of a deeply held principle recognizing the salvific potential of other religions. As we have seen, the history of Jewish attitudes regarding this question is far more complicated, but there is an element of truth

---

[11] For a discussion of the scholarly debate about these matters, see my "On the Image and Destiny of Gentiles in Ashkenazic Polemical Literature," pp. 74–91. Several participants in that debate also pointed to a medieval hymn in the High Holiday liturgy that describes in recurrent, celebratory language how all the world's inhabitants will gather to worship the true God. For an English translation of this hymn, see, for example, *The Complete Artscroll Machzor: Rosh Hashanah* (New York, 1986), pp. 495, 497.

[12] For a translation and discussion of the relevant passage, see, for example, Steven Schwarzschild, "Do Noachides Have to Believe in Revelation?" in *The Pursuit of the Ideal*, ed. by Menachem Kellner (Albany, 1990), p. 36.

[13] *Tiferet Yisrael* to Avot 3:14 (*Boaz #1*).

in this assertion even with respect to the pre-modern period. As Allen Friedman has put it in an oral communication, medieval Christians and Muslims did not expect to meet anyone who was not a co-religionist in heaven; even Jews with a restrictive view of salvation expected to meet a few righteous gentiles.

Thus far, I have addressed the views of Jews in a traditional society and their Orthodox successors in modern times. It goes without saying that almost all non-Orthodox Jews maintain that Christianity provides its adherents with the ability to find favor in the eyes of God, and those non-Orthodox Jews who believe in an afterlife affirm that good Christians have a portion in the World to Come. For such Jews, proselytizing is a symptom of an intolerant, even immoral theology of exclusion. While Reform Judaism has, after much soul-searching, affirmed the desirability of outreach to non-Jews with the hope of attracting them to Judaism, these efforts are restricted to "unchurched" gentiles or—sometimes—to Christians who have married or plan to marry Jews. Committed Christians remaining within their own community remain beyond the scope of such initiatives for reasons not only of pragmatism but of principle.

Before attempting to assess how Jewish attitudes toward missionizing may affect current interactions between Christians and Jews, we need to turn, however briefly, to historic Christian approaches toward missionary activity directed at Jews. It is hardly necessary to say that classical Christianity strove to spread the good news and that Jews were not excluded as objects of this effort. At the same time, a theology developed that granted Jews special, even unique toleration both because they were seen as witnesses to the truth of Christianity and because Romans 11, however one reads it, speaks of their continued separate existence when the fullness of the nations arrives.[14] Thus, although it was clearly desirable for individual Jews to save themselves through conversion, systematic efforts to convert large numbers of Jews were rare before the thirteenth century. An article on Jewish conversion in thirteenth-century England in a recent issue of *Speculum* asserts that even at this relatively late date, Robert Grosseteste "view[ed] Jewish

---

[14] For a detailed analysis of Christian readings of this difficult chapter, see Jeremy Cohen, "The Mystery of Israel's Salvation: Romans 11:25–26 in Patristic and Medieval Exegesis," *Harvard Theological Review* 98 (2005): 247–281.

conversion as a consequence of the end of history rather than as a current possibility or even a desire."[15]

Though the vision of Jewish conversion at the end of days persisted, the thirteenth-century saw the exponential growth of efforts to convert the Jews en masse. As time passed, some of these efforts developed an eschatological perspective linked to the belief that Jewish conversion must precede the imminent end of days, while others resulted from the desire to establish a uniformly Christian Europe. The earlier absence of conversionary programs does not bespeak a strong interest in the welfare of Jewish souls, and I see little indication that the primary motive of the new policy was a sudden concern for the fate of Jews who would otherwise be condemned to hellfire, though some missionaries undoubtedly took satisfaction in the benefit that they brought to the objects of their ministry. The treatment of new Christians in *this* world certainly left much to be desired. They were sometimes deprived of their property, the conditions in the halfway houses for converts were often lamentable, and other efforts to meet the needs of individuals removed from their families and support systems were sporadic and generally inadequate.[16]

When converts were suspected of judaizing in late-medieval-and-early-modern Iberia, they were of course subjected to terrible consequences. Here we confront the logic of imposing one's faith on an unwilling other in its most acute form, since the torments inflicted by the Inquisition were imposed at least in part for the sake of the immortal souls of the unfortunate judaizers. But the souls of unconverted Jews are presumably just as destined to damnation as those of insincere converts, so that as a matter of cold logic the policies of the Inquisition could just as well have been applied to the former. But they were not. The tradition of toleration, even in an age of expulsions and intense missionary pressures, maintained some modicum of its original standing.[17]

And so we return to modern and contemporary times. The question of the propriety of a Christian mission directed at Jews depends first of

[15] Ruth Nisse, "'Your name will no longer be Asenath': Apocrypha, Anti-martyrdom, and Jewish Conversion in Thirteenth-Century England," *Speculum* 81 (2006): 738–739.

[16] See, for example, Robert C. Stacey, "The Conversion of Jews to Christianity in thirteenth-century England," *Speculum* 67 (1992): 263–283.

[17] For a discussion of both elements constituting the tension in the Church's position, see Kenneth Stow, *Alienated Minority* (Cambridge, Mass. And London, 1992), pp. 242–273.

all on the underlying theology of salvation maintained by the Christian group in question. Such theologies range across a broad spectrum:

- Jews, like all other non-Christians, are condemned to eternal hellfire.
- Non-Christians, including Jews, are at a distinct disadvantage in the struggle for salvation, but such salvation is not ruled out.[18]
- Jews, uniquely among adherents of non-Christian religions, can be saved no less readily than Christians because they are already with the Father.
- Salvation is readily available to all good people irrespective of religion.

Even the last two positions do not in themselves rule out proselytizing since spreading the good news could be desirable or obligatory because of the inherent value of ultimate truth without reference to the eternal destiny of the non-Christian. Still, the first two positions, and especially the harsher of the two, greatly strengthen the argument for an active mission.

How then does a Jew, or at least this Jew, respond to such an argument? As long ago as 1983, I expressed strong opposition to Jewish efforts to instruct Christians about what to believe regarding their own religion, and I have repeated this position on numerous subsequent occasions. I confessed, however, that with respect to missionizing, "even Jews who hesitate most about intervention in the internal affairs of Christianity have some mixed feelings." I went on to say that "the Jewish mandate to protect Jews from conversion is no less a religious requirement than any Christian mandate to convert them, and, although my basic sympathies are with the 'non-interventionists,' in the case of aggressive missionizing aimed specifically at Jews, the overriding principle of *pikkuah nefesh*, or preventing danger to life (including spiritual life), may well prevail."[19] In short, if I could persuade a Christian uncertain of his or her position regarding mission to the Jews that proper Christian belief

---

18 This is the position expressed in the controversial Catholic document *Dominus Iesus*. See my analysis in "*Dominus Iesus* and the Jews," *America* 185:7 (September 17, 2001): 7–12, also available at http://www.bc.edu/research/cjl/meta-elements/texts/cjrelations/resources/articles/berger.htm. Reprinted in *Sic et Non: Encountering Dominus Iesus*, ed. by Stephen J. Pope and Charles C. Hefling (New York, 2002), pp. 39–46.

19 "Jewish-Christian Relations: A Jewish Perspective," *Journal of Ecumenical Studies* 20 (1983): 17–18.

should affirm the possibility of salvation for unconverted Jews, I would try to do this.

Nonetheless, I do not regard honest advocates of proselytizing who adhere to the harshest position regarding Jewish salvation as evil in any sense. Thus, I take the position that someone who has declared war on me and my people is nonetheless a fine person whom I can embrace as a friend in other contexts. There is, of course, an emotional tension in this position, and I ask myself whether an argument for Jewish exceptionalism can be formulated that does not impinge on Christian doctrine. I think it possible that this question can be answered in the affirmative. Christians in the modern world, including those with exclusivist views of salvation, definitively reject coercive methods, whether physical or economic, to enforce conformity to Christian belief and practice, and they do this not only because such methods would be ineffective but because they abhor them in principle. This appears to mean that even saving another's soul does not outweigh all competing considerations. One who refrains from religious coercion recognizes that the apparently transcendent benefit does not outweigh the harm done to the coercer's moral personality, to that of his or her collective, or to civil society as a whole, not to speak of the immediate suffering of the presumed beneficiary.

In light of these considerations, we are now in a position to ask if there is any moral harm inflicted by non-coercive proselytizing. It can certainly damage, even poison, intergroup relations, and it renders respectful dialogue about religious matters next to impossible. These concerns apply to proselytizing directed at any group; the question is whether they are serious enough to set aside the salvific advantage of conversion to Christianity. At the very least, they may persuade Christians who believe that the other party's salvation is not at stake to eschew active missionizing.

In dealing with Jews, the moral objections to conversionary efforts increase exponentially. First, even in an open society, there is a tinge of pressure, if not genuine coercion, when members of a majority religion carry out sustained campaigns to convince the minority to abandon its faith. In 1988, the *New York Times* published a letter in which I objected to their accepting advertisements from "Jews for Jesus" containing biblical prooftexts for Christian doctrines. Setting aside the well-known issue of the ethically objectionable misappropriation of Jewish symbols, the letter argued that publishing such religious polemic puts a Jewish respondent in an untenable position. Jews would either have to explain in a counter-ad why the verses in question cannot legitimately be understood christologically, which "would pollute the atmosphere of interfaith relations and create concrete dangers for the Jewish minority," or they would have to remain silent, thus accepting "a quasi-medieval position of being bombarded by public attacks on their faith without opportunity for candid response."[20]

Second, the history of Christian treatment of Jews is genuinely relevant to this moral calculus. The Jewish community reacts to missionary efforts by Christians through the prism of crusades, Inquisition, blood libels, accusations of host desecration and well poisoning, depictions of Jews as instruments of the devil, and assorted massacres. This reaction is not merely understandable; it is thoroughly legitimate. The Jewish people managed to survive these religiously motivated efforts to destroy it, but contemporary efforts to wipe it out by kinder means are tainted by this history. Like it or not, the Christian missionary to the Jews is continuing the work of Count Emicho, Vincent Ferrer, Torquemada, and Chmielnicki. "Jews for Jesus" can proclaim as loudly and as often as they wish that these persecutors of Jews were not Christians, but there is no avoiding the fact that they acted and were perceived as acting in the name of Christianity. Even if proselytizing other groups is appropriate, proselytizing Jews is arguably not.

Let me end more softly by returning to my anti-interventionist mode. In a contemporary context, it is a matter of the first importance to recognize that belief in eschatological verification is very different from mission. I have made this point in several essays, but it bears repetition here. Participants in dialogue often affirm that even the assertion that your faith will be vindicated at the end of days constitutes morally objectionable triumphalism. I regard this position as itself morally objectionable. Both Jews and Christians are entitled to believe that their respective religions are true in a deep and uncompromising sense, and that this truth will become evident to all the world in the fullness of time.

[20] "Jews for Jesus Ad Poses Painful Choices," *The New York Times*, January 9, 1988, p. 26.

ON *DOMINUS IESUS* AND THE JEWS

From: *America* 185:7 (September 17, 2001): 7–12.

The Declaration *Dominus Iesus*, issued in September 2000 by the Congregation for the Doctrine of the Faith, aroused deep concern among many Jews and not a few Catholics. Let me first survey the specific areas of concern, proceed to address the question of whether or not Jews can plausibly be said to lie outside the effective scope of the document, and finally express some personal views about the propriety or impropriety of the objections that have been raised and examine the implications for Jewish-Catholic dialogue.

Jewish criticisms of *Dominus Iesus* have focused on several central points. The declaration maintains that the salvific grace of God is given only by means of Jesus and the Church. Though "individual non-Christians" can attain this grace in a manner that remains difficult to define, it is a certainty that the process cannot take place without "a mysterious relationship with the Church." This appears to mean that other religions, presumably including Judaism, have no independent salvific power. The text goes on to emphasize that although "followers of other religions can receive divine grace, . . . *objectively speaking* [emphasis in the original] they are in a gravely deficient situation in comparison with those who, in the Church, have the fullness of the means of salvation." Thus, Jews, if they are included in this assertion, are apparently far less likely to be saved than Catholics.

Moreover, interreligious dialogue is described as part of the "evangelizing mission" of the Church, "just one of the actions of the Church in her mission *ad gentes*" (no. 22). The declaration goes on to emphasize in this context that though "equality . . . is a presupposition of interreligious dialogue, [it] refers to the equal personal dignity of the parties in dialogue, not to doctrinal content" (no. 22). For many Jews, the denial of doctrinal equality is objectionable, even deeply objectionable, in and of itself, and the ascription of evangelical intent to the dialogue appears to be a dagger thrust into its very heart.

The most comprehensive approach to neutralizing these objections is the assertion that Jews, who received the initial divine revelation and entered into a covenant with God before the rise of Christianity, are *sui generis*. Not only was *Dominus Iesus* not formulated with Jews in mind; Jews, we are sometimes told, are entirely excluded from the purview of its controversial assertions.

I do not find this position plausible.

To begin with, the declaration contains one explicit reference to Jews, and it comes in the section entitled "Unicity and Universality of the Salvific Mystery of Jesus Christ," a title almost identical with the subtitle of the document as a whole. "It was," declares *Dominus Iesus*, "in the awarenesss of the one universal gift of salvation offered by the Father through Jesus Christ in the Spirit (cf. Eph 1:3–14), that the first Christians encountered the Jewish people, showing them the fulfilllment of salvation that went beyond the Law and, in the same awareness, they confronted the pagan world of their time, which aspired to salvation through a plurality of saviours" (no. 13). The following passages make it crystal clear that this encounter with the Jews is to be seen in the context of the firm belief that "the universal salvific will of the One and triune God is offered and accomplished once for all in the mystery of the incarnation, death, and resurrection of the Son of God" (no. 14).

It is almost superfluous to pursue the argument further. Though one short section, which declares "the canonical books of the Old and New Testament" fundamentally different from the sacred writings of other religions, clearly places Judaism and Christianity in the same category, it needs to be stressed that the central theme of the entire declaration, underscored on virtually every page, is that salvation comes in only one essential fashion for all humanity, and that is through the triune God of Christianity and his embodied Word. To suggest that Jews, who reject belief in both trinity and incarnation, attain salvation outside this otherwise universal system is to render the document virtually incoherent.

The principal author of *Dominus Iesus* is Joseph Cardinal Ratzinger. Last year on December 29th, the Cardinal wrote a conciliatory piece in *L'Osservatore Romano* emphasizing that "the faith witnessed by the Jewish Bible" is special to Christians because it is the foundation of their own; consequently, the dialogue with Jews takes place on a different level from all others. The article appeals to this special relationship to assert that the Nazis "tried to strike the Christian faith at its Abrahamic roots in the Jewish people." As a Jewish observer has pointed out, this is a deeply objectionable effort to transform the Final Solution into a primarily anti-Christian campaign, but it is peripheral to our main concerns. The key point is that Cardinal Ratzinger's affirmation of a unique Jewish-Christian relationship, which also includes the prayer that the paths of Jews and Christians will eventually converge, in no way contradicts of even modifies the unflinching message of *Dominus Iesus*. To understand the Cardinal's position more clearly, we need to look at his other writings about Jews and Judaism, collected in a slim volume entitled *Many Religions—One Covenant*.[1]

In these essays, he speaks of reconciliation, emphasizes the ongoing role of the Jewish people, and defends the value of the Hebrew Bible. It is clear, however, that he understands these positions as a rejection of the quasi-Marcionite position that the Hebrew Bible and its God embody reprehensible moral and religious qualities. On the contrary, argues the Cardinal, the God of the Hebrew Bible is the same as that of the New Testament, and the Law of the Hebrew Bible, seen through the prism of the new covenant, does not really stand in conflict with it. But all this is simply classic, pre-modern Christian doctrine recast in a spirit of friendship.

"The Sinai covenant," writes Cardinal Ratzinger, "is indeed superseded. But once what was provisional in it has been swept away we see what is truly definitive in it . . . . The New Covenant, which becomes clearer and clearer as the history of Israel unfolds . . . fulfills the dynamic expectation found in [the Sinai covenant]."[2] And in another formulation, "All cultic ordinances of the Old Testament are seen to be taken up into [Jesus'] death and brought to their deepest meaning . . . . The universalizing of the Torah by Jesus . . . preserves the unity of cult and ethos . . . . The entire cult is bound together in the Cross, indeed, for the first time has

---

[1]   San Francisco, 1999.
[2]   Pp. 70–71.

become fully real."[3] Cardinal Ratzinger, then, who has also declared that despite Israel's special mission at this stage of history, "we wait for the instant in which Israel will say yes to Christ,"[4] is a supersessionist.

At this point, we need to confront the real question, to wit, is there anything objectionable about this position? In a dialogical environment in which the term "supersessionism" has been turned into an epithet by both Jews and Christians, this may appear to be a puzzling question. We need to distinguish, however, between two forms of supersessionism, and in my view Jews have absolutely no right to object to the form endorsed by Cardinal Ratzinger. There is nothing in the core beliefs of Christianity that requires the sort of supersessionism that sees Judaism as spiritually arid, as an expression of narrow, petty legalism pursued in the service of a vengeful God and eventually replaced by a vital religion of universal love. Such a depiction is anti-Jewish, even antisemitic. But Cardinal Ratzinger never describes Judaism in such a fashion. On the contrary, he sees believing Jews as witnesses through their observance of Torah to the commitment to God's will, to the establishment of his kingdom even in the pre-messianic world, and to faith in a wholly just world after the ultimate redemption.[5] This understanding of Jews as a witness people is very different from the original Augustinian version in which Jews testified to Christian truth through their validation of the Hebrew Bible and their interminable suffering in exile.

For Jews to denounce this sort of supersessionism as morally wrong and disqualifying in the context of dialogue is to turn dialogue into a novel form of religious intimidation. As the pre-eminent Orthodox rabbinical authority Rabbi Joseph B. Soloveitchik understood very well, such a position is pragmatically dangerous for Jews, who become vulnerable to reciprocal demands for theological reform of Judaism, and it is even morally wrong. To illustrate the point from the perspective of Orthodox Judaism, I will not shrink from mobilizing the most telling illustration.

The cardinal theological sin in Judaism is *avodah zarah*, literally "foreign worship." I became embroiled in a controversy several years ago when I carelessly used the usual translation "idolatry," which is in fact sloppy and misleading in our context. Properly understood, *avodah zarah*

---

3   P. 41.
4   *National Catholic Reporter*, Oct. 6, 2000.
5   *Many Religions—One Covenant*, pp. 104–105.

is the formal recognition or worship as God of an entity that is in fact not God. For Jews, the worship of Jesus of Nazareth as God incarnate falls within this definition. Because of the monotheistic, non-pagan character of Christianity, many Jewish authorities denied that worship of Jesus is sinful for non-Jews, though many others did not endorse this exemption. Now, let us assume that I respect the Christian religion, as I do. Let us assume further that I respect believing Christians, as I do, for qualities that emerge precisely out of their Christian faith. But I believe that the worship of Jesus as God is a serious religious error displeasing to God even if the worshipper is a non-Jew, and that at the end of days Christians will come to recognize this. Is this belief immoral? Does it disqualify me as a participant in dialogue? Does it entitle a Christian to denounce me for adhering to a teaching of contempt? I hope the answer to these questions is "no." If it is "yes," then interfaith dialogue is destructive of traditional Judaism and must be abandoned forthwith. We would face a remarkable paradox. Precisely because of its striving for interfaith respect and understanding, dialogue would become an instrument of religious imperialism.

Once I take this position, I must extend it to Christians as well. As long as Christians do not vilify Judaism and Jews in the manner that I described earlier, they have every right to assert that Judaism errs about religious questions of the most central importance, that equality in dialogue does not mean the equal standing of the parties' religious doctrines, that at the end of days Jews will recognize the divinity of Jesus, even that salvation is much more difficult for one who stands outside the Catholic Church. If I were to criticize Cardinal Ratzinger for holding these views, I would be applying an egregious double standard. I am not unmindful of the fact that these doctrines, unlike comparable ones in Judaism, have served as a basis for persecution through the centuries. Nonetheless, once a Christian has explicitly severed the link between such beliefs and anti-Jewish attitudes and behavior, one cannot legitimately demand that he or she abandon them.

We are left, however, with the profoundly troubling passage about mission as a fundamental component of inter-religious dialogue. Is it possible that at least this assertion does not apply to Jews? Once again the answer must be negative. Here too the language of the declaration is thoroughly universal. In the very paragraph describing dialogue as an expression of mission, we read that "the Church, guided by charity and respect for freedom, must be primarily committed to proclaiming to all people the truth definitively revealed to the Lord, and to announcing the necessity of conversion to Jesus Christ and of adherence to the Church through baptism and the other sacraments in order to participate fully in communion with God, the Father, Son, and Holy Spirit" (no. 22). To say that this sentence, complete with its references to baptism and conversion, does not apply to Jews is to say they are not included among "all people" and are already "fully in communion" with the triune God.

Moreover, in an essay on dialogue dealing primarily with Jews and explicitly including them in the key passage, Cardinal Ratzinger wrote that missionary activity should not "cease and be replaced by dialogue . . . . This would be nothing other than total lack of conviction . . . . Rather, mission and dialogue should no longer be opposites but should mutually interpenetrate. Dialogue is not aimless conversation: it aims at conviction, at finding the truth; otherwise it is worthless." In a world where other people already know something about God, "proclamation of the gospel must be necessarily a dialogical process. We are not telling the other person something that is entirely unknown to him; rather, we are opening up the hidden depth of something with which, in his own religion, he is already in touch."[6]

In sum, we now have an official document of the Catholic Church, "ratified and confirmed" by the Pope himself, declaring that a key purpose of interfaith dialogue is mission, which includes the message that conversion is necessary to attain full communion with God. There is overwhelming evidence that the author intended this to apply to Jews as well. Are there any considerations capable of mitigating the impact of such a statement sufficiently to enable a self-respecting Jew to continue to pursue this enterprise?

The answer, I think, is yes, but it is a highly qualified yes. First, it is very likely that a substantial majority of Catholics involved in the dialogue disagree with this assertion in *Dominus Iesus* despite its official standing. Second, Cardinal Ratzinger himself asserts in his other writings that the teachings of the Church Fathers instruct us that before the end of days "the Jews must remain alongside us as a witness to the world."[7] And speaking about dialogue among religions in general, he says that unification "is hardly possible within our historical time, and

---

6   *Many Religions—One Covenant*, p. 112.
7   *Many Religions—One Covenant*, p. 104.

perhaps it is not even desirable."[8] Finally, if dialogue avoids discussion of core doctrinal issues and focuses on shared moral, social, and political concerns, it may well be justified even with people whose conversionary objectives are much sharper that those of *Dominus Iesus*. Many Jews hold discussions about such issues with evangelical Protestants who conduct overt missions to the Jews, and Rabbi Soloveitchik, who did not believe that such objectives had been abandoned by the Catholic Church, endorsed discussion of these matters with full awareness that theological content would play a significant role.

Orthodox Jews are routinely subjected to criticism for conforming to Rabbi Soloveitchik's guidelines by resisting dialogue with a primarily theological focus. The appearance of an official Catholic assertion that a major objective of dialogue is mission is a striking, unwelcome, and, for me at least, unexpected validation of the rabbi's much-maligned concerns. At the very least, criticism of the avoidance of dialogue about doctrinal issues should be suspended as long as this passage of *Dominus Iesus* remains in force without a formal assertion by the Commission for the Doctrine of the Faith or the Pope himself that it does not apply to dialogue with Jews.

Many of the criticisms leveled against *Dominus Iesus* strike me as unwarranted, and I greatly admire Cardinal Ratzinger's profound commitment to his faith. Despite huge gaps in implementation, the Catholic Church as a whole and the Pope in particular have taken steps to improve relations with the Jewish people that merit our highest regard. Generally speaking, criticisms of these initiatives from both Jewish and Christian quarters, even when technically valid, diminish their moral significance and sometimes cross the line into blinkered, almost churlish petulance. For all its imperfections, I see the statement on the Shoah as a historic act of genuine ethical stature, and the Pope's apology for Christian antisemitism and his behavior during his trip to Israel fill me with unalloyed admiration. But a climactic paragraph of *Dominus Iesus* effectively expects Jews to participate in an endeavor officially described as an effort to lead them, however gently and indirectly, to accept beliefs antithetical to the core of their faith. Many Jews will no doubt swallow their self-respect and proceed as if nothing has happened. But it is not clear that they should, and they should surely not be criticized if they do not.

---

8   *Many Religions—One Covenant*, p. 109.

REVISITING "CONFRONTATION"
AFTER FORTY YEARS
A Response to Rabbi Eugene Korn

From: http://www.bc.edu/research/cjl/meta-elements/texts/center/
conferences/soloveitchik/Berger_23Nov03.htm.

———————

*On November 23, 2003, the Center for Christian-Jewish Learning at
Boston College held a conference on the fortieth anniversary of Rabbi Joseph
B. Soloveitchik's "Confrontation." Originally a public lecture responding to
the second Vatican Council's ongoing discussions on the Jews and Judaism,
"Confrontation" criticized the nascent movement encouraging interfaith
dialogue on theological issues. Rabbi Soloveitchik argued that such dialogue
is unwise, dangerous, and, in the deepest sense, not even possible. Eugene
Korn, the main speaker at the event sponsored by the Center, pointed to some
of the problems in Rabbi Soloveitchik's presentation and maintained that his
opposition to religious dialogue should be modified in light of significant changes
in the Jewish-Christian relationship. I was asked to respond at the conference,
and that response follows.*

*The full text of "Confrontation," Rabbi Korn's lecture, and a series of
additional responses and exchanges appear at http://www.bc.edu/research/cjl/
meta-elements/texts/center/conferences/soloveitchik/#2.*

"Confrontation" is a characteristically brilliant, highly influential, and
notoriously problematic work. While Rabbi Soloveitchik addresses
a number of pragmatic issues clearly and to my mind presciently, he
also makes an apparently unqualified assertion that matters of religious
faith cannot in principle be communicated. Thus, interfaith dialogue
should not and really cannot deal with theological issues. Its only proper
subject is the realm of the secular order, expressed in the pursuit of social
justice and related concerns.

As Dr. Korn notes, serious readers have raised two fundamental
and apparently insuperable objections to these formulations. First, the
assertion of the intrinsic incommunicability of matters of faith leads

to, or is already, a *reductio ad absurdum*. Great religious works have been written through the ages by members of disparate faiths, and Rabbi Soloveitchik himself read many of them. Indeed, he was influenced by many of them—and not just on the level that he describes as cultural, a level where even secular thinkers can "enjoy and cherish" religious insights. To make matters worse, he says that the individual "encounter between God and man" cannot even be communicated to another individual in the same faith community. Thus, theological discussion among Jews would also be impossible. Second, the much-quoted footnote that Dr. Korn describes as "the assumed Achilles heel" of "Confrontation" affirming that to the man of faith the so-called secular order is also sacred underscores the artificiality of any sharp division between theological and non-theological matters.

Great thinkers do not write transparent nonsense. They do sometimes engage in rhetorical hyperbole, and the more obvious it is that the literal understanding of a hyperbolic assertion cannot be intended, the more an author has the right to rely on the reader to understand this. But one must also be careful not to denude the rhetoric of all meaning, to the point where it says something so removed from its presumed intent that the formulation misses the point entirely.

Dr. Korn, then, is surely correct in his contention that the plain meaning of Rabbi Soloveitchik's assertion of total incommunicability must somehow be limited. He suggests, then, that the objection to theological dialogue was restricted to full-fledged religious polemic. Thus, Rabbi Soloveitchik assumed that the modern dialogue would differ very little from the medieval model in which Christians attempted to prove that Jesus was the messiah and that Jewish law has no ongoing validity. This would be a "theological duel to the death." Rabbi Soloveitchik's assertion that dialogue is absurd refers only to efforts to prove or disprove faith rationally. He objected, then, or objected primarily, to "doctrinal disputation." (We are not told what the secondary objections may have been.) This is a neat and clean resolution of the problem, but, as we shall see, I think it does too much violence to Rabbi Soloveichik's language as well as to other evidence.

Dr. Korn goes on to argue that the major changes in Catholic teachings about Jews and Judaism since "Confrontation" largely neutralize Rabbi Soloveitchik's concerns. *Nostra Aetate* itself confirmed the irrevocability of the election of the Jews, Pope John Paul II made clear that the Old

Covenant is not revoked, the establishment of diplomatic relations with Israel effectively recognizes the right of the Jewish people to its historic homeland, anti-Semitism has been repudiated and denounced, mission to the Jews has been eliminated, influential Catholics consider Judaism salvific for Jews, and even Cardinal Ratzinger, who looks forward to the acceptance of Christianity by Jews, does not anticipate this before the end of days. Thus, there is no triumphalism, no effort to convert, no disputation, no serious problem.

Let me begin by conceding that Rabbi Soloveitchik was not entirely unconcerned by the residual problem of outright polemic. Dr. Korn correctly notes that he uses the term debate at one point, and I agree that the term is revealing. It is also clear that Rabbi Soloveitchik assumed that he was dealing, even on the eve of *Nostra Aetate*, with a thoroughly supersessionist Catholicism whose adherents were interested in converting Jews. But I cannot agree that the full intent of "Confrontation" is exhausted by depicting it as a warning against engaging in old-fashioned disputation. First of all, Jews did not need such a warning. Second, it was perfectly clear even in 1963 and 1964 that the call for dialogue was not framed in disputational terms. Indeed, that is precisely why Rabbi Soloveitchik had to caution against it. Thus, the preliminary text "On the Attitude of Catholics toward Non-Christians and especially toward Jews" distributed at the second session of the Council on November 8, 1963 declared that "since the Church has so much of a common patrimony with the synagogue, this Holy Synod intends in every way to promote and further mutual knowledge and esteem obtained by theological studies and fraternal discussions" (Arthur Gilbert, *The Vatican Council and the Jews*, p. 262). Third, Rabbi Soloveitchik provided guidance to the interfaith representatives of the Rabbinical Council of America for many years after *Nostra Aetate*. By then it was perfectly evident that interfaith dialogue was not Barcelona-style disputation, that the parties were not engaging in medieval polemics about Isaiah 53 or the rationality of the incarnation. And yet Rabbi Soloveitchik, on the whole, held to his guidelines. The entire thrust of "Confrontation"'s inspirational rhetoric about the private character of the religious experience is incommensurate with an interpretation that sees it as a straightforward injunction against trying to "prove" your faith; the issue is explicitly communicating an experience, not demonstrating the truth of a position. In other words, though the existential character of R. Soloveitchik's stance correctly noted by Dr. Korn is indeed inimical to the notion that religious positions can be definitively proven, the larger argument is that the personal experience of faith cannot even be communicated. What *can* be communicated is intellectual apprehension of faith. The problem is that such communication is pitifully inadequate.

This, I think, is the real thrust of R. Soloveitchik's position. Of course many elements of religious *doctrine*, of the *content* of religious belief, can be conveyed. The assertion that the great encounter between God and man cannot be communicated, applied in the same breath even to individuals of the same faith, cannot mean that no theological discourse is possible. It means that the deepest levels of the faith experience are inaccessible to outsiders, and Rabbi Soloveitchik applies this to a collective of believers as well as to individuals. Thus, as much as theological propositions can be conveyed, as much as even religious emotions can be partially expressed, that which ultimately commits a person to God or a faith community to its particular relationship with God remains essentially private, leaving not only a lonely man of faith but a lonely people of faith—a nation that dwells alone.

Since Rabbi Soloveitchik believed that untrammeled interfaith dialogue presumes to enter into that realm, he declares it out of bounds. Even though dialogue among believers concentrating on social issues has a religious dimension, it does not presume to enter that innermost realm, and its value therefore outweighs its residual dangers. If I am correct, then even theological discussion that knows its place would not be subject to the most radical critique in "Confrontation," and in this general sense I am in agreement with Dr. Korn. But it is critically important to recognize that the incommunicability of the ultimate religious commitment is not the totality of Rabbi Soloveitchik's argument. The very fact that he goes beyond that point lends credence to the view that he did not mean it as an all-encompassing delegitimation of any theological discussion. If he did, there would have been little reason to go further. But he does go further, and here his argument moves from the extreme rhetoric of philosophical absolutism to the penetrating, pragmatic, prescient insights that make "Confrontation" an essay of ongoing relevance.

Rabbi Soloveitchik worried that theological dialogue would create pressure to "trade favors pertaining to fundamental matters of faith, to reconcile 'some' differences." He argued against any Jewish interference in the faith of Christians both on grounds of principle and out of concern that this would create the framework for reciprocal expectations. Now, the changes in Catholic attitudes detailed by Dr. Korn are real, welcome, and significant, but they do not undermine these concerns. Quite the contrary. The trajectory of dialogue to our own day has confirmed the validity of Rabbi Soloveitchik's analysis to an almost stunning degree.

It is precisely friendly theological discussion and not religious disputation that generates these dangers, all the more so when the discussion is formalized as a theological encounter not between individuals but between communities. As I noted in a paper on *Dabru Emet*, a prominent participant in the dialogue with as positive an attitude toward Jews and Judaism as one could hope for congratulated the Jewish theologians who authored that declaration. "The dialogue," he said, "will be stymied if Christians affirm a theological bonding with Jews . . . without an acknowledgement of such bonding from the Jewish side." Several years ago, I criticized The New York Board of Rabbis for inviting its members to participate in an interfaith prayer service in the main sanctuary of St. Patrick's cathedral, asserting in an interview with *The Jewish Week* that although many Jewish authorities maintained that classical Christian theology is not considered idolatry for Christians, it is for Jews. In light of this, prayer in such a setting raises the most serious of issues to the point where no Orthodox rabbi should even consider participating. An important official in the New York Archdiocese wrote a strong letter of protest to the paper, and in a private letter to me, he complained about my expressing such an assessment of Christianity after all that Catholics had done to reassess their negative image of Judaism. In an article on *Dominus Iesus*, I have already expressed my regret at using the term idolatry, which is easily misunderstood in this context, but my correspondent was not mollified even after he understood very well that I was not suggesting that Christians attribute divinity to icons. Rabbi Soloveitchik's concern about the trading of favors pertaining to fundamental matters of faith could not be more clearly illustrated.

In that reaction to *Dabru Emet*, I also cited an example of the sort of Jewish demand upon Christians that Rabbi Soloveitchik opposed and that can so easily lead to reciprocal demands. A prominent Jewish ecumenist denounced a Catholic document for implying that at the end of days, Jews would discover that the Messiah is after all Jesus of Nazareth. Such a denunciation is, in my view, a virtual *reductio ad absurdum* of the sort of interference in the faith of the other that Rabbi Soloveitchik warned about. As Dr. Korn notes, and as I emphasized in my reaction to *Dominus Iesus*, Cardinal Ratzinger's expectation that Jews will recognize the truth of Christianity at the end of days is entirely unobjectionable, and it indeed parallels Rabbi Soloveitchik's assertion of the eschatological confirmation of Judaism. While this assertion does not necessarily mean that non-Jews will, in Dr. Korn's formulation, "adopt the current practices" of Judaism, it does mean that they will recognize its truth and adopt its creed.

Cardinal Ratzinger's vision, however, is not confined to the *eschaton*. He appears interested in bringing individual Jews to a recognition of Christian truth even before the end of days, and he sees interfaith dialogue—though that is not its only purpose—as one means of accomplishing this end. (It is worth noting that even in the Middle Ages, the survival of a Jewish collective until the Second Coming was seen as part of the divine plan.) I argued for this understanding of the Cardinal's position in that article on *Dominus Iesus* and cannot revisit it now, but at least as I see it, even Rabbi Soloveitchik's concern about a missionary aspect of dialogue has not been rendered altogether obsolete by the developments underscored by Dr. Korn.

The assertion that the caveats expressed in "Confrontation" bear continuing relevance does not mean that they carry the authority of Sinaitic revelation or that they are easy to apply. I have already emphasized my understanding that Rabbi Soloveitchik was not asserting the categorical impossibility of all theological communication. Persuasive anecdotal evidence indicates that he worried about the lack of qualifications for such dialogue among most Orthodox rabbis, a concern that comes to the fore in Dr. Korn's eloquent peroration. One of the rabbis most committed to enforcing Rabbi Soloveitchik's guidelines has told me on more than one occasion that his revered mentor had said that he trusted Rabbi Walter Wurzburger to deal with theological issues in conversation with Christians. Discussions of anti-Semitism, which Orthodox representatives consider kosher and even essential, lead to the most sensitive issues involving sacred Christian texts. For pragmatic reasons, Orthodox Jews want Christians to understand the theological importance that Judaism assigns to the land of Israel. Because of these blurred boundaries, I have prepared several presentations on such issues in a dialogical setting with the approval, sometimes enthusiastic, sometimes ambivalent, of Orthodox organizations. This is not an exact science, and Dr. Korn's own caveats toward the end of his talk may mean that our positions are not that far apart. However that may be, the value of interfaith discussion is real, and its dangers, especially to traditionalists, are no less real. The forty-year old document that we are addressing today is very much alive.

DABRU EMET:
SOME RESERVATIONS ABOUT
A JEWISH STATEMENT ON CHRISTIANS
AND CHRISTIANITY

From: http://www.bc.edu/research/cjl/meta-elements/sites/partners/ccjr/
berger02.htm
Read at the first annual meeting of the Council of Centers on Jewish-
Christian Relations. Baltimore, October 28, 2002

Shortly after the publication of *Dabru Emet: A Jewish Statement on Christians and Christianity* in *The New York Times* of September 10, 2000, I was contacted by the Union of Orthodox Jewish Congregations of America to formulate a brief reaction. What emerged was the following paragraph, which was posted on the Union's website and later adopted by the Rabbinical Council of America as its official position on the document.

> This is in many ways an admirable statement composed by people for whom I have high regard. I agree with much of it, including the controversial but carefully balanced passage denying that Nazism was a Christian phenomenon. However, I did not agree to sign it for several reasons. First, for all its exquisitely skillful formulation, it implies that Jews should reassess their view of Christianity in light of Christian reassessments of Judaism. This inclination toward theological reciprocity is fraught with danger. Second, although it is proper to emphasize that Christians "worship the God of Abraham, Isaac, and Jacob, creator of heaven and earth," it is essential to add that worship of Jesus of Nazareth as a manifestation or component of that God constitutes what Jewish law and theology call *avodah zarah*, or foreign worship—at least if done by a Jew. Many Jews died to underscore this point, and the bland assertion that "Christian worship is not a viable religious choice for Jews" is thoroughly inadequate. Finally, the statement discourages either community from "insisting that it has interpreted Scripture more accurately than the other." While intended for the laudable purpose of discouraging missionizing, this assertion conveys an uncomfortably relativistic message.

On this occasion, I have the opportunity to address these and other issues raised by this very important document more fully. Let me begin with reciprocity, which I consider the most dangerous problem generated by interfaith dialogue. *Dabru Emet* formulates this expectation in its most benign form, but I am uneasy with any document that accepts such a framework. For Jews, the dynamic of interfaith dialogue has produced pressure from within or from without to see Jesus as a prophet, or even as a Messsiah for non-Jews; to see the incarnation as a theologically acceptable, even if erroneous belief; to downplay the problem of "foreign worship" (*avodah zarah*); and to engage in interfaith prayer services. For Christians, it has produced pressures to deny the historicity of sections of the Gospels; to see the New Testament as an antisemitic work; to demand that it be revised; to question even eschatological confirmation of Christian truth, an issue to which I shall return; to see Judaism as an absolutely equal religion and to regard as morally abhorrent the denial that it can provide salvation just as effectively as Christianity.

Let me elaborate briefly on this last point. In the ecumenical arena, Christians who will not grant Judaism full salvific force are denounced by both Jews and Christians in language appropriate for characterizing moral miscreants. But the reason given for granting Judaism such status has nothing to do with morality at all but rather with the assertion that the first covenant remains in force—a purely theological point. A Christian who rejects this position may or may not be making a theological error from an inner Christian perspective, but he or she is not guilty of a moral defect unless one is prepared to posit a universal moral principle that every religion must be granted full salvific efficacy.

While I do not believe that anyone has the right to tell someone else what that person's own religion teaches, or should teach, in matters of belief, there is a right to level criticisms, even demands, of a universal moral sort. This creates the temptation to make theological demands on the grounds that the issue in question has moral consequences. There is sometimes truth, even overwhelming truth, in such assertions, but I am a very strict constructionist on this matter. Once Christians are prepared to break the link between a doctrine and its possible anti-Jewish consequences, Jews should refrain from any further intervention. Since pressing such points can—and does— generate backlash, and the only reason for pressing them is pragmatic, the wisdom of intervention must be scanned even without reference to the moral imperative of leaving Christian doctrine to Christians. Participants in the Christian discourse may, of course, wish to address these issues out of an internal moral dynamic. Jews can and should express appreciation for this, but they should do so as engaged observers, not as aggressive participants.

Once we become accustomed to arrogating to ourselves the right to intervene in the other's faith, we can lose our sense of proportion even when dealing with moral issues where some expression of opinion is appropriate. Jewish reactions to the Catholic Church's treatment of its own heroic and not so heroic figures are a case in point. I do object (mildly) to the canonization of Pius IX. I object vehemently to the proposed canonization of Isabella, whose transformation into a saint would be the rough equivalent of canonizing a deeply pious early-twentieth-century Catholic who had been instrumental in carrying out lynchings. But I do not object to the canonization of Edith Stein. I thoroughly disapproved of Jewish pressures to open the Vatican archives in the hope of demonstrating Pius XII's moral deficiencies. Within the International Jewish Committee on Interreligious Consultations (IJCIC), I argued vigorously both orally and in writing against going ahead with the joint commission on Church behavior during World War II, a project whose bad end should have been perfectly evident to anyone who thought the matter through.

Despite my aversion to any gesture toward expectations of theological reciprocity, I am of course aware that perceptions of the other are affected by interaction. Sometimes Jewish perceptions of Christianity have become more favorable because relations improved, sometimes even because they became more tense. The latter point is counterintuitive, but medieval Christian attacks on anti-Gentile discrimination in the Talmud led Jews to insist on a legally significant distinction between Christians and the pagans of old, a distinction some came to believe in full sincerity—and one which I believe to be correct in the eyes of God. Nevertheless, the expectations generated in contemporary theological dialogue have become institutionalized, part of the structural warp and woof of the enterprise, and they are deeply threatening to a traditionalist. John Pawlikowski may well be correct in his appreciative comment about *Dabru Emet* in a commencement address at Hebrew Union College in Cincinnati in May, 2001: "The dialogue will be stymied if Christians affirm a theological bonding with Jews . . . without an acknowledgement of such bonding from the Jewish side." To the degree that this observation is true, however, it reinforces my concerns.

Let us now turn to the actual content of *Dabru Emet*. "Jews and Christians," it asserts, "worship the same God. " This statement, I believe, is simultaneously true and false. In *Christianity in Jewish Terms*, the volume that emerged out of *Dabru Emet*, David Novak writes, "Idolatry is the worship of a 'strange god' (*el zar*). The wrong worship of the right God is 'strange service' (*avodah zarah*), which means the worship of God by humanly constructed rather than by divinely revealed means." This is not flatly incorrect; there are indeed rare forms of *avodah zarah*, notably the worship of the golden calf according to some interpretations, that fit this definition. Nonetheless, it is misleading. Jewish legal and theological terminology make no use of the term *el zar* despite its appearance in Psalm 81. *Avodah zarah* almost always refers to the formal recognition or worship as God of an entity that is in fact not God. For one who denies the divinity of Jesus, classical Christianity is clearly included in this definition. Thus, it is *avodah zarah* not merely because of the means of worship but also because of the object of worship.

Even medieval Jews understood very well that Christianity is *avodah zarah* of a special type. The tosafists assert that although a Christian pronouncing the name of Jesus in an oath would be taking the name of "another god," it is nonetheless the case that when Christians say the word "God," they have in mind the Creator of heaven and earth. Some later authorities took the continuation of that *Tosafot* to mean that this special type of *avodah zarah* is forbidden to Jews but permissible to gentiles, so that a non-Jew who engages in Christian worship commits no sin. One medieval authority, Rabbi Menahem ha-Meiri, may even have believed that a Jew engaging in Christian worship is not guilty of *avodah zarah*, though no other rabbi of any standing endorsed this position. In the final analysis, then, virtually all Jews understood that Christian worship is distinct from pagan idolatry because of its belief in the Creator of heaven and earth who took the Jews out of Egyptian bondage, revealed the Torah at Sinai and continues to exercise his providence over the entire cosmos. Some asserted that the association (*shittuf*) of Jesus with this God is permissible for non-Jews. Virtually none regarded such association as anything other than *avodah zarah* if the worshipper was a Jew. Do Jews and Christians, then, worship the same God? The answer, I think, is yes and no.

It bears noting that this issue is not entirely a one-way street. Some evangelical Christians object to interfaith prayer even with monotheists on the grounds that it is idolatry to participate in a service with those who worship anyone but the triune God. I have difficulty understanding how this position can survive scrutiny from a purely biblical perspective. While Christians have traditionally believed that the Hebrew prophets understood and even alluded to the triune nature of God, it is difficult to assume even from a Christian perspective that the Israelite masses during the First Temple period were aware of this, and yet prophetic denunciations of idolatry allude only to the worship of pagan deities. At the very least, a nontrivial number of Israelites must have worshipped the God of Israel without understanding the trinity, and yet the prophets never refer to this form of idolatry. Nonetheless, I can construct a (weak) response to these objections, and even if I could not, my difficulty in understanding this position would not justify my denying others the right to maintain it. They have this right, and I do not harbor the slightest resentment at their exercising it.

If Christianity is *avodah zarah* even for non-Jews, does that mean that Judaism denies Christians salvation? I do not believe that this is so. The question of salvation for Christians—or even the relationship of Christianity to what Jewish tradition calls the Noahide covenant binding on all of humanity—is not addressed in *Dabru Emet*. I suspect that one reason for this is that raising this question would have been very uncomfortable in a document that does not even want to say that Judaism is true in a way that Christianity is not. In *Christianity in Jewish Terms*, Prof. Novak does address the matter, suggesting that Christians, because they meet the key Maimonidean criterion of believing that the Noahide laws are divinely revealed, are the quintessential example of non-Jews who attain salvation. This suggestion, for all the attractiveness of its central insight, requires the adoption of the "liberal" view about the permissibility of "association" for non-Jews and fails to address other complicating features of the Noahide laws that make the assertion that Christians observe, or even endorse, all of them less than certain. It needs to be supplemented by the position of Rabbi Jacob Emden, who asserted in a responsum that non-Jews, even those who engage in technical *avodah zarah* because of mistaken adherence to ancestral tradition, can attain salvation if they observe the key moral laws in the Noahide code. Non-Jews need not attain a perfect score in observing their obligations any more than Jews need to do so in observing theirs.

We move now to the final concern that I expressed, namely, unease with *Dabru Emet*'s "uncomfortably relativistic message." "The humanly irreconcilable differences between Jews and Christians will not be settled until God redeems the world as promised in Scripture." The paragraph that follows this heading goes on to assert that the key difference regarding the proper way to serve God "will not be settled by one community insisting that it has interpreted Scripture more accurately than the other." Here again Prof. Novak's remarks in *Christianity in Jewish Terms* illuminate both the careful thought that went in to this document and the stubborn problems that remain. In providing guidelines for Jewish-Christian dialogue, he counsels the avoidance of both relativism and syncretism. The section on avoiding relativism is formulated with admirable vigor. It sits, however, very uneasily with the section on avoiding triumphalism, which asks, "What . . . of those Jews who assert that it is precisely at the end of days that the triumph of Judaism will be manifest, and what of those Christians who assert that at the Second Coming Christianity will triumph?" And it answers, "We must answer that the final judgment of all human history is not yet in."

For many traditionalists of both faiths, the affirmation that the key tenets of one's religion will be verified at the end of days follows ineluctably from the conviction that they are true. The dialogical environment has created such distortions that basic religious affirmations of this sort have become suspect, even morally unacceptable. As I wrote in an article on *Dominus Iesus*, "We . . . face a remarkable paradox. Precisely because of its striving for interfaith respect and understanding, dialogue would become an instrument of religious imperialism."

On this last point, let me cite a letter of mine published in the *Forward* in response to an article by Rabbi James Rudin:

> Jews engaged in dialogue with Christians succumb all too often to the temptation to tell Christians what to believe about their own religion. While Christian revision of teachings that contain the potential of spawning antisemitism is very much in the Jewish interest, Jews need to be cautious about making demands that can create resentment and backlash and even legitimize Christian demands for reciprocal revisions in Judaism.

Though this is a longstanding problem about which I have often expressed concern, I was stunned by Rabbi Rudin's assertion ("While the Messiah Tarries," February 22, 2002) that Catholics must not only assert that the Jewish longing for the Messiah is "valid"; they must assert that "the messiah's identity remains unknown, and Jesus, whom Christians believe to be the messiah, is not waiting at the end of days for Jews to recognize the 'error of their ways.'" How does one believe that Jesus is the messiah and simultaneously refrain from asserting that Jews will discover this at the end of days?

Rabbi Rudin apparently believes that Jews have the right to demand that Christians reject one of the core beliefs of Christianity. We have no such right, any more than Christians have the right to demand that traditional Jews give up their conviction that at the end of days all the world will recognize the messiah—and that he will not be Jesus of Nazareth.

Finally, at this delicate moment in history, I need to add something about *Dabru Emet*'s passage on Israel even though I did not address it in my initial single-paragraph reaction. "Christians," say the authors, "can respect the claim of the Jewish people upon the land of Israel." This statement is surely true, and its validity is demonstrated by the many instances of manifest Christian enthusiasm for the Jewish state. Nonetheless, Christian attitudes toward Israel in the current crisis have once again raised serious questions in Jewish minds about the value of dialogue. Support for Israel in the organized Christian community comes primarily from those who eschew theological dialogue and support conversionary efforts aimed at Jews. Churches and organizations most involved in dialogue are far more ambivalent and even hostile. The very habits of mind that produce the dialogical imperative—the desire to redress grievances and achieve justice for the historically oppressed— produce sympathy for Palestinians. In the view of most Jews (myself decidedly included), this sympathy has led to an inversion of morality in which mass murder in response to an extraordinary peace proposal, education toward *jihad* in the bloodiest sense, and mass dissemination of the vilest antisemitism evoke next to no protest or even diminution of sympathy. Rather, it is Israel's efforts at self-defense, usually carried out with exemplary concern for innocent life, that arouse passionate moral disapproval.

As long as this state of affairs persists, the Jewish-Christian relationship, at least on the level of the Jewish street, will not be determined by theological documents on either side. It will be determined by an assessment of who cares about the survival of a Jewish state and the fate of its citizens—and who does not.

JEWS, CHRISTIANS, AND *THE PASSION*

From: *Commentary* 117:5 (May, 2004): 23–31.

Mel Gibson's *The Passion of the Christ* opened on February 25, Ash Wednesday. I planned to catch a noon showing that Friday, and I was a nervous wreck. Even setting aside the question of anti-Semitism, reviewers had depicted a movie so horrific, with clawed whips sending chunks of bloodied flesh flying across the screen, that I was not sure I could endure the experience. (In the aftermath of childhood nightmares, I have assiduously avoided fictional horror and cinematic gore alike.) But one can hardly undertake to write about a film whose controversial nature rests in part on its violence and close one's eyes when the going gets tough. And so I entered the theater in fear and trembling.

As the film unfolded, my reactions taught me something about one of the key issues in this entire affair—the critical role played by expectations and prior experience in molding a viewer's response. *The Passion* is indeed saturated with anti-Jewish motifs; and yet my expectation of anti-Semitism had been set at so high a level that I could barely muster more than a trace of indignation. The violence is interminable, central, and utterly graphic; but my trepidation had been ratcheted up to a point where I emerged from the theater with a sense of relief. Essentially, a film drenched in blood, suffused with sublime sentiments of sacrifice and forgiveness, and replete with images of venomous Jews left me neither uplifted nor viscerally outraged. Though I am more than capable of leaving a movie in tears, I left this one curiously unmoved.

My reaction no doubt resulted in part from the need to steel myself against surrendering to an experience that might rob me of sleep for months to come. But there was more to it than that. Despite its powerful cinematic effects, this is a film whose capacity to move depends in large measure on the viewer's ability to identify with Jesus of Nazareth for reasons that are not presented in the film itself. If you come with love and admiration for its hero, and all the more so if you come with faith in his divinity and his supreme self-sacrifice, every lash, every nail, every drop of blood will tear at your psyche. But for a viewer with neutral sentiments, or with little knowledge—or with the mixed emotions of a Jew acutely aware of the role of this story in unleashing persecution— the film provides little basis for empathy. Its unremitting violence remains just that.

Thus, I had great difficulty—and still do—in assimilating the assertion of some viewers that they had seen an Oscar-winning performance on the part of the film's Jesus (played by Jim Caviezel). Because of the very nature of Mel Gibson's faith, his Jesus must be a one-dimensional figure. After the first moments in the garden of Gethsemane, this is a man without inner conflict, without inner development, without complex, evolving relationships with others. Aside from a few flashbacks of the briefest duration, the task of the actor is to deliver melodramatic pronouncements and to writhe in agony. No one, however talented, could turn this into an Oscar-winning role. God is not a candidate for an Academy Award.

* * *

The disputes swirling around the movie are remarkably complex, conforming to conventional lines and at the same time cutting across them. With respect to the interfaith tensions spawned by this affair, Dennis Prager's observation that Jews and Christians have been seeing different movies is the beginning and perhaps even the middle of wisdom. But the film has also exacerbated divisions among Christians themselves—and among Jews—as well as confrontations between secular and religious Americans, with the potential to create new alliances and damage old ones. These shifting fault lines reflect and emerge out of a constellation of deeply entrenched Jewish fears, a half-century of Jewish-Christian dialogue and rapprochement, Christian attitudes toward the Israeli-Palestinian conflict, the ambivalent alliance of Orthodox Jewry with the Christian Right, secularist and liberal Christian concerns about ascendant fundamentalism, traditionalist Christian resentments at widespread mockery of their beliefs and values, and more.

Thus, an entire essay could be devoted to the cultural politics of the Gibson affair, on exhibit in a vast multitude of opinion pieces in the news media, on television and radio, on the web, and in magazines occupying every point of the ideological spectrum. For purposes of manageability, but also because I believe this to be the most important issue of all, I mean to concentrate here on the aspect of the controversy touching directly on Christian-Jewish relations.

Gibson's project entered public consciousness when, last year, a group of Catholic and Jewish scholars reviewed a preliminary version of the screenplay and expressed deep reservations. When their suggestions for massive changes were transmitted to Gibson, his representatives charged that the script had been obtained improperly. The United States Conference of Catholic Bishops (USCCB), which had encouraged the review, then backed away, failing to offer even a modicum of support to the authors, who came to be subjected to savage attacks.

The scholars had approached the screenplay from a perspective shared by only a handful of observers. They knew that the passion narrative had played a central role in fostering and unleashing anti-Jewish sentiments through the ages. They also knew that it had loomed large in the dramatically positive transformation of Jewish-Catholic relations ever since the declaration of the Second Vatican Council in 1965 that, "even though Jewish authorities and those who followed their lead pressed for the death of Christ, neither all Jews indiscriminately at that time, nor Jews today, can be charged with the crimes committed during his passion." They knew that the Pontifical Commission for Religious Relations with the Jews had issued "guidelines" and "notes" about how to apply the Council's declaration in liturgy, education, and preaching. Finally, they knew that in 1988 the USCCB's Committee for Ecumenical and Interreligious Affairs had issued "Criteria for the Evaluation of Dramatizations of the Passion."

The scholars can hardly be blamed for having assumed—naively, as it turned out—that the Conference took its own published standards seriously. Among other things, these criteria affirm that dramatizations of the passion should present the diversity of Jewish communities in Jesus' time; that Jews should not be portrayed as avaricious or bloodthirsty; that any "crowd scene" should reflect the fact that some in the crowd and among the Jewish leaders supported Jesus, and that the rest were manipulated by his opponents; that Jesus' opponents should not be made to look sinister while he and his friends are depicted in lighter tones, thus isolating Jesus and the apostles from the Jews as a group; that "if one cannot show beyond reasonable doubt that the particular Gospel element selected or paraphrased will not be offensive or have the potential for negative influence on the audience . . . , that element should not, in good conscience, be used"; and that Pontius Pilate should be presented as the "ruthless tyrant" that we know he was.

That the screenplay of *The Passion* violated the Conference's criteria in all these particulars was self-evident. But changing it to conform to the Conference's official positions would have required Gibson to start over from scratch, and there was no way he would accede to such a request. Instead, he took the offensive. One Catholic figure who supported him issued the preposterous statement that the screenplay did conform to established guidelines. Another declared that everything in the film was historically accurate. Spokesmen for the producers indicated that the film was a faithful presentation of the Gospel accounts, so that any criticism of the screenplay was a criticism of the Gospels themselves. Sympathetic commentators, including several Orthodox Jews, dutifully repeated these assertions, although very few of them had read the screenplay or seen the film.

* * *

At this point in the controversy, I felt both sympathy and antipathy toward the arguments of Gibson's defenders. For two decades, I had publicly expressed strong reservations about the tendency of Jews engaged in interfaith dialogue to tell Christians what to believe about their own religion.[1] This same caveat had been issued in the 1960's, in the midst of the excitement surrounding the Vatican Council, by Rabbi Joseph B. Soloveitchik, the renowned Orthodox scholar, who was not only committed on principle to nonintervention but was also concerned about the dangers of reciprocal expectations. In general, it is because their own instincts enable them to empathize with the deep, unalterable convictions of fundamentalists that Orthodox Jews are particularly reluctant to propose revisions in the faith of others. By contrast,

---

[1]   See my "Jewish-Christian Relations: A Jewish Perspective," *Journal of Ecumenical Studies* 20 (1983), and my articles on *Dominus Iesus, Dabru Emet,* and "Confrontation" [reprinted in this volume].

secularists, liberal Christians, and non-Orthodox religious Jews, even with the best of intentions, cannot quite grasp the full dimensions of an unwavering commitment to the literal truth of a sacred text.

Of course, the word "literal" is not subject to precise definition; but it is not without meaning, either. Thus, to argue (as some critics of *The Passion* have done) that Pontius Pilate could not have been successfully pressured by a Jewish mob is to argue that the Gospel accounts—all four of them—are incorrect. To argue that the Gospels contradict each other regarding the scourging of Jesus, with John placing it prior to the final decision to have him crucified and Matthew and Mark placing it later, is to misapprehend the approach of a fundamentalist, who will assert that he was scourged both before and after.

There is a fascinating irony in the understanding that many Orthodox Jews exhibit toward the sensibilities of the most traditional Christians. After all, the Orthodox retain deeper anti-Christian instincts than liberal Jews—avoiding interfaith prayer, shrinking from theological dialogue, affirming an ancient obligation to undergo martyrdom rather than embrace Christianity, and in many cases seeing Christian anti-Semitism as a metaphysical, unchangeable condition captured in the formula, "Esau hates Jacob." And yet, several Orthodox Jews have gone so far as to ask me whether even hostile non-Scriptural material in *The Passion* may be justified in light of authoritative Catholic traditions. I doubt that this question would even enter the mind of the non-Orthodox.

Beyond empathy with believers who resist the questioning of Scriptural accuracy, many traditionalist Jews feel a commonality with traditionalist Christians on a range of other issues as well: abortion, sexuality in the public sphere, homosexuality, aid to denominational schools, protection of religious rights, and the claim of Jews to the land of Israel in its entirety. Lengthy tracts could be written to qualify the simplistic, homogenizing implications of this list, but it does help explain the fact that Gibson's most enthusiastic Jewish defenders have come from the ranks of the Orthodox. This is not to say, however, that a majority of Orthodox Jews think that the film is a good idea. Quite the contrary: Gibson's apologists among the Orthodox are far outnumbered by those typified, in extreme fashion, by a relative who told me that once this movie appeared he would be careful not to stand close to the edge of a subway platform. What the apologists and the fearful straphangers do have in common is a tendency to regard vigorous Jewish *criticism* of the film as incendiary and self-defeating.

I do not wish to be misunderstood. While I strongly believe that Jews should not instruct Christians about the proper parameters of Christian faith, I do not regard alleged faithfulness to the Gospel narratives as a valid defense of a decision to present those narratives without elaboration or nuance. In a newspaper piece that appeared well before the film's release, I put the point as follows:

> The pre-modern Catholic Church—and Gibson is after all an unreconstructed Catholic who pines for the good old days—actively discouraged any reading of Scripture by the laity. While few people today would endorse this approach, it reflects the healthy understanding that the text of Scripture cannot stand alone. It needs to be explicated—and not by the proverbial Devil so famous for quoting it. Gibson and his defenders imagine that the film's adherence to the words of the Gospels with nothing added provides their most effective defense. In fact, along with the sadism and gore, it is precisely what justifies severe indictment.

In short, respect for the power and history of this story requires that it be placed in a framework that elucidates its message in light of the teachings of contemporary mainstream Christianity, Catholic and Protestant alike.

* * *

In the months leading up to the film's release, the war of words intensified, and with it, the anticipation. The most vocal Jewish attacks came from the Anti-Defamation League (ADL), whose leader, Abraham Foxman, became the prime target of both Gibsonites and anti-anti-Gibsonites. In the wake of intense criticism and a more realistic assessment of potential consequences, the ADL moderated its rhetoric. But the damage could not be entirely undone.

This episode deserves a brief comment, if only because it continues to provoke debate. Although the decibel level of the ADL's initial reaction was clearly a serious misjudgment, other factors need to be taken into consideration. First, the organization did try to act behind the scenes, but encountered a stone wall. Second, some of Gibson's rhetoric, as well as his apparent doubts concerning the large-scale gassing of Jews by the Nazis in World War II, understandably raised Jewish hackles. Third, it was evident early on that his assertions about the absolute fidelity of the film to the Gospels were questionable. Finally, and despite what some of

Foxman's detractors implied, this movie would hardly have disappeared into the void had the ADL and others kept silent. Although its success would almost certainly have been more limited, Gibson's name, the technical quality of the production, the mobilization of the evangelical and traditionalist Catholic communities, and the intrinsic significance of the story to countless multitudes would have guaranteed a very wide viewership throughout the world and for many years to come.

In any event, when Ash Wednesday 2004 finally arrived, the film's reception rapidly demonstrated the near irrelevance of the framework within which much of the earlier discussion had taken place. Did viewers base their reaction to *The Passion* on the degree of its deviation from the criteria established by the Bishops' Conference? The very question is comical. While the earlier debate did alert filmgoers to the specter of anti-Semitism, the vast majority reacted through the filter of their religious commitments. To the degree that the movie was evaluated against some other standard, that standard turned out to be—other movies.

Thus, the question raised was not whether Gibson's depiction was "better" or "worse" than that of the Oberammergau passion play, or of the Gospels themselves, but whether it was more or less violent than *The Texas Chain Saw Massacre.* That film, which I have mercifully never seen, has become a main point of comparison in traditionalist Christian discourse about *The Passion,* to the extent that it was invoked by a twelve-year-old preacher interviewed on Fox News who, I hope, has also not seen it. In a similar vein, many fundamentalist Christians have pointedly wondered why secular commentators have fallen silent at best and been supportive at worst when it comes to gangsta rap and other abhorrent manifestations of popular culture while subjecting a film about Jesus to withering attack.

This argument, for all its force, is persuasive only as an ad hominem riposte (and, as we shall see, it can be easily reversed). Nonetheless, it is of central importance in explaining the emotions unleashed by criticism of the film. Since I empathize with some of those emotions, let me try to formulate the key points as vigorously as I can.

Straightforward logic and elementary intuition inform us that books, films, songs, theater, and art can exercise a profound influence over readers, listeners, and viewers. And yet, out of ideological or financial motives, intelligent people have regularly delivered themselves of the most transparent absurdities regarding this matter. Producers of violent or pornographic films tell us that what happens on screen is not transmuted into actual behavior, an assertion that, while surely true for most viewers, is unquestionably false for a nontrivial minority. Distributors of gangsta rap assert with straight faces that the unspeakably vile lyrics of the songs they disseminate reflect a regrettable reality but surely do not exacerbate it. After all, they intone, no listener, whatever his age, would ever dream of actually carrying out any of the horrific acts that the songs explicitly encourage—and besides, it is not the responsibility of these pillars of society but rather the obligation of parents to monitor every piece of music to which their children are exposed.

The most vigorous critics of this debased ethos and its products have been traditionalist Christians. For their efforts, they have been pilloried for narrowness, intolerance, and worse. When, for example, a dung-splattered Mary appeared in an exhibit at the Brooklyn Museum, their objections were dismissed not just on First Amendment grounds but on the supposed principle that it is the *task* of a museum to exhibit "cutting-edge" art. Not surprisingly, unequivocal moral support for Christian concerns came predominantly from Orthodox Jewish organizations.

It was pent-up grievances of this kind that exploded in traditionalist Christian circles in the face of attacks on the film by secularist liberals— attacks that often extended to Christian conservatives themselves. Here, for example, was Stuart Klawans in the *Nation*:

> However much you might play at seeing his work as just another movie, Gibson has gone outside the normal bounds of show business and into the territory of America's religious absolutists: John Ashcroft anointing himself with oil, gay-hating lawmakers attempting to write Leviticus into the Constitution, antiabortionists shooting to kill, generals declaring holy war against the Muslim infidel. Our country has a great, great many such people who do not consider their convictions to be open to discussion. They maintain a significant hold on power; and since a lot of them have an antinomian streak, I doubt the rule of law would stand in their way, should we manage to loosen their grip. The ever-boyish and ingenuous Gibson, with his simple faith, has made *The Passion of the Christ* as a gift to such people.

To retain one's equanimity in the face of such rhetoric is no easy task. Nonetheless, grievances do not provide a license to suspend one's own moral code. It is decidedly true that people who routinely ignore the damage that popular culture can cause, who wrap themselves in the

First Amendment to guard against the need to think seriously about the consequences of music and films, and who then speak of the dangers inherent in *The Passion,* may justly be denounced as hypocrites. But so can those who routinely rail against the dangers of popular culture and then turn a blind eye to this film's brutality and its potential for harm.

To speak repeatedly about the psychological damage to children who are exposed to cinematic violence, and then take high-school classes to see *The Passion,* is problematic in the extreme; perhaps, indeed, a form of child abuse. (It should be unnecessary to add that peer pressure strips the option to stay home of any meaning.) In assessing the potential consequences of popular culture, traditionalist Christians do not ask if those attending a rap concert will seek out women to rape immediately upon leaving the theater. Similarly, the question of whether crowds will pour out of multiplexes to initiate immediate pogroms is hardly the proper criterion for evaluating the potential effect of *The Passion* on attitudes toward Jews. Those who understand the power of films to mold behavior, and who worry about their impact upon even a minority of susceptible viewers, should be the first to recognize the danger.

* * *

Finally, then, we turn to the message of the film itself. I do not believe *The Passion* was made with the purpose of arousing or increasing hostility to Jews, but it exudes indifference to this prospect. The litany of its anti-Jewish motifs, many of them not required by the Gospel accounts and sometimes even standing in tension with them, is lengthy and impressive. No filmmaker who actually cared about avoiding anti-Semitism could have produced anything resembling it.

To begin with, the high priest and his wicked associates wear costumes that evoke contemporary prayer shawls. They are bedecked with precious metals. Judas's thirty pieces of silver are thrown to him in slow motion; they scatter on the floor, and he greedily picks them up. The Jewish boys who pursue Judas are transformed into little demons— the metaphoric progeny, as Andrew Sullivan has noted, of Satan himself (or herself), who flits menacingly among the Jewish crowds.

In describing Jesus' arrest by Jews armed with swords and staves, the Gospels themselves simply assert that he was led away—in John, bound and led away—to the Jewish authorities. In *The Passion,* he is beaten vigorously and repeatedly during his forced march to the point where he falls off a cliff, is brought to a sudden halt by the chain around his neck, and must then clamber back up. It is not enough to remark that the Gospels tell us nothing of the sort. It strains credulity to believe that the Gospel writers could have known of such extreme mistreatment without allowing the slightest hint of it to enter their accounts.[2]

Once Jesus is delivered to the high priest and his associates, the Gospels do speak of his being buffeted, spat on, and slapped after or just before his condemnation. Here too, though, the depiction in the film is much stronger than that of the Gospels. Then, when he is handed over to Pilate, the sensitive Roman governor of the movie asks: "Do you always punish your prisoners before they are judged?" This question, which does not appear in the Gospels, is left unanswered, but its implications are unambiguous. If the Jews behave this way as a matter of course, they are routinely vicious; if not, they have singled Jesus out for special cruelty.

And so we come to Pilate. Before seeing the film, I had vigorously defended the right of believing Christians to affirm that Pilate was reluctant to execute Jesus but was successfully pressured by a Jewish crowd to override his own preference. I continue to adhere to that position in principle, but the film has impelled me to moderate it. The inner struggle ascribed to the morally conflicted governor goes beyond what the Gospels require, and its inconsistency with what we know about this man's character from extra-biblical sources becomes a legitimate basis for criticism.

In the context of the film, Pilate's (biblically unattested) complaints to his wife about the rotten outpost to which he has been assigned and the stinking rabble that he must deal with appear eminently reasonable. The viewer, then, is led to identify with a perspective that sees Judea and its undifferentiated population, taken as a whole, through the prism of this bloodthirsty crowd. Pilate's moment of discomfort while viewing the lashing his men inflict on Jesus—a reaction also unrecorded in the Gospels—forms an acute contrast with the unmoved cruelty of the Jews. In still another scene, both unbiblical and implausible, Pilate attempts but fails to quiet the crowd, whereupon the high priest sarcastically

---

2 "And they that had laid hold on Jesus led him away to Caiaphas the high priest" (Matthew 26:57); "And they laid their hands on him, and took him . . . . And they led Jesus away to the high priest" (Mark 14:46, 53); "Then took they him, and led him, and brought him into the high priest's house" (Luke 22:54); "Then the band and the captain and officers of the Jews took Jesus and bound him and led him away" (John 18:12–13).

asks—to appreciative laughter—if they have no respect for the Roman governor. Thus, the Jewish crowd does more than manipulate Pilate; it subjects him to open mockery.

Finally, in a controversial scene that is indeed in one of the Gospels, Pilate washes his hands of guilt, and the crowd apparently exclaims, "His blood be on us and on our children." I say "apparently" because Gibson has, in a fit of philo-Semitism, removed the subtitle at this point, and, as he told Diane Sawyer, the Aramaic exclamation is partially obscured by other noise. (I heard the Aramaic "His blood be on us," but could not make out the curse on the children; since Gibson has indicated that it is there, I am prepared to take his word for it.)[3]

There is, in any case, no realistic way to prevent the addition of the relevant subtitle in English, in Arabic, or in any other language, as the film makes its way through the world, through the years, and through a variety of electronic formats. This is a paradigmatic example of a passage that a Christian has every right to believe but no right to present in such a film without some dialogue expressing a disavowal of the sentiment by figures with whom the audience will identify. Yes, the crowd said it; but God, for one, did not agree with it. Jesus' later generic "Father, forgive them" does not begin to suffice.

At this point we must screw up our courage to examine the scourging and all the rest. For the last hour and fifteen minutes or so, this is a film depicting a man beaten to a bloody pulp and then nailed to a cross. In another controversial choice, Gibson here endorses John's account of the scourging of Jesus on Pilate's orders before the final cries of "Crucify him, crucify him." I have already noted my defense of Gibson's right to make such a choice, but once again the film impelled me to qualify my position. The relevant verses in John—in their entirety—read only as follows: "Then Pilate therefore took Jesus, and scourged him. And the soldiers platted a crown of thorns, and put it on his head, and they put on him a purple robe, and said, 'Hail, King of the Jews!' and they smote him with their hands" (John 19:1–3). Out of this raw material, there emerge ten almost unrelieved minutes of unremitting whipping with implements of varying cruelty, leaving Jesus a welter of blood.

---

3   Considering the effort that went into preparing an Aramaic script and teaching it to the actors, the errors in pronunciation reflect a startling degree of sloppiness. To cite but one example in a very important word, the high priest pronounces the word "messiah" more than once in a grotesque conflation of Hebrew and Aramaic *(meshiaha).*

Since no one could have stood erect or perhaps even lived after such treatment, it is self-evident that the scene is untrue to the intent of the Gospel. What this means is that the subsequent scene, in which the Jews have one more opportunity to change their mind, takes on a dimension that even the admittedly harsh Gospel account does not convey. The crowd now beholds a man who has visibly been subjected to unspeakable torment. The rabbis of the Mishnah say that Jews are "merciful people descended from merciful people." Not here. Not a fleeting scintilla of mercy. "Crucify him! Crucify him! Crucify him!"

So Pilate sends him off to be crucified. At this point, direct responsibility for the violence shifts entirely to the Romans. And here in large measure is the basis for my tentative assertion earlier that Gibson did not intend to foment hostility toward Jews as such. I am referring to the consistent bestiality of the Roman soldiers, plus a few small but significant positive indicators of another kind.

The sadism of the Romans underscores Gibson's consuming desire to maximize the depiction of Jesus' torment and to highlight the contrast between the evil forces of the film's villains and the pure, self-sacrificing goodness of Jesus and his followers. When evil is embodied in Jews, they are depicted in the worst possible light; when it is embodied in Romans, *they* are.

* * *

For Gibson, who was raised in an anti-Semitic household, the images of avaricious, bloodthirsty, gold-bedecked Jewish monsters are no doubt standard means of symbolizing Jewish evil, and may be used with no concern whatsoever for their larger impact. Perhaps, just perhaps, he really does not understand what some of his clearly decent defenders also do not understand—that the depiction of Jewish monsters has a potential for evil consequences that the depiction of Roman monsters does not. It should not be necessary to make an argument for this assertion, but apparently it is.

We have been assured that, just as there is no reason to suppose the film will cause hatred for Italians, there is no reason to suppose it should cause hatred for Jews. The differences, however, are numerous and compelling. The Roman soldiers are not the leaders of their people; the high priest and his associates are. The depiction of the Romans does not reinforce a hostile stereotype that has persisted over centuries; the depiction of the

Jews does. The Italians atoned for their sin by embracing Christianity; the Jews did not. There is no history of persecution directed against Italians as a consequence of this story; there is a history of persecution—a long and bloody one—against Jews. There is no longstanding theological argument for punishing Italians for their role in these events; there is a deeply influential one for punishing Jews. No non-Jewish Italian has ever been called "Christ killer" while suffering a beating at the hands of classmates or mobs; Jews—Italian and otherwise—have lived through this experience, and sometimes failed to live through it, on countless occasions from medieval times through the 20th century.

Even on a purely cinematic level, a profound difference obtains. The Romans in the movie are "innocently" sadistic. They simply enjoy smashing bones, scourging flesh, making blood flow. They cannot help it; it is their animal nature. The Jews, by contrast, are villainous out of conviction; theirs is a thoroughly conscious, thoroughly intentional, thoroughly satanic evil. There is a distinction, and Gibson cannot but make it palpable even if he does not consciously mean to.[4]

Why, then, am I still inclined to see the Roman monsters as an indication that Gibson's assault on Jews in this film results not from intentional anti-Jewish malice but from a Manichaean vision reinforced by the anti-Semitic stereotypes that he imbibed with his father's milk? What nudges me in this direction is the presence of a few touches that are inconsistent with systematic anti-Semitism.

The most striking of these is a single word spoken by a Roman soldier to Simon of Cyrene, the Jew forced to help Jesus carry the cross. Simon himself is depicted more sympathetically than the Gospels require; when he asks the Romans to show Jesus some mercy, a soldier dismisses him with the epithet, "Jew." Here, then, the film underscores the Jewishness of a sympathetic character where the Gospels do not.

Another such touch appears in the very brief flashback to the Sermon on the Mount, where some of those present wear prayer shawls, thus reminding us of the Jewishness of Jesus' followers. While these tiny flourishes do not even begin to neutralize the extended anti-Jewish motifs and images at the core of the film, they do not sit well with the assumption that it was made with the conscious purpose of fomenting hatred against Jews.

---

4   I am indebted to Neal Kozodoy for the point made in this paragraph.

For me, an unexpected consequence of watching this movie was a new regard for the Gospel writers' restraint. Gibson shows us the interminable beating of Jesus as he carries his cross to the crucifixion. We have already seen that John asserts in but a single unelaborated verse that Jesus was scourged before his final conviction. In Luke, there is no scourging at all. The only references to scourging after Pilate's final decision appear in Matthew and Mark, and in each case the information is contained in the briefest of subordinate clauses: "and when he had scourged Jesus, he delivered him to be crucified" (Matthew 27:26); "and delivered Jesus, when he had scourged him, to be crucified" (Mark 15:15). That is all.

Since the flogging implied here is no small matter, and might well have merited greater emphasis, it appears that the Gospel writers consciously marginalized this element of the story, that they did not want the sacrifice of Jesus to turn into a horror movie. In light of this, the very core of Gibson's film—which reflects his conviction that, in order to appreciate Jesus' sacrifice, one must wallow in his agony—runs counter to the intentions of the Gospels.

Pondering this point, I have come to understand why a Catholic priest who has been prominently involved in ecumenical activities both in the United States and in Rome told me before the film was released that its reported concentration on the flaying of Jesus was in his view blasphemous.

* * *

It is no surprise that the early reactions to showings of *The Passion* should have mirrored the positions held before it was released. Nonetheless, they have been instructive and occasionally troubling.

The scholars who criticized the early screenplay, Christian and Jewish, reaffirmed their first assessment. Since the film was not changed in any fundamental way, this was inevitable. As for Catholics of a traditional bent, most embraced the film enthusiastically. Thus, William Donohue, president of the Catholic League for Religious and Civil Rights, described it in an open letter to the Jewish community as "magnificent beyond words." Anyone who subscribes to the notion of collective guilt, Donohue wrote, or who believes that today's Jews are responsible for the behavior of some Jews 2,000 years ago, is demented.

Since not many people are insane, Donohue's remark was clearly intended to reassure, as well as to reinforce his denunciation of the film's critics. Unfortunately, however, the Catholic teaching that all sinners are responsible for the crucifixion was once seen as perfectly consistent with the doctrine that the Jewish collective, and the Jewish collective alone, suffered specific, grave, and ongoing punishment for its role. Although it is a comfort to know that Donohue, a mainstream Catholic holding a responsible position, cannot even conceive of the rationality of this position, still, the "demented" view was held by major Church authorities through the ages and by masses of Catholics even in the United States through the mid-20th century, and its permanent demise can hardly be celebrated with confidence.

I was particularly interested in seeing the official review of the movie by the USCCB's Office of Film and Broadcasting. It was no doubt to be expected that the movie's great popularity among the laity would affect the positions of Catholic leaders, and so it did. While the review contains some mild criticisms, it is on the whole laudatory; more to the point, it contains not a single reference to the "Criteria for the Evaluation of Dramatizations of the Passion."

Michael J. Cook, one of the Jewish scholars involved in the original evaluation of the screenplay, has seen this as no less vexing than the movie itself. "The solid bridge of trust Jews thought they had with the Catholic Church now lies exposed as merely a drawbridge, readily placed in raised position when it is most needed." My own emotional reaction is identical to Cook's; no measure of internal communal dynamics can justify this betrayal of decades of Catholic-Jewish dialogue. But if Donohue's view is too rosy, Cook's may be too despairing. In moments of crisis, ecumenical work can indeed be ignored in favor of larger concerns, but the quotidian activity of ecumenists effects slow, gradual, deep change. The most fervent partisans of this movie have couched their defense as a denial that it blames the Jews. Two generations ago, certainly three generations ago, Jewish responsibility was taken for granted.

And evangelical Christians? Despite the Catholic provenance of the movie, and despite its concentration on themes that Protestants have historically deemphasized, these denominations have embraced it with unbridled enthusiasm—to the point of construing criticism of "Mel's" work as enmity toward them and their values. In fact, a de facto alliance between fundamentalist Protestants and traditional Catholics has developed around the movie, with consequences that are difficult to foresee.

Because uncritical devotion to the film has become a virtual religious obligation for them, fundamentalist Christians regularly attest that it is entirely faithful to the biblical account. Interviewing Rabbi Daniel Lapin, the most outspoken and uncompromising Jewish apologist for Gibson, Rev. Pat Robertson asked, "What is the story here [regarding Abraham Foxman's criticism]? This movie is anything but anti-Semitic. It is the four Gospels that Christians believe is inspired Scripture. There is nothing that is departing from this narrative." To which the rabbi responded: "It is breathtakingly arrogant. What he is saying is that the only way to escape the wrath of Foxman is to repudiate your faith."

Similarly, Patrick J. Buchanan, serving as guest host on the MSNBC program *Scarborough Country,* asked Rev. Franklin Graham whether it is not the case that the film "is extraordinarily faithful to the Gospels." The reply: "Of course, Mel has a little bit of Hollywood artistry in the film. But it's very accurate . . . it's extremely close." Buchanan then posed a similar question to James Kennedy, described as the most widely watched Presbyterian minister in the country: "Could Gibson have portrayed it any other way and remained faithful to the Gospels?" Kennedy replied: "[W]ith a few tiny little dramatic licenses that he added, no, he could not have, because that's the way the story goes."

Thus have the culture wars impelled biblical literalists to display so little concern for the Gospel accounts that major deviations and invented scenes, to say nothing of the larger vision transforming the narrative into a bloodbath, become "tiny little dramatic licenses."

The nastiest vignette so far appeared a bit later in Buchanan's program, when he interviewed Rabbi Shmuley Boteach in the presence of Revs. Graham and Kennedy. In an effort to trap the rabbi into declaring that Jesus was a charlatan, Buchanan began by asking, "Do you believe Christ rose from the dead?" The rabbi had to reply in the negative, but made a point of adding that he considered Jesus to have been a devout Jew. Buchanan proceeded to ask: "If he was a devout Jew, why did he, in effect, say that before Abraham was, I am, and in effect say, 'I am the messiah'? And as a consequence of what he said, he not only laid down his life, but others laid down their lives. Now, if he was not the son of God, how can he be a good man if he sent men to their deaths on behalf of something that was not true?"

In other words, a Jew has no choice but to regard Jesus as less than a good man. This was a despicable attempt to foment religious enmity, and in Buchanan's case it may even have been more than that: an effort to create discord between Jews and evangelical Christians in the hope of weakening the support that the evangelical community has extended to Israel. This, after all, has been a major stumbling block to Buchanan's ability to achieve agreement with evangelicals across a broad range of issues.

Whether or not that was Buchanan's intent— and I put nothing past him—this same issue is also at the heart of Jewish concerns about the dangers of criticizing *The Passion*. To be sure, some liberal Jews—liberal in both the political and religious sense—are deeply ambivalent about the alliance established with the evangelical community regarding Israel, and welcome the opportunity to disengage. But more conservative Jews regard evangelical support for Israel as a virtual lifeline, valuable in and of itself and especially crucial at a moment when that community forms a key constituency for a conservative Republican administration in Washington . Many Jews worry that the moderate, potential danger posed by *The Passion* has been allowed to outweigh the acute and present danger that currently confronts the Jewish people—and who is to say that they are wrong?

* * *

This brings us back to the thesis with which I began: the battles over this film have struck deep and dangerous chords. Reflecting and intensifying old antagonisms, they have pitted conservative Christians against liberal ones and religious fundamentalists against secularists. They have divided Jews along both familiar and unfamiliar lines, forcing them to confront the paradoxes of their current engagement with the Christian world: a world in which fundamentalists who work to convert them in order to prevent their otherwise likely (or certain) damnation extend desperately needed support to Israel, while many religious liberals, recognizing the ongoing value of Judaism and sensitive to manifestations of old-style Christian anti-Semitism, vehemently denounce almost any efforts by Israel, no matter how manifestly necessary, to defend its citizens against mass murder at the hands of terrorists.

In the face of the deep emotions stirred by this controversy, the challenge of maintaining a posture of measured criticism is especially daunting. In the Jewish case, total suppression of criticism would not only constitute a craven abandonment of self-respect; it would betray Christian friends who have devoted much of their lives to the welfare of the Jewish people. But neither can criticism be allowed, on either side, to descend into self-righteous condemnation of all who disagree. If amity is to prevail, traditionalist Christians will have to force themselves to understand that reasonable people have grounds for genuine concern about this movie, that its critics do not necessarily hate them, and that some like them very much indeed. Jews for their part will have to force themselves to recognize that the fervent embrace of the film by traditionalist Christian audiences is not necessarily a sign of hostility or even indifference toward them, that it emerges out of positive religious emotions as well as understandable resentments flowing from the demonization of the religious Right by influential sectors of American public opinion. Jews must also force themselves to continue tending ecumenical vineyards even as the limitations of previous achievements have become painfully evident.

The reservoirs of good will that have been painstakingly accumulated in the last generation are being sorely tested. They cannot be allowed to run dry.

INDEX OF SOURCES

INDEX

Unelaborated references in footnotes are not listed in the index.

LaVergne, TN USA
20 December 2010
209594LV00002B/25/P